Engaging the Other: 'Japan' and Its Alter Egos, 1550–1850

Brill's Japanese Studies Library

Edited by

Joshua Mostow (Managing Editor)
Caroline Rose
Kate Wildman Nakai

VOLUME 65

The titles published in this series are listed at *brill.com/bjsl*

Engaging the Other:
'Japan' and Its Alter Egos,
1550–1850

By

Ronald P. Toby

BRILL

LEIDEN | BOSTON

Cover illustration: Revelers in the Hōkoku Festival of 1604 arrayed in Nanban fashion can be identified as Japanese masqueraders by the sandals on their feet. Kano Naizen, *Hōkoku sairei-zu byōbu*. Pair of six-panel folding screens, color and gold leaf on paper. Detail, left-hand screen, 5th panel. Courtesy Toyokuni Jinja, Kyoto

Library of Congress Cataloging-in-Publication Data

Names: Toby, Ronald P., 1942– author.
Title: Engaging the other : 'Japan' and its alter egos, 1550–1850 / by Ronald
    P. Toby.
Description: Leiden ; Boston : Brill, [2019] | Series: Brill's Japanese
    studies library, ISSN 0925-6512 ; volume 65 | Includes bibliographical
    references and index.
Identifiers: LCCN 2018057774 (print) | LCCN 2018060452 (ebook) | ISBN
    9789004393516 (ebook) | ISBN 9789004390621 (hardback : alk. paper)
Subjects: LCSH: Japan—Ethnic relations—History. | Aliens—Japan—History. |
    National characteristics, Japanese—History. | Other (Philosophy)—Social
    aspects—Japan—History. | Japan—Foreign relations—1600–1868.
Classification: LCC DS832.7.A1 (ebook) | LCC DS832.7.A1 T63 2019 (print) |
    DDC 305.800952/0903—dc23
LC record available at https://lccn.loc.gov/2018057774

Typeface for the Latin, Greek, and Cyrillic scripts: "Brill". See and download: brill.com/brill-typeface.

ISSN 0925-6512
ISBN 978-90-04-39062-1 (hardback)
ISBN 978-90-04-39351-6 (e-book)

For Yuko

∵

Contents

Acknowledgements

Souls of poets dead and gone,
What Elysium have ye known—
Happy field or mossy cavern
Choicer than the Mermaid Tavern.
JOHN KEATS[1]

∴

We historians inevitably pass many days and months in silent conversation with "souls of poets dead and gone," figures of the near or distant past about whom we write, time alone with their diaries, letters, and random jottings; with their paintings, prints, maps, and artifacts. We often imagine ourselves as solitary searchers in the archives, and to an extent, of course, we are. Yet our work is also highly social, a tapestry woven of relationships, not only by our engagement with both our subjects and our audience, but even moreso by engagement with family, friends, colleagues, students, and the larger world in which we live and work. They sustain and enrich our work with their interest, encouragement, and criticism, often without fully realizing how critical their contributions are.

All scholarship therefore rests on a foundation of countless moral and intellectual debts, great and small, and my own is no exception in this regard. In researching and writing his book, which has matured over the course of many years' inquiry, I have been exceptionally fortunate to benefit from wisdom generously offered by friends and colleagues, whose patience, insight, and criticism have helped me beyond measure.

A chance suggestion in 1985 from Michael Cooper, then editor of *Monumenta Nipponica*, that I take a look at some "newly discovered" Edo-era paintings of Koreans that had recently been covered in the Japanese press, began me on the winding path that led eventually to the writing of this book. I had, of course, been aware for many years of early modern Japanese paintings, prints, and book illustrations depicting Korean, Ryukyuan, and other foreign sojourners in Japan, but had seen them primarily as exceptionally interesting and vivid

---

1 Keats, "Lines on the Mermaid Tavern," at www.poetryfoundation.org/poems-and-poets/
poems/detail/44476.

illustrations—examples that could tell me and my readers, e.g., "this is what a Korean embassy parade looked like." Michael's suggestion, which bore fruit in an article for *Monumenta* the following year, opened my eyes to these works of art as a discursive medium which, with appropriate theoretical and methodological rigor, one might interrogate to learn what it meant—in Japanese eyes—to be something other than Japanese.

The late Sin Kisu, the independent scholar, *zainichi* activist, and art collector who had found the paintings that Michael Cooper set me to investigating, was ever-generous with ideas, insights—and *sake*—granting access to his collection, introducing me to other collectors, and to people all around Japan who have preserved or revived festival performances rooted in Edo-period variations on the theme of "Koreans embassies visiting Japan."[2] Mr. Sin was instrumental in organizing the first exhibit of art and artifacts related to those embassies, at the Tokyo National Museum (1985) and Korean National Museum (1986), which heightened Japanese and Korean awareness, and catalyzed the discovery of many more textual, visual and folkloric resources that have energized my own research as well as that of many others.

I had not anticipated, however, all the tricky reefs, shoals, and undercurrents that were hidden beneath the surface of this inquiry. The reaction of a Korean-American undergraduate attending an early presentation of this work at Cornell in 1986 brought some of the dangers home to me. It should not surprise anyone that early modern Japanese ideas about Korea and Koreans were neither unambiguously positive, nor congruent with Koreans' self-image, and in my talk I had tried to explain how some of those views—early modern Japanese seeing Korea as a vanquished tributary state, for example—had come into being, and how they affected Japanese attitudes and actions toward Korea. The student's comment made it clear that she had understood me as *advocating*—rather than *analyzing*—what were often deprecatory attitudes toward Korea, which was, if anything, the very antithesis of what I had hoped to do. To that student, and interlocutors like her in other forums, who have questioned and challenged me both to better understanding and to clearer exposition, I am forever grateful.

1   Signs/Meanings

Appointment to a Faculty Fellowship in a Second Discipline from the College of Liberal Arts and Sciences at the University of Illinois enabled me to spend the

2   The term *zainichi* ("in Japan"), short for *zainichi Chōsenjin* or *Zainichi Kankokujin*, generally refers to ethnic Koreans who are long-term residents in Japan.

1987–1988 academic year across the Quad, in the Department of Anthropology, reading cultural anthropology, and auditing seminars with Edward Bruner, Alma Gottlieb, and Ann Anagnost. The pathways revealed in those seminars, and in conversations with Ed, Alma and Ann, and the larger community of anthropologists, especially David W. Plath, have led me to the essential, critical avenues along which I have pursued the sometimes elusive meanings Japanese invested in the system of signs they developed for representing non-Japanese, and generating the shifting boundaries of identity.

Nancy Abelmann, Aoyagi Masanori, Asano Shūgō, E. Taylor Atkins, Misha Auslin, Jim Barrett, Mary Elizabeth Berry, James Boon, Kai-wing Chow, Martin Collcutt, Laurel Cornell, Kevin Doak, Paul Droubie, Byron Earhart, Joshua Fogel, Poshek Fu, Fujii Jōji, the late David Goodman, Alma Gottlieb, the late JaHyun Kim Haboush, Jeffrey E. Hanes, Hashimoto Hiroyuki, Tom Havens, Mette Hjort, David Howell, Rania Huntington, the late Marius B. Jansen, Kanda Yutsuki, Janet D. Keller, Cornelius J. Kiley, Kinoshita Nagahiro, Kinoshita Naoyuki, Kurushima Hiroshi, Harry Liebersohn, Paisley Livingston, Joshua Mostow, Murai Shōsuke, Kate Nakai, Nakao Hiroshi, Oka Eri, Ōkubo Jun'ichi, David W. Plath, Brian Platt, David Prochaska, Jacob Raz, Kenneth Robinson, Sata Yoshihiko, Satō Masayuki, the late Shin Kisu, Henry D. Smith II, Sugimoto Fumiko, Bob Tierney, Royall Tyler, Constantine Vaporis, Kären Wigen, Rod Wilson, Yamaji Hidetoshi, Yamamuro Shin'ichi, Yoshida Mitsuo and Yoshida Nobuyuki have offered advice, read and commented on all or part of the manuscript at critical junctures along the way; their generosity of spirit and acuity of insight have helped me to refine arguments, to focus ideas, and to improve my prose.

In the critical final stages of preparing the manuscript to send if off to Brill, Kate Babbitt, historian, documentarist, and editor extraordinaire, went through the entire draft with what I can only call dispassionate commitment. Kate rendered out excess, leaving a leaner text, with subtler textures and flavors than my efforts alone might have served up.

Curators at museums, archives, and private collections in Japan, Korea, the U. K., and the United States, who have opened their collections to me deserve special mention, for without their remarkably generous willingness to grant access to the treasures they contain, little of this work would have been possible. I am especially grateful to Norma and Howard Lee; the late Mary Griggs Burke and her curators, Stephanie Wada and Sandy Williams; Money Hickman and Ann Morse (Museum of Fine Arts, Boston); Yamamoto Yūko (Nagoya City Museum); Tanaka Atsuko (Kawagoe Museum); the late Sin Kisu; Miyoshi Tadayoshi and Oka Yasumasa (Kobe Museum); Takafuji Harutoshi (Nikkō Tōshōgū); Barbara Brennan Ford (Metropolitan Museum of Art); Margaret Glover (New York Public Library); James Ulak (Freer Gallery). Janice Katz (Art Institute of Chicago) invited me to curate a small exhibition at the Institute in

2007, "Alien Images: Foreigners in Japanese Prints, 17th–19th Century," which stimulated further articulation of my ideas about the perception and representation of non-Japanese in Japanese discourse. Roger Keyes introduced me to a key work of Suzuki Harunobu (Fig. 7.14) that catalyzed profound changes in the way Chapter 7 has evolved.

In Japan, I have been uncommonly fortunate in the hospitality afforded me over many years by the Historiographical Institute (*Shiryō Hensanjo*) at University of Tokyo, both during several extended periods of formal affiliation as a Visiting Scholar, in the 1970s, 80s and 90s, as a frequent short-term visitor during brief trips to Japan over the years, and during my tenure as a professor in the University of Tokyo's Graduate School of Humanities and Sociology. The faculty of the Historiographical Institute—more than fifty immensely erudite and talented historians of premodern Japan—were always welcoming, and the unfettered access to their remarkable library. It is surely the most comprehensive collection of both manuscript and printed original source materials and historical journals and monographs, and a resource I have learned to rely on more than any other. Gonoi Takashi, who had the dubious pleasure of sharing his office with an ever-changing parade of visiting overseas scholars at the Institute, graciously guided me to important Jesuit correspondence I would not likely have found otherwise; I am ever grateful for his quiet erudition and unfailing good cheer, as I am to his assistant, Ōhashi Akiko. Over the years, Hotate Michihisa, Ishigami Eiichi, Katō Tomoyasu, Komiya Kiyora, Kurushima Noriko, Miyachi Masato, Miyazaki Katsumi, Sata Yoshihiko, the late Takagi Shōsaku, the late Tanaka Takeo, Tsuruta Kei, Yamamoto Hirofumi, and Yokoyama Yoshinori have been uncommonly generous with their expertise and advice.

It is a particular pleasure to acknowledge my profound intellectual and personal debt to Kuroda Hideo, who has been generous beyond measure with ideas, sources, and criticism. I was particularly fortunate to encounter Kuroda, who has been a pioneer in the reading of visual materials as historical texts—what he terms *kaiga shiryō*—in the early stages of my project. Kuroda shares not only an interest in the visual as historical, but in the construction and representation of boundaries—difference—in Japanese history. In *Medieval of the Boundary; Medieval of the Symbol*,[3] Kuroda had begun to "deconstruct the map" well before J. B. Harley's exhortation.[4] Whenever I was in Tokyo, daily conversations in our favorite *Mermaid Tavern*—the "Mrs. Moa" coffee shop,

3   Kuroda (1986).
4   Harley (1989).

itself now dead and gone, opposite Tokyo University's *Akamon* ("Red Gate")—gave me the benefit of his immense interdisciplinary erudition, seemingly limitless familiarity with both written and visual texts, piercing Socratic interrogation, and insatiable appetite for knowledge and understanding. His methodological and interpretive rigor, his intellectual passion, relentlessly probing questions, and his introductions to entirely new sorts of materials, have immeasurably enriched this work.

If, as Tip O'Neill observed, "Money is the mother's milk of politics," the same is true of scholarship. Without the generosity of the University of Illinois and a number of foundations, this project would never have come to fruition. I began the project while on a Fulbright Fellowship-Hays Faculty Research Fellowship at Keio University in 1984–85. Much of the research was done during several extended research visits to the Historiographical Institute at Tokyo University, and a year as Visiting Professor at the Institute for Research in the Humanities at Kyoto University. I am grateful to both institutes for providing a stimulating, intellectually rewarding environment in which to work. Research for this paper has been supported by a travel grant from the Northeast Asia Council of the Association for Asian Studies, a William & Flora Hewlett Summer Research Grant from the Office of International Programs and Studies, University of Illinois; a Japan Foundation Professional Fellowship, a Senior Research Fellowship and a Summer Research Fellowship from the National Endowment for the Humanities, and a Japan Society for the Promotion of Science Fellowship; the Institute for Research in the Humanities of Kyoto University; grants from the Toyota Foundation, the University of Illinois Research Board, the Center for East Asian & Pacific Studies of the University of Illinois, and the Cultural Affairs Agency, Japan, provided funding for research assistants, travel, and photography, and other research needs. I am deeply grateful to these organizations for their generosity.

Earlier versions or sections of several chapters in this volume have appeared previously in either English or Japanese, but have been substantially revised and expanded here. An earlier version of Chapter 2, "The Ragged Edges of State and Nation," was published as "Kyōkai ryōiki no kinsei-teki ninshiki: Nihon-zu o chūshin ni," in *Chizu to ezu no seiji bunkashi* (Kuroda Hideo *et al.*, ed. 2001), Chapter 3, "Imaging and Imagining Anthropos," is a revised and expanded version of an article that appeared in *The Visual Anthropology Review* (Toby 1998a); parts of Chapter 4 appeared as "The Indianness of Iberia and Changing Japanese Iconographies of Other," in *Implicit Understandings* (Toby 1994b). Chapter 5, "Parades of Other, Reaffirmations of Self," has been substantially revised from "Gaikō no gyōretsu/gyōretsu" (Toby 1994a); Chapter 6, "The Birth of the Hairy Barbarian," has been revised from "'Ketōjin' no tōjō o megutte" (Toby

1997); and parts of Chapter 7, "The Mountain That Needs No Interpreter," appeared in much shorter form as "Kan-Nihonkai no Fugaku enbō" in a volume I co-edited with Aoyagi Masanori, *Kanryū suru bunka to bi* (Toby 2002), further revised as Chapter 6 in *"Sakoku" to iu gaikō* (Toby 2008).

In the end, of course, even the best efforts of friends and colleagues can help an author only so far in improving the work and steering clear of error, interpretive or empirical. As I have watched my own understanding of both—of seemingly minor empirical details, and broad interpretive frameworks—form and re-form over the years, I have become even more intensely conscious of the fragile nature of the interpretive enterprise. Interpretation is, after all, an inevitably inexact and provisional endeavor. For whatever errors may remain, whether matters of fact or of interpretation, I alone am responsible.

Finally, to my wife Yuko, whose wit, warmth, and love have sustained me throughout the many years this book has gestated, evolved, and—yes—occasionally seemed to stall in its tracks, I owe far more than a few dedicatory words can possibly measure.

2   Some Practical Matters

At the practical level, I use the standard Romanization systems, Modified Hepburn for Japanese and Ryukyuan, McCune-Reischauer for Korean, and Pinyin for Chinese, throughout, except when quoting a western-language text that employs its own transcription, e.g., contemporary European writers like Engelbert Kaempfer or Rutherford Alcock who, in any case, predate the invention of standard, systematic transcription schemes. All Japanese, Korean, Chinese and Ryukyuan names in the text, notes, and references appear in standard order, i.e., with the family name preceding the given name; an exception is made for names of modern authors writing in English and signing themselves in Western name-order. I omit macrons for terms that have entered the English dictionary, such as "shogun" and "daimyo," and common toponyms like "Osaka" and "Tokyo." All translations are my own, unless otherwise noted.

Words in Chinese orthography can be pronounced as "Chinese," "Korean," or "Japanese" words, and transliterated as such. Even in "Chinese," the Pinyin system transcribes only the pronunciation of standard modern Chinese ("Mandarin"), which is but one of many regional dialects. A Japanese word like *Tōjin*, for example, would be read *Tangren* in modern Mandarin, but *T'angin* in modern Korean, though seventeenth or eighteenth century pronunciation was surely different in each of these languages, as well as from region to region within each. Moreover, the Chinese who came to Japan were for the most part from Fujian, where a distinct dialect was spoken that was (and is) quite different from the Beijing standard. Representing the parlance of early modern maritime China in modern Mandarin is no more than a convention and convenience, but it will have to do.

A Word about Language

Producing, or reading, any work of history or ethnography is fundamentally a series of translation acts—across time and space, across language and culture. Both authors and readers must constantly remind themselves that language is constantly changing. To paraphrase the medieval poet, critic, and priest Kamo no Chōmei (1153?–1216), the flow of language is ceaseless, and yet the words are never the same:[1] Writing about peoples or cultures of one time and place, for an anticipated audience of another, writing in one language of lives or practices lived in another, inescapably entails choices of language and representation that are, each of them, multiple acts of translation.

Some would argue as well that writing from the subject position of an American academic about aspects of a Japanese past entails still further translations, and I would be the last to dispute that; still, I would argue that no-one writing today about the distant past can claim to be writing as anything but an outsider. The past is, decidedly, "another country," all of whose inhabitants are gone; only their words, acts, and artifacts remain. It is the historian's craft to fashion meaning from those leavings, and this is above all an exercise in translation. An extended inquiry into the practice of history as a series of translation acts will have to await another opportunity, but some acknowledgement of the process is essential if we are to maintain some self-awareness of our own agency in the work.

The texts, artifacts, and practices examined in these essays were mediated, in the main, by the symbolic field of early modern Japan, both linguistic and non-linguistic, a field in which multiple, shifting registers of discourse necessarily cohabited, but the modes of cohabitation shifted over time. The explosive expansion of literacy beyond the religious and ruling elite, the emergence of a vast and highly ramified and specialized publishing industry, and the growth of reading not only as a consumer practice—the consumption of books as cultural commodities producing new forms of cultural capital—were both products of and precursors to a proliferation of linguistic registers. Texts were produced in "Japanese," of course, but even that seemingly simple label belies the varieties of language it entailed; it is no accident that language itself became an arena of ideological and political contestation.

---

1   Kamo (1956), *Hōjōki*, opens with a sentence known to every Japanese schoolchild: *Kawa no nagare wa taezu shite, shikamo moto no mizu ni arazu* (In Donald Keene's [1955, 197] rendering, "The flow of the river is ceaseless and [yet] its water is never the same." Kamo, born into a prominent line of Shinto priests, took the tonsure as a Buddhist priest at age fifty.

But more importantly, for our purposes, even texts that were "Japanese" might simultaneously be "in Chinese." Writing, of course, first appeared in the Japanese archipelago in the form of written Chinese—legal, religious, diplomatic, administrative, and literary; to be a "literate Japanese" at the highest level, even in the early modern era, meant the ability to produce and consume texts, not only in any register of written Japanese, but in Chinese, as well. At the same time, as David Lurie, Emanuel Pastreich, and others have shown, the production or reading by Japanese of what appears on the surface to be a Chinese text—no matter how seemingly fluent—is inevitably a form of "Japanese language." And even among those who "knew" Chinese, knowledge was invariably limited to the literary language or, from the late seventeenth century, the written vernacular of popular Chinese fiction; almost no-one learned to speak Chinese.[2]

From earliest times, Japanese readers and writers developed what one might call "translation machines," or at least, a "mechanics of translation," to turn a grammatically, syntactically, and graphically Chinese text into Japanese. The nexus of practices through which this was accomplished are known collectively as *Kanbun*, a term which seems simply to mean, "Chinese text," but refers to this translation system. My late mentor Herschel Webb distinguished *Kanbun* from "Chinese," by suggesting—perhaps a bit too broadly—that whenever the seemingly Chinese text was operated upon by a Japanese actor, either as writer or reader, the product was *Kanbun*.

Early modern Japanese writers and readers took full advantage of *Kanbun*, often without consciousness of the linguistic boundary transgressions inherent in the practice. Indeed, both the official language of legal texts, and the informal language in daily use had long since incorporated *Kanbun* locutions, phrases taken wholesale from Chinese but assigned domesticated significations, and purely Japanese locutions that came to be written in *faux* Chinese grammar and syntax. By the seventeenth century if not earlier, Japanese were producing entire texts in *faux* Chinese—not texts that tried but failed to be "proper" Chinese, but texts that consciously exploited the grammar and syntax of Chinese, and the translation practices of *Kanbun*, to create texts that *looked* Chinese, but were intended to be read as Japanese, and to exploit the Otherness of Chinese for comic purposes.

---

2 Best known of these is the Confucian scholar Ogyū Sorai (1666–1728), though it is not certain how well he had mastered spoken Chinese. Less well-known, but surely more fluent, was Amenomori Hōshū (1668–1755), a Confucian scholar employed by the daimyo of Tsushima, who studied spoken Chinese in Nagasaki, and Korean in Pusan.

I dwell on this *faux* Chinese because it became a favored medium for messages about the Other: Prose and poetry *about* the Other, in what might be mistaken for the language of the Other, to be read as comic prose or verse *in Japanese*. Ōta Nanpo (1749–1823), for example, a minor bakufu official but a major wit and prolific writer, was a master of comic expression in *faux* Chinese, both prose and poetry, and often chose that medium as the *langue* for his scathing commentary on Japan's Others. Much of what Nanpo wrote in this vein—or any vein, for that matter—we would find outrageously discriminatory or "racist" (if "race" were a meaningful notion in eighteenth-century Japan), but Nanpo's wit was "no respecter of persons," and happily roasted all sacred cows to a crisp.

This brings me to the most delicate of linguistic matters. My own linguistic range is relatively limited—the brand of American English on which I was raised, nearly fifty years' more-or-less daily use of Japanese, an atrophying knowledge of Korean, a reading knowledge of literary Chinese, and the smatterings of Latin, French and a few other languages imperfectly acquired in youth, and mostly forgotten, that remain with me today. In none of these languages can I think of a term for outsiders—foreigners, outcasts, minorities—that is not, at least potentially, freighted with deprecation. Even a seemingly simple and straightforward word like "foreigner," with an appropriately sneering inflection, quickly becomes a pejorative. Even a term for the Other that seems to be chosen as neutral or respectful seem invariably to morph quite quickly into a term of opprobrium or disrespect, so long as the underlying disrespect and discrimination persist.

The historical engagement of Japan with its Others inevitably brings with it the baggage of pejorative vocabulary in which the Other was spoken in popular discourse. Chapter 6, "The Birth of the Hairy Barbarian," explicitly engages one of the best known of these pejoratives, but other unhappy terms for Other bob through the texts examined here like flotsam on a stormy sea. Most problematic is the Japanese term *Tōjin* (Ch., *Tangren*), the most common term for Chinese in particular and for foreigners in general in the broad parlance of the early modern age. At its most benign and "literal,"[3] in Japanese discourse *Tōjin* meant a "Chinese person," and more narrowly, a person from Tang dynasty China (618–907). In the maritime world of early modern China, overseas Fujian merchants identified themselves as *Tangren*, but it is unlikely that

---

3 To assert a "literal" meaning is to suggest that there is a precise one-to-one correspondence between signifier and signified; only one "correct" translation for each word. (*The American Heritage Dictionary*, 4th ed. [2000], defines "literal" as, "Being in accordance with, conforming to, or upholding the exact or primary meaning of a word or words.").

Japanese in early modern times referred to Chinese and other foreigners as *Tōjin* simply because that is what Fujianese called themselves.

But *Tōjin* had an independent life as a Japanese term. It appears in late eleventh century texts, for example, over a century and a half after the fall of the Tang dynasty in China, and a century after the establishment of the Song.[4] A witty mid-sixteenth century Japanese dictionary notes that, "Even when the *Tōjin* blows his nose, he does it in rhyme";[5] a few years later, a more sober-minded Buddhist prelate records an exchange of gifts with some *Tōjin*;[6] while an early seventeenth century wit's list of "high things" (*takaki mono*) included "Mt. Sumeru [the Buddhist *axis mundi*], kingship, the Heavenly Realm of Non-cognition, the pagoda at Tōji, [and] the *Tōjin*'s nose."[7] The attribution of a tall (*i.e.*, "big") nose to *Tōjin* suggests that by the turn of the seventeenth century, *Tōjin* had already enlarged its capacity to envelop all "foreigners," for it was the recently-encountered Europeans (*Nanban*; "southern barbarians") who were usually seen—and represented—as having large noses.

In common parlance, then, *Tōjin* was both a specific name for "Chinese," and an *omnium gatherum* for the generic Other. In most contexts, though, as a term for people from Ming and Qing China, from Korea, the Ryukyus, or Southeast Asia, it was unquestionably pejorative, much as "Chinaman" is in English. I have wrestled with the question of translation, and have chosen to offer this brief explanation of *Tōjin*, rather than to render it into an English equivalent. To translate it as "Chinese" or "foreigner" is to be both too "literal" and too narrow, on the one hand, and over-determined on the other, for any single translation effaces the penumbra of other significations. And to translate it as "Chinaman," it seems to me, is not only needlessly offensive to our ears; at the same time it merely emphasizes the pejorative, while eliding the more-or-less neutral valences of the term.

I have therefore chosen to carry *Tōjin* across (*trans-latus*) the linguistic divide; its very strangeness to our ear emphasizes that it signifies Otherness, and recalls the multivocal valences of strangeness that it signified to Japanese as they wrote or spoke, read or heard, painted or viewed, images of the Other. It was precisely in dialogic engagement with *Tōjin*, writ large, that Japanese constructed and confirmed identity: Just as there is an almost limitless inventory of deprecatory visions of the *Tōjin* in all registers of Japanese discourse, from comic routines (*rakugo*) to scholarly debate, there were also many who

---

4   The Mother of Jōjin, *Jōjin Ajari Haha no shū* (1073), quoted in NKD (2: 982).
5   *Gyokujinshō* (1536), quoted in *ibid.*
6   Shōnyo (1966–1968, 1: 545), entries of Tenbun 16/8/13; 16/6/20 (1547/9/26; 1546/10/3).
7   Uzumasa Munemura, *Inu makura* (1606), quoted in NKD (2000–2002).

spoke with either admiration or detachment of foreign—especially Chinese, but Korean as well—ideas, institutions, and cultural models. While the word *Tōjin* was rarely the term of choice for those who held up Chinese ideas and institutions as ideals, it seems best to let context determine content; otherwise, we would need a half-dozen translations for it.

1   **Some Practical Matters**

At the practical level, I use the standard Romanization systems, Modified Hepburn (Japanese), McCune-Reischauer (Korean), and Pinyin (Chinese) throughout, except when quoting a western-language text that employs its own transcription, e.g. European writers like Engelbert Kaempfer or Rutherford Alcock who predate the invention of standard transcription schemes. I omit macrons for terms that have entered the English dictionary, such as "shogun," and common toponyms like "Osaka" and "Tokyo." All Japanese, Chinese, and Korean names in the text, notes, and references appear in standard order, i.e., family name preceding given name; an exception is made for names of modern authors writing in English and signing themselves in Western name-order. All translations are my own, unless otherwise noted.

Figures

Between Engagement and Imagination

Identity is a psychic sense of place. It's a way of knowing that I'm not a rock or that tree. I'm this other living creature over here…. I am not necessarily what's around me. I become separate from that even though I'm a part of that. And it's being able to make those differentiations clearly that lets us have an identity.

NTOZAKE SHANGE[1]

• • •

So basic is the cleavage that a decisive component of the self-identity of Jews and Arabs [in Jerusalem] alike is not who they are, but rather, who they are not….

MERON BENVENISTI[2]

• • •

When you turn the corner and run into yourself, then you know that you have turned all the corners that are left.

LANGSTON HUGHES[3]

∴

Identities, collective as well as individual, are constructed in complex dialectical processes that we are only beginning to understand, processes that entail a constant tension between discourses of identity and similitude—of community and shared characteristics and interests on the one hand ("I am human, just like you; you are Greek, just like me") and discourses of difference and dissimilarity, conflict and uniqueness ("I am a unique individual; you are a foreigner") on the other. Without the former, we and our communities

---

1 Shange (1992).
2 Benvenisti (1988, 34–37, 66–72).
3 Hughes (1958/1990); Hughes (1959).

are atomized, isolated, anomic; without the latter, we are submerged, over-whelmed, autistic.

> THE JUDGE: Look here: you've got to be a model thief if I'm to be a model judge. If you're a fake thief, I become a fake judge. Is that clear? ...
>   THE JUDGE: (*To the Executioner, going up to him*): Ah! Ah! your plea-sure depends on me.... (*He pretends to look at himself in the Executioner.*) Mirror that glorifies me! Image that I can touch, I love you.... (*To the Thief*) And without you too, my child. You're my two perfect complements.... Ah, what a fine trio we make! (*To the Thief*) But you, you have a privilege that he hasn't, nor I either, that of priority. My being a judge is an emana-tion of your being a thief. You need only refuse—but you'd better not!—need only refuse to be who you are—what you are, therefore who you are—for them to cease to be ... to vanish, evaporated. Burst. Volatilized. Denied.[4]

Genet's judge knows he cannot be his Self without his Others. For Freud, among many psychoanalytic philosophers, such discourses of difference are primary, fighting, as it were, against discourses of similitude. The formation of the "individual" is a constant process of self-differentiation, of the discovery and the achievement of separations—from mother/father, from home—to the constitution of a unique, autonomous, and "healthy" individuated self. At the collective level, as well, Freud returns often to a discourse of difference, stated most forcefully in *Civilization and Its Discontents*. Freud sees in the formation and maintenance of identities a "narcissism of petty differences" (*Narzissmus der kleinen Differenzen*), a compulsion to distinguish oneself—one's collective self—from those one feels are most uncomfortably proximate and similar. For Freud, the exemplars were "communities with adjoining territories, and related closely to each other in other ways as well, who are engaged in constant feuds and in ridiculing each other—like the Spaniards and Portuguese, for instance, the North Germans and South Germans, the English and Scotch, and so on."[5]

But there are other, equally powerful, discourses at work in making us and our communities—"with-nesses"—who we are. As David Plath has shown, people situate themselves, constitute the narratives through which they "tell"

---

4 Genet (1960, 15; 19).

5 Freud (1961, 72). Genet, Freud et al. would have appreciated the "Classification of Visible Minority," promulgated in Canadian administrative law, June 15, 2009, which likewise defines by negation, by who is *not* a visible minority: "This category includes persons who are non-Caucasian in race or non-white in colour and who do not report being Aboriginal." (http://www.statcan.gc.ca/eng/concepts/definitions/minority01a, accessed 2016/09/20).

themselves "who they are," in discourses of commonality, of shared experience and affective bonds, particularly those with whom we partake of "long engagements," those interactions and interdependencies—or hostilities—that take place over the *longue durée* of our lives.[6] As identities are socially constructed, it is these "consociates," Plath argues, with whom we "convoy" through the years, who share and affirm our narratives of selfhood, and without them we are unlikely ever to form an identity at all. The protective convoy of consociates buffers us from atomization and anomie, fixes us in the body social, and constitutes meaning in our lives.

Collectivities and "affinity groups," as they are now called, likewise form consociative discourses of similitude—we Manhattanites/Yalies/Medes/police are an indivisible, yet beleaguered community sustained by narcissistic discourses of difference—we are better than Brooklynites/Harvard/Persians/lawyers.[7] Some sets of symbolic community may simultaneously transcend a single group and join it to others—"Jewish," "Christian," "Muslim," "Hindu," "Buddhist"—while at the same time separating its elements—"Ashkenazi/Sephardi," "Catholic/Protestant," "Shiite/Sunni." Freud's *Narzissmus*, of course, can further fragment any collective identity: "Ashkenazi" into "Litvak/Galicianer," "Catholic" into Roman vs. Eastern Rite, "Orthodox" Christianity into Greek and Russian....

While language, territory, and power may ultimately have separated France from England, Christianity united them, at least until Henry VIII took England out of the Church, in a discourse of similitude vis-à-vis Muslim difference. On the other hand, a community of Confucian and Buddhist heritage did little to inhibit intense and sometimes virulent discourses of distinction and mutual disdain between Japan and Korea in premodern times. Nor did it prevent Japan from claiming a serendipitous effacing of distinction when it claimed to be liberating "fellow Asians" from European domination—only to introduce new modes of domination.

---

6 Plath (1980).

7 From a distance, the Brooklyn/Manhattan dichotomy may be invisible, Yale and Harvard merge into an undifferentiated "Ivy League" or "Eastern elite schools," and, as a wag once observed, "One man's Mede is another man's Persian." But from up close, those petty differences are the ones that matter: Manhattan-bound subway entrances in Brooklyn and Queens still bear the legend, "To the City," or "To New York," recalling an earlier time when today's "outer boroughs" were independent of a "New York" that was coterminous with Manhattan Island. One of my college roommates was from Brooklyn, another from Oregon; I was from a Westchester suburb so close that the Empire State Building was visible on clear days. To the Oregonian, I was a New Yorker; to the Brooklynite, I was from "upstate."

As communities, peoples or "nations," then, ultimately we are united, find similitude and community, in this process of differentiating a collective identity from both proximate and distant Others, and at the same time we construct ideologies of mutual equivalence within the collectivity. We exist in a set of concentric and sometimes overlapping spheres of consociative identity, narcissistically separated from imagined Otherness(es) constituted by an imagination of Freud's "petty differences." This process, "the "inscription of alterity within the self ... [means that] the self has to come to terms with the fact that it is also a second and a third person,"[8] that the self is also an Other.

In the chapters that follow, I attempt to unravel some strands of this interplay of similitude and difference in the popular culture of early modern Japan (ca. 1550–1850). My focus will be on the construction of difference between an "imagined community" of Japanese similitude and those I term "proximate Others," those more familiar Others in nearby lands—China, of course, but also the peoples of Korea and Manchuria/Mongolia, Ryūkyū (Okinawa), and Ezo (Hokkaido).[9] The imagined "Japanese" community, of course, was not itself imagined as internally homogeneous; rather, it was structured around its own schemes of internal difference: Legally sanctioned distinctions of status (*mibun*) and rank (*kakushiki*), as well as age, gender and occupation (*shoku*), distinctions often rendered visible in hairstyles, clothing, accessories and body language, as well as audible in finely graded patterns of diction—from grammar and vocabulary to modulations of voice.[10]

Yet the urgency with which Japanese confronted difference in the early modern era, while perhaps less pressing than the discourses of difference between what were constructed as "white" and "black" in the formation of American literature and identity,[11] was substantively greater than it had been

---

8   Young (1990, 124).

9   Anderson (1992). I arrive at the notion of "proximate Other" as a contrast to what Todorov (1985) has called "radical difference," a sense of separation beyond the limits of existing discourse.

10   On *mibun*, see Asao Naohiro (2004); Tsukada, (2006); Wakita Osamu (2001). Two multivolume series, Yoshida Nobuyuki, *et al.* (2000); Yoshida, *et al.* (2006–2008), offer a good summario of the state of the art in *mibun* studies. In recent English-language scholarship, Howell (2005); Ooms (1996).

11   See especially Toni Morrison's compelling elucidation of the indispensability of "Africanist" others to the formation of American literature: "What Africanism became for, and how it functioned in, the literary imagination is of paramount interest because it may be possible to discover, through a close look at literary 'blackness,' the nature—even the cause—of literary 'whiteness.' What is it for? What parts do the invention and development of whiteness play in the construction of what is loosely described as 'American'?" (1992, 9).

in the previous millennium and the confrontation was far more urgent as a consequence of the encounter with new, more extreme forms of alterity, what Todorov has termed the "radical difference" that characterized the Age of Encounter (ca. 1450–1650). In that era, Japanese merchants, pirates, and adventurers voyaging as far afield as the Gulf of Bengal crossed paths with the Europeans who had entered East Asian waters in the wake of Columbus, da Gama, and Magellan. These early overseas encounters have left no impression in the Japanese record, however. It was only when the new European Other arrived in Japan in the 1540s that these radical alterities impinged sufficiently on the consciousness of record-keepers—diarists, chroniclers, letter-writers, artists—to be inscribed in durable form.

In the encounter, cosmologies clashed all around the globe, as one people after another discovered the "brave new world" beyond earlier imagining. What the encounter with radical difference meant to Europe or Africa, the Americas or China, for example, is beyond the scope of this brief study. In Japan, the confrontation with the radical alterities of Europe, of the Americas, and of a maritime and continental Asia beyond China undermined long-standing cosmologies, introduced a theretofore unimaginable multitude of possible Others and provoked a crisis of collective identity. That crisis required, or at least precipitated, the collapse of previous distance and difference between what was constructed as Japan and its familiar, long-known Others—principally articulated as "China" (*Shintan* or *Kara*). Conventional Japanese cosmology posited a world comprised of the "three countries" (*sangoku*) of *Honchō* ("this country"; also *Wagachō*, "our country"), *Shintan* or *Kara* (both "China" and "the continent"), and a distant *Tenjiku*, often rendered "India," but perhaps more appropriately envisioned as a cross between the land of the Buddha and a sort of trans-*Kara*—everything beyond China.[12]

The Age of Encounter was characterized by a fragmentation of identities for virtually every player in the first drama of globalization. Japanese, as much as Spaniards and Caribs, English and Algonquians, French and Iroquoians, Portuguese and Goans, experienced the collapse of long-established cosmologies under the weight of a suddenly expanded universe of Others. The challenge to identity, never a simple binary relationship between monolithic selves and others, was profound, for Other became myriad in its varieties and itself

---

12   In the 1590s and early 1600s, at least, to mean "Siam." (Collegio 1603; Doi 1980, 554; 654) Japanese were of course aware of the Korean kingdoms, both ancient and contemporary. In the metaphor of *Sangoku*, however, Korea was most often subsumed within *Shintan* and, as we shall see below, Koreans were visually represented as indistinguishable from Chinese.

more internally differentiated. For Japan, as both the geographic and epistemic distance from "China" suddenly imploded under the impact of "Southern Barbarians," "Red-Hairs," and "Blacks," Japanese strove to reestablish distance and difference from those familiar, proximate Others of Korea, China, Ezo and Ryukyu, and move them discursively further from the boundaries of Japanese identity.

From about the turn of the seventeenth century, consequently, Japanese displayed an urgency to reestablish a sense of distance and difference from those familiar Others, from "Chinese" (*Tōjin*) of every stripe—Ming, Korean, Ryukyuan, Mongol.... Meanwhile the notion of "Chinese" (*Tōjin*), polyvocal to begin with, expanded its compass to subsume all forms of human alterity: The German physician Engelbert Kaempfer, a sojourner in Japan in 1690–1692, was just one of many European or American visitors between the seventeenth and nineteenth centuries to report being tagged a *Tōjin*.[13] Visual, verbal, and performative modes of expression were absorbed as never before in the representation of Other, both to carve out a buffer zone of difference between what it meant to be "Japanese" and not-"Japanese" and to begin differentiating Other more finely.

Prior to the turn of the seventeenth century, for example, Japanese artistic conventions made no clear distinction between representations of "Chinese" and "Korean" subjects. In the opening chapter of *Tale of Genji* (ca. 1000) a fortuneteller from *Koma* (the Korean state of Koryŏ) warns of a dire future for the infant prince if he is not removed from the royal line of succession.[14] Yet when artists rendered that scene, their representation of the prognosticator was invariably indistinguishable from representations of Chinese. And indeed, it was common to think of Koreans as a sort of subspecies of Chinese: When the merchant Enomoto Yazaemon (1625–1686), one of the thousands of spectators when a Korean diplomatic parade entered Edo in 1655, recorded the

---

13   Kaempfer (1727/1906). Etymologically, *Tōjin* (Ch., *Tangren*) means "a person from Tang [dynasty China]" (618–907); as such, it was anachronistic in the context of the seventeenth to nineteenth centuries, but even after the fall of the Tang, Japanese continued to use the word to signify "Chinese." See examples in NKD, 9: 982. Exactly when the signification of *Tōjin* broadened to include other sorts of foreigners—not only Kaempfer, but Koreans, Ryukyuans, and others—is uncertain. Cf. Alcock (1863, 123), de Fonblanque (1863, 117), and Hall (1992, 84; 88–89; 269; 271), for similar encounters.

14   The *Genji* text calls the man a *Koma-udo*, i.e., a person from Koryŏ (i.e., Korea; 936–1392). Koryŏ sent no embassies to the Heian court, so some commentators identify this "Koma" with Parhae (J., *Bokkai*; Ch., *Bohai*; 698–926), also called *Koma* in Japan (Yanai Shigeshi *et al.*, ed., [1993]: 1: 19, n. 26; NKD, 5: 1035). But it hardly matters, since the *Genji* is fiction, and the last Parhae mission visited Japan in 919/920—a half-century before Murasaki Shikibu's birth. Ishii (1979–97), 12: 747; Taigai (1999): 103–105.

experience in his diary, he described them not as "Koreans" but as "Chinese from Korea" (*Chōsen Tōjin*).[15]

Yet over the first half of the seventeenth century, a concern for differentiating "Koreans" from "Chinese" became increasingly visible in Japanese discourse. Korean embassies to Japan were a subject that attracted the attention of painters as early as the second decade of the century, but artists lacked a visual rhetoric, a vocabulary of identifying characteristics and a grammar for combining them, that announced the distinctly "Korean" identity of the persons represented. The result was that in the earliest attempts, the "Koreans" emerged as a mélange of signs—"Chinese," "Portuguese," and "Tatar" clothing, hairstyles, and accoutrements—decidedly Other, yet thoroughly generic in their alterity. Not until the second half of the century did painters and printmakers achieved some consensus about what a "Korean" should look like in Japanese art.[16]

This book, then, following Ntozake Shange's and Meron Benvenisti's notions of identity, is as much about what it is not as about what it is. Rather than a monograph that builds along a single line of narrative and argument to a conclusion that resolves a single informing hypothesis, it is a series of interlocked essays, deep soundings in the shifting shoals of identity and difference that emerged in early modern Japan. While each chapter both builds on and undergirds its companions, their relation to each other and to the larger project has more in common with the spokes that sustain a wheel—all radiating from a common hub, supporting a common rim—that may be steered in many directions, than they do with a road or rail line that goes only in one.

Sixteenth- to nineteenth-century Japan forms the empirical stage for this exploration; yet what "Japan" signifies in those centuries is by no means identical to what it signifies today. Setting aside, for the moment, such matters as political structures and legal frameworks—which, of course, were not constant in any case—questions of what constituted Japan, in terms of both human and territorial geography, were resolved quite differently in both Japanese and foreign consciousness. At a fundamental level, therefore, I propose arguments that will, I hope, advance or clarify our understanding of the dynamics of cultural production and reception, the processes of identity formation, and the domains of ideology and belief that inform not only the construction of national identities and differences but also the ways in which Japanese—whether

---

15   Ōno (2001, 294).
16   See Toby (1996a, 1:120–129 and accompanying plates, 42–45, 51–53).

as individuals; as communities of residence, craft, or belief; or as political collectivities (the "state"[17])—interacted with what was constructed as Other.

1   Blues and Roots

At the same time, this book both emerges from, and is addressed to, three overlapping and increasingly intertwined domains of theory and practice: history,
anthropology—especially visual anthropology—and art history. My own professional training has been principally that of the historian, schooled primarily
in analysis and narrative of a particular slice of time and space—in my case,
"early modern" time in the spaces of "Japan," "Korea," and "East Asia"—and it is
there that I suppose myself most comfortable.[18] But engaging people of times
gone by solely through the corpus of written records they produced—even
taking "records" here in the broadest possible sense—necessarily limits the
scope of inquiry to the concerns of the literate.

Now, to be sure, by the late seventeenth century, the community of "the literate" likely constituted a proportion of the adult Japanese populace greater
than in almost any other contemporary society.[19] Diary-keeping and letter-
writing were widespread practices even among the (upper) peasantry and
urban bourgeoisie, and reading was a practice that was increasingly taken
for granted, so much so that a *sake* shop in early Edo could announce "We
have *miso*" by posting a written sign to that effect and expect customers to be
able to read it.[20] Prolific writers such as Asai Ryōi (d. 1691) and Ihara Saikaku
(1642–1693) could support themselves in modest luxury on income from their
books, while a haiku master such as Matsuo Bashō (1644–1694) could cover his

---

17   Whether the early modern Japanese polity was a singular "state" under the shogun, or plu-
      ral, sovereign daimyo "states," is the subject of ongoing scholarly debate. For the former
      view, see Toby (2001b); for the latter, Roberts (1998) and Ravina (1999).
18   Such terms as "early modern," "Japan," etc., are contingent and contested; hence the
      scare quotes. Still, they will have to serve, subject to the caveat that they are terms of
      convenience and approximation. Even the ambit of territory labeled "Japan" was a shape-
      shifting (Chapter 2), contested quality in the centuries under discussion—and remains
      so, to a degree, in our own time.
19   On literacy, Dore (1965); Rubinger (2007).
20   A *sake* shop in the Kanda area displays a simple sign, *miso ari*, in the *Edo-zu byōbu* (pair
      of six-panel screens, ca. 1634–1635, color and gold leaf on paper; National Museum of
      Japanese History). A painting of a shop sign is not, of course, a shop sign, yet there is
      little reason to doubt the underlying realism of the depiction of social practices in the
      Edo-zu byōbu. See, for example, Ozawa and Maruyama (1993). On early modern diaries,
      Plutschow (2005); Komiya (2006); Fukaya (2003).

considerable travel expenses with gratuities from poetry circles in rural communities from one end of the country to the other.[21]

Still, privileging the written word obscures much in the lives and consciousness of a large swath of any historical population, not only those who cannot
write but many whose writings are either inherently evanescent or suppressed.
Women's voices, especially, of every social class are so rarely heard—except as
reported by men—as almost to seem systematically effaced from the written
record. A recent search for diaries, letters, or other echoes of women's voices
from the city of Edo in the seventeenth century left me astounded by the pau-
city of traces written by women themselves, the more so since there is so much
from earlier centuries.[22]

This brings me to the question of gender, where it is necessary to note that
in large measure the Other of early modern Japanese imagining was all male.
It is indeed remarkable how few the images of women appear in Japanese representation of Other peoples and Other lands. After a brief dalliance with a bi-
gendered world of Other in late sixteenth and early seventeenth century visual
texts, artists largely effaced women from the vision of the peoples there. There
are important exceptions, to be sure, most significantly in the corpus of eth-
nographic/exotic writing and pictorial representation of the Ainu inhabitants
of Ezo that accumulates from the latter third of the eighteenth century,[23] in
occasional reiterations of seventeenth-century schemas of the peoples of the
world,[24] and in eroticized fictionalizations and visualizations of an imaginary
"China."[25]

Perhaps the most fully realized Edo-period ethnography of a single country,
Nakagawa Tadateru's *Shinzoku kibun* (Customs of the Qing),[26] is a remarkable
work. Tadateru (1753–1830), a mid-level *bakufu* functionary, compiled *Shinzoku
kibun* while serving as magistrate of Nagasaki. Much like Ruth Benedict, who
had to produce an ethnography under conditions that did not allow her access

---

21   On personal and official diaries, Plutschow (2005); Komiya (2006); Fukaya (2003); Barnhill
      (2005, 5) notes that Bashō's journeys were "good for business."

22   Inoue (1682/1973) is the only seventeenth-century Edo diary I have found by a woman;
      there are surely others, but there are surely others as yet unpublished.

23   For example, Mogami (1791/1969, 4:439–484); Hata, Murakami, and Mamiya (ca. 1801,
      4:545–638); for a fuller discussion, Igarashi (2003).

24   An example is Nishikawa (1720/1898), which essentially replicates exemplar male-female
      pairs of late-sixteenth- to mid-seventeenth-century tabular presentations. See Chapter 2
      for a discussion.

25   For an example of such fiction, Hiraga (1770/1961); for a visualization, Kitagawa (1788–1790).

26   Nakagawa (1799) has appeared in a modern annotated (Nakagawa [1966]), and in Chinese
      translation (Nakagawa [2006]). For a provocative use of *Shinzoku kibun* as a source on
      customs of the Qing, see Bray (1997); see also Yamamoto (1994); Muramatsu (1996).

to the country she was studying, Tadateru mobilized the magistracy's interpreters to interview Chinese merchants in Nagasaki for trade, questioning them about kinship and family relationships, social and religious customs, rituals, housing, daily life, agricultural practices, and so on.[27] Since Fujian merchants dominated the Nagasaki trade, it is not surprising that the picture that emerges centers on customs of that region. Though Nakagawa intended only to produce a handbook for port officials in their dealings with Chinese merchants, when *Shinzoku kibun* was published, it proved quite popular well beyond official circles, an index of rising interest in foreign peoples and customs in the early nineteenth century.

Yet voices inaudible in the written record may be recovered, heard in a chorus of nonverbal utterances. "Reading" the nonverbal text, whether the artifacts of daily life, the costumes and implements of popular performance or performance itself, or the extensive visual record created by both professional and amateur artists—or even the very ground over which historical actors walked[28]—has not always been part of what Bloch called "the historian's craft." Learning to do that has entailed a few disciplinary boundary crossings.

Interrogation of Japan's engagement with the Other was the starting point of my academic career, a search for historical roots of the conflicting and conflict-laden ideas that Japanese and Koreans professed about each other in the nineteenth and twentieth centuries and how they interacted with/reacted to each other politically, diplomatically, strategically, and culturally. The historian's desire to explain, to find underlying causes of phenomena, led me to search for early modern roots to the modern Korea-Japan dilemma and ultimately to an exploration of the structures and processes of early modern Japan's relations with the rest of East Asia and the ideologies informing them. That inquiry left no doubt that actors on all sides were motivated as much by received ideas about each other—culturally constructed visions of the Other, though at the time I did not articulate it in quite that way—as by "objective" assessments of "actual" qualities of the Other.

From the first, of course, I was aware that early modern artists, printmakers, and book illustrators had produced images of aliens who had visited Japan—Europeans, Koreans, Ryukyuans, Chinese, and others. The parade of Korean diplomats entering Edo Castle in the *Edo-zu byōbu* (ca. 1634–1635) or marching into the shrine to Tokugawa Ieyasu at Nikkō in the *Tōshōsha engi emaki* (1640)[29]

---

27   Benedict (1946).
28   I have attempted to read that ground and the paths people walked upon it in Toby (2005).
29   *Edo-zu byōbu* (pair of six-panel screens, ca. 1634–1635, National Museum of Japanese History); Kanō Tan'yū, *Tōshōsha engi emaki* (five scrolls, ink and color on paper, Nikkō Tōshōgū Hōmotsuden).

were my news photographs, a chance to see what the historical actors or event "looked like," rather than a set of signs or messages. They were representations not just of the object but also of the producers' and audience's ideas about the object of representation, of "Koreans" or "Ryukyuans," or "Chinese." The choice to foreground the Korean arrival at Edo Castle or at the Nikkō shrine to Ieyasu as central events in the history of those sites or to place "tribute" objects from the Korean or Ryukyuan courts, or the Dutch trading mission, in prominent, publicly visible locations at the shrines to the first and third shoguns were, of course, significant and figured in my analysis as signifying acts. But the depiction of the Koreans or Ryukyuans themselves, the manner of their representation, the representational codes instantiated in those depictions—these did not yet seem to me at the time to hold their own messages.

It was not until the mid to late 1980s that these images spoke to me as more than illustrations of the political, diplomatic, or ideological phenomena that had theretofore interested me most. A chance request from Michael Cooper, then editor of *Monumenta Nipponica*, transformed my approach to the visual archive. The *Asahi shinbun* and other leading Japanese dailies had recently reported a series of "discoveries": several Edo-period paintings had come to light depicting Korean diplomats parading through early modern Japan. Michael's invitation led me to Sin Kisu, a *zainichi Chōsenjin*—an ethnic and juridical Korean born and raised in Japan, an activist, and a self-trained scholar—who had made it his mission to transform contemporary Japanese historical consciousness of the importance of Korea to the national past, and particularly to discover and publicize cultural artifacts generated by the impact of Korea on early modern Japanese consciousness.

Sin, a successful filmmaker and entrepreneur, had edited a volume and produced a documentary film on Edo-era Korean missions to Japan that introduced what, it was becoming clear, was a vast and variegated range of representations across the entire spectrum of early modern expressive culture—not only in painting and sculpture, but in kabuki and festival performance, in fiction and verse.[30] Korean embassies were not simply diplomatic and political events but were also cultural sites where Japanese articulated their own ideas about themselves and the Other, about identity itself.

What I had expected to be a brief note on the two paintings transformed my understanding of visual representation. Where I had earlier seen little more than interesting, off-the-beaten-path images that were handy as *illustrations* in an otherwise verbal article or monograph began to speak to me as *sources* that

---

30   Both the volume and the film shared the same title, *Edo jidai no Chōsen tsūshinshi*, the film produced by Eizō Bunka Kyōkai (1980), the book published by Mainichi Shinbunsha (1979).

embodied the discourse of identity that was to become my central concern. The brief research note grew as I encountered more and more visual representations and began to understand their significance as alternatives or counterpoints to the usual textual sources into a 40-page article that appeared in 1986.[31]

Further exploration and study revealed the not-entirely-unsurprising degree to which representations of "Korea" and "Koreans" in Japanese expressive culture were part of a broader discourse of identity and difference in which Korea/Koreans were but a subset of generic Otherness that was linked to a multiplicity of other specific Othernesses. Korea, that is, appeared on a continuum with "Ryukyu," "China," "Jurchen," and "Ainu," proximate Others who were joined in their difference from Japan and yet increasingly differentiated from each other; they, in turn, shared broad features of alterity with the more radical Others from Europe, South Asia, the Americas, and so forth.

2   Inhabiting

Though it may well be that "a picture is worth a thousand words," the hermeneutic problem remains: For any picture, exactly *which* "thousand words" is it worth? To arrive at a "historical interpretation of pictures"[32] that is not simply idiosyncratic or arbitrary but is rather, in some substantial way, both responsive and responsible to the moment of production or reception is not a straightforward task. If reasonable interpreters can arrive at mutually irreconcilable readings of the same written text that each sees as "true" to the "intentions of the framers" of the text (the recent history of constitutional jurisprudence in the United States comes readily to mind), how can one hope to elicit from nonverbal texts a verbalized interpretation of their meaning(s) or significance?

My approach to nonverbal texts, not just pictures but also parades, dramas, and other forms of performance as well as artifacts, costumes, and fashion, owes a significant debt to earlier work in my original discipline of history and to the disciplines of anthropology and art history. I have been, I suppose, more eclectic and idiosyncratic in grazing those neighboring fields, an eclecticism informed more by the needs of practice than by a unitary theoretical or philosophical stance. Throughout, that is, I have proceeded from the materials that confront me and the questions that compel me to examination of theorists, methodologists, and other practitioners whose work seems to offer the promise of pathways to the goal.

---

31   Toby (1986).
32   Baxandall (1985).

In the first instance, I have found Bourdieu's notion of "the *habitus*" helpful:

> The structures constitutive of a particular type of environment (e.g. the material conditions of existence characteristic of a class condition) produce *habitus*, systems of durable, transposable *dispositions*, structured structures predisposed to function as structuring structures, that is, as principles of the generation and structuring of practices and representations which can be objectively "regulated" and "regular" without in any way being the product of obedience to rules, objectively adapted to their goals without presupposing a conscious aiming at ends of an express mastery of the operations necessary to attain them and, being all this, collectively orchestrated without being the product of the orchestration of a conductor.[33]

One need not share Bourdieu's Marxian materialism to believe that material and nonmaterial cultural products both emerge from and embody or re-produce structures of "practices and representations" and that they signify, have meaning—in the historical or ethnographic sense—only when read as products and producers of those structures of practice and representation. I take this to require the outside interpreter—whether from another time, another place, or another social class—to *inhabit* the context in which practices and representations were either produced or, particularly when reception is at issue, consumed.

This is not to enjoin other modes of interpretation, as the way van Gogh and other early Impressionists interpreted, say, a print by Suzuki Harunobu, or how Picasso saw a Yoruba mask. At that level, all signs have the potential to be "empty" and invested with whatever meaning a serendipitous encounter with radical alterity might call forth—the ignorance of the producers' sign systems and codes of representation with which van Gogh and Picasso approached, interpreted, and appropriated Japanese or African art in no way diminishes the significance of the new modes of representation each was inspired to reach for.

It is only to say that a *historically* or *ethnographically situated* interpretation, one that strives to approach and represent the signification attached to a text in its moment of production or reception, demands a thoroughly different battery of commitments. Those commitments are both empirical and hermeneutical. An empirical commitment to attempt to understand the structures of practice and representation informing a text: With what common sense (in Geertz's sense of "common sense") did the producer(s) or receiver(s) of the

---

33   Bourdieu (1977, 72).

text (performance, print, painting ...) approach and derive meaning (pleasure, pain, amusement, insight ...) from it? How, for example, did they reckon time or space[34]? How did they construct gender? Conceive of power? And so on. This may be an ideal, but it is not entirely unattainable.

Though it may seem tautological, at one level, the need to inhabit moments in which particular texts were produced or consumed entails immersion in myriad texts from those moments. Much as the acquisition of language ultimately—actually, quite early—leads to the production of entirely new, unique utterances that nonetheless signify meanings, producer and receiver are quite likely to agree on and share the vocabulary inhabited by the participants, precisely because they are informed by the rules of grammar and syntax. Words that seemed strange become familiar, significations that were obscure become apparent through repeated, ceaseless participation in the production and consumption of texts.

At the practical level, therefore, I have striven when possible to ground readings of nonverbal texts in verbal ("written") texts as well as in a multiplicity of other nonverbal texts. I do so not because the verbal is necessarily more "true" or "accurate" than the nonverbal but simply because our habits of mind, as well-schooled producers and readers of the written word, *seem*—I underscore "*seem*" here—to make meaning more explicit and less ambiguous in word than in image.

The outlines of a method for deconstructing art in a historically or ethnographically responsible fashion, informed by and reflecting the habitus of production or consumption,[35] have been sketched by the art historian Michael Baxandall, throughout his provocative and important œuvre, but most explicitly in *Patterns of Intention* (though Baxandall does not, to my knowledge, invoke either Bourdieu or "the *habitus*").[36] My encounter nearly thirty years ago with Baxandall's reading of the first railroad bridge to span the Firth of Forth as a "historical object" produced though processes of "purposefulness," embodying agendas ("charge" and "brief" are his terms) of both patron (the North British Rail Company) and producer (architect Benjamin Baker), marks

---

34   See Satō (2004) for a most provocative cross-cultural and cross-temporal exploration of the structure of both temporal and spatial consciousness and the translation of time and space into meaning.

35   "Or": I have a personal aversion to the slashed "and/or" and hope to avoid it at all costs— though I know it is a lost battle in the larger language. Throughout this work, therefore, I use the conjunction "or" in the dual meanings it carries in symbolic logic, where it may signify either exclusive "A or B, but not both," as well as "either A, B, or both A and B."

36   Baxandall (1985).

an important turning point in the development of my own thinking about the ways that pictures and other historical objects mediate not only action but meaning, how they may be not only the products of purpose but the producers of action and ideas.

Baxandall crossed Baker's Forth Bridge as the route to a method applied, in later chapters and succeeding works, to the deconstruction of pictures— of Picasso, della Francesca, and Chardin, among many others. The apparently nonsignifying (but hardly insignificant) bridge, precisely because it seemed on the surface to be merely instrumental, practical, mechanical, industrial— anything but a sign or embodiment of signification—becomes, in Baxandall's hands, the perfect palette to delineate the ways that made objects (and pictures of course among them) embody purposes and messages. Further, though this is less explicit, the bridge's public nature—it is out there at all times, for all to see—and the public, joint-stock nature of the patronage illuminate questions of reception as much as they do issues of production and intention. Both Baker and the directors of North British who employed him were intensely conscious of the bridge as public proclamations of their respective identities that was produced for an anticipated structure of reception that they knew informed public consciousness. The bridge, no less than the *Portrait of Kahnweiler*, could *mean something* only in the context of its reception; to that extent, the bridge and the *Portrait* were co-productions not only between patron and producer but also between them and their audience.[37]

Occasionally a specific verbal text, or a series of verbal texts, quite directly illuminates a nonverbal text. A series of textual utterances in eighteenth- and early-nineteenth-century dramaturgy and poetry, for example, confirms the legitimacy of (that is, authorizes) reading a painting by Hanabusa Itchō that likely dates from the second decade of that century and a print by Suzuki Harunobu that was almost certainly produced in 1763 or 1764 as assuming a direct, unmediated engagement of the Other by Mt. Fuji. This is not an attempt at "intentionalism," imputing to the producer of the text a specific set of intentions not stated in the text, but at attempt at approaching the "systems of durable, transposable *dispositions* ... [the] principles of the generation and structuring of practices and representations,"[38] of producers (consumers) of

---

37 Baxandall's argument, of course, leads inevitably to the problem of authorial intent, and the question of 'intentionalism'—hotly debated in philosophy, literary criticism and art criticism. For a sampling of views, Livingston (1996; 1998); Byrne (2001); Bevir (2002); Brown (2002).

38 Bourdieu (1977).

the text in the context of its production (consumption). That is, not necessarily *did* a particular producer *intend* or a particular consumer *understand* the text in *this way*, but *could* she have done so? Did the discourse in which the creative or hermeneutic act occurred support such a set of meanings as *possible*? This is, after all, the closest we can come to an identity between sign and signification.

CHAPTER 1

Interlude: A Pair of Parables

"In the reign of a certain emperor, it matters not when," His Majesty arose from his slumbers in the Pure Cool Pavilion (*Seiryōden*) and stepped out onto the verandah running under the eaves at the east side of the building.[1] As the imperial gaze swept north along the verandah his eyes rested first on the Pond-of-Brilliance Screens (*Konmei-chi no sōji*, Fig. 1). The south face of the screen allowed the emperor to gaze across the seas and back a millennium or more, to look upon the Pond of Brilliance built at the command of the Chinese emperor Wudi of the Han dynasty (r. 140–86 BCE) on the outskirts of his capital city of Chang'an. Looking beyond the Pond-of-Brilliance Screens, he took in the Wild-Sea Screen (*Ara-umi no sōji*, Fig. 2), at the north end of the verandah, a painted screen that blocked the north end of the corridor from intrusive eyes. The Wild-Sea Screen presented to the emperor's eyes yet another strange, but long-familiar vista of fantastic creatures on a rocky, storm-tossed shore.[2]

1　"In the reign …" (*izure no o'on-toki ni ka*) is, of course, the opening phrase of the *Tale of Genji*.

2　Some authorities read 障子 here as *shōji*; I follow Sei Shōnagon (late 10th c.), who writes it phonetically as sōji さうし. (Ikeda [1963, 43–44]) For placement of the *Wild-Sea Screen*, the *Pond-of-Brilliance Screen* in the Pure Cool Pavilion, and the bamboo plantings in the courtyard, Ōtsu (2001, 317); for the palace compound, ibid., p. 307, or Tyler, trans., (2001, p. 1122). The screens Sei Shōnagon describe, and several subsequent reiterations, were lost to fire; yet each time the imperial palace burned, painstaking efforts were made to reproduce the lost screens as faithfully as possible. The current iterations date from 1855. For a brief discussion of the *Wild-Sea, Pond-of-Brilliance*, and *Sages and Worthies* screens, see Chino (2003, pp. 23f; cf. Chino 1993, 6), who notes that many of the doors and screens surrounding the emperor's quarters paired scenes of "Chinese subject matter" on the side facing the emperor's living quarters, while the reverse sides presented depictions of "Japanese subjects." These screen paintings, she argues, "were based on a double-layered structure of 'Kara' and 'Yamato,'" i.e., China and Japan, that also characterized "Heian cultural identity" writ large. Ōtsu (2001, 323) sees both screens' deployment of Chinese themes as evidence that the mid-Heian emperors were undergirded by a vague but ever-present "something Chinese" (*Chūgoku-teki na mono*). The screens are believed to date from 818 (Eiyū 1965, 185); Heldt (2008, 251) suggests that the subject matter of the *Pond-of-Brilliance Screen* may reflect emperor Saga's (r. 809–823) "desire to see the new urban landscape of Heian-kyō as a modern equivalent to [capitals] of neighboring realms." Chino and Heldt, that is, read the screens within the ambit of what Pollack (1984, 3) calls the "dialectic [of] *wakan* (Chinese-Japanese)." A desire to equate Heian-kyō with an ancient Chinese capital may have been a factor, but since the *Pond-of-Brilliance Screen*, like the *Wild-Sea Screen*, paired the foreign scene on its obverse with a domestic hunting scene on the reverse, one might suggest that the program was at least as concerned with the dichotomy of self and other as with claims to equivalence with the Han capital. These

FIGURE 1   "Pond of Brilliance Screen," as depicted in the *Ban Dainagon emaki* (color on
paper, late 12th c., Idemitsu Museum), is visible behind the man on the veranda.
It depicts a view of the "Pond of Brilliance: (J., *Konmei-chi*; C., *Kunming-chi*)
in the Han Dynasty capital of Changan—a quintessentially alien scene—on
the side facing us, and on the reverse side a scene of falconers at the hunting
grounds of Saga, just west of the Heian capital. The screen was placed at one
entrance to the Japanese emperor's sleeping quarters, with the scene of Changan
facing in toward the emperor's quarters, and the domestic scene at Saga facing
outward, where it greeted persons approaching the emperor's presence.

These scenes were familiar, for Japanese emperors had gazed upon them daily
for time out of mind, yet strange, for the screens were populated by creatures
seen nowhere else. As the Emperor Juntoku (r. 1210–1221) wrote of the Wild-Sea
Barrier he awoke to each day, "On the north [side of the Pure Cool Pavilion]
are the Wild Sea Screens. On the south face is [toward the emperor's cham-
bers], a depiction of Long-arms and Long-legs (*Tenaga; Ashinaga*); on its north
face, net-fishing at Uji. It is painted in ink on silken screens."[3] Two centuries
earlier Sei Shōnagon, an attendant of the empress, had recorded her own and
her peers' response to the untamed scene of what Juntoku calls "Long-arms
and Long-legs": The south face of the screens presented, she wrote, "a scene of
wild seas, and terrifying creatures, [one] long-legged, [the other] long-armed.

---

two readings are not, of course, mutually exclusive and—as Heldt aptly observes—Heian
painting and poetry relied heavily on incorporating multiple, sometimes contradictory
meanings. For further discussion of the screens, Ienaga (1966, 29–30).

3   Emperor Juntoku, *Kinpishō* (1213), quoted in Suzuki (1994, 20).

It's hateful that they're always in view when the doors of Her Majesty's chambers are open."[4]

The south face of the Wild-Sea Screens depicted three deformed man-like beings, naked save for primitive skirts about their waists, who stood upon a rocky shore, the wild surf crashing at their feet. No, to be more accurate, one stood—on long, spindly legs—carrying another on his shoulders, a wild-eyed, shaggy-bearded creature, gripping his burden with stubby, spindly arms that seemed useful for nothing else. Opposite this pair squatted a creature who mirrored the deformities of the first two: his legs were as stubby, but his arms were as long as his companions' legs. Like Jack Spratt and his wife, they complemented each other's shortcomings, "and so, betwixt themselves," they sought shellfish in the surf. The emperor confronted—guarded against—distorted, wild and even threatening, primitive, almost-but-not-quite-human creatures, who lacked even the most rudimentary of technologies; their only means of survival was to gather what food they could with their bare hands.

Daily, since the ninth century, Japanese emperors had thus confronted the Other upon arising in the morning and before lying down at night, symbolically protecting Japan from foreign dangers. Ironically, the outer face of the screen presented to the would-be voyeur a more familiar vista, of Japanese fishermen casting their nets in the rushing waters of the Uji River just southeast of the Heian capital. Consistently throughout the palace, indeed, the subject matter of painted screens surrounding the emperor's person maintained this pattern: arrayed so that the emperor always confronted images of the Other (*Kara-e*), whether fabulous creatures like the *ashinaga* and *tenaga* of the Wild Sea Screens, peaceful scenes of the ancient Chinese capital of Luoyang, or "Chinese" playing polo (*dakyū*), while anyone looking toward the imperial chambers from the outside—the *Oni-no-ma* and *Daiban-dokoro*, for example—saw only "Japanese" scenes (*Yamato-e*).[5] While the emperor, the ideological center of Japanese discourse and politics, looked outward and saw images of the Other, any of his subjects seeking to look in on him were reassured by the sight of things most familiar and domestic: the realm peaceful and secure; its people sustaining themselves through the mediation of technology and civilization.

The emperor next swept his gaze out east across the gardens, one area planted with "Chinese Bamboo" (J. *Kara-take*; Ch., *Hanzhu*), another with "South

4   Sei (1958, 58); Ikeda (1963, 43–44). My italics. My rendering differs from McKinney (2007) and Morris (1967). Sei Shōnagon served in the chambers of the imperial consort Fujiwara no Teishi (976–1000); the screens would have been visible from there.
5   Iwama (2012); Uramatsu (1993).

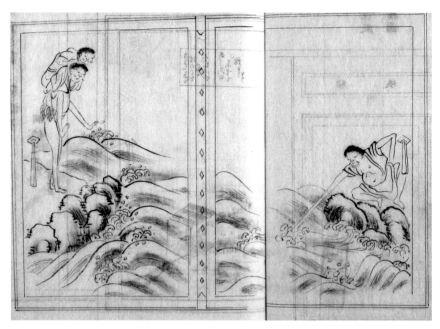

FIGURE 2   The "Wild Sea Screen," sketched here in a late 18th century catalog (Minamoto
1861) of the architecture and artifacts of the imperial palace complex in Kyoto,
like the "Pond of Brilliance Screen," pairs a scene of the Other—in this case
wild "long-legs" and "long-arms" creatures first adumbrated in the *Shanhaijing*
("Classic of the Mountains and the Seas"), a late Zhou dynasty Chinese text, with
a scene of domestic tranquility, in this case weir fishing at Uji, just south of the
capital.

China Bamboo" (J. *Kure-take*; Ch., *Wuzhu*), past the Purple Pavilion (*Shishinden*)
where he would later attend to matters of state, and back south along the verandah, where he took in the Pond-of-Brilliance Screens (*Konmei-chi no sōji*,
Fig. 2). The south face of the screen allowed the emperor to gaze across the
seas and back a millennium or more, to look upon the Pond of Brilliance built
at the command of the Han Dynasty Chinese emperor Wudi (r. 140–86 BCE) on
the outskirts of Chang'an, his capital city. To anyone approaching the Japanese
emperor's chambers from the outside, however, the reverse of the screen offered again a safely domestic view of falconers on the fields of Sagano, just west
of the Japanese capital, offering no hint of the alien scenes that confronted the
emperor within the hall.

His morning ablutions completed, the emperor was dressed by his attendants and partook of a light breakfast before proceeding along roofed corridors to the Purple Pavilion. He entered and arranged himself on the raised dais,
within the half-revealing curtains of state. His presence blocked from view the

fabulous lions (*koma-inu*, or "Korean dogs") and felicitous tortoises, Daoist portents of divinity and longevity, that occupied the central panels of the Barrier of Sages and Worthies (*Kenshō no sōji*).[6] Thus, as his ministers attended him, they saw instead, arrayed on the screen on either side behind the emperor, images of thirty-two Chinese paragons of wisdom and virtue, wise and valued advisers to exemplary emperors from high antiquity to the Tang dynasty (618–907 CE), each standing as if in service to the Japanese emperor, looking on and counseling him from their Other worlds.[7]

Japanese monarchs had never left the Japanese islands. Indeed, after the ninth or tenth century, they rarely left the comfortable precincts of the capital city—or, for that matter, of the palace compound—until the Meiji emperor, a millennium later, was moved to the newly renamed "Tokyo" and mobilized for imperial progresses, parades, and visits around the country, all in service of the building of a modern imperial nation-state.[8] Emperors neither led armies abroad nor even—again, after the tenth century—received foreign visitors with any regularity.

Yet the most mundane rhythms of the emperors' lives were punctuated daily by confrontations with the Other, fabulous creatures at the limits of belief, like the pick-a-back "long-legs" and "long-arms" combining their not-quite-humanness to pluck fish from the waves, "Korean dogs," and alien landscapes, exemplars of virtue from across the seas. Further, each portrayal of the alien was painted, quite literally, back-to-back with representations of "self," of things familiar, close at hand, like the fisherfolk at the Uji River and the imperial falconers at Sagano, in eloquent testimony to the inseparability of Self from Other, of their co-existence in a mutually generative process.

The monarch, who claimed descent from the supreme deity of the Shinto pantheon and was ideologically imbued with the essence of "Japanese" identity, was situated, waking and sleeping, throughout the day, in constant reference to images and representations of the Other. In his bedchambers and in his chambers of state he confronted and controlled Other, by regular, regulated juxtaposition with himself. To put it in reverse terms, from the ninth to the

---

6   For the *Kenshō no sōji*, Suzuki (1994, 267ff).

7   My interpretation of these screens import differs from—but does not negate—the readings of Ōtsu, Heldt and others, who view them through the lens of the so-called *Wa-Kan* (Japan-and-China) dialectic. Rather, I approach the screens along a different vector of significations that emphasizes the need for an ever-present Other in the construction of identity.

8   On the transformation of the emperor through public spectacle, Fujitani (1966). Retired emperors, however, were freer to move about. The retired emperors Go-Toba (1180–1239; r., 1183–1198) and Go-Saga (1220–1272; r., 1242–1246), for example, both made chronicled pilgrimages to the shrines and temples of Kumano after their respective abdications.

nineteenth century, Japanese emperors existed *only* in relation to their own—and Japan's—acknowledged Others.

By the late sixteenth century, long after Japanese emperors had begun to situate themselves in reference to representations of the Other, their temporal power had been reduced to nil, overwhelmed and absorbed by a series of martial monarchs—shoguns—who derived their authority first from the sword and only later from less martial sources. In the latter sixteenth century, military hegemons began to claim for themselves a growing aura of (usually, but not invariably, postmortem) 'Shinto' divinity—to be revered as gods—to strengthen the foundations of their rule. As they did so, they commissioned their own programs of public architecture, in which scenes and symbols of alterity were liberally deployed. Oda Nobunaga (1532–1582), who laid the military basis for political unification in the late sixteenth century, surrounded himself with Chinese and Indian symbols of divinity in the decorative program of his castle at Azuchi.[9] Nobunaga was assassinated just six years after completing Azuchi Castle, and most of his monuments—including the castle—were razed; but his deployment of the Other to buttress sweeping claims to domestic political authority serves to underscore the underlying power of the Other in the construction of self.[10]

Tokugawa Ieyasu, founder of the last dynasty of shoguns, not only brought a definitive end to over a century of civil war and instituted two and a half centuries without domestic or foreign warfare—the longest era of peace in Japanese history—he also tamed the emperor and his court, reducing them to little more than a bureau within his own government. When Ieyasu died in 1616, his heirs and publicists followed his wishes and enshrined him the following year on the slopes of Mt. Nikkō, about seventy-five miles north of Edo, as a Japanese deity and rival to the sun goddess who—putatively—begat the imperial line. At Nikkō, he was apotheosized as Tōshō Daigongen, the "Great Avatar Who Illumines the East." Though Ieyasu was enshrined as a Shinto—that is, "native"—deity, the architectural and iconographic program of his shrine largely ignored Japan, instead situating him, like the emperors in Kyoto, in juxtaposition to the Others he was to control. In life, after all, his official title

---

9   On the program of paintings in Azuchi Castle, see Wheelwright (1981, 87–111); on the architectural program, Coaldrake (1996, Ch. 5).

10   Nobunaga was also apparently fond of dressing in 'foreign' garb, amassed a large wardrobe of *Nanban* ('Southern Barbarian,' i.e., Portuguese) garments; his successor, Toyotomi Hideyoshi (1536–98), also enjoyed dressing in both *Nanban* and Chinese outfits: On an excursion with his leading generals to view the fabled cherry blossoms of Yoshino in early 1594, for example, Hideyoshi arrayed himself as a Chinese emperor, while some of his generals donned *Nanban* robes. Kano (1991, 108–111).

had been *Sei-i taishōgun*, the "Barbarian-Quelling Generalissimo," who—in theory—protected the country from external threat.[11]

Ieyasu's shrine at Nikkō—most of the complex as it stands today dates from the 1630s–is quite literally encrusted with a sculptural program of alterity.[12] On the south face of the Yōmei Gate, main entrance to the shrine, carvings depict the Prince of Zhou, who is credited with foundational elements of Chinese civilization, hearing subjects' suits; to his left, Confucius, accompanied by a retinue of scholars; to the right, a sculptural group engaged in the four essential accomplishments of the cultured Confucian gentleman— zither, chess, calligraphy, and painting (J., *kin-ki-sho-ga*; Ch., *qin-qi-shu-hua*). The program and all its elements proclaim by analogy that Ieyasu had established the Kingly Way (J., *ōdō*; Ch., *wangdao*) of government in Japan, administering justly and wisely, in accord with the Will of Heaven. Confucius and Mencius, Daoist immortals, and Buddhist deities; fabulous birds and beasts— dragons, tigers, giraffes, phoenixes, and, of course, monkeys—all testified to the cosmic potency of Ieyasu both to situate Japan against all Others and to protect Japan against the threat they pose.

Just three years after Ieyasu's death and apotheosis, in 1619, his son Hidetada (1579–1632) arranged the marriage of his daughter Masako[13] to the reigning Emperor Gomizuno'o; Hidetada lived to see his granddaughter succeed as emperor[14] in 1629. When Hidetada and his own successor, Iemitsu (1604–1651), made a grand progress to Kyoto in 1626, they ordered a special Visitation Palace (*Gyōkō no goten*) constructed within the precincts of Nijō Castle to receive the emperor, his consort Masako, their four-*sai* daughter (the future empress Meishō), and their entourage.[15] The Visitation Palace was luxuriously appointed and decorated throughout with paintings on alien themes—scenes of Chinese paragons from the late Ming *Dijian tushuo* (Mirror for instructing

---

11   Ieyasu's initial, temporary resting place was atop Mt. Kunō, towering more than 700 feet above the shores of Suruga Bay, and just 8 km east of Ieyasu's retirement castle at Sunpu (modern Shizuoka). On the deification of Ieyasu, see Ooms (1985) and, more recently, Sonehara (1996; 2008.

12   See Takafuji (1996, 113–221) for a detailed discussion of the Chinese references in the program of Ieyasu's shrine. Also, Coaldrake (1996, 138–1925); Gerhart (1999, Ch. 3).

13   Authorities disagree on the pronunciation of this name; Asao (1996: 747) reads it "Masako," while Yoneda (2003: 307; 310) reads it "Kazuko."

14   *Tennō*, the Japanese emperors' title, was gender free (or bi-gendered) and applied equally to male and female sovereigns (eight women have held the office in recorded history). *Tennō* applies only to the sovereign, never to consorts; therefore, a title like "empress," which might also denote the consort of a *tennō*, seems inappropriate.

15   For contemporary accounts of the five-day imperial family sojourn in the Visitation Palace at Nijō Castle, *Tokugawa jikki* (1964, 2: 377–387).

the emperor, 1573), of Mongols at the hunt, of Chinese engaged in the four accomplishments of the gentleman; of the Chinese poet Tao Yuanming (3rd–4th c.), famed for his "Record of the Peach-Flower Spring," a parable of journeying to the Other World.[16]

Now it may be partly true that, as Karen Gerhart suggests, Hidetada's advance team specified this program of the Other for the Visitation Palace because "Chinese themes [were] favored] for the public and ceremonial halls" of the imperial palace, while scenes of Jurchens (*Dattan*, i.e., Mongols or Manchus) at the hunt or playing polo might have "served as generalized celebrations of the warrior spirit" which in Japan was embodied in shogun and samurai.[17] However, it is equally true that the program once more placed the emperor and his entourage in confrontation with Japan's multiple Others and that it was their hosts, the shogun and the retired shogun, to whom had been entrusted the "quelling of barbarians."

Further, both shogun and emperor were aware that just two years earlier, latter-day Jurchen (J., *Joshin* or *Dattan*, whom we commonly identify as "Manchus") had invaded Korea and the shogun had dispatched an envoy to offer military aid to the Korean king.[18] Japanese discourse quite readily associated these new Dattan with the Mongols who had twice attacked Japan in the thirteenth century, so it is not inconceivable that the scenes of Jurchen cavalry were calculated to elicit a sense of threat and to remind the court that it was the shogun and his minions alone who could defend Japan.[19]

Whether Hidetada's agenda was indeed motivated by the immediate international and strategic environment of the late 1620s, or simply a collection of stock figures of the Other from the artists' inventory of standard models, cannot be finally determined. In either case, however, the program of the Visitation Palace reminds us that for at least a millennium, Japanese authority constituted itself discursively in reference to clear, explicit representations of the Other. For a thousand years, Japanese emperors and shoguns had reminded themselves and their subjects that they were all Japanese, and Japan was Japan, only when engaged with and juxtaposed to its Others.

---

16 For a detailed discussion of the program of paintings in the Visitation Palace, see Gerhart (2004, 171–186).
17 Ibid., 175–177.
18 See Toby (1984, 116–118).
19 On the equation of the Manchus with the thirteenth-century Mongols of in seventeenth-century Japanese discourse, ibid., 166–167.

CHAPTER 2

Mapping the Margins: The Ragged Edges of State and Nation

> Who knows where that country is? Is it Japanese territory, or Chinese—it's hard to tell.
>
> CHIKAMATSU MONZAEMON[1]

∙ ∙ ∙

> The power to map or narrate, or to keep other forms of mapping at bay, is a key element in the ability to claim a territory.
>
> GEOFF KING[2]

∙∙
∙

"Space has values peculiar to itself," Claude Lévi-Strauss observes, "just as sounds and scents have their colours and feelings their weight."[3] The values invested in space are rendered visible through representation produced through the collective processes of social judgment—not just in maps but also in art, in oral and written narratives, in land deeds, in boundary disputes.[4] "The social value accorded to maps and globes [in Europe] throughout the late fifteenth and sixteenth centuries ... was not predicated on their scientific accuracy alone. Whilst they were valued for their demonstration of learning, they were also valued for their ability to operate within a whole range of intellectual, political and economic situations, *and to give shape and meaning* to such situations."[5]

The spatial "value" that often seems most important to social and political groups, the value that is most frequently contested, is the boundary, the place—whether clearly or ill-defined—where difference confronts itself,

---

1 Chikamatsu (1711/1993–1995, 348).
2 King (1996).
3 Lévi-Strauss (1961, 126).
4 See Yonemoto (2003) for a provocative discussion of spatial discourse in early modern.
5 Brotton (1997, 19), italics added.

where "we" exclude "them." Making and maintaining ethnic groups, states, or nations entails imagining boundaries—producing, projecting, and rendering them visible—as much it does the imagining of communities. If nations are "imagined communities,"[6] claimed identities of people, culture, language, and land, they can be imagined only against excluded others, and others can be excluded only by the imagining of boundaries, both human and territorial.[7] The construction of contrast, of the excluded others against whom the community is imagined, takes a variety of discursive forms, from a politics of the body and gesture[8] to assertions of race and genetics[9] to the mapping of the spaces claimed for the body social—what Thongchai Winichakul calls the "geobody of the nation."[10]

Each of these discursive genres attempts to construct, represent, and maintain (or subvert) boundaries—divisions between imagined ethnic, cultural, social, and geographic communities. When these boundaries are contested at a particular historical moment, which boundaries are contested, and how they are contested, as Thongchai, Anderson, and others have made clear, is symptomatic of larger questions of the contestation over identity and very construction of "the nation" itself. States and nations are the products of human artifice and conflict, not spontaneous generation. Japan is not a "natural region," immanent in its geographic circumstances, as Delmer Brown suggested over sixty years ago.[11] Rather, Japan has been produced through a series of dialogic processes pitting the positive (inclusionary) and negative (exclusionary) urges of human communities—communities both within, without, and straddling the margins of the territorial, social, and cultural communities that constitute the ongoing, multiple narratives that we call "Japan."

Maps have proved a crucial arena for the production of states and nations in many different cultural, historical, and political contexts, a venue for contesting and articulating not only the territorial extent of the geobody but the locus and nature of the transition "in" and "out."[12]

---

6   Anderson (1992).
7   See Barth (1985); Batten (2003).
8   Burke (1997, 60–76).
9   Toby (1998).
10   Thongchai (1994).
11   Brown (1955), quoted in Morris-Suzuki (1998).
12   For example, Thongchai (1994).

1   Mapping Japan

Precisely when the peoples of the Japanese archipelago first began making maps is unclear; the earliest extant map of Japan itself dates only from the early fourteenth century,[13] yet, according to the *Nihon shoki*, as part of the Taika Reform program the state commanded, as early as 646, that "boundaries of the provinces should be examined and a description or map prepared" for presentation to the court.[14] Extant *shōen* (estate) maps of the mid eighth century reveal a set of sophisticated cartographic conventions, suggesting that they are the products of an already-well-advanced culture of both surveying and mapping the land,[15] while the *Shoku Nihongi* records the presentation of maps of "all the provinces and districts in the country" to the court in 738.[16] In the more inclusive sense of mapping, what Kuroda Hideo has termed "'Japan maps' as the inscription of the 'national territory,'"[17] a set of what has been termed "spatial and geographic discourses inher[ing] in the political practices and cultural forms"[18] of a particular time and place, mapping "Japan," is evident in the earliest extant writings—the land-creation (*kuni-umi*) myths of the *Kojiki* and *Nihon shoki*, the province-by-province *fudoki* (gazetteers), and even the "frontier guard" (*sakimori*) poems of the *Man'yōshū*.[19]

The mapping projects of the Tokugawa bakufu and the prodigious outpouring of commercially published maps of Japan have been the subject of scholarly inquiry for some time.[20] Yet with rare exceptions, scholars have taken Japan as a self-evident geographic or cartographic entity and have not asked how mapmakers—even in the provocatively expanded sense of "mapping" as a set of visual and textual practices Marcia Yonemoto has proposed—conceived the limits of that "Japan" or the nature of the transition from "Japan" to "not

---

13   Map dated 1305 (Ninnaji archives). While no earlier Japan maps survive, there is a copy of a no-longer-extant Japan map dated (according to the Edo-period copyist) 805. See Unno (1990, 202); Kuroda (2003).

14   Aston (1896/1956, 225). There is no evidence that these "descriptions or maps" were actually produced, but the attribution of mapping by the compilers of the *Nihon shoki* (712) suggests, at least, that by the early eighth century the state saw mapping as part of its brief.

15   Kinda et al. (1996); Kuroda (2000).

16   Kuroda (2001).

17   Ibid.

18   Yonemoto (2003, 2).

19   The *Kojiki* (712) and *Nihon shoki* (720) are the oldest extant histories of Japan; the *Man'yōshū* (759), the earliest collection of Japanese poetry.

20   See Kuroda (1977, 1980, etc.); Kawamura (1984, 1990); and Sugimoto (1994, 12:303–325; 1999) for the Tokugawa mapping projects. For the history of commercial maps, see Yonemoto (1995, 2003).

Japan."[21] Bruce Batten offers the a perceptive analysis of those areas of transition, distinguishing between a "'frontier'... a vague, spatially diffuse division between social groups"; a "'boundary'... also a social interface, but one that is relatively well defined—a line that can easily be drawn on a map, as opposed to a zone." "Border," he uses "as a generic term for social divisions regardless of degree of geographic clarity."[22]

We must be mindful, of course, that the very notion of states and nations, boundaries and territories, like discourses of space more broadly, are themselves inevitably historically situated constructs. In the discourse of the twentieth and twenty-first centuries, territory is univocal: It "belongs" only to one state or another. The modern world system abhors the vacuum of unclaimed territory, on the one hand, and the contradiction of joint sovereignty, on the other. With the exception of Antarctica, every parcel must—ideally—belong to one state, and only one, while the distinction between claimed territories must be along clear linear borders.[23]

Early modern Japan and its neighbors shared notions of "territory" and "sovereignty" quite different from their European contemporaries, ideas and practices that admitted of multiple, complex, layered claims of authority (even "sovereignty" is problematic in this context). Territory might be simply unassigned, not subject to the sovereign claims of any state; it might also "belong," like Tsushima or the Ryukyus, to more than one state at a time.[24] Japanese authorities, for example, were well aware that the Chosŏn state regarded Tsushima as "belong[ing] to Kyŏngsang Province," and as a "dependency and borderland of our country."[25] Likewise, while Edo mapped the kingdom of Ryukyu in 1644 as a Japanese province and received tribute missions from its "alien" king, the shogun's minions evinced not the least discomfort that the

---

21   Morris-Suzuki (1994, 1998) and Batten (2003) question the self-evidence of Japan as a cartographic entity. See also Yonemoto (2003).

22   Batten (2003, 16). As Batten notes, however, some historians of Japan's northeast (Howell 1995; Walker 2001) have questioned the applicability of the notion of "frontier" to early-modern Ezo/Hokkaido.

23   This is not to say, of course, that modern states have outgrown border disputes; Trieste/Trst and Alsace/Elsass, Israel and Palestine, Kashmir, and the Crimea are only a few of the best-known recent instances. Japan, too, asserts claims to islands occupied and claimed by Russia and the Republic of Korea, while Japan occupies islands just north of Taiwan (J., Senkaku; Ch., Diaoyutai) that are claimed by China.

24   The Ogasawara Islands, a tiny (104 km²) western island group now administratively part of Tokyo today, are known in English as the "Bonin Islands," a name derived from the Japanese term *Bunin-tō* (*Mujin-tō*), an Edo-period designation meaning "unpeopled islands."

25   *Sejong Taewang sillok*, entry for Sejong 2[1419]/11; (*Sŭngjŏngwŏn ilgi*, 25: 10ba [1710]). The Korean text uses *sok* (属; J., *zoku*), "to belong"; to "appertain to."

king also sent missions to Beijing, where he presented his realm as a dutiful vassal of Ming and Qing.

In this chapter, I offer an initial examination of the practices of mapping the margins of Japan in early modern cartography and cartographic/geographic discourse, as an approach to understanding where "Japan" was in early modern discourse.

2   *Where* Was Early-Modern "Japan?"

Historians of Japan have recently opened a vigorous debate on the nature of sovereignty and the locus of both state and nation (or "proto-nation"[26]) in the early modern era, when authority was divided—in sometimes fluid and ill-defined ways—between the central (?) Tokugawa bakufu and some 250 territorial daimyo domains. The polity has been characterized in the English corpus as, inter alia, "centralized feudalism," "federal," and "compound."[27] I have argued for seeing the Tokugawa state as powerful and sovereign.[28] James White sees the central state as "the primary context" of early modern Japan; and Sugimoto Fumiko argues that the early modern regime was the most powerful national state yet seen in Japanese history.[29] By contrast, Philip Brown, Mark Ravina, and Luke Roberts each argue that sovereign authority, and the emergent "nation" are more properly located at the level of the local domains of daimyos—at least the most powerful, who controlled the territories comprising one or more entire provinces.[30]

A parallel question in early modern Japanese history, less often addressed but equally critical, might be stated as Where does "Japan" end? or *Where* is Japan? It might seem, in the spirit of what that Brown saw as the "natural entity" of Japan, that the boundaries of an island realm are self-evident; yet through most of the Edo period there was neither clear agreement nor much explicit discussion about the geographical limits of "Japanese" authority. The "sixty-six provinces and two islands" (*rokujūroku-shū ni-tō*, a common epithet for Japan in early modern times) were—for the most part—undisputedly part of "Japan," but were they *all* of "Japan"[31]? Where did Japan end and not-Japan

26   Mitani (1997, 5–350).

27   See Hall (1996); Berry (1982); and Ravina (1999).

28   Toby (1991, 2001a).

29   White (1995); Sugimoto (1994).

30   Brown (1993); Ravina (1999); Roberts (1998).

31   The term "two islands" (*nitō*) refers to Iki and Tsushima, north of Kyushu, which were not among the original eighth-century tabulation of the sixty-six provinces of Honshu, Shikoku and Kyushu.

begin? And how, exactly, did one describe or experience the transition from Japanese to not-Japanese territory? Was the kingdom of the Ryukyus in or out—or both? Was Ezo (now Hokkaido) "ours" or "theirs"? Was Tsushima beyond dispute?

The question of the Ryukyus—as the playwright Chikamatsu Monzaemon put it, "Who knows where that country is, Japanese territory or Chinese?"— was never clearly settled in the early modern period, nor do modern historians agree as to the locus and nature of early modern Ryukyuan sovereignty. The same was true of Ezo, though a mounting sense of threat from Russia, beginning in the final decades of the eighteenth century, brought new urgency to the question of what John Harrison (1953) called "Japan's northern frontier." Indeed, when the Jesuit Heronymo de Angelis crossed from Tsugaru to Matsumae—i.e., from the northern tip of Honshu to the southern tip of Ezo— in 1618 to evade the recent order to expel all Jesuits from Japan, the local lord, Matsumae Kimihiro allowed him to stay, explaining that, "It's no big deal (*daiji mo nai*) if a padre appears in Matsumae, for though the Realm (*tenka*) has ordered the padres out of Japan, Matsumae is not [part of] Japan."[32] Indeed, until the 1770s, at least, in part because the Matsumae domain strictly limited access to Ezo, "Japanese intellectuals regarded Ezo as a foreign land unrelated to Japan," while even Matsumae domain's personnel "had no interest in the geography of Karafuto (Sakhalin) and the farther of the Chishima Islands."[33]

As I have argued elsewhere, the guide to its diplomatic practice that the bakufu compiled in the early 1850s, *Tsūkō ichiran*, treated the Ryukyus as a distinct overseas kingdom for purposes of foreign policy, including Edo-Naha relations, trade, and the disposition of castaways, and expressed no reservations about the conclusion of a French treaty with the Ryukyus in 1844.[34] Daimyos from all across the "sixty-six provinces and two islands" were uniformly subject to the constraints of the alternate attendance (*sankin kōtai*) system, and required to spend half their time in Edo, for example, while the king of Ryukyu, by contrast, sent periodic *diplomatic* missions to the shogun; he maintained

---

32   Quoted in Kikuchi (2013, 20). Kimihiro's declared independence of "Japan" must be balanced against the fact that his father, Kakizaki Yoshihiro, had sought—and was granted— exclusive trading rights in Ezo, from both Toyotomi Hideyoshi (1593) and Tokugawa Ieyasu (1604). Kimihiro's declaration reflects the still-nascent integration of the Matsumae house into the early modern political and status order.

33   Akizuki (199, 138).

34   Toby (1990, 1991); Hayashi (1852/1967). Ezo, however, was not treated as a foreign land; except for its role as the site of interactions with Russia, it did not figure in *Tsūkō ichiran* at all.

no Edo residence and—with one exception—never set foot on the Japanese mainland.[35]

Yet Edo ordered the Ryukyus mapped as if it were one of Japan's provinces in the *kuni-ezu* (province map) project of the 1640s and the head of the Shimazu clan was often informally labeled the "Lord of Four Provinces," which again seems to count the Ryukyus a province of Japan.[36] Indeed, some historians have argued that Ryukyuan foreignness was merely a pose, that the islands were fully "Japanese."[37] But bakufu mapping practices do not consistently support their argument, while public (commercial) mapping practices undermine it. On the other hand, even though it ordered "province maps" (*kuni-ezu*) of the Ryukyu Islands to be produced, beginning in the 1640s, Edo did not include Ryukyu in its national maps of Japan (*Nihon-zu*) until the early eighteenth century, suggesting that it was not until Genroku that the bakufu began to see the Ryukyus as "Japanese." And only fifteen years after one shogun's minions incorporated the Ryukyus in the bakufu's map of Japan, another shogun ordered production of a new Japan map that excluded the Ryukyus—and Ezo.

Ezo, like the Ryukyus, was an ambiguous object of the bakufu's cartographic gaze. The southern tip of Ezo was home to the daimyo house of Matsumae, whose eponymous castle town on the Oshima Peninsula was the northernmost outpost of the Tokugawa polity. The area surrounding the castle town was labeled *Wajinchi* (Japanese people's territory), and the vast area beyond, *Ezo-chi* (Ezo, i.e., Ainu territory). The radical alterity of the indigenous Ainu people was underscored by a synonym for *Wajinchi*, to wit, *Ningenchi* ("human territory").[38]

Like the Ryukyus, the bakufu first commanded a *kuni-ezu* for Ezo in the Kan'ei era (completed in 1644), but the map is entirely schematic, owing far more to the mythic topos of *Ezo ga Chishima* (the "thousand isles of the eastern barbarians") than to any serious engagement with cartographic positivism. It conforms not even minimally to the uniform standards of scale and representation Edo mandated for all other province maps. Unlike the Ryukyus, however, the *Tsūkō ichiran*, compiled between 1851 and 1853, after decades of mounting concern over growing Russian incursions in Ezo, Karafuto (Sakhalin), and the Chishima (Kuril) islands, significantly does not deal with relations with Ezo—except as a site of contestation and Ainu trade with Russian forces.

---

35   Toby (1990; 1991). The lone exception entailed Satsuma's presentation of the captive King Shō Nei (r. 1589–1620) to the shogun in 1610, a year after Satsuma "pacified" the Ryukyu kingdom.

36   Okinawa-ken & Ryūkyū Kuni-ezu Shiryō Henshū Iinkai (1992–1994).

37   Arano (1988); Elisonas (1991).

38   On the *Wajinchi-Ezochi* distinction, Howell (1995, 25; 191 n. 2); Walker (2001). For the epithet *Ningen-chi*, Tabata Hiroshi, "Wajinchi," in *Nihon dai-hyakka zensho* (Shōgakukan) on line via *Japan Knowledge* (www.japanknowledge.com).

Ezo was remapped in 1700 as part of the Genroku *kuni-ezu* project, and even then, the further from the Japanese base at Matsumae one went, the more clearly the map partook of the mythic genre. As Brett Walker notes, the Ezo *kuni-ezu* are detailed only for what Japanese termed *Wajinchi*, the "Japanese territory" at the south, and indicate only in iconic fashion most of the land to the north.[39] "They are maps of foreign lands," he observes, "and betray a fundamental interest in trade, rather than becoming part of a homogenized geographic space." Ezo was depicted in the bakufu's *Shōhō Nihon-zu* (ca. 1651),[40] but only in perfunctory, iconic fashion, with a clear emphasis on *Wajinchi* territory and ports where Japanese might trade.[41] The map extended to Karafuto and Chishima ("thousand islands") as well, but again in only schematic fashion: The bakufu simply reproduced the map of "Ezo" produced by the Matsumae daimyo, with the "thousand islands" as a matrix of dots floating off the northeast coast of Ezo.[42]

Whether Ezo—at least beyond *Wajinchi*—and Ryukyu were "Japanese" or "foreign," that is, was an ambiguous, unsettled question even to the bakufu; it was clear to both commercial mapmakers and geographers—whatever the bakufu's viewpoint—that both were foreign territory.[43] The "conquest of Ainu lands" in geographical discourse, the cartographic assertion that Ezo was part of Japan, was an artifact of the contestation of what has been called "Japan's northern frontier" that began in earnest in the last third of the eighteenth century.[44]

It is from this perspective that I approach the question. The mapping practices of the early modern regime embody contradictions that mirror both these tensions: between the local or provincial level and the larger "national," or "Japan-wide," level, on the one hand, and indeterminacy of "national" boundaries, on the other. From its inception, and four times subsequently,[45]

---

39   Walker (2001).

40   See Nanba, Muroga, and Unno (1973, 32–33); Kawamura (1984, 312–313).

41   Walker (1997, 88–89).

42   *Nihon sōzu* (ca. 1655; MS color on paper. Ōsaka Furitsu Toshokan).

43   On the other hand, the *haikai* poet Matsue Shigeyori's (1638/1943, 174–176) *Kefukigusa* listed "Matsumae" as part of the "north-country circuit" (Hokurikudō), beyond Sado Island, suggesting that he considered at least the *Wajinchi* portion of Ezo part of "Japan" proper. Neither Matsue's *haikai* métier nor *Kefukigusa*'s character as a *haikai* handbook suggest that Shigeyori considered himself a geographer. Rather, he was offering aspiring *haikai* poets a province-by-province catalog of terms they could marshal as poetic epithets for various parts of the country, analogous to the more "refined" word-associations (*utamakura*) for sites/sights canonized as *meisho* (famous places) in the classical poetic tradition. On *Kefukigusa*, NKBD, 2: 383–384.

44   Harrison (1953).

45   The standard count is four iterations of the *kuni-ezu* project, commissioned by shoguns Ieyasu (Keichō era [1596–1615]), Iemitsu (Kan'ei [1624–1644]), Tsunayoshi (Genroku [1687–1704]), and Ieyoshi (Tenpō [1830–1844]). Kuroda (1996), however, argues that there

the bakufu commanded that maps be produced of each of the sixty-eight prov-inces of Japan (*kuni-ezu*, or "province maps"), an act of "claiming the land" by subjecting its parts to the cartographic gaze of the state, insinuating central authority into local, domain territories in an act that is consistent with other practices, such as nationwide land surveys. *Kuni-ezu* were—like Hideyoshi's land surveys—ideally, if not actually, composed to uniform standards of scale and logic, effacing daimyo domains under the withering intensity of a hege-monic shogunal gaze. These maps were acts of possession rather than acts of registration: Once the *kuni-ezu* were compiled, they were stored in state archives—merely possessed—and neither displayed nor made public. It was the act of mapping, like the act of surveying the land, that asserted shogunal sovereignty and possession.

The bakufu—which I take to be the "state," and the subject that asserted sovereign claims over all "Japan" (however conceived)—compiled nation-al maps of "Japan" as well as provincial maps that constituted "maps of the complete territory under the administration of the bakufu"[46] and staked an aggregate claim to national authority through "the power of maps."[47] These "official" national maps, too, were secret state documents, kept in the shogu-nal archives, the Momijiyama Bunko, and were not generally accessible to the public. Individual mapmakers, on the other hand, had produced maps of Japan in medieval times, and publishers began producing commercial Japan maps in the seventeenth century.

Indeed, the relationship between state-produced maps of "Japan" and com-mercially published ones is problematic. Marcia Yonemoto argues that the producers of the earliest commercial maps, such as Ishikawa Ryūsen, must have had access, directly or indirectly, to the bakufu's official "national" maps, though there is no direct evidence to demonstrate (or falsify) that inference.[48] But—as I shall argue below—there are good reasons to believe the contrary, and some of those reasons rest at the ragged edges of "Japan" in the representa-tion of boundary sites and ambiguous territory, such as Ezo and Ryukyu.

For despite Yonemoto's suggestion and Kawamura's declaration that the bakufu's national maps were "maps of the complete territory under the

---

were five *kuni-ezu* projects, that the second shogun, Hidetada, also commissioned a set of *kuni-ezu* in the Genna era (1615–1624) as one in a series of acts proclaiming his "new" reign immediately after the death of Ieyasu. Earlier, in the Tenshō era, Toyotomi Hideyoshi had commanded provincial maps for at least twenty-nine provinces, though only thirteen were actually mapped in this project (Kawamura 1984, 23). Kawamura (2005a, 353–368) provides a nearly comprehensive bibliography of research on *kuni-ezu*.

46   Kawamura (1984, 512).
47   Wood (1992).
48   Yonemoto (2003).

administration of the bakufu,"[49] even the "Japan" that those maps asserted was constantly in flux and not consistently congruent with the sum of the bakufu's province maps, while commercially published maps were never congruent with the "national" territory the bakufu's mapping practices claimed. No two bakufu maps of "Japan," moreover, ever asserted the same territorial claims. Though the bakufu extended the gaze of its *kuni-ezu* to both Ezo and Ryukyu in its Shōhō-era (1640s) province-mapping project, Ezo was not mapped onto "national" maps until the 1650s–and then only perfunctorily, along with Karafuto and the Kurils. Ryukyu did not appear on the bakufu's own "national" maps until the early eighteenth century—and then only once. Yet just fifteen years later, in the maps commissioned by the eighth shogun, Yoshimune, Ryukyu had disappeared from the bakufu's official maps of "Japan" (see Figs. 3 & 4).

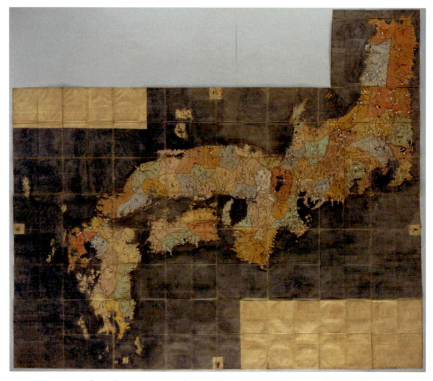

FIGURE 3   "Keichō Nihon sōzu" (Keichō-Era Complete Map of Japan, National Diet Library),
             compiled from the first round of bakufu-ordered province maps, ca. 1605–15, in
             a copy of ca. 1653 that reflects at least two rounds of editorial emendations, in
             ca. 1639 and ca. 1653.

---

49   Kawamura (1984): 516.

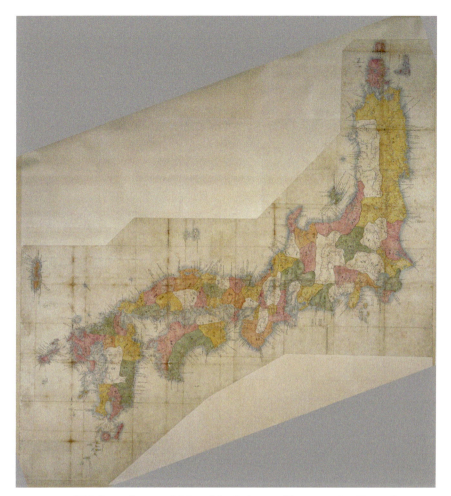

FIGURE 4   "Kōkoku michinori zu" (Map of the Highways of Japan. ca. 1670, National
             Museum of Japanese History), based on the province maps of the Shōhō era
             (1644–48), is the first official map to include both Ezo and the Kurils (*Ezo ga
             chishima*), though only schematically.

Not only were the bakufu's own representations of "Japan" in "maps of the
complete territory under the administration of the bakufu" inconsistent from
one to the next, they were only once consistent with the sum of the *kuni-ezu*,
whatever their flaws. Territories at the geographic margins of bakufu authority,
some mapped—hence claimed—in *kuni-ezu*, some not, were excluded from
the "Japan" of most published national maps, producing a "ragged edge," a dis-
juncture between bakufu claims and public discourse as to the range of territory and people(s) subsumed in "Japan." The Ryukyuan kingdom in the southwest

and the island of Ezo in the northeast were treated in most published national maps of Japan as if they were ontologically analogous to Korea—that is, as if they were offshore foreign territories—an ambiguity found also in bakufu policy toward some of these territories.

It is in this sense that both cognitive and graphic early modern maps of Japan evinced a sense of the country whose boundaries were to a degree vague and indeterminate, with "ragged edges," rather than clear and fixed borders. Kären Wigen has called the result "a malleable map," one that reflects "the plurality of [early modern] Japan's cartographic cultures." I quite agree with this characterization, but would go farther and argue that maps of Japan were malleable and mapping cultures plural precisely because there was no clearly defined set of boundaries to what constituted "Japan." Indeed, as will become clear below, it was only when external forces—first Russia, then other Euro-American powers—were seen to contest the edges of Japan, and even to make incursions into what all agreed was "Japanese territory," that Japanese cartographers and political authorities began to articulate clearly defined national boundaries.

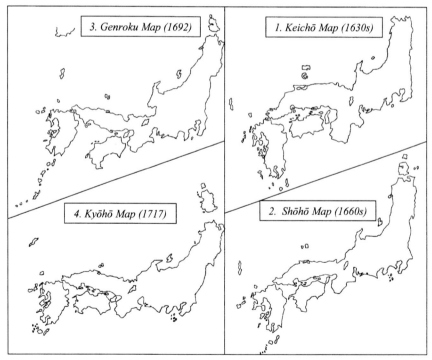

FIGURE 5   Comparison of the territorial coverage of the four successive "complete maps of Japan" compiled by the bakufu, adapted from Kawamura (1984). The changing treatment of Ezo, the Ryukyus and Korea suggests the fluid attitude of Edo authorities toward these sites on the outer margins of Japan.

FIGURE 6   The "Jōtokuji Map of Japan" (color & gold leaf on paper, one of a pair of
             six-panel folding screens, Jōtokuji Collection, Fukui Prefecture), a late
             16th-century work, executed in the "Gyōki" style, enhanced with mountains in
             the northeast. shows the sea lanes from Hideyoshi's Kyushu command center,
             Nagoya Castle, via Iki and Tsushima, to Pusan, and the indicates in red the
             route from Hideyoshi's invasion command headquarters at Nagoya in northern
             Kyushu, to the port of Pusan, where Hideyoshi's forces began their invasion in
             1592. The inclusion of southeastern Korea adumbrates Hideyoshi's continental
             ambitions, while the southern tip of Ezo peeks in from the north.

Even before the bakufu first compiled "national" maps, the conventions of representation in public—that is, unofficial—discourse for those ambiguous territories at the ragged edge were coming into view. The late-sixteenth-century
"Jōtokuji Japan Map" surrounds most of the seas around Japan with the gold-
leaf clouds characteristic of no-space/no-time in *emaki* and *rakuchū-rakugai*
screens.[50] "Ezo" bleeds off the screen at the upper right (northeastern) margin,
while "Kōrai" (K., Koryŏ, *i.e.* Korea) bleeds off screen at the upper left (northwestern) corner. "Pusan" is indicated as well, connected by a line indicating the
sea route to Tsushima, Iki, and Hideyoshi's command post at Nagoya, in Hizen
Province (see Fig. 6). A map of northeast Asia rendered for Hideyoshi on a folding fan—also likely reflecting his continental ambitions—locates Ezo on the
Asian mainland northeast of "Kōrai" about where one might expect to see the
Amur River, clearly beyond the frontiers of Japan.[51] (see Fig. 7)

50   Nanba, Muroga, & Unno (1970).
51   The map bears the seal of the artist Kanō Eitoku (d. 1590), but the linking of Pusan to
      Hideyoshi's base at Nagoya suggests that the map dates from the years of his invasion
      of Korea, 1592–1598. See Nanba, Muroga, and Unno (1973, 182–183; fig. 20). It may not
      be appropriate to classify this as an "unofficial" map, as it was likely commissioned by
      Hideyoshi.

FIGURE 7   Map of Japan, China and Northeast Asia drawn on a folding fan for Toyotomi
Hideyoshi. Like the Jōtokuji map (Fig. 6), this work also reflects Hideyoshi's
ambitions to conquer Korea and China: Iki and Tsushima, crucial staging areas
for the Korean campaigns, are drawn in exaggerated scale. The fan map
indicates the Korean capital, "Kyŏng" (J. *Kyō*, now Seoul, the only Korean
toponym on the map), and Ming capitals of Beijing and Nanjing. Ezo,
still largely *terra incognita* for most Japanese, is mapped on the eastern
Manchurian coast, rather than as an island north of Honshu. (formerly in
the collection of Mutō Sanji).

But other unofficial maps of Japan from the late sixteenth and early seventeenth century are quite random about their treatment of Japan at the ragged
edge. The *Nansen bushū Dainihon-koku shōtō-zu*, a Gyōki-type manuscript map
ca. 1557 shows China (*Daitō*) to the west (upper left) and the mythic Rasetsu-
koku, where "[t]here are women; but if men go [there] they do not return," to
the south (lower left).[52] The equally legendary Gandō is indicated north of the
San'in region (i.e., the provinces of western Honshū on the Japan Sea coast;
right margin) but is not identified as such. Some of these maps identify Gandō
as an island, a "country where [the creatures] do not have human shape."[53]

Yet other maps of this period, such as those in the first print editions of
the medieval encyclopedia *Shūgaishō*, reproduce a completely disconnect-
ed Japan that ends at Tsugaru in the northeast, Tsushima in the west, and

52   Cortazzi (1986, 70). Ōji (1996) has an excellent discussion of the "Gyōki-type" map, which
      is characterized by a spatial logic that was concerned with the relationship of provinces'
      locations rather than their actual shape. Rasetsu-koku, the land of the female *rasetsu*
      (Skt., *rākṣasa*) demons, who had supernatural powers, and were believed to bewitch and
      devour men—hence, men who "go there do not return." See Inagaki (1984, 243).
53   On "Gandō" and "Rasetsu," see Ōji (1996, 25–46).

Satsuma in the southwest, with no indication of Korea, Ryukyu, or Ezo (the map places "the land of the northern barbarians" (*emishi-chi*) *inside* northern Mutsu Province.[54] (Fig. 8) The *Dai Nihon jishin no zu* (Earthquake map of Great Japan, 1624), a printed single-sheet map published that same year, represents a "Great Japan" protected by a great sleeping dragon, and Ezo, Matsumae, and Hachijōjima as outer-boundary *topoi*, floating on the body of the dragon but not connected to Dai-Nihon. Islands and island provinces such as Sado, Iki, and Tsushima straddle the inner, fully Japanese area and the liminal back of the dragon (Fig. 9)—but so do the nine Kyushu provinces, parts of Shikoku, and "Matsumai" (Matsumae).[55]

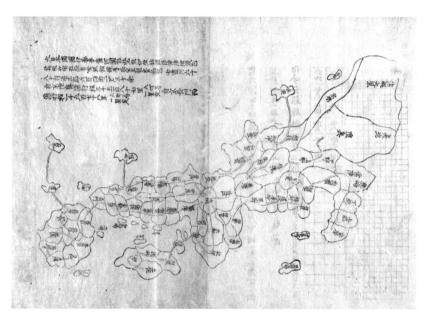

FIGURE 8   "Map of Great Japan" (*Dai Nihon-koku zu*, in Tōin, 1656), which bills itself as "The map made by the bodhisattva Gyōki," is typical of "Gyōki-style" maps of Japan: There is no effort to approximate the shapes of the "sixty-six provinces and two islands," only to show their relative sizes and spatial relationships along the highways connecting provinces to the capital. It also gives no indication of anything lying beyond shores of "Great Japan," save for "Izu Ōshima" and "Mitsukejima" lower right page, and "Tane" (Tanegashima), south of Kyushu (lower left). There is no indication of Ezo, Ryūkyū, or Korea.

---

54   Tōin Kinkata (1656). Tōin Kinkata (1291–1360) was a high-ranking courtier, rising to Junior First Rank (*juichi'i*), and a prolific scholar.
55   See Kuroda (2003); Nanba, Muroga, & Unno (1970); Dolce (2007).

FIGURE 9

The *Dai Nihon jishin no zu* (1624)
squeezes a "Gyōki-style" map of
Japan into the space delineated by
the scaly body of the great dragon
that lies beneath the country and,
when restless, causes earthquakes.
Provinces that are home to ports
for Japanese and foreign ships, i.e.,
Kyushu and the islands of Iki and
Tsushima, are mapped on the body
of the dragon at the bottom of the
map, suggesting their liminal status; "Matsumai" (Matsumae), the
outpost projecting Japanese power
in southern Ezo (Hokkaido), also
sits upon the dragon's body. Unlike
other maps of the time, the *Dai
Nihon jishin no zu* makes a nod to
some of the boundary conditions
to the northeast and southwest:
Ezo, on the neck of the dragon; and
Tanegashima, Iōgashima ("sulphur
island"), and Kikaigashima ("isle
of demons"), beyond the dragon's
body at the bottom of the map.

Indeed, the representation of Ezo, Ryukyu, and Korea on Nakabayashi Kichibei's
Fusō-koku no zu ("Japan map," 1666) and Ishikawa Ryūsen's *Honchō kōmoku
zukan* ("Map of Our Country") maps two decades later (Figs. 10 & 11)[56] were
semantically and grammatically identical to the representation of the mythic,
mysterious island "countries" (*kuni*) of "Gandō" and "Rasetsu" that had appeared in so-called Gyōki-type maps from medieval times, a cartographic rhetoric on which these new mapmakers clearly drew. As deployed in medieval

---

56   *Fusō-koku no zu* (1666), reproduced in Cortazzi (1983, 104). Ishikawa Ryūsen, *Honchō
      zukan kōmoku* (Edo, Sagamiya Tahei, 1687, Mitsui Map Collection, C.V. Starr East Asian
      Library, University of California, Berkeley; also Kyoto, Hayashi Yoshinaga, collection Kobe
      City Museum); *Nihon kaisan chōriku zu* (1689, Mitsui Map Collection, C.V. Starr East Asian
      Library, University of California, Berkeley); *Honchō zukan kōmoku* (1691, Kyoto); and *Dai
      Nihon-koku ō-ezu* (Edo: Yamaguchiya Gonbei, 1712; collection Kobe City Museum). For
      reproductions, see, Kobe Museum (1994, 32–33), and Cortazzi (1983, insert at 114–115).

FIGURE 10   Nakabayashi Kichibei, *Fusōkoku no zu* (1666; National Diet Library)
Nakabayashi places the proximate coasts of Korea, Ezo and Ryūkyū as
boundary conditions, at the margins of his map.

FIGURE 11   Ishikawa Ryūsen, "Annotated Map of Our Country" (*Honchō zukan kōmoku*,
Sagamiya Tahei, 1687; National Diet Library). In Ryūsen's treatment, following
Nakabayashi Kichibei's map (Fig. 10), Ezo bleeds off the map at the right
margin, as does Ryūkyū, along the lower margin, and Korea at the upper left
corner. The mythical islands of Gandō and Rasetsu intrude from the upper
margin (center) and lower margin (just to the right of the dark circle with the
character *minami* in it), respectively. *Gandō* was normally written with the
characters 雁道 ("goose road"); Ryūsen uses nearly homophonous characters
韓唐 for "Korea" (*kan*; K., *han*) and "Tang [China]" (*tō*), equating Gandō with
China and Korea.

maps they operated as what I term "boundary conditions," territories that—like Rasetsu and Gandō—floated offshore: Gandō and Rasetsu bracketed Honshu in the seas to the north and the south of Japan, with no clear signs whether they were in "Japan" or out. In Kichibei's and Ryūsen's maps, Ezo, Ryukyu and Korea similarly bled off the margins of the map, implicitly indicating that they were not actually part of "Japan" but only "boundary conditions" representing what was immediately beyond the outer limits of "Japan."[57]

The representation of boundary conditions in the Nakabayashi and Ishikawa maps are distinct from each other only insofar as Ryūsen treated Matsumae—the base of the trading daimyo's "domain" on the southern tip of Ezo—as a separate island (it was not) between "Ezo" and the northernmost Japanese province of Mutsu. In contrast, Nakabayashi treated Matsumae as a distinct site (point) on the large boundary-condition land-mass off in the sea to the northeast (Ezo). Both Ryūsen and Nakabayashi also identify Pusan, the site of the Japanese trading factory in Korea (J., *Wakan*; K., *Waegwan*). Ryūsen connects it to Tsushima with a "48 *ri*" line indicating the sea route connecting them. (He does not connect Matsumae in this fashion, indicating at the mouth of Mutsu Bay only that "From here it is two days by sea to Matsumae.")

An unsigned printed map of Japan, ca. 1683—that is, roughly contemporaneous with Ryūsen's—likewise floats Korea and Ezo offshore, bleeding off the sheet in the upper left (northwest) and right (northeast) corners, respectively.[58] The castle of "Matsumae" is indicated by a red square onshore in Ezo, just as "Fusan-kai" (Pusan, location of the Japanese trading post in Korea) is noted onshore in Korea, suggesting, perhaps, that these were outposts of "Japanese" presence on "foreign" soil. Rasetsu bleeds off the lower margin. A single island labeled "Ryukyu" floats just within the lower margin south of Satsuma—which might be read as including Ryukyu as part of *Dai-Nihon* ("Great Japan") for its treatment links it with Tanegashima, Iki, Tsushima and other offshore Japanese islands, and distinguishes it from places such as Ezo and Rasetsu that bleed off the map.[59]

The anonymous *Shinsen Dai-Nihon zukan* ("Newly Compiled Map of Great Japan"), published the same year as Ryūsen's map, also in the Gyōki-type idiom of bale-shaped provinces, likewise treats Korea (*Chōsen-koku*), Ezo, and

---

57   This is not to suggest that Kichibei's maps were identical to Ryūsen's in other respects or that Ryūsen's map remained stable through its various iterations and editions.

58   Cortazzi (1983, 106–107).

59   The caption, however, a roster of Japan's provinces, in the canonical "Five Home Provinces and Seven Circuits" (*Goki-shichidō*) taxonomy, counts Iki and Tsushima as provinces in the "Western Maritime Circuit" (*Saikaidō*), clearly marking them as constituents of a common entity (Japan).

Ryukyu as boundary conditions to Japan, bleeding off the margins of the map.[60] Matsumae is a location in Ezo rather than a separate island—as in Ryūsen's earliest maps—but it is connected by indications of the sea route to northern Honshu. Neither Korea (*Chōsen-koku*) nor Ryukyu is connected to Japan, and there is no indication of Pusan, though a ship wandering in the open sea between Tsushima and Korea suggests that there is commerce between them. There is no such suggestion of a link between Ryukyu and Japan. Also, unlike Ryūsen, the mapmaker excludes the mythic isles of Gandō and Rasetsu. Cortazzi notes that "Ezo, with its fief of Matsumae, is clearly labeled in the extreme upper right, running off the map (conveniently obscuring the relationship of Ezo to the mainland, a matter of some doubt at the time)."[61] It is actually unlikely, however, that the nature of Ezo—whether island or part of the mainland—was unclear at the time. As Cortazzi observes, "Korea— *Chōsen-koku*—[also] protrudes from the upper left border," but the same is true of Ryukyu. Indeed, it is clear from the bakufu's 1651 and 1679 "Japan" maps that Edo recognized Ezo was an island; one wonders whether it is only coincidence that the Matsumae lord's courtesy title was that of "governor of Shima Province," for *shima*—written with a different character—also means "island." Rather, it is the ambiguity of Ezo's status—"Is it domestic or foreign?"—that most likely accounts for the way it is represented in these published maps.

Similarly, Ryukyu was invisible in an unsigned Kanbun-era (1661–72) atlas of Japan, *Nihon bunkei-zu* (Maps of Japan in segments), which likewise omitted Ezo—though the map of Mutsu Province has a notation off Nobeji, in Mutsu Bay, that "Matsumae is two days' voyage from here."[62] Korea, too, was unmapped, though a disembodied notation for "Kōrai" floated significantly in the waters north of Tsushima, and an appendix notes that "from Tsushima to the Korean port of Pusan is twenty-five *li*."[63] The atlas makes no mention of Ryukyu whatever, but the declaration that, "Forty-eight *li* southwest of the

---

60   Cortazzi (1983, 99).

61   Ibid.

62   Anonymous (1666). Matsuda (1865), a province-by-province atlas published in the waning days of Tokugawa rule, opens by listing of Japan's provinces, followed by maps of each. It similarly excludes both Ezo and Ryukyu from Japan—but specifies "Matsumae" off the coast of Mutsu Province, something the *Bunkei-zu* does not do. This is ironic, since by Matsuda's time the bakufu had assumed complete control of Ezo, and the port of Hakodate was open to foreign trade.

63   Anonymous (1666, appendix). Japanese continued to refer to Korea anachronistically as Kōrai (K., Koryŏ, 918–1392), well into the Edo period, though they also used Chōsen (K., Chosŏn, 1392–1897), the name of the state that ruled Korea in their own time.

Gotō Islands are Onjima and Meshima. It is Japanese territory as far as here. South of there are the islands of Takasago."[64]

Indeed the anonymous author's preface explicitly limited Japan to the islands of Honshu, Shikoku and Kyushu, plus the supernumary islands of Iki and Tsushima:

> Now our country of Japan is on the east side of the world, in the midst of the eastern ocean. It is several thousand *ri* across the western sea from Great Ming, while the [Southern] Barbarian countries are several tens of thousands of *ri* distant. The sea to the north ends at Korea [*Chōsen*], more than two thousand *ri* away. Its shape is long from east to west, but short from north to south, like that of a sleeping dragon. It is as if the beaches of Satsuma in the southwest were the head, while Mutsu, in northeast, was the tail. In all, it is 4,200 *ri* from east to west. It comprises the Capital District and the Seven Circuits.[65]

If the command to produce a *kuni-ezu* of the Ryukyus signaled that at some level Edo considered the Ryukyuan kingdom to be within the ambit of its authority, that consciousness had not been communicated even to the educated elite beyond the bakufu's inner circle.

Ihara Saikaku (1642–93), best known as the leading author of *ukiyo-zōshi* (fiction of the "floating world"), also dabbled in geography and cartography.[66] His *Highways at a Glance* (*Hitome tamaboko*) is a rough gazetteer and map of *meisho*, famed sites/sights canonized in the classical poetic tradition.[67] Saikaku's tour is organized along the course of Japan's highways, starting with the fanciful "Sunrise Beach" (*Hinode-no-hama*) in the far northeast where, "Our country is also called 'the origin of the sun' (*hi-no-moto*) because it is descended from the god Amaterasu (the sun goddess)." Beyond the northern reaches of Japan he depict the southern edges of "the thousand barbarian islands"

---

64   Ibid. The final appendix, "The Five Home Provinces and Seven Circuits, with Distances, Directions ..." lists the sixty-six provinces by circuit, plus Iki and Tsushima, with their assessed productivity; but since "Tsushima is near the boundary of a foreign country (*ikoku*), and therefore we do not count its productivity." (67a)

65   Ibid. (preface). "Great Ming," of course, had fallen to the Qing two decades earlier. The distances in this passage are all overstated. At 3.9 km/*ri*, they would put the length of the Japanese archipelago from Mutsu to southern Kyushu at over 16,000 km; from Japan to Korea at 7,800 km.

66   *Ukiyo-zōshi*, the term for a genre of popular fiction that began with Saikaku's *Kōshoku ichidai otoko* (1682) and continuing to the mid-18th century, is not attested until over a decade after Saikaku's death. NKD, 2: 154; NKBD, 1: 263–264; Moretti (2010).

67   Ihara (1689).

(*Ezo-ga-chishima*) and the "Sea-Otter Isles" (*Rakko-jima*), as well as Matsumae Castle and the port of Esashi, peeking into view from the upper margin, but they are beyond the ambit of the Sixty-Six Provinces and Two Islands; to the north of these islands, he says, lies Korea (*Kōrai*). Saikaku concludes in the southwest with a bird's-eye view of a jumble of islands off northwest Kyushu, from the "Temple-Island of Oki," Hirado and the Gotō Islands, to Iki and Tsushima. Like *Nihon bunkei-zu*, that is, Saikaku excludes the Ryukyu islands from "Japan."

This contradiction between the bakufu's fluid assertions of sovereignty, on the one hand, and public understanding on the other, was one source of the playwright Chikamatsu's confusion—more likely irony—in wondering "where" Ryukyu belonged. It embodies the ragged edge of Japan, a discontinuity between two simultaneous and overlapping systems of asserting, visualizing, and mapping "the realm"—the discontinuity between the sum of the provinces and "the realm" as a totality. It is this contradiction that I propose to interrogate.

3   Reprise

If "geography, like the nation, is very much a state of mind," then mapping—the systematically encoded, schematic, graphic representation of the uses of space and the spatial distribution of power, authority, and resources and the entire gamut of "things" and "actions" humans can imagine—might be conceived as a "state of mind about a state of mind."[68] This is what Kären Wigen calls a "geographic imaginary," in which peoples organize the cognition of identity and activity against grids of spatiality and territoriality.[69] But mapping, as J. B. Harley and Denis Wood write, is also fundamentally about power, "a form of political discourse concerned with the acquisition and maintenance of power" creating maps as "weapons in the fight for social domination."[70] Who makes the map and for what purpose and what ideologies of sovereignty and possession, spatiality and boundary, inform their making—by estate owners or manorial lords, villages, or governments—profoundly determine the nature of the map and the stories it tells.

As peoples "imagine" themselves as "communities," they may concomitantly begin to imagine—assert—an isomorphism of their community to a defined geographic space they possess exclusively; yet as Thongchai

---

68   Doak (2001, 85).
69   Wigen (1992).
70   Harley (1988, 57); Wood (1992, 66).

Winichakul persuasively shows, "the terrain" itself is equally problematic.[71] It is socially constructed and represented—graphically, verbally, discursively—in frames that are negotiated through historically, culturally, and politically particular contingencies. The terrain itself may be contested by other external communities that have been equally "imagined" into being (by both the internal and external communities, a point Anderson overlooks, but one that Thongchai notes).

In early modern Japan, I have argued, the notion of "zones" of decreasing inclusion, or mutual frontiers across which entities imperceptibly fade into one another, may be more appropriate.[72] As the narrator in Japanese playwright Chikamatsu's dramatic text vividly observed, cultures may apply other notions of boundary than a clearly demarcated line between cultural, political, or ethnic territories.[73]

In the early modern age (ca. 1550–1850), Japan experienced a veritable boom in mapmaking as a newly unified "national" polity (I use the term here strictly to denote a regime that claimed authority over all "Japanese" territory, rather than in the sense of the modern nation-state), the Tokugawa bakufu established hegemonic control over "the realm" (*tenka*), subjugating daimyos (territorial lords) who had maintained autonomy through warfare since the late fifteenth century. The Tokugawa bakufu, the most powerful state Japan had yet known, established domestic and international sovereignty through legislation, ritual, and diplomacy, as well as through the exercise of raw, material power—both military campaigns and the attainder, reduction or transfer of recalcitrant daimyos. They further insinuated their authority into hitherto autonomous domains through cadastral surveys that revealed the economic power base of every daimyo, revealing them to the gaze of the new Tokugawa state.

The Tokugawa state went farther in casting its constitutive gaze upon the territory, commanding detailed maps of all Japan's sixty-eight provinces—which were rarely congruent with any of the 250 or more daimyo territories—each to the same scale and using uniform conventions of representation.[74] Each of the first three Tokugawa shoguns commanded the compilation of a set of province; as an assertion of his authority, maps (J. *kuni-ezu*) cast a hegemonic gaze across "the realm." Later shoguns repeated the exercise in the late seventeenth and early nineteenth centuries. These maps effaced daimyo authority, taking

71   Anderson (1992); Thongchai (1994).
72   Toby (1990).
73   Chikamatsu (1711/1985–1990).
74   Kawamura (1990).

as their referent a set of "provinces" that had been established in the seventh and eighth centuries but that by the sixteenth century were little more than literary or cultural conventions that corresponded to no functioning units of political administration.

Yet, ironically, the sum of the "provinces" compassed by the *kuni-ezu* project was never congruent with "the realm" as constituted by cartographers outside the bakufu—and only once, in 1702, was it congruent with the "Japan" of the bakufu's official, if secret, "national" maps. Though the bakufu extended its cartographic gaze to the kingdom of Ryukyu by commanding a *kuni-ezu* of that territory in 1644, its inclusion of Ryukyu within "the realm" remained ambiguous—at least when the bakufu compiled its maps of the entire country.[75] The bakufu had authorized the southwestern province of Satsuma to invade the Ryukyus in 1609 yet continued to allow the Ryukyuan kings to engage in tributary relations with China, while treating its own relations with Ryukyu as diplomatic relations with a foreign country.[76] The ragged edge of Japan was produced in discourse and politics, perhaps from a propensity for "fluid boundaries" in East Asian ideology.[77]

The contradiction extended to mapping practices, and it is this contradiction that I interrogate here: though the state began to produce maps of "Japan" in the late sixteenth century and continued to do so irregularly thereafter,[78] these maps were rarely congruent with the sum of territories the state claimed under its authority, nor were the sovereign claims of the state identical for all parts of the territory it claimed. Moreover, these "official maps" were held as secret documents in state archives and not a public proclamation of either the state's authority or its cartographic vision. Private cartographers had begun mapping the realm as early as the fourteenth century,[79] and in the seventeenth century, commercially published maps began appearing, such as Nakabayashi Kichibei's *Nihonzu* of 1666 (Fig. 10) and Ishikawa Ryūsen's *Honchō zukan kōmoku* of 1687 (Fig. 11),[80] and the maps of Nagakubo Sekisui (1717–1801), *Kaisei Nihon yochi rotei zenzu*, first published in 1775, and reprinted frequently thereafter (Fig. 12).

These "Sekisui maps" (J. *Sekisui zu*), which became the standard maps of "Japan" to the mid-nineteenth century, were the first "national" maps to indicate

---

75   *Ryukyu kuni-ezu*, ca. 1690, in Okinawa-ken and Ryūkyū Kuni-ezu Shiryō Henshū Iinkai (1992–1994).

76   Toby (1991).

77   Smith (1997).

78   Ōtani (1932); Unno (1994).

79   Unno (1994); Cortazzi (1986).

80   1687, collection Kobe City Museum.

longitude and latitude as well as points of the compass—adoptions of western cartographic techniques.[81] Yet, ironically, none of these "national" maps corresponds to the territory the bakufu "claimed" through the cartographic gaze of the *kuni-ezu*. Ryūsen and Sekisui both exclude Ryukyu, treating it identically to Korea and "Ezo" (today's "Hokkaido"). Indeed, what is noteworthy is that both Ryūsen and Sekisui treat Ryukyu, Ezo, and Korea, alike as "foreign" territory external to the realm. They are depicted not as part of but as external limits of the realm despite their mutually quite different relationships to Tokugawa authority and to "realm" itself. In Kichibei's and Ryūsen's maps, corners of Ryukyu, Ezo and Korea bleed in from beyond the margins of the map; Sekisui treats Korea and Ezo in much the same fashion as his predecessors, but of Ryukyu notes simply, in the lower left corner of his map, "one-hundred-twenty *ri* (ca. 470 km) south of here is the land of Ryukyu," beyond the boundaries.[82]

4   Taxonomic Boundaries

The ambiguities in mapping practices, the inconsistency of the bakufu's own assertions of boundary (first between the range of sovereignty the *kuni-ezu* claimed and in the "national" maps and then in the shifting margins from one national mapping project to the next), and the apparent contradiction between the bakufu's cartographic representation of the ambit of its authority and the unchallenged representations of private, commercial mapmakers' published and widely disseminated efforts are replicated in the analyses of "Japan" as a coherent (or incoherent) space in the writings of encyclopedists and geographers from the early eighteenth century on. All seemed to agree that there was a unitary geographic entity known as "Japan" (Nihon), and public geographers and cartographers seemed likewise to agree on the extent of "Japan"—the coherent (?) "nation" that subsumed them all.

And from the Kyōhō period (1716–1736) onward, there was a growing congruence between the understanding of public geographers and the assertions of the "state" about the map of "Japan." Yet the "Japan" of that official map continued to be incongruent with the sum of the bakufu's mapped "provinces." These cartographic contradictions would not be fully resolved until after the Meiji Restoration—indeed, one might argue that with disputes ongoing at the northeastern, southwestern, and northwestern edges of what the Japanese

---

81   Iizawa (1979–1996).

82   *Kore yori minami hyaku nijū-ri, Ryūkyū-koku ari.* Sekisui's calculation is remarkably accurate: It is ca. 471 km from Yakushima to the center of the island of Okinawa.

government claims as its sovereign territory,[83] the contradictions are unresolved even today.

Two encyclopedists of the late seventeenth and early eighteenth centuries, Nishikawa Joken (1648–1724) and Terajima Ryōan (1654–??), took somewhat differing approaches to the question of Japan's geographic limits—though they did so implicitly, for neither explicitly addressed the question of boundaries and inclusion. Nishikawa, a prolific scholar who worked most of his life in Nagasaki, wrote extensively, including books of advice and wisdom for merchants (*Chōnin-bukuro*, 1692) and peasants (*Hyakushō-bukuro*, 1720).

5   Nishikawa Joken's "Japan"

Nishikawa twice undertook to catalogue much of the world beyond Japan, in two works, *Ka'i tsūshō-kō* ("On Trade between the Civilized and the Barbarians," 1692/1708) and *Shijūni-koku jinbutsu zusetsu* ("Illustrated guide to the peoples of forty-two countries," 1720); by implication, what he left uncatalogued may perhaps be taken as his notion of "Japan." In both works, Nishikawa reflects the fluidity of Japan's boundaries. He clearly regards Ryukyu as a "foreign country" (*gaikoku*) equivalent to Korea, Taiwan, Tonkin, and Cochin in that "although they are outside Chinese territory, they follow China's orders, use Chinese writing, and have received the Three Teachings [*sankyō*, i.e., Confucianism, Daoism, and Buddhism]." *Ka'i' tsūshō kō* gives no indication of whether Nishikawa considered Ezo a part of Japan or a foreign territory. On his world map, "Japan" could be construed to be comprised of four islands corresponding to Kyushu, Shikoku, Honshu and Ezo. *none of* the islands is individually identified, but Ezo is ambiguously placed, halfway between northern Honshu and the Siberian coast. Ryukyu, by contrast, is clearly labeled, in a manner suggesting that Nishikawa saw it as having the same relationship to Japan as Taiwan or Luzon. Nishikawa does not include the Ainu people of Ezo among the "forty-two" peoples in his abbreviated ethnographic catalog. Here too, however, Ryukyuans are represented as the people of a foreign land, just as Chinese, Manchus, and Mongols were.

However, Nishikawa resolves all ambiguity about the northeastern and southwestern margins in his *Nihon suido kō* ("On the Geography of Japan," [Nishikawa 1720]), which opens with a pair of maps, a "Map of the Asian

---

83   I refer, of course, to the "northern territories" dispute with Russia; with China over the Diaoyu/Senkaku islands to the south; and with Korea over Takeshima/Tokto, tiny islands in the "Sea of Japan" (or "East Sea).

Continent", and "Map of the Directional Orientation of Japan" ("Nihon hōgaku no zu," Fig. 12). The map of Japan, in a representation reminiscent of the *Dai Nihon jishin no zu* of a century earlier, depicts the islands of Japan afloat in an ocean enclosed in a circle of the compass points of the Chinese zodiac. Both Ezo and Ryukyu, neither of which is either depicted or mentioned, lie beyond the encircling zodiac ring, implicitly excluded from "Japan." The companion "Ajia daishū zu," with Nishikawa's "Asia" constituting roughly what is often termed the "eastern hemisphere," follows the conventions of his world map of two decades earlier: "Ryukyu" is labeled and clustered far south of Kyushu, along with—and ontologically equivalent to—the foreign countries of "Luzon" and "Taiwan," while "Ezo" (here it is named—as a foreign land) floats ambiguously equidistant from the northern tip of Honshu and the coast of Siberia. For Nishikawa, that is, as for his contemporaries Nakabayashi

FIGURE 12   Nishikawa Joken's map of "The Directional Orientation of Japan" ("Nihon hōgaku no zu," in Nishikawa 1720; reprinted in Takimoto, 1928–1931, 4: 537) excludes Ezo and Ryukyu from the territory of Japan; in the companion "Map of the Asian Continent" (Fig. 13), Ezo and Ryukyu are treated as analogous to Korea, Luzon (i.e., the Philippines), Taiwan, i.e., as foreign territories beyond the ambit of Japan.

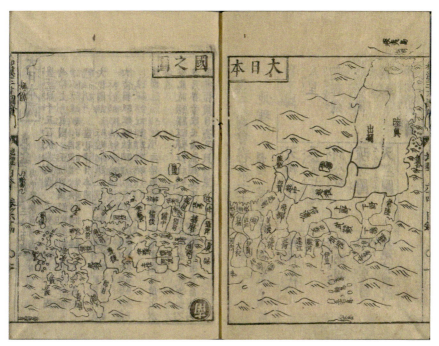

FIGURE 13   Terajima Ryōan (1712, 64: 1b–2a) maps Ezo and Matsumae beyond the frame of his "Map of Great Japan" (upper right), and the Ryukyuan kingdom so far off that he only offers a verbal comment (lower left) that it is, "This way to Ryūkyū." Korea (upper left corner), Tsushima (left border), Hachijōjima (lower border, right-hand page), and Kinkasan, a small island (12 km²/4.7 mi²) about 700 meters offshore from the tip of the Oshika Peninsula in Mutsu Province (right margin) as boundary conditions.

Kichiei, Ishikawa Ryūsen and Terajima Ryōan, Japan comprised only the three main islands of Honshu, Shikoku and Kyushu, and a few offshore islands like Sado, Oki, and Hachijō, but excluded both Ezo and Ryukyu, which he regarded as foreign countries.[84]

---

84   In his *Shijūnikoku jinbutsu zusetsu* (Nishikawa 1720), cataloging the peoples of forty-two foreign lands—including the mythic countries of the giants and the dwarves—Nishikawa includes Ryukyu as one of these foreign countries. In his earlier *On China's Commerce* (Nishikawa 1708, 3: 1) he groups Ryukyu with Korea, Taiwan, Tonkin and Cochin, as foreign countries (*gaikoku*) that are "outside of China, but obey its commands" (*Migi no kuni wa, Tōdo no soto nari to iedomo, Chūka no mei ni shitagai, Chūka no moji o mochiu*).

6   Terajima Ryōan and the *Wakan sansai zue*

In contrast to Nishikawa, his contemporary encyclopedist Terajima Ryōan, like
Ishikawa Ryūsen before him and Nagakubo Sekisui after, excluded both Ezo
and Ryukyu from Japan, separating them into categories analogous to Korea—
and to Japan as well.[85] The larger organization of Terajima's "Geography" (*Chiri-
bu*) section of Terajima's *Illustrated Encyclopedia of Japan and China* (*Wakan
sansai zue*, 1713) underscores the foreignness of Korea, Ryukyu and Ezo, and
their equivalence with "Japan" as countries, with no suggestion that Ryukyu
and Ezo, much less Korea, are somehow part of Japan. After an extended discussion of Chinese geography,[86] which he illustrates with maps of both China
as a whole, and individual maps of each province, Terajima proceeds to a map
of what he calls "Great Japan."[87] (Fig. 13) The sequence in which he organized
them is telling: geographically, "Great Japan," Korea (Chōsen), and Ryukyu are
all 'countries' (*kuni*), while Ezo is an "island" (*shima*); but in the section on
"Human Society" (*jinrin-rui*), Japan, Korea, Ryukyu and Ezo each has a "national language" (*kokugo*). Interposing the larger, more important, and most
indisputably "foreign" Korea between "Great Japan," on the one hand, and
Ryukyu and Ezo on the other, renders their equivalence (foreignness) unmistakable. The equivalence is clear even in the table of contents. Terajima concludes his "Geography" chapters by mapping Central Asia and India (based on
Buddhist cosmography), Europe ("Northern Barbarians"), and Southeast Asia
("Barbarians of the Southwest"), though his maps suggest to a modern eye just
how little he knew of these distant and unfamiliar lands.

   As a mode of representation, Terajima's "Map of Great Japan," *Dai Nihon-
koku no zu*,[88] relegates Ezo and Matsumae to the status of marginalia. Not only
do they float offshore to the north, but they are unnamed and lie outside the
frame of the map itself. They are more foreign than Korea (Chōsen), which is
suggested by a perfunctory squiggle of coastline at the upper left corner (northwest), directly above Tsushima. Tsushima, too, like Hachijōjima, to the south
of Izu, floats dangerously close to alienation, dancing on the left margin of the
map, but Ryukyu is even more "out of it": At the lower left (southwest) corner
of the map of "Great Japan," he notes only that "Ryukyu is in this direction"
(*Kono kata, Ryūkyū ari*). That is, the way Terajima organizes his cartographic
representation of the relationship of Korea, Ryukyu, and Ezo to "Great Japan"

---

85   Terajima (1712, *kan* 64).
86   Ibid., *kan* 62–63.
87   Ibid., *kan* 64.
88   Ibid., *kan* 64, lvs. 1b–2a.

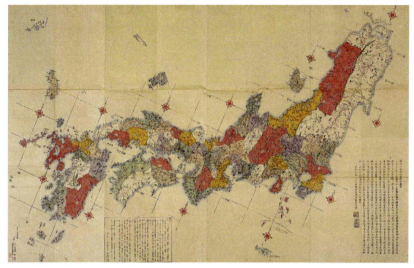

FIGURE 14   Nagakubo Sekisui, "Complete Route Map of Japan, Revised" (1779) maps only
the Japanese communities (*wajin-chi*) along the southern coast of the Oshima
Peninsula in Ezo, *chi*, upper right. The southeast corner of the Korean
peninsula, and the trading port of Pusan appear as a boundary condition,
upper left. A brief note inscribed just offshore of Erabu Island, in the lower
left corner, gives the distance (120 *ri*, ca. 470 km) to Ryūkyū—which is well off
the map.
COURTESY OF THE GEORGE H. BEANS COLLECTION, UNIVERSITY OF
BRITISH COLUMBIA

leaves little doubt that he regards as them as ontologically equivalent, foreign
territories.

While he marginalizes and "alien"-ates them in his "Great Japan" map,
Terajima gives each of the three "border condition" countries detailed attention in its own map and brief accompanying explanation in his chapters on geography, and rudimentary ethnographic treatment in his chapters on human
society. "Ryukyu is an island [country] in the midst of the sea, southeast of
Fujian," he writes, and further, "The qualities of its people are detailed in [the
section on] foreign peoples."[89] The landscape of Terajima's "Map of the Country
of Ryukyu" (*Ryūkyū -koku no zu*) is littered with architectural landmarks that
are indelibly inscribed with the iconographic markings of "Chinese"—that is,
foreign—architecture, further marking Ryukyu as external to "Japan." A legend in the northeast quadrant further proclaims, "[To the] northeast is the
province of Satsuma in Japan." Lest there be any doubt about the status of

---

89   Ibid., p. 754.

Ryukyu in Terajima's taxonomy, he concludes his brief discussion by noting, "The historical fortunes of the people of this country are [recounted] in detail in 'Peoples of Foreign Lands' [*ikoku jinbutsu*], Part 2 (chapter 13)," a notation not paralleled in his notes on either Korea or Ezo. Terajima does not share the confusion of his contemporary, Chikamatsu (1711), about the identity and location of Ryukyu. While for Chikamatsu, Ryukyu is *neither* Chinese nor Japanese, for Terajima it is a completely foreign topos—no matter that the bakufu had mapped it (for the first and last time) as part of "Japan" only ten years before. Ten years later, under the eighth shogun, Tokugawa Yoshimune, the bakufu would map Ryukyu "out" of Japan once more.

In his map of Ezo, Terajima situates Japan and Sakhalin ("Karafuto-jima, a dependency of Tartary") as external boundary conditions of Ezo, just as Ezo was a foreign boundary condition of "Great Japan." Ezo, he writes, "is an island in the sea northeast of Japan.... For the quality of its people (*jinpin*), the details appear in the section on 'Peoples of Foreign Lands.'"[90] The treatment of Korea is identical to that of Ezo and Ryukyu in this regard: "The quality of its people is detailed in 'Peoples of Foreign Lands Part 2.'" Like his predecessor Ryūsen and his successors Nagakubo Sekisui and Hayashi Shihei, Terajima implicitly repudiates the bakufu's claims—asserted in its mapping strategies—to both Ezo and Ryukyu, classing them with Korea and China as foreign lands, rather than with Japan's domestic provinces. Indeed, the refutation of Japanese possession borders on the explicit, for the northern tip of Honshu bears the label, "part of Tsugaru territory in Japan" (*Nihon Tsugaru chinai*), while the large land mass to the north is labeled "The Island of Sakhalin, i.e., a dependency of the Manchus" (*Karafuto no shima, sunawachi Dattan no zoku*). Ezo, for Terajima, is like Ryukyu: neither Japanese nor Chinese but sui generis and yet thoroughly foreign.

Despite their inclusion in the *bakufu's* mapping project, Terajima's exclusion of Ezo, Ryukyu and Korea from "Great Japan" in the "Geography" (*chiri*) chapters of his encyclopedia, and his treatment of them as ontologically equivalent "foreign" territories is reaffirmed in his "Gazetteer" (*chibu*), which follows. This detailed province-by-province gazetteer of Japan, which comprises sixteen of the 105 chapters of the total work, proceeds across the land from northeast to southwest, an organization familiar to users of modern Japanese geographical reference works, from Michinoku (Mutsu) and Dewa to the provinces of Kyushu, Iki, and Tsushima, includes the sixty-six classical provinces of Japan

---

90   For a discussion of the significance of the trope of *jinpin* in Japanese imaginings of the foreign, see Toby (1998a, 1998b); Chapter 4, below.

and the two supernumeraries.[91] Each regional subsection begins with a map of the region but devotes substantial space to detailed accounts of major towns and focuses on Shinto and Buddhist religious sites, and on local products.

Where Terajima's map of Japan, *Dai Nihon-koku no zu*, relegates Ezo and Matsumae to the status of marginalia—floating not merely offshore to the north but outside the frame of the map itself—his *Map of Michinoku and Dewa*, like Ryūsen's "Japan" maps, brings Matsumae into the frame, offering a perfunctory line north of Honshu to indicate a coastline, which he labeled "Matsumae." A legend at the mouth of Mutsu Bay notes that "[i]t takes two days by sea to reach Matsumae," just as Terajima's "Great Japan" map noted "[t]his way to Ryukyu" as a border condition rather than an essential element of what was to be mapped. The detailed, written information in the gazetteer chapters begins with Michinoku, making mention—but asserting no claim of "Japanese" status or dependency on Japan—of Matsumae or Ezo. In the southwest, "Japan" ends with Iki and Tsushima.[92] The only mention of either Korea or Ryukyu are a notation on one of the "local products" (*miyage*) of Tsushima: "[g]inseng (Korea)"; and a brief epilogue that explains that "[t]he Japanese [province] of Satsuma is opposite Jejiang; Tsushima is opposite Korea, five-hundred *ri* [away]." Ryukyu is completely invisible to Ryōan's cataloging "gaze"-etteer of "Japan," and Korea is only dimly visible, "one day's [voyage], if the winds are right."[93]

7   Hayashi Shihei and the "Three Countries"

Likewise, the geographer and military strategist Hayashi Shihei's (1738–93) gazetteer of Japan's three nearest foreign neighbors, *Sangoku tsūran zusetsu* (Illustrated Guide to the Three Countries, 1786), covered Korea, Ezo and Ryukyu as ontologically equivalent entities—that is, as foreign countries—though each had a distinct relationship to "Japan" and "Japanese" authority.[94] But Shihei's focus as a cartographer, geographer and military strategist in this work was less on what was *within* Japan than in what lay immediately outside Japan's boundaries, precisely how to define those boundaries and—as he

---

91   Terajima (1712, *kan* 65–80). In contemporary parlance these were the *Rokujūroku-shū nitō* ("sixty-six provinces; two islands").

92   Ibid., *kan* 80).

93   Ibid., p. 1139.

94   Hayashi (1786), reprinted in Hayashi (1979, 2: 15–113; 2: supplement). On Hayashi see Keene (1952, 39–45 *et passim*); Taira (1977); Noguchi (1991, 204–211).

argued in a companion work *Kaikoku heidan* (Military Lectures for A Maritime Country)—how to defend, or even expand, those boundaries.[95]

As he wrote in a colophon to his unpublished "Complete Map of the Foreign Countries around Japan" (*Nihon enkin gaikoku no zenzu*, Hayashi 1782),

> Our country is in the midst of the sea, while the borders of the three countries of Korea, Ryukyu and Ezo abut our country. There are maps in circulation where one can see the approximate directions of those neighbors, but while one can get a general idea about them, one cannot learn accurate details of the sea lanes, distances or topography. Therefore I have compiled this new complete map, with our country at the center, and Korea, Ryukyu and Ezo around it, inscribing their boundaries correctly, and clarifying their directions [vis-à-vis Japan]....[96]

Japan's boundaries—at least the "northern frontier"—had quite suddenly become much more than a purely academic questions, but rather an urgent issue of Japanese security, for mid- and late eighteenth-century Russian activity along the Siberian littoral had brought what Donald Keene aptly termed "tales from Muscovy," and fears of a Russian invasion from the north.[97] In the early 1770s, the self-styled "Baron" or "Count" Moritz von Benyowsky, who had

---

95   Hayashi (1791), reprinted in Hayashi (1979, 1: 77–312). *Kaikoku heidan* criticized Japan's defense policies which, based on Chinese military science, were oriented primarily to defense against land-based threats. These were inapplicable to a "maritime country" like Japan, Hayashi argued, and proposed strategies prioritizing naval warfare and coastal defense. In 1792 Shihei was arrested for publishing a critique of state policy, and for producing "maps of Japan and foreign countries [that] are contrary to geography," i.e., inaccurate. The bakufu's response was likely based on Furukawa Koshōken's charge in *Tōyū zakki* (1789), which he presented to Matsudaira Sadanobu, head of the *rōjū* (the bakufu's highest executive council), that Shihei's geography of northeastern Japan was inaccurate, and that, "if he doesn't even know the geography of his own country, it's even more [likely that he is ignorant of] foreign countries' [geography]." (Furukawa 1789, 499). Ironically, Furukawa's own 1788 map of Ezo and the northern tip of Honshu (Takagi 2011, fig. 5) is itself hardly more accurate than Shihei's. Itasaka Yōko (1979, 24), Matsuzaka Toshio (2005) and Marcia Yonemoto (2003, 82), agree that it was likely Furukawa's critique that brought down Shihei. Shihei was sentenced to domiciliary confinement in Sendai, where he died, while both *Sangoku tsūran zusetsu* and *Kaikoku heidan* were banned, copies of the books and printing blocks confiscated and destroyed; his publisher was fined and put out of business. For details on the case, Taira (1977, 247–250). In a further irony, six decades after Shihei's death bakufu officials negotiators appears to have used Shihei's maps to assert Japan's claims to the Bonin (or Ogasawara) Islands, and rebut those of Commodore Matthew C. Perry. (Nagata 1943, 6–8).

96   Hayashi (1782), quoted in Takagi (2011, 84).

97   Keene (1969, 31–58); the term "northern frontier," I take from Harrison (1953).

escaped from captivity in Kamchatka, sent letters to the Dutch in Nagasaki the last of which, dated 20 July 1771, warned that Russia had deployed "two galleons and a frigate" to Kamchatka, and planned "an attack on [Matsumae]... for next year."[98] Benyowsky's assertion had no basis in fact, but that did not prevent it from stirring up urgent concern among Japanese intellectuals, though Harrison may go too far in characterizing it as "a condition of near hysteria."[99]

Hayashi Shihei shared the widespread sense of foreign threat that Benyowsky had stirred up, but Taira Shigemichi sees Shihei's conversations in 1775 with the Overseer of the Dutch Factory in Nagasaki, Arend Willem Feith, as the more proximate cause of his alarm, and the motivation for writing both *Sangoku tsūran zusetsu* and *Kaikoku heidan*. Taira calls this Shihei's "Nagasaki awakening."[100] Feith explained the European pattern of colonization, of "seducing and subduing countries tens of thousands of *li* distant and making them their own possessions, to the long-term benefit of the home country," as Shihei put it.[101]

For Shihei, just as for Ryūsen and Sekisui, there was no isomorphism between the "Japan" he mapped as a "realm" and the "realm" claimed in the *bakufu*'s practices of province mapping. Shihei chides earlier geographers and cartographers because,

> Now, there are no small number who speak of geography, but they either hurriedly [draft] maps of the whole world [*bankoku no zu*], or limit themselves to the territory of our country [*honpō no chi*]. This is but my personal opinion, but aren't they all quite inadequate? It is for this reason that my humble intent is now to compile a new map, centered on Our Country (*honpō o naka ni shite*), clarifying [the positions of] Korea, Ryukyu, Ezo, and the Ogasawara [islands] (these are the uninhabited isles [*mujintō*] of Izu). That is because these three countries' territories are contiguous to Our Land, and in truth are [its] neighbor states (*rinkyō*). Truly, what everyone in Our Land should know, noble and base, samurai and civilian alike, is the geography of these three countries.[102]

Shihei also agreed with Terajima, Ryūsen and Sekisui that Ezo and Ryukyu, as well as the Ogasawara Islands, were ontologically equivalent to Korea as

---

98   Quoted in ibid., p. 34.
99   Harrison (1953, 17).
100   Taira (1977, 94–95).
101   Hayashi (1786), quoted in Taira (1977, 64–95).
102   Hayashi (1786, 1: 1a); parenthetical comment in the original.

foreign places. He repeatedly distinguishes them from other foreign lands because they are "neighboring countries," on the one hand, but unquestionably *not* part of Japan, on the other.[103] Rather, they were lands that, while outside Japan's authority, were strategically essential to Japan in ways that other, more distant—non-"neighbor"—lands were not.[104] Hayashi continues with a critique of the practices of commercially available maps of Japan that treated his "three countries" as an afterthought—recall that *Sangoku tsūran zusetsu* appeared only a few years after Sekisui's much-heralded map—noting that,

> Maps of Our Land chart only the ports (*minatoguchi*) whence one crosses the seas in the four directions, but they do not show their entire shape [*zenkei o agezu*]. Now, there have always been many complete maps of Our Land (*honpō*) [circulating] in society; most recently we have the detailed map compiled by [Nagakubo] Sekisui of Mito. Those who wish to know the [domestic] geography of Our Land should rely on Sekisui's map.[105]

Yet even Sekisui's maps, which Shihei holds in high regard for their comprehensive detail about *domestic* geography, he charges, were inadequate precisely because they offered no useful information about those "neighboring lands" that Shihei considered strategically crucial to Japan's own survival. He goes on to note significant differences in the length of the unit of distance—the *ri*—in these three countries, saying that he has corrected them to the standards of "Our Country": "I have recorded all land and sea route distances [*kairiku dōhō*] in the three countries using the 36 *chō*=1 *ri* that is standard in Our Country; I have not used the route-distances of foreign countries [*ikoku*]. This is so that it will be readily comprehensible to people of Our Country."[106] For Shihei, as for Ryūsen and Sekisui, Korea, Ryukyu, and Ezo were not *part of* "Our Country"

---

103   Hayashi restates this equivalence in the afterword to *Kaikoku heidan* (1791, vol. 16): "I recently wrote *Sangoku tsūran* [*zusetsu*]. In that work I published maps of Korea, Ryukyu and Ezo, Japan's three neighboring countries...."

104   Hayashi's *Little Map for the Purpose of Seeing How the Several Countries of Korea, Ryūkyū,Ezo, Karafuto, Kamchatka, Rakko, etc., Connect [to Japan]* (*Chōsen, Ryūkyū, Ezo narabi ni Karafuto Kamusasuka, Rakko-jima nado, sūkoku setsujō keisei o miru tame no shōzu*) confirms in its labeling and color-coding that he sees Korea, Ryūkyū, and Ezo as equivalent "countries" (*koku; kuni*). Only the southern tip of Ezo is color-coded as part of *Dainihon* and is labeled "Matsumae." See Hayashi (1786), appendix, "Sūkoku setsujō ichiran no zu." To the southwest, Hayashi's color codes Tokara-jima as part of Japan, and labels Kikai-jima, "From here on is Ryūkyū territory" (*Kore yori Ryūkyū no chi*).

105   Hayashi (1786, 19).

106   Ibid., 20.

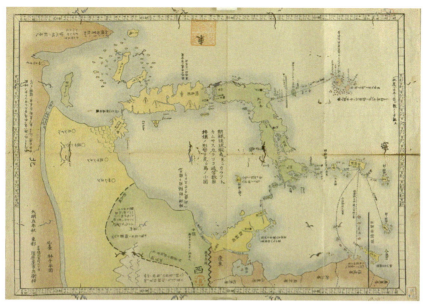

FIGURE 15   Hayashi Shihei, "Sangoku tsūran yochi rotei zenzu" (Hayashi 1786): Territory
Hayashi considers Japanese is color-coded green; countries he considers
non-Japanese—Ezo, the Ryukyus, Korea, and the "Uninhabited Islands"
(*Mujin-tō*, i.e., the Bonin, or Ogasawara, islands)—are in contrasting colors.
The text at the center of the map explains that it is, "A small map to see the
shapes of the several nearby countries, [i.e.] Korea, the Ryukyus and Ezo, as
well as Karafuto (Sakhalin), Kamchatka and the Sea Otter Islands (i.e., the
southern Kurils)," making explicit Hayashi's notion of the boundaries of Japan.
1 Immediately above Kikai-jima, regarded as a boundary island since early
medieval times, is the notation, "Beyond here [is the] territory of Ryūkyū"
(*kore yori Ryūkyū no chi*). 2 In a notation that has implications in the present,
Hayashi labels two small islands ""Takeshima," and explains that "[These] are
possessions of Korea" (*Chōsen no mochi nari*); "From these islands one can gaze
at the Oki Islands [in Japan] and also see Korea" (*Kono shima yori Onshū o
nozomi, mata Chōsen o mo miru*). Hayashi is correct that Korea—at least the
summit of Sŏnginbong, at 984m, the highest point on Ullŭngdo—is visible
from Dokdo/Takeshima on a clear day. The Oki Islands, however, 162 km to the
southeast, are never visible from Dokdo/Takeshima.

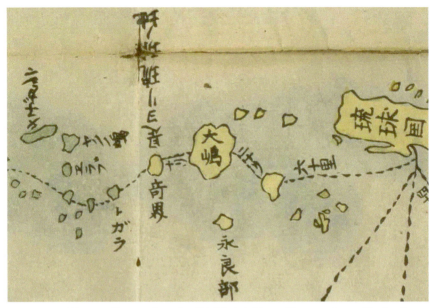

FIGURE 16   Kikaijima ("strange boundary") is labeled, "Beyond here, territory of Ryūkyū."

FIGURE 17   Hayashi labels the "Takeshima" islands "Korean territory," and notes that "from
             here one can see Oki Island."

FIGURE 18

The land at the southern tip of Ezo, centered on Matsumae Castle (black square) is color-coded as "Japanese" territory, while yellow distinguishes "the country of Ezo," as foreign territory.

FIGURE 19   Hayashi Shihei, "Ezo-koku zenzu" ("Complete Map of the Land of Ezo"): On his map of Ezo, Hayashi not only uses color-coding to distinguish "Ainu lands" (*Ezo no chi*) from Japanese lands, but adds notation, at Usubechi on southwest coast, and Haraki on the southeast, where, "from here [is] Ainu territory" (*kore yori Ezo-chi*). See Fig. 20 for detail.

FIGURE 20   Hayashi Shihei, "Ezo-koku zenzu" (detail of Fig. 19): In his "Complete Map
of the Land of Ezo," Hayashi repeats the color-coding used in his "Sangoku
tsūran yochi rotei zenzu" (Fig. 15), adding the legends.

but rather its limiting or boundary conditions, as Shihei's term *rinkyō* clearly
implies.

What distinguished Shihei—a teacher of "military science" (*heigaku*)—
from those earlier cartographers, however, was his belief that Japan's geography, and especially its archipelagic nature, presented important strategic
challenges that were beyond the capacity of existing military science which
was based, after all, on Chinese traditions oriented to China's historical pre-
occupation with defending extensive land borders. He articulated those concerns further in a companion work, *Kaikoku heidan* (1791):

> What is a "maritime nation?" It signifies a country with no neighboring
> countries whose lands adjoin it; a country entirely surrounded by the sea.
> Therefore, there are defensive preparations appropriate to a maritime
> country that are categorically different from [those set forth in] Chinese
> books of military strategy and from those transmitted in Japan from
> ancient times to the present.[107]

This ambiguity regarding the territories that comprised Japan was not restricted to private scholarship but was mapped onto public practice: When France
sought to conclude a treaty with the Ryukyuan kingdom in 1844, Edo authorized the negotiations—which Europeans might see as a Japanese disavowal

---

107   Hayashi (1791, preface).

of sovereign claims to the Ryukyus under the principles of "international law." And when the *bakufu*'s own chief of diplomatic protocol, Hayashi Fukusai, compiled a guide to Japanese diplomatic precedents that treated Ryukyu as a foreign country with which the *bakufu* had diplomatic relations, he must surely have known of the "province maps" of Ryukyu.[108]

It is my initial hypothesis that, just as in Siam and China, Japanese notions of territorial sovereignty were not linked to clearly delineated borders; rather, as suggested earlier, they were conceived as zones of gradation—both gradients of decreasing "civilization" as distance from the "civilizing" Japanese "center" increased and as a nautical gradient across an *ao-unabara* (blue-green sea), *shiozakai* (tidal boundary), or *chikura-ga-oki* (the waters between northern Kyushu and southern Korea).[109] Though never encoded cartographically, the *shiozakai* was vividly represented in Zhu's (n.d.) depiction of Ryukyuan vessels bound for China: "Ryukyuan" waters were divided from "Chinese" by a diagonal line of white-capped waves, on either side of which quite fragile-seeming ships were tossing about.

Further, although daimyos mapped their provinces as extensions of the *bakufu*'s cartographic gaze—producing the maps that became *kuni-ezu*—they did so as objects of the *bakufu*'s hegemonic gaze rather than through an independent hegemonic eye. Certainly daimyo often mapped the boundaries of their domains, a practice essential for resolving inter-domain jurisdictional disputes. Yet the daimyos' acceptance of *bakufu* authority to map the provinces, even in the Tenpō era, argues more eloquently for the overarching sovereignty of shogunal authority and for the *bakufu* as a "state" than for nascent "states" and "nationalities" at the local level of daimyo, even the *kuni-mochi* daimyo, domains.

It was only in the mid-nineteenth century—though pressures were building from the 1770s on—that Japan was unavoidably confronted with the "modern world system" that aggressively pushed its notions of unitary sovereignties and exclusive territorial claims on all the peoples and states of the earth. In order fully to understand how Japan negotiated that confrontation and ultimately assimilated to the Congress of Vienna system that embodied those notions, we must better comprehend—as Thongchai has for Siam—the discourses of space and authority, and the cartographic sign system in which they were expressed, that produced a "ragged-edged" Japan.

---

108   Hayashi (1913/1967).
109   Toby (1985).

8   Margins and Maps

The "ragged edge" of early modern Japan becomes visible only at the frayed margins, at the "tidal boundary" between Japan and its nearest neighbors. As Thongchai has argued for Siam, Smith and Howland for China, "national" borders were fluid, malleable, and perhaps intentionally vague for the early modern Japanese state.[110] The bakufu made clear assertions of sovereignty over Ezo and Ryukyu through the imposition of cadastral surveys, anti-Christian policies, population registration, and the bakufu's cartographic gaze in *kuni-ezu*. Yet the bakufu was both slow to assert the inclusion of these "claimed" territories at the margins and inconsistent when it did: Neither Ezo nor Ryukyu appeared on the earliest maps of Japan the bakufu prepared. Eventually the bakufu included Ezo (in the 1650s), and then Ryukyu (in 1702), but later excluded Ryukyu from the map of Japan prepared at Yoshimune's order in 1717.

Cartographers, geographers, and encyclopedists outside the bakufu—the ones who produced geographic knowledge for dissemination through commercial and intellectual networks—seem never to have accepted the *bakufu's* claims over Ryukyu and Ezo (if they even knew of them at all) and treated both as either ill-defined boundary conditions, as Sekisui did, or as foreign countries, as Terajima and Hayashi did. Throughout the eighteenth century, mapmakers, encyclopedists and geographers treated Ezo and Ryukyu as "foreign" territory, ontological equivalents of Korea. They knew, to be sure, of the Matsumae presence on the Oshima Peninsula at the southern tip of Ezo (and sometimes inscribed it as part of Japan) and of Satsuma's virtually complete control of Ryukyu, yet they continued to treat both as *ikoku*. The mass of people who saw Ryukyuans on the nearly twenty occasions when they paraded through Japan, from Satsuma to Edo and back, also regarded them as no less "foreign" than Koreans. If even an exceptionally well-informed daimyo such as Matsura Seizan, lord of Hirado, or the geographer Nishikawa Joken could regard Ryukyuans as foreigners (*Tōjin*), ordinary folk could be forgiven for doing so as well.[111]

One is tempted by the hypothesis that the ragged edges in the "national" maps in the collective (i.e., combined state and private) mapping project of early modern Japan were not there by oversight but by choice. It is certainly

---

110   Thongchai (1994); Smith (1996); Howland (1996).

111   Matsura (1979–1981, 7: 291–8:29), writing in 1832, consistently distinguishes "Ryukyuans" (*Ryūjin*) from "people of our country" (*wagakuni-bito*). Nishikawa (1720/1898–1907), like Terajima Ryōan (1712), counts Ryukyuans as aliens in his forty-two country taxonomy of foreign peoples.

not the case that Japanese were unable to conceive of clear-cut boundaries; indeed, there is ample evidence that a concern with clear boundaries at the local and provincial levels was well established from ancient times. Boundary disputes—between estate proprietors, between villages, or between peasants—were among the most frequent matters of litigation.[112] Certainly, the *kuni-ezu* are unambiguous about provincial boundaries—but evinced little concern for what lies beyond the edge of the province. And *shōen* maps were often concerned with little else *but* boundaries,[113] and often rendered anything beyond the estate boundary in perfunctory, iconic fashion, in much the same way that Ryukyu, Ezo, and Korea were noted, rather than mapped, in all—"Japan" maps—as boundary conditions, whose particular status was a matter of little concern to the nature of "Japan" itself. If the bakufu allowed the ambiguity to persist, not correcting Ryūsen and Sekisui, Terajima and Hayashi, perhaps it was because a ragged-edged "Japan" was as comfortable a notion to Japanese, as a ragged-edged Siam was to Siamese, until Western notions of absolute demarcations of sovereignty, forced a transformation in Japanese practice in the nineteenth century.

Several things, however, are clear from this discussion. First, Tosa and Hirosaki—to take but two examples—may have articulated seemingly autonomous identities in the eighteenth century, which Edo did not contest so long as they were not flagrantly flaunted. But Edo asserted unrefuted claims to the entire country along many avenues, not least of which was its penetrating cartographic gaze, which on the one hand probed microscopically, in the *kuni-ezu* into each province, effacing even the daimyo domain itself, and quite literally collected the realm piece by piece in the Momijiyama Bunko, the shogunal archives in the precincts of Edo Castle. On the other, the gaze was broadcast macroscopically, gathering all provinces, into a single project, as the *Nihon sōzu* ("complete map of Japan"), and asserted a *unified* shogunal claim to every village and farm, every highway and mountain, as a single object of sovereign possession—and again locked up the realm in the Momijiyama Archive.

Second, though the *bakufu* might be—or at least pretend to be—master of all it surveyed in its various national mapping projects, it was unclear about the boundaries of the object of its gaze. As Kawamura has shown, no two of the national maps the *bakufu* generated from *kuni-ezu* treated what I call "the ragged edges"—the marchlands of Ezo and the Ryukyus—quite the same.[114]

---

112   Kuroda (1986b, chapter 3).
113   See, for example, Kuroda (1986b); Kinda, et al. (1996).
114   Kawamura (1990).

The *bakufu*, like Siam, was content to leave uncontested boundaries undefined, or at least, from a modernist perspective, only vaguely defined.

And further, whatever boundary claims the *bakufu* might assert as state secret, the general public had little idea what those claims were, and when mapmakers like Ryūsen and Sekisui, encyclopedists such as Terajima and Hayashi, got it "wrong"—if the *bakufu*'s maps are somehow the definition of what was officially "right"—the *bakufu* made no attempt publicly to correct the error. The authorities, that is, evinced no interest in asserting a public consciousness of where Japanese territory gave way to something else. We can only speculate whether these mapmakers and geographers had access, direct or indirect, to the *bakufu*'s "truth" about boundaries, and chose to ignore them— treating Ezo, Ryukyu, and Korea as equivalent boundary conditions of Japan, rather than distinguishing between "Japanese" and "foreign" territory in exactly the same way as the *bakufu*—or whether they were making independent assertions, which the *bakufu* allowed to go unchallenged.

What is certain, however, is that the question of national (i.e., Japanese) boundaries remained ragged at the edges—in the same way as Siam's—until the re-encounter with the "West" in the nineteenth century forced the question, and knitted up the raveled sleeve into the sort of neat, clear boundaries that "modern" international law and practice demands. We must remember, with Denis Wood, that "National boundaries," ultimately,

> "are not sensible," and that at the margins, the boundary, maps may "just be ... *opinion*, somebody's *idea* of where your property began and ended, a good *guess* at where the border was.... What is elided in this way is precisely the social construction of the property line, the social construction of the border ... which—like everything else we map—is not a line you can *see*.... But no sooner are maps acknowledged as social constructions than their contingent, their conditional, their *arbitrary* ... character, is unveiled."[115]

The contingent, conditional, and arbitrary mappings of something styled "Japan" throughout the Edo period reveals just how fragile any consensus might be on where that Japan began and ended, on what it was that visibly signified the transition from the realm of the domestic to the domain of the Other. The

---

115   Wood (1996, 8, 19).

indeterminacy and fluidity of the outer limits asserted and inscribed in contemporary maps is vivid testimony of the ragged edges of Japan.[116]

9   Coda

The indeterminate, malleable and ragged "national" boundaries characteristic of both official and unofficial maps of Japan in the seventeenth and most
of the eighteenth centuries articulated well with fluid conceptions of border
or frontier lands, and notions of overlapping sovereign or suzerain claims—
especially with regard to the Ryukyus, but also with reference to Korea and
Ezo—that were intrinsic to Edo-era ideological constructions of political, diplomatic, and cultural space.[117] To reverse the terms, a Japanese discourse that
simultaneously asserted some form of sovereign or suzerain claims—however
specious—over Ryukyu and Korea, on the one hand, yet recognized that both
were tributaries first of Ming and, later, Qing China, on the other, could only
cohere by constructing graded, nuanced ragged-edged frontier zones.

Beginning with the Benyowsky letter of 1771, however, perceived threats of
Russian aggression and actual encroachments in Ezo, occasional armed confrontations between Russian landing parties and both Ainu and Japanese, and
Russian attempts to open direct trade with Japan, provoked a growing sense
of foreign threat, in both government circles and among the politically aware
population more generally.[118] That sense of alarm was soon magnified, in the
early nineteenth century, by the incursion of the British frigate *H. M. S. Phaeton*

---

116   If commercially published maps are any index of the public conception of the extent
       of "Japan," a land whose territory was conceived as excluding Ryūkyū and Ezo, then
       there is ample cartographic evidence that Europeans shared—indeed received—that
       vision. European maps of Japan from the late seventeenth to the early nineteenth cen-
       turies generally derived from published Japanese maps brought to Europe by men such
       as Engelbert Kaempfer and Franz Phillip von Siebold. Kaempfer's Japan map, a virtual
       tracing of *Shinsen Dainihon zukan* (1687), treats Ezo, Ryūkyū, and Korea as boundary
       conditions. My assessment of Kaempfer's sources differs from that of Marcia Yonemoto
       (2000), who links Kaempfer's map directly with Ishikawa Ryūsen's *Honchō kōmoku zukan*.
       J. G. Scheuzer's copy of Kaempfer's (Kaempfer, 1727) map, however, suggests reliance on
       the *Shinsen Dainihon zukan* (1687; see Cortazzi, p. 99) map in its treatment of Matsumae
       and "Jesogasima" (*Ezo-ga-shima*), "Liqueio" (Ryūkyū), the island of Oki, and several
       other details. For an excellent introduction to European cartographic understandings of
       "Japanese" territorial sovereignty, see especially Walter (1994), Boscaro and Walter (1994),
       and Kreiner (1994).
117   Toby (1985, 1990, 1991); Walker (2007); Wigen (2010); Oguma (2014).
118   On the petition of Catherine the Great's 1792 envoy Adam Laxman to open direct trade
       with Japan, and Nikolai Rezanov's expedition to Nagasaki in 1804, Lensen (1959, 96–176).

into Nagasaki Harbor in 1808, by increasingly frequent sightings of American whalers and China clippers off the Pacific Coast, and by occasional landings by western crews seeking food, fuel and water.[119]

The earliest published attempt to inscribe a northern boundary on maps, and indeed the boundaries of "Japan" in all directions, as we have seen above, appeared in Hayashi Shihei's *Sangoku tsūran zusetsu* of 1786, discussed above.[120] Hayashi traced the urgency about the vulnerability of Japan's ill-defined borders and his desire for better maps directly to the Russian advance: "Recently, it seems, many from Muscovy have settled on the island of Uruppu [Urup]. From that base, they come to Iturup to trade. But their real purpose in the trade is hard to gauge. Might they really have their hearts set on swallowing Etorofu [Iturup]?"[121]

While Hayashi's maps may at first glance seem a bit imprecise about the boundary between Japanese territory (*Wajinchi*) and foreign territory, more a zone where the color-coded *Wajinchi* faded into *Ezochi* than a line clearly separating one from the other, on closer examination we see notations at both Usubechi on the southwest coast, and Haraki on the southeast, "From here is Ezochi" (*Kore yori [e]zochi*). Just inside the limits of *Wajinchi* he notes both the distance from Matsumae Castle, and the presence of a checkpoint (*sekisho*), controlling passage between *Wajinchi* and *Ezochi*. And in his main text he notes: "Kumaishi is the northern limit of Japanese territory."[122] At the opposite end of "Japan" he was equally unambiguous, labelling Kikai-jima as the place where Japanese territory ended and that of Ryūkyū began: "From here [it is] Ryūkyū territory" (*kore yori Ryūkyū no chi*).

Hayashi's boundary claims were perhaps more aspirational than descriptive, and may not, of course, have accorded with official thinking, either in Matsumae or—as his later arrest and the banning of his books suggests—in Edo. Yet just at the moment Hayashi was compiling and publishing his work, the bakufu, under the leadership of *rōjū* Tanuma Okitsugu, had begun casting its gaze to the north, with an eye to colonization of Ezo. In 1785 Tanuma

---

      Lensen calls the Laxman mission "the opening wedge." See also Keene (1952); Harrison (1953); Toby (1984; 2008).

119   Here it is worth recalling that Melville (1851) speaks of "the Japanese Whaling ground," which "first became generally known" in 1819; and that it is there that the Pequod finally encounters Moby-Dick. On the Phaeton Incident, see especially Wilson (2010).

120   Hayashi had earlier produced a hand-drawn draft map, Hayashi (1782), now in the Sendai City Museum.

121   Hayashi (1786).

122   *Kumaishi o motte Nihon fūdo no kagiri.* Kumaishi, at N42°7′45″ N, 139°57′59″ E, is about 75 km north of Matsumae.

dispatched an official team of inspectors to survey Ezo's economic prospects, and proposed a scheme to incorporate the island into the political economy of Japan by sending tens of thousands of outcastes as agricultural colonists. His inspectors' reports in 1786 included a "Complete map of Ezo" which encompassed Ezo and Karafuto, and was at the same time the first map to represent the Kurils as an island chain. The plan envisioned adding nearly six million *koku* (about 1.8 million kiloliters) of rice-equivalents to the Japanese economy, but was repudiated by Tanuma's successors, led by Matsudaira Sadanobu, after he was ousted from office in 1786.[123]

Yet after Tanuma's downfall, and the apparent reversal of his plans to colonize Ezo, however, the pace of both exploration and mapping of the northern frontier zone stretching from Matsumae to Karafuto, north of Ezo, and the Kurils to the east, accelerated as concern over Russian encroachment mounted. In 1790 Matsumae domain dispatched Takahashi Sōshirō to explore and map Karafuto. The following year Katō Kengo, also of Matsumae, drafted a new map of Ezo that, though flawed by modern standards, came much closer to approximating the shape of the island, as well as extending its range to Iturup (J., Etorofu) in the east, and Karafuto—however distorted—to the north. In the context of competition with Russia for control of the Ainu populations in these outlying islands, one can see these mappings as adumbrating territorial claims.

Soon thereafter the bakufu began to dispatch its own expeditions to Ezo and beyond, recording both geographical and ethnographic observations, and making maps. In mid-1798 Kondō Jūzō, while on just such a bakufu expedition, planted a signpost on the island of Iturup proclaiming it, "Etorofu in Great Japan";[124] that same year he drafted a map of Ezo which, however, did not include any of the offshore islands.[125] The following year the bakufu embarked on a program for the direct administration of Ezo, posting a magistrate in Hakodate in 1802, and extending its reach to the north (Sakhalin) and east (Urup and Iturup).[126]

By the turn of the nineteenth century, as the Japanese discourse of indeterminate boundaries increasingly confronted both Russian inroads in the north, and whalers and merchantmen off the Pacific coast, with occasional

---

123   Keene (1952): 39–41; Hall (1955): 67; Ooms (1975): 120; Walker (2001): 164–165;

124   Kansei 10/7/28 (1799/8/27), quoted in Tōkyō Daigaku Shiryō Hensanjo (1989–1993, suppl., p. 32). See also Stephan (1970, 68–69); Kikuchi (1999, 84–86). Kondō's *Ezo-chi ezu*, drafted a year earlier, indicates neither Urup, nor the Kurils closer offshore of northeastern Ezo, i.e., the westernmost of the Kurils. Tōkyō Daigaku Shiryō Hensanjo (1989–1993, *fuzu* 6).

125   Tōkyō Daigaku Shiryō Hensanjo (1989–1993, Suppl., Map 6).

126   Walker (2001, 150–153).

landings to demand water, fuel and other supplies. The challenge of Euro-American notions of sharp, clearly delineated claims of territorial authority and sovereignty—backed by the economic and military might of the Industrial Revolution—forced Japanese authorities gradually to recognize the need to respond with assertions of exclusive sovereign claims to territory. The first moves to knit up the raveled sleeve came in the north, naturally enough, where Russian inroads in northern Ezo were seen as a threat as early as the 1770s.[127]

In negotiations with a Russian mission to Ezo in 1813–1814, the bakufu's representatives, Kōjimoto Sukeyuki and Takahashi Shigekata, reported that the Russians had proposed setting a "contact boundary" (*sekkyō* 接境) between Russia and Japan in the Kurils, and were instructed to respond by saying that it would "be difficult to establish relations [between the two countries] within the framework of either diplomacy or trade (*tsūshin; tsūshō*)."[128] They were further instructed to say that although they might want to negotiate a boundary between the two countries through correspondence, it would be impermissible under Japan's ancestral law (*sashiyurushigataki kokuhō nari*). Yet at the same time, Kōjimoto's and Takahashi's reports note proposing that the limit of Japanese territory in the western Kurils was the island of Etorofu (which Kondō Jūzō had proclaimed part of "Great Japan" in 1798), and that the limit of Russian territory should be Simushir Island, 110 km northeast of Etorofu. They explicitly proposed that neither Japanese nor Russians should build houses on any of the small islands in between, creating a buffer zone that would minimize contact and conflict.[129]

The earliest attempt to inscribe a clear, delineated northern boundary on Japanese maps, and indeed the boundaries of "Japan" in all directions, as we have seen above, appeared in Hayashi Shihei's unpublished manuscript map, *Nihon enkin gaikoku no zenzu* ("Complete Map of Foreign Countries Near and Far to Japan," 1782), and subsequently his *Sangoku tsūran zusetsu* of 1785. Hayashi's motives were complex, but, as adumbrated in *Kaikoku heidan* (1787–1791), his greatest concern was the perceived Russian (*Mosukobia*) threat from the north, to which Japan, a "maritime nation"(*kaikoku*), was particularly

---

127   Keene (1952); Harrison (1953).

128   The notion that Japanese "ancestral law" recognized only two forms of foreign relations, i.e., state-to-state diplomacy (*tsūshin*) and non-state trading relations (*tsūshō*), which was conducted without state-to-state diplomacy, is a construct first proposed by Matsudaira Sadanobu in his response to Russian approaches in 1792 (Adam Laxman) and Nikolai Rezanov (1804), and then read back onto the Tokugawa dynastic founders. See Toby (1984, 240–242; Toby 2008, 90–91)

129   Hayashi Akira (1913/1967 119–121).

vulnerable because its military policies focused solely on land warfare, while totally ignoring naval defenses and tactics.[130]

Where exploration and administration led, of course, cartography was to follow. In 1799 the bakufu placed Ezo under its direct administration, motivated by the need to "control the boundaries with foreign countries" (*ikoku sakai torishimari*), and took over supervision of the Ainu-Russian trade, though there was no immediate official move actually to delineate those "boundaries" in any direction.[131] The assumption of bakufu administration, however, and the perceived threat from Russia, helped to instigate the most ambitious mapping project to date, led by Inō Tadataka (1745–1818), a retired sake brewer, to produce the first systematically surveyed scale map of the complete Ezo coastline in 1800. Ironically, his primary motivation was to survey at a large enough scale to calculate the precise length of a degree of latitude; the map of Ezo was simply a by-product. Inō funded his own survey of Ezo, but presented the completed map to the bakufu.[132] Comparison of Inō's Ezo map to the one drafted only eight years earlier by Katō Kengo (1762–1822), a Confucian scholar in the employ of Matsumae domain, is suggestive.[133] Katō lacked Inō's training in astronomy, triangulation techniques, and precise measurement, so his map is less precise; and while he comes closer to approximating the general shape of Ezo than previous map-makers, he is no match for Inō's precision. But the timing of Katō's mapping project, immediately after Adam Laxman's mission to Nemuro—where Katō was one of the Matsumae officials dealing with Laxman—suggests that his motivation (or the domain's) was also to make explicit territorial claims vis-à-vis the Russian advance.[134]

As the sense of foreign threat increased, cartographers worked to produce ever more precise maps of Japan. Yet even as pressure from Europe and

---

130   Hayashi Shihei (1787–1791).

131   Walker (2001, 150–153).

132   From then until his death Inō worked under bakufu sponsorship, mapping the entire coastline of the Japanese archipelago and logging over 33,000 kilometers on foot (Hoyanagi 1974, 6). Inō's project has since made him something of a culture hero in Japan, the subject of numerous scholarly studies, popular biographies and television biopics. A title search for books on Inō yielded more than sixty items. For a technical analysis of Inō's maps, Hoyanagi (1974); for more recent evaluations see Tōkyō Chigaku Kyōkai (1998); Hoshino (2010); Watanabe & Suzuki (2010). In English Ōtani (1932), and especially Wigen (2010, 93–97).

133   Katō's map, now in the Northern Studies Collection, Hokkaido University Library, at www.lib.hokudai.ac.jp/northern-studies/digital-exhibitions/antique-maps-1/ (accessed 2018/01/25). Weblio at https://www.weblio.jp/content/加藤肩伍 (accessed 2018/01/25), for biographical information on Katō.

134   Katō, op. cit.

America grew, and more foreign countries attempted to force Japan to accept foreign trade, the bakufu made no apparent attempt to define a set of national boundaries, nor did the foreign powers demand such a clear definition of Japanese territory. The "Convention between the United States and Japan" (the "Treaty of Kanagawa," 1854), for example, while expressing the mutual desires of the two countries "to establish firm, lasting, and sincere friendship between the two nations," made no reference to the question of limits of Japan's (or America's) territory,[135] nor did the subsequent treaties with Holland, France, Great Britain, and other Western powers.[136]

It was not until the Treaty of Commerce with Russia, signed on 7 February 1855 (N. S.), that the Russo-Japanese boundary question was explicitly encoded in an international agreement—the first time that the limits of Japanese territory were officially defined. Yet even then, the treaty left part of the boundary vague:

> Article 11.
>
> The boundary between Russia and Japan shall pass henceforth between the Islands of Etorofu and Uruppu. The Island of Etorofu belongs entirely to Japan, while the Island of Uruppu and other islands of the Kurils north of this island belong to Russia. *With regard to the Island of Karafuto (Sakhalin or Saghalien), it remains as in the past a joint possession of Russia and Japan.* (emphasis added)[137]

The following year, after the treaty settled the Russo-Japanese boundary in the Kurils, the bakufu hired the explorer Matsuura Takeshirō to survey and map Ezo. Matsuura's "Survey Map of the Mountains, Rivers and Geography of East and West Ezo" (*Tōzai Ezo sansen chiri torishirabe-zu*, 1859), perhaps for the first time, mapped Etorofu (Iturup) as part of greater Ezo, reflecting in his map the territorial claims agreed upon in the Russo-Japanese treaty of 1855. While the treaty was clear about the Russo-Japanese boundary in the Kurils, however, it effectively placed Sakhalin under an ill-defined dual sovereignty, roughly analogous to the implicit status of the Ryukyus as simultaneously a tributary of both Japan and China.

At the other end of the archipelago, neither Japan nor China explicitly acknowledged the other's suzerain status over the Ryukyus, where—as

---

135   The text of the treaty is in Beasley (1967, 119–122).
136   Of course, it is equally true that the treaties said nothing about the boundaries of the counterparty countries.
137   The full text of the treaty is in Harrison (1956, 165–168).

Chikamatsu had quipped in 1711—it was "hard to tell" whether they were "Japanese territory, or Chinese." Sovereignty over the Kingdom of the Ryukyus remained both ambiguous (or bifurcated) and disputed between the Qing and Japanese governments until the Meiji period. The Meiji government proclaimed the abolition of the Kingdom of the Ryukyus, unilaterally repositioning it as "Ryukyu Domain" (*Ryūkyū han*) in 1872, while simultaneously re-titling the last king of the Ryukyus as the "King of Ryukyu Domain," thus eliminating—from Japan's perspective, at least—the ambiguity of dual suzerainty.

The previous year, when a Ryukyuan ship was shipwrecked on the southwest coast of Taiwan, the local Mou-lan tribe had killed fifty-four of the sixty-six men on board. In 1874, the Meiji government sent an expeditionary force to avenge their deaths, arguing that the Ryukyuans were Japanese subjects, as a way of further asserting Japan's claim to the Ryukyus. What Japanese call the "disposition of the Ryukyus" (*Ryūkyū shobun*), i.e., the full annexation of the Ryukyus, was a process that proceeded sporadically between the "restoration" of direct imperial rule (*ōsei fukko*) in 1868, the abolition of the Ryukyuan monarchy and, in 1879, the formal incorporation of the archipelago into Japan as "Okinawa Prefecture," now firmly under Japanese sovereignty.[138]

While vaguely defined boundaries were unproblematic to the authorities, as well as cartographers, under the Tokugawa regime, they were incompatible with the notions of territorial sovereignty underlying the "modern" state system. Resolving the contradictions between the practices of the Tokugawa period and those of the Treaty of Westphalia—which posited states with clear and explicit boundaries, and exclusive sovereignty over the territories so inscribed—was a project that would take several decades to achieve.

---

138   Gordon (1965); Mizuno (2010); Makihara (2008, 217; 235).

CHAPTER 3

Imagining and Imaging "Anthropos"

> Our world has just discovered another one: and who will answer for its
> being the last of its brothers, since up to now its existence was unknown
> to the daemons, to the Sybils, and to ourselves?
>
> MONTAIGNE (1987)[1]

∴

The age of encounter provoked cosmological tremors for many peoples around
the world, Caribs and Spaniards, Goans and Portuguese, Algonquians and
English. Japan, too, was shaken by shifting cosmologies in the sixteenth and
seventeenth centuries, when Japanese and Europeans first encountered each
other, initially in the waters of Southeast Asia and later in the Japanese archipelago itself. If Shakespeare could see himself, England, and all of Europe as a
Miranda awakened to a "brave new world" of myriad unimagined new peoples
and customs, Japanese likewise had to reorder not only their cosmology but
their imaginings and imaging of the range of human variation they encountered in the wake of Columbus. What emerged was a variety of new modes
of imagining and the visual imaging and representing of peoples—domestic
and foreign—that apprehended and visualized a new, and newly universal,
category of "anthropos" in Japanese discourse.[2]

Japan's first encounters with Europeans surely predated the arrival of a few
Portuguese on a small island in southwestern Japan in 1543 or the landing of
Francisco Xavier, who first preached in Japan in 1549, for Japanese had been
voyaging to Southeast Asia at least since the late fifteenth century and we know
that some had gotten as far as Goa before Xavier left for Japan.[3] By the 1560s,
Portuguese merchant ships, with their mixed crews of Portuguese, Goans,
black Africans, and, occasionally, native people of the Americas, were a regular

---

1 Montaigne (1991, 1029).
2 Foucault argues that the category is even newer in Europe, unaffected by the Encounter for
   nearly three centuries. (Foucault 1970, xxiii).
3 Xavier took on a Japanese Christian convert in Goa as his interpreter for his missions to
   Japan, so some Japanese, at least, had voyaged that far from home. On the initial Japanese-
   Iberian encounters, see Boxer (1951), the classic treatment.

© KONINKLIJKE BRILL NV, LEIDEN, 2019 | DOI:10.1163/9789004393516_005

FIGURE 21   Kano Naizen, *Nanban byōbu*, late 16th–early 17th c., right-hand screen of pair of
             six-panel folding screens, color & gold leaf on paper.
             COURTESY KOBE CITY MUSEUM

sight in Japanese ports. Jesuits, starting with Xavier himself, proselytized in the
capital of Kyoto, and in 1560 the order established a church there—commonly
called the "Southern Barbarian Temple" (*Nanban-ji*)—which brought an ongoing alien presence to the very center of Japanese cultural production. Japanese
artists quickly began both to represent these newly discovered aliens and to
learn from their modes of representation, as Jesuit mentors taught young
men under their tutelage the essentials of Iberian and Italianate painting (see
Fig. 21).

    Yet more was at stake in these initial encounters in Japan than simply learn-
ing new and alien ways of painting and finding new aliens to paint. A cosmology, too, was up for grabs. Prior to the Xavierian moment, as noted above the
predominant cosmological frame for Japanese imaginings of the world had
been that of *sangoku*, or "three realms": *Wagachō* ("Our Land"; also *Honchō*,
"This Country"), *Shintan* or *Kara* (the continent, conceived as a "China" that
subsumed all other continental lands and peoples, such as Korea), and *Tenjiku*,
often rendered as "India," but conceived theologically as the land of the Buddha
and topologically as what lay beyond Kara.[4] I think of Tenjiku as "trans-Kara"; it
was a realm with which "Our Land" had no contact; no Japanese was known to
have gone to Tenjiku and returned alive to tell the tale, nor did palpable, visible

4   Japanese also imagined quasi-human creatures along the island chains to the northeast and
    southwest, but these, like the "peoples" of *Tenjiku*, were recognized as fanciful and fantastic.
    See, e.g., "Onzōshi no shimawatari," in (Ichiko 1958, 102–123). Ainu, the indigenous people of
    the far northeast, were not fully realized as a distinct iconographic representation until the
    mid-eighteenth century.

people come from Tenjiku to Japan.[5] Thus, the real world consisted largely of two possible identities: people of "Our Land" and people from "China"—which was comprised of "the Continent," with which there was a long history of contact and commerce.

In a universe of two possible "real" identities, all alterities were radical: Everything human and yet "not Japanese" might be subsumed within the "Chinese" identity. Thus, it is difficult to find visual iconographic codes in Japanese painting and sculpture prior to around 1620 that clearly distinguish a "Korean" identity from a "Chinese" one. Both were subsumed in the identity of Kara. After 1550, however, Japanese were inundated with a bewildering array of newfound Others, "unknown ... to the Sybils," in Montaigne's phrase, who came in a hitherto-inconceivable variety of colors, shapes, hirsuteness, and habiliments. These were no longer simply people of the *sangoku* but denizens of *bankoku* ("myriad lands"; "myriad countries"), nearly infinite in their variety.[6]

A *bankoku* cosmology demanded new geographies and new taxonomies of the peoples in them. The new geographies would quickly take shape, but here we are concerned principally with the ways Japanese integrated the stupefying variety of human-like creatures suddenly impinging on their consciousness. Among the earliest imagings of the rich new assortment of aliens were two parallel but related forms, both dating from the 1590s. One, a form of genre painting unified by subject matter rather than style, principally included large-format folding screens with paintings depicting foreigners of all colors and descriptions arriving in Japanese ports and parading in the streets of Japanese towns, as well as imagining them in foreign settings such as Goa and Macao.[7] Less dramatically, but more systematically, Japanese painters also adapted

---

5   There are occasional, though quite rare, records of men from *Tenjiku* visiting Japan, notably a few Buddhist priests in the mid-eighth century, a lone merchant in the mid-fifteenth, see Toby (1994, 328). Only in the late sixteenth and early seventeenth centuries did Japanese venture as far as Siam, which, according to the contemporary Jesuit dictionary of Japanese, is what Japanese then understood as *Tenjiku*. (Doi 1980, 551; 645). The most famous of these voyagers in early modern popular culture was a man known as "Tenjiku Tokubei" (1612–??), whose account, *Tenjiku tokai monogatari* (Tale of a voyage to Tenjiku, 1707) was adapted into a series of kabuki plays popular in the eighteenth and nineteenth centuries.

6   Arano (1988). Dening (1994), however, has recently argued, if unconvincingly, that Japanese intellectuals became increasingly concerned with the West in the early modern era, and that we do better to see Japanese cosmology moving from a *sangoku* of Japan, China, and Tenjiku, to another *sangoku* in which Tenjiku is superseded by "the West" as an undifferentiated distant Other.

7   Other formats were employed as well, ranging from paintings on folding fans, to ivory carvings, lacquer inlays, and ceramic figurines. For a typology, see Okudaira (1991, 65–66).

several schemata informed by Portuguese and Spanish (and, later, Dutch) "discoveries" of peoples that Japanese had not yet encountered directly, imaged through the lenses of Renaissance cartography and Italianate painting in the decade or so after 1592.

It is important to recall, too, that Japanese visual culture prior to the Xavierian encounter rarely took account of aliens *in Japan*. In the decades after Xavier, however, as Portuguese, Spaniards, Goans, Javanese, and other newfound aliens came more and more commonly to tread the streets of Japanese ports and towns, they were represented visually in genre paintings of urban life. Not only did Japan discover the Other "out there"; now, Other had landed "in here" as well. The very presence of the new foreigners forced not only a confrontation with distinctions of "Japanese" self from Other generally but a refinement of the distinctions among the burgeoning variety of Other as well.

This process of re-differentiating a collective "Japanese" identity from proximate Others, I argue elsewhere, partakes of Freud's "narcissism of petty differences," a compulsion to distinguish oneself—collectively—from those felt most uncomfortably proximate and similar.[8] This critical moment in the social psychology of collective Japanese identities expressed itself also as a recognition and visualization of a broad new category of *jinrui*—"anthropos"— infinite in its variety and populating a limitless universe of "myriad countries," *bankoku*, spread across the face of a now global world.[9] The articulation of this newly discovered "anthropos," moreover, was part of a larger project in the organization and rationalization of knowledge in Japan and more broadly in East Asia, an "encyclopedic" movement that had roots in late-sixteenth-century China but incorporated both European elements and indigenous Japanese forms to organize and represent knowledge.[10]

---

8   Toby (1994b). See above, pp. 2–4.

9   *Jinrui* has a long lexical history in the sense of "ethical relationships." Here, the referent is clearly "anthropos," the modern meaning, and as far as I can tell, this is the first instance where *jinrui* has this sense.

10   The Wanli era (1573–1620) in late Ming China witnessed a proliferation of encyclopedias— more than in the two prior centuries of the Ming dynasty—for both elite and popular audiences. Prominent among the former is Wang Chi (1607); the *Wanjin bujiuren* (1604) and *Xuefu chuanbian* (1607) are representative of the more popular encyclopedias. See Tanaka (1996, 38–88; 199–264) on the representation of Japanese in these encyclopedias. For a brief introduction in English to Ming encyclopedism, see Sakai (1970).

1   **Imaging Difference at Home**

As Europeans and other Others became more prominent on the streets of
Japan, late-sixteenth-century Japanese artists, who had rarely represented foreigners in explicitly "Japanese" settings before, began to place Europeans, and
with them Africans, Indians, and Chinese, in the Japanese landscape. This efflorescence of an art of Otherness focused initially on the radically different
figure of the "Southern Barbarian" (Nanban, signifying Iberians) in scenes both
Japanese and foreign.[11] Not only were they already radically Other; because
the Iberians did not come alone but brought the culturally and racially diverse
crews that were characteristic of their project and their newfound empire,
Japanese artists were compelled to distinguish not only *between* "Japanese"
Self and "Southern Barbarian" Other but *among* a newly numerous variety of
radically different Others. At the same time, they had to develop schemata for
comprehending yet differentiating "Japanese" selves from these new Others
while also comprehending these new Others within a satisfying taxonomy of
alterity that distinguished them from the old, familiar Others, both of Kara
and of the Japanese imaginary. This immediately posed the problem of distinguishing among a panoply of Others, no longer singular but plural, no longer
a comfortably dyadic distinction between us/not-us but among a multitude of
not-us-es.

Fascinatingly, the labor of differentiation took place first in Japanese scenes
of the harbor and market, as artists represented the newly plural Other on
the piers of Nagasaki and Sakai and on the streets of Osaka and Kyoto. As
I have argued elsewhere, though foreigners had been common visitors to Japan
from earliest times, they had been "invisible"; Japanese had not previously visualized foreigners as present *in Japan*. When visually represented, foreigners were, with rare exceptions prior to 1550, depicted as "out there," in foreign
lands (Buddhas in *Tenjiku*; Chinese in Kara). The encounter between Japan and
Europe in the sixteenth century, that is, brought about a fundamental transformation in the relationship between Japan and its Others, allowing—one
might say, compelling—Others to be visible for almost the first time. Kanō
Dōmi, Kanō Naizen, and other artists populated their late-sixteenth-century
street scenes with an astounding variety of foreigners, often at the limits of
credibility—though "credibility" here must be understood as "common sense"
(after Geertz), as a culturally systematized set of understandings about what

---

11   For excellent introductions to "Nanban" art and culture, see Okamoto (1972) and Cooper
        (1971). In positing "radical difference" for the "Southern Barbarians," I follow Todorov
        (1984, 3–4), who casts the Columbian encounter in these terms, an encounter between
        peoples who had not even imagined each other's existence.

can happen or exist in the "real" world. Some seemed "over seven feet tall and black in color"; others had noses "like a wartless conch shell, stuck onto [their] face[s] as if by suction ... eyes ... like a pair of telescopes, but the irises were yellow ... [with a small head and] long claws on its hands and feet."[12]

At the same time, "Koreans," "Tatars," "Ryukyuans," and other familiar, proximate Others emerged from the shadow cast by China in the *sangoku* cosmology and were rendered consistently distinct and visible to Japanese visual imaginings for the first time. This re-imaging was catalyzed not only by the Iberian irruption of the sixteenth century but was further prompted by a massive confrontation with Korean difference when Japanese armies invaded Korea in the 1590s. Hundreds of thousands of Japanese troops fought a Korean-Chinese alliance in Korea, and thousands of Koreans—sometimes whole villages—were brought to Japan, more as war booty than as prisoners of war. Despite this, however, the first attempts to represent Koreans as distinct from Chinese were faltering, even comic at times, as Japanese artists assembled bits and pieces from other newfound representations of Other, much like a child dressing a paper doll with an incongruous assortment of cutout clothing: Portuguese *mombaxas* (trousers) and a Korean topknot might adorn a single figure. It was not until the middle of the seventeenth century that Japanese settled on a consistent set of representational codes to distinguish "Koreans" from "Chinese."

2   Brave New World: The Panopticon of Peoples in the Myriad Realms

The imaginings and imagings of genre-screen painters, though they portrayed "many goodly creatures" on ships at anchor and in the streets and shops of the towns, however, did little to order the new knowledge of Other in any coherent, systematic fashion. Rather, they absorbed Other indiscriminately into the Rabelaisian disorder of the street, the market, and the carnival. The first steps toward the subordination of impressions to a disciplined taxonomic schema came as artists joined with cartographers—producers of disciplined knowledge par excellence—to produce ordered knowledge of both the world and its peoples: the hand-painted *mappa mundi* efflorescence of the late sixteenth and early seventeenth centuries. Dozens of these world maps were produced between around 1590 and 1640, often painted on large (approximately 175 × 390 cm) folding screens, some paired with a map of Japan, others with

---

12   Anon. (n.d.). See, e.g., the Kanō Naizen screen in the Kobe Municipal Museum, reproduced in Cooper (1971, fig. 94); Kanō Dōmi screen (ca. 1593–1600); Kanō Naizen screen (ca. 1603–1610, collection Museu Nacional de Arte Antigua, Lisbon), reproduced in Mendes Pinto (1986).

FIGURE 22 (L, R)   Map of Japan & Mappa Mundi, with cartouches of the peoples of the
                    world. Pair of six-panel folding screens, color & gold leaf on paper. After
                    1607. Nanban Bunkakan, Osaka.

representations of Nanban, of European cities, or European battles.[13] Several
of these maps incorporate tabular images of the peoples of the countries of the
world—numbering from sixteen to forty-two countries (see Fig. 22).

The Europeans brought with them "round-earth" knowledge of the myriad
realms of Trans-Kara as well as strategies for mapping that world and representing its myriad of peoples. I leave the question of mapping strategies, per
se, to a separate occasion, concentrating here on Japanese attempts over the
succeeding century to impose a seeming order on the remarkable proliferation
of "peoples" in the myriad realms now revealed to them. While the emergence
of an "anthropology"—as *jinruigaku*, a "science of humanity"—remained but
an unimagined possibility for future fulfillment (in the "west" as well as in
"Japan"), one can imagine in these movements toward an ordering of knowledge of Other in sixteenth- to eighteenth-century discourse a groping toward
an "anthropology" of sorts. Indeed, as will be seen below, I am led to the notion
of an "anthropology" of representation—imperfect though it is—by the self-
description of a series of printed mid-seventeenth-century one-sheet tables
depicting all the peoples in the myriad realms as a display of *jinrui* composed
to aid the reader in determining the relative qualities of each of these peoples—an ambition not unlike the pleasure nineteenth-century physical anthropologists took in measuring and classifying peoples in order to place them
in a Darwinian evolutionary hierarchy.

The tabulations of the "peoples of the myriad lands" that first appeared as
marginalia to Japanese world maps composed in the late sixteenth and early
seventeenth centuries adapted both taxonomic and representational schemas
directly from their European models, sometimes representing only Catholic
Europe and its "New World" conquests.[14] Often, as in the forty-two cartouches,

---

13   For a tabulation and typology of twenty-eight of the extant Japanese world-map screens,
      see Unno (1994, Appendix 11.4).

14   This is the case with the sixteen cartouches spread across the lower edge of the world-
      map that is paired with the screen depicting the Battle of Lepanto, *Repanto sentō-zu/*

most depicting male-female couples, from all around the world in the Imperial Household *mappa mundi*, even the apparently "Japanese," "Chinese," and "Tatar (?)" couples are painted through the mediation of a European iconographic vision (see Fig. 23).[15] The peoples of the world are arrayed in two tables flanking the world map and devolve from the lighter-skinned, fully clothed, "civilized" peoples of the world at the right margin to darker-skinned, half-naked peoples at the left. Of particular interest is the representation of Japanese in this example, for it makes clear that the vision informing these representations is European, even if the hand of the painter was Japanese. The painter uses Italianate techniques of shading to produce the illusion of rounded three-dimensionality in his figures; the woman in the Japanese couple is portrayed in robes worthy of nineteenth-century Japonoiserie and long, wavy tresses hanging well below the shoulder—though curly hair was a mark of great ugliness in Japanese culture.[16] Not only was the cartographic vision of these early maps—with their Atlantic-centered geography—European, derived from a variety of late-sixteenth- and early-seventeenth-century models, their ethnographic knowledge and the painterly vision embodying it were markedly European as well.[17] The earliest maps were Eurocentric, placing the Atlantic Ocean and Europe ("Battle of Lepanto/Mappa Mundi Screen"), or Jerusalem ("Twenty-Eight Cities/Mappa Mundi Screen") at the center, thus relegating Japan and the rest of East Asia to the extreme orient at the far right-hand margins of the map (Fig. 23). It was only with the introduction of Matteo Ricci's China-centered

---

Sekai chizu byōbu (pair of six-panel screens, color on paper, 153.5 × 370.0 cm., Kōsetsu Bijutsukan, Kobe), reproduced in Sakamoto et al. (1990, fig. 5). For a European example that places visual representations of foreign peoples in tabular array at the margins of the map, see, e.g., John Speed, *The Kingdome of China Newly Augmented by I.S. 1626*, reproduced in Cortazzi (1983). The almost Roman quality of Speed's "Souldier of Iapan" may dissuade us from being too dismissive of the empirical inaccuracy of Japanese imagings of the foreign.

15   *Bankoku ezu (mappa mundi)* (color on paper, 177 × 483 cm, Imperial Household Collection, Tokyo). For a brief discussion, Unno (1994, fig. 23); Oda, Muroga & Unno (1975).

16   *Nijū-hachi toshi-zu/Bankoku-zu byōbu* (pair of eight-panel screens, color on paper, 179 × 490 cm, Imperial Household Collection, Tokyo), reproduced in Sakamoto et al. (1990, fig. 23).

17   Ibid., p. 40. For examples of earlier European *mappae mundi* with arrays of the peoples of the world, see, for example, Pieter van den Keere's *Nova Totius Orbis Mappa, ex Optimis Auctoribus Desumta* (Amsterdam, ca. 1611), or Claes Janszoon Visscher, *Orbis Terrarum Typus De Integro In Plurimis Emendatus, Auctus, Et Iunculis Illustratus A° 1614* (Amsterdam, 1614), both of which are reproduced in Shirley (1983, plates 216 and 225). The Visscher *mappa* depicts twenty-five peoples in cartouches along the upper and lower borders, including "Iaponi," "Chinenses," and "Tatari," as well as "Brasilienses," "Peruvaiani," and "Magellani"; the vertical borders offer an array of twenty of the world's cities, ranging from Amsterdam and London, to Havana and Cusco, Goa and Macao. Interestingly, neither Hirado, the Dutch trading post in Japan, nor Nagasaki, the Portuguese port, is depicted.

FIGURE 23 (L, R)   Depictions of peoples of forty-two countries around
                    the world, arrayed around a mappa mundi, detail of
                    Nijū-hachi toshi bankoku ezu byōbu, early 17th c.,
                    San-no-Maru Museum.

adaptation of the European world map that the center of the world shifted
cartographically to East Asia, and Japanese were quick to note the shift.[18]

18   *Repanto sentō-zu/Sekai chizu byōbu, op. cit.; Nijū-hachi toshi-zu/Bankoku-zu byōbu, op cit.*
      On the Ricci map, see Baddeley (1917) and Ayusawa (1953).

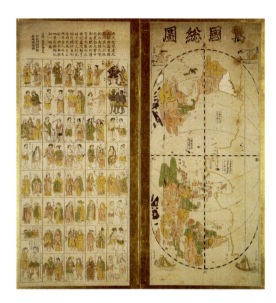

FIGURE 24
Bankoku sōzu & *Bankoku jinbutsu-zu*, 1647. Hand-colored wood-block prints on paper. Kobe City Museum.

A printed Ricci-style world map—the first printed European-style map in Japan—appeared from an unidentified Nagasaki publisher in 1645 (Shōhō 2) under the title *Bankoku sōzu* (Complete Map of the Myriad Countries) in tandem with an accompanying table of forty different peoples of the world, arrayed in a grid five cells across and eight cells high. Several unsigned editions were published over the next few decades though the visual information deteriorated as cheaper versions appeared (see Fig. 24).[19]

The table, commonly called the *Bankoku jinbutsu-zu* (Pictures of the Peoples of the Myriad Countries; the 1649 version carries a title *Sekai jinkei-zu* (Pictures of the Forms of the Peoples of the World]), bears a legend at the top, which reads as follows:

---

19   Anonymous (1645) *Bankoku sōzu*; Anonymous (1647a) *Bankoku sōzu*; Anonymous (1647b) *Bankoku sōzu*; Anonymous (1649) *Bankoku sōzu*; Anonymous (1671 [1670]) *Bankoku sōzu*. On the significance of published world maps in the context of 1645, see Kawamura (2005b). Ishikawa Ryūsen (1688) lacks the accompanying table of peoples; Kobayashi Kentei (1710) abbreviates the table to only sixteen examples, and replaces the Ricci-style *mappa mundi* with a pair of hemispheres in polar projection—complete with graticules for longitude and latitude. Elena Polovnikova's study (2013a; 2013b) of world maps in home encyclopedias (*setsuyōshū*)—which were nearly ubiquitous in Edo-period homes—suggests that Indiocentric *sangoku* world maps prevailed in early editions, but were displaced by Ricci-style maps after 1699.

The world is broad; the variety of its peoples [*jinrui*] is without end. Just as its countries differ, the peoples are likewise different. In appearance, some are tall and some short; they appear in paired opposites: black and white; male and female. If we represent their body types as specimens, this is what they are generally like. One can distinguish at a glance their systems of clothing and headgear; the manufacture of their bows, swords, and weapons. [Using this chart one can] instantly discriminate the quality of each people [*jinpin shabetsu*] in the regions of the world. Thus we have prepared this [chart] solely that it may serve as an aid to the investigation of things and accomplishment of knowledge [*kakubutsu shichi*].[20]

The Shōhō *Bankoku jinbutsu-zu*, that is, makes explicit claims to an authoritative and didactic gaze that offers a visual array of representations designed to assist in the attainment of a systematic knowledge of the peoples of the world—claims that were only implied, but unstated, in the earlier tabular arrays accompanying folding-screen *mappae mundi*. It proposes the beginnings of a global "anthropology," a visual ethnography allowing the reader to "discriminate" among peoples and arrange them in a meaningful, systematic order, a hierarchy of "quality." The chart accomplishes this, in the first instance, by simple—though not entirely consistent—tabular arrangement of peoples: in a geographic order, from the "nearer" people of eastern and northeast Asia, at the top, to peoples from "faraway places with strange-sounding names," such as "Ingeresu" (England), "Amerika," and "Perusha" (Persia), at the bottom and in an implicitly descending order from Japanese at the upper right to the barbarous, savage, and grotesque at the lower left. This organizational scheme relies on iconographic cues as well as location in the tabular arrangement of information. It signifies "civilization" and "savagery" through the deployment of signs such as clothing and nakedness, whiteness or blackness of skin, decoration of the body with tattoos (by "savages"—*dojin*) or with recognizable animal products (furs, feathers, or unprocessed leaves), hair texture and hairiness.[21]

---

20   "Bankoku sōzu" (1645, 1647a, 1647b, 1649, see n. 19). My transcription follows the phonetic glosses of "Bankoku sōzu" (1647b), which reflect the seventeenth-century Nagasaki area dialect. At least four versions of this chart were published between 1645 and 1649, though it is not certain they were all produced by the same publisher. The versions vary slightly in internal detail, since they are all hand painted, but they share the basic same gaze, directed at the "variety of peoples" to "discriminate the quality of each people."

21   Perhaps because it is difficult to depict tattoos on a figure only a few inches high, the people of "Rataran," mapped as an island south of Japan and east of Luzon (likely the "Island of Thieves" [Ilha de Ladroes] in early Nanban-style world maps), are also explained verbally: "These savages figure their bodies with ink, and like only to steal and raid" (*dojin sumi o motte bunshin, moppara tōzoku o konomu*). The tattooing is invisible in all examples of the 1647 edition I have seen but is clearly marked in the 1652 version,

The successive iterations of the *Bankoku jinbutsu-zu* represent a tentative move away from European vision and toward a Japanese vision. The taxonomic "ethnographies" of the earlier painted screens placed Europeans at the pinnacle, devolving through European peoples, white-skinned and fully clothed, to familiar non-Christians like Turks and Persians on to the peoples of Asia signified as advanced peoples by their clothing and accoutrements, skin color, and bearing. Japanese were the last pictured among these cultured, non-savage peoples. Only then did the taxonomy proceed to Europe's true exotics, those peoples who, as signified by wild hair, unadorned weapons, and either nakedness or the use of unprocessed natural products (tobacco leaves, etc.) were rendered savage and totally Other. In the *Bankoku jinbutsu-zu*, by contrast, the Japanese appear as the first among peoples (upper right), the normative human type (*jinrui*) against whom all else is Other. It then proceeds to elevate Japan's familiar, proximate others (China, Korea, Manchus, and Mongols) from the lowest rank to the highest—ahead of all Europeans and the more remarkably strange "cannibals" and eaters of snake flesh (see Figs. 2 and 24).[22]

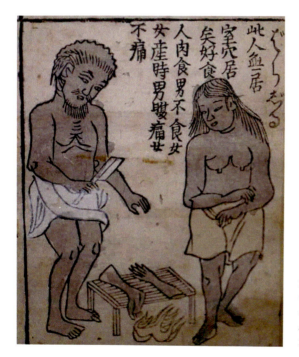

FIGURE 25
Cannibal denizens of "Brazil" as depicted in the *Bankoku sōzu* & *Bankoku jinbutsu-zu*, 1647.

Bankoku sōzu, sekai jinkei zu, (hand-colored woodblock print, 65.5 × 41.5 cm; 65.5 × 41 cm, collection Kobe City Museum); see Oda Takeo et al. eds. (1975).

22   Japanese sometimes ate snake flesh, but it was considered medicinal rather than culinary.

FIGURE 26   Detail of Fig. 25, showing human hand and foot being grilled over an open fire.

Thus, the lower corners of this *National Geographic*-style display of comfortably lesser Others are anchored by quite antipodal depictions of savagery and
alterity: At the lower right, a nearly naked "Amerika-n" couple wear tobacco-
leaf headdresses and the man wears a skirt. Below them, a cannibal couple
from "Barajiru" (Brazil) stand over a (remarkably well-crafted) grate, where a
human hand and foot roast over an open fire: "They live in holes, and like to
eat human flesh. They eat men, but they don't eat women. In childbirth, the
men have labor pains; the women do not have pain" (see Fig. 3.7).[23] The image

---

23   This image is similar to those in cartouches at the center of the lower margins of the
      mappae mundi in both the Kōsetsu Museum's (see fig. 9) and the Imperial Household
      Collection, in Oda, Muroga, and Unno (1975), and to an undated Kanō-school hanging
      scroll (likely early seventeenth century) in the late Mody Collection (Mody 1939, fig. 1)
      depicting a black "Barajiru" couple standing by a grate with three white human limbs
      roasting over a roaring fire: "The people of this country do not make houses; they clear
      away earth, make a hole, and use that for their residences. They eat human flesh; but
      they [only] eat men, and do not eat women. They use birds and the seven beasts (?) to
      make their clothing." Ultimately, European models surely lie behind this image, as they
      do behind most of the unfamiliar *jinrui*. For example, two illustrations in volume 3 of de
      Bry's *Great Voyages* (1592), show naked "savages" grilling a collection of human arms and
      legs on a grate over an open fire—prefiguring the cannibals in the *mappae mundi* and
      the various iterations of the Shōhō *bankoku jinbutsu zu* (see fig. 10). And similarly, "One

of the people of Brazil as cannibals, indeed, this very image, drew on a line of predecessor images inserted as cartouches in Japanese *mappa mundi* screens executed in so-called *Nanban* style in the early seventeenth century (Figs. 27 & 28). These images, in turn, unquestionably derive, via undetermined intermediaries, from images in Theodor de Bry's *Voyages* (Fig. 29) illustrating his account of the captivity of the German soldier Hans Staden (c. 1525–1579) at the hands of the Tupinambá.[24]

FIGURE 27   Cannibals from "Brazil" roasting human body parts over an open fire, depicted in a cartouche at the bottom center of a mappa mundi folding screen. Pair of six-panel folding screens, color on paper, early 17th c., Kōsetsu Museum, Kobe.

---

of the earliest known examples [of European illustrations of the peoples and customs of the Americas] showed naked men and women dressed in plumed collars standing under a palm-leafed roof from which human limbs were dangling." (Bucher 1981, 5) The earlier *mappae mundi* isolate the scene of cannibalism from the more clearly taxonomic array of cartouches of peoples of the world; it is only in the Shōhō *bankoku jinbutsu zu* that cannibalistic denizens of "Barajiru" are subsumed in the same taxonomy of "anthropos" as the other peoples of the world.

24   de Bry (1598). De Bry's illustration is itself loosely derived from two woodcuts in Staden's (Staden 1557; 2008, 133; 136) account of his captivity. It is likely that the Japanese painters who executed these screens saw a copy of the *Voyages*, probably brought to Japan by a Jesuit missionary, or in a European *mappa mundi*.

FIGURE 28   Cannibals from "Brazil" roasting human body parts over an open
fire, depicted in a cartouche at the bottom center of a mappa
mundi folding screen. Pair of six-panel folding screens, color on
paper, early 17th c., San-no-Maru Museum, Tokyo.

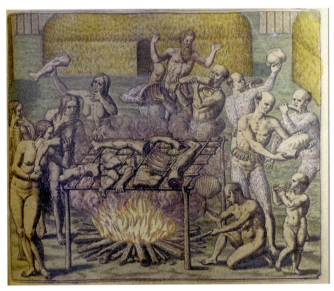

FIGURE 29   Cannibals from "Brazil" roasting human body parts over
an open fire, in a hand-colored print in de Bry's *Dritte Buch
Americae* (1593).
COURTESY OF RARE BOOKS & SPECIAL COLLECTIONS,
UNIVERSITY OF ILLINOIS LIBRARY

At the lower left are two men from the land of the Giants (*Chōjin*), "people" (*hito*), who are "one *jō* and 2 *shaku* [about 15 feet] tall; because they don't have letters, they use ropes to govern." The "giants" leave just enough space to show four men, "people" from the land of "Dwarves" (*Shōjin; Kobito*) strolling arm in arm; they are "one *shaku* and two *sun* [ca. 36 cm] tall; because they're likely to be captured if they walk alone, they walk in large linked groups" (see Fig. 30). With the exception of these last two antipodal peoples, all these "varieties of people" emerge either from Japanese experience in east and northeast Asia or from the implicit ethnography of the earlier Nanban screens. The "Giants" and "Dwarves" emerge from a confluence of the European imaginary with the parallel world of the *Shanhaijing* (Classic of the Mountains and the Seas).[25] Their native lands are even identified on the accompanying *mappa mundi*, located at the antipodes: the dwarves north of "Hinma" (Finland), the giants southeast of Tierra del Fuego, on the rim of a giant circumpolar continent.[26] Curiously invisible are the peoples of both Ezo (i.e., Ainu) and Ryukyu (Okinawans), Japan's nearest outer bounds, both of which were increasingly closely bound to—though not part of—Japan at this moment, while maintained as boundary "Others."[27]

Yet the Shōhō *Bankoku jinbutsu-zu*'s system of organization remains curiously unsystematic, though it seemingly takes geographical distance from Japan as its underlying organizational principle rather than the "discrimination of qualities" proclaimed in its caption. Japan serves as the starting point for these peoples/countries. The remainder of the top row is devoted to Japan's more or less "familiar" others in Northeast Asia: China, Korea, Tartary (*Dattan*), and Manchuria (*Orankai*)—though China was archaized as Dai-Min ["Great Ming"], a dynasty that had fallen in 1644, and Korea as Kōrai [the Koryǒ dynasty], overthrown in 1392, rather than the contemporary names for China (*Dai-Shin*, "Great Qing") and Korea [*Chōsen*; K., *Chosǒn*]). All the East Asian peoples are clothed in garments firmly grounded in the iconographic and ethnographic intersection of Japanese "sight" and "representation" that Gombrich (1969) suggests we should expect from Japanese artists. So far so

25   On the *Shanhaijing* in Japan, see Kōma (1994). The *Shanhaijing* appears in the *Nihon-koku genzaisho mokuroku* (ca. 891), but the earliest Japanese printed edition dates from 1670. Takeda (1984).

26   The 1645 edition locates only the "Dwarves," though it is likely that this only reflects the map's state of preservation. Later editions locate both the "Dwarves" and the "Giants."

27   The ambiguity of Ezo and Ryukyu and their peoples in Japanese cognition is symbolized by the exclusion of both from the first "official" maps of Japan, compiled by the bakufu in 1655, while only a decade earlier the bakufu had commanded the mapping of Ryukyu as a Japanese province; see above, Chapter 2; Toby (1994) and Dening (1994).

FIGURE 30
Dwarves and Giants populate the
antipodes in the 1645 *Bankoku jinbutsu-zu*
and subsequent iterations. Here, from a
1647 printing.
COURTESY KYOTO UNIVERSITY MUSEUM

good. But, interestingly, Iberians, now a taboo subject of sorts in Japan[28]—are identified and located nearby, in Luzon and Macao, rather than in "Spain" and "Portugal," while "Holland," whose bases in Taiwan and Java were of great concern to Japanese, was located far off in Europe, nestled between "Zerumaniya" (Germany) and "Furansa" (France). Represented in this way, however, the Iberians appeared more "outland-"ish, their clothing marking them off more radically from their neighbors (in the chart) than their location in East Asia might suggest.

Publishers in Nagasaki and Kyoto produced and reproduced these tabular representations of *Bankoku jinbutsu-zu* frequently for the next quarter-century, as we have seen, with but minor variations. The forms of "anthropos" imagined in these "myriad realms" differed significantly from the anthropologies of the cartouches and tabulations in the earlier Nanban-genre maps in several respects:

1. The specific peoples represented in the earlier Nanban-genre schemata of peoples themselves constituted the elements of an "anthropology" that had initially been constructed by an Iberian gaze, and only later adopted by Japanese artists. This was especially true for the "peoples" of Catholic Europe and lands in Africa, the "Indies," and the "New World" that had been the fixed in the colonizing gaze of Portugal and Spain. The "peoples of the world" sees Brazilians, that is to say, but not the peoples of North America; it *recalls* the "Tartarians" of the Mongol invasions and Marco Polo's *Travels*, yet is blind to the Manchus, Mongols. Other peoples of continental northeast remained Asia, hidden "beyond Cathay," as did two of Japan's nearest neighbors, Ezo and Ryukyu.[29]

2. The "peoples" portrayed in the *Bankoku jinbutsu-zu* of 1647–1671 are, by contrast caught in the focus of a *new* gaze, one that combines Iberian, Japanese, and Chinese cosmological and "anthropological" lenses, through which it "sees" the peoples of Korea, Manchuria, and Mongolia,

---

28   With the expulsion of the Iberians and the complete suppression of Christianity, in 1639, Iberian themes and images were banned from public replication and display, see Toby (1994) and Dening (1994).

29   Nishimura (1958) identifies the countries of the sixteen peoples represented as Spaniards, Romans, Muscovites, Abyssinians, Senegalese, Greenlandians (?), Turks, Sumatrans, Brazilians, French, "Irelandians," "Tartarians," "Canarians," Malabarians, People of Ilha de Ladroes (*Nusuhito-jima no hito*, "Thieves' Isle," an island in the Marianas that appears in Magellan's log in March 1521), and "Magalanicans" (depicting what Nishimura identifies as an "Australoid" people). Each is identified as the object of an anthropological, rather than a geographical, gaze—that is, as "the people of" such-and-such place (*XX no hito*) rather than as the place itself.

peoples invisible to sixteenth-century Portuguese, who never strayed far
enough from the sea lanes of eastern Asia to "see" peoples beyond China
and Japan. It also "sees" peoples the Iberians had never encountered,
"giants" (*Chōjin*) and "dwarves" (*Shōjin*)—absent from the tabular array
of the Imperial Household *mappa mundi*—who "lived" only in the mythic cosmology of the *Shanhaijing* and its rehearsals in late-Ming encyclopedism. Yet the maps remain blind to Ryukyu and Ezo.

The vision underlying the first edition (1645) of the Shōhō *Bankoku jinbutsu-zu*
is a gaze that—however much it finds its *objects* in Iberian imports—is constituted in a mixture of Iberian/Italianate and Sino-Japanese iconographic
tradition quite separate from the purely Iberian vision of the Imperial *mappa
mundi*. If, as Gombrich suggests, "an existing representation will always exert
its spell over the artist even while he strives to record the truth," training the
artist, "to see what he paints rather than to paint what he sees"; if, that is, iconographies are "a selective screen which admits only the features for which
schemata exist,"[30] the Imperial *mappa mundi* represents either a nearly total
cooptation of Japanese artists to an alien gaze, even when seeing themselves,
or more likely a playful engagement with new ways of visualizing both self
and other. The gaze that the Shōhō *Bankoku jinbutsu-zu* levels at "China,"
"Korea," and northeast Asia, and reflexively at "Japan," by contrast, increasingly
derives its "view" from Japanese and Chinese iconographic models, while the
"Europeans" and others from the "brave new world" have been assimilated—to
a Japanese iconography and gaze not found in the earlier Nanban-genre vision.

One or two examples will suffice to clarify some of these differences of
gaze. First, and most significant, the position of the "Japanese" couple in the
compendia attached to Nanban-style painted *mappae mundi* suggests that
they were modeled on European examples in which Japan was a peripheral,
perhaps antipodal, country, recognized as civilized but marginalized nonetheless. European peoples were positioned first; in the Imperial Household
Collection *mappa mundi*, the Japanese couple appears only in the seventh
row—making them twenty-first of the forty-two peoples represented—after
fifteen unmistakably European couples, several of whom are apparently
Turkish or Persian, as well as Chinese and Tatar couples. In the printed versions from the Shōhō era, by contrast it is the Japanese couple—now labeled
as such—that leads the parade of peoples, followed by the familiar peoples of
East and Northeast Asia: Chinese, Koreans, Tartars, and "Orankai" (a people
in eastern Manchuria). Europeans are now represented as peripheral, only
midway through the forty peoples depicted. The Armenians—whom Japanese

---

30   Gombrich (1969, 82, 85–86).

had never encountered—were twenty-first, the Portuguese ("Macao; same as Goa") were twenty-third. The Spanish were thirty-eighth of forty, just before the "dwarves" and "giants."

Second, there is a fundamental shift in viewpoint; a European gaze, translated through Japanese hand and brush, is gradually replaced by a Japanese eye. The "Chinese," "Tatar" (?), and "Japanese" couples[31] of the *mappa mundi* screen in the Imperial Household Collection—like all the "peoples" illustrated—are constituted in a sixteenth-century Italianate style, as replicated by the anonymous Japanese artist, rather than in a "Japanese" painterly vision. The "Japanese" woman, apparently intended to be an aristocrat, is dressed in robes more prescient of the nineteenth-century Japonisme of the impressionists than reflective of a Japanese vision—indeed, one might wonder whether the artist had actually *seen* an aristocratic Japanese woman, so alien are her garments in both "design" and illustration—and she sports long, flowing, curly raven tresses down to her waist, unthinkable in a Japanese aristocratic woman of the time.[32] Her "spouse," likewise, is displayed in a pose not common in Japanese portraiture, a standing full figure, and is stylistically more evocative of the representations of Japanese visitors to Europe in the illustrated press of the nineteenth century than of any Japanese models I can identify.[33] Further, he is depicted as clean-shaven, which would have been regarded as unmanly in turn-of-the-seventeenth-century Japan. He is likewise outside the parameters of Japanese portraiture.[34]

In the Shōhō *Bankoku jinbutsu-zu* series (1640s), by contrast, the Japanese couple are products of a more Japanese vision, both iconographic and observational, though here we are dealing with a transition in vision and representation away from European mediation. The underlying outline print in all three mid-century versions is consistent with Japanese modes of representation, but

---

31   The Lepanto screen-map represents most "peoples" in bi-gendered pairs, likely spousal couples, as the Eskimo (?): the man supports a kayak in his left hand; holds a bow in his right; a woman nuzzles an infant. There is one adult triad (one man; two women) among the peoples coded, by (un)dress and skin color, as barbarous. In the 1645 "anthropology," also, some "peoples" are represented by same-sex pairs; and some, like *Toroko* (Turkey) by two men and one woman.

32   Three centuries later, Etsuko Inagaki Sugimoto (1966, 15–16) recalled how the pain she felt as a child due to her wavy hair, caused her to separate herself from "the little girl who was myself, when I remember how many bitter trials she had to endure because of her wavy hair ... 'Etsuko,' [Mother] said, 'do you not know that curly hair is like animal's hair? A samurai's daughter should not be willing to resemble a beast ...'".

33   Yokoyama (1987) examines representation of Japan and Japanese in the Victorian-era British popular press.

34   Kuroda (1988); Toby (1997).

the over-painting in the 1645 version still uses European-derived techniques of shading to evoke rounded three-dimensionality in some of its figures. The general treatment of the body and its drapery, as well as the coloristic techniques of the painter—especially the use of shading in faces and exposed parts of the body and in drapery—are of a generic southern-Renaissance style, reflecting either an underlying European model or a European eye. The Japanese man is represented as a seated warrior in full battle regalia, grasping a halberd in his left hand. He sports a beard and moustache and reminds the viewer of the memorial portrait of Honda Tadakatsu, a general of fierce repute in the armies of Tokugawa Ieyasu at the turn of the seventeenth century.[35] His spouse, too, has begun to be iconographically repatriated from the alien vision of the Imperial House screens: her hair (painted, not printed) is still perceptibly wavy, but it flows down the shoulders of her multi-layered kimono, itself a sign of a woman of rank. In the hand-colored Kyoto University example (1647), the sartorial signs of her status are replicated by the chalk-white skin of her face and hand—a left hand that dutifully holds a long sword (*tachi*), as if her husband is about to go off into battle.[36] Both are represented in "correct" garments, garments that would be recognized by contemporary "native" observers as "authentic" and in a painterly idiom that would be convincingly "real" to them.

Only in the 1647 version is her hair free of its Italianate curlers, and it flows straight and smooth down her shoulders. Both "Japanese" figures are fully liberated from the European vision that initially informed the tabular taxonomic genre and are firmly rooted now in a Japanese iconography. Indeed, though it is difficult to make comparisons between the tempera overpainting of the 1645 version and the simple, almost transparent, pastel wash overpainting in later editions, it is safe to say that by 1647, both the essential vision and the overall technique in execution of the figures in the tables of "the peoples of the world" had been thoroughly naturalized to Japan. Only the range of peoples catalogued there continued to depend on the ethnographic information gleaned from European explorers of continents and islands Japanese had never visited, though the addition of cartouches of Korean and *Orankai* (eastern Manchurian) couples—but not Ainu or Ryukyuan—began the move toward assimilating preexisting Japanese cultural categories to the new taxonomies of anthropos.

---

35   See Shimizu (1988).

36   See Wagatsuma (1967) on the cultural signification of skin whiteness. The Japanese woman is not the only whitened figure in the *Shōhō Bankoku jinbutsu zu*, however: The woman of *Da-ming* (China) is likewise whitened, as are two men (or a man and a woman, it is hard to be sure) from the "Land of Giants" (*Chōjin-koku*).

The Shōhō *Bankoku jinbutsu-zu* and *Bankoku sōzu*, with its "anthropological" panopticon of forty "peoples" reappeared in several variant editions at least until the late seventeenth century. Even as late as the first decade of the eighteenth century, *Nendaiki shin'e shō* replicated the geography and "anthropology" of the *Bankoku sōzu* and *jinbutsu-zu*. At the same time, Inagaki Kōrō attempted to combine an abbreviated and somewhat revised "anthropology"—one that saw people in Ryukyu, if not Ezo, but also bodhisattvas in Tenjiku—with a dual polar-projection world map.[37]

Inagaki's vision included the people of Ryukyu, who had been invisible in earlier iterations of the "myriad" peoples of the world, even though the country of Ryukyu appeared unmistakably—and color-coded, like Ezo, as a "foreign" country—in an accompanying *Bankoku sōzu*. As a cartographer, Inagaki recognized Ezo as a foreign country, while excluding the people of Ezo from his gaze. He likewise declined omitted the people of Korea, even while presenting the country (*Chōsen*) on his map.[38] "Brazil," whose people were cannibals in earlier iterations, became denizens of "Cannibal-land" (*Shokujin-koku*), fiercer and hairier than their iconographic forebears and far more obviously eager to sate their cravings for human limbs roasting on an open fire. These were joined by new "peoples" from "Blackpeople-land" (*Kokujin-koku*) and a rediscovered Tenjiku, the latter looking for all the world like the bodhisattvas that inspired them.[39] Ishikawa Ryūsen's *Bankoku sōkai-zu* of 1688, published after the Kangxi Emperor's final defeat of the last remnants of Ming resistance, maps *Dai-shin* ("Great Qing"), rather than the *Dai-min* ("Great Ming"), of earlier maps. Inagaki omits the name *Dai-min* from his map; yet in his "anthropology," he insists on picturing a couple from "*Dai-min*" but not "*Dai-shin*." His concession to the Qing triumph, is to distinguish "Tatars" and "Jurchens" in his "anthropology," though this may be a renaming of "Orankai." *Nendaiki shin-e shō*, likewise, refused to concede the Qing conquest, picturing only *Dai-min* in its "anthropology" and further dissociated lands and peoples by picturing a Korean couple from the anachronistic *Kōrai* while noting the nautical distance to contemporary *Chōsen*.

---

37   Inagaki (1708), in Oda, et al. (1975, 1: 151); Anon. *Nendaiki shin-e shō*. Polar projections had been known for about a century in Japan.

38   The anachronistic designation of Korea as *Kōrai*, that had appeared in *bankoku* maps and "anthropologies," is corrected to *Chōsen*, in Inagaki's map, as well as Ishikawa's 1688 *Bankoku sōkai-zu*.

39   These "black people" (*kokujin*) were not necessarily representations of Africans, for there was a mythology of black-skinned peoples, derived from the *Shanhaijing*, that long predated contact with Africans. See Toby (1995).

At the same time, the encyclopedist Nishikawa Joken began to reorganize anthropological knowledge from those "myriad" countries; he returned to the forty-two of the Imperial *Bankoku sōzu* screen—a number that would become canonical in later iterations well into the nineteenth century.[40] Divorcing his anthropology from cartography, Joken adopted a format that was replicated in later iterations, accompanying each illustration of a people with a brief explanatory text. He "saw" the people of Ryukyu—but not Ezo—and clearly distinguished Ming, by which he meant "real" Chinese who had not adopted Manchu customs, and Qing, who, "because the emperor [of China] (*tenshi*) is originally from Tartary, they have amended the customs of Ming; for this reason, I have divided the countries into two [separate] illustrations, in order to show the reader the customs of the past and present (*kokon no fūzoku o shirashimu*)." Within this frame, Nishikawa introduced new "knowledge," such as the distinction between Ming and Qing, and the existence of a people in Ryukyu who were distinct from both Japanese and Chinese. He also divided the world into "five continents" (*go-daishū*, one of which included both the northern and southern continents of Amerikiya), though, interestingly, he located Africa (Rimiya, i.e., "Libya") and Europe by reference to direction from Tenjiku—by which he meant India. The giants and dwarves of his anthropology were the ultimate antipodalities, the last of his forty-two peoples, just as they were the last of the *Bankoku* charts' peoples, at the corner diametrically opposite the warrior-general and elegant woman of Japan.

Nishikawa's vision, however, contrasted sharply with the earlier *Bankoku* vision in two crucial respects. First, his forty-two countries were *all* foreign; that is, they excluded Japan. This was exclusively an anthropology of Other, designed to catalog and order the foreign as categorically distinct from—rather than inclusive of—a Japanese self. And where *Bankoku* representations sought only to depict, but not to describe, its objects of knowledge, and did not attribute to them the least social and cultural subjecthood, Nishikawa, in adding prose descriptions, gave each people a history, if only momentary, and an identity, however fanciful. Nishikawa moved toward an encyclopedism—another "technique of knowledge"—reflective of a parallel universe of rationalist analysis.

---

40   Keene (1952). For a nineteenth-century descendant of Nishikawa's anthropology, see, for example, Sugiya (1827), which replicates illustrations from *Shijūnikoku jinbutsu zusetsu*, and preserves the distinction between "Ming," now nearly two centuries gone, and "Qing" of his own time. Cf. Nishikawa 1720/1898–1907 and Nishikawa 1720/1917.

3   The Encyclopedic Vision: Articulate Selves and Typed Others

Nishikawa Joken traveled, as it were, in two epistemological universes; the finite universe of the Nanban/*Bankoku* vision, and the limitless, panoptic universe of encyclopedism, a technique of knowledge that had expanded rapidly in China from the late sixteenth century and with growing force in Japan since the middle of the seventeenth century.[41] The encyclopedist urge to organize all knowledge intersected with a reflexive ethnography of Japan itself, *Shokunin uta-awase* and *Shokunin e-zukushi* ("pictures and songs of artisans"; "pictures of all the artisans") through which, since medieval times, Japanese who had mastered "techniques of knowledge" classified themselves, i.e., aristocrats, and their internal Others—craftspeople—in song and picture.[42] In the earliest Japanese encyclopedias, the Sinocentric ethnographies of *Sancai tuhue* (Illustrated encyclopedia) and *Xuefu chuanbian* (Complete encyclopedia) are turned back on themselves.[43] Chinese encyclopedists represented Chinese as a fully articulated people, with a range of occupational and status types that devolved from the Yellow Emperor through actual emperors to ordinary people, and reduced each foreign people to a single, single-gendered (usually male) type. By contrast, Nakamura Tekisai's universal encyclopedia, *Kinmō zui* ("Illustrated encyclopedia for instruction and enlightenment," 1666), "humanity" (*jinbutsu*) represented Japan as an articulated—if limited—set of nearly sixty statuses, genders (though construed as statuses), and occupations, derived from the *Shokunin uta-awase* tradition.[44]

Nakamura's "humanity" is divided into two groups, a main group and an "appendix," and each contains some foreign peoples as well as Japanese. The Japanese run from the highest nobility (*kō-kyō-shi-jo*) through the canonical "four classes" of warrior, peasant, artisan, and merchant (*hei-nō-kō-shō*) and life stages (infancy, [male] youth, and old age (both male *okina* and female *ōba*), to a wide variety of occupations, including such "despised" occupations as actor, beggar, and prostitute (see Figs. 31, 32 & 33). Each of the two sets of

---

41   Wang (1607) was especially influential in Japan. For a brief introduction to these encyclopedias, see Tanaka (1993).

42   See especially Amino (1992, 1993, 1994); Iwasaki (1993); Umeda and Hayashi (1983).

43   Wang, *Sancai tuhue* (1607); *Xuefu* (1607), reproduced, in part, in Tanaka (1996).

44   Nakamura (1666, 1668). A later unsigned encyclopedia, *Jinrin kinmō zui* (1690), covers 496 Japanese statuses, crafts and occupations, reflecting the rapid occupational specialization of the seventeenth century—but includes no alien identities. The emergence of new crafts and occupations is underscored by comparison with *Nanajū-ichiban shokunin uta-awase* (ca 1500), which depicts 142 (in 71 pairs), and Kaihō Yūsetsu's (ca. 1650) vision of "all the occupations," which was limited to 120 occupations.

statuses/occupations seems to be arranged hierarchically. After each group of Japanese comes an assortment of foreign peoples: a fur-covered Ezo (Ainu) archer, Nanban (here Portuguese), Chinese (*Chūgoku*, or "central kingdom"), Korean, Mongol, and Jurchen in the main section; then a Ryukyuan, Luzonese (Spaniard, here distinct from Nanban), Annamese, and so forth; grading into the Giants, Dwarves, and so forth of the *Shanhaijing* in the second half of the appendix. In an interesting transition, however, Nakamura (1666) retreats from the bigendered visual schema of the Nanban world maps and the Shōhō *Bankoku jinbutsu-zu*, offering only a single male specimen for each of the foreign peoples he covers, while Japanese alone are bigendered, represented in the full range of their statuses and occupations. In this, he returns to the Chinese encyclopedic pattern set by the *Sancai tuhui, Xuefu chuanbian*, and so forth, in which domestic society is fully ramified by gender and occupation while alien peoples are represented only by individual types, nearly all of them male.

Nakamura's foreigners have a variety of iconographic and anthropological forebears. His denizens of "Nanban" and "Luzon," for example, peoples not noted in any case in the late-Ming encyclopedias, are heavily indebted to the images in Shōhō *Bankoku jinbutsu-zu*. But his Korean—here the contemporary *Chōsen*, rather than the archaic *Kōrai*—owes everything to *Sancai tuhui*, as do his Jurchen and Mongol ("Xiongnu" in the *Sancai tuhui*) as well as his

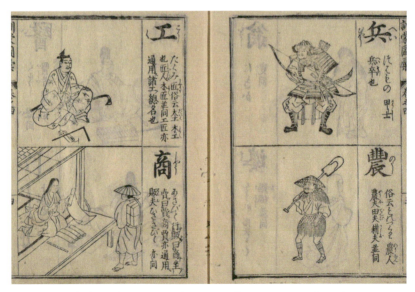

FIGURE 31   Clockwise from upper right: Warrior, farmer, artisan and merchant.
             Nakamura (1666).

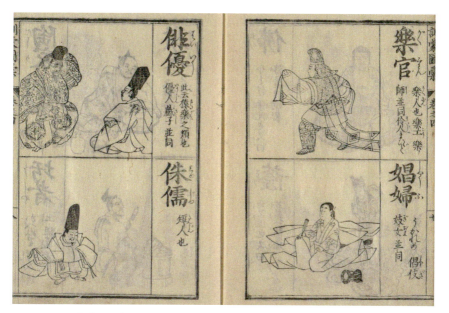

FIGURE 32   Clockwise from upper right: Court dancer, prostitute, actors and dwarf. Nakamura
(1666).

FIGURE 33   Clockwise from upper right: Hunter, diver, Ainu and Nanan. Nakamura (1666).

man from "Tenjiku." Even his "Buddha," for whom there were nearly infinite models available, is clearly copied from the *Sancai tuhui*. The taxonomy of the "human," however, remains quite puzzling: demon, Taoist immortal, Buddha, and bodhisattva are both "Japanese" and "human" in Nakamura's scheme, if I understand him correctly. They follow, in Nakamura's logic, upon Shinto and Buddhist ritual specialists (shaman, priest, monk, nun), who communicate with them, and precede others who traverse the boundaries between the human world and other sorts of alien realms: hunters who roam the mountains and diving women (*ama*) who enter the Dragon King's realm beneath the waves. They serve as a transition to the truly foreign peoples, beginning with Nanban and the border Ezo (Ainu), China (here *Chūgoku*, the "central kingdom"), Korea, and beyond.

Nakamura's scheme of representation is a straightforward combination of the visual and the nominal; a picture of each "thing," accompanied by a name tag that includes all the names by which the thing was known. Thus, for example, China is "named" as follows: "Central country; *Kara. Morokoshi*. Same as Central civilization (*chūka*). Here, we call the Central country Han or Tang. Central Asians call it *Shintan* or *Shina*."[45] His schema for humans is the same as for other phenomena such as wind and rain (vol. 1); features of the natural or built landscape such as valleys, rivers, and bridges (vol. 2); buildings and architectural features (vol. 3); clothing (vol. 6); and insects (vol. 15).[46] The human is a comprehensive ontological and epistemological category, to be ordered and imaged along with other observable phenomena.

A half-century after *Kinmō zui*, in 1712, Terajima Ryōan published his monumental illustrated encyclopedia, *Wakan sansai zue* (Illustrated encyclopedia of Japan and China), a domestication of the *Sancai tuhui* in which, like much contemporary discourse, Japan and Japanese toppled China from centrality and took over center stage.[47] Unlike the *Sancai tuhui* (Wang, 1607; "Illustrated encyclopedia"), however, and *Kinmō zui*, which saw even demons, buddhas,

---

45   Nakamura (1666/1668, 4:10b).

46   The only exception is "The Body," vol. 5, which includes some bare-bones explanations that might be useful to a physician.

47   Terajima (1712). There is a modern facsimile edition (Terajima 1970). The two modern print editions, Terajima (1985–1991, 1980), reproduce all illustrations, but their text transcriptions are not always reliable, and should be used with caution. Terajima (1998) is a CD-ROM version. It is not clear when the *Sancai tuhui* was first imported into Japan, but as noted above, some of the illustrations in *Kinmō zui* clearly draw on illustrations in the Ming encyclopedia, so it was in circulation well before Terajima adapted it. Ōba (1967, 242) says an edition of *Sancai tuhui* was imported to Japan in 1714, but this is clearly not the first copy seen in Japan. See Ōba (1967), for a discussion of imported Chinese encyclopedias in early modern Japan.

giants, and dwarves as "people" (*jinbutsu*), Terajima's "anthropology" is more exclusive. He begins his examination of the species with Japanese, apparently the only people to know proper human relations (*jinrin*): he examines "categories of human relations" (*jinrin-rui*), "kinship in human relations" (*jinrin-shinkoku*), "offices and ranks" (*kan'i*) and "the utilities of human relations" (*jinrin no yō*). All are Japanese, from the emperor to thieves (*nusuhito*), from prostitutes (*keisei*) and wet nurses (*menoto*) to beggars (*kotsujiki*) and boy-lovers (*nanshoku*). Even angels (*tennin*) were Japanese. Terajima's analysis of Japanese "human relations" follows on a tradition of representing and imaging occupations—from nobility to thief, prostitute, and outcaste—that had itself recently made a transition to encyclopedism.[48]

Terajima proceeds to foreign peoples, who are also "people" (*jinbutsu*). But as if they were distant biographically, as much as geographically or culturally, he interposes two volumes on the human body (*keiraku*) between *jinrin* and foreign peoples. He further divides the foreign world into two subcategories, "peoples of different/strange [i.e., "foreign"] countries" (*ikoku jinbutsu*), in what is among the briefest of all his 105 chapters, and "outer barbarian peoples" (*gai'i jinbutsu*). His criteria for distinguishing between "countries" and "barbarians" are not entirely clear, though most of the eleven "countries" are familiar—China and Korea, for example, as well as Ryukyu and Ezo. Each has a history—of sorts—a language, and customs—including, for example, the Tatar (Manchu) queue, which is discussed in great ethnographic detail.[49] Not all the "foreign countries" have relations with Japan, so it is not that alone that distinguishes them from the "outer barbarians," but all are in what we would call northeast Asia—they are Japan's familiar Others.

The "outer barbarians," however, are a complex lot. There are over one-hundred-sixty of them, beginning with Champa, including Cambodia, Siam, Spain, and Portugal (in the guise of Luzon and Macao) and ending—not including the appendix—with Holland. Many of these "barbarians" are, clearly, "real." But many more of the "countries" of the *Bankoku jinbutsu-zu* have fallen through the cracks, replaced by "people" from the *Sancai tuhui*, who in turn owe their existence to the *Shanhaijing*: the "long-armed" and "long-legged" people (*tenaga; ashinaga*) and (my favorite) the "hole-in-the-chest" people (*senkyō*), whose aristocrats ride on poles through the hole in their chest, borne by porters.

All these peoples, however, are apprehended in the universal gaze of Terajima's encyclopedia, completing, as it were, the project begun at the margins of the world maps of the late sixteenth century. Ironically, Terajima's

---

48 Amino (1992, 1993, 1994); Iwasaki (1993).
49 See Toby (1997).

marriage of the *Bankoku jinbutsu-zu* to the encyclopedic traditions of both *Sancai tuhui* and *Kinmō zui* led to the complex ramification of gender difference within Japanese society but the effacement of any gender distinction whatever in the envisioning foreign peoples. Each of the foreign "peoples" and "barbarians" is pictured only as a male specimen; women disappear from view. This was not the case in later, more complex single-country ethnographic works,[50] which attempted a more thorough representation of the diversity of cultural experience, extending to both sexes, the family, and stages of the life course as well as a range of economic activity—such as farming practices, bathing, or rites of passage.

4 Toward a Visual Ethnography of a Myriad Lands

While some of this knowledge of the myriad countries of the world may be quite fanciful—seventeenth- and eighteenth-century European "knowledge" of the foreign was not consistently empirical, either—and hardly either "modern" or "scientific," not to say empirical in any sense that we would accept, it is "rationalist" in its urge to classification and order. And it is fundamentally informed by a highly visual, almost tactile, concern with rendering its objects of knowledge as directly accessible to the sense of sight as is possible, a compulsion to rely on visual representation as the primary vehicle of communication. Before there was the world, in the earliest Nanban world maps, there was the picture, sometimes without so much as a caption to name it. The picture still dominated printed representation of the peoples of the world throughout the seventeenth century, though words increasingly crept in as labels for the growing literate audience. Accompanying maps might locate the peoples pictured appropriately on the surface of the globe, but little verbal information was offered to help the reader decode the image or to inform the image with substantial ethnographic content. It was only with Terajima's encyclopedia of 1713 that a logocentric mode of representation overwhelmed the visual imaging of other peoples, adding significant proto-ethnographic detail about political and social organization, culture and customs. But by then, the visual forms of imagining and imaging, an iconography of "anthropos" first adumbrated in cartouches on world maps, in late-Ming encyclopedias, and in tabular arrays of "peoples of the world" had become the established, familiar form of imagining and imaging the unfamiliar in the Japanese search to acquire and order knowledge of the Other.

---

50   For example, Nakagawa (1799).

The framework was one of rationalization and organization, yet the approach to the acquisition or constitution of knowledge to be ordered in the frame is neither entirely empirical nor skeptical, and it is certainly not "scientific." Yet I would argue that the attempts to order knowledge, particularly to reinscribe boundaries of Other around a circumference of Japanese identities that is represented in the *Bankoku sōzu* and *Jinbutsu-zu*, in *Kinmō zui* and *Wakan sansai zue*, marks a radical change in cosmologies and epistemologies from anything visible prior to around 1550. As important, for our purposes, the principal medium for representing Other in Japanese discourse was the visual image and each image was a specimen, much like museum dioramas or specimen villages at a world's fair. The specimen "Chinese" or "Brazilian" couples imaged in the *Bankoku sōzu* stood for all "Chinese" or "Brazilians," cataloging the variety of possible alterities while effacing all difference within categories of the Other. As such, these early Japanese tabulations and encyclopedias are part of a movement toward a visual representation of other peoples imagined as a new category of "anthropos," in which "Japanese" was but one of an explicitly "myriad" possible identities ("ethnicities" seems anachronistic) placed around the newly global world.

Certainly the explosion from *sangoku* to *bankoku* brought new knowledge of Other and Self, imagined, imaged, and inscribed in these texts. It is a knowledge that could not conform to imagination. The proliferation of peoples and continents, especially the irruption of Other into Japanese spaces, required the invention of new practices, new forms of constituting both Self and Other, that marked an irreparable discursive break with the nature of that knowledge and its modes of representation. The discovery of "myriad countries" beyond Japan's shores did not incite an age of expeditions to confront and catalog peoples—there were no Japanese explorers with artists in tow to paint Australians and Hawaiians for the edification or titillation of an audience back home. Indeed, from the 1630s to the 1850s, Japanese rarely voyaged more than a few hundred miles from home. The visualizations of anthropos introduced to Japanese imagination in the sixteenth and seventeenth century were reproduced and reimaged by people who had never seen the "peoples" they represented, much as engravers transformed the sketches of travelers or missionary photographers in Africa.

The new visual arrays of "anthropos," while not perhaps anthropological in the strictest sense, approached a mode of visual ethnography, "mediating the strangeness" of the bewildering variety, the myriad potential othernesses of the post-encounter world.[51] They constructed a visible/visual taxonomy

---

51   Dening (1994, 477).

of a not-quite-perfect continuity between "Japanese"-ness and Otherness, establishing a "petty difference" between "Japanese" and formerly distant but familiar Others, what we might today call "East Asians," in the old Shintan, and the newer, more radical alterities "discovered" through Japanese voyaging and the post-Xavierian encounter with "Southern Barbarians" and their brave new world.

It is important to note, too, that Japanese culture became quite radically more visual in the aftermath of—though by no means because of—the age of encounter. The visual arrays of the Shōhō *Bankoku jinbutsu zu* and the efflorescence of Japanese encyclopedism that began in the last third of the seventeenth century were part and parcel of an explosion of literacy, print culture, and commercial publishing that swept the country, beginning in the great urban centers of Kyoto, Edo, and Osaka but spreading quite rapidly into the provinces. This publishing revolution brought visual representation—heretofore largely the privileged domain of aristocrats and wealthy merchants with the means to patronize painters and commission luxurious works such as the Imperial *Bankoku sōzu*—within reach, and hence into the cognitive realm, of a growing mass audience. Cheap printed images circulated among urban commoner classes and even among the peasantry, who never before had confronted the visual "arts" and the power of the images they propagated. The imaged Other became part of the everyday cognitive world.

The imaged "anthropos" of the Shōhō *Bankoku sōzu* and *Wakan sansai zue* resonated with the visual imaginary of people throughout Japanese society. It permeated consciousness at a level hitherto unimaginable and was translated into a "knowledge," a visual taxonomy that both joined collective Self and Other in a common bond of shared identity as *jinrui* and distinguished and displayed difference between Self and all Others, between Other and Other, in a potent didactic form. The images of imagined *jinrui*, conjoined as they were from their inception with a geographic and cartographic imaginary that transformed the habitat of *jinrui* from *sangoku* to *bankoku* and the shape of the world from a single massive continent floating in a cosmic sea to a set of continents on the face of a globe, circulated and regenerated over time. Without the benefit of independent Japanese "voyages of discovery," the imaged/imagined "anthropos" took on a discursive life of its own.

Iterations of the "Peoples of the Forty-two Lands," early adumbrated by Nishikawa Joken, continued to appear well into the nineteenth century, with "Hollanders" and "English" still dressed in seventeenth-century garb, even as post-Napoleonic Hollanders traded in Nagasaki. And world maps published in the mid-nineteenth century, too, frequently illustrated selected countries around the world with visual images of these same taxonomies, locating the "Hollanders" in "Holland" and the "English" in "England" (complete with the Union Jack) not to mention the "Giants," still south of Patagonia, and the "Dwarves," arm in arm for mutual protection in the cold and frozen north beyond "Finlandia." The collective project of an imaginative cultural and human geography that was begun in the sixteenth century and first articulated as such in the seventeenth continued to inform Japanese visualization of "anthropos" even as Japan confronted a reemergent "West" in the middle of the nineteenth century.

CHAPTER 4

Indianizing Iberia/Performing Portugal: Responses to the Iberian Irruption

Miranda
O! Wonder!
How many goodly creatures are there here!
How beauteous mankind is! O brave new world
That has such people in't.

SHAKESPEARE, The Tempest, V. i, 182–185

∙∙∙

Caliban
Do not torment me! O!
Stephen
What's the matter? Have we devils here? Do you put tricks upon me
    with salvages and men of Inde?

SHAKESPEARE, The Tempest, II. ii, 56–58

∙∙∙

Along the way we met a squadron of many men, armored from head to foot, and carrying bows and arrows, and lances, ready for battle, who called us Indians; they said that hostilities had erupted because we had spoken ill of their pagodas, and so we should be killed and driven from this land."

FR. JOÃO FERNANDEZ TO FRANCISCO XAVIER (1551)[1]

∙∙
∙∙

---

1   Irmão João to Francisco Xavier," in *Nihon kankei kaigai shiryō Iezusu-kai Nihon shokan-shū genbun-hen* (1990), p. 174. My thanks to Gonoi Takashi for this reference. My translation is from the Japanese text in *Nihon kankei kaigai shiryō Iezusu-kai Nihon shokan-shū yakubun-hen* (1994), 1: 63f.

Japan's most significant Other, China, as well as Japan's other Others, Koreans and Mongols, Ryukyuans and Ainu—not to mention "devils ... salvages and men of Inde"—had populated the universe of Japanese consciousness for centuries before the Age of Encounter brought Iberians and Italians, English and Dutch, Africans and Javanese, Indians and Amerinds to Japan.[2] Chinese, Koreans, and others from the East and Northeast Asian mainland, had voyaged to the Japanese from at least the third century of our era,[3] and Japanese had ventured abroad. Chinese and Koreans, especially, had migrated permanently to Japan, either in communities or as individual Buddhist missionaries. And the Mongols had twice attempted (and failed at) invasions of Japan.

These old Others inhabited—indeed constituted—a world of Japanese iconography and representation, of performance, and of rich oral and written literatures. Yet despite the large numbers of Others in Japan prior to the Iberian irruption in the sixteenth century, the Other of Japanese representation was overwhelmingly marked as "Chinese" and Chinese in ultimate referent. Other was nearly invariably represented as being "out there," in China or India (the land of Buddha, and venue of much Buddhist representation, hence inherently Other) rather than "here" in Japan. Save for visual representations of the Mongol invasions (1274; 1281), there are precious few representations of Other *in Japan* in art (drama, or literature) of the Japan that greeted Xavier on his arrival in 1549.[4] Typically, Japanese artists depicted their Chinese figures in Chinese landscapes, and indeed, in profoundly Chinese painterly styles, like Sesshū Tōyō's *Winter Landscape*, or Tenshō Shūbun's *Studio of the Three Worthies*.[5]

The Iberian irruption transformed all this. Other was no longer safely "out there." Japanese art and festival masquerade responded to the "salvages and men of Inde" who arrived by the hundreds, if not thousands, after 1549, with a new interest in, a new excitement with, the "Southern Barbarians,"[6] who were depicted with great zest in the vibrant genre painting of the late sixteenth

2 The literature on China in Japanese consciousness is too vast for complete inclusion here. See especially Pollack (1986), who examines the literary trope of China over a millennium; Harootunian (1980) and Nakai (1980) examine the seventeenth to nineteenth centuries.

3 I use the terms "Japanese" and "Korean," strictly as geographic markers when referring to an age before their respective peoples had coalesced into the more-or-less unified precursors of their modern nation-states.

4 As distinct from depictions of Chinese in China. See Wakabayashi (2009) for an insightful analysis of the representation of the invading Mongol forces in a series of fourteenth- and fifteenth-century illustrated shrine and temple histories (*jisha engi*).

5 See Paine & Soper (1955, 77–78) for Sesshū (1420–1456) and Shūbun (d. ca. 1544–50).

6 Nanban (Ch. *nanman*); the character *ban/man* means "fierce, savage, uncivilized," as well as "foreigner."

and early seventeenth centuries. Portuguese and Spaniards, and their African, Indian and Mesoamerican slaves, peopled Japanese cityscapes, as well as being represented in an Iberia of Japanese artists' imagination. After an initial infatuation, Japan's nearly allergic reaction to Counter Reformation Catholicism brought the Iberian interlude to an end after less than a century, and a wave of Christophobia and attendant Iberophobia obliterated the image of Iberians from Japanese art and performance—indeed, from nearly all modes of discourse. By 1650, Christianity was a capital offense, and the representation of Iberians taboo.

Yet the disappearance of the Iberian (read Catholic) Other from the painter's palette, the performer's stage, and the masquer's dance did not mean reversion to an iconography in which Other was only "out there." Rather, as the new Other was cast out of Japan, nearly expelled from consciousness, and totally obliterated from view, the niche it had carved for itself in the Japanese landscape was appropriated by other Others, the old Others of Korea, the Ryukyus, and China.

This absence of Other from the iconographic/cognitive landscape of Japanese prior to the Iberian irruption, the intensity with which Japanese art and masque adopted the Iberian trope during the Nanban (Iberian) interlude, 1543–1640, and the assumption by old, familiar Others (formerly excluded from the Japanese landscape) of the place the Iberians had made for themselves are suggestive of transformations in consciousness wrought by Japan's experience of Other in the Nanban century.

Before the encounter, recall, the dominant Japanese cosmology was one of "three realms" (*sangoku*)—Our Country, China, and "India" (*Wagachō/Honchō, Shintan/Kara*, and *Tenjiku*).[7] Since *Tenjiku* was conceived more as "the land of the Buddha" than geographical "India," within a few years of the encounter, the cosmology of "three realms" was quickly displaced by a world of "myriad countries" (*bankoku*), represented cartographically and discussed in learned and popular texts, and a nearly infinite range of human and cultural variation. Since one of the "three realms" in the earlier cosmology had been not only inaccessible, but perhaps not "real," Japan had been enmeshed, *de facto*, in a binary cosmology; the only Other that made a significant impression in mainstream discourse was "China," while all other Others were subsumed within it.[8] It is in the nature of binaries, of course, that everything is either "A" or "B";

---

7   See Ōji (1996, 121–150) and Kawamura (2003, 9–17) for concise discussions of *sangoku* cosmology in pre-encounter Japan.

8   What I am here rendering "China" was, more properly, "the continent," so dominated by China in mainstream Japanese cognition that "Korea" disappeared into it. Japanese were, of

thus, in the binary logic of pre-encounter Japan, all continental Others were absorbed in *Shintan*. The encounter with "C," "D," and so on, which could not be subsumed as special cases of "China," as Korea had been, required major cosmological and cognitive surgery. The Japanese art and performance of the late sixteenth and early seventeenth centuries that we now call "Nanban art" was part of that process—attempts to re-integrate a coherent picture of the world and its peoples in the aftermath of encounter.

1   **Implicit Others and Manifest Men of Inde**

"During the reign of Emperor Gonara-no-in [1526–1557]," wrote a Japanese chronicler nearly a century later,

> the hundred-eighth sovereign since the Emperor Jinmu [mythic found-er of the imperial line], around the Kōji era [1555–1558], there came on a Nanban merchantman a creature one couldn't put a name to, that [appeared to have] human form at first [glance], but might as well be a long-nosed goblin, or a long-necked demon of the sort that disguise themselves as Buddhist lay-priests in order to trick people. Careful in-quiry [revealed] that the creature was called a "Padre." How big its eyes were! They were like a pair of telescopes, but the irises were yellow. Its head was small; it had long claws on its hands and feet. It was over seven feet tall and was black in color, [but] its nose was red; its teeth were lon-ger than a horse's teeth, and its hair was mouse-grey. Above its forehead it'd shaved a spot on its pate about the size of an overturned sake cup. Its speech was incomprehensible to the ear; its voice resembled the screech of an owl. Everyone ran to see it, mobbing the roads with abandon. They thought this phantasm more terrible than the more ferocious monster.[9]

---

course, conscious of Korea, but it wasn't accorded the ontological status of "country"-hood in popular discourse. I have elided here the presence of a variety of mythic maritime Others, who were not recognized as fully human in any case, the cannibal peoples of islands to the south, the horse-headed people of islands to the northeast, etc. See, especially, Murai (1988).

9 *Kirishitan monogatari*, in *Zokuzoku Gunsho ruijū* (17 vols., Zoku Gunsho Ruijū Kanseikai, 1969–1978), 12: 531–550. For a full, but slightly different translation, see Elison (1974, 319–347), who regards "[t]his alien apparition [as] altogether unnatural" (30), but it is unlikely that the realm of demons and goblins, of fox and badger spirits capable of assuming human form were entirely un-"natural" to most Japanese of the sixteenth and seventeenth centuries, who rather saw an animate continuum from "Japanese human" at the last remove through "alien human" on one axis, through "birds, beasts, and fishes" on another, and through "demons and

FIGURE 34   The first thing one noticed was how long its nose was! It was like a wartless
conch-shell, stuck onto [his face] by suction. Detail from a folding screen,
early 17th century.

FIGURE 35
An officer in the retinue of a Korean diplomatic mission, portrayed as
exceptionally hirsute. Ishikawa Toyonobu, "Korean Smoking," woodblock
print, 1748.

Well, indeed, might Japanese be puzzled by the arrival of the new manner of creature (Europeans, specifically Portuguese) that in 1543 landed on the island of Tanegashima, southwestern Japan, the first Europeans ever to visit Japan, or by the strangely frocked Francisco Xavier, a founder of the Society of Jesus and the first Jesuit to proselytize in Japan, who arrived in Kyushu from Goa six years later. Equally confusing, surely, were Xavier's colleagues Cosme de Torres (1551), Luis de Almeida (1552), and Allessandro Valignano (1566), their merchant and military companions, and the huge "black ships" (*kurofune*) that bore them.[10]

Yet if the Japanese were confused by these new men, their faces and bodies, their clothing, their language, and their "black ships" (and "black" slaves), imagine the Europeans' amazement when their Japanese hosts mistakenly (or so *they* thought) greeted them as a Tenjikujin—"men of Inde!"[11] What a sweet irony: At the very moment—broadly speaking—that westbound Europeans were "discovering" "men of Inde" at their first landfall in the New World, their eastbound compatriots were being construed as "men of Inde" at their farthest landfall, beyond the eastern rim of Asia. Xavier and his confreres at least "knew" where they were, and whom they saw—but they had the advantage of "knowing" where they were going: to Zipangu/Iapam, and of an awareness that none of their kind had preceded them. The Japanese who found these "devils ... salvages, or men of Inde" clambering upon their shores were rather more like Miranda than Ferdinand: The landscape was—they thought—unchanged and it was only "such people" that made it brave and new. Little wonder, then, if Japanese had trouble mapping this brave new world.

---

gods" (*kishin*) along the third. This schematized typology of Others was developed in conversations with Kuroda Hideo.

10   Kuroda (1986b) examines why the "black ships" were black and significations of black in sixteenth-century Japanese color symbology.

11   Tenjiku, the Buddhist term for "the land [whence] the law of the Buddha was transmitted to China ("Morokoshi") over a span of three-hundred years." *Kojiki* (Record of Ancient Matters), entry of 13th year, 4th month, reign of Empress Suiko (605). The Jesuit Japanese-Portuguese dictionary of 1603, *Vocabulario da Lingoa Iapam*, which I used in the translation by Doi et al. (1980, 216) lists Tengicu—which he equates with Siam—as one of the *tres reinos* (Sangocu) constituting the Japanese cosmos, i.e., "China, Sião, Iapão." For example, Fr. Cosme de Torres (1598/1972, 18) wrote Xavier from Yamaguchi on 20 October 1551 that the Japanese "*nos disserão chensicus*" (that they "call us 'Tenjikus'"—i.e., "Indians"). This passage in the Portuguese translation was dropped in the Spanish text in *Cartos que los Padres y Hermanos de la Compania de Iesus* ...(1575; Biblioteca Nacional, Madrid, ref. no. R-6654), 50. My thanks to Professor Gonoi Takashi for his guidance with these passages in the Jesuit letters.

But Stephen's first reading of Caliban offers the beginnings of a map from our own, and Xavier's, first bemusement at the "confusion" through the implicit ethnographies that inscribed these newfound aliens upon an already densely charted (if little visited) Japanese iconography of Other, a map "known" to encode "all the world," and all "such people [as were] in't." For though the Portuguese were hardly the first aliens the "Japanese" had met, they were the first "new" aliens encountered in nearly a millennium, nearly the first to come from beyond the familiar "human" realm of Japan and China, from the largely mythic Tenjiku where Buddhas and Bodhisattvas abode.[12]

We might follow Pirandello and suggest that the Iberian arrivals were characters in search of an author for their text.[13] Even more apt is Marshall Sahlins's provocative direction to "consider what happened to Captain Cook. For the people of Hawaii, Cook had been a myth before he was an event, since the myth was the frame by which the event was interpreted."[14] By contrast with Captain James Cook and Hawaiian myth as represented by Sahlins, however, Japanese encounters with the Other in legend and tale more commonly occurred offshore, in the mode of Momotarō, the "Peach Boy," or Minamoto no Yorimitsu, hero of the *Shuten dōji* legend. Both Momotarō and Yorimitsu went "out there," confronted the bestial/demonic Other, bested them, and returned with their treasure, their captives and their magic.[15] In the "Xavierian encounter," by contrast, Other was not more-or-less safely "out there," but invasive, *here*, more closely analogous narratologically to the fictitious confrontation of Hakurakuten, i.e., the Tang poet Bo Zhuyi, with the Japanese god Sumiyoshi Daimyōjin off the coast of northern Kyushu.[16] In the nō play *Hakurakuten*, the

---

12   A monk often identified as an Indian (in *Zokuzoku gunsho ruijū* [11:214ff.], the *Tōdaiji zoku yōroku* identifies him as being from "Linyi"—probably part of what is now northern Vietnam) had a role in the ceremonies vivifying the Great Buddha in Tōdaiji (temple) in Nara in 752, but "[men] of Inde" were rarely on Japanese soil thereafter. A "Tenjikujin"— that is, an alien clearly not from China, Korea, or Ryukyu—merchant, most likely was from southeast Asia, came to Japan in the late fourteenth century, residing in area of what is now Osaka long enough to leave behind two sons. One of the sons, known by his Japanese name, Kusuha Sainin (1395–1486), distinguished himself in the service of the great Nara temple Kōfukuji, making two trade voyages to Ming China, 1432 and 1453. Since Sainin's childhood name is recorded as "Musuru" (Japanese phonetic equivalent of Musul—Musulman?), it is likely that his "Inde"-ish father was a Muslim, suggesting Malacca as a likely origin. The definitive study on Sainin is Tanaka (1959).

13   Pirandello, 1954.

14   Sahlins (1985, 73).

15   For a basic version of the Momotarō tale, see Ichinose (1960, 2:30–34); for *Shuten dōji*, see Ichiko (1958, 361–384). *Otogizōshi shū* contains several other tales of the "conquest-of-Other" or "encounter-with-Other" type, but in each case, the encounter occurs "out there," offshore (or under the sea, in the case of Urashima Tarō).

16   On Bo Zhuyi's status in Japan, see Pollack (1986); and Brower and Miner (1961, 180–181).

poet, as archetypal Invasive Other, was sent by the Tang Chinese emperor to spy on Japan—only to be beaten at his own game, bested by Sumiyoshi in an offshore poetry contest and driven off before ever landing in Japan by a divine wind (*kamikaze*) summoned by the god.[17]

What kind of cosmology, what "implicit iconography" (if not ethnography) of all the "goodly creatures" of the world mapped the known, the expected, and the unexpected for Japanese in the pre-encounter age? Why were the first Jesuits "men of Inde" even before they were "southern barbarians" (*Nanban*)? And if the Jesuits were "men of Inde," then why were their ships "black ships" (*kurofune*) rather than "Indiamen" (*Tenjikubune*)? Chinese ships, after all, were simply "Chinese ships" (*Karafune*) and Korean ships just "Korean ships" (*Komabune*). In the new few pages I explore the Japanese cosmology/iconographic realm into which the Iberians sailed at mid-century, to suggest how they fit (or failed to fit) into it, and to speculate that their sojourn in, and expulsion from, Japan made for lasting changes in Japanese notions of ethnic Self and in their iconography of Other. The discussion is preliminary, speculative, and suggestive and makes no claim of exhaustiveness or definitiveness.

2   Setting the Stage

In understanding the radical transformations that the arrival of these Iberian "men of Inde" wrought upon the deployment of iconographies of Other in Japanese elite and popular culture, we need to note two central characteristics of the stage onto which the Iberians walked.

It should be no surprise that Japanese iconographies had developed a highly articulated code of markers for Otherness, a (set of) code(s) formed over centuries of contact with the other peoples of continental and archipelagic northeast Asia.[18] As Japanese notions of Self and Other changed, iconographies were re-encrypted to accommodate them; yet the relationship was, as we have

---

17   For the *nō* play *Hakurakuten*, see Yokomichi and Omote (1960–1963, 41:305–308). Sumiyoshi's invocation of the *kamikaze* serves as a prelude to divine winds that defeated the archetype Invasive Other in Japanese historical consciousness, the two attempted Mongol invasions of 1274 and 1281. A popular puppet play of early 1719, the eve of an expected visit by a Korean mission, represents "Mashiba Hisayoshi," a thinly masked Toyotomi Hideyoshi, as reversing the scheme, making a pilgrimage to four Sumiyoshi shrines to pray for the success of his planned invasion of Korea. Chikamatsu (1928, 11:733).

18   It is important to note that this environment of Others included fellow inhabitants of what we now regard as the Japanese archipelago: unassimilated overland and island neighbors to the northeast and southwest who shared grosser genetic, cultural, and linguistic characteristics with "the Japanese," and more clearly "alien" Others, such as the ancestors of the Ainu and the Okinawans. As the boundaries of "Japan" and "the Japanese"

seen already in the arrival of the Portuguese, intersubjective and intertextual: Perceptions of both old and new Others were constrained by received codes of Other, while newly discovered Others provoked further articulation of those codes. Further, however, because Japan is an archipelago distant (75 km at nearest landfall in Korea; 340 km from the Chinese coast) from the continent, and because of the relative disinterest of Chinese and Koreans in journeying to Japan, there were long periods when foreign traffic was rare indeed. Even at times of relatively intense foreign contact, prior to the 1630s, more contact came from Japanese going abroad, than Others coming to Japan. Consequently, perhaps, iconographies of Other seem less contested than they might otherwise have been.

When the Portuguese stepped off their ships onto Japanese soil, they were dressed for the role: their skin was dark, sunburned from months at sea; they had curly hair and heavy beards and were generally more hirsute than any people previously encountered in Japan. Observable bodily characteristics of the Nanban, that is, were already heavily signed in Japan as markers of alienness and barbarianness.[19] Likewise, the ruffled collar of the elite of Iberia (and much of contemporary southern and western Europe) in the mid-sixteenth century conformed almost perfectly to a rich Japanese iconography that, at least since the eleventh century, had used frilled and ruffled collars, sleeves, and hems as explicit markers of the Other.

But what interests us most in this encounter is the transformation in the iconographic venue of Other that, apparently, was wrought by the European irruption and the century (ca. 1550–1640) of dense Euro-Japanese contact. It is difficult to be precise about dating and about the transformation of content, but broadly speaking, Other, the clear-cut foreigner, with a few rare exceptions, is portrayed in pre-Nanban art only abroad—in China (often in essentially Chinese-style painting) or Tenjiku/India—and not in Japanese settings. The major exceptions to this iconological generalization seem to be portrayals of kinds of Other-in-Japan as invaders, objects of border subjugation, or tributaries, on the one hand, and portraits of Chinese Buddhist monks who came to Japan as missionaries, on the other. The latter, however, are generally portrayed in the conventional manner assigned to the category of "Buddhist monk," and so decontextualized that there is no "setting" as such.

After 1550, Other becomes omnipresent, a permanent and pervasive feature of Japanese iconography. For nearly a century, Japanese artists and sculptors

---

        remained less-than-fully determined, so too, did these Others occasionally cross boundaries in the iconography.

19   Murai (1988) discusses the signed quality of skin color, hair texture, and meat-eating (and imputed cannibalism) in medieval Japanese cosmology.

enthusiastically, prolifically painted Nanban-jin, not only in a native European habitat the artist had never seen (Japanese art had a long tradition of depicting idealized Others in idealized foreign settings that the artist, poet, or writer knew only through the art or writing of others) but also in Japanese ports, inland towns, and buildings of every description. Japanese took to the "new-wave" Other in many ways, adopting "Nanban" clothing styles, masquerading as "Nanban-jin" in festivals and plays, mimicking "Nanban" tastes in furniture, food, and clothing.

Many of the revelers in the great Hōkoku Festival in 1604 commemorating the seventh anniversary of the death of Toyotomi Hideyoshi (1536–98, deified as Toyokuni/Hōkoku Daimyōjin) arrayed themselves in Nanban-style outfits (Fig. 36). Though contemporary spectators' accounts write of men in "Tōjin" garb, it is clear that these revelers had wrapped themselves in costumes derived from contemporary European models.

In 1635, in the initial celebration of the annual festival at the newly rededicated Hachiman Shrine in the provincial castle town of Tsu, we see the conflation of Nanban and Tōjin: All verbal texts, from the festival's inception to the present day, agree that the residents of the wealthy merchants' quarter of Wakebe-chō, just outside the castle walls, presented themselves in the guise

FIGURE 36   Revelers in the Hōkoku Festival of 1604 arrayed in Nanban fashion can be identified as Japanese masqueraders by the sandals on their feet. Kano Naizen, *Hōkoku sairei-zu byōbu*. Pair of six-panel folding screens, color and gold leaf on paper. Detail, left-hand screen, 5th panel.
COURTESY TOYOKUNI JINJA, KYOTO

of Tōjin. Nowadays, residents of the ward dance in iconographically orthodox Tōjin garb, accompanied by orthodox instruments, and parade as a stylized version of a seventeenth-century Korean ambassador's retinue, complete with correct pennants and regalia. They too believe that they have "always" been Tōjin and Koreans in the festival performance.[20] (Fig. 37) Yet pictorial records of the early festival, believe to date from the inaugural celebration in 1635, show these Wakebe-chō Tōjin in unmistakable Nanban costume, wearing high-topped boots, billowing pantaloons, button-front jackets, some in flowing locks with a reddish tinge, others with thick, black side-whiskers, beards, and moustaches. They carry straight-blade swords, and one, most tellingly, shoulders a harquebus; a bit later in the retinue, a little-boy Tōjin (in garb

FIGURE 37   "Korean Procession" presented by Wakebe-chō annually in Tsu City's Hachiman Festival. While modeled on the parades of Korean embassies to Japan in the Edo period, the main character, the bearded figure, center, is a "Korean general" (*Chōsen taishō*), rather than an ambassador, evoking associations with the many captives brought back from the Japanese invasions of 1592–98 by Tōdō Takatora, the first daimyo of Tsu domain.

PHOTO BY THE AUTHOR, 1990

20   Field notes, Tsu, Mie Prefecture, 9–11 October 1990.

FIGURES 38–40   Wakebe-chō's Hachiman Festival "Chinaman" (*Tōjin*) masquerades in the
                        1630s and 1640s incorporated Nanban, rather than Korean, clothing styles,
                        and red wigs evocative of Japanese ideas about the English and Dutch,
                        who were called *Kōmō* (red-hairs). Contemporary texts identify this as a
                        Tōjin performance. It is unclear precisely when the transition to "Korean"
                        costumes occurred. *Tsu Hachiman sairei emaki*, ca. 1640.
                        COURTESY SPENCER COLLECTION, NEW YORK PUBLIC LIBRARY

distinct from the Nanban style) plays a *charumera*, a double-reed instrument
associated with the Other, while farther back, another little-boy Tōjin brings
up the rear (see Figs. 38, 39, 40).[21]

It seems likely that this revaluation of overtly Nanban clothing as Tōjin, perhaps the reemergence of the Tōjin from the shadow of the Nanban, is but another side-effect of the rising fear of Christianity, and concomitant suspicion
of Portuguese, that had led to edicts prohibiting evangelization as early as 1587.
Hideyoshi's edict of 1587 was honored in the breach, but in 1612, Ieyasu had issued a more explicit proscription that in fact resulted in the expulsion of many
missionaries and Japanese Christians; in 1619, over sixty Christians had been
executed in Kyoto; and on Genna 8/8/5 (1622/9/10), just four months after the
festival for the seventh anniversary of Ieyasu's death, fifty-five Christians were

---

21   Anonymous (circa 1645). See Tsu-shi (1989, front matter) for a color reproduction showing
      a section of the Wakebe-chō Nanban/Tōjin masquerade; other details, and bibliographic
      data in Murase (1986, 173–175); Sorimachi (1978, 26–27). When a facsimile of this scroll was
      displayed during the 1990 Tsu Hachiman Festival, several local participants remarked that
      the costumes seemed "all wrong," that they "didn't look like Tōjin or 'Korean' costumes."
      An ethnic Korean born in Japan who was active in identifying and studying "Korean-
      embassy masquerades" was perplexed that these "Koreans" looked like Nanban (Field
      notes). The Tōjin quality of costume in all later depictions I have seen, whether in Tsu
      or elsewhere, has lost any hint of Nanbanness. *Charumera*, from Portuguese *charamela*,
      a sort of shawm, was also known in Japan as the *Tōjinbue* ("Chinaman flute"; "foreigner
      flute"); the instrument had long been known in East Asia.

executed in Nagasaki.[22] It was becoming dangerous to "play" Nanban, it was safer to call this rose by another name, *Tōjin*.

Indeed, in the rising tide of Christian persecution and xenophobia, it becomes increasingly difficult to find either visual or textual evidence of the Nanban in Japanese iconography. But as the "blurred genre" of the Tōjin-in-Nanban clothing in the festivals of 1604, 1622, and 1635 suggests, the desire both to masquerade as Other, and to represent Other visually, was more enduring than the specifically Nanban style. The representation of Other was essential to the perpetuation of community, to the inscription of boundaries, and to the reconstitution of categories of Self and Other, in the aftermath of the Nanban interlude. As the Nanban were driven from Japan (ultimately in 1639), and Christianity virtually extirpated, or driven underground thereafter, the Other had to find new clothes. The re-clothing of Other found convenient sources in a different, more familiar direction, also suggested by the *Tōjin* tags of 1622: Japanese masquers and artists alike turned back to the Other they had known all along, the Other of the continent and archipelago (primarily Korea and Ryūkyū), for themes and tropes of Alterity.

The initial Japanese ascription of Indianness to Iberians recorded in Cosme de Torres's letter to Francisco Xavier accords with the analogous Iberian "error" in their "New World," or the Hawaiian inscription of Captain Cook in earlier texts of Alterity. In each case, the earlier text (Tenjiku; India; the Hawaiian god Lono) had been a text "read" vicariously, not directly: No Japanese had been to Tenjiku; Columbus had not seen "India"; Lono had not (likely) visited Hawaii in memory of those who greeted Cook. The nomination of the Iberians as Indians, as Tenjikujin/Chensicus, inscribed them in a sacred text, the land of the Buddha, and hence sacralized and exalted this Other. The ready renaming of Chensicus as Nanban, too, represents but their re-inscription from sacred text (India) to profane, for the Nanban were one of the barbarians of the four directions (*shi'i*) in a Chinese cosmology that had been mapped onto Japan.

The assimilation of a new, inadequately known form of Other, Iberians, to a prior category of indirectly experienced Other is one thing. Their subsequent absorption to a category of well-known Other, Tōjin, evident in the naming of the masqueraders in the memorial festivals for Hideyoshi and Ieyasu, is somewhat different, yet no less unprecedented. John Saris, the envoy who bore the letter of James I of England to Japan reported in 1613, for example, that "the

---

22   The increasingly severe suppression of Christianity (or rising tide of persecution, in most accounts sympathetic to the evangelical enterprise) is outlined in Boxer (1951) and Elison (1973).

place [was] exceedingly peopled, [and they were] very Civill and courteous,"
with one exception:

> Onley that at our landing, and being here in Hakata [a major port in
> Kyushu], and so through the whole Countrey, whithersoever we came,
> the boyes, children, and worser sort of idle people, would gather about
> and follow along after us, crying Coré, Coré, Cocoré, Waré, that is to say,
> You Coreans with false hearts: wondering, hopping, hallowing, and mak-
> ing such a noise about us, that we could scarcely heare one an other
> speake, sometimes throwing stones at us (but that not in many Townes),
> yet the clamour and crying after us was every where alike, none reproving
> them for it.[23]

Tens of thousands of Koreans ("Coré," Saris's rendering of *Kōrai*, the Japanese
pronunciation of *Koryŏ*)[24] had passed through Hakata as captives during the
Japanese invasions (1592–1598), and thousands, at least, still lived in the region,
forming the core of potters' communities, acting as Confucian advisers, and
the like. There is no reason to believe that "Coré" was just a vicarious text for
the "boyes, children, and worser sort of idle people" there. Further, we should
recall that the term Kōrai itself was a deliberately alienating archaism in
Japanese discourse. The Koryŏ state had fallen in 1392, some 200 years earlier.
Its successor state, Chosŏn (J. *Chōsen*, 1392–1910), while recognized in official
correspondence, was unrecognized in popular discourse.

Eighty years after Saris, long after the Iberians had been expelled, Engelbert
Kaempfer, a German physician to the Dutch trading factory in Nagasaki, likewise reported that during his two journeys to Edo,

> In some towns and villages only we took notice, that the young boys,
> who are childish all-over the world, would run after us, call us names,
> and crack some malicious jests or other, levell'd at the Chinese, *whom
> they take us to be*. One common, and not much different from a like sort
> of compliment, which is commonly made to Jews in Germany, is Toosin
> bay bay [*Tōjin baibai*], which in broken Chinese, signifies, Chinese, have
> ye nothing to truck?[25]

---

23 Diary of John Saris, in Samuel Purchas, *Purchas, His Pilgrimes in Japan*, ed. Cyril Wild
    (Kobe, 1939), 148–149, quoted in Cooper (1965, 287–288).
24 Saris's "Coré," from *Kōrai*, the Japanese pronunciation of the name of the medieval Korean
    kingdom of Koryŏ (935–1192).
25 Kaempfer (1727/1906, 2:357; emphasis added). The close parallels between Kaempfer's
    phrasing and Saris's suggests either that Kaempfer had read Saris (which is unlikely) or

Catalyzed by Christophobia and Iberophobia, Europeans were reinscribed as subcategories of less-threatening Others, as a variant form of "Chinese."

3   Alter Others: Koreans, Okinawans, and Chinese in the Japanese Text

Japanese cosmologies were amply supplied with Others prior to the Iberian irruption of the mid sixteenth century. I have alluded to a core Japanese Self, bounded to the east by limitless seas and to the west by China (*kara/moro-koshi* = continental, and including Korea), with Tenjiku (the "chensicus" of Cosme de Torre's letter to Xavier), the land of the Buddhas, beyond it. Unlike Japan's Iberian encounter, however, most previous Japanese meetings with the Chinese and Indian Other had occurred "out there," in China and Tenjiku, not just in iconographic conceit but also in historic practice.[26] With some exceptions, of course, Japanese monks made the pilgrimage to China, rather than the reverse, and Japanese merchants who bore them there.

The Xavierian moment, the mid-sixteenth-century era of Iberian irruption into East Asia and Japanese consciousness, coincided with a half-century of low ebb in Japan's relations with nearby East Asia. Civil war in Japan had unleashed "Japanese" piracy up and down the East Asian coast, which had provoked Ming China to embargo direct trade with Japan, banning both Japanese voyages to China and Chinese voyages to Japan.[27] Relations with all East Asia reached a nadir with Japan's invasion of Korea in 1592 and the ensuing seven-year war between Japan and a Sino-Korean alliance.

The devastation of Korea was accompanied by an enrichment of Japan. Countless Korean cultural treasures were taken as booty by Japan's generals,

---

that a corpus of lore circulated among the Japanese of early modern Europe, a European iconography of Other, in which this was a common trope. It reappears in writings of other westerners in Japan in the nineteenth century, as well; for example, de Fonblanque (1863, 15), Fortune (1863, 96). There is little doubt that both de Fonblanque and Fortune had read Kaempfer.

26   The ninth-century Japanese monk Shinnyo set out from China by sea for Tenjiku in 865, but reportedly died en route in Luoyue, near today's Singapore. Later legend had it that he was eaten by a tiger. (Terajima 1712, 982) Other than Shinnyo, I know of no Japanese claims to have visited Tenjiku before the seventeenth century. A seventeenth-century mariner gained notoriety as "Tenjiku Tokubei" for his fabulous claims to have visited Tenjiku and came to personify the evil potentialities of the foreign in numerous popular plays of the eighteenth and nineteenth centuries.

27   Murai (1993) argues that these "Japanese" pirate crews were in fact multi-ethnic affairs, including Koreans and Chinese, as well as Japanese.

and entire communities of potters and other craftsmen were uprooted and taken captive to Japan, where they established new centers of ceramic arts in Japan or reinvigorated old communities. These tens of thousands of Koreans constitute the largest documented immigration to Japan before the twentieth century. Some of the communities they established remained ethnically distinct into modern times.[28] Moreover, judging from depictions of Korean-descended potters in nineteenth-century Satsuma gazetteers, the men continued to follow the "Korean" tonsorial practice of wearing full beards and mustaches.[29] Yet these communities of eternal internal Others do not appear to have excited artists' brushes.

In the decade after the war, when Korea and Japan had resolved their overt differences, Korea sent an embassy of nearly 500 men to the Tokugawa capital of Edo, the first of seven such missions in the seventeenth century. Likewise, after a short, Granada/Panama-style Japanese invasion of Ryūkyū (Okinawa) in 1609, the Ryukyuan king was brought to Edo in 1610, followed by six other Ryukyuan missions to Edo that century.[30] Just as the Europeans were, Koreans and Ryukyuans, too, were objects of curiosity, confusion, and wonder.

Each embassy was a major popular cultural event, a once-in-a-lifetime tourist attraction for people along the route.[31] Along the Inland Sea, people rode out into the channel to get a closer look when the flotilla passed; at each port town where they spent the night, hundreds would gather to gawk and stare. At Osaka in 1682, wrote a Korean diarist in the entourage, "A million onlookers swarmed like ants on the riverbanks ...; pontoon bridges spanned the water, and countless thousands lined up on them to watch us." And the spectators and gawkers were neither solely the lower classes, who could afford no loftier entertainment, nor exclusively those a few minutes or hours' walk from the route, for whom the trip was no expense:

---

28   For example, the Korean potters of Naeshirokawa in Satsuma (southern Kyushu), who remained identified as Korean for at least two and a half centuries after originally being transplanted to Japan as captives in the 1590s. See Haraguchi and Sakai (1975, 199–200 [original]; 88–89 [translation]).

29   Illustration in *Sangoku meishō zue* (1843), reproduced in *Nihon Kinsei Seikatsu Ebiki Minami Kyūshū-hen* Hensan Kyōdō Kenkyū-han (2018, 112).

30   See Toby (1984) for a fuller account.

31   Embassies traveled by ship through the Inland Sea to Osaka, then up to the Yodo River on galleys to the castle town of Yodo. They entered Kyoto by foot, horseback, or palanquin and traveled to Edo by road, passing through four of the five largest cities in the land (Osaka, Kyoto, Nagoya, and Edo). For a discussion of the tourist appeal of these events, see Toby (1986).

At the arrival of the Ryukyuan tribute mission [of 1832] ... great numbers
of spectators, both male and female, flocked to see, lining both sides of
the river, and even floating boats out into the middle of the river, clog-
ging the channel ... when they went upriver by boat ... to Fushimi ... it's
said the spectators lined the route all the way. What's more ... Imperial
Princes, members of the Regent's House, and senior courtiers were
pleased to [watch], and it's even rumored that the Retired Emperor
secretly made an Imperial Progress to watch.[32]

A half-century of Nanban art and performance practices had firmly established a canon of representing Other in Japanese settings from Kagoshima and
Nagasaki to Kyoto. A half-century of Nanban fashion had generated new forms
of Other in festival performance, as we have seen in the festivals at the seventh anniversaries of the deaths of Hideyoshi and Ieyasu. The reappearance
in Japan of its other Others, ambassadorial entourages from Korea and the
Ryukyuan kingdom beginning in the first decade of the seventeenth century,
was quickly translated into visual representations of Other-in-Japan. At least
by the early 1620s, Kyoto artists (likely on commission from daimyos or wealthy
merchants) began to fill the spaces of the Kyoto landscape with Koreans,
depicting members of the Korean embassy of 1617 in paintings as they march
through the streets of the city, and mill about gawking in the precincts of great
Hōkōji temple complex on the outskirts of town.[33]

The Koreans depicted in both the Hayashibara and Burke *Rakuchū-rakugai*
screens are readily distinguishable from the Japanese around them: most
wear hats, shoes, ballooning trousers, and ruffled collars; the hatless pages
have unshaven pates. Indeed, in both screens several figures in the "Korean"
entourage at Hōkōji are arrayed in *Nanban*-style garb, and one of the figures
in the Hayashibara screen is black-skinned. There is little emphasis on the
Koreans' beards, as would characterize later representations, both visual and
performative, perhaps because Japanese law had yet to proscribe facial hair
the clean-shaven face had yet to dominate *Japanese* men's fashion.[34] Many
of the Japanese are represented sporting moustaches and full heads of hair,

---

32   Anonymous (1846, 11:239).
33   Unsigned *Rakuchū rakugai-zu byōbu*, six-panel painted screen (Mary Jackson Burke
       Collection, Minneapolis Museum of Arts); unsigned *Rakuchū rakugai-zu byōbu*, pair of six
       panel painted screens, ca. 1619–1623 (Hayashibara Bijutsukan, Okayama). These screens
       can be dated to 1619–1623 on the basis of internal evidence, and are likely products of the
       same atelier. For details, see Toby (1996a).
34   See below, Chapter 6, on the significance of hair and tonsorial practices in Japanese law,
       identity, and discourse.

which were soon to be outlawed. In the absence of pictorial codes specifying that the men depicted here as Koreans—as distinct from Chinese, Okinawan, or Portuguese—the artists have mobilized a combination of signs for Other, Chinese and *Nanban*, in particular.

Shortly after the Korean Other appeared in Japan, that is, came to be located in explicitly Japanese cityscapes, and after the 1630s gradually dis-/re-placed the expelled and tabooed Iberian Other. This process, we have seen, began in the confusions of genre implicated in the Nanban-costumed Japanese of the Hōkoku Festival(1604), the Wakayama and Tottori Tōshōgū festivals in memory of Ieyasu (1622), dubbed "Tōjin" (Chinamen) by the priest Gien, and in written records of the program of march; in the visual representations of Koreans in the Hayashibara and Burke *Rakuchū-rakugai* screens; in the epithet "Coré" hurled so often at Saris, and later "Toosin" (Tōjin) spat at Kaempfer.

By the time the last Iberians were expelled from the country (1639), Koreans and Okinawans, bearded, in plumed hats, frilled or ruffled costumes, boots or shoes (in some cases) and trousers, were being incorporated into particular cityscapes and landscapes in Japan. In 1640, Kanō Tan'yū, the premier painter in the shogun's entourage, executed the illustrations for Tenkai's history of the shrine to Tokugawa Ieyasu, *Tōshōsha engi*, in response to shogunal command. Most of the verbal and pictorial text recounts the pre-life and life of Ieyasu; the final chapters expand on the great reverence he has received since his deification. Heavily-tagged in the codes that had marked the invasive Iberian Other, East Asian Others who had formerly been kept safely Out There (iconographically) usurped their predecessors' place In Here, in overtly Japanese settings. Where the Nanban screen paintings had depicted Iberians sightseeing in the shrines and temples of Miyako (Kyoto), Tan'yū showed them entering the Tōshōsha (later Tōshōgū) shrine in Nikkō, 115 km north of Edo, as if to worship the deified Tokugawa Ieyasu.[35] The place is indisputably *Japan*, the entrance to a quintessentially *Japanese* sacred space, a *torii* shrine gate; the pine trees are *Japanese* pines, and the spectators are dressed in styles characteristic of particular *Japanese* social statuses and life-stages: The Koreans are clearly Other; they are clearly in *Japan*, as they had rarely been in pre-Nanban representation.

---

35   I argue (Toby 1984, 204) that the "worship" of Tōshō Daigongen (Ieyasu) by foreigners (the Koreans were told it was a "sightseeing trip") was part of a program to universalize the sacral reach of Ieyasu-the-god, an element in the ideological agenda of the early Tokugawa state. There is no evidence that the Koreans, for their part, regarded themselves as worshipping Ieyasu's numen. The idea that the Koreans went to "worship" was entirely a Japanese conceit, an ideological ploy by Tokugawa Iemitsu and the monk Tenkai. On the deification of Ieyasu and promotion of the Tōshō Daigongen cult, Sonehara (1996; 2008); Ooms (1984, 50–62); Boot (2000).

Similarly, the centerpiece of the *Edo-zu byōbu* (ca. 1634–1635), a panoramic Edo cityscape painting, most likely produced for display before the shogun, is the march of the 1624 Korean embassy parading through the streets of the shogunal capital and into Edo Castle for their audience with the shogun, Tokugawa Iemitsu.[36] Here, too, the Koreans are signed Other with frilled collars and sleeves, plumed hats, beards, shoes and boots, and the like. They, more even than the parade of Korean "pilgrims" to the shrines at Nikkō, are inscribed in a richly signed Japanese scene, passing through the streets of Japan's most populous city, crossing the moat to enter the walled and ramparted shogunal castle, before clusters of gawking, staring, pointing Japanese—again in rank- and status-coded dress and hairstyles. The scene is richly evocative of the scenes of a Nanban-peopled Kyoto a few decades before, and entirely at variance with the nearly totally Other-less Japanese landscape that preceded the Iberian arrival a century earlier. Iberian fashion, especially for ruffled collars, at the moment of encounter had been a fortuitous conformity with the iconographic text of Other that anticipated their arrival; the absence of Other on the Japanese domestic scene—or at least in representations of it— enabled them to enter an open role already costumed. By the time the Iberians left, the role of Other was established in the text of the Japanese landscape; in the absence of Iberians, Koreans, Okinawans, and other Others were asked to stand in their stead.

A further playing field for the iteration of Other-On-Our-Shores, which again continued tropes rehearsed in the representation of the Nanban, was the adoption of Nanban-Tōjin/Korean-coded costume for a broad range of itinerant acrobats, jongleurs, and monkey-trainers, some of whose activities remain a part of the encoding of Other on the Japanese scene today. Other-as-acrobat likely predates the Iberians; at least, I am not certain it does not, and the clothing of acrobats and jugglers in temporally or spatially alien garb is as familiar as the Ringling Brothers' Circus. But clearly the representation of Iberian

---

36   Unsigned pair of six-panel painted screens, each 162.5×366.0cm., color and gold leaf on paper; National Museum of Japanese History, Sakura City. For full reproductions, see Suzuki (1971); high-resolution images on-line at https://www.rekihaku.ac.jp/education_ research/gallery/webgallery/edozu/index.html. Kuroda (1993, chapter 1) has shown that this screen was painted sometime in late 1634 or early 1635 to celebrate the early years of the reign of the third shogun, Iemitsu (r. 1624–1651), and was likely commissioned by one of his closest advisers. The Korean procession shown, therefore, depicts the mission of 1624, the first of three Iemitsu received. The importance Iemitsu attached to the Korean mission is reflected in the fact that the scene of their arrival at Edo Castle is at the center of the overall composition, and the most densely populated scene in the entire panorama. See Toby (2008c, p. 6).

sailors, and more often, the dark-skinned men who accompanied them (most likely Africans and Goans), at work in the rigging of "Black Ships" as acrobats, sometimes nearly simian in aspect, performing tricks on the high-wire, was a favorite motif of the artists of the Nanban screens. It is no accident that the ruff-collared, puff-sleeved, elongated crew members doing handstands on the bowsprit, hanging from the yards, and sliding down the stays of the ship riding at anchor are deeply, darkly black, in Kanō Naizen's screen-painting of the Portuguese *kurofune* in Nagasaki harbor. The "Nanban" acrobats in the ship's rigging in another Kanō-school screen are likewise nearly all portrayed as dark-skinned (see Figs. 41, 42).[37]

FIGURE 41   Black-skinned men in Nanban garb climb in the rigging of a "black ship" (*kurofune*), i.e., a Portuguese carrack, anchored in Nagasaki harbor. Detail from Kano Dōmi, six-panel folding screen, color and gold leaf on paper.

---

37   Kanō Naizen, *Nanban byōbu*, pair of six-panel screens, each 154.5×363.2cm., color and gold leaf o paper; collection Kobe Municipal Museum, reproduced in Cooper (1971, fig. 94); images on line at http://www.city.kobe.lg.jp/culture/culture/institution/museum/meihin_new/405.html. Kanō-school screen (collection Suntory Museum), ibid., fig. 1. These are typical, rather than exceptional, representations.

FIGURE 42   "Picture of Koreans Crossing the Sea by Ship" portrays Koreans performing
acrobatics in the rigging of the ambassador's ship in this single-sheet print
of 1811.
COURTESY OF THE SIN KISU COLLECTION, OSAKA MUSEUM OF HISTORY

Itinerant peddlers, too, particularly ones who dealt in products—like candy
or medicine—often assimilated to acrobatics, Other-masqued dress, Other-
marked musical instruments, to announce themselves and attract an audience for their patter (Fig. 40). The association of itinerant peddlers of certain
products, such as "*Tōjin*-candy" (Tōjin-*ame*; also *Kanjin ame* and and *Sankan
ame*) with Other, seen, for example, in Hanabusa Itchō's *Ameuri* (candy peddler), was so well established that a comic poet wrote, "It's the *Tōjin* he shout-
ed, pointing at the candyman." Itchō's *Tōjin*-candyman wears a blatantly false
beard, a plumed, conical hat, frill-cuffed pantaloons, and a frilled girdle from
which hangs a giant chili-pepper (*tōgarashi*, "China pepper");[38] on his trunk
rests a *charumera* (from Port. *charamela*), a kind of oboe signed as Other, that
was a regular part of the musical troupes accompanying Korean and Okinawan
visits to Japan; also on his trunk dances a mechanical doll, a *karakuri ningyō*,
in the shape of a *charumera*-playing monkey in Dutchman's clothing! Only the
candyman's straw sandals, and the obvious falseness of his whiskers, reveal his
underlying identity as Japanese.[39]

---

38   Called *Tō-garashi* (the *Tō* of Tōjin, "foreign pepper"), the chili pepper was introduced from
the Americas in the sixteenth century. Not merely "domesticated" but "indigenized" in
Korean and many regional Chinese cuisines, it remained, true to its new name, an "exotic"
item in Japanese cuisine, tagged "foreign" and used sparingly.

39   Several of Hanabusa Itchō's (1652–1724) paintings were later reproduced as a three-
volume collection of prints (Hanabusa, 1770), models for the aspiring young artist. There
are two painting on this theme attributed to Itchō, one in the Museum of Fine Arts,
Boston, the other in a private collection in Tokyo. But in its reincarnation as an illustration

FIGURE 43   A "Chinese" *Candy-peddler* sports a false beard and mustache, while his mechanical doll (note the gear-wheel behind it) in faux Chinese garb is adorned with
chin-whiskers. "Ame-uri," from Hanabusa, 1770.

4   The Invasive Other: Fear of Foreigners and the Changing
         Iconographic Field

The ironic interplay of tropes[40] in the assumption of roles and niches in
Japanese iconography and folklore, by Iberians and their border-crossing,
genre-bending entourage, who assumed (appeared in) the garb of *Chensicus*
and Tōjin, of demons and goblins (and of monkey, dogs and other animals[41])
in which guise they entered Japan after a millennium offshore; by Coré and
Tōjin, who stepped into the onshore places of Iberians and Englishmen
(and later Dutch and Germans, but almost invariably men, not women); and
finally by Koreans, Okinawans, and later again Dutch, bespeaks a profound
continuity in the iconographies of Other in late-medieval and early modern

---

in a collection of monochrome reproductions and variations on several of Itchō's works
        (ibid., 2: 5–6), that it received wide circulation.
40   I adapt this phrase from Fernandez (1984).
41   The position I take here contests assertions by Emiko Ohnuki-Tierney of an unalloyed
        "positive attitude towards foreigners" (1987, 146) and an implicit separation of the alteri-
        ties of bestial and of human Others. John W. Dower (1986), too, implies that bestialization
        of Other was more characteristic of U.S. constructions of its Other, Japan, before and
        during the Pacific War, than it was of Japanese constructions of the West.

Japan. Yet also the inescapable contrast between the absence of Other from Japanese iconographic soil prior to 1550, and the pervasive presence of Other in the performative, literary, and artistic Japanese landscape after 1550—even after the expulsion of the Iberian interloper—represents a profound transformation of the field on which Japanese dialogues of Self and Other were played out.

The sense of vulnerability to the foreign engendered by the Iberian irruption and its aftermath made it impossible to keep Other safely "out there," sapped the evocative power of the god Sumiyoshi Daimyōjin, and the Divine Wind (*kamikaze*) he invoked to repel Hakurakuten; the Divine Wind that had twice protected Japan from the Mongol onslaught. The Iberians stepped into an iconographic, cosmological, and cognitive text in Japan long in the writing, well-rehearsed in the reading, and ironically filled a space available in the text: There were many Others Out There, but few had come In Here; the Iberians filled that space, added to the text. After the Iberians were expelled—indeed the few remaining Europeans were virtually imprisoned in Nagasaki—the text continued to demand a presence of Other In Here, but denied the reader an Iberian image for reading.

Readers, however, transposed other Others into the text, rewriting the Iberian part for Koreans, Chinese, Okinawans, and others, who had largely been formerly excluded from the domestic text, but were now essential to its reading. As the Iberians had so conveniently arrived in costume at the first, now, too, their costume—and role—could be conceded to these other Others, keeping Others In Here, reminding readers of the Intrusive Other, sustaining fear of foreigners (along with fascination, excitement, titillation) long after the Other had been defanged of its horse-teeth, and sent packing away.

5   Performative Possibilities in the Age of Encounter

If one response to the Iberian Other was fear and eventual expulsion, another was played out in the universal human diversion of mimesis, a medium for becoming the Other and thereby constructing the Self—what David Napier has called "the assimilation of what one takes to be foreign into one's cultural sphere.... the tactical use of the foreign in manipulating cultural canons."[42]

Japanese, like many peoples around the world, had been assuming Other identities since earliest times, long before the Portuguese encounter, masquerading for purposes of both entertainment and deception, while foreign

---

42   Napier (1992, 108).

clothing styles have been "fashionable," as well. Particularly as "fashion," foreign style continues to be incorporated in everyday life—even the "indigenous" kimono is today a performance, a statement of a kind of Other identity, that of "traditional Japanese." And, just as few revelers at Carnival or Halloween forego the opportunity to slip into another, largely imagined identity, in which they can make up the rules as they go along, so, Japanese have for centuries worn Other identities as a form of diversion.

In mid-943, for example, courtiers who had found the recently departed ambassador from Parhae somewhat amusing and more than a bit exotic, put on a masque to recapture that sense of Otherness: "The court entertained itself by masquerading as barbarian visitors (*bankaku*). The Middle General ... played the Ambassador, while all the other roles were assigned to someone or another...."[43] The one identity a masquerader is least likely to perform, after all, is her own.

The Japanese-Iberian encounter of the mid-sixteenth to mid-seventeenth century—primarily with Portuguese merchants, military, and religious adventurers—caught the Japanese imagination. Within the first few years of the encounter, the enthusiasm of Japanese, at least those elite courtiers, warriors and merchants whose habits are recorded, for this new form of exotica, had produced a craze for Nanban ("Southern Barbarian"—that is to say, Iberian) fashion that persisted for decades.

Oda Nobunaga (1532–1582) and Toyotomi Hideyoshi (1536–1598), who dominated national politics for the last third of the sixteenth century—the golden age of Nanban culture—were both avid aficionados of dress-up, refashioning themselves new personae befitting their emerging status as masters of the realm. Thousands of lesser samurai, not to mention courtiers and commoners, were only too glad to follow suit, not only experimenting with fashion, but currying favor with their new masters. A sort of sartorial Lusimania took Japan by storm in the closing years of that century, and continued well into the next.

We may never know the precise moment when the very first Japanese draped himself—herself?—in some version of Lusitanian robes, but it is quite likely that when Francisco Xavier first arrived in Satsuma in 1549, his interpreter "Paolo" (formerly Yajirō) was arrayed in Portuguese fashion, as a catechist. By the 1570s, Japanese Christian converts were adopting aspects of

---

43   Tachibana (1966, 121). Narisue compiled *Kokon chomonjū* ("a collection of ancient and modern tales") in the mid-thirteenth century from a variety of sources. This diversion is also recorded in the *Nihon kiryaku*, a history of Japan most likely compiled in the mid-eleventh century. The state of Parhae (the modern Korean pronunciation; Ch., Bohai; J., Bokkai), which was formed by remnants of the state of Koguryŏ, spanned eastern Manchuria and what is now northeastern Korea from the eighth to the tenth centuries.

Portuguese dress, while warriors had refashioned the Portuguese coat as a jacket to be worn over armor—known as the *jinbaori*—adapted the shapes of Portuguese hats as helmets, and otherwise incorporated Nanban form as Japanese fashion. Nobunaga, who was moving toward national hegemony just as the Portuguese were becoming well established in Japan, himself possessed a substantial wardrobe of *jinbaori*, and was said to be fond of wearing the sort of neck ruffle that was fashionable in sixteenth-century Europe. For better or for worse, however, Nobunaga's fondness for performing Portugal did nothing to save him from an assassin's attack in 1582, before his armies had brought all of Japan under his sway.

Hideyoshi, who avenged Nobunaga's death, then replaced his mentor as hegemon and "completed" the unification of Japan with the destruction of the Hōjō, the last daimyo to resist him, in 1590.[44] His contemporary biographer, Oze Hoan, reports that Hideyoshi marched to the siege of Odawara Castle, the headquarters of his last remaining enemy, "in a procession of such strange form (*igyō*) I know no words adequate to describe it.... It was all put together hastily, so everyone casually threw together costumes in the foreign [Portuguese] fashion...."[45] Hideyoshi himself added "false whiskers blackened with iron" to complete the array, because his natural tonsorial endowments were inadequate to the standards of manliness—Nobunaga was said to have called him a "bald rat" (*hagenezumi*)—for in their day, a man without a beard was no "man" at all.[46]

Hideyoshi's delight in the mimesis of alterity was not limited to Nanban fashion, of course. When he received an embassy from Ming in 1596, trying to reach a settlement of the war in Korea, he rejected the proffered appointment by the Wanli Emperor of Ming China as "King of Japan," but took obvious pleasure in parading about in the Ming monarchic robes that Wanli had sent as the visible symbols of new office Hideyoshi repudiated. He might not wear foreign titles, but foreign robes were just his style.

Hideyoshi's "fashion passion" (*furyū*[47]) was infectious—what monarch's whims are not?—and was quickly imitated by daimyos and others, though the fashion was hardly new with Hideyoshi, as we have seen. Some of his Nanban

---

44   The best full-length English-language treatment of Hideyoshi is Berry (1982). For a superb, though briefer, treatment, see Elison (1981).

45   Oze (1944, 2:17).

46   Ibid. On the changing semiotics of male facial hair in this period, see below, Ch. 6.

47   On *furyū* (also read *fūryū*), which I am defining rather loosely here, see especially Okazaki (1943–1950, vol. 2); and Sano (1997). Sano, with a nod to Okazaki, gives a fair definition of *furyū*: "For example, *furyū* in clothing might be described as something that renders visible evidence of the self (*watakushi*) through competition in originality (*shukō*)" (59).

outfits survive, such as a gold-colored velvet cape, for which the fabric—or per-haps the cape itself—was imported, embroidered with the figures of fabulous creatures of felicitous portent.[48] When Hideyoshi resided briefly at Nagoya Castle in northwest Kyushu, the command center for his invasion of Korea, and all the daimyos of the land followed suit, Luis Frois reports, the demand for Nanban fashions was so great that all the tailors of nearby Nagasaki were kept busy day and night creating *cappa, mombaxas, zubon,* and all manner of other Nanban favorites.[49]

Hideyoshi's entire life might be seen as mimetic, of course, for he was after all the perfect performer parvenu. Born a peasant, he rose to the heights of both the warrior *and* courtier elite, something no one before had accom-plished. He was, thus, constantly engaged in the mimesis of alterity, his rise attributable not only to his military and organizational genius, but to his abil-ity to assume roles that *should* have been denied him, and performing them so well his "audience" arrived at the willing suspension of disbelief. Perhaps to impress and overwhelm those who had been his "betters," but were now his subjects, Hideyoshi enjoyed role-playing that reminded others of his superior-ity—in fact, if not by birth. In these performances, more familiar alterities—of indigenous class and status—sometimes were more effective than the radical alterities of (what we might today call) "ethnicity."

Hideyoshi's own flamboyance was widely celebrated—though sometimes also ridiculed—described by one modern biographer as the "Golden Taikō,"[50] and when he was in the "Other" mood, he expected his courtiers, that is, the se-nior daimyos of the realm, to join him. One fine Spring day in 1594, Hideyoshi decided to take in the cherry blossoms at Yoshino—across the mountains from Osaka, and the paradigmatic site for *hanami,* or flower-viewing outings. His biographer doesn't comment on Hideyoshi's attire for the outing—though he again makes a point of mentioning that "Lord Hideyoshi wore his usual false whiskers, and blackened his eyebrows with iron-blacking," and goes on to recount that "the people in [his] retinue competed to take splendor to the

---

See also Berry (1994), who defines *fūryū* as "refer[ring] to a showy elegance, particularly in dress, although it could also indicate splendor in music or poetry" (245).

48 Hideyoshi's cape (collection Nagoya City Museum).

49 Luis Frois, *Literae Annuae Iaponenses anni 1591 & 1592,* cited in Cooper (1974, 104). Hideyoshi's "Nagoya" is a few dozen kilometers west of Fukuoka and is unrelated to the modern city of Nagoya, which is written with a different character for *go.*

50 Yamamuro (1992).

limits. So splendid was the entourage as it departed that a crowd of spectators gathered [to watch]."[51]

However, we have some idea of what the outing may have looked like, from a contemporary screen-painting. (Figs. 44 & 45)[52] Hideyoshi himself is pictured clothed as a Chinese emperor, seated on an imperial palanquin of Chinese (or faux Chinese) design, while the accompanying courtiers and daimyos are shown wearing Nanban trousers, capes and hats, or draped in other strange garb, getting "outside themselves" for the expedition. Date Masamune (1567–1636), a powerful northeastern daimyo who had sworn fealty to Hideyoshi only four years earlier, can be identified by his red velvet Nanban cape, embroidered in gold filigree; he also sports a white ruffled collar, and tops out the array with a Nanban hat, a rakishly daring high-crowned, broad-brimmed affair with what looks like a feather hatband.[53] Some of the others in the train are likewise bedecked in Nanban fashion, though none quite so strikingly. None, however, has Othered himself head-to-toe: all those whose feet are visible are shown wearing Japanese-style sandals. Perhaps the point was to be clearly seen to mix-and-masque—to let some of both identities, overt/"mimetic" and covert/ "real," show through—for without that, the performative, intentionally artificial (in the sense of "artifice," rather than "false") might go unappreciated by viewers.

Hideyoshi's mania for Nanban fashion survived his own demise in 1598. Hideyoshi was deified posthumously as Toyokuni Daimyōjin ("the great deity who brings prosperity to the country) and was enshrined in an expansive Shinto complex just southeast of Kyoto—near the site of the current Kyoto National Museum. In Japanese memorial practice, the anniversary of a death is commemorated by special observances, with the first, "third," and "seventh" anniversaries carrying special importance.[54] The seventh anniversary of Hideyoshi's death, commemorated at his shrine in 1604, was especially significant to the celebrants, for his heirs had been displaced by Tokugawa Ieyasu—

---

51   Oze (1996, 456). Hideyoshi's retinue included many senior Kyoto courtiers as well as the most powerful daimyos, including Tokugawa Ieyasu, Ukita Hideie, Maeda Toshiie and Date Masamune. The names of the men in Hideyoshi's entourage are listed in ibid., pp. 458–468, as authors of the poems they composed during the excursion.

52   Unsigned, *Yoshino hanami-zu byōbu* (pair of six-panel screens, color and gilt on paper, each 171 × 384 cm, private collection, Osaka), published in Kano (1991, 108–117).

53   Masamune's cape (collection Sendai City Museum). Another Nanban cape from Masamune's wardrobe is pictured in Tanno (1994, 44, fig. 3).

54   The "first anniversary" (J., *isshū-ki*; "one [annual] mourning cycle") is indeed one year after the death; thereafter, however, the death itself is counted as "first," so that the "third anniversary" (*sankai-ki*; "third time to grieve") is actually two years after the death, and the "seventh" is six calendar years after. On Japanese bereavement practices in modern times—which include these anniversaries—are analyzed in Smith (1974).

FIGURE 44 Toyotomi Hideyoshi, dressed in Chinese court garb, and
sporting his signature false whiskers, on his 1594 flower-
viewing excursion to Yoshino. *Yoshino hanami-zu byōbu*,
unsigned, color and gold leaf on paper; detail, left screen.
Hosomi Bijutsukan.

FIGURE 45 Daimyos and courtiers accompanying Hideyoshi on his
Yoshino excursion. The figure in the Portuguese-style hat,
ruffled collar and red mantle is believed to represent the
daimyo Date Masamune. The mantle is extant today. *Yoshino
hanami-zu byōbu*, unsigned, color and gold leaf on paper;
detail, left screen. Hosomi Bijutsukan.

named shogun in 1603—whose ascent ultimately stripped the Kyoto-Osaka area that had been the heart of Hideyoshi's power base of any semblance of real authority. Hideyoshi had revived, reorganized, and rebuilt war-ravished Kyoto in his brief tenure, and the anniversary was an unimpeachable opportunity for Kyotoites to look back to better days, when their town *really* mattered.

The celebration was an occasion for unrestrained revelry, characterized by music, masquerade, and wild dancing in the streets, rivaling even the annual celebration of the Gion festival. As described by a contemporary, the noble-born priest Gien (1558–1626), who had close ties to Hideyoshi, "The performances included the Four Deva Kings, as well as Tōjin, Daikoku, Ebisu, and Mt. Kōya holy men—all sorts of masquerades." (*Gien Jugō nikki*, Keichō 9/8/15). Though Gien's verbal descriptions merely speak of Tōjin—narrowly, "Chinese," but generically "foreigners"—the visual representations are of unmistakably Nanban-clad Japanese reveling in the street-dances of the festival. "Performing Portugal" was one of the high moments of the festivities, perhaps recalling the way Hideyoshi enjoyed the company of Lusitanians such as the Jesuits Luis Frois and João Rodrigues when he was alive—not to mention the prosperity their custom brought to the city.

There is no way of knowing whether the Nanban masquerades in the Toyokuni Memorial of 1604 were unprecedented in a religious context, but thereafter, Nanban *furyū* became a fixture of both fashion and festival for about forty years—until the proscriptions on Christianity made anything that smacked of Nanban suspect. (Fig. 46) Tokugawa Ieyasu, who had destroyed the last of the Toyotomi and their partisans in the Battles of Osaka (1614–1615), was himself likewise deified on his death in 1616. First enshrined on Kunōzan, a peak just east of his retirement castle of Sunpu (modern Shizuoka), Ieyasu's remains were transferred a year later to a newly-built shrine on Mt. Nikkō—about 115 kilometers north of Edo—as *Tōshō gongen*, the "Great Avatar Who Illumines the East."

Moreover, since Ieyasu's heirs remained as shoguns—for another two-and-a-half centuries—his cult survived and flourished. Tōshōgū shrines were consecrated all over the country; virtually every daimyo's castle town had one, and Edo had several. Kunōzan, the initial interment site, remains a Tōshōgū to this day, as does Nikkō. Among the first to follow suit were Ieyasu's junior sons, daimyos ensconced in Nagoya (not Hideyoshi's "Nagoya," but the one we are familiar with as a modern industrial city), Wakayama (south of Osaka), and Mito (northeast of Edo). In each of these growing castle-towns, too, Ieyasu's sons endowed and constructed their own Tōshōgū, while two—later several more—others were built in Edo itself, one in the precincts of Edo Castle itself, and another in the shogunally-sponsored Kan'eiji, in what is now Ueno Park.[55]

---

55   The Tōshōgū shrines in Edo Castle and in the Kan'eiji and Zōjōji temple precincts are depicted in the panoramic *Edo-zu byōbu*. See above, n. 34.

FIGURE 46   Japanese dandies dressed in a mixture of Nanban and Japanese clothing.
Detail of unsigned pair of six-panel folding screens, color and gold leaf on
paper; left screen panel 1. Imperial Household Agency.

And, as had been the case with Hideyoshi, the seventeenth day of the fourth
lunar month of 1622, the seventh anniversary of Ieyasu's death, was the occasion of great memorial celebrations at *each* of these shrines that rivaled and
perhaps even eclipsed the Toyokuni Festival of 1604. In Wakayama, as had been
the case in the Toyokuni Festival, the written record speaks of several China-
mimes, of both Tōjin, and a *karafune* (China boat) filled with treasure from
abroad. There is no suggestion in these written texts that anyone performed
Portugal.

Yet, as Sumiyoshi Jokei's representation in the *Illustrated History of the
Waka[yama] Tōshōgū* (*Waka Tōshōgū engi emaki*) makes clear,[56] these
"Chinese" preferred Nanban dress, from the Portuguese-style broad-brimmed

---

56   Sumiyoshi Jokei, *Waka Tōshōsha engi emaki* (color on paper, four scrolls, collection Waka
Tōshōgū, Wakayama). For a reproduction of the scene, see *Kobijutsu* 73 (1985): 18–19. On
the history of the Waka-matsuri, see Tanaka (1979).

hats on their heads, to their buttoned jackets and ballooned *mombaxas* trousers. The only thing "Chinese" about them was the accident that *Tōjin* was the generic term for "foreign." The *Illustrated History* of the Nagoya Tōshōgū was commissioned to another artist, Sumiyoshi Gukei; we find there, as well, that Nanban fashion ruled the day of Ieyasu's memorial, just as it did in Wakayama, and probably in Edo and Nikkō, Mito and Kunōzan, as well, though we lack the pictorial evidence to be sure.[57]

Nor was it just at memorials for "great men" like Hideyoshi and Ieyasu that people were inspired to perform Portugal. In the annual *Sanja matsuri*, the festival celebrating the three deities of Edo's Asakusa Shrine—associated with the Sensōji temple—too, performing Portugal was the order of the day, at least in the Kan'ei era (1624–1644).[58] The scene of a Sanja Festival from this period has been depicted (represented) in one corner of a panoramic screen painting of Kan'ei-era (1624–44) Edo that takes a commoner's point of view, the *Edo meisho-zu byōbu* ("Famous Sites of Edo Screens").[59] Nine figures—it is difficult to tell whether they would have seen themselves as celebrants or sightseers, though they clearly were dressed to *be seen*—are arrayed in a variety of elaborate Nanban outfits. Though one might suspect on first glance—I did, though only for a moment—that they are "real" Portuguese, visiting the shrine to enjoy the goings-on; on closer inspection, there can be no question who they are—"Japanese" performing Portugal. Not only has the artist been at pains *not* to use the highly-developed conventions of "othering" the faces and bodies of "real" Portuguese—fierce eyes, large noses, dark skin and sometimes wild hair—but at equal pains to equip several of them with Japanese swords, and show in loving detail that they are shod in *tabi* (socks) and *waraji* (straw sandals), not in the boots that would have been appropriate to the "real" thing (see Fig. 45).

In Kyoto, where Nanban *furyū* had been most firmly established, performing Portugal had likely infiltrated the performances of the Gion Festival long before, for the mimesis of alterity was at the core of the festival. In a depiction of the festival from the Kan'ei era, contemporary with the *Edo meisho* screen depiction of the Sanja Festival noted just above, one group of child revelers is seen

---

57   Sumiyoshi Gukei, *Nagoya Tōshōsha engi emaki* (color on paper, four scrolls, collection Nagoya Tōshōgū).

58   For an introduction to the religious life of Asakusa, though it focuses primarily on Sensōji and Buddhist religiosity, see Hur (2000). For his brief but valuable discussion of the Shinto sites that were part of what Alan Grappard calls the "shrine-temple complex" and the Sanja Festival, see especially 120–122. On the Sanja Gongen Shrine (today called the Asakusa Shrine), see Saitō (1835/1966–1967, 5:234–236).

59   *Edo meisho-zu byōbu*, pair of unsigned six-panel screens in color and gold leaf on paper, each 107.2×488.8cm. Idemitsu Museum Collection.

FIGURE 47   Groups of revelers in Edo's Sanja Festival wearing Nanban costumes; their straw
sandals identify them as Japanese masquerading as foreigners. *Edo meisho-zu
byōbu*, pair of eight-panel screens, color and gold leaf on paper. Detail, right-hand
screen, panels 1–2.
COURTESY IDEMITSU MUSEUM

performing an *ishibiki*, or stone-hauling, usually associated with castle construction projects, but here—according to one modern commentator—likely
an evocation of Hideyoshi's construction of the Hōkōji, conventionally called
the "Hall of the Great Buddha" (*Daibutsuden*), just southeast of the capital.[60]

The *ishibiki* itself is reminiscent of the scene in the *Chikujō-zu byōbu*
(Castle-building screen, Fig. 49), a panoramic painting of a castle construction site, a painting that appears to depict a "real" construction site—however festive it appears.[61] At the construction site depicted in the *Chikujō-zu
byōbu*, the group of men dancing atop the huge block of stone are dressed
quite outlandishly, in a mimesis of alterity—perhaps it is the association

60   *Gion sairei-zu byōbu* (pair of six-panel screens, color and gold leaf on paper, collection
Kyoto National Museum), reproduced in Kano (1991, 4: 17–39); for Kano's comment and a
detail of this scene, see page 30.

61   *Chikujō-zu byōbu* (six-panel folding screen, color and gold leaf on paper, 55.8cm × 210.2cm,
collection Nagoya City Museum), reproduced in Kano (1991, 3:43–63); for the *ishibiki*
scene, see page 62. On this screen, Naitō (1978); Shintani (1982).

FIGURE 48   A group of boys masquerading as Nanban in a Kyoto festival, as depicted in a
             "scenes of the capital" panoramic screen painting.

with superhuman (extra-human) strength needed to move such massive stone—but there is nothing especially Nanban in their attire. (Fig. 48) At this Gion festival, however, several of the children are in unmistakably Nanban fashion; but some are in a hodgepodge of styles and mixed messages. The main character in the tableau, the child riding the ox, and several of his attendants, are done up in clear Nanban style.

6   Disengagement and Code-Switching

What precisely the children performing Portugal in the Kan'ei-era Gion Festival—at least as represented in the *Gion sairei-zu byōbu*—were enacting, we can of course never be quite certain, for neither the artist, nor the children, have told us directly.[62] (Fig. 48) That is precisely the problem with reading non-verbal text. An image is surely a system of signs, but can we be sure of

---

62   *Gion sairei-zu byōbu* (Gion Festival screens), pair of unsigned six-panel folding screens,
      color and gold leaf on paper, early seventeenth century. Kyoto National Museum.

FIGURE 49   Musicians *Chikujō-zu byōbu*

the signified, especially when we are observing one representation, a performance, through a meta-representation in the form of a painting?[63] Reading these images, that is to say, is rather like attempting an ethnography solely through someone else's field-notes.

Yet it is more: The underlying practices are performative and mimetic representations of altered states of being through an ever-changing set of codes and fashions; the images are therefore second-order representations, ostensibly (we hope, at least) instantiating the underlying performance they depict. But the images participate in a second set of protean practices, codes, and fashions. Further, genre paintings are, for the most part, at least, retrospective, the practices being antecedent to the image. An artist—or a patron—may well be more interested in a nostalgic presentation of what Peter Laslett once called "a world we have lost," adding further difficulty to the reading of pictures as historical "evidence."[64]

---

63   These questions are stimulated, in part, by Peter Burke's provocative chapter, "Beyond Iconography?" in Burke (2001).
64   Laslett (1966).

At the least, as just noted, their codes are mixed. The main character rides an ox or water-buffalo—not particularly associated with the Portuguese—and wears a stupendously long Japanese sword. While the cut of his clothes, and those of his retinue, may be Nanban, the fabric patterns clearly are not; some are "purely" Japanese and others are a Japanese idea of "Chinese." One could go on, but it may be more profitable to turn to some other examples.

As is well-known, Japan expelled the Portuguese entirely in 1639, after several decades of increasingly severe restrictions on their secular activities, and stringent proscriptions on Christianity. In that atmosphere, even *performing* Portugal became not merely exotic, but dangerous. To the state, it was subversive; to the performer, it might bring severe punishment. Performing Portugal was no longer simply fun, or a way to play with identities; it was a challenge to public order. The signal event prior to the 1630s may well have been the martyrdom of fifty-five Christians at Nagasaki in 1622. But by that time, other sorts of Others had emerged as mimetic material—particularly Koreans, whose embassies began visiting Japan in 1607.[65]

Performing Portugal, however, continued beyond the suppression of Christianity—if the pictorial archive is indeed evidence of contemporary *festival* practice, rather than simply *painterly* convention—into the 1630s and 40s, though not likely beyond that. As noted above, Nanban *furyū* was conspicuous in the seventh-anniversary memorial festivals for both Hideyoshi (1604) and Ieyasu (1622). A few years later, in 1645, the recently installed daimyo of Tsu (in modern Mie Prefecture) completed construction of a shrine to Hachiman, patron deity of the Genji and god of war, and ordered a grand festival to inaugurate the shrine as the reigning local deity. Among the masquerades were several that were described as Tōjin by chroniclers, including that of Wakebe-chō, a ward just outside the castle gates that was occupied by the town's wealthiest merchants (see Figs. 38, 39, 40).[66]

But a contemporary *emaki* (painted scroll) saw things differently. Wakebe-chō's performance, led by the ward's golden sunburst *machijirushi* (the ward's crest, sculpted in three dimensions, Fig. 38), shows a group of men in what looks—at first glance—like Nanban *furyū* garb, broad-brimmed hats, ruffle-collared jackets with gold buttons, and trousers, all decorated with gold embroidery. Several wear long, straight European-style swords (rapiers?), in black scabbards. Like many "real Portuguese," as depicted in countless Nanban genre screens, they are accompanied by animals, and carry what looks—one cannot be sure—like the head of some large beast, suspended from a pole. But, there

---

65   See Toby (1984) for a discussion.
66   "Hachiman go-sairei gyōretsu no shidai," reprinted in Yamanaka 1656/1968.

are two stark, striking differences between these Nanban and all the others we have encountered. First, where Nanban, both "real Portuguese" and *furyū* celebrants performing Portugal, are invariably dressed in ornate, colorful, almost gaudy array, this *furyū* is monochromatic: Except for the gold embroidery, their entire complement are dressed in black—none of the scarlet and vermilion that show conspicuously in nearly every other "normal" Nanban getup (save, of course, priests and friars). And second, these not-quite-right Nanban all wear bright orange-red wigs; Portuguese, by contrast, were always represented with black hair.

Beginning in 1600, of course, other sorts of Europeans than Iberians and Spaniards had begun to appear in Japan, from the Protestant Netherlands and England. Not only were they distinguished their religious conviction; in Japanese eyes, these new aliens looked physically different, as well: The most profound perceived difference was hair color: The newcomers were labeled *kōmō*, or "red-hairs," a verbal representation that we see here—I believe— translated into performance. The Portuguese had just been expelled, and Japanese suspected of Nanban—or at least *Kirishitan* (Catholic)—sympathies were being hunted down and subjected to excruciating punishments. As Japan disengaged with Iberia, even performing Portugal could be dangerous. But masking the masque as *Kōmō* gave an acceptable gloss to Nanban mummery, and perhaps allowed Nanban costumes, still too new to discard, to be recycled as some other Other.

CHAPTER 5

Parades of Difference/Parades of Power

The Korean Tōjin (*Chōsen Tōjin*) entered [Edo] at Shinagawa at noon on the 2nd day of the [10th] month in the first year of Meireki [1655], passing Honchō at four o'clock. I [went to] watch. The Tōjin who stayed in Bakuro-chō and Honchō, including their Great General (*taishō*), numbered three-hundred-sixty-seven men. Two-hundred-eighty of them were on horseback. The rest were foot soldiers or lancers; the lancers numbered thirty. Their lances were shaped like this: Also, there were another hundred-thirty men who stayed behind in Nagasaki [*sic*].

ENOMOTO YAZAEMON, *Sansai yori no oboe*[1]

∵

One late summer's day in 1643, a grand procession of 462 Koreans, escorted by well over a thousand Japanese samurai and porters, paraded through Kyoto—the old capital and Japan's second-largest city, en route to the shogun's capital at Edo. The Koreans, the third embassy dispatched by Korea's King Injo (r. 1623–1649) to the court of Tokugawa Iemitsu (r. 1623–1651), was sent to congratulate the shogun, now in his fortieth year, on the long-awaited birth of his son and heir, later known as Ietsuna (r. 1651–1680).

Five Korean embassies had visited Kyoto in the previous four decades, and one, in 1617, had spent several weeks in the old capital, yet they were a rare enough sight that thousands of spectators flocked the roadsides to watch, to see their unfamiliar pennants fluttering in the sultry summer breezes and their other regalia and gilded palanquins but even more to gape at their literally outlandish clothing, beards, and hairstyles, as the foreigners passed in parade.[2]

---

1   Enomoto (2001, 294). Enomoto was misinformed. Korean embassies never passed through Nagasaki, sailing from Pusan to Tsushima, Iki, and Ainoshima, and thence through the Seto Inland Sea to Osaka. They left their ships and sailors in Osaka, proceeding to Edo and back overland—except for a 30 km stretch by boat up the Yodo River from Osaka to Yodo, in what is now in the city of Kyoto.

2   At the same time, Koreans also gathered to watch when embassies to Japan traveled the Korean countryside from Hansŏng to Pusan, as Kim Ingyŏm (1999, 51), for example, noted in his *Iltong chang'yu-ga*, a diary-in-verse of his mission to Japan in 1763–64: "Spectators

As the parade passed through the streets of Kyoto on the 14th day of the 6th month, wrapped in a protective envelope of Japanese guards, the courtier Kujō Michifusa noted in his diary, "Has the shogun's might already extended to foreign countries! They seem to send an embassy whenever there's a felicitous occasion."[3] In Michifusa's eyes—and he was no political naïf, for he was a court minister and would later be imperial regent—the arrival of a Korean embassy proclaimed that the prestige (*go-ikō*) of the shogun's authority shone as brightly abroad as it did at home. It had become customary for foreign monarchs, fearing shogunal power and swayed by shogunal virtue, to send embassies to the shogun whenever there was an event worthy of celebration. That is how Michifusa, at least, interpreted the arrival of the Koreans as they journeyed to the shogun's court.

1 Parade Diplomacy

It was not the nobility alone in Edo-period Japan but commoners as well for whom a diplomatic parade was their best opportunity to gaze upon the Other face to face. Indeed, these parades were the public face of shogunal diplomacy, as Korean, Ryukyuan, and Dutch emissaries to the shogun, always escorted by a far greater number of Japanese guards, passed through Japan from Kyushu to Edo and back with varying regularity during the 268-year span of the Tokugawa hegemony: Koreans, twelve times; Ryukyuans, eighteen times; Dutch, annually or biennially. The Dutch "missions," headed by the chief of the Dutch trading post at Nagasaki, were not formal embassies from a foreign "state," but they were equally—perhaps more—as alien as the Koreans and Ryukyuans. But diplomatic or commercial, these grand processions of foreigners through Japan made their way across the country in the format of a parade, usually called "alien parades" (*ijin gyōretsu*) or "*Tōjin* parades" (*Tōjin gyōretsu*) in the common parlance of the day.[4]

Profoundly exotic in the public mind, the Korean and Ryukyuan embassies, in particular, which paraded to and from the shogun's capital thirty times during the Tokugawa era, were a grand entertainment for tens of thousands of spectators who lined the shores and the roadsides all along their routes from

---

thronged all around us, carrying their lunches, spread out to our left and right. I couldn't count them in their tens of thousands."

3 Kujō, n.d., vol. 5 (Kan'ei 20/6/14).

4 The term "Tōjin," on the surface meaning "Chinese" or "Chinamen," was both a mildly pejorative term for Chinese and a broad-gauged epithet for virtually all foreigners, whether Chinese, Korean, or even European, in Edo-period parlance.

Kyushu to Edo and back. For the *bakufu*, the "alien parades" were an opportunity to impress on the populace the belief—a fantasy, but an important ideological projection of shogunal authority—that its prestige "extended to foreign countries" beyond the seas. But for the vast crowds of onlookers enjoying the spectacle for its grandeur and exoticism, it was not just an opportunity to be impressed with shogunal power, it was also a site for constructing a rhetoric of difference, creating a vocabulary of images of alterity, and reaffirming core notions of what it meant to be "Japanese"—and, of course, *not* "Japanese."

2   Watching the Watchers: Intersecting Gazes in Procession and
       Parade

Parading, strutting before others, is so widely shared a form of human behavior that we may rarely give it a thought. Yet however universal, parades are highly constrained, rule-governed group behavior with culturally specific differences that are worthy of close attention. Though most cultures might subscribe to the proclamation "I love a parade" and many authors have described parades, whether in Yuzawa, in northern Japan, in medieval Bali, or nineteenth-century Philadelphia, the parade as a form of behavior has yet to receive adequate theoretical attention.[5] Of course we love a parade, and know one when we see one, but what, after all, is a parade? In an attempt to move in that direction, I will first indulge in a perhaps-too-Foucauldian general theory of the parade form.

Not every procession is a parade.[6] To focus the distinction I hope to make, let us examine the question, "Why was John Kennedy's funeral procession a *parade* while most family funerals are not?" The mere movement of a group of people (including, perhaps, animals, vehicles, or other paraphernalia) arrayed in lines, moving in a common direction, even toward a common destination, even though the group progresses in a seemingly rule-governed manner, need not constitute a parade. For a procession to become a parade, *spectators*

---

5   Geertz (1980); Geertz, "Centers, Kings, and Charisma: Reflections on the Symbolics of Power," in Geertz (1983); Davis (1986).

6   Here, I differ with Meyerhoff (1986, 269–271), for whom what appears to have been an only loosely organized protest march in Venice, California, was a "parade." Princess Elizabeth's 1559 progress through London on the day before her coronation, by contrast, was a "parade," closely choreographed for both marchers and spectators to display the power and majesty of the woman who would be queen, while the constant progresses of Hasan about Morocco seems too diffuse and unpredictable to be a "parade." See the discussion in Geertz (1983, 121–146).

must be present, and their behavior must be constrained in an equally rule-governed fashion.

My emphasis on spectators as an essential part of the parade, rather than mere external observers, differs from the conceptualization of Michael Ashkenazi, who writes that "parades exemplify events midway between rituals and festivities.... They 'mediate' between the two, being formal in their performance and organization and informal and festive in their interaction with the audience that lines the parade route." This situation is highlighted by Yuzawa's major parade, the *Daimyō gyōretsu* ("daimyo parade"), which is the highlight of the town's major annual festival. "Here the body of the parade is ritually ordered, serious, and uncompromising in its roles. At the tail, in contrast, formal roles are nonexistent, and interaction with the public is the order of the day. Those who watch a parade are drawn into participating in it in a variety of ways. The mere existence of a crowd lining a parade route is a measure of a parade's success and *part of the parade itself*."[7]

Thus, it takes more than simply a group of people, organized in rows or columns and moving in the same direction to make a parade. A "parade," as I use the term, is a particular form of collective human behavior, a mode of public performance and display constrained by a complex set of rules. While some of the rules governing a parade are surely specific to local culture, certain characteristics are common to the parade form, as I conceive it. In a parade:

- A group or groups ("marchers") who share in common a certain form of identity maintains a formalized column structure and a set style of progress ("marching") to proceed along a predetermined route to a fixed destination.
- A group whose purpose is to watch the marchers lines the predetermined route; their behavior constrained by a set of formal or informal rules for "spectators."
- As much as the spectators view the marchers, the marchers also view the spectators. They interact; both are simultaneously viewers and viewed.
- The organization of both the marchers and the spectators is regulated by the cultural canons and systems of power within which they exist. That is, authority renders itself visible by the manner in which it *displays* the marchers and spectators to each other.
- This interaction of display and observation, of watching and being watched, occurs at the conscious level more markedly among the marchers than the spectators, but as the marchers are conscious of *being watched*, they also consciously *display* themselves and by extension display the prestige and authority under which they march. That is, the authorities that set the

---

7   Ashkenazi (1993, 49). Emphasis added.

marchers to marching—in this case, foreign monarchs—display their minions and through them display their own authority. At the same time, the
marchers' behavior is informed by an intense consciousness that they are a
means for displaying the dignity and power of their sponsors.
– But in diplomatic parades, the authorities that have brought foreign missions to their shores, that have, in effect, caused—or appear to have
  caused—foreigners to come at their call, display the marchers as a sign that
  their own authority "extends to foreign countries." In Edo-period Japan, the
  bakufu consciously and purposefully displayed "alien parades" to the imperial court, the daimyo, and the general populace who were spectators.
– The marchers, watching the spectators, observing the scene as they pass
  through it, are also spectators.
Early-modern Japanese culture presented, represented, and understood itself
and its environment in a wide variety of cultural forms. Yet among these the
parade occupies a unique space in the performative representation of both self
and Other in early modern Japan.

3   Edo Culture as Parade

Edo-period Japan was a culture both on and of parade:[8] Monarchic power
paraded itself before the populace whenever the emperor, surrounded by
hundreds of attendants and bodyguards, went forth from the palace to visit a
shrine or summer villa and whenever a shogun left Edo Castle to hunt, visit a
favored vassal, or pray at family shrines and graves. The shogun's senior vassals,
the 260 or so daimyos, or territorial barons, displayed themselves twice annually, parading in ornate, highly determined trains of hundreds, even thousands,
of armed warriors, standard-bearers, hostlers, and porters as they journeyed to
and from Edo for their mandatory attendance upon the shogun (*sankin kōtai*;
"alternate attendance").[9] In doing so, they constituted an intermediate form
of monarchical display, for the shogun, by requiring baronial attendance at
court, manifested his monarchical power to command, while at the same time
daimyo constituted themselves publicly as puissant princes, demi-monarchs
in their domains and in the national aristocracy of baronial power.
    Even for brief outings in the city of Edo or longer journeys through the
countryside—such as mandatory days of attendance at the Castle—daimyos,

---

8   See Kokuritsu Rekishi Minzoku Hakubutsukan (2012) for a broader analysis of "early modern
     Japan seen through parades."
9   On *sankin kōtai* see Vaporis 1989; 2008.

bannermen and lesser samurai traveled *en suite*, with retinues scaled to their respective stations. Samurai traveling on official business, too, were accompanied by a company of armed men and porters graded to the status of their offices, rather than their own rank and station.[10]

Yet monarchic and baronial display was but a small sampling of the culture of parade in Edo-era culture. Ordinary folk constituted themselves in parade in *matsuri* celebrations—the thousands of grand and petty linear performances centered on Shinto shrines in communities ranging from the greatest of cities to the smallest, most remote hamlets in the land. The greatest of these, the Sannō and Kanda festivals in Edo—together known as the "festivals of the realm"—or the Gion and Tenma festivals of Kyoto and Osaka, involved literally tens of thousands of celebrants in parades that wound through the cities' streets and wards to bring the deity to every corner of the area it protected. The Sannō and Kanda festival parades also marched through the Edo Castle compound. Courtesans of the licensed quarter, again, not just in Edo's Yoshiwara district, but in every major town across the land, displayed themselves publicly in impromptu parades (*niwaka*) that often parodied performances in local festivals.

Nor does this begin to exhaust the rich variety of paraded presentation that punctuated the civil and ritual calendar of daily life in Edo-period Japan. Yet my interest here is not in Japanese, no matter what their rank, status, or position, parading *themselves* before their compatriots. Rather, I shall interrogate some of the meanings of parades of Other: Alien, non-Japanese visitors to Japan; foreigners, principally Korean and Okinawan ambassadors and their retinues, who paraded from their overseas homelands to southwestern Japan and thence by sea, river, and overland to Edo and back some thirty times during the 265-year reign of the Tokugawa shoguns.

4   Alien Parades

Korea and Okinawa, the two foreign countries with which Edo maintained formal, if asymmetrical, diplomatic relations, sent mammoth diplomatic goodwill missions to the shoguns in Edo, usually to congratulate a new shogun on his succession; Okinawan kings also sent missions to announce their gratitude for the grace of the shogun in sanctioning their own royal succession. These missions, entourages of anywhere from one hundred or so to more than

---

10   On alternate attendance processions see Vaporis (1994; 2008); Kokuritsu Rekishi Minzoku Hakubutsukan (2012).

five hundred aliens, men—they were all men—in quite literally outlandish dress and hairstyles, paraded half the length of Japan to the accompaniment of marching bands playing weird, foreign music, flying unfamiliar flags and pennants, proclaiming their alienness to all who watched.

And watch they did: All great parades were major tourist events, attracting thousands, tens of thousands, perhaps even hundreds of thousands of spectators from far and wide. If spectators lined the route of *matsuri* parades, which were at the least an annual event in even the smallest village, for once-in-a-decade, even once-in-a-lifetime alien parades, the crowds were often reputed—spuriously, to be sure—to reach into the millions. Watching exotically accoutered aliens traipse the length of the country was not only good fun, it provided a venue for ordinary folk to reaffirm, or indeed to reconstitute, their mutual identity by contrasting it with manifestly different visitors from abroad. If Koreans and Okinawans were not quite for Japanese what Todorov has called "radical alterities"—that role was played by Europeans—everything about them, from clothing and hairstyles to language and culinary choices, fell well beyond the range of anything apprehended as a "Japanese" identity.[11]

Part of the charge of each Korean mission dispatched to Japan—as is the case with most diplomats posted abroad—was to observe Japan and report their observations on such factors as politics, social conditions, and the economy to the Korean government on their return home. They were not merely visitors and spectators but inspectors as well. Yet at the same time, every member of a Korean mission to Japan was intensely conscious of the national prestige of Korea, which considered itself a "microcosm of civilization" (*sohwa*) that tended the flame of Confucian rectitude during the long, dark days of "barbarian" (i.e., Qing) rule in China. As such, they were expected to behave on parade—and at all times—in a manner that would impress Japanese spectators with Korea's high level of Confucian culture.

On the other hand, the Japanese authorities were intensely conscious that their realm was likewise on display, open to the gaze of their foreign guests and were therefore at pains to ensure that they and their subjects gave a favorable impression. To that end, as we shall see, both the appearance of all public spaces and the behavior of ordinary folk anywhere the foreigners might possibly be expected to cast their eyes were subjected to strict constraints, an attempt to produce—in the theatrical sense—a performance of "Japan" that would engender the impression abroad of a prosperous, civilized, and well-ordered realm.

---

11   Todorov (1984).

Thus, when foreign envoys paraded along Japan's roads and waterways, both the visiting aliens and the local spectators were players in a public performance with two competing producer-directors, each trying to structure the performance as a display of its own prestige and authority. The *bakufu*, of course, which brought the foreign visitors across the seas to visit Japan and displayed them to the assembled spectators, as well as the Korean and Ryukyuan monarchies, who sought to display the radiance of their own authority and prestige abroad, and the daimyos of Satsuma and Tsushima, whose prestige were greatly enhanced by their ability to bring alien visitors to the shogun's court, were all, in different, competing ways, the producers and directors of this multi-layered performance of power, authority, and identity.

Further, the alien parade—the Tōjin *gyōretsu*—was far more than a political event, more than a site for the visible display of identities and difference in the popular culture of Edo-period Japan. For in a popular culture that cherished display, parade, and parody as core performative modes, the alien parade offered a replicable stage where Japanese could enact identities and difference even when "real" aliens were unavailable. In towns and villages all across Japan, people adopted the alien parade as a site where they could perform their visions of what it meant to be "Japanese" by enacting what they understood to be *not* "Japanese"—constructing a performance of identities on parade for people who might never see a "real" foreigner even once in the course of their lives. Though the referent of the alien parade might not necessarily even be a Korean embassy or Ryukyuan embassy, but a mythic Japanese conquest of Korea or the journey of a legendary Japanese hero to the palace of the Dragon King, these encounters with the Other were performed *in the style* of these diplomatic parades, borrowing their structures and regalia to represent alien, non-"Japanese" identities and in the process reaffirming common conceptions about "being Japanese."

5   The Internal Structure of an "Alien Parade"

What was the scale and form of a diplomatic mission's parade through early modern Japan? Korean and Ryukyuan missions differed from each other somewhat in form—and Ryukyuan entourages were quite a bit smaller than the Korean ones—but both were enacted on a grand scale that required over a year's preparation both for both hosts and visitors. Dutch "missions" to Edo were far more frequent than Korean and Ryukyuan embassies but neither so grandiose nor so closely watched. Missions varied somewhat in style over course of the Tokugawa period, but their basic format remained largely intact for more than two centuries. Since these missions were the most important stage for presenting foreigners directly to Japanese observers and the performative style of the "alien parade" became a metaphor for expressing identity and difference throughout Japanese popular culture, it is worth taking a moment to examine synchronically the structure of "alien parades" that are visible to us through both documentary and pictorial sources.

Fortunately, perhaps, the parade as a mode of public display that is performed on a linear stage—the sea, rivers, and roads—is singularly suited to representation in narrative scroll paintings (*zukan; emaki*), some examples depicting Korean embassies stretch forty meters or more in length. Artists and patrons were quick to take advantage of this ready correspondence of medium to message and from the seventeenth to the nineteenth centuries produced a wealth of scrolls depicting "alien parades." At the same time, it should be recalled that there had been an efflorescence of *Nanban* ("southern barbarian") art in Japan from the last third of the sixteenth century, representing the *Nanban* ("southern barbarians," i.e., Iberians) in Japanese ports and cities as well as in an imagined vision of their native habitat. With the complete suppression of Christianity and the final expulsion of the Portuguese in the 1630s, the fevered pitch of "southern Barbarian" art quickly cooled, yet the passion for the exotic, whetted by sixty years of unfettered expression, was as heated as ever. Unable any longer to portray the radically Other Portuguese, Japanese sought to slake their thirst for the exotic with representations of Korean, Ryukyuan, and other sorts of "*Tōjin* parades." Not content with the limitations of the narrative scroll format, which tended to elide both site and spectators, artists also produced an outpouring of painted screens, cityscapes of Kyoto and Edo, and both painted and print depictions of classic famous places such as Lake Biwa or Mt. Fuji, now populated with exotic parades of aliens traipsing across the Japanese landscape.

6   A Documentary Painting Is Not a Sketch

There are only a few pictorial representations of the earliest Korean embassy parades, but from as early as the last third of the sixteenth century, in the "Southern Barbarian" period, Japanese artists began to depict aliens passing through the streets of Japan. "Southern Barbarians," however, did not organize themselves as a parade, in the sense we have defined it; at least, Japanese documentary and visual records make no attempt to represent them as moving in an organized and structured progress, nor is there any suggestion that the

Portuguese followed prescribed routes between publicly announced origins and destinations.

It was only in the seventeenth century that Japanese public culture became obsessed with the parade form. The alternate attendance of daimyos at Edo ensured that upwards of two hundred parades, some covering more than 800 kilometers by ship and overland, crisscrossed the country each year. Meanwhile, the resumption of diplomatic relations with Korea in 1607, nearly 120 Dutch missions from Nagasaki to Edo between 1609 and 1850, and the regularization of Ryukyuan missions to Edo in 1634 ensured a steady stream of alien parades, grist for artists and essayists and great entertainment for tens of thousands of spectators.

With the regularization of diplomatic parades, the *bakufu* and the many daimyos who were mobilized to support and facilitate foreign embassies began keeping voluminous records, reference for use in the reception of future missions. Records took the form not just of documents and records, but of visual representations as well, recording—through the conventions of Japanese art, to be sure—the foreigners' regalia, their clothing, and their general equipage as well as their facial features. Yet we cannot always take these documentary paintings as objectively descriptive, realist images of what the artist observed. The earliest visual representations of Korean embassies give no indication that an army of artists carefully observed the hundreds of alien visitors and prepared detailed sketches from which to compose their grand compositions. Rather, they painted within the conventions of the genre of "alien" as it had developed in earlier Japanese art, and amplified by representations of *Nanban* in the Late sixteenth and early seventeenth centuries. "Aliens" had to look like what conventional Japanese vision *expected* aliens to look like, an effect the earliest accomplished by mixing Japanese conventions for representing *Nanban*, "Chinese," and Tatar (Mongol or Manchu) figures.[12]

The earliest attempts to represent Koreans as distinct from other forms of *Tōjin*, works executed in the first half of the seventeenth century, portray them only as isolated scenes in larger works, either screen paintings or narrative scrolls in which the Koreans were not the subject, per se, but as one event

---

12   For the known earliest Japanese attempts at representing Koreans in a mixture of signs, ca. 1620, see the unsigned *Rakuchū rakugai byōbu* (Mary Griggs Burke Collection, Minneapolis Museum of Art; below, Figs. 6.6, 6.7, 6.8a–c); on dating this screen, Toby (1996a); the unsigned *Edo-zu byōbu* (ca. 1634–35; National Museum of Japanese History); Kano Tan'yū, *Tōshōsha engi emaki* (1640; Nikkō Tōshōgū Hōmotsukan). It is only with Kano Masunobu's *Chōsen tsūshinshi kantai-zu byōbu* (1655; Sennyūji, Kyoto) that we can distinguish a set of conventions to represent Koreans as distinct from other East Asian ethnicities or nationalities. (Toby 2016)

among many portrayed within the overall work.[13] Korean embassy personnel are depicted in four paintings reliably dated to the first half of the seventeenth century, the Hayashibara Museum *Rakuchū rakugai-zu byōbu* (ca. 1620) and the Minneapolis Museum of Art/Burke Collection *Rakuchū rakugai-zu byōbu* ("screens of sites in and around the capital," ca. 1620), the *Edo-zu byōbu* ("Edo Panorama Screens," ca. 1634–35), and the final scene in the *Tōshōsha engi emaki* ("illustrated history of the Tōshō shrine," 1640), but in each case, as noted above, the Koreans are only scenes in much larger works.[14] And, in each case as well, the "Koreans" are depicted only as a mélange of painterly codes for Chinese, Tatars, *Nanban*, and generic codes of foreignness, a strategy necessitated, as I have argued elsewhere, by the absence of specific iconographic models for representing Koreans.[15] It was only in the second half of the seventeenth century that Japanese artists began to construct iconographic models specific to the representation of Koreans, and many of their paintings began to show a more explicitly documentary character, suggesting commissions from members of the political elite.[16] At the same time, beginning with the Korean embassy of 1682, artists who played to the popular market began to depict Korean embassies, sometimes for elite patrons, on the one hand, but also for publishers of popular prints, sold to a broader market.[17]

---

13   The National Library of Korea has a Japanese painted scroll depicting a Korean embassy procession in Japan which it dates to 1624, *injo inyŏn t'ongsinsa hangnyŏl t'o*, but the tonsorial practices of the Japanese men it depicts, especially the predominance of clean-shaven faces, suggest a much later date, in the second half of the seventeenth century or even the early eighteenth. For the 1624 dating, Kungnip Chung'ang Pangmulgwan (1986, 25). A second painted scroll depicting a Korean embassy parade, in the National Museum of Korea, has been attributed to Kim Myŏngguk (1600–1662), the official painter attached to the Korean embassy of 1636; as a Korean work, its dating does not affect the chronology of Japanese representations. Kungnip Chung'ang Pangmulgwan (2002, 117–118).

14   For the Koreans depicted in the Hayashibara Museum *Rakuchū rakugai-zu byōbu*, Sin & Nakao (1993–1996, 37); for the Minneapolis Museum of Art/Burke Collection *Rakuchū rakugai-zu byōbu* ("screens of sites in and around the capital," ca. 1620), ibid. pp. 42–45; for the *Edo-zu byōbu* ("scenes of Edo," ca. 1634–35), Suzuki (1971); for the *Tōshōsha engi emaki* ("illustrated history of the Tōshō shrine," 1640), Tenkai & Kano Tan'yū (1640); Komatsu & Kanzaki (1994).

15   Toby (1996a).

16   Ibid.; Toby (2016).

17   For commissioned works, Kano Masunobu, *Chōsen tsūshinshi kantai-zu byōbu* (pair of eight-panel screens, color and gold on paper, 1665; Sennyūji Collection, Kyoto), I argue, is the earliest example of an attempt to represent Koreans with something approaching documentary realism; also Kano Eikei, *Chōsen tsūshinshi gyōretsu zukan* (ink and color on paper, 1682; Spencer Collection, New York Public Library). The earliest depiction by an *ukiyo-e* artist is Hishikawa Moronobu, "Korean Embassy Parade" (ink and color on paper, 1682; Sin Kisu Collection, Osaka Museum of History), which was the basis for a

The most comprehensive example of such documentary realism is a set of four scrolls depicting the parades of the Korean embassy of 1711, commissioned by the bakufu while the embassy was still in Edo.[18] The *bakufu* ordered the daimyo of Tsushima, who was responsible for day-to-day dealings with Korea and for escorting Korean embassies from Pusan to Edo and back, to prepare a set of four documentary scroll paintings (*zukan*) representing the Koreans' parades—as they appeared on the road to Edo; proceeding through Edo to the shogun's castle; returning from the shogun's castle to their Edo lodgings; and on the road back to Korea. The artists employed by the daimyo of Tsushima had just the previous year prepared a set of documentary scrolls for the daimyo of Satsuma to present to the shogun that represented the Ryukyuan embassy of that year. These were their baseline sketches for their documentary scrolls of the "Korean" parades. The "documentary scroll" of the Korean embassy's parade homeward, representing what they "looked like" heading west on the road after their departure from Edo, was completed and presented to the shogun *before the Koreans had even left the city*, a concession to the impatience of the shogun to receive the paintings.[19] Comparison of the "Korean parade" paintings shows that the studio produced the later set by copying the Okinawan paintings, substituting the conventions for representing Korean faces, hairstyles, clothing, regalia, and so forth for the painterly canons for "Okinawans" onto a template used for both processions. They were a "record" only of what Japanese discourse predicted rather than of what "happened."

Korean and Okinawan parades were not uniform in their self-presentation. For their journeys to and from the shogunal court, they wore travel dress, and the length of the journey—several months' round trip—dictated that they carry immense amounts of baggage. Again, when traveling along the Inland Sea, the Koreans rode in large ocean-going Korean ships, while from Osaka they went upriver to Yodo in Japanese riverboats supplied by various daimyos in the Kansai region, presenting quite a different aspect from their appearance on the road. From Yodo overland to Kyoto, and thence to Edo and back, they proceeded in parade formation. But when they went from their Edo lodgings to and from their audiences at the shogun's castle, they wore court dress, which was far more ornate and formal than their traveling clothes.

---

woodblock-printed scroll of which only two panels survive, "Korean Embassy Parade" (monochrome woodblock print, 1682; Art Institute of Chicago).

18   Kuksa Pʼyŏnchʼan Wiwŏnhoe & Chosŏn Tʼongsinsa Munhwa Saŏphoe Chiphang Wiwŏnhoe, comp. (2005) for complete reproductions of all four scrolls.

19   Tashiro (1990). The scroll painting of the Ryukyuan embassy parade is now in the Hawley Collection, University of Hawaii at Manoa Library.

But whether on sea or overland, these alien parades proceeded in linear fashion, unfurling past thousands of eagerly waiting spectators like Enomoto Yazaemon, cited above, a Kawagoe merchant who made the trip up to Edo in 1655 especially to watch the Koreans enter the city, or Matsura Seizan, daimyo of Hirado, who rented the second story of a shop along the route to gaze down upon the Ryukyuans parading through Edo in 1632. Seizan (1760–1841), an inveterate recorder of the world around him, adds detailed sketches of the Ryukyuans' equipage and regalia, and a multi-sheet polychrome print peddled to spectators, as well as his own descriptions of the event as he saw it. Most of all, he seems to relish recording the rumors and speculation circulating in the streets of Edo about these strange and alien visitors.[20]

7   Parade in Review

Let us review a Korean parade, taking as our examples the processions of 1682 and 1711, the embassy dispatched by King Sukchong (r. 1674–1721) to congratulate Tokugawa Tsunayoshi (r. 1680–1709) and Ienobu (r. 1709–1712) on their respective accessions as shogun. By relying on both the "order of march" (*shidaigaki*), which verbally details the sequence of elements of the procession, and the extensive pictorial evidence, it is possible to reconstruct with some confidence a sense of how these parades appeared to spectators and participants.[21]

The first thing to strike the spectator about the structure of the parade is the fact that from vanguard to rearguard, a phalanx of Japanese guards escorted the alien marchers as they proceeded through Japan, while hundreds of porters carried their luggage and bore the ambassadors' palanquins.[22] Whether on highways through the countryside or on the streets of Japan's cities, the

---

20   Matsura (1979–1981, 7:0291–361).

21   This reconstruction of the parades of Korean embassies is based on official and unofficial records of the order of march as well as the extensive pictorial record. Especially useful have been the documents included in Hayashi (1913/1967, 2:111–223, 477–545); and "Kondo Chōsen-koku yori raihei no shinshi, shukkyō no toki jinba" (1682), reproduced in Hayashi (1913/1967, 3:62–63).

22   When the Korean mission of 1711 (the first for which figures are available) paraded along the highways of Japan, they were supported by 816 porters; more than 300 of whom bore the Koreans' palanquins or steadied their pennants and regalia, while nearly 500 were needed just to carry the Koreans' luggage. The porters served in relays, levied as corvée from "assisting villages" along the route. In all, nearly 13,000 porters and 10,000 horses were corvéed for the transport of the 1711 Korean delegation. Hayashi (1913/1967, 2:132). On "assisting villages," see Vaporis (1989); for a study of mobilization of corvée for Korean missions, see Kobayashi (1967).

foreigners were never left unexposed but were virtually wrapped in an envelope of Japanese escorts everywhere they went. Several dozen Japanese samurai, *chūgen, ashigaru*, and porters formed both the vanguard and rearguard of
the entire parade, surrounding the visiting Koreans. Indeed, it was not until
more than a hundred men in service of the daimyo of Tsushima had passed—
a company of *chūgen*, followed by the daimyo's bow and arrows, his equipage,
his horse, and his standard (*matoi*)—that the first Koreans appeared.

Two parallel columns of three mounted Korean military officers headed the
procession, flying large red-bordered blue flags bearing the legend "purify the
path" (K., *ch'ŏngdo*; J., *seidō*) in red characters, the tops of some of the six-foot-
long poles decorated with pheasant plumage, others with spear points. These
pennants preceded royal or imperial progresses in both Korea and China,
ritually removing any impurities that might otherwise sully the royal presence—a presence here represented by the official letter from the Korean king
to the Japanese shogun. Next, following a pair of mounted standard-bearers
carrying ceremonial tridents, came two more horsemen, each flying a silken
flag so large—about nine feet by six, atop an eighteen-foot staff—that four
Japanese had to walk before and behind stabilizing it with guy ropes. These
brilliantly colored flags portrayed dragons—one ascending into the sky, the
other descending from the clouds—that literally "gave form to the name"
(K. *hyŏngmyŏng-gi*; J. *keimei-ki*) of the Korean king, symbolizing the royal presence, the producer behind this performance.

These pennants, public signifiers of monarchic authority and grandeur in
Korea—and of the arrival of the exotic Other in Japan—were followed by four
spare horses, escorted by Japanese hostlers. There followed Korean foot soldiers marching in two columns, bearing decorated halberds and spears, and
smaller military pennants with the legends, "inspection" (K., *sunsi*; J., *junshi*)
and "command" (K., *yŏng*; J., *rei*), announcing the symbolic royal presence, embodied in the king's state letter (K., *kuksŏ*; J., *kokusho*) to the shogun.[23] After
a small party of Korean musketeers and military officers and a number of
Japanese samurai escorts and porters came a Korean military band, a troupe
of equestrian acrobats who would offer an entertainment for the shogun, and
a further group of military officers, all marching in twin columns and all surrounded by Japanese escorts and porters. The military band alone consisted of

---

23   These pennants became the object of controversy in 1711, when the shogun's adviser,
      Arai Hakuseki (1657–1725), protested that they were based on the pretense that the
      Korean monarch was sending an inspection mission to Japan as if it were inspecting a
      dependency. Hakuseki's writings on the Korean embassy question are collected in Arai
      (1905–1907, vol. 4).

over a hundred musicians on horseback, spread out in several groups along the route for hundreds of meters. The musicians were occupied with their instruments, so each horse was led by a pair of Japanese hostlers and was surrounded by guards and porters carrying baskets of luggage. In all, the hundred musicians were wrapped in an envelope of over five hundred armed Japanese escorts. The band's members wore high-crowned, wide-brimmed hats decorated with pheasant plumage and fastened with gold-beaded chinstraps that were partially hidden by the men's luxuriant beards, and pink or pale-blue jackets over white trousers and blouses. They played marching music whenever the parade was on the road, proclaiming the advance of the procession to those not yet in sight but within earshot. On the day of the three ambassadors' audience with the shogun, 1682/8/27, the band "played their music all along the road from [their lodgings at] Honseiji to the dismounting station at the Ōte Gate [of the Castle]."[24]

Yet the 170 or 180 Koreans and hundreds more Japanese escorts, as well as the band itself, were merely the prelude to the main body of the procession, which consisted of the Korean king's letter of greetings to the shogun and the king's three ambassadors (K., *samsa*; J., *sanshi*) and their immediate retinue. To those watching the parade, the band, consisting of brass, reeds, percussion, and strings, announced the immediate approach of these central elements of the entire parade.

On the open highway, a cluster of eight to twelve Japanese carried the king's letter, itself in hidden within a lacquered box, in a splendid roofed cerulean and vermilion palanquin, reliquary for the king's letter, hidden within in a lacquered box. (When the mission went for its audience at the shogun's castle, Koreans would carry the palanquin with the state letter.) As an embodiment of the king, this letter and its palanquin were the heart of the Korean parade. It was for the king's letter that it had been necessary ritually to "purify the path" with the pennants at the vanguard of the procession. The dragon's-head finials on the shafts of the palanquin once more proclaimed the royal presence embodied within. When the mission got to Edo, the ambassadors would present this letter along with a catalog of the King's ceremonial gifts and the gifts themselves to the shogun at Edo Castle and receive the shogun's state letter and gifts in return.

Following the king's letter came the three ambassadors and their immediate party, which consisted of scribes, guards, servants, and interpreters. Among these, Japanese showed the greatest interest in the "young boys" (K., *sodong*; J., *shōdō*), young, unmarried men of good family who served as pages to the

---

24   *Onikki*, reproduced in Hayashi (1913/1967, 2:482).

ambassadors. Among all the Koreans, they alone were bareheaded and beard-less; unlike the others, who wore their hair bound up and hidden under their headgear, the pages wore their hair down, either straight and unbound or tied in a braided or unbraided tail that hung well down their backs.[25] A ma-ture Korean man always wore his hair in a tightly bound topknot, and—like men in medieval Japan—always wore a head covering of some kind, usually coded to social status.[26] Since the standard—the legally mandated—public face of adult Japanese men under the mature Tokugawa regime was hatless and beardless with a shaved pate (see Chapter 6), the lavishly bearded faces of the Korean men drew much curiosity and comment. Yet the pages, who were sometimes mistaken for women or the Korean equivalent of the Japanese *wakashu* (youths), attracted even more intense interest. They were the subject of comic verse and comic paintings and prints—some mocking the Japanese themselves.

Each of the three ambassadors was surrounded by his own party of as-sistants and servants, including four to six *sodong* who waited on him. The ambassadors rode the entire way in palanquins borne by a dozen Japanese por-ters. The ambassador's palanquin was cushioned with tiger skins, and the vice-ambassador and first minister were seated on leopard skins. Neither tigers nor leopards were native to Japan, and they seemed terribly exotic to the specta-tors along the way. For the open road, the ambassadors had roofed palanquins, trimmed in black lacquer and gold; for shorter official journeys between their lodgings and the shogun's castle, for example, they had open sedan chairs and enormous pastel silk parasols. On the open road, the empty sedan chairs and their parasols preceded the roofed palanquins in which the Ambassadors rode.

Still to come after the three ambassadors passed were interpreters, scribes and scholars, the embassy's physician, and dozens of lesser officials. Some rode in palanquins or on horseback, but the lower-ranked officials marched the

---

25   Bird (1898/1986, 1: 128–129) describes "The [Korean] youth, with long abundant hair divid-ed in the middle and plaited at the back, wearing a short, girdled coat, and looking as if he had no place in the world though he may be quite grown up, and who is always taken by strangers for a girl, is transformed by the formal reciprocal salutations which constitute the binding ceremony of marriage. He has received the tonsure, and the long hair sur-rounding it is drawn into the now celebrated 'top-knot.' He is invested with the mang-kun, a crownless skull-cap or fillet of horse-hair, without which, thereafter, he is never seen. He wears a black hat and a long full coat, and his awkward gait is metamorphosed into a dignified swing. His name takes the equivalent of 'Mr.' after it; honorifics must be used in addressing him—in short, from being a 'nobody' he becomes a 'somebody.'

26   Ibid., 2: 174, for a detailed, if brief account of the topknot and its socio-cultural signifi-cance in late Chosŏn Korea: "To the Korean the Top-Knot means nationality, antiquity … sanctity derived from antiquity, entrance on manhood socially and legally…."

FIGURE 50   Korean military band at the vanguard of the 1655 Korean embassy crossing
              Tokiwabashi to enter Edo Castle. Kano Masunobu, *Chōsen tsūshinshi kantai-zu*
              byōbu, pair of eight-panel folding screens, color and gold leaf on paper. Detail,
              right screen, panels 1 & 2.
              COURTESY SENNYŪJI, KYOTO

entire way. Several of these, particularly the scribes and physicians, were often sought out by Japanese who wanted to engage the doctors in discussions of the latest medical knowledge or acquire from the scribes samples of their calligraphy, which was eagerly desired by Japanese connoisseurs and collectors. The indiscriminate pursuit of Korean calligraphy was so pervasive that at least one artist, Hanabusa Itchō (1652–1724), satirized the calligraphy-seekers in a painting showing an obviously intoxicated Japanese spectator getting a sample of calligraphy from a *sodong* as he rode by on horseback (Fig. 53)!

8   How to Wrap a Parade

The Korean embassy that visited Edo in 1682 had a complement of 363 men—they had left 112 in Osaka with their oceangoing vessels—yet they were but a small part of the total array on parade. On the Japanese side, the parade included "fifty mounted samurai who accompanied them, fifty archers, fifty musketeers, and fifty lancers, as well as some 1,700 foot soldiers," not to mention a vast company of porters.[27] A glance at the *zukan* depictions of the embassy of 1711—which brought 371 Korean officials to Edo—gives the immediate impression that this was not so much a "Korean parade" as a parade of Japanese,

---

27   *Tenna Kanpei ki*, quoted in Hayashi (1913/1967, 2:320).

decorated with a smattering of Koreans—about one Korean for every five or six Japanese—mixed in. Most of the Japanese were either porters, hostlers or samurai, a military escort provided by the daimyo of Tsushima (or Satsuma, in the case of Ryukyuan missions), who formed protective clusters around each group of foreigners wherever they went, whether along the highways or in town, as if wrapping the alien element in a protective envelope (Fig. 53).

It is not clear whether the escort was protecting the foreign visitors against the unlikely event of rowdy spectators—though once, in 1764, a Tsushima samurai actually did murder a Korean visitor—or protecting Japan from possibly baneful influences from abroad.[28] There has been a great deal of scholarship, much of it inspired by the folkloric work of Orikuchi Shinobu on "the stranger" (*marebito*), to suggest that Japanese regarded strange visitors at the same time as immensely interesting and potentially beneficial, but also potentially quite dangerous.[29] At the least, the authorities went to great lengths to prevent Japanese from interfering with the aliens on parade.

According to both pictorial and documentary evidence, especially records of the order of march, it is clear that every alien parade was led by several dozen Japanese, led by the minions of the daimyo of Tsushima or Satsuma. On the road, the first 150 to 180 marchers in the parade were Japanese. Standard-bearers displayed the regalia of the daimyo while an hostler led his leopard skin-blanketed horse, a symbol of the daimyo's presence even when he was absent; archers, lancers, and musketeers; five of the daimyo's senior ministers (*karō*) on horseback; and the daimyo's principal Confucian adviser, each attended by his own cluster of porters—and palanquin-bearers, in case of rain—as well as their own military escort. Spectators were thus treated to a grand parade of the familiar before the main show, the unfamiliar aliens who were the meat of the parade.

Only then, after these nearly two-hundred Japanese had passed, did the first Koreans appear, beginning with the twin columns of mounted officers flying *ch'ŏngdo* pennants. Each of the vividly colored pennants was surrounded by a cluster of Japanese samurai. Four or five Japanese samurai and porters surrounded each of the two Korean horsemen carrying tridents festooned with horsehair, proclaiming the approach of the spectacular, brocaded dragon flags. And the Korean horsemen flying the banners, as well, were likewise surrounded

---

28   On this incident, Ikeuchi (1999).

29   Orikuchi articulated his *marebito-ron* (theory of the stranger) in numerous articles, including "Kokubungaku no kenkyū, dai-san-kō," reprinted in Orikuchi (1954–1959, vol. 1). Orikuchi's fascination with the subject has fostered an academic cottage industry of what might be termed "stranger studies," among them Komatsu (1985), Akasaka (1985), and Sumiya, Tsuboi, Yamaguchi, and Muratake (1987).

by an escort of seventeen or eighteen Japanese, a quarter of them using guy-ropes to keep the huge, heavy banners from toppling over.

Horses—either presents to the shogun, or spare horses for the parade; mounted Korean military men carrying muskets, spears, or fearsome halberds, with scimitar-like blades glistening in the sun; more pennants with a variety of legends ... Each of the Korean visitors seemed almost to float in his own pool of Japanese escorts, each was surrounded by Japanese. The ornate palanquins bearing the Korean King's state letter, as well those of each of the three ambassadors—and their empty spare palanquins—were each surrounded by a cluster of Japanese escorts. In short, the entire parade of aliens was completely surrounded, piece by piece, in a protective envelope of Japanese guards wherever they went on Japanese soil, from Kyushu to Edo, and back again.

9   Why Wrap an Alien?

If we pause to examine two particularly graphic visual documents, this "wrapping" comes into clearer focus. One, a brief manuscript entitled *The Parade of the Ryukyuans to [Edo] Castle and Their Pilgrimage to The Shrine [to Tokugawa Ieyasu] in Ueno* (1796), is particularly vivid (Fig. 53).[30] The manuscript opens with an explanation of its internal code before proceeding to a graphic representation of the entire order of march for the Ryukyuan parades: "△—this symbol for Satsuma (i.e., Japanese) people; ○—this symbol for Ryukyuans." In the diagram of the parade that follows, what is striking is that every "○" is preceded by "△," followed by "△," and enveloped in a cluster of "△." The entire Ryukyuan parade was wrapped in an envelope of Japanese wherever it went.

FIGURE 51   The "Three Ambassadors" of the 1655 Korean embassy, borne along Honchō street
as they approach Edo Castle. Kano Masunobu, *Chōsen tsūshinshi kantai-zu byōbu*,
pair of eight-panel folding screens, color and gold leaf on paper. Detail, right
screen, panels 5, 6, 7 & 8.
COURTESY SENNYŪJI, KYOTO

30   *Ryūkyūjin tojō narabini Ueno o-miya sankei goretsu* (1796, MS, collection Historiographical
Institute, Tokyo University).

Similarly, just over a century earlier, in 1691, when the German physician Engelbert Kaempfer journeyed to Edo for the first time in the retinue of the chief of the Dutch trading factory in Nagasaki, he made a sketch of the procession as it made its way across Japan for its audience with the shogun. There were only four Hollanders in the procession, including Kaempfer and the captain, but they were escorted, guarded, and surrounded by about a hundred Japanese, including samurai who marched as a vanguard and clustered around each of the Hollanders, interpreters, and dozens of porters. Each of the Hollanders had a Japanese hostler who led his horse by the bit and a protective envelope of Japanese to guard him—though from what, it was not clear to Kaempfer, who found the Japanese along the road polite to a fault.

Kaempfer wrote, "They supply us with far more horses and porters for our luggage than we need; they assign four Japanese escorts and guards to each of us."[31] In fact, in addition to the escort for the alien parade, the behavior and appearance of the spectators, too, was tightly controlled, both physically, by the presence of what Hong Mallang, Third Ambassador in the Korean mission of 1636, saw as a "hedgerow" of guards and legally, by a series of detailed edicts regulating the behavior of spectators and even the appearance of the streets themselves. As Hong, wrote in his diary, not only did the visitors have a massive escort, but "[Japanese] officers armed with staffs line the street like a hedgerow, blocking the road" (Figs. 60, 61), for not only was the alien parade itself closely guarded: the spectators, too, were heavily guarded and strictly controlled.[32]

If anything, the mobilization of this strict and overprotective envelope of guards and escorts was far beyond anything needed for physical security or to prevent spectators from breaking away from the crowd and either mingling with the marchers or somehow threatening them with violence. Rather, this massive "security" detail was a visible manifestation of the power of Japanese authority—the shogun and the daimyo of Tsushima or Satsuma—to control the alien contingent who "came to pay court" (raichō) and was marshaled to create the impression that the visitors had been *brought* to the shogun as foreign petitioners.[33] But it also, and just as importantly, offered spectators a visible contrast as hundreds of aliens, with their exotic dress and hairstyles, their flowing beards, and their strange music, were framed by the familiar. Exotic and familiar, side by side, was a moving diorama of difference, an embodiment of identities in clear and visible form.

---

31   Kaempfer (1727/1906).

32   Hong (1624). Hong served as *Chongsagwan*, which translates roughly as "Chargé d'Affaires," the third-ranking of the *Samsa* ("three ambassadors") who led each mission.

33   For a discussion, see Toby (1984).

10   How to Watch a Diplomatic Parade

One sunny midsummer's afternoon in 1748, Tame'emon, the headman of Ōtaki Village in Mino Province (now part of the town of Tarui, Gifu Prefecture), took his family on an outing to the nearby post town of Tarui, where the Mino Road branched off from the Nakasendō. The procession of the Korean ambassador and his retinue of nearly four hundred was scheduled to pass through Tarui, just a few kilometers from home. The embassy, sent by King Yŏngjo to congratulate Tokugawa Ieshige on his accession as shogun, was the first Korean mission to Edo in nearly thirty years and provided a rare opportunity for Tame'emon and his neighbors to see exotic foreigners for themselves.

The parade route for Korean missions to the shogun's court in Edo was fixed early in the seventeenth century and did not vary thereafter; from Kyoto to Nagoya, Koreans did not follow the main Tōkaidō highway—as Ryukyuan missions did—but took the Nakasendō and Mino Road. This was not the Koreans' choice, but the *bakufu*'s, which wanted the foreigners to pass through larger towns, where they could impress more spectators like Tame'emon.[34] We have no way of knowing how many other spectators joined Tame'emon and his family in Tarui that afternoon but if the impressions of the Korean visitors of the crowds that came out to see them are to be credited, the town must have been alive with the vibrant energy of the expectant multitude.

Such an occasion was not to be missed. Tame'emon was accompanied by his wife, their three sons and a daughter, and three servants. "We rented three-mats in a tatami room from Yasubei [whose shop faced the highway], at 120 *monme* per mat. We had steamed eggs and burdock root, iced *konnyaku*, pickled ferns, and pickled plums."[35] The nine of them, along with hundreds of other spectators, sat and watched as the vast parade of exotics passed through Tarui on their way from a midday stop in Imasu to their planned lodgings in Ōgaki, where they spent the night.[36] Perhaps, like contemporaries in Osaka and Edo, Tame'emon and his family found the foreigners somewhat comical and more than a little strange. More than one Edoite wrote that even after the Koreans had left the city and headed for home, the air was still rank with the smell of the meat they were imagined to have eaten.[37]

34   Kodama, ed. (1990). When the bakufu mapped the national highway system in 1800, the map of the route from Toriimoto (in Ōmi Province) to Hachimanchō

35   *Chōsenjin raichō ni tsuki shoji oboe* (1748, collection Nakasendō Mini Hakubutsukan), quoted in Gifu City Museum of History (1992, 94).

36   For the route of the embassy, see Hayashi (1913/1967, 2:282–283).

37   Tsuji (1748); Ōta (1985).

Dozens of parades passed through Tarui every year; the grandest in most years were those of daimyos on their way to and from Edo on their annual *sankin kōtai* (alternate attendance) journeys between their domains and the shogun's court, though major local festivals were also organized around parades.[38] But this parade was different: The grand procession of foreigners, with strange hairstyles and outlandish clothes, and playing exotic, foreign music, was for most spectators a once-in-a-lifetime experience. For of the three sorts of foreign missions that visited the shogun from time to time— Korean, Ryukyuan, and Dutch—only the Koreans passed this way, and they came to Japan but a dozen times during the 268-year reign of the Tokugawa shoguns. It had been nearly thirty years since a Korean mission had passed through Tarui, and who knew how many more years it would be before they passed that way again.

Japanese spectators, whose images of the Other were more likely to come from folktales, popular prints or fiction, or from festival performances or the theater, were always eager for a glimpse of "real" foreigners, a chance to observe their features and their habits, to hear their speech and music, even— if they were lucky—to meet them and exchange some calligraphy, poetry, or learned "brush conversations."[39] By the time the Koreans reached Tarui, they had been in Japan for weeks, traveling by ship from Tsushima to northwest

---

38   Engelbert Kaempfer, traveling from Nagasaki to Edo in both 1691 and 1692, remarked of these grand processions that "the train of some the most eminent among the Princes of the Empire fills up the road for some days" (1727/1906, 2:331). For a study of the alternate attendance system, see Tsukahira (1966). On urban festival parades in early modern Japan, see especially Sakumi (1996), Tōkyō (1939), Chiyoda (1970), and Kinoshita (1985). On festivals in two modern Japanese towns, see Ashkenazi (1993) and Nelson (1996).

      Just a few miles east of Tarui in Ōgaki, the annual Hachiman festival, inaugurated in 1645, paraded through the town; the residents of Takeshima-chō performed a Korean masque.

39   The "brush conversation" (J., *hitsudan*; K., *p'ilt'am*; or C., *bitan*) was a medium for those who did not share a spoken language but were literate in classical Chinese. They could "converse" in writing on whatever subjects caught their fancy. The brush conversation, the favored medium of conversation between Korean visitors and Japanese intellectuals— unless they were fortunate enough to have an interpreter present, but the interpreters' knowledge of abstruse points of Confucian theory were likely to be inadequate to the task— was a common occurrence when Korean missions came to Japan. For example, Sin Yuhan reports that on 1719/9/1, during an overnight stop in the Inland Sea port of Ushimado, the Tsushima Confucian scholar Amenomori Hōshū brought several local scholars from Bizen Province to his lodgings for a poetry exchange. "The next morning, the scholars came back. Our *hitsudan* ran to several pages. They asked about our civil service examinations, the ages I took the major and minor exams, and what the exam questions were then, as well as the examiner's name. I replied through a *hitsudan*"; Sin (1974, 103). The definitive study of *hitsudan* during Korean embassies to Japan is Yi (1997, esp. part 2, chapter 1, 69–126.

Kyushu and through the Inland Sea to Osaka; then upriver from Osaka to Yodo on boats provided by daimyos in the area, and overland through Kyoto, Hikone and Nagoya, and thence on to Edo.

Ōtaki, where Tame'emon was headman, was an "assisting village" (*sukegō*) assigned to provide men and horses to the post town of Sekigahara, just west of Tarui on the Nakasendō, which means that Tame'emon must have had to mobilize—or tax—his village for support of the Korean mission as it passed. Perhaps the chance for a little sightseeing today was all the sweeter because the heavy burden was behind him. Tame'emon had spent 360 *mon*—about the price of two to three liters of sake—just for some good seats to watch for a few hours as the Koreans parade through Tarui and for an elaborate lunch. He even brought along three servants. Not only were he and his party spectators who watched the foreigners as they passed; when he rented prime seats for the show and brought servants as well as family—no doubt decked out in their best finery—Tame'emon was also *displaying* himself and his family, his status, and his wealth. He impressed his friends, to be sure, but he also displayed Japan as a place of wealth and luxury, which was calculated to impress the visiting Koreans.

The members of the Korean mission seem to have been fully aware that they were quite an attraction, that seats along the route and service for the spectators was an active and profitable business. Sin Yuhan, who visited Japan as a senior scribe (*chesulgwan*) with the mission of 1719, described the scene when the Korean ships paraded into Osaka harbor:

> On either side of the river, fishing boats and merchant ships lined the banks for over 1,000 rods, as if strung together bow to stern. The spectators, both men and women, stood in rows on both sides, most of them wearing brocade garments. The women wore flower-like *kanzashi* (hairpins) in their lustrous black hair, or else combs of tortoise shell, and fine powder on their faces. They wore long, flowing robes decorated with pictures in crimson and green, their long, slender waists wrapped in jeweled sashes. It looked like a Buddhist painting. The more splendid of the men were even flashier than the women in the color of their garments and the style of their decorations. None of them over the age of eight was without a precious sword thrust into the left side of his belt. Infants in diapers were scattered on [spectators'] laps like precious bits of jade. It was as if a grove of thousands of trees and a myriad flowers, all crimson and azure, yellow and purple, were arrayed before us.
>
> Some spread cushions, while others spread woven mats, and still others lay out wine, tea, and delicacies on splendid brocaded cloths. From

FIGURE 52
A Japanese man holds up a sheet of paper to get
a sample of calligraphy from a mounted Korean
page (*sodong*) in the midst of an embassy procession. Hanabusa Itchō, *Bajō kigō-zu*, hanging scroll,
color and ink on paper, circa 1711–1719.
COURTESY SIN KISU COLLECTION, OSAKA
MUSEUM OF HISTORY

what I hear, there's a master for each spot, who rents it out for cash. The
charge for a seat is two silver coins, but there are different rates depend-
ing on whether [the seat] is close or far away, good or bad.[40] (Figs. 55–57)

Hong Ujae, an interpreter with the 1682 Korean mission, described the spectators in Osaka as "a million onlookers [who] swarmed like ants on the riverbanks … [while] countless thousands line up on the bridges that spanned
the water."[41] And elsewhere, Sin continues the metaphor of swarming insects
when he speaks of the spectators watching his mission parade into Edo Castle

40   Sin (1974, 113–114).
41   Hong (1624, 4:30).

as "crowded together like silkworms."[42] Forty-five years later, another Korean mission brought out vast crowds when they landed at Osaka, where a Japanese observer noted, "There is nothing to compare with the parade of the Korean embassy's flotilla sailing up the [Yodo] River. Vast numbers of people, young and old, male and female, even monks and nuns, flocked to watch. It goes without saying that they came from all over the Osaka area, but they came from other nearby provinces as well."[43]

Hosts and visitors were mutual spectators at their shared parade, carefully—though sometimes playfully—observing each other's appearance and behavior. It is little wonder that each found the other rather strange.

11   "'Festival Chinamen' Are More Convincing 'Chinamen'"

As we have just seen, the Japanese lining the route of a parade of Koreans or Ryukyuans were as giddy as spectators at a festival parade. In fact, while the Korean embassy that had brought Tame'emon and his family out to watch was in Edo—they were there for more than three weeks—a minor samurai by the name of Tsuji Jihei likened the atmosphere in town to the effervescence of a festival in a satiric poem he wrote for the occasion:

> Their music's dull—play with the *ch'ŏngdo* pennants.
> The pages (*sodong*) ain't pretty, but their hair's sure weird!
> With their lutes and zithers, trumpets and flutes echoing about,
> The parade is just like a festival day![44]

If Tsuji thought it was "just like a festival day," that was largely due to the simple fact that it was a day out of time, a moment when ordinary routines were suspended and special—indeed, for most, once-in-a-lifetime—ceremonies were unfolding before his eyes. But more than that, since the suppression of Christianity in the 1630s, the practice of dressing up and masquerading as Southern Barbarians that had become popular in the late sixteenth century and was a fixture in many urban festivals was suppressed along with the southern Barbarians' religion. But Japanese revelers had come to delight in dressing up as foreigners—as evidenced by the costumed dances (*furyū odori*) seen in

---

42   Sin (1974, 1:281); cf. Kang (1974, 196).
43   *Hōreki monogatari* (1764, 27: 299), in Tanigawa (1968–1984), 27:299.
44   Tsuji (1748). Tsuji composed his poem in a faux classical Chinese, even seeming to follow a proper Chinese rhyme scheme.

the festivities in 1604, commemorating the seventh anniversary of Toyotomi Hideyoshi's death, or those in 1622, commemorating the anniversary of Tokugawa Ieyasu's death.[45]

Having discovered the joys and pleasures of masquerading in outlandish foreign dress—at least as they imagined it—however, folk all around Japan proved unwilling to give it up just because they could no longer dress up as Portuguese. Perhaps looking for an equally outlandish style to take the place of their Southern Barbarian fashions, Japanese celebrants reinvented their Other as Korean or Ryukyuan and replicated the fashions and format of their diplomatic parades as "festival Chinamen."

It is not precisely clear when the first "festival Chinamen" appeared in Japanese public celebrations, but there are scattered references to *Tōjin* masquerades long before the Edo period—as early as the tenth or eleventh century.[46] And sometime in the mid- to late-seventeenth century, the now-lost "Southern Barbarians" were replaced by parades that modeled themselves on Korean and Ryukyuan embassy parades—though their stated themes were often taken from Japanese history or legend. By the 1630s, *Tōjin* performances were a common secular accompaniment to the sacred elements of great urban celebrations like the Sannō and Kanda festivals in Edo, as well as in a growing number of provincial towns like Nagoya, Tsu and Wakayama; by the late seventeenth century, both "*Tōjin* parades" and "Korean parades" (*Chōsenjin gyōretsu*) were regular fixtures in dozens of other urban festivals around Japan.[47]

45　For the festivities in memory of Hideyoshi, see *Dai Nihon shiryō*, Part 12, Vol. 2: 496–518; for those in memory of Ieyasu in Wakayama, see ibid., Part 12, vol. 51: 27–50; for Nanban masquing in a festival of the 1630s in a provincial castle town, see Yamanaka (1656/1968).

46　*Nihon kiryaku* (1964, 11: 43), entries for Tenkei 5 (943)/5/17 and 5/5/19.

47　*Tōjin* and *Nanban* mummery was part of the Edo Sannō Festival from the early seventeenth century, judging from the appearance of a half-dozen separate *Tōjin* and *Nanban* masques depicted in the unsigned *Tenka sairei-zu byōbu* (private collection). For reproductions, see the special issue of *Kokka*, 104.4 (1998, frontispieces); for discussions by three art historians, see Hatano (1998), Iwasaki (1998), Sakakibara (1988; for a historian's take, Kuroda (2010). Like most screen paintings, the *Tenka sairei-zu byōbu* is undated: Iwasaki dates it to 1635–1658; Tsuji, to 1656; Hatano to the early eighteenth century, and speculates that the patron was the eighth shogun, Tokugawa Yoshimune; Sakakibara only to 1635–1657; and Tsuji to 1656. Kuroda convincingly dates it to 1659. *Tōjin* masques were seen in local festivals Tsu and Wakayama, on the west and east shores, respectively, of the Kii Peninsula, by the 1640s. For depictions of "Chinamen" performances in the annual Tōshōgū festival in Nagoya, see Naitō Seisan's mid-eighteenth-century *Chōshū zasshi* (Naitō, 1975–76, 3: 92–93; 120–123; 136–137; 294–301). For Wakayama, Sumiyoshi Gukei (ca. 1640, scroll 5), *Tōshōgū engi emaki*, scroll 5, reproduced in Kyōto Bunka Hakubutsukan (2001, 125), and attributed to Hanabusa Itchō, *Kishū Waka gosairei emaki* (ca 1690), reproduced in Kano

Contemporary comic routines (*rakugo*) even had it that the "Chinamen" performed by Japanese celebrants at their festivals were more convincing, more realistic, than the Koreans and Ryukyuans who came from abroad. One of them, recounting a conversation between a courtesan and her guests at a house in the Yoshiwara licensed quarter went:

> Guest: "Hey, did you see the Okinawans? They're splendid … and the Koreans in all their numbers are real fancy, too. But for music, the festivals of Edo are much more interesting."
> Courtesan: "Yeah? Really? The Chinamen of Edo are much more splendid than the Chinamen from China!"

And another:

> Guest: "I got up around four yesterday morning and went to see the Ryukyuans at Takanawa. Wasn't any fun at all. After all, they're Chinamen, so they're just like festival Chinamen. The Chinamen of Toshima-chō are far more splendid."[48]

For comic routines like these to have any punch, "*Tōjin* parades" had to have become a fixture in festivals—not only in Edo, but also nationwide. Toshima-chō, a small ward in central Edo, had become famous for its "Korean parade" in the biennial Kanda Festival, and was celebrated in guidebooks and popular prints—and, as seen here, in popular humor.

12   Parade-Watching as Festival

Perhaps, then, Tame'emon was in the same festive high spirits watching the Koreans march through Tarui as Tsuji Jihei was when he wrote his satiric verse. But there was something missing from Tame'emon's lunch menu that must have dampened his spirits: Tame'emon's lunch was dry—he had no alcohol to lubricate his feelings that day. In the context of Japanese revelry, this is certainly odd. Unless Tame'emon was a teetotaler, why would he forego sake on a

---

et al. (2005, 1–55; esp. pp. 39–44); for Tsu, *Tsu Hachiman sairei gyōretsu zukan* (Spencer Collection, New York Public Library).

48   Mutō (1988, 352). Toshima-chō, which has been absorbed into the Higashi Kanda area of central Tokyo, was famed for its "Korean" performance in the Kanda Myōjin Festival.

wonderful day like this? I will take this up in more detail in a moment, when I look at the constraints on the spectator.

The day Tame'emon and his family came to Tarui to watch the Koreans, the foreigners had arisen that morning in Hikone, on the shores of Lake Biwa; stopped for a lunch at Imasu Station, provided by the daimyo of Hikone; and were scheduled to stay that night in Ōgaki, which was both a post town on the Mino Road and the castle town of the local daimyo, Toda. The parade was comprised of 392 Koreans (another eighty-two were left with the ships in Osaka) who were guided by house elders and samurai posted by the daimyo of Tsushima as well as hundreds of other escorts and guards and porters for the equipage of both the Korean embassy and their Japanese escort. In all, the magnificent, vast parade that passed through Tarui, as Tame'emon and his family looked on in delight, consisted of more than two thousand men and hundreds of horses.

No pictorial sources survive to illuminate for us how Tarui might have appeared that day, as the Korean parade marched through the post town, its pennants fluttering in the heavy summer breeze. An anonymous artist of the late seventeenth century has given us a vivid idea of what the scene might have been like in a rendition of both a parading Korean mission and the massed spectators who watched, as it passed through the post-town of Okitsu, on the Tōkaidō highway about 134 km west of Edo.

The *Korean Parade through Suruga Province* depicts—in quite obviously deformed and parodic fashion—marchers and sightseers in Okitsu during the passage of the Korean mission on the morning of 1682/8/17.[49] The artistic conventions for representing Koreans were well established by the 1680s, but so was the tradition of visual parody (*mitate*), and much in this huge painting is parody—not only in its representation of the "aliens" but in its depiction of "Japanese" spectators and their behavior as well. The clothing and hairstyles, the flags and regalia of the Koreans are wildly, intentionally exaggerated, while the depictions of the spectators and the town are an ironic comment on the *bakufu*'s attempts to present Japan as a land of high public morals and decorum.

The commoner family kneeling humbly in the dust on the far side of the road and the samurai family stiffly seated in formal fashion—probably on reed mats—on the near side remind us of the politely deferential scene one senses in Tame'emon's diary. But the sake-besotted monk, his young boyfriends gathered around him, violates not only every rule of public decorum but the explicit edicts of the *bakufu*, a contrast to Tame'emon's more temperate family

---

49   Unsigned, *Fujisan Seikenji Miho no Matsubara zu byōbu* (single six-panel folding screen, ca. 1682, color on paper, collection Amagasaki-shi Kyōiku Iinkai).

outing. And, as if public drunkenness and debauchery were not enough, a pair of samurai are dueling in the compound of Seikenji, the temple up the hill behind the town, in flagrant violation of edicts demanding public order.[50] If there actually were rowdies and drunks such as are depicted in this remarkable painting, the Koreans seem not to have noticed, for as one of the ambassadors described the scene passing through Okitsu in 1655, "There was no telling how many thousands of spectators there were today. But they were quiet, and didn't run around raising a racket."[51] (Figs. 55, 56, 57)

Foreigners were no great rarity for people living in the immediate vicinity of Nagasaki, the only port in Japan regularly open to foreign trade. Hundreds of Chinese and numerous Hollanders lived there—though they were restricted to residential compounds—and ships called regularly. But for people living anywhere else in Japan, whether along the shores of the Inland Sea or along the highways and in the great and small towns between Osaka and Edo, an alien was a rare sight indeed after the 1630s, once in a lifetime for most. Indeed, save for these grand alien parades and the less-splendid processions of the

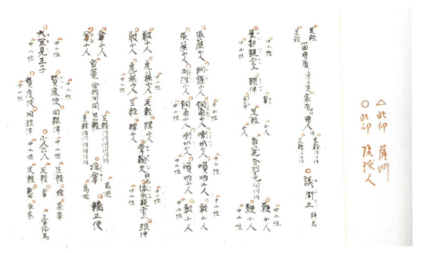

FIGURE 53   This schematic of the 1796 parade of the Ryukyuan embassy across Edo, from their lodgings in the Satsuma domain compound to the shrine to Tokugawa Ieyasu in Ueno, graphically depicts the way all the Ryukyuan participants were enveloped by their Japanese guards. *Ryūkyūjin tojō narabini Ueno o-miya sankei goretsu* (1796, MS).
COURTESY HISTORIOGRAPHICAL INSTITUTE, TOKYO UNIVERSITY

---

50   Seikenji, a Rinzai sect Zen temple founded in 1261, received financial support from the Ashikaga and Tokugawa shoguns. Korean and Ryukyuan embassies to the Tokugawa shoguns frequently stopped there on their journeys to and from Edo.

51   Hong (1655).

FIGURE 54

Spectators lining a Nagoya street to
watch the passage of the Ryukyuan
embassy of 1832. Odagiri Shunkō,
Ryūkyū gashi (MS, 1832).
COURTESY TŌYŌ BUNKO, TOKYO

FIGURE 55 A monk and his pages (l) and a group of women with a child (r) who have
hired prime locations to watch a Korean embassy as it paraded through
the post town of Okitsu. Unsigned *Okitsu Chōsen tsūshinshi gyōretsu-zu
byōbu* (six-panel folding screen, color on paper, ca. 1682).
COURTESY AMAGASAKI BOARD OF EDUCATION

FIGURE 56

Parents and children bowing
respectfully at the Korean embassy
as it moves through Okitsu. Unsigned
*Okitsu Chōsen tsūshinshi gyōretsu-zu
byōbu* (six-panel folding screen, color
on paper, ca. 1682).
COURTESY AMAGASAKI BOARD OF
EDUCATION

Dutch to Edo, virtually the only time Japanese might see a foreigner was after a shipwreck. Thus, whenever a Korean or Ryukyuan embassy's flotilla of alien ships passed through the Inland Sea, it inevitably attracted a lot of attention and thousands of spectators from near and far. The Korean flotilla generally stayed close to the Honshu coast as it sailed through the Inland Sea; locals and visitors, who had never before had a chance to see foreigners or their exotic ships, clustered on shore, picnicked on small islands, or went out into the channel in small boats to gain the best views possible.

For a hint of what it was like for spectators along the Inland Sea, we have a remarkable 1748 scroll painting by a local headman in Tamano, on the eastern coast of Bizen Province (modern Okayama Prefecture), which he called his *Memorandum of the Koreans Coming to Pay Court*.[52] With more wit, perhaps, than technical polish, the amateur artist shows clusters of spectators picnicking on hillsides, while others in small boats have rowed out into the channel to get a closer look at what he called the "Chinese ships" (*Kan-sen*), pointing and shouting, "Hey, look at that! Looks like the sails of the Vice-Ambassador's ship got burned up. It ain't got cotton sails like the baggage ship," commenting on the difference between what the spectator had expected and what he actually saw. These expectations were formed partly by rumor, partly by word of mouth, and partly by broad cultural ideas of what foreigners and foreign ships "should" look like. But more important, spectators could purchase illustrated guides to the event, and become instantly well-versed in the arcana of alienness.

By the late seventeenth century, spectators with enough spare change in their purses were purchasing illustrated guidebooks to the Korean or Ryukyuan embassy, their personnel, their regalia, and even their language, as well as the purported reasons why foreign monarchs sent embassies to Japan, programs to help them understand what they were watching. These guides, published as single- or multi-sheet pictures or bound as guidebooks, were available both in publishers' shops and on the streets, where peddlers hawked them for a few coppers, shouting out patter like this, recorded by the playwright Chikamatsu Monzaemon in 1711, "The *Tōjin* parade! The *Tōjin* parade! A guide to the interpreters' words. A guide to the treasures, gifts and tribute. All recorded in detail in two sections. Six coppers a copy! For three coppers you can learn all there is to know about the lands ten thousand leagues distant."[53]

---

52   *Chōsenjin raichō oboe Bizen gochisō-bune gyōretsu-zu* (MS scroll, 1748, color on paper, 14.8 × 849 cm, private collection). For a brief discussion of this scroll, see Toby (1986, 438 and fig. 5); the entire scroll is reproduced in Shin and Nakao (1993–1996, 6:24–33).

53   *Tōjin no gyōretsu! Tōjin no gyōretsu! Tsūji kotoba no shidai. Shinmotsu miyage takaramono no shidai. Tsubusa ni shirushi jōge wa rokusen issatsu. Sanzen banri no anata made tsubusa ni shireru.* Chikamatsu (1985–1990, 10:439). Among other things, Chikamatsu's play is a

FIGURE 57   A three-generation family gazing at the Korean embassy as it moves through
              Okitsu. Unsigned *Okitsu Chōsen tsūshinshi gyōretsu-zu byōbu* (six-panel folding
              screen, color on paper, ca. 1682).
              COURTESY AMAGASAKI BOARD OF EDUCATION

Publishers apparently paid dearly for the privilege of publishing, with one
reportedly paying the daimyo of Satsuma over one hundred *ryō* in gold for the
rights to print a guide to the 1832 parade of the Ryukyuan embassy.[54] While
there is no indication whether Tame'emon purchased such a guidebook, they
were both common and inexpensive by 1748, and it is likely that they were
available all along the route.

13   The Spectator's Condition

Folks throughout western and central Japan looked on these alien parades as
one of the finest spectacles available to them, an entertainment of unparalleled
exoticism, and just plain fun. Yet in the social world of early modern Japan, the
dress, deportment, and behavior of all people was closely regulated according to their status and was constrained to conform to the dictates of time and
place. Spectators at the visits of foreign dignitaries intruded themselves into

parody of the *bakufu*'s handling of the Korean embassy of that year, which had been quar-
tered in Osaka until just weeks before *Taishokan* opened.

54   Matsura (1979–1981, 7:302).

a time and place where they were themselves objects of display, visible to the aliens just as the aliens were visible to them. The behavior of Japanese spectators therefore reflected upon the dignity of Japan and the shogun.

Since spectators watching an alien parade were, by definition, watching the strange and exotic, people and things rarely seen, it is readily understandable that they would reflect their surprise and wonder at the strange in words and gestures—sometimes crude and even insulting words and gestures that could prove an embarrassment or even provoke a diplomatic incident. The testimony of John Saris, an envoy from James I of England to Tokugawa Ieyasu who arrived in Japan in 1613. Saris landed in Kyushu, and after stopping in at the English trading factory in Hirado, made his way to Ieyasu's retirement castle at Sunpu (modern-day Shizuoka). This was long before the English and Spanish had abandoned the Japan trade and the Portuguese had been expelled, a time when there were still thousands of Koreans who had been brought to Japan as prisoners of war in the 1590s and when Chinese still resided in several Kyushu ports. Foreigners ought not to have been such a strange sight in Hakata (part of the modern city of Fukuoka) when Saris and his party passed through. And yet,

> The place exceedingly peopled, very Civill and courteous, onely that at our landing, and being here in Hakata, and so through the whole Countrey, whithersoever we came, the boyes, children, and worser sort of idle people would gather about and follow after us, crying Coré, Coré, Cocoré, Waré, that is to say, You Coreans with false hearts: wondering, hooping, hallowing, and making such a noise about us, that we could scarcely heare one another speake, sometime throwing stones at us (but that was not in many Townes) yet the clamour and crying after us was every where alike, none reproving them for it.[55]

If Saris's passage through Hakata, only fifteen years after the end of the Japanese invasions of Korea, at a time when both southern and northern Europeans were a fairly common sight in Kyushu, could provoke such outbursts of contumely and misbehavior, it is little surprise that the Japanese authorities soon sought to control the crowds that gathered to watch foreigners passing through their midst on diplomatic business. Someone who appeared as strange as Saris

---

55   Saris quoted in Cooper (1965, 287–288). What Saris heard as "Coré, Coré, Cocoré, Waré" would be *Kōrai Kōrai, kokoro warui* in modern standard Japanese. His rendering of the phrase is accurate, however. But it is interesting is that Kōrai (K., Koryŏ) is an anachronism, the name of a Korean dynasty that had been overthrown over two centuries earlier. The contemporary Korean dynasty was Chosŏn (J., Chōsen, 1392–1910). The endurance of "Kōrai" in Japanese parlance has parallels in the term "Tōjin" (people of Tang) for Chinese.

must have, who was different in physique, hair and skin color, hairstyle, clothing, and speech, would have been a marvel in any society, but when the object of such curiosity is a foreign diplomat, a state guest, then the public reaction is also a matter of state.

Behavior was closely regulated in early modern Japanese society for people of all stations in life even in the everyday world of work, play, and family, so it is not surprising that there were special constraints placed on the behavior of spectators to diplomatic parades, which bore directly on the dignity of the shogun, state, and country. The *bakufu* could hardly be expected to countenance the sort of public rudeness and derision that Saris experienced. If this was so for the occasional English or other envoy who happened to appear at court, there was no question that public decorum and customs would be strictly regulated on the occasion of major diplomatic missions from the Korean and Ryukyuan courts, which came at the official invitation of the *bakufu*.

14   The Well-Tempered Spectator

The *bakufu* issued edicts regulating public behavior, especially the deportment of spectators along the route, in advance of the arrival of every foreign mission to the shogun's court. It is particularly instructive to examine these shogunal edicts in the light of the pictorial evidence of public conduct and the diaries of the foreign visitors, who often noted their observations of the crowd's behavior.

It is not certain when the *bakufu* first attempted to regulate spectators' conduct, though Saris's experience suggests that it could never have been too soon. On the other hand, the *bakufu* recognized that foreigners might well misunderstand Japanese customs and respond in ways Japanese found rude, noting in 1711, "Foreigners are unfamiliar with our customs, and may seem rude."[56] In short, not only did the *bakufu* foresee—and attempt to forestall—Japanese rudeness; the authorities were also concerned that simple miscommunication might be taken as impoliteness.

The earliest extant example of official restrictions on the conduct of the crowds of spectators witnessing an alien parade dates from the eve of the Korean mission of 1655 to Edo. Beginning months before, the *bakufu* proclaimed a series of edicts ordering people to clean up and beautify the house fronts and shop fronts facing the streets and then to clean up public behavior:

---

56   Hayashi (1913/1967, 2:66).

1655/3/6

− This Summer the Koreans will be coming here [to Edo]. Therefore, repair all damaged barracks, repaint any unsightly places on walls, repair any roof damage, so that there is nothing unsightly and repairs are done beforehand. Let there be no mistake about this. And it goes without saying that when the Koreans arrive, nothing unsightly should be left on the rooftops.[57]

Four months later, on 1655/7/5, and once more on 9/19, edicts again commanded that walls be repainted, roofs be re-thatched or re-tiled, and damaged roads be repaired. Streets were to be cleaned and unsightly gear removed from public view. Major diplomatic events, particularly the visits of Korean embassies, were regularly the occasion for broad public works programs, with the *bakufu* ordering repairs of roads and bridges on the overland route and commanding owners to spruce up any buildings that might come under the passing visitors' gaze.

Then, the day before the Koreans' arrival in Edo, the shogunate issued a set of regulations designed to temper the enthusiasm and curiosity of the crowd with a measure of restraint to preserve the public dignity of both the foreign visitors and the shogun's realm. The order is in the form of instructions to the heads of each of Edo's wards, which were to be passed on to the residents under their responsibility.

1655/10/1

− Tomorrow the Koreans will finally arrive here [in Edo], so all house-owners, of course, and renters likewise, should be strictly warned to be careful about fire.

− The guards [*jishinban*] in each ward shall be at their posts and vigilant, night and day. The officer of the month in each ward shall station himself at the gates of the ward from dawn, and shall see to it that there are no arguments or fights. And of course, he should order [residents] to be especially careful about fire.

− When the Koreans pass, it is forbidden to watch from second-story windows. Second-story [windows] are to be shuttered.

− At the hour the Koreans pass by, there shall be no laughing or finger-pointing.

− You are to order [people] not to watch from upon the bridges. Nor are there to be spectators beyond the eaves of the roofs [along the route]. In all events, order [people] that they are to be well-behaved, and not disorderly.

− If [spectators] put out box seats [*sajiki*] under the eaves, the space under the *tatami* should not be visible.

− There should be a bucket of water placed in front of every house for putting down the dust, and you shall clean the street, sprinkling water just before the Chinamen [*Tōjin*] pass by. And while the Koreans are in town, keep the

---

57   Hayashi (1913/1967, 2:57–58).

rain-barrels full of water and place buckets of water in front of each house, and if a fire should break out, run and extinguish it.[58]

The above was circulated to every ward where the Koreans [were scheduled to] pass on the first day of the tenth month, the Year of the Ram.

In later years, rules for both the spectators' conduct and maintaining the public face of the street, became ever more detailed, if not always more restrictive. In 1711, for example, wards along the route of the Korean ambassadors' parade were ordered,

– Assiduously to sweep the streets throughout the wards; to put out water-buckets at regular intervals; to sprinkle the streets [for dust] just before the Koreans pass by....

– When the Koreans pass by, unless it is an emergency, passersby both noble and base shall be pulled over to the left or right [side of the street] and stopped; if there are those who wish to cross the parade route, they must be detained; if you ascertain clearly that it is an emergency, pass them across quickly when there is a break in the parade.

– At the hour when the Koreans pass by, if there are spectators watching from the second story, or from windows, they should [watch from behind] hanging screens and be well behaved. They may of course watch from clothes-drying platforms. However, they may not watch from the rooftops.

– Even when spectators watch from storefronts or second stories, they must not raise their voices, laugh loudly, or point their fingers; they must watch in complete silence. Spectators must put up screens or curtains to separate men from women, priests from nuns. They must not sit all mixed together. They must not scatter their refreshments about; they must not comport themselves in a disorderly fashion; it goes without saying that fighting, arguing, and disorderly drunkenness are prohibited, and at all events rowdiness is prohibited....

– Spectators who happen upon the parade as they cross a bridge or walk on a side street are different [from those watching from] galleries; so long as they are well behaved spectators, there is no objection to men and women, priests and nuns, watching together....

– Trading with members of the Korean retinue, whether high-ranking or low, is strictly forbidden. If [such actions] come to light in the days to follow, [violators] will be prosecuted.[59]

---

58 Hayashi (1913/1967, 2:58–59). The *furegaki* was the most common form of legislation, "circulated writings" that notified the populace of an edict or directive. Nearly every major public event—including the impending arrival of a foreign delegation—was the subject of numerous *furegaki*.

59 Hayashi (1913/1967, 2:65–66).

But it is clear that long before 1655, the *bakufu* had begun explicitly to regulate spectators' behavior—and that the visiting Koreans were aware of the restrictions. As early as 1624, a Korean visitor noted that for the final thirty *ri* (approx. 118 km, or 73 miles) before they reached Shinagawa (the entrance to Edo proper), "The spectators [K., *kwangwang*; J., *kankō*], both male and female, blocked the roadsides to the left and the right. Officers armed with staves lined the streets like a row of shrubs, to prevent fights," referring to the warders stationed along the route to restrain the crowds from fighting, rowdiness, or anything else the *bakufu* considered "bad behavior."[60] (Figs. 58, 59 & 60)

FIGURE 58
A group of outcasts—a blind *biwa* player, a *yamabushi*, an *izari* (paraplegic) and others—whose presence at a Korean embassy procession was banned by the authorities, are shown at the side of the road through Okitsu station as the embassy parades past. Unsigned *Okitsu Chōsen tsūshinshi gyōretsu-zu byōbu* (six-panel folding screen, color on paper, ca. 1682).
COURTESY AMAGASAKI BOARD OF EDUCATION

FIGURE 59   The Korean vice-ambassador's ship passing through the Inland Sea off Bizen Province. *Chōsenjin raichō oboe Bizen gochisō-bune gyōretsu-zu* (MS scroll, 1748, color on paper, 14.8 × 849 cm, private collection).

60   Kang Hongjung, *Tongsarok*, entry of Injo 2[1624]/12/12, in *Haehaeng ch'ongjae* (1914), 2:252–253; Kim Seryŏn, *Haesarok*, in *Haehaeng ch'ongjae* (1914), 2:436–437.

FIGURE 60   A squatting guard with his staff, and a man sprinkling
            water to hold down the dust along the route of the 1655
            Korean embassy. Behind them, a group of spectators
            who have hired ringside seats. Kano Masunobu, *Chōsen
            tsūshinshi kantai-zu byōbu*, pair of eight-panel folding
            screens, color and gold leaf on paper. Detail, right screen,
            panel 5.
            COURTESY SENNYŪJI, KYOTO

The authorities circulated edicts like these "regulations of public morals" every
time Korean or Ryukyuan embassies came to Japan, not just for the crowds
in Edo, but for Osaka, Kyoto, and everyplace along the route the foreigners'
parades were to travel. The regulations varied from time to time in their se-
verity, but they invariably "strictly" (*kitto*) prohibited any "breach of etiquette"
(*busahō*) on the part of spectators—and specified in detail the particular im-
proprieties that were banned.

Nor was the *bakufu* satisfied merely with regulating the spectators' deportment. For months before the anticipated arrival of a "foreigner's parade," the
bakufu was busy ordering the repair of riverbanks, roads, bridges, buildings,
and the planned lodgings of the visitors all along the route. Householders were
directed to "remove laundry racks from the rooftops," while shopkeepers were
required to "take down any unsightly shop signs ... and shop signs with replicas
of [the goods for sale] or pictures that make no sense, for the duration while
the Koreans pass"; special mention was made in this regard of the signboards

of gynecologists' shops. All this to prevent anything that might be embarrassing from catching the eye of these state guests from abroad.

It was *bakufu* policy not to maintain bridges over the Nagara, Kiso, and other major rivers, so the *bakufu* constructed pontoon bridges especially for the dignitaries' grand parades—a luxury not afforded daimyos on their annual journeys to and from the shogun's court.[61] In 1711, for example, the *bakufu* ordered the daimyos in the area around Ōgaki to prepare a pontoon bridge across the Ibi River so the Korean embassy could parade across without getting its feet wet. The bridge, 218 meters (715 feet) long, was supported by eighty boats anchored in the stream, and the entire structure was anchored with great hawsers at each end.[62]

Japanese authorities were assiduous about presenting the face of a well-ordered country to state guests from abroad. Just as campaigns to "beautify and purify public spaces and public morals" and to "improve public infrastructure" have been commonplace in contemporary Japan when receiving foreign dignitaries or when a particularly large influx of foreign visitors is expected—for the Olympics or a World's Fair—the Tokugawa regime was deeply concerned about the public face of their realm (*kokutai*).

15   Watching the Spectators

What can we learn of spectators' behavior from the pictorial evidence we examined in looking at the structure of the parade? How did the spectators look to the visiting dignitaries, who were observing them as intensely as they were watching the foreigners?

Most of the "parade scrolls," unfortunately, are single-mindedly focused on the foreigners and their escorts and turn a blind eye to the crowds of spectators. But from the early seventeenth century, many of the great cityscape folding screens, beginning with several of the "scenes of the capital" (*rakuchū rakugai*) screens, take great delight in depicting the mass of spectators looking on with great curiosity at the foreign dignitaries and their retinues parading through Kyoto and Edo. Interestingly, the behavior of the crowds as represented in the

61   See Vaporis (1994, 48–55) for the most reliable discussion of the reasons why there were no bridges over the major rivers. Frequently it was because they were prone to bursting into powerful torrents after a heavy rain upstream. Bird (1881) describes the destruction of a great bridge over the Hirakawa River in Yamagata.

62   *Shōtoku-do Minoji Sadogawa funahashi ezu* (1711, MS, ink and color on paper, 72.3 × 343.0 cm, Kasamatsu Jin'ya Tsutusmi-kata Monjo, Gifu Kenritsu Shiryōkan). Reproduced in Gifu City Museum of History (1992, fig. 35).

screens does not often comport with the strict regulations handed down by the authorities.

The luxuriously gilded *Edo-zu byōbu* (Edo Panorama Screens), most likely painted between late 1634 and early 1635, celebrates the great events in the early years of the reign (*miyo-hajime*—the start of the august reign) of Tokugawa Iemitsu the third shogun (r., 1623–1651), grandly laying them out across a panoramic view of the Edo cityscape, centered on the vast compound of Edo Castle and its towering central keep.[63] The screens are dotted with parades, large and small, representations of Iemitsu's progresses to the hunt, to a falconry expedition, or to war games on the outskirts of Edo. But one parade, more spectacular than all the rest, occupies center stage: Clusters of spectators stand at every street corner, pointing and gawking at the procession of the Korean ambassadors of 1624 curling through the streets, crossing a bridge over the outer moat, and entering Edo Castle to present King Injo's greetings to the shogun. Because the screens were commissioned and executed a decade after the Korean embassy's visit to Edo, the artists likely had no sketches to work from, which may help to account for the disconnect between an actual Korean embassy's raiment, regalia and gifts, on the one hand, and the way they are represented in the screens.

It is entirely fitting that the Korean embassy parade be at the center of this grand screen commemorating Iemitsu's *miyo-hajime*, for its mission was

FIGURE 61

A guard, and a man with a broom who is ready at a moment's notice to sweep up any droppings from horses in the Korean embassy retinue. Kano Masunobu, *Chōsen tsūshinshi kantai-zu byōbu*, pair of eight-panel folding screens, color and gold leaf on paper. Detail, right screen, panel 5.
COURTESY SENNYŪJI, KYOTO

---

63   Suzuki (1971). See Kuroda (1993, Part 2, Chapter 1) for a detailed discussion of the dating of the *Edo-zu byōbu*.

to congratulate the young shogun on his accession to office. And from the shogunate's point of view, much of the rationale for staging this grand and opulent public spectacle was to proclaim to one and all the recognition and legitimation of both this particular shogun and the Tokugawa dynasty to everyone in Japan.

King Injo's gifts for the shogun—tiger and leopard skins, and other less readily identifiable furs, bolts of silk damask and brocade, and precious medicines in brightly colored porcelain urns—are already arrayed on the plaza inside the main gate; the vanguard of the parade, its dragon flags and "purify the road" pennants fluttering in the chill winter breeze. The ambassadors'—only two are portrayed in this much-abbreviated representation—open vermilion palanquins, each borne by four Koreans, and sheltered under huge gold-brocaded parasols, approach the bridge over the outer moat, surrounded by civilian members of their retinue; some of the military attachés are already in the courtyard, while others are crossing the bridge. Their facial hair, whiskers, and headgear, as much as their regalia, call attention to their alienness. A troop of samurai brings up the rear, carrying the standards of the daimyo of Tsushima. Their bare heads, shaved pates (*sakayaki*), and starched *kataginu* jackets set the alienness of the Koreans off against normative "Japaneseness"—as does the bare-headedness, dress, and hairstyles of the spectators along the route.

FIGURE 62   Bird's-eye view of 1624 Korean embassy entering Edo Castle for its audience with Tokugawa Iemitsu. *Edo-zu byōbu* (pair of six-panel folding
screens, color & gold leaf on paper, ca. 1634–1635). Detail, left-hand screen
panels 1–2.
COURTESY NATIONAL MUSEUM OF JAPANESE HISTORY

FIGURE 63   Samurai on duty in Edo Castle running to see the Korean embassy as it ar-
             rives in the main compound. *Edo-zu byōbu* (pair of six-panel folding screens,
             color & gold leaf on paper, ca. 1634–1635). Detail, left-hand screen panels 1–2.
             COURTESY NATIONAL MUSEUM OF JAPANESE HISTORY

FIGURE 64   Crowds of men, women and children gather in the Edo streets to watch the
             Korean embassy parade. *Edo-zu byōbu* (pair of six-panel folding screens, color &
             gold leaf on paper, ca. 1634–1635). Detail, left-hand screen panels 1–2.
             COURTESY NATIONAL MUSEUM OF JAPANESE HISTORY

FIGURE 65   Members of the Korean embassy on the plaza of Edo Castle arranging the Korean
king's gifts for the shogun while, at left, bearers of the vanguard flags stand to
attention. *Edo-zu byōbu* (pair of six-panel folding screens, color & gold leaf on
paper, ca. 1634–1635). Detail, left-hand screen panels 1–2.
COURTESY NATIONAL MUSEUM OF JAPANESE HISTORY

At every stage, spectators engage in what would later be decreed "unseemly
behavior," and expressly prohibited by the authorities. Clusters of samurai in
the courtyard and crowds of commoners on the public streets gather to stare;
they point their fingers at the Koreans and are probably laughing and chuck-
ling audibly—though even the most talented painter could not record that.
Inside the courtyard, one samurai—readily identified by the two swords thrust
through his belt—points at the Koreans as he beckons a friend while running
to get a better look.

The spectators seated between the moat and the official mansion of
Tsuchiya Toshinao, daimyo of Kururi, watch the Korean parade politely, with
"well-behaved" self-restraint, but one of the women in the crowd of spectators
to the left of the bridge and two of the samurai in the castle courtyard are finger-pointing, misbehaving in ways that would soon be prohibited. The pictorial
evidence, not to mention the nearly universal reactions of people everywhere
to the strange and different, suggest that such edicts were not terribly effective.

A vast and opulently gilded screen painting of the embassy of 1655 parading
through the Streets of Edo, and being received by the fourth shogun, Ietsuna
(r. 1651–1680)—which he later presented to his Great-Aunt Tōfukumon'in, em-
press-consort to Emperor Gomizuno'o (r. 1611–1629)—suggests much greater
compliance with shogunal edicts.[64] Perhaps this is to be expected in a work

---

64   Kanō Masunobu, *Chōsenjin kantai-zu byōbu* (pair of eight-panel screens, each 166.7 ×
501.6 cm, color and gold leaf on paper, collection Sennyūji, Kyoto). Reproduced in Toby
(1994b, 46–47).

commissioned by the shogun; yet even here, some of the spectators are represented as pointing fingers, and two samurai actually turn their backs on the parade, facing a blank wall to spurn the alien visitors. Of course, it is not just Japanese spectators who are caught up in the drama of difference embodied in this parade: Several Koreans, too, are shown finger-pointing, commenting to each other on the strangeness of their hosts, who find them strange in return.

A much earlier, and less lavish, screen painting depicting the Korean embassy of 1617 parading through the streets of Kyoto, passing west of the imperial palace compound on their return from an audience with the second shogun, Hidetada (r. 1605–1623), at Fushimi Castle, represents the spectators as uniformly polite and reserved.[65] In fact, most remarkable—and un"realistic"—is the fact that there are so few spectators, and none lining the street.

Yet other, later artists leave no doubt that they saw the spectators and their conduct as flagrantly violating the shogunal edicts that were supposed to keep the crowds "well-behaved" for the visiting foreign dignitaries of the aliens' parade. A *rakuchū rakugai* (scenes of the capital) screen dating from the late seventeenth or early eighteenth century, which compresses the distance between the Katsura River and Kyoto to show the Korean parade both approaching the city and marching past Nijō Castle, depicts most spectators as watching quietly, even respectfully, as the foreigners pass, but others at some of the intersections are laughing and pointing at them, while children play in the street just before the parade.[66] In a more elaborate screen painting of the same vintage, spectators watch not only from seats in the shops and houses and on the street itself but also from the bridges, even standing knee-deep in the water of the Horikawa Moat, behavior "strictly forbidden" by shogunal edict.[67]

The testimony of Sin Yuhan, a scribe with the Korean embassy of 1719, described the behavior of the spectators watching the embassy's boats parade into

---

65   Though Sennyūji, the Kyoto temple where the Masunobu screens are held, has no record of their provenance, Kōriki Tanenobu, *Enkōan gasshū 5-hen* (MS, collection Nagoya Shiritsu Hakubutsukan) quotes the patter of a shill describing the screen at a 1785 Nagoya exhibit of Sennyūji's treasures: "This folding screen was beloved of Tōfukumon'in [consort of Emperor Gomizuno'o]; it is a painting of the Koreans coming to pay court, from the brush of Masunobu, of the house of Kano, and was a gift from the shogun." Tanenobu's sketch of the screens leaves no doubt that the shill is describing this same screen—though his sketch is only about 12 cm high, less than one-tenth the size of Masunobu's screens, it is instantly recognizable. On Tōfukumon'in and her place in the art world of her day, see Lillehoj (1996; 2007; 2011); on the screens themselves, Toby (2016).

66   Unsigned pair of six-panel screens, Boston Museum of Fine Arts.

67   Unsigned, *Rakuchū rakugai-zu byōbu* (pair of six-panel screens, color and gold leaf on paper, private collection, Takaoka City); below, *Takaoka-bon Rakuchū rakugai-zu byōbu*, reproduced in Toby (1994, 48).

Osaka Harbor, even proscribed behavior, with some affection. "Sometimes a child cries, or a young woman laughs. When a young woman laughs, she makes sure to cover her mouth with a handkerchief," just as many women do in Japan today. "Their laughter jingles, as if precious stones were clinking together, and sounds like a delicate birdsong."[68] Far from being offended by these minor sorts of what the *bakufu* called "misbehavior," Sin found it quite affecting.

"Watching from atop the bridges," or "watching from a point beyond the eaves of the buildings" along the route were specifically prohibited to spectators in the towns, as we saw earlier. Yet, just as clearly, the ban was required precisely because such spectators were given to such unsightly conduct. Hong Ujae had noted that "countless thousands line up on the bridges that spanned the water" when he and his embassy arrived at Osaka in 1682.[69] Of course, it is possible that the townspeople of Kyoto were in fact well behaved and conformed fully with the *bakufu*'s rules of conduct for spectators and that the artist was merely parodying forbidden follies, but the likelihood is high that not everyone was quite so compliant.

It was not only the sophisticated urbanites of Osaka, Kyoto, and Edo that gazed upon these "Chinamen" as if they were some strange, rare creatures, "pointing their fingers and laughing out loud." Thousands of the curious put out in small boats when alien ships paraded up the Inland Sea, or gathered—like Tame'emon and his family—in all the post towns along the highway, paying their hard-earned money for good seats. In Okitsu, a post town about 150 kilometers west of Edo on the Tōkaidō, an artist reports, an old man watching the Korean parade from a boat offshore and a mother squatting with her child in the dust by the roadside to get a look were among those who risked shogunal retribution for finger-pointing at the passing foreigners.[70]

Many groups of spectators along the Inland Sea put out into the channel in small pleasure boats to watch the parade of oceangoing Korean "great ships" (*ōbune*), whose alien hulls and cotton sails, prows brightly decorated with lurid demon mask motifs, and brightly colored pennants whipping in the breeze offered almost as much excitement as the strangely dressed, bearded aliens on board. Since winds and Inland Sea currents were unreliable, Korean crews also rowed the ships, while dozens of large and small Japanese tow boats helped to pull them along with great hawsers.[71] When the Korean Ambassador's convoy

---

68   Sin Yuhan, *Haeyurok*, in *Haehaeng ch'ongjae* (1941, 1:248); cf. Kang, tr., *Kaiyūroku*, p. 114, entry of (Sukchong 37 [1719]/9/4).

69   Hong Ujae, *Tongsarok*, in Hong (1941, 4:30).

70   Unsigned, *Fujisan Seikenji Miho no Matsubara zu byōbu*.

71   *Chōsenjin raichō oboe Bizen gochisō-bune gyōretsu-zu?*

hove out of Mitajiri Nishinotsu, in Nagato Province, "assisted by a fast-running tide" on the morning of 1719/8/25, "there was a strong west wind. The Tsushima ships, the escort vessels from [the daimyo of] Nagato, and the supply ships all hoisted sail at once. The sails, oars, pennants and flags covered the sea for several tens of *ri*," reported Sin Yuhan.[72] It must have been a spectacular sight to see. There were "finger-pointing, loudly laughing" spectators in these crowds, as well. (See Fig. 57)

To be sure, the parading alien visitors returned the curiosity of the Japanese spectators measure for measure, for foreigners were at least as uncommon a sight in early modern Korea as they were in Japan: Japanese traders in Korea were confined to a compound in Pusan, while trade with China and the peoples of Manchuria were all conducted on the northern border.[73] *Tōjin* parades offered a rare opportunity to test the limits of identity by comparison with what was constituted as clearly alien.

16   Seeing and Showing

Spectators were as much the objects of an alien gaze; that is, they were observers of the alien visitors passing in parade before them, whether on sea or on land. As such, the authorities were quite conscious that they were both displaying the aliens at home and putting their realm on display, showing their well-ordered land to foreigners and through them to foreign potentates. And since the dominant Confucian discourse held that public morals were directly a symptom of the morals of the monarch, the behavior of the crowd—as well as of every individual involved in the reception of foreigners—was a critical matter of state, a reflection of the "face of the state" (*kokutai*) projected abroad.

Controlling public decorum was thus essential to the project of showing the realm abroad as a well-ordered manifestation of shogunal virtue. Not only did this entail regulating the conduct of those who gathered to see the aliens' parades, it also involved regulating even who could see the parade—and necessarily be seen by (shown to) the foreign dignitaries. Early modern Japan's was a society in which status distinctions—not merely of degree but of kind as well—were central to the state's vision of public order.[74] Within the status system, some social groups were constituted as either permanently or temporarily outside truly human society—one such group was actually called

---

72   *Haeyurok*, in Hong (1941, 1:239 passim, 93 passim).
73   See James B. Lewis (2003).
74   Hall (1974); the best recent treatment is Howell (2005).

"un-persons" (*hinin*, i.e., outcasts)—and subject to severe and systematic discrimination, both in law and in popular practice. The *bakufu* chose not to show such people to foreign dignitaries, barring them from seeing the foreigners' parades, no matter how well behaved they might be:

– As the route of the Koreans shall be cleared of *hinin*, they are not even to be lodged in the *hinin* shelters of the towns along the way.[75]

Similarly, when the 1832 Ryukyuan mission was scheduled to pass through the post town of Okoshi, on the banks of the Kiso River athwart the Mino Road, in the Owari domain a half-day's march west of Nagoya, the domain not only proclaimed that spectators "are strictly forbidden to laugh out loud or point their fingers" and enjoined them to "be properly well-behaved," but went beyond this to note,

– *Hinin* and beggars must, of course, not be allowed to stay in the post towns and villages; they are also barred from the precincts of Noma and Matsubara.[76]

That is to say, *hinin* and others who were excluded from the core, "straight" status groups of samurai, peasants, artisans, and merchants, much like "unsightly shop signs," were something the authorities tried to conceal from the visiting aliens. Regarded as not fully human and marked off by legally mandated distinctions of dress, deportment, and hairstyles—and in some cases, inscribed with tattoos or disfigurement in punishment for a crime—though having human form, they were incompatible with the vision of the well-ordered realm that the *bakufu* sought to put on international display.

Yet outcasts and pariahs, too, were curious about the aliens, people who were different, but in different ways, and sought to join the crowds of spectators—hence the authorities' prohibitions. Whether the *bakufu* enjoined outcast spectators earlier than 1748 is uncertain, but a late-seventeenth-century artist reports a group of outcasts—a wandering mendicant, a blind story-teller (*goze*), a paraplegic (*izari*), a beggar, a blind musician, and a mountain ascetic (*yamabushi*)—squatting beside the road in the post-town of Okitsu among the spectators as the Korean embassy paraded past in (Fig. 58) 1682.[77] Perhaps this is simply artistic license or evidence that the *bakufu* did not yet regard these excluded groups as too unsightly to allow them to be visible abroad; it is also possible that the artist was consciously parodying those things the *bakufu* sought to hide from sight, for much of the behavior he represents, even among

75   Hayashi (1913/1967, 2:79), edict, third month of Kan'en 1 (1748).
76   "Owari-han murakata furegaki-shū," quoted in Yokoyama (1987, 182).
77   Unsigned, *Fujisan Seikenji Miho no Matsubara zu byōbu.*

the spectators whose status did not exclude them, was conduct that the *bakufu* had proscribed.

In any event, however much the authorities tried to control public behavior and to display Japan and its society in a favorable light when foreign visitors were passing in parade, the thousands of spectators who hurried from the provinces to watch the alien parade were unfazed, intent on enjoying the rare opportunity to see for themselves these exotic visitors from abroad.

17   Four Lines of Sight

Looked at in this fashion, diplomatic parades were not merely important state rituals but had much broader social, cultural, and ideological significance.

The *bakufu*, conscious that foreign dignitaries would observe Japan, and spread their impressions beyond the seas, exerted itself to display Japan—its roads and towns, but also, and more important, its people—in the best light possible, to put on a show of Japan as it *ought* to be rather than as it was. Not only did the authorities regulate the behavior of spectators in great detail, but they also worked to conceal those who by status or deformity were excluded from mainstream Japanese society. For the *bakufu*, the diplomatic parade was a site where it could display to the outside world—the world of East Asia, which mattered most—a stable, well-ordered society that reflected the "virtuous rule" of the shogun.

For the most part, the alien guests—who were themselves spectators in reverse, watching the watchers—reported that the crowds were indeed "well behaved," apparently conforming themselves, in the main, to the *bakufu*'s regulations for the public behavior of spectators. At the same time, the foreigners were clearly aware that public order was not spontaneous.

Yet for the spectators, when foreigners came to Japan, "The parade was just like a festival day!" Indeed, the "foreigner parade" became an integral part of many Japanese festivals, where the dramas of difference revealed when "real" foreigners came calling could be rehearsed and reinforced on a regular basis. Artists captured the festival mood of the crowd, unconstrained by the rules of public behavior. The pictorial evidence, the product of careful observation, conventions of representation, and artistic license, suggests that the edicts were often more honored in the breach than the observance.

The Birth of the Hairy Barbarian: Ethnic Slur as Cultural Marker

> Why does [the prime minister], who's always got an obsequious grin even when his eyes aren't smiling, ecstatically hug and shake hands with these—I shouldn't call them hairy barbarians (*ketō*), but—white men? If I were prime minister, I'd just stand there with both hands stuck in my pockets.
>
> ISHIHARA SHINTARŌ, MP, 1993[1]

· · ·

> It is the greatest hardship to mix among these hairy barbarians (*ketōjin*); it feels terrible, and I shall resent it for the rest of my life.
>
> SAIGŌ TAKAMORI, exiled in the Ryukyus, 1859[2]

∴

The body is a potent cultural metaphor, not merely a biological or physical given but a key site for the construction of both individual and collective identities, and for distinguishing between members of the community—however defined—and the Outsider or Other. Bodies and their perceived characteristics (size, shape, color, texture, odor, hairiness/smoothness, etc.) are markers of cultural inclusion and exclusion and as such have been the object of countless epithets and pejoratives identifying the excluded or deprecated Other. Bodies have been exposed or covered (anywhere from complete nudity to total coverage), as well as decorated, molded or modified (enhanced; mutilated), to serve as indelible or ephemeral markers of ethnic or cultural in/exclusion, of gender, age or social status within the ambient cultural system, and as personal "fashion statements."

---

1 Quoted in the *Mainichi shinbun*, July 11, 1993.
2 *Kono ketōjin no majiwari, ikanimo nangi shigoku, kimochi ashiku, tada zansei uramubeki gi ni gozasōrō.* Saigō Takamori to Ōkubo Shōsuke (Toshimichi) et al., Ansei 6/2/7, in Ōkawa (1926, 1:162).

© KONINKLIJKE BRILL NV, LEIDEN, 2019 | DOI:10.1163/9789004393516_008

Hair and beards, among the most visible, malleable, and oft-manipulated of bodily features, are particularly potent signed sites; they are sites, that is, that can be invested with particular cultural meanings precisely because of their susceptibility to shaping, grooming, or neglect (non-grooming); to cutting or shaving (or not); or to or coloring—into articulate expressive forms.[3] As such, hair is often a locus for the expression of gender and sex identities, life course stages, or other identity niches within a culture. Hair is therefore both intensely personal and highly political.[4] Likewise, hair can readily become the focus of pejoratives to characterize foreigners or other despised groups, thus setting up boundaries to a particular cultural identity.[5]

Japanese are not, of course, unique in deploying tonsorial practices as one of many markers distinguishing members of the body social from the excluded Other, or among various status, gender or other subject positions within the larger community. The commandment that, "Ye shall not round the corners of your heads, neither shalt thou mar the corners of thy beard,"[6] still informs tonsorial practices in many orthodox Jewish communities today. Indeed, male tonsorial practices more broadly were important signs of social standing and ethnic identities across the Near East in biblical times.[7] The Greek tragedian Aeschylus was commemorated in an epitaph that used hair—or hairiness—as the sole marker distinguishing Athenian from Persian:

> Under this monument lies Aeschylus the Athenian,
>> Euphorion's son, who died in the wheatlands of Gela. The grove
>> of Marathon with its glories can speak of his valor in battle.
>> The *long-haired Persian* remembers and can speak of it too.[8]

---

3   Oldstone-Moore (2016, 2) argues that, "*The language of facial hair is built on the contrast of shaved and unshaved.* Using this basic distinction, and its many variations, Western societies have constructed a visual vocabulary of personality and social allegiance." (italics in original)

4   Vigorous public debate generated by Michelle Obama's hair, to take one recent example, spawned a long-running blog ('Michelle Obama Hair Project, http://blacksnob.blogspot.com/2008/05/michelle-obama-hair-project.html), articles in major on-line news outlets (Williams, 2009), as well as coverage in the more established media (Desmond-Harris 2009, etc.). Her hairstyle makeover in early 2013 also prompted comment, including Parker (2013), who opined that "Hair is the frame we choose for the portrait we project to the world. Hair conveys messages we don't even consciously recognize." More recently, controversy erupted over the intersection of race and the U.S. Army's regulations regarding women's hairstyles. Byrd & Tharps (2014); Cooper (2014a; 2014v); Staples (2014).

5   The literature on hair, beards, and regimes of tonsorial practice as indicia of ethnic or national identity is too vast for comprehensive listing here. I have found especially helpful Cheng (1998); Dikötter (1998); Entenmann (1974); Firth (1973); Horowitz (1997); Nelson (1998).

6   Translation from Hertz (1961, 289) of Leviticus 17.29.

7   See especially Bloch-Smith (2003); Niditch (2008).

8   Quoted by Richmond Lattimore, "Introduction to the *Oresteia*," in Lattimore (1959): 1. Emphasis added. Aeschylus had fought in the defense of Athens against Darius's Persian

The Sikh anti-depilatory taboo (*kuraht*), and the concomitant practice of *kesh*—letting one's hair grow naturally without cutting or trimming it—Uberoi argues, should "be understood as a specific inversion in symbolic terms of the custom of total depilation" practiced by other sects from which the founder sought to distinguish his followers.[9] Mughal hostility to the *kesh* often led to quite gruesome torture: in the eighteenth century Zahariya Khan, governor of Lahore, is said to have offered the reward of a blanket to anyone who cut off a Sikh's hair, and fifty rupees for a Sikh scalp (presumably with the hair attached).[10] Similarly, the tonsorial practices of English colonists in Wales and Ireland emerged as a critical marker of identity—in the eyes of the English, at least—during the twelfth to fourteenth centuries. The parliament of 1297 addressed this problem: "'Englishmen,' it declared, 'as if degenerate, wear Irish clothing and, having their heads half-shaved, grow their hair long at the back of the head and call it a cúlán, conforming to the Irish both in dress and appearance....[therefore,] all Englishmen in this land [Ireland] shall wear, at least on the head, *which they display the most to view*, the custom and tonsure of the English, and shall no longer dare to turn their hair in a cúlán.'"[11]

And just as official regimes have deployed the force of law to prescribe or proscribe particular hair styles, dissident groups have responded with countervailing—self-identifying or self-othering—tonsorial modes. From ancient Egyptian reliefs and Biblical pre/proscriptions to the Beats in the 1950s, from hippies in the '60s and '70s to skinheads, Rastafarians, and Hare Krishna, not to mention, more recently, Sikhs serving in the American military, and the contestation of tonsorial practices in the Muslim world, many have mobilized hair/no-hair as visible signs of identity.[12] In the ancient world as in the modern,

---

armies at the Battle of Marathon, 490 BCE. My thanks to David Sansone for pointing out that Lattimore's "Persian" is Μῆδος, or "Mede," in the original Greek.

9   Uberoi (1967, 94).

10 From *Sikh Wiki: Encyclopedia of the Sikhs*, http://www.sikhiwiki.org/index.php/Zakariya_Khan (accessed 2013.02.28); see also, e.g. Gächter (2010).

11 Quoted in Duffy (1997, 88); emphasis added. Similarly, R. R. Davies (1996, 13–14) has noted that, "Gerald of Wales had devoted a whole chapter to describing Welsh customs with regard to hair styles and moustaches," and for Bartholomew Angelicus, "Frisians could be distinguished from Germans by the cut of their hair. But it was in Ireland, significantly, that ethnic differences were statutorily defined by hair style. Already in 1297 it was decreed that anyone who wore the cildn (the Irish hair style) could forfeit his English status. Nor was this an empty threat: when a Gaelic lord came to terms with the English in 1333 he "had the hair of his cúlán cut in order to hold English law," while more than a century later it was agreed that any man who wished to be considered English must "have no hair upon his upper lip so that the said lip be shaven at least once within two weeks."

12 See, e.g., Naguib (1990); Stager (1998); Niditch (2008); Bromberger (2008); Delaney (1994); Ghufran (2001); Rigdeon (2010); etc. Agrawal (2015).

that is, whether in East Asia or Africa, Europe or the United States, tonsorial regimes have stood as markers of identity, of inclusion and exclusion from "society," across time and space.[13]

Anthropologist Raymond Firth eloquently sums up the potency of hair as public symbol:

> It is striking to note how out of this sluggish, physiologically almost func-tionless appurtenance of his body, man has imaginatively created a fea-ture of *such socially differentiating and symbolic power*. But in contrast to other appurtenances hair has a number of qualities which *recommend it as an instrument for social action*. Though personal in origin, it is mul-tiple, any single hair of a person tending to be like any other. It is detach-able, renewable, manipulable in many contexts, so to some degree can be treated as an independent object. Yet there is some variation in tex-ture and colour, *so it offers scope for social differentiation*. And it is associa-tive, *tending to call up important social ideas*, especially concerning sex.[14]

The symbolic power of hair may help explain why, of the many Japanese pejo-ratives for "foreigner" (has any people/language a lexicon of favorable terms for aliens?),[15] none has made a deeper impression on English-speaking observers than "hairy barbarian" (*ketō; ketōjin*).[16] And the term has shown a durability in

---

13   In the Meiji period, tonsorial practices became less a marker of ethnic, national or status (*mibun*) identity than of the transition from the "base practices of the past" (*kyūhei*) to "civilization and enlightenment." See, e.g., Howell (2005, 164–166); *idem* (2009); O'Brien (2008).

14   Firth (1973, 263). Italics in original.

15   I do not wish to suggest that Japanese culture is somehow more given to xenophobia, or what Bob T. Wakabayashi (1986) has called "anti-foreignism," than other cultures. It is precisely by asserting difference from groups posited as Other, and superiority to that differentiated alterity, that human collectivities constitute themselves as distinct "eth-nic" or "cultural" identities. The posited differences need not be profound; indeed, Freud speaks frequently, in *Civilization and Its Discontents* and elsewhere, of "a narcissism of petty differences" (*Narzissmus der kleinen Differenzen*) at the core of the construction of identities. See Freud (1953–1974, 9: 199). I prefer to render *kleinen Differenzen* as "petty dif-ference," a small difference from Strachey's "minor differences."

16   This chapter deals with racial and ethnic epithets in Japanese discourse. Consequently, it will be necessary from time to time to render these terms into appropriately valenced English words that are not—or ought not be—acceptable in ordinary English-language discourse. I use these translations in the interest of preserving the tone of the discourse represented. While *Tōjin*, in seventeenth- to nineteenth-century Japanese speech and popular discourse, has a valence close to the pejorative nuance of "Chinaman" in English, I have—as outlined in "A Note on Language"—chosen to avoid that term.

Japanese discourse—despite innumerable waves of change in both Japanese and foreign hair styles and tonsorial practice over the decades—precisely because hair is a convenient site for deploying the exotic in the interest of codifying (Japanese) identity.

Joined with exaggerated visual representations of the beards, side whiskers, and flowing wavy locks that, in Japanese eyes, at least, seemed to characterize European and American male fashion in the nineteenth century, the hirsute Caucasian became a fixture of mid- to late-nineteenth-century Japanese popular culture. As recently as the summer of 1993, we were reminded of the ongoing currency of "hairy barbarian" mythologies when Ishihara Shintarō, then a prominent right-wing M. P., speaking to a group of his supporters, publicly castigated the prime minister—who took his internationalism and fluency in English as a point of pride—for being too cozy with foreigners. He could think of no more stinging barb than to say that the prime minister's cordiality to the visiting Russian foreign minister was a form of obsequiousness to "hairy barbarians."[17] The epithet Ishihara used—*ketō*—seems etymologically to mean "hairy Chinese" (*ke*, "hair"; *tō*, "Chinese" or "foreign" is the Japanese pronunciation of the Chinese character Tang, meaning "China"), yet the term is universally understood in contemporary Japan as indicating what Japanese parlance lumps together as "Euro-Americans" (*Ō-beijin*).

The circumstances of cultural practice that call forth this, and other, ethnic and racial pejoratives, the moments and instances of their production, however, are little studied.[18] *Why* does a particular epithet or pejorative emerge at a specific moment in the ongoing discourse of identities? Does it reflect new-found notions of difference? New-found sites of contestation? Changes in cultural practice within the cursing culture? In the pages that follow, I examine such questions by interrogating the common Japanese epithets, *ketōjin* and *ketō*, "hairy barbarian," for the "hairy barbarian" may not be quite who

---

17   Ishihara's remark in Japanese: *Herahera tsuijū warai o shitemo, me de waratte inai hito ga, ketō to itcha ikenai ga, hakujin ga kuru to ureshisō ni dakitsuite akushu suru no? Watashi ga sōri dattara, poketto ni ryōte o tsukkonde damatte tatteru.* Reported in the *Mainichi shinbun*, 93/7/11. Ishihara was then an M.P. from Tokyo, and later served as governor of Tokyo (1999=2012). He has a long history of provocative comments about race and ethnic difference that have generated hundreds of letters, articles and blog posts. A Google search for "Ishihara Shintaro racist" (2016.12.12) yielded 11,800 hits. Mizuho Aoki, for example, writes that, "Ishihara's often racist remarks may have cost Tokyo votes in its previous attempts to host [the Olympics]...." (Japan Times, 2012.12,17, accessed 2013.02.20).

18   But see Lenneberg (1964), especially E. R. Leach's stimulating approach to invective, unprepossessingly entitled "Anthropological Aspects of Language," and Sørensen (1983).

he seems:[19] When and how did the terms *ketōjin* and *ketō* first appear? What were the contexts of cultural identity and social or cultural practice from which they appeared? What, therefore, did they mean, and how do they illuminate the processes of the production and re-production of *Japanese* cultural identities?

In crude Japanese discourse in the late 20th/early 21st century, as Ishihara's indelicate comment suggests, and as noted above, the epithet "hairy barbarian" refers to Caucasians, and Japanese today seem generally to believe that this once-common racial and ethnic pejorative derives from the generally denser facial and body hair thought to distinguish Caucasians from Japanese. Indeed, the widely used *Kenkyūsha's New Japanese-English Dictionary* (Masuda, 1974: 805) defines *ketō* as, "a white person; a Westerner." Morohashi Tetsuji's authoritative dictionary of Chinese and Sino-Japanese likewise defines *ketō* as, "A word deprecating foreigners. So-called because they are hairy" (*kebukai kara iu*).[20] In modern usage, that is, "hairy barbarian" has come to denote Caucasians, and is seen to derive from the seemingly empirical happenstance that, as a group, Japanese have less pronounced body and facial hair than most Caucasians. Seki Akiko, perhaps following *Kōjien* and Morohashi, states flatly that, "*Ketō* ... is a word that *originates* in the belief that Europeans were 'hairy foreigners.'"[21] As we shall see, this is contradicted by evidence of the earliest usages of the word.

Indeed, both the notion—and the epithet—of the "hairy barbarian," emerged in a specific historical and cultural context in which, ironically, the initial referent, the first "hairy barbarians" of Japanese discourse, were not Caucasian, but neighboring peoples in East Asia, particularly Koreans and Chinese. This is the meaning of the *tō* in *ketō*, the name of the Chinese Tang dynasty (618–935), which had become a generic Japanese term for "China," and by extension, for all East Asian peoples, long before 1600.[22] *Ketōjin/ketō* thus means, literally, "hairy Chinese" (*ke* = "hairy" + *tōjin* = "Chinese"; often abbreviated to *ketō*), and, as we shall see, the initial usage of the epithet unmistakably

---

19   It will be apparent from the discussion below that *ketō/ketōjin* refers almost exclusively to males, and emerged in response to changes in male tonsorial practices in Japan and China.

20   Morohashi (1955–1960, 6:816).

21   Seki (2012, 81). Emphasis added.

22   Sometime in the late sixteenth or early seventeenth century, the capacity of *Tōjin* expanded to become a generic term for "foreigner," as well as referring specifically to "Chinese," but it is uncertain when this shift took place. The earliest usage in this sense cited in NKD, 9: 982, is a line in Hata Sōha, *Inumakura* (ca. 1600).

refs to "Chinese" of "Koreans"—at least as constructed by Japanese discourse (i.e., including Koreans and other East Asians).[23]

1   Initial Encounters and Radical Others

Japan's initial encounters with Europeans, in the middle of the sixteenth century, fundamentally challenged existing Japanese cosmologies. The dominant *Sangoku* ("Three Realms") cosmological frame, derived from Buddhist cosmologies, posited a tripartite universe comprising the "Three Realms" of *Wagachō/ Honchō* ("Our Land"), *Shintan* (the Continent, equated with Kara), and *Tenjiku* (the land of buddhas and bodhisattvas, often equated with *Indo*, or India).[24] Japanese traveled to and from *Kara* or *Morokoshi* (China, which included Korea cognitively), and people came to Japan from there; Kara was "real," in that it was within the realm of potential quotidian experience.[25] Tenjiku, however, was beyond ordinary human experience, for no Japanese was known ever to have journeyed thither and returned to speak of it; nor did Tenjiku-ites visit Japan. Tenjiku, that is, comprised all that was "trans-Kara." Kara was *ikoku*, "the other country"; Tenjiku, by contrast, was part of *ikai*, "the other world," inhabited by buddhas and demons alike.

Kara-ites were thus "familiar" Others. And in a Sangoku cosmology where one "realm" was beyond experience, they were the modal Other against which identity could be measured.[26] The "discovery" in the sixteenth century of lands "beyond Kara," to which people might actually travel, and whence people arrived—in small droves—fundamentally challenged the viability of the Sangoku cosmology, and introduced a multitude of new, radically different "realms," that had never been imagined; it also produced new and radical

---

23   Early Heian texts refer to the inhabitants of northeastern Honshu who had not submitted to the authority of the court as "hairy people" (毛人, glossed both *mōjin* and *Emishi*). See Araki (1993); Kojima (1984).

24   J. *Shintan* (Ch. *Zhendan*) is a Chinese coinage used to render the Skt. *Cīnasthāna* ("China") in Chinese translations of Buddhist texts. *Cīnasthāna*, in turn, is believed to derive from Ch. *Qin*, the name of the first unified Chinese empire, 221–206 BCE). *NKD* (7: 665).

25   *Kara* and *morokoshi* are indigenous Japanese words that could denote either "China" or "Korea," and were assigned the character *tang/tō*.

26   Other alterities might be recognized from time to time, particularly the Emishi or Ezo identities north and east of Wagachō and island peoples either beyond Ezo or south of the seas south of Wagachō, but I would argue that they were, by the mid-sixteenth century, marginalized alterities that were not highly valenced in the discourse of Japanese identity. These identities, too, became more highly charged particles in the discourse after the Iberian irruption.

alterities, not only European, but African, Southeast and Southern Asian, and even American, into Japanese consciousness. This explosion of new alterities, I believe, collapsed the cognitive and psychological distance between "Our Realm" and the old, familiar "proximate Others" of Kara, and provoked a burst of energy devoted to the production of new distance between the peoples of "Our Realm" and those of the old, no-longer-quite-viable Kara.

That these radical Others, the first Europeans in Japan, Portuguese and Spaniards, were greeted by a host of epithets on their arrival, should not be surprising. That they were called, inter alia, "Indians" (*Tenjikujin*), is high irony, considering Columbus's error in "Indianizing" the peoples he had encountered in the Caribbean a half-century earlier, and half a world away; later, they came to be called "southern barbarians" (Nanban), a name that remains with them. These *Tenjikujin*-as-Southern Barbarians were often *pictured* as heavily beard-ed in the so-called "Nanban art" that flourished between ca. 1560 and 1630; but their perceived hairiness gave rise to no "hair-rhetoric." Nor were north-ern Europeans (Hollanders and Englishmen) called "hairy" when they came to Japan in substantial numbers in the early seventeenth century, though they were marked rhetorically by the ascribed *color* of their hair: they were labeled Kōmō, or "red-hairs." Though the representation of difference by reference to hair was established in both Chinese and Japanese discourse long before the arrival of the Iberians,[27] hirsuteness, *per se*, was not initially a key signifier of the alienness of the European intruders.

The birth of this new "hairy barbarian" is thus not attributable simply to the thicker beards and body hair (if indeed they are) of Caucasians. Indeed, pejorative characterizations of what Napier calls "foreign bodies" are *not* based on empirical observations of objective physical characteristics of those bod-ies "as they are."[28] Rather, they are representations produced, in this instance, by Japanese and then inscribed upon the image of the foreign—the Korean, Chinese, Ryukyuan, Ainu, or "western"—body. The fact that Chinese, Japanese, Ryukyuans and Koreans may *seem*—at least to "our" eyes—to be hirsute in more-or-less equal degree, i.e., to have about the same volume or density of fa-cial and body hair, merely reinforces this point: representations are generated by the representing culture; they are produced at the representing Center and imposed upon the represented margins; they are not merely inert stereotypes derived from "objective" or "dispassionate" observation of the Other (for the moment assuming that to be possible). As such, these representations tell us

---

27   Kojima (1984) examines the construction in Nara- and Heian-era discourse of "hairy east-
      ern barbarians" at the Japanese frontier. See also Araki (1993).
28   Napier (1992).

nothing about the bodies being inscribed, but rather, speak eloquently about the culture that is doing the inscribing.

In Edward Said's terms, seventeenth-century Japanese were "Orientalizing" the foreign Other.[29] Said is persuasive in arguing that there is no empirical basis for the representation in the represented itself, and in showing that European Orientalists got their representations of "the Orient" somehow "wrong." He does not, however, say much about what the process of representation tells us about the culture of the *marginalizing* Center, the represented, beyond stating the obvious, that the act of representation is an act of power, and that Centers demonstrate that power by the fact of representing. In this discussion, by contrast, I accept as given that representations are instrumental and constitutive. Almost by design, representations "get it wrong" in the empirical sense, precisely because their aims are not empirical, but instrumental: they are concerned with the construction of objects of representation—the "self" as well as the "other"—as such, and as amenable to manipulation. In the seventeenth century, Japanese were confronted with an epistemological and cosmological crisis of unprecedented scale, the collapse of the earlier "Three Realms" cosmological frame that represented the world, and its replacement by a cosmology of "Myriad Realms" (*bankoku*). I am concerned in this chapter most particularly with the production of ethnic identity and cultural difference through the representation of difference in hairiness or tonsorial practices; however, hair is but one site of many where identity, difference and boundaries were represented and contested in Edo-period popular practice.

These representations of China, Korea, and other Others, are constitutive, most importantly of *Japanese* identities. They perform this operation by displaying characteristics that invert the believed or desired cultural identity of Japan and Japanese, the represented. In doing so, they reveal in the representation of what is beyond the margins, the discovery in Other of what Susan Stewart has called "antipodal expectations" in alterity.[30] Japanese representations marginalize or Other China (as well as Korea, Ryūkyū and, later, the Ainu)—a rhetorical strategy I have discussed elsewhere—by focusing a constitutive gaze on, imposing a representation upon, the Chinese body in the Japanese imaginary. Further, Japanese are reflexively articulating a *Japanese* identity by negating "China," as an excluded Other, and distinguishing themselves from it.[31] Later, of course, in the eighteenth and nineteenth centuries, the West also became the object of this negation/inscription, as Japan Orientalized the West. The point here is that these representations are *dynamic* and *effective*, and that

29   Said (1978).
30   Stewart (1989).
31   See Toby (1985).

in studying them, we learn much about the *represent-er*, but next to nothing about the represent-*ed*.

The process of representation is for many historians firmly embedded in the objective qualities of the thing being represented. The Korean and Chinese origins (as *represented* or *signified* quantities) of the "hairy" barbarian underscore the absurdity of this: The seeming "empirical" absurdity of Japanese calling Chinese "hairy barbarians" serves to detach the representation from the represented, and turns the reader's focus to the issue of why Japanese produced this particular representation of alterity at a given historical moment.

If we were to accept, hypothetically, that Morohashi's etymology is correct, the emergence of this racial epithet ought to reflect contact with Caucasians, who first appeared in Japan in the mid-sixteenth century.[32] Caucasian hair, its color and consistency, as well as European hairstyles, beards, etc., caused great comment, and generated the term *Kōmō* (red-hairs), to distinguish the English and the Dutch "red-hairs" from the Iberians, who had come earlier—and who were not tagged with a "hairy" pejorative. Morohashi to the contrary notwithstanding, the "hairy barbarian" does not spring from a European genealogy.

To the contrary, I shall show that the *ketōjin* epithet is true to its apparent literal meaning, that it emerged as a term of contempt for "Chinese" (understood broadly, as it was in seventeenth and eighteenth-century Japan to include Koreans, Ryukyuans, and Southeast Asians), as the embedded term *tōjin* suggests, at the historical conjuncture of specific changes in Japanese, Chinese (and perhaps Korean) cultural practice, and political conditions, at a particular moment in Japanese and, more broadly, in East Asian and world history. In the mid-seventeenth century, both the Chinese (more precisely, Qing/Manchu) and Japanese states attempted to produce populations of what Foucault has called "docile bodies," human bodies/subjects made to conform by a "new micro-physics of power" imposed upon them.[33] Within the calculus of that

---

32   It goes without saying that it is not, however. Since Japanese dictionaries generally give "examples" (*yōrei*) rather than a true *locus classicus*, it is sometimes difficult to credit their explanations of the earliest meaning of a term. The best lexicographer's explanation I have seen of why the word *ketōjin* first appeared is in Ōtsuki (1891/1984): "*Tōjin* means foreigner; in an age when Japanese [*hōjin*] shaved their beards, they were so-called because they grew beards. Said equally of Chinese, Hollanders, and other Europeans. *Later*, a pejorative term" (emphasis added). Ōtsuki, too, is slightly off the mark, and his exemplum is not helpful about origins—either in timing or in meaning—as it is an eighteenth-century apocryphon falsely attributed to Bashō. Ono (1975, 18–19), in a rather confused passage entitled "Kōmō; ketōjin," seems to suggest agreement with Ōtsuki.

33   Michel Foucault (1995, 135–169), proposes a "micro-physics of power" applied in the creation of "docile bodies," part of a transition from a penal regime of corporal punishments to one of confinements. Some of the applications of power in Japan and China were more brutally macro- than micro-physical, for bodies that refused to be gentled might lose

micro-physics, both the Tokugawa and the Qing states inscribed their hege-
monies on the docile bodies of their subjects—more precisely, attempted to
render wild and resistant bodies docile by inscription—most visibly in the imposition of constraints on male hair-styles and tonsorial practice. It is this moment, and these changes in cultural practice and mutual perception in Japan
and China, I shall argue, that were the instance—though not necessarily the
agent—prompting the emergence of the epithet and notion of the "hairy barbarian," in Japanese imagination and expression.

The first half of the seventeenth century were years of momentous change
in East Asia, comprising both the dénouement of a century of civil war and
beginnings of the Pax Tokugawa in Japan, and the Qing, i.e., Manchu conquest
of China—not to mention the impact of the post-Columbian wave of global
exchange of the previous century. The Tokugawa and Qing states each sought
to inscribe submission onto male bodies in the most visible of places: legislation regulating and prescribing normative (mostly male) hairstyles—and proscribing non-normative ones—in both Japan and China signified new systems
of domination and subordination for all to see.[34]

Ironically, the practices imposed on Japanese and Chinese male bodies were
mutual mirror-images: From the seventeenth century to the mid-nineteenth
most adult Japanese males were required to depilate—by either shaving or
plucking—the center of their pates, from the hairline back to the crown, leaving the sides long, and were prohibited from wearing facial hair. The depilated
pate, known as the *sakayaki*, was not new in the seventeenth century; what
was new was that it became legally mandatory for adult samurai and commoner males.[35] (Figs. 66, 67, 68 & 69) The Manchu rulers of China required
Chinese men to shave the entire head, back to the ears, *except for the crown*.
Japanese men bound their hair in an oiled, unplaited topknot; Manchu and
(after ca. 1644) Chinese men braided theirs.[36]

---

more than their hair; both life and limb were, quite literally, at stake, in China as well as
in Japan.

34 The gentling of Japan's martial caste is the subject of Eiko Ikegami's stimulating work
(1995). Ikegami briefly mentions hairstyles in her discussion of deviance (203–211) but
does not analyze them in depth. Significantly, there were no changes in the male tonsorial
regime in Chosŏn (Korea).

35 These rules applied to most adult male samurai and commoners; there were different,
but distinct, tonsorial regime for the Kyoto nobility, for physicians, Confucian scholars,
Shinto and Buddhist religious, and outcast/outcaste (*hinin* and *kawata* [or *eta*]) males. To
my knowledge, the earliest reference to the *sakayaki* is a comment in *Gyokuyō* (Kujō 1969,
592) dated Angen 2.7.8 (1175/8/14). For a brief note on the origins of the *sakayaki*, Ōhara
(1988, 39).

36 For concise discussions of the tonsorial practices entailed by the queue, Entenmann
(1974); Cheng (1988).

FIGURE 66   A samurai has his *sakayaki* shaved at an outdoor barber stall
             at the west end of Gojō Bridge, Kyoto. Iwasa Matabei, *Rakuchū
             rakugai-zu byōbu*, pair of six-panel folding screens, early
             seventeenth century. Color on gold-leafed paper, Tokyo National
             Museum. Detail, left screen, panel 5.

The adult male tonsorial regime of Chosŏn Korea, in contrast to both Qing
China and Tokugawa Japan, mandated preserving both hair and beard, as prescribed in the *Classic of Filial Piety*: "Our body, skin and hair are all received
from our parents; we dare not injure them. This is the first priority in filial duty."[37] Continued adherence to this corporeal expression of the central
Confucian precept of filiality, especially after the Manchus imposed the queue
on their Chinese subjects, became a point of Korean pride; the contrast with
Japanese tonsorial practice, too, reinforced a self-image of Korean cultural superiority and Japanese barbarity.[38]

37   de Bary & Bloom (1999, 236). *Xiaojing*, "Kaizong mingyi," 1: *Shen ti fa mu, shou zhi fumu,
      bugan huishang, xiao zhi shi ye* (身體髮膚、受之父母、不敢毀傷、孝之始也).
38   Kim Igyŏm, a secretary in the 1764 mission to Edo wrote of "the Japanese spectators" as
      they marched by, "the men shave their heads, leaving only the [hair] at the back, which

FIGURE 67   A range of male hairstyles depicted at the west end of Gojō Bridge,
Kyoto. Iwasa Matabei, *Rakuchū rakugai-zu byōbu*, pair of six-panel
folding screens, early seventeenth century. Color on gold-leafed paper,
Tokyo National Museum. Detail, left screen, panel 5.

FIGURE 68   Nearly all the samurai in this retinue of a person of rank have unshaved pates,
and many have facial hair. Iwasa Matabei, *Rakuchū rakugai-zu byōbu*, pair
of six-panel folding screens, early seventeenth century. Color on gold-leafed
paper, Tokyo National Museum. Detail, Right screen, panel 5.

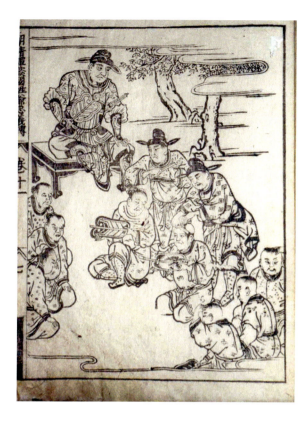

FIGURE 69
Chinese men in Beijing
being forced to go under the
razor and adopt the Manchu
tonsorial regime. From Ukai
(1717, vol. 11).

It is important, also, to note that the contexts from which the *ketōjin* epithet
emerged seem to have been highly gendered. The congeries of cultural practices that surrounded the appearance of *ketōjin* were primarily engendered in
inscriptions of the state's domination on *male* bodies: One does not find comparable attempts at state control of *female* tonsorial practice.[39] And the cultural productions through which the new term of opprobrium was recorded,
re-produced, and visually re-inscribed, were overwhelmingly statements *by*
and *about* men and men's bodies. *Ketōjin*, that is, was articulated by *male* gaze
directed at *male* bodies; the world of women was largely invisible.

Similarly, we can detect a gendered shift in the Japanese gaze across the seas,
at the "world's peoples," or peoples of "strange" or "foreign" lands (*bankoku;*

they shape like a chili pepper (*goch'u*); they go barefoot, nor do they wear trousers ..."
Kim (1999, 123).

39   This is not to say there were not distinctive female hairstyles and other forms of inscrip-
      tion on the female body, in both China and Japan. The most distinctive of these, perhaps,
      was the Chinese practice of female foot binding. Women's hairstyles serve as signs of eth-
      nicity in *Kokusen'ya kassen*. For a brief discussion, see Toby (1996b).

ikoku), between the vision of the late sixteenth to mid-seventeenth centuries, and the century to follow. Earlier taxonomies of the world's peoples, a common theme in maps, paintings, and prints, presented a bi-gendered universe of couples from "all the countries" of the world. But toward the end of the seventeenth century, representation of the "world's peoples," or peoples of "strange" or "foreign" lands, shifted to representations that excluded women—except in the mythic Amazonian "land of women" (*nyonin-koku*).[40] In the late eighteenth century, women reappeared in *bankoku* taxonomies, and remained visible to the end of the Edo period. It is difficult to explain these gender shifts in gaze. Foreign women were almost never seen in Japan, until the 1860s, but their empirical absence does little to help us understand their discursive appearances and disappearances.

2   The First Hairy Barbarians

The first step in an archaeology of *ketōjin* must begin with its own beginnings. When did the word first appear, and what did it purport? The now-common racial epithet *ketōjin* is absent from the authoritative *Vocabulario da Lingoa de Iapam* (1603), published by the Jesuit mission in Japan.[41] The *Vocabulario*, compiled by foreigners, is understandably sensitive to Japanese terms for aliens; the absence of *ketō* or *ketōjin* is strong evidence that the term had not emerged in the first half-century of contact with Caucasians. (*Kōmō* is also absent from the *Vocabulario*.)

The earliest written example of the term I have found thus far is in the chanter's script for a puppet play (*jōruri*) of 1665, *Usa Hachiman no yurai* (The history of the god Hachiman): "Hairy *Tōjin*!" the legendary empress Jingū declaims, as she prepares her invasion of the continent, "Mere mortals cannot prevail [against the power of the divine command]. The gods command that we rout them...."[42] Ironically, the "hairy *Tōjin*" in question are not "Chinese" at all, but "Koreans" (from Silla and Paekche), who are foolish enough to resist the

---

40   The "humans" (*jinbutsu*) in the *Bankoku jinbutsu-zu* (1647) and the encyclopedia *Kinmō zui* (1665) were depicted in male-female couples, as were the peoples decorating late-sixteenth-century Japanese world maps; Terajima Ryōan's massive encyclopedia, *Wakan sansai zue* (1712), by contrast, depicts only male types for each country.

41   Doi *et al.*, trans. (1980), translation of Collegio de Iapam da Companhia de Iesus (1603).

42   *Kimi eibun atte sayō ni shinzū o wataru. Ketōjin! Shin no chikara nite utsu koto kanōmaji. Ōi o motte taiji sen to no senji nite, katajikenakumo mizukara yumiya wo taishitamatsurite, toki no itaru o machitamō. Dewa no Jō* (1665).

empress's divinely ordained—though thoroughly mythic—"conquest" of the Three Kingdoms of ancient Korea.

It is important to note that the world of *jōruri* is the world of orality: *Jōruri* playwrights wrote for an audience of *listeners*—playgoers—rather than readers of a written text. A vocabulary not intelligible on the audience's first hearing, therefore, would communicate no meaning. It is therefore reasonable to infer that the word *ketōjin* had been well-established in streetcorner parlance quite some time before the first performances of *Usa Hachiman no yurai* in 1665—though how long before, we cannot be sure.

By the mid-1670s, a decade after *Usa Hachiman no yurai* first appeared in print, the association of hairiness/beardedness with foreigners was so well-established that a thesaurus for *haikai* poets listed *Tōjin* as one of the words appropriate to link with *hige* (beard). This poets' guide to beard associations includes: "Shrimp, yams, white radish, mountain potato, ginseng, whales, catfish, rats, cats, katydids, dragons, moss, Tenjin, *Tōjin, ebisu, Ezo-jin* ("peoples of Ezo," i.e., the Ainu)."[43] Writing for an oral medium (the audience, of course, did not have the script), the *jōruri* playwright—whether Chikamatsu, or the author of *Usa Hachiman*, was limited to vocabulary already well established in popular discourse, in order for the audience to understand: *ketō/ketōjin* was part of Japanese oral discourse well before 1665, when it first appears in writing.

Ketōjin—along with *higetōjin* (bearded *Tōjin*)—also appears frequently in the dialogue of Chikamatsu Monzaemon's puppet plays whenever Japanese characters encounter Chinese, particularly in *Taishokan* (1711), *The Battles of Coxinga* (1715), and *The Latter-day Battles of Coxinga* (1716). *Battles* was perhaps the greatest first-run hit of the puppet stage, running from 1715 to 1717 at Osaka's Takemoto-za; it recounts the highly fictionalized exploits of Zheng Chenggong, better known in Japan as Kokusen'ya ("Coxinga" is how he appears in Dutch records.) Chikamatsu's hero Watōnai (Coxinga's "real" name in the play, meaning "betwixt Japanese and Chinese") in China.[44] Tonsorial tropes figure in several of the source works Chikamatsu drew on for his *Battles* and,

---

43   Takase (1677/1969): 520. Tenjin: apotheosis of the Heian courtier Sugawara no Michizane (845–903); *Tōjin*: Chinese/foreigners; *ebisu*: both "northern barbarians" and one of the "seven gods of good luck" (*shichifukujin*); *Ezo-jin*: "people of Ezo," i.e., Ainu.

44   Chikamatsu's Watōnai/Coxinga is based on Zheng Chenggong (1624–62), born in the Japanese port town of Hirado to the Chinese merchant/pirate Zheng Zhilong (1604–61) and his Japanese wife, whose natal surname was "Tagawa." In an earlier *Coxinga* play that Chikamatsu would almost certainly have attended, Nishiki Bunryū's *Kokusen'ya tegara nikki* (Nishiki 1701), the chanter's text speaks only of Chinese taking on "Japanese customs" (*Nihon no fū*), but the corresponding illustration prefigures Chikamatsu's tonsorial imagery even though hair plays no role in the *text*. On Coxinga and his father, see Ishihara (1942; 1945; 1986), Guo (1979), Yuan *et al.* (1957), Terao (1986), etc.; in English, Keene (1951,

as I have argued elsewhere, tonsorial images and epithets are a recurring trope throughout Chikamatsu's entire *Coxinga* cycle—indeed, in almost every iteration of the Coxinga legend in Japanese fiction, drama and art, both before and after Chikamatsu.[45]

Tonsorial imagery is a less frequent trope in Ejima Kiseki's *Coxinga and the Great Pacification of Ming China* (1717), an *ukiyo-zōshi* (prose fiction) almost certainly written to capitalize on the "Coxinga" craze Chikamatsu's hit play had engendered. Still, Kiseki's preface sets the tone of his *Coxinga* tale, not coincidentally highlighting a moment in Chikamatsu's play that underscores the significance of tonsorial practice in distinguishing self from Other:[46]

> "How pleasing (*kokochiyoshi*) to see the papier-mâché tigers from beyond Senri lined up in the doll-makers' shops, [the tigers] Watōnai tamed and *shaved off their three-finger beards.*[47] The pattern-makers and *ukiyo-e* artists are all big fans of Watōnai, who is all the rage; [they depict] Coxinga transforming ancient Chinese style to Japanese customs, forcing the *ketōjin* to shave themselves into a *sakayaki* [Japanese-style shaved pate; see Figs. 69 & 70] and to put their hair up in a [Japanese-style] topknot.... Puppet theaters, of course, but even the merchants working temple fairs (*kaichō*) make money off [Watōnai's father] Old Ikkan.[48]

76–85) explores the literary sources from which Chikamatsu worked, but makes no mention of Bunryū's *Kokusen'ya tegara nikki*.

45   Toby (1996b). More than twenty Edo-period works of narrative history, drama or prose fiction are grounded in the exploits of the historical Zheng Chenggong (1624–1662), the model for Watōnai. Among the most important, Ukai (1661), was reprinted in an illustrated edition to exploit the success of *Battles* (Ukai 1717); see, e.g., Ukai (1717, 11: 6b–71) for an account of Dorgon imposing the queue on Chinese officials. Tonsorial imagery also figures in Nishiki Bunryū's 1701 puppet play, *Kokusen'ya tegara nikki* (A Diary of Coxinga's Exploits, Nishiki [1701]).

46   Ejima (1717/1933, 377); cf. Ejima (1717/1933, 341). On the relationship of Kiseki's *Kokusen'ya* fiction to Chikamatsu's hit play see Ishikawa (1988).

47   Where Chikamatsu's Watōnai tames one tiger, Kiseki's bests two of them. Kiseki (1717): 365–366.

48   Ejima (1717, 3). "Ikkan" was an epithet for Watōnai's father, Zheng Zhilong (1604–1661). In contemporary European texts he is often known as "Nicholas Iquan." The *sakayaki*, or shaved male pate, apparently originated in medieval battlefield practice, when samurai shaved their pates the better to secure their helmets. In times of peace, they regrew their hair, which they covered with an *eboshi*, or court cap. In the endemic warfare of the Warring States era (1467–1573), however, when samurai had to be battle-ready at all times, the *sakayaki* became the standard samurai hairstyle. See Itō (1997, 53) for a discussion.

Although Watōnai is the son of a Chinese father and a Japanese mother, throughout the play Chikamatsu consistently identifies him as quintessentially Japanese; it is his Japaneseness, and the protection of Amaterasu, the Japanese sun goddess, that give him heroic qualities. Chikamatsu's (and the audience's) contempt for Chinese, who have accepted an alien sovereign in the Manchus, expresses itself in an array of epithets, *ketōjin* and *hige-tōjin* most prominent among them. Hair, as noted above, and men's hair in particular, is an important, recurring trope throughout Chikamatsu's *Coxinga* cycle for signifying ethnic identification, not only in the words of the script, but in the way the play is presented on both the puppet and *kabuki* stages, and re-presented in playbill illustrations, illustrated printed texts, festival performances, prints and paintings, so we will return to examine the themes of hair/no-hair in that text below.[49]

A century later, however, the signification of *ketōjin* was becoming confused. For some authors, like Hiraga Gennai, and his equally irreverent contemporary, Ōta Nanpo, the *ketōjin* remained "Chinese," but for others, the notion had begun to wear European dress. In Gennai's *jōruri* play *Shinrei yaguchi no watashi* (1770), the *ketōjin* was still Chinese: "Hey! Blabbermouth *ketōjin*, with your wordy classical quotations! Justifying your surrender to the enemy/barbarian (*teki*)."[50] That same year Nanpo predicated his entire *Neboke Sensei bunshū* (The collected works of Prof. Sleepyhead) on the oppositional identity of "hairy-barbarian" Chinese, from its attribution to a "Mr. Nonsense, the Hairy *Tōjin*" (*Ketō no* Chin Punkan) as author, through the opening line of the text, "Mr. Chin Punkan, the *ketō*, likes to decorate his rhetoric with cut-and-paste quotations from the classics," to its conclusion that, "*Ketō* of later ages may use this collection to finish their sleep-talk, I have [recorded] all that I talk-in-my-sleep."[51]

---

49 For a brief discussion of tonsorial metaphors in *Kokusen'ya kassen*, see Toby (1996c). Chikamatsu continued to exploit these tonsorial themes in his sequel, *Kokusen'ya gonichi kassen*, which opened to a brief run in Osaka in 1716. Fujii (1925–1928, 10: 1–128).

50 *Namanuruki ketōjin no hikigoto. Ima teki e kudatte.* Hiraga (1961, 339). *Teki*, "enemy," is homophonous with *teki*, "northern barbarian," referring to the Manchus. A few years later, in a *kabuki* play reprising Hideyoshi's Korean invasions of 1592–98, "Katō Masakiyo" (i.e., Katō Kiyomasa, whose actual name was banned from the stage) announces that he will "'head for Kyūshū, join the massed armies conquering the Three Korean kingdoms (*sankan*), and tear off the heads of those *ketōjin*,' and so saying, grabbed a *Tōjin* doll from the candy-vendor's goods and tore it in half." Nakamura (1786/1931, 1:315–316).

51 Ōta Nanpo, *Neboke Sensei shū*, in Hamada, Nakano, Hino, and Ibi (1985–1990, 1:341–366). *Chinpunkan*, in Nanpo's text, is one of many nonsense terms in the lexicon of what I call *wasei Tōjin-kotoba*, made-in-Japanese babble that sounds "Chinese"; it was a favorite of poets, playwrights, and fiction writers in the Edo period. *Ketō* also makes an appearance

Yet the signification of *ketōjin* was in flux, for in an anonymous *senryū* (comic verse) of just three years earlier, *Ketōjin! hadaka ni naru ni kohanji*: "Hairy *Tōjin*! It takes you half an hour to strip to the buff!" which the commentator takes to refer to Hollanders, whose mysterious buttons must surely have impeded quick undressing when they visited the brothels of Nagasaki's Maruyama district.[52] And yet more jingoistically: "The *ketōjin*'s unrequited love: Sakuyahime" (*Ketōjin oyobanu koi wa Sakuyahime*: Sakuyahime is the divinity of Mt. Fuji, the divine representation of Japan, for which the Westerners longed.[53] Mitamura Engyo (1870–1952), that tireless chronicler of the customs of the "Edo" he was born just too late to experience firsthand, underscored the confusion with a quotation from a play of 1799: "Dutch red-hairs or hairy Chinamen, what's the difference!"[54]

3   With a Flick of the Razor

As I shall show below, the context from which the *ketōjin* emerged was not solely dramatic or verbal: there were changes in *both* Chinese *and* Japanese tonsorial practice, in Chinese domestic and international politics, and in Japanese notions of China, that constituted the milieu in which this racial epithet would rise and flourish.

Men's cultivation of facial hair had been socially acceptable—even mandatory—in Japanese practice from the twelfth to the sixteenth centuries. Indeed, as Murai has shown, deviation from "Japanese" hair style practices were signs to the traveler that he/she had strayed beyond "Japan."[55] For the "manly" (*otokodate*), at least, in the late Sengoku era and into the earliest years of Tokugawa rule, a lush beard was so important that those who could not grow them bought them or made them. Toyotomi Hideyoshi, described by Oda Nobunaga as a "bald rat" (*hagenezumi*), for example, was only one of the—likely—thousands of his tonsorially challenged contemporaries in the late sixteenth century who made up for pilatory inadequacy by decorating their faces with false beards. As Hideyoshi's biographer observed, "Besides his usual false beard (*tsukurihige*),

---

in Nanpo's comic fiction *Koitsu wa Nihon* (1784), as does *keshi-bōzu*, another tonsorial image likening the Manchu queue to the fruit of the poppy: "The young lord Fu-wang of Great Ming surrendered to the Tatars and became a *keshi-bōzu*." Ōta (1784/1985. 224).

52   Hamada (1968, 154), dates this verse to 1767.
53   Okada (1984, 312).
54   *Kōmō da no ketōjin da no*, from Namiki Senryū and Nakamura Gyogan, *Morokoshi ori Nihon tekiki*, quoted in Mitamura (1975–1978, 19: 74).
55   Murai (1988).

Lord Hideyoshi also ordered false eyebrows, blackened with iron."[56] False whiskers of waxed, *sumi*-blackened paper covered the inadequacies of many a tonsorially inadequate rake in the late sixteenth and early seventeenth centuries.[57]

Whiskers, whether raised from the follicle or cosmetically produced, were much more than vanity, however, for a false beard might also save a warrior from an ignominy worse than death itself: Yamamoto Tsunetomo, writing at the turn of the eighteenth century, claims to have heard "an aged samurai" relate that—in the days when samurai actually went into battle—"The reason [samurai] wax up their mustaches is that when they take heads on the battlefield, they slice off the ears and noses of the fallen; to avoid any confusion whether it was a man or woman, they sliced off the mustache and all. At that moment, a head without a drooping mustache would be mistaken for a woman's, and just be thrown away. [Waxed whiskers] were a custom they adopted so their heads wouldn't just be thrown away [on the battlefield] after they died."[58] It is not difficult to understand, then, that a handsome beard might earn the sobriquet, "a bearded man of fearsome mien," while a beardless face brought a man such derisive epithets as "girl-face."[59] What worse fate might a samurai imagine than to be dismissed as an adversary in battle because his head would not be deemed a prize that might bring a battlefield reward.

The bearded quality of late-Sengoku Japanese notions of manliness is well captured in the late sixteenth-century *kyōgen* (farce) play, *Higeyagura* ("Beard-tower"), whose protagonist introduces himself as,

> I am a person who lives in the capital (*rakuchū*). For the upcoming Daijōe festival in the Imperial court, it was said that they wanted to give the role of carrying the rhinoceros halberd to the man with the biggest beard. But after searching everywhere in and around the capital (*rakuchū rakugai*), they found that there was no-one with a bigger beard than mine…. and

---

56   Oze Hoan (1996, 458); also quoted in Ema (1976, 262).

57   See Kitajima (1977, 139).

58   Yamamoto (1974, 575). Even if Yamamoto (1659–1721) was recalling a tale heard in his youth, his "aged samurai" must have been extremely old to recall these battles, since there had been no warfare since the Siege of Osaka, 1614–1615. This passage is far from clear. Ujiie (1995, 187) infers that the old warrior's worry is being discarded as unworthy of reward. Yamamoto's concern—which Ujiie, writing on Eros, ironically overlooks—was with male beauty in death: "If you wash your face with water every morning, then when you are cut down [*uchijini no toki*] it will not change color."

59   Ema (1976, 261–262), citing *Keichō kenbunshū*. This recalls that in medieval Iceland to charge a man with "beardlessness" was an insult to his sexual or gender identity so severe it might lead to legally justifiable blood vengeance. See Sørensen (1983, 9, 25ff.).

so I have been commanded to [perform] the role of [bearer of] the rhinoceros halberd.

The protagonist is filled with pride that his manliness has been recognized by
the Court. But his wife is less delighted, for in order to perform the role, he
will have to outfit himself with expensive clothes, present gifts to important
people, and probably entertain his friends, expenses the hard-pressed family
budget can hardly sustain. Besides, she says, "Actually, I find your beard suf-
focating, myself. Just shave it off and be done with it!" Her shocked husband,
however, cannot stand the thought of parting with his manhood, and, with
ironic echoes of Nobunaga, replies, "Whose beard do you think this is?" It is
no longer merely the beard of one man, he proclaims, "It is now the beard of
the entire realm! Anyone who lays so much as a finger on it won't get away
unscathed." To protect himself from his wife's razor, he encases his face in a
wood-lattice watchtower (*yagura*), for he would rather bankrupt his family
than lose his beard.[60]

It is not clear *why* facial hair assumed such symbolic importance in the
Sengoku era, nor why it came to be viewed as a sign of resistance to authority in the years of transition from Sengoku to Tokugawa. Yet it is clear that by
the mid- seventeenth century, facial hair, and rough-and-ready hairdos, which
had been "manly" and "heroic," for Hideyoshi and his contemporaries, had
been symbolically—and legally—transformed. As portraits of emperors, shoguns, daimyos, and depictions of commoners, attest, "straight" Japanese men
(men not beyond the margins of society; homoeroticism was quite "straight" in
seventeenth-century Japan)—or at least men in positions of political power,
capable of imposing their preferences on others—began to prefer a cleaner
mien, while lush whiskers and full heads of hair became symbols of marginal-
ity and cultural resistance. The "beard of the entire realm," sought after even by
the imperial court, had become the beard of the ruffian (*yakko-hige*), the sign
of the resister, to be suppressed by shoguns and daimyos.

Thus, although portraits of emperors and male courtiers, shoguns and lesser
warriors, from the late Heian period to the turn of the seventeenth century,
nearly without exception depicted their subjects with beards or mustaches,

60   *Higeyagura*, in Koyama (1960–1961, 43:208–212). *Higeyagura* was performed at Shōkokuji
      in Kyoto in 1563; it may be an adaptation of an earlier play, *Hige kaidate*, performed as
      early as 1464. Kitagawa (1984). In the end, of course, the man's wife and her women win,
      overwhelming his defenses with long-handled blades, rakes and tweezers; he ends up
      beardless. The women's attack is visualized in an early Edo period *Ko nō kyōgen no zu*
      (no. BK016-004), and Tsukioka Kōryū, "Higeyagura," in his album *Kyōgen gojūban* (n.d.),
      both searchable at www2.ntj.jac.go.jp/dglib/collections/ (accessed 2016/5/27).

precisely the reverse is true for their descendants after the 1630s.[61] Nobunaga and Hideyoshi, Ieyasu and Hidetada, all are rendered as bearded in the memorial portraits we have of them, as are the emperors Ōgimachi and Goyōzei, not to mention Ieyasu's loyal general Honda Tadakatsu, whose beard would be the pride of any demon of the imagination.[62] In bald contrast to these, the portraits of all shoguns from Tokugawa Iemitsu, and emperors from Gomizuno'o, to the end of the Tokugawa era show their subjects clean-shaven.

As peace reduced the opportunities for samurai to show their manliness in battle, at the same time it produced large numbers of unemployed and masterless samurai for whom their swords, and the status they symbolized, were the only remaining vestiges of pride. Masterless *rōnin*, bored *hatamoto*, and plain ruffians alike roamed the streets of Edo and lesser castle towns, starting fights, and terrorizing the innocent. For these "ruffians" (*yakko*), men who were "bent out of shape" (*kabukimono*), at mid-century, a beard—soon called a *yakko-hige* ("ruffian's beard")—and either a lush, full head of hair (*nadetsuke; sōhatsu*), or its inversion, the *ōbitai* ("large forehead"), a radically over-done *sakayaki*,[63] became proclamations of their untamed, unbowed resistance to regimentation and order. Somewhere between the 1580s and 90s, and the 1630s, beards and full heads of hair became transvalued from marks of orderly manliness, into signs of resistance to the newly established order. By the 1660s, not only was the *yakko-hige* illegal, but the *sōhatsu* (full head of hair) had likewise been outlawed for adult males in the four main status groups, in favor of a mandatory shaved pate, i.e., the *sakayaki*.[64]

These tonsorial "re-inscriptions" of state authority on the bodies—pates and faces—of the subject population were articulated in public law, at both the *bakufu* and the domain level, from at least the Genna era (1615–1623).[65] In the late Spring of 1615, and again in 1623, the *bakufu* proscribed a broad array of

---

61   Kuroda (1993, Part 3, Chapter 1) makes this point.
62   See the portraits of "Minamoto no Yoritomo," Nobunaga, Hideyoshi, Ieyasu, Tadakatsu, and Emperor Gomizuno'o in Shimizu (1988). Yonekura (1995) and Kuroda (2011; 2012) have demonstrated that the "Yoritomo" portrait is more likely a depiction of Ashikaga Tadayoshi, though some art historians dispute their conclusions.
63   The *sakayaki*, the shaved pate of adult males, was mandatory for samurai and commoners in the Edo period. The *sakayaki* was first used by medieval courtiers as a cure for fevers; the practice spread to samurai on the battlefield during the Muromachi period, and is pictured in the *Yūki kassen emaki* (c. 1490). Endō (1985).
64   Different tonsorial constraints applied to outcastes, religious professionals, physicians, Confucian scholars, and a few other status groups and occupations. On the significatory power of non-practice, see Boon's (1994) study of "circumcision/uncircumcision" in Bali.
65   Kikuchi (1991, 56–70) traces the legislation on the "customs" (*fūzoku*) that prescribed this inscription on the male body.

accoutrements and body-decoration deemed resistant to public order, including both radically overdone *sakayaki and* full heads of hair (*ōbitai; sōhatsu*), as well as a variety of exaggerated styles of swords and scabbards.[66] In mid-1645, "It was decreed [again] that swords shall be no longer than 2 *shaku* 8 *sun*, daggers no longer than 1 *shaku* 8 *sun*. Further [radical hairstyles], and large beards have been prohibited from before. Since [these prohibited hairstyles] have been seen around lately, they are re-prohibited."[67]

Daimyo domains quickly followed suit. In Tottori domain, on the Japan Sea coast of western Honshu, an edict of 1648 prohibited "Stand-up hair [*tategami*, "mane," or long hair on an unshaved pate] and hang-down whiskers [*sagehige*]," proscribing at the same time a wide range of public self-presentation deemed inimical to public order.[68] Tokushima domain, likewise, prohibited "everyone from younger kept-boys to minor samurai, [from wearing] stand-up hair, and large beards (*hige*)." And the following year, once more, "'stand-up hair' and 'hang-down beards' are prohibited.... Anyone found violating these measures shall be removed from the rolls of [the lord's retainers]."[69] *Bakufu* edicts issued between 1664 and 1680—probably repeating earlier proclamations—extended some of these tonsorial proscriptions to commoners, as well.[70]

Edicts like these had a logic of their own, given that long hair and beards had become as much signs of social rebellion in Japan, by the early 1600s, as they were in the United States and elsewhere in the capitalist world in the 1960s. The beard and the *sōhatsu*, in the aftermath of Sekigahara and Osaka, were translated into signs of resistance. What had been admired as *otokodate*, or "manliness," was transformed into *yakko-buri*, the "ruffian style"; *machi-yakko* ("town ruffians") and *hatamoto-yakko* ("bannerman ruffians") sported

---

66　*Tokugawa jikki* (1974): 39:249, entry for Genna 9 (1623) /3/26. Violators were subject to imprisonment, and their masters to a fine of two pieces of silver.

67　Ibid., 40:408, entry for Shōhō 2/7/18. Interestingly, the outrageous, prohibited hairstyles specified in the legislation are ones in which the shaving of the pate (the *sakayaki*) is too radical.

68　Ishii (1961, 52, doc. 16, Keian 1 [1648]/8/1)

69　Ishii (1962, 7, doc. 5, Shōō 2 [1653]/2/9; 9, doc. 12, Shōō 3[1654]/6/1). Both in these edicts and in the Tokushima edict noted above, the prohibitions on beards and wild hair are items in long lists of other "arts of resistance" (to use James C. Scott's [1990] term) displayed by aggressive samurai at mid-century. Other forms of "resistance" catalogued in these edicts included wearing vermilion-lacquered scabbards, swords, or dirks beyond prescribed lengths or even wearing certain kinds of kimono collars. The irony is that the "resistance" comes in this instance from members of what Scott would see as the ruling elite.

70　Takayanagi & Ishii (1958, 133; [doc. 213 {1664}]; 135 [doc. 217 {1680}]; 1241–1242 [docs. 2699 and 2700 {1670}]). Ōkurashō (1922–1925, 3:469). The tone of these edicts, however, suggests that the goal was to suppress too-blatant pandering by male prostitutes.

remarkable tonsorial constructions to demonstrate their non-submission to this new attempt at the inscription of authority on their persons. After about 1650 the hegemonic order took hold, and it became extremely difficult to survive with "stand-up hair" and "hang-down mustaches."

Nor were samurai the only targets of the authorities' regime of tonsorial discipline, which was merely one element in a much broader regulatory program aimed not only at taming the samurai. Tonsorial prescriptions and proscriptions, coupled with a network of rules correlating social station with clothing, down to the cloth used in clothing, as well as matters such as the architectural details of one's residence, were aimed at rendering one's place in the normative order of juridical status (*mibun*) regime instantly legible.[71] Prescribed hairstyles for peasants and urban commoners (i.e., merchants and artisans) were sufficiently distinct from those for samurai that contemporaries had no difficulty reading one's status position within the core four-status system (i.e., samurai, peasant, artisan & merchant)—not to mention outcasts (*hinin*) and outcastes (*kawata; eta*), Buddhist clergy, and other "marginal" status groups.[72]

Yet tonsorial distinctions within the core paled in comparison with the radical difference between the core and the status periphery—particularly outcasts (*hinin*) and outcastes (*eta*)—who were also residentially segregated both from the core status groups *and* from each other.[73] In an edict of 1723, for example, the Edo Town Magistrates observed that, while male *hinin* had long been prohibited from binding their hair in topknots, "Somewhere along the line, *hinin* began to bind their hair, and look just like *ordinary people* (*tsune no*

---

71 See, e.g., Shively (1964–65); Coaldrake (1996).

72 In late 1725, for example, the town magistrates (*machi-bugyō*) ordered Edo's *hinin* males to crop their hair short, with their pates unshaven and their heads uncovered. They noted that *hinin* men had ceased following laws banning them from wearing the topknot, and "somewhere along the way" (*itsu to naku*) had begun to look "like ordinary folk" (*tsune no mono*), causing social confusion. *Kyōhō sen'yō ruishū*, in NSSSS, 25: 150. Some Buddhist clergy and other professional religious were of relatively high social standing, and could be quite powerful, yet were outside, and hence also "marginal," in relation to the four status groups. "Marginal status" (*shūen-teki mibun*) has become a central question in recent scholarship on early modern Japan, e.g., Tsukada, Yoshida & Wakita (1994); Tsukada *et al.* (2000; 2007–08); Toshi-shi Kenkyūkai (2002); Tsukada (2010), though the concept has been expanded to include not only groups juridically excluded from the core body social, but village headmen and others who mediated between status groups.

73 The early modern regime distinguished the marginalized *hinin* and *eta*, not only from the four core *mibun* groups, but from each other, legally, functionally, and even residentially. *Zōho kaisei Sesshū chizu*, a commercially printed map of Osaka (1806), for example, locates an "*eta* village" (*eta-mura*) on the southern outskirts of the city, but a cluster of blocks near Osaka Castle as "*hinin* huts" (*hinin koya*). Discussed in Toby (2011).

mono dōzen), so that, in the end, there is *no visible sign*, so they can be mistaken for ordinary good-for-nothings (*itazuramono ni aimagire sōrō*)...."[74]

The Tokugawa bakufu and daimyos ultimately succeeded in inscribing submission on the bodies of their subjects. Much of this inscription was performed by the invisible hand of tonsorial fashion, as men shaved their scalps and their chins, seemingly in pursuit of style and good looks, rather than out of visible compulsion. Yet adult males who failed to find adequate inducement in the following winds of fashion soon faced quite severe sanctions, and were shorn of their beards, mutton-chop side-whiskers and full heads of hair, on pain of criminal penalties: as the Tottori edict put it, "violators shall be punished under criminal law."[75] Punishment could be quite severe, including fines, exposure in the public stocks, imprisonment, and even disfigurement: "Violators ... will be imprisoned; their masters subjected to a fine of two pieces of silver for each [violator in their employ]. For [masters] who keep [servants] with goatees, the fine shall be three pieces of silver," the bakufu proclaimed in 1615.[76] The lord of Okayama, Ikeda Mitsumasa, noted in his diary in late 1642 that some ruffians, "who were arrested on the first [of the month], with stand-up hair and [over-]long dirks, had both their thumbs cut off," while two of the most egregious offenders, "Had both their thumbs, and their noses, sliced off. They were banished from the province ... and exposed at Kyōbashi for two days."[77]

Now, if Tokugawa practice seems sometime Draconian, emerging practices in China under the new Manchu (i.e., Qing) regime were quite literally Dorgonian. At the very moment the bakufu and various domain regimes were beginning to regulate tonsorial practice in Japan, the Manchus likewise inscribed their hegemony on gentled Chinese bodies by the imposition of the tonsorial regime we call the "queue" (Manchu, *soncoho*; Ch., *bianzi* or *bianfa*) as a sign of submission.[78] The Manchu armies had imposed the queue, the standard hairstyle for adult males in Manchu custom, on Chinese in the areas

---

74 Kobayashi (1981, 116), emphasis added. Separate edicts pro/prescribed hairstyles for *eta*; e.g., an 1840 edict, ibid., 338, that specified permitted hairstyles for both men and women of the *eta* status group.

75 Ishii (1961, 52, doc. 16).

76 Ishii (1959–1961, 4:226 [entry dated Genna 1{1615}/5/15]).

77 *Ikeda Mitsumasa nikki* (Tokyo: Kokusho Kankōkai, 1983): 43.

78 Chinese chroniclers from Sima Qian in the early Han labeled the braided coiffures of various northern border peoples *bianfa*. On the pre-Qing history of the *bianfa* see Godley (1994); Kuwabara (1913/1968); Shiratori (1929). "Queue," from the Latin *cauda* ("tail"), by way of Old and Middle French, and Anglo-Norman, was applied to the braided tail of men's wigs by the early eighteenth century—as was "pigtail." I am uncertain when "queue" was first applied to the Chinese *bianzi*; the OED cites an 1874 reference to the "black pig-tails" of Chinese. On-line *Oxford English Dictionary*.

they conquered from early on, at least as early as the capture of Liaoyang in 1621. There was strong Chinese resistance to the queue, for it violated core tenets of Confucian belief that since the body, including the hair, was a gift from one's parents it was an act of filial piety to preserve it intact, so enforcement was uneven before 1644.[79]

Upon capturing Beijing in the Spring of 1644, however, the Manchu regent and supreme commander, Prince Dorgon, commanded his officers to shave the heads of the people; he even decreed death for those who merely memorialized against the queue.[80] "All should shave their heads," Dorgon commanded in mid-1644, "If there are willful offenders, then we shall surely exterminate them!"[81] The prefect of Jiangyin, on the south bank of the Yangzi, was perhaps more poetic, announcing, "Keep your head, lose your hair; keep you hair, lose your head!"[82] There are some provocative debates as to how the Manchus themselves read the queue; ample evidence suggests that the Manchus saw shaving and braiding in the pattern of the queue as a sign of manliness—it was the standard adult-male hairstyle—while Chinese in the sixteenth century may have read it as a denial of masculinity.[83] "Ironically," as Philip A. Kuhn observes, "what to the Manchu warriors symbolized manliness, to the Chinese symbolized effeminacy."[84]

Yet, however Chinese read the Manchu tonsorial regime, one thing is clear: there were radical changes in the ways that the two emergent hegemonic orders of seventeenth-century East Asia, the Tokugawa and Qing regimes, inscribed their power onto the normally visible parts of the male body, at approximately the same moment, demanding that subjects exhibit signs of conformity and submission. The hairstyles required of men in Japan and China were diametrically opposed, and Japanese noticed this tonsorial inversion very quickly.

In the mid-1640s, as the Southern Ming was attempting to survive, even seeking military aid from Japan, merchant ships arrived in Nagasaki, both from Southern Ming "loyalist" areas, and from Manchu-controlled areas of China. The Nagasaki authorities decided which of these ships would be permitted

---

79   See n. 37 above. On resistance to the queue in the Jiangnan region see Wakeman (1975).
80   Entenmann (1974). I am grateful to Prof. Entenmann for providing me with a copy of his
        paper.
81   Wakeman (1985, 1:414).
82   Wakeman (1975, 58).
83   Entenmann (1974); Struve (1984); Wakeman (1975; 1985); Kuhn (1990, esp. 53–56). It is iron-
        ic, as Ryū (1990) reminds us, that for many Chinese at the end of the Qing dynasty, such
        as Lu Xun's "Ah-Q," the queue had been revalued as a positive sign of Chinese identity,
        threatened by new Western encroachments.
84   Kuhn (1990, 58).

to trade, and shogunal sympathies were clearly with the pro-Ming loyalists: Ships whose crews wore the queue were "northern barbarian" ships, and were barred from trading; ships whose crews wore a full head of hair were admitted. As early as 1646, Japanese regulations barred Chinese traders from Manchu-held areas, whom they identified by their queues: "The Nanjingese who came with their hair done in the *prohibited* Tatar style were allowed to trade their goods, this time only, but are prohibited from voyaging here again," the Dutch *Opperhoofd* noted on 27 July. and on 10 September, "Some junks entered port. But as the crews of both ships have shaved their heads, as in accordance with the previous case, they will not be allowed to trade."[85]

The Japanese authorities, that is, almost instantly recognized this "strange" hairstyle, ironically almost the reverse of that which Japanese "order" demanded domestically, as a marker of a new cultural and ethnic distinction.[86] The culture of the Japanese streets and stage soon noticed the tonsorial boundary, as well, transforming beards and hair into signs of ethnic identity as never before.

4   Bearded Boundaries

As Japanese tonsorial practice with regard to hair was transformed by both legal compulsion and evolving fashion, visual media and performance moved to the representation of Other as increasingly hirsute, contrasting starkly with more clean-shaven Japanese. In earlier seventeenth-century representations of Korean, Chinese, and other Asian visitors to Japan, the iconographic master trope centered on clothing rather than on corporeal characteristics. Yet with the imposition of Japanese restrictions on male hairstyles at mid-century, one can detect an increasing emphasis on the beards, eyebrows, and general hairiness of Other in Japanese popular art. By the middle of the eighteenth century, Koreans, Chinese, and others were identified as Other by cues such as full

---

85   Murakami (1938–1939, 3:34, 50). See Toby (1984, 139–140). Emphasis added: This suggests that there had been a specific bakufu proscription on trading by queued Chinese, though I have yet to find the text of that edict. The *Opperhoofd* was the chief of the Dutch trading outpost in Nagasaki

86   The queue/*bianzi* also became a marker of both self-identity and othering when Chinese formed émigré communities in Southeast Asia, Europe and the Americas. See, e.g., Skinner (1957) on Chinese in Thai society, later challenged by Tejapira (1992); Ross (2013); etc. Marshall (2011) argues that Chinese in Manitoba abandoned the queue as a repudiation of the Manchus, and adopted "Western" hairstyles to proclaim their identification with the 1911 revolution and embrace of a "modern" identity.

heads of hair, bushy eyebrows, mustache and beard, and even by a hint of fur
on their garments.

The radical changes seen in Japanese male tonsorial practice in the seventeenth century imparted new dimensions of ethnicity to the signifying power
of hair and beards as cultural practice. Facial hair had been a feature of the
secular adult male visage for a millennium, as we have seen, and, in the sixteenth century, a mark of virility and bravery so essential to male identity
that tonsorially challenged men—like Toyotomi Hideyoshi—wore fake paper
beards blacked with India ink, and stiffened with wax.[87] Yet as, from the early
seventeenth century, state power and the winds of fashion moved to depilate
the Japanese male face, even while requiring the shaving of the pate, Japanese
popular culture began resorting to tonsorial difference as a marker of ethnic
identity. As early as the first decade of the seventeenth century, chroniclers
began likening a bearded face to "northern barbarians" (*Ezo-ga-shima no hito*).
Edicts became progressively stricter, proscribing facial hair and side-whiskers,
and requiring men to shave their pates, and by the 1660s, on the eve of the earliest recorded use of the term *ketō*, the proscription had been extended beyond
samurai, and commoner men, as well, were prohibited from wearing beards
or full heads of hair. The depilation of Japanese men contrasted starkly with
the continuing fashion for beards in Korea, China, Ezo, and the Ryukyus, in
the seventeenth century, and with the queue that had been imposed in China,
sparking a reinvention of these new male tonsorial practices as markers of ethnic identity—even of being fully "human."[88]

It was in this archaeological stratum between 1640 and 1660, I believe, that
Japanese culture and rhetoric inscribed this tonsorial distinction as a particular mark of Chinese (and, though less commonly, Koreans or Ryukyuans), i.e.,
Tōjin, particularly in the epithet *ketōjin*, but also in its companion terms *keshi-
bōzu* ("poppy-headed monk") and *keshi-atama* ("poppy-head")—drawing an
analogy between the shape of the queue hairstyle, and that of the stem of the

---

87   Kashiwara (1922, 70–73).
88   Kikuchi (1991, 70–71) goes so far as to argue that "the *sakayaki*, topknot, and beardlessness
      were evidence of being human, and at the same time, a sign of the Japanese as a member
      of the nation." I am not as ready as Kikuchi seems to be to apply the terminology of the
      modern nation-state to seventeenth-century Japan, but I find his overall argument quite
      convincing. Particularly revealing is the bakufu's tonsorial distinction between *hinin* (lit.,
      "un-persons," an outcast [thrown-out] status not necessarily hereditary), and *eta* (which
      I render a "outcastes," a hereditary caste outside fully human society). The former, who
      might be restored to membership in society, were ordered to conform to the tonso-
      rial strictures of the *sakayaki* and shaved-face standard that applied to "straight" status
      groups; the order did not apply to *eta*.

poppy flower.[89] *Ketōjin/ketō* did not refer to Europeans until at least the late eighteenth century, and *keshi-bōzu* never referred to Europeans—though it did also describe a children's hairstyle that left only the hair at the center of the scalp, while the surrounding pate was shaved clean.

In the late eighteenth century, *ketō* seems to have begun to expand its range of signification to include Europeans, but usage is ambiguous, at least as late as ca. 1770, as to whether the referent is Chinese or European. Pictorial evidence is suggestive of the growing confusion, as a copy book illustration of 1770 (*Ameuri*, Fig. 70), based on earlier paintings (Fig. 71) by Hanabusa Itchō (1652–1724), demonstrates. Itchō's original painting depicts a Japanese candy-vendor, a street peddler of *Chōsen-ame* or *Tōjin-ame* ("Korea-candy," or "*Tōjin*-candy"), a popular confection, dressed in *Tōjin-fuku* ("*Tōjin* clothes").[90] He sports a set of luxuriant—yet unmistakably false—whiskers fastened to the chin-cord of his broad-brimmed, feather-topped *Tōjin-gasa* ("*Tōjin* hat"), modeled on the hats of Korean military officers in the retinues of visiting diplomatic missions. A crowd of children gather around him excitedly, attracted by the sound of his *charumera*, a double-reed instrument associated with foreignness.[91] His umbrella-shaded peep-show chest (*nozoki karakuri-bako*), and the mechanical doll (*karakuri*) done up as a *Tōjin* further reinforce the suite of visual and auditory *Tōjin* images.

---

89   Both terms appear in Chikamatsu's *Coxinga* plays, *keshi bōzu* in *Battles*, and *keshi atama* in *Tōsen-banashi ima Kokusen'ya* (Chikamatsu 1722). It is clear that foreigners recognized the *sakayaki* as a distinctively *Japanese* hairstyle well before this, for Luis Frois reported that during the Japanese invasions of Korea in the 1590s, "Some Koreans, in desperate straits, shaved their pates and put their hair up in Japanese fashion, so that they might attack their brethren with threats and a mimicry of the pillaging of the Japanese." Frois, *Historia da Iapam*, quoted in Kikuchi (1991, 67). The *sakayaki* and clean-shaven face were not yet, however, either mandatory or universal male practice in Japan itself at this early date, as the bearded visages of several of the invading generals attest. It is only in the mid-seventeenth century that tonsorial legislation made these practices nearly universal, and hence fully significative of a "Japanese" identity.

90   These China- and Korea-signed confections were sold under a number of other names as well: *Sankan* (三韓飴 "Three Korean [kingdoms]") *ame; Sankan* (三漢飴 "Three China") *ame; Sankan* (三官飴 "Third Officer" *ame*). See, e.g., Kuroda, 1994b; Yao, 2008.

91   *Tōjin ameuri zu* (ink & color on silk, 32.3 53.8 cm., Museum of Fine Arts Boston, painted sometime between 1709 and the artist's death in 1724) is among several of Itchō's works exploiting the *Tōjin ameuri* trope; see, e.g., *Ferry Crossing* (*Watashibune zu*, n.d., in Kobayashi Tadashi 1988, fig. 6). Miriam Wattles doubts the MFA is an authentic Itchō (personal communication). The association of the *charumera* and both Chinese and candy-peddlers is epitomized in a line in Kawatake Shinshichi II's 1862 kabuki play, *Kamiarizuki iro no sewagoto*: "Japanese China-boys gather 'round the candyman and his *charumera*." (*Charumera no ame e torimaku Wa no okeshi*), quoted in *NKD*, 2: 1086. Okeshi ("poppy-head") is a "Chinese" hairstyle common for young boys in the Edo period.

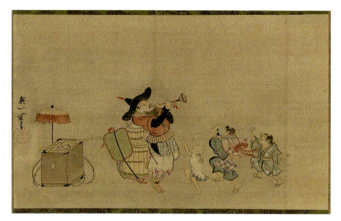

FIGURE 70   A peddler of "Chinaman candy" (*Tōjin-ame*) sports a false
             beard and mustache, which—along with his plumed,
             broad-brimmed hat, ruffles at on his collar, waist and
             ankles, and the *charumera* that he plays to attract custom-
             ers, mark him as performing the foreigner; only his straw
             sandals remind us that the man under all this costumery
             is actually Japanese. Hanabusa Itchō, *Tōjin ameuri-zu*
             (Chinaman candy-seller), hanging scroll, ink and color on
             silk, early eighteenth century. Fenellosa-Weld Collection,
             Boston Museum of Fine Art.

FIGURE 71   Itchō's *Tōjin ameuri-zu* reprised in a printed album of
             Itchō's works published forty-six years after his death.
             Here, the false beard and mustache are even more
             evident, and the later artist has added a bearded
             mechanical doll (under the umbrella) playing the
             charumera. "Ameuri," in Hanabusa (1770, 1: 5b–6a).
             The editor, Suzuki Rinshō, has reworked Itchō's
             composition.

The depiction of the *ameuri* in the 1770 copy book illustration alters Itchō's original composition in several ways: the peddler still attracts a gaggle of children, and his whiskers are still blatantly false; but the draughtsman has added a mechanical doll *Tōjin*—also bearded—dancing to the music of its own *charumera*, which appears in a second Itchō *ame-uri* painting.[92] The *Tōjin* doll is a mixed, transitional metaphor: His hat and beard are iconographically "Chinese"/foreign, but his buttoned coat owes more to Dutch than Chinese models, perhaps suggesting the expansion of *ketō* to include the Dutch.[93]

The *Tōjin*, i.e., "Chinese" or "Korean," candy-man remained a popular figure, a brilliant branding and marketing strategy in the highly competitive early modern pharmaceutical market throughout the Edo period—and perhaps beyond: The inveterate diarist Kōriki Tanenobu comments on "the peddlers of 'Korean Fragrant-Cinnamon pills'" who danced in the streets of Nagoya in early 1780. Nearly forty years later, in late 1818, Tanenobu records cake peddlers who dressed in *Tōjin* clothes, and played tunes on the *charumera* as a way to attract customers, while in 1823 he remarks on singing street peddlers in "*Tōjin* hats" (*Tōjin-gasa*) selling didactic texts.[94] In a similar vein, the obscure but prolific writer Kanwatei Onitake (d. 1818) wrote, "As we crossed Asakusabashi, two candy-peddlers came toward us from the other end [of the bridge] dressed in the now-popular *Tōjin* style. They stopped, holding parasols and spreading folding fans with one hand, [calling out] 'Here we are, here we are, with that famous Jakarta-sugar candy from the Maruyama district of Nagasaki in Kyūshū.... It'll lengthen your life.' Clearly, alterity sold well, and the bearded, ruffled, hatted *Tōjin/Chōsenjin* was a great way to sell it—but, as one character observes, and Onitake's illustration confirms, these *faux* foreigners were defective: "Hey, if they're *Tōjin*, why don't they have beards?!"[95]

---

92   Some will recall the itinerant peddlers of so-called *Shina-soba* ("Chinese noodles"), who used the *charumera* to announce their approach. The second painting is in a private collection. Thanks to Miriam Wattles for introducing me to this painting.

93   *Itchō gafu*, 3 vols. (Hanabusa 1770). I have used copies in the Tokyo University Library, National Diet Library and Art Institute of Chicago collections. *Itchō gafu* is a copybook of line-drawings, by Suzuki Rinshō (d. 1802), working nearly fifty years after Itchō's death; it is based—quite loosely, in many cases—on paintings by Itchō. Comparison of *Itchō gafu* drawings, *Ameuri* among them, with the extant Itchō paintings underlying them reveals that Rinshō often took significant liberties in both composition and setting. For a discussion, see Wattles (2013, 181–185)—though she does not address this image specifically. *Tōjin ameuri zu* (ink and color on silk, 32.3 53.8 cm., Museum of Fine Arts Boston), is among several Itchō paintings in which the *Tōjin ameuri* trope appears, another is *Ferry Crossing* (*Watashibune zu*, n.d., in Kobayashi Tadashi 1988, fig. 6).

94   Hanzawa (1996), following Kōriki (1756–1831).

95   Kanwatei (1805–06, 2.1: 5a). Onitake was the nom-de-plume of Kurahashi Ra'ichirō, a low-ranking retainer in the retinue of the Hitotsubashi branch of the Tokugawa house. (Koike

5   Coxinga's Pate/Chinese Bodies/Tatar Hair

Kokusen'ya kassen ("Battles of Coxinga), Chikamatsu Monzaemon's hit play of
1715 is quintessentially a dramatization of emerging Japanese identities, identities that are articulated in explicit contrast to a generalized "China," seen as
both militarily weak and morally bankrupt.[96] What is not widely recognized,
however, is the centrality of hair and tonsorial distinctions to Chikamatsu's
construction of ethnicity and identity in the world of *Coxinga*. Precisely because *Coxinga* was written a half-century after the first recorded use of the
terms *ketō, ketōjin, hige-tōjin,* etc., which we have been examining in this discussion, and represents more a culmination and crystallization of the process
of bearding the barbarian, the play is an excellent lens to examine the discursive shift that the diffusion of *ketōjin* into common usage portends. Hair is
a critical marker of alterity and identity in the rhetorical field of *Kokusen'ya
kassen*. Not only Japanese hair, but Tatar—*Dattan*—hair, and Chinese hair,
beards, and bodies.[97]

The play recounts the exploits of Zheng Chenggong, the Japanese-born son
of a Chinese pirate-merchant and his Japanese spouse, who journeys from
Japan to China seeking to overthrow the Qing, and restore the "legitimate"
Ming dynasty. The hero is known in the play as Watōnai, a name meaning "betwixt Japanese (*wa*) and Chinese (*tō*)"; he is performed on the puppet and kabuki stage beardless, with a shaved pate; totally *Japanese*, while Chinese like
Kanki, the General of the Army of the Five Constants (*Gojō-gun shōgun*), who
had gone over to the Tatar cause, but later joined forces with Coxinga, wear
so-called "*Tōjin* topknots" (*tōjin-wage*) and—in Kanki's case—a full, flowing
beard that reaches to mid-chest.

On his arrival in China, Watōnai finds himself in the Bamboo Groves of
Senri. There, in what is perhaps the most famous scene in the play, the hero
confronts a ferocious tiger, but because of his Japanese parentage—on his
mother's side—he is able to tame the beast without suffering so much as

---

1984). Though little known today, he was a close friend and collaborator of Jippensha Ikku
and other major literary figures of his day. (Nakayama 2009).

96   This observation is, of course, hardly novel, having been made by, *inter alia* Keene (1951)
and Jansen (1980; 1992), but it bears repeating here. Keene's masterly translation was done
without the aid of the annotated editions that are standard now; it remains the best text
for those not practiced in reading *jōruri* scripts. Several annotated editions have appeared
in recent decades, including *Shigetomo* (1958, v. 1); Shibata Minoru (1984).

97   See above, n. 27. *Kokusen'ya kassen* is not unique in deploying the imputed hairiness of
the Other as a sign of ethnic difference. In an earlier play, *Taishokan* (1711), Chikamatsu
puns on *ketōjin*, and later describes a Chinese general as being, "eight feet seven inches
tall; [he] divides his beard to the left and right," when he makes his initial entrance on
stage. Chikamatsu (1711), 7: 333; 437.

a scratch. Watōnai tames the tiger, first cowing the beast by holding up an amulet from the Ise Shrine, then by throwing the tiger about to complete the subjugation, so that the fierce beast starts meekly mewing and cuddling up to him. Watōnai straddles the ferocious beast in complete triumph. He then confronts a gang of Chinese, followers of the traitorous Chinese general Ri Tōten (Li Zicheng, murderer of the last Ming emperor) who had been hunting the tiger. The Chinese threaten to take Watōnai's prize from him, but are no match for the bravery and prowess they confront. After Watōnai has killed the leader of the gang, and scared off most of the rest, he proclaims to the remaining survivors, "You speak contemptuously of Japan as a small country, but perhaps now you'll realize that even tigers cower before Japanese prowess! ... If you value your lives, then become my allies; if you say no, you're tiger-bait!" The three "Chinese" throw themselves on the ground before him, in fear for their lives, and Coxinga accepts their fealty, but with a set of conditions:[98]

> Chinese officers: We beg to become your vassals!
> Narrator: [As they] say this, they bow so low their noses scrape the ground.
> Watōnai: It worked! But if you're to be my vassals, I'll have to shave your pates in Japanese style, put you through your coming-of-age ceremonies, and change your names.
> Narrator: And, so saying, he draws his short sword, which serves as an improvised razor ... [Watōnai and his mother] give them a rough shaving. They give them wide cuts and narrow cuts, whatever the sword dictates, and in the blink of an eye, they're finished shaving: *Heads: Japanese; beards: Tatar; bodies: Chinese.*

While Chikamatsu's scene of Coxinga and his mother shaving the *sakayaki* to make his newfound vassals partly "Japanese" is fictional, it is not without foundation in fact—whether the playwright knew it or not. Some of Hideyoshi's generals on the battlefields of Korea in the 1590s imposed the Japanese tonsorial regime on captured Koreans they took into service. As Ankokuji Ekei wrote to one of his vassals in mid-1592, he had begun converting some of his Korean captives to Japanese identities: "I have taught these Koreans the *kana* syllabary, plucked out their hair [i.e., given them a *sakayaki* hairstyle], and for the youths,

---

Kokusen'ya kassen, 2: 255. In performance, all the parts, as well as the narration, are chanted by the narrator, who indicates by vocal technique whether he is "narrating" or being a "character." Following Donald Keene's practice, I have arranged the lines as they might be in an English-language script.

FIGURE 72 Watōnai and his mother shave his new Chinese retainers' pates into the
sakayaki (right); one of the men sobs, "I miss my forelocks!" The newly-shaven
retinue marches off to the left, as one of the men rubs his bare scalp. From
Chikamatsu (1715), *Zashiki ayatsuri otogi gunki*, vol. 2.

shaved the center [of their scalps] in Japanese fashion.... Now, I have taken on
two or three of them [as vassals]."[99]

A bit later in the play, Kanki, the "General of the Army of the Five Constants,"
proclaims that the "Tatar king" had sought a hero who could stand up to
Coxinga, and announces that he, himself is that very hero, and will defeat the
foreigner, and bring his head before the emperor: "I'll chase him down in a
single battle, and return dangling Watōnai's shaved pate!"[100] Kanki's challenge
receives a quick response, as Watōnai appears before his castle gates, offering
his own mother as a hostage, to entice the general to repudiate the evil Tatars,
and join Watōnai's cause. To the guards, he shouts, "Hey, you hairy Chinamen!
(*ketōjin*)! Where do you have your ears stuck on! Can you hear me?" Shortly
after, receiving what he thinks is a sign that Kanki has refused, Watōnai confronts Kanki in his castle, and shouts in rage, "Yo! You bearded *Tōjin* (*hige-tōjin*),
Kanki of the Five Constants Army!" while reaching for his sword.[101]

---

99   Quoted in Kitajima (1982, 92).
100 *Watōnai ga sakayaki-kubi hissagete kitaran to. Kokusen'ya kassen, op. cit.*, 2:267.
101 *Kokusen'ya kassen*, in *Chikamatsu jōruri shū*, 50: 269. The intricacies of plot, the mi-
     raculously complex relationship between Watōnai and Kanki, are too convoluted to be

It is also in Kanki's castle that the tonsorial and sartorial inscription of ethnicity on women's bodies is revealed. The maids serving in the women's quarters of Kanki's castle remark that, "Have you ever seen a Japanese woman before? Her eyes and nose aren't any different from ours, but what an odd way of binding up her hair! What way of sewing her clothes!" And, as if to confirm the superiority of Japanese identity, one laments that "If I must be [re]born as woman, at least I want to be a Japanese woman, like her!"[102]

Thus, *Coxinga* reveals an ethnographic imaginary of Japan and East Asia, the contestation of Japanese identity(ies) and ethnic boundaries, and most of the conflicts in East Asia, expressed in the bodies of the people on stage, and in the rhetoric that describes them. The three Chinese who beg to become Watōnai's vassals are a virtual map of Japanese ethnic representation, with "Japanese heads, Tatar beards, and Chinese bodies." Kanki is Othered by his beard, a spectacular tonsorial display on stage, and—though not mentioned in the text—by a "Chinese topknot" (*Tōjin wage*) piled atop his head. He responds, from the opposite side of that boundary, which is symbolic of the inherent complicity of changing Qing/Chinese practice—identities of the "excluded other—in the articulation of Japanese identities. The *sakayaki*, the shave-pate hairstyle mandated by bakufu law, serves as an ongoing sign of Japanese ethnicity, as set against other—in this case, Chinese and Manchu— identities. Each identity/ethnicity is signified by a particular tonsorial or corporeal sign. The *sakayaki* sits at the very center of this tonsorial rhetoric, and the re-construction of ethnicity in Japanese discourse, virtually calling the *ketōjin* into being.

The success of *Kokusen'ya kassen* on the Osaka puppet stage was so monumental that it became what might be called a "pop-culture" phenomenon. Even during the initial run on stage, publishers reprinted illustrated versions of the story as a prose war-tale,[103] and Chikamatsu's rival Osaka playwright, Kino Kaion, brought out his own version, set in a brothel quarter. Chikamatsu wrote his own "Coxinga II" (*Kokusen'ya gonichi kassen* "Coxinga fights again,"), which opened but weeks after the final curtain on his original hit.[104] "Coxinga II" likewise plays with Tatar queues, and Kanki's "great beard right down to his belt," a beard that casts a shadow like the trees.[105] With the move into visual

---

unpacked here; the discovery of a common bond through Kanki's marriage to Watōnai's Chinese half-sister is a key to the resolution of their confrontation.

102   *Kokusen'ya kassen*, p. 262–263; cf. Keene (1951, 133).

103   E.g., Ukai (1661; 1717). Keene (1951, Ch. 4) reviews much of this flood of me-too fiction, drama, and publishing.

104   Chikamatsu (1717), 10: 1–128.

105   Ibid., pp. 60; 61.

media, illustrators had a field-day with Watōnai's *sakayaki*, and queued and wild-bearded aliens.

Chikamatsu's hit play immediately became a nationwide cultural icon, and its tonsorial symbolism permeated consciousness across the country. As it spread into festival performance around the country, Watōnai's *sakayaki*, and its contrast to the *ketōjin*'s bearded, queued mien, were produced, performed, and re-produced, in festival performances and local productions from one end of Japan to the other.[106] No later than 1718, Watōnai was performed—most likely by *karakuri ningyō* (mechanical dolls)—in the mountain fastness of Takayama, about 225 km. northeast of Osaka as the crow flies, and about the same time in Sendai, 800 km. northeast.[107] While it is not clear which scene was the attraction in Takayama, a handbill from the Sendai festival shows that the scene of Watōnai "taming the tiger" was what all the fuss was about. His shaven pate and clean cheeks and chin proclaim his Japanese identity. The juxtaposition of Watōnai's *sakayaki* and the bearded faces of *ketōjin* became a stock trope of identity, reproduced in votive tablets (Fig. 73) and woodblock prints (Fig. 74), helping to fix the tonsorial boundary in popular consciousness.

6   Playing the Hairy Barbarian

Increasingly, then, hair became a marker of difference and distinction. Also, we must remember another aspect of Japanese cultural practice—or social practice—that changes in the early Edo period: Prior to the Sengoku ("warring states") period (1467–1568), virtually all adult Japanese males, except for Buddhist clergy, always wore *eboshi* (court caps) of one sort or another: starched, black-lacquered hats that were coded to status and occupation, even while sleeping. In a *kōwaka-mai*, a medieval chanting text, a Japanese who is blown by the winds into the south seas—probably the Ryukyus—says, "Though there were men, they wore no hats; though there were women, they did not let their hair down."[108] Bareheaded men—the absence of hats—and

---

106   Similarly in the preface to his *Chōsenjin raihei ki* ("A record of the Koreans coming to court," MS, 3 vols., 1748), Watanabe Zen'emon (1701–62), a retainer in the Yodo domain just south of Kyoto, rehearsed the contrasts between the "unkempt beards" and "silly mustaches"(*mushakusha hige; rachi no akanu higegao*) and "poppy-head" (*keshi-bōzu*) mien of the visitors from "distant lands," and the "shaved pates of our country (*wagachō no sakayaki*)." Kyōto-shi Rekishi Shiryokan, 2010: 3–4.

107   *Uehara Kisoemon-dono kakitsuke* of 1718, copied in 1786 in *Yuzuhara-ke nikki*, repr. in Takayama Yatai Hozonkai (Takayama, 1959, 21).

108   *Iōgashima no uchi*, quoted in Murai (1988, 44). At the other "end" of Japan, similarly, *Onzōshi no shimawatari*, the tale of Minamoto no Yoshitsune's travels across the islands to the north of Japan, the young hero confronts a variety of truly "outlandish" creatures,

FIGURE 73   A Japanese warrior shaving the pates of "Chinese who have surrendered, performing their coming-of-age (*genbuku*) rite, and turning them into retainers."
From Terasawa (1790).

unkempt women's hair were what alerted the castaway to the fact that he was
no longer in "Japan." But hats, by their nature, cover a variety of sins, including
hiding hairstyles.

By the seventeenth century, however, Japanese men no longer wore *eboshi*,
and so hair, which had been to some extent rendered invisible—it's difficult
to tell whether a pate hidden under a hat is shaved or not—became a visible
sign. Hair, that is, was a public inscription of identities, and therefore, became
a site for establishment of who one *was*, and equally, who one *was not*. I am

from centaur-like "people" (?), shaped like horses from the waist up, and like people
below" to the little people of the Island of Dwarves (*Chiisagoshima*) and a variety of
monsters. Yoshitsune takes his leave of Japan, "which is the land of the gods," wearing
his *eboshi*—as do all the men in this scene—and never loses his cap throughout his
entire perilous journey. It is the barbarians he meets who are uncapped, thus exposing
the variety of their barbarous hairstyles; but it is Yoshitsune's *eboshi*, not his hairstyle,
that marks him as "Japanese." The only exception is a demon-king who has the power
to transform himself into other shapes, and transforms himself into a "Japanese," sitting
on raised tatami and wearing an *eboshi*. See the text and illustrations in Ichiko (1958,
102–123). Kuroda Hideo (1990) argues that the illustrations in the early-eighteenth-cen-
tury Shibukawa edition (reproduced in the *Nihon koten bungaku taikei* edition) preserve
late-medieval iconographic keys.

FIGURE 74 A votive plaque of 1843 portrays a beardless, shaved-pate Coxinga, astride the tiger, subduing a group of bearded Chinese into submission simply by waving an amulet from the Ise Shrine. Murakudō Bakin, *Watōnai-zu*, ink and color on wood.

COURTESY TENMA JINJA, SABAE CITY, FUKUI PREFECTURE

FIGURE 75

Ichikawa Danjūrō VII as Watōnai Sankan (Coxinga) and Ichikawa Ebizō V Goshōgun Kanki in a performance of *Kokusen'ya kassen* at the Nakamura-za in 1850. Coxingas's clean-shaven face and pate, decorated in *kumadori* (kabuki makeup), contrast with General Kanki's full beard and lush head of hair. Kanki's alienness is underscored by the ruffles of his collar and sleeves. Utagawa Toyokuni, "Actors Ichikawa Ebizō V as Goshōgun Kanki and Ichikawa Danjūrō VIII as Watōnai Sankan," woodblock color print. William Sturgis Bigelow Collection, Boston Museum of Fine Art.

reminded of Meron Benvenisti's comment on Arab and Jew in Jerusalem: "Increasingly," he wrote, "people identify themselves by who they are not."[109] What we find then, in the transformations of Japanese tonsorial practice, and in the discovery of its inversion in Qing practice, is the deployment of inscriptions of negative identities, surrounding an *undefined* remnant, which is a Japanese "identity."

As this bearding of the Other, in and out of his lair, proceeded in verbal rhetoric, it also was articulated on parallel tracks in visual and performance media. The construction of a hairier, more bearded alien, that is, was furthered by representation and re-presentation in a wide variety of expressive forms, from the costumes of itinerant peddlers, such as the one portrayed in Hanabusa Itchō's painting, "Candy-man" (*Ameuri*), to festival and stage performance, and the imaginative world of painting and prints, as well as in fiction and poetry.

7   Envisioning Hair

I turn now to the visual representations that served to inform vision, to tell people how to see the Other, and by contrast, how not to see themselves. It is important to note, following Gombrich, that none of these representations was intended as—or could be—a "photographic" or "realistic" record, for painters do not merely "paint what they see"; they also paint from other paintings, what the discursive field allows them to see, and to expect the viewer to understand and decode.[110] Rather, these visual expressions are to be understood as "representations," as productions of the meaning of Japanese identity through its Others.

I begin with an early seventeenth-century screen-painting depicting the capital city of Kyoto (*rakuchū rakugai-zu*), and a wide variety of social activity

---

109   Benvenisti (1988). Or, consider the third *bracha* uttered by the observant male Jew each morning: *Shelo asani goy*: "Thank God you didn't make me one of *them!*" This and the two succeeding *brachot, shelo asani yever* (a slave), and *shelo asani ishta* (a woman), construct identities by exclusion of negated exteriors, rather than inclusion of affirmed interiors. The last mentioned of these *brachot*, it goes without saying, have been the subject of quite a bit of controversy in the last few years; Reform and Reconstructionist Judaism have rewritten this text. Or, as R. D. Laing puts it, "Every relationship implies a definition of self by other and other by self" (1969, 69). Similarly, Peter N. Dale's argument hinges on the notion that Japaneseness "[is] the anti-image of foreignness" (1986, 39). Characteristically contrarian, William Safire, who probably grew up on the *brachot* cited above, is incapable of understanding this: "Why should anybody want to define himself [*sic*] by what he is not?" (Safire, 1988).

110   See, for example, Gombrich (1969, 189–193ff.).

at famous sites around the town. While the focus of the work is the broad range of street life, it also presents two views of foreign visitors, most likely the Korean embassy that Tokugawa Hidetada, the second shogun, received at Fushimi Castle in 1617.[111] This is, I believe, the earliest attempt to represent a "Korean" identity in Japanese art as distinct from a broader "continental" identity of *soi-disant* "China" (*Kara/Tō/Morokoshi*). What interests us here is that many of the "Japanese" men pictured about town are shown with mustaches—still fashionable, and for practical purposes, legal in the Genna and Kan'ei eras—while most of the Koreans are shown with virtually no visible facial hair. By contrast, however, most of the Koreans (eighteen of twenty-nine) wear hats of various sorts, while most of the Japanese—with the exception of a nun and some travelers—are bareheaded, in reversal of medieval social practice and pictorial rhetoric.[112] The bareheaded Korean figures display three distinct hairstyles. The ambassadors' pages (*sodong*) are shown wearing their long hair hanging down beyond their shoulders, but there is not enough detail to tell whether their hair is straight or plaited, bound or unbound.[113] Four other hatless figures (one carrying the ambassador's palanquin; three in the

---

111   *Rakuchū rakugai-zu byōbu* (six-panel folding screen, color and gold leaf on paper; Mary Jackson Burke Collection, Minneapolis Museum of Art); *Rakuchū rakugai-zu byōbu* (pair of six-panel folding screens, color and gold leaf on paper; Hayashibara Museum, Okayama). For a discussion of the basis for dating these screens to around 1619–1623 see Toby (1996a), where I also discuss the mixed metaphors of alterity they contain. Cf. *Injo i-nyŏn t'ongsinsa hangnyŏl-to* (also known as *Kan'ei Chōsenjin raichō zukan*; color on paper, 32.1 × 984.2 cm, collection Seoul National Museum). The Seoul and Tokyo national museums do not agree on a title for this work, but they do agree on dating it to 1624. Tokyo National Museum (1985, 8), and Korean National Museum (1986, 25–26). Despite the agreement of the two museums, there are serious questions about the dating, both at the iconographic and ethnographic levels and at the levels of technique and composition, but we will hold those in abeyance for the moment. I believe the work is at least sixty years later, and perhaps nearly a century, as late as Tenna (ca. 1682) or even Shōtoku (ca. 1711), and that its hairy/hairlessness is retrospective rather than descriptive. It is not a particularly good work of art, but our interest here is its ethnographic rather than its esthetic or technical qualities.

112   Bird (1898/1986, 2: 114–115) observes that after his coming of age ceremony the Korean man of the Chosŏn dynasty, "He is invested with the *mangan*, a crownless skullcap or fillet of horsehair, *without which, thereafter, he is never seen*. He wears a black hat and a long full coat ...," symbolic of his adulthood. Suzuki (1994, 79–80) notes that prior to the fifteenth century, similarly, "for noble and base alike ... for [Japanese] a man to show his uncovered head to another was considered shameful."

113   The normative hairstyle for Korean youths prior to coming-of-age rites (K. *kwallye*) was a plaited braid called *ttahun mŏri*. http://terms.naver.com/entry.nhn?docId=1761738&cid=4 9278&categoryId=49278 (accessed 2014/08/05). My thanks to Yoonjeong Shim for pointing me to this reference.

precincts of Hōkōji temple) have their hair done in a *sangt'u* (topknot), the modal Korean hairstyle for married adult males. Two of the three flag-bearers leading the ambassador's parade through town, and one in the precincts of Hōkōji, are hatless, but their hair is close-cropped in the style of Japanese catechists (*irmaõ*) serving the (Portuguese) Jesuits.[114] Hats/no-hats had reversed its ethnic valence since the days of the *kōwaka-mai* quoted earlier, but hair/no-hair had not yet been firmly fixed in modes that comported with the emergence of a *ketōjin*—"hairy *Tōjin*" or "hairy barbarian"—other.

The *Tōshō-sha engi*, the illustrated history of the apotheosized dynastic founder, Tokugawa Ieyasu, similarly embodies a vision of Other in which the ethnic significance of hats and hair were still in flux.[115] When Tokugawa Iemitsu commissioned Kanō Tan'yū to illustrate the *Tōshō-sha engi*, he specified inclusion of the first visit of a Korean diplomatic mission to Tōshōgū, in the winter of 1636–37, an event of which Iemitsu was particularly proud.[116] Tan'yū represented an entourage of "Othered" Koreans, parading past Japanese spectators to the *torii*, or ritual gate, of the shrine. (Fig. 80) Predominant in the crowd of spectator-Japanese are bearded, *eboshi*-capped men, virtually indistinguishable from their counterparts in crowds of spectators depicted along the roadsides of 13th-century *emaki* processions of warriors and courtiers. The "Koreans," by contrast, are not particularly hirsute—some are beardless—nor are they clothed in anything a Korean would recognize as a being a "Korean" style; rather, they are shown in a Japanese notion of "Tatar" fashion, consistent with the representational conventions familiar to Tan'yū and his contemporaries from a genre of "Tatars at the Hunt" screens.[117] Tan'yū, like his peers, was familiar with—indeed, had hand-copied most of—the iconographic tradition in which he was trained, and drew both his "Japanese" and "foreign" identities from his models. We have to be careful how we read this, but in these and other early seventeenth-century examples, Japanese continue to be

---

114   Bird (1898/1986, 2: 174), writing shortly after the Korean king cut off his own topknot and issued an edict calling on all men to do likewise—provoking nationwide protests and revolts—notes that, "To the Korean the Top-Knot means nationality, antiquity ... sanctity derived from antiquity, entrance on manhood socially and legally...."

115   Tenkai & Kanō (1641). Tenkai wrote the text; Tan'yū painted the illustrations. For a color facsimile, see Komatsu & Kanzaki (1994); for convenience, see the reproduction of this scene in Toby (1984, 98–99). On Korean clothing styles, see Son and Kim (1984); on the official dress of Korean embassies to Japan in the seventeenth to nineteenth centuries, see Kung (1982).

116   Discussed in Toby (1984, 97–103, 203–209). Iemitsu was likely guided in his choices by the Tendai priest Tenkai.

117   See, for example, Kanō Jin-no-jō, *Tatars Playing Polo & at the Hunt* (pair of six-panel screens, 153 × 348 cm collection, Freer Gallery of Art); reproduced in Doi (1978, fig. 46).

FIGURE 76   The Korean embassy of 1617 depicted parading through
Kyoto. In the absence of established painterly conven-
tions for depicting Koreans, the artist used a variety of
"foreign" tropes, such as the "catechist"(J. *iruman*, from
P., *irmão*) hairstyles on the two pennant-bearers at the
far left, and the crucifixes on the two flags at the corner.
Rakuchū rakugai-zu byōbu, single six-panel screen, ca.
1620, color and gold leaf on paper.
COURTESY MARY GRIGGS BURKE COLLECTION,
MINNEAPOLIS INSTITUTE OF ART

FIGURE 77   The bakufu arranged for the Korean embassy of 1617 to stop at Hōkōji, a
temple founded by Toyotomi Hideyoshi, for lunch on their return from
their audience with the shogun in Fushimi Castle. The artist depicts the
ambassador in *Nanban* (i.e., Portuguese) garb, and the two other
Koreans without their hats—unthinkable, in practice—to show their
foreign hairstyles, contrasted with the Japanese man's shaved *sakayaki*.
Rakuchū rakugai-zu byōbu, single six-panel screen, ca. 1620, color and
gold leaf on paper.
COURTESY MARY GRIGGS BURKE COLLECTION, MINNEAPOLIS
INSTITUTE OF ART

FIGURE 78

Two Korean pennant-bearers depicted with the hairstyles of Portuguese catechists, and ruffled collars, in an attempt to make them look foreign. *Rakuchū rakugai-zu byōbu*, single six-panel screen, ca. 1620, color and gold leaf on paper.

COURTESY MARY GRIGGS BURKE COLLECTION, MINNEAPOLIS INSTITUTE OF ART

FIGURE 79   The bearded Korean ambassador, riding on a sedan chair, as well as his Korean porters and retinue, are all designated foreign by their ruffled collars. *Rakuchū rakugai-zu byōbu*, single six-panel screen, ca. 1620, color and gold leaf on paper.

COURTESY MARY GRIGGS BURKE COLLECTION, MINNEAPOLIS INSTITUTE OF ART

FIGURE 80   Kano Tan'yū depicts the arrival of the 1636 Korean embassy at the Nikkō
            Tōshōgū. The main body of the embassy retinue approaches the shrine through
            town streets, while the vanguard passes through the *torii* (detail). In the absence
            of models for depicting Koreans, Tan'yū mixes Ming and Tatar images. Kano
            Tan'yū, *Tōshōsha engi emaki*, five-part handscroll, color and gold leaf on paper;
            vol. 5. Tōshōgū Hōmotsuden, Nikkō.

represented as bearded and hatted, while Others needed not be particularly
hirsute, and are more fully set off by their clothing than by their corporeal
characteristics.

Illustrative in this regard is the schematic representation of "all the peoples
of the world," the *Bankoku jinbutsu zu* (Nagasaki, 1645), a Noah's ark of peoples,

FIGURE 81
A Japanese (right) and Ming couples depicted in
a table of the peoples of the world. At this early
juncture, the *Bankoku sōzu; Jinbutsu-zu* (1647).
COURTESY KOBE CITY MUSEUM

two-by-two, from around the known, unknown, and imagined world (Fig. 81).
First among them are a Japanese couple, who appear as a bearded medieval
warrior in full armor, and a kimono-robed woman. Compared to the Japanese
warrior, who sports whiskers that would have made him a competitor for the
role of carrier of the rhinoceros halberd in *Higeyagura*, the men of "Ming"
(China), Kōrai (Korea), and Dattan (Tartary), even those of Engeresu (England)
and Zerumaniya (Germany), are not remarkably hirsute.[118] The break between
bearded- and unbearded-ness was not yet an unambiguously valenced signifier of alterity.

Alternatively, we might compare two parade prints of the mid-1680s by
Hishikawa Moronobu, one of a daimyo's procession, the other, of a Korean
diplomatic mission under Japanese escort.[119] There is no question that by
1685, no daimyo or hatamoto would dare appear in Edo Castle sporting the
beard Moronobu depicts in this daimyo procession; nor would he be escorted
by retainers wearing the mutton-chop whiskers he portrays. That they have
been inscribed that way, in their mutton-chop whiskers, *sōhatsu*, etc., is in a
sense nostalgic, rather than descriptive. Yet in his prospective presentation of
the *Procession of the Koreans* (Fig. 82), where "Japanese" and "foreigners" appear side-by-side, Moronobu stresses more fully the bearded/unbearded contrast—though some of the "Japanese" are still bearded. Here, a very few of the
Japanese porters and escort still show hints of facial hair, token mustaches,
on some of them, wispy beards on others. But in Moronobu's rendition, the
Korean ambassador is more thickly bearded than his pictorial predecessors;
and in Okumura Masanobu's 1711 "Korean procession" series (Fig. 83), though
there remain some nostalgic hints of the beard that once was on Japanese

118   Examples are in the collections of the Bungakubu Hakubutsukan, Kyoto University, and
       the Kobe Municipal Museum (hand-colored woodblock print, 136.4 × 58.9 cm, Nagasaki,
       1647). See Kobe Shiritsu Nanban Bijutsukan (1972, 5:77 [fig. 76]). A Kyoto publisher
       re-rendered this schema in an inexpensive print of 1671, reproduced in Mody (1939/1969,
       fig. 24). Interestingly, the samurai who represents "Japan" seems to have been shorn of his
       beard—as best as I can tell from the reproduction in Mody—though his companion is
       still depicted as a Heian beauty.
119   Both are in the Buckingham Collection of the Art Institute, Chicago.

FIGURE 82   By the 1680s, the contrast between Japanese and foreign
             tonsorial practices had become firmly entrenched, and
             Japanese artists began emphasizing foreign beards in
             contrast to clean-shaven Japanese; foreign hats in contrast
             to bare-headed Japanese. Hishikawa Moronobu, "Korean
             Embassy Procession," hand-colored woodblock print, 1682.
             COURTESY ART INSTITUTE OF CHICAGO

FIGURE 83   The Korean ambassador, depicted
             in one sheet of a twelve-sheet
             woodblock-print published for sale
             during the visit of an embassy to Edo
             in 1711, probably intended to be glued
             together as a handscroll. Okumura
             Masanobu, "Korean Embassy Parade,"
             hand-colored woodblock on paper.
             ©TRUSTEES OF THE BRITISH
             MUSEUM

faces, the faces of the Koreans are distinctly more heavily bearded, as the beard
of the ambassador himself shows.[120]

　　Similarly, in some late seventeenth-century *Rakuchū rakugai-zu byōbu*, or
the *Chōsen tsūshinshi byōbu*, the artists depict—bearded, to be sure—Koreans
marching through the streets of Kyoto, but they march past Japanese spectators

---

120   Okumura (1711). Three panels from the British Museum example are reproduced in Tokyo
       National Museum (1985, 82).

many of whom still sport facial hair, side-whiskers, and even *sōhatsu* hairdos—signs of transgression or resistance.[121] Though the law has shorn Japanese men of their foliage, iconographically, they have yet to reach the barber shop. This is in part a reflection of the fact that Japanese—and other painters—paint from earlier examples and an iconographic tradition, which may sometimes be more resistant to change than other media.

These tonsorial indices of identity/difference also appeared elsewhere throughout Japanese expressive culture, other than in depictions of "foreign" embassies to Japan. In *Kōshoku ichidai otoko* (The Life of an Amorous Man, 1682), Ihara Saikaku's picaresque rake Yonosuke makes his way to Nagasaki, whence he will take ship to look for the Isle of Women (*Nyōgo ga shima*). Before his departure, he makes a detour to Maruyama, the Nagasaki licensed quarter, frequented by Chinese and Dutch merchants, as well as by local Japanese. Yonosuke window shops in front of a brothel, along with a group of *Tōjin* strolling by (Fig. 84): Yonosuke, signed as a proper Japanese swell by his glistening *sakayaki* and clean-shaven face, is set against *Tōjin* Other-marked both by their costumes and, particularly, by their spiky, almost goat-like beards. Though the *Tōjin* denizens of Nagasaki were all-but-exclusively Chinese, these *Tōjin* are clothed in Korean-inspired, iconographically—if not ethnographically correct—*Tōjin* fashions: These are not attempts at empirical replications, but discursive representations, intended to signify alterity, and to reinforce identity: To announce Yonosuke's first brush with the territory of the Other.[122] In a similar, though more erotic, vein, Saikaku imagines a visit to Nagasaki's Maruyama licensed quarter in his "Great mirror of the varieties of Eros" *Shoen ōkagami* (Fig. 85): a young Japanese dandy, clean-shaven, and with his exposed, dome-like *sakayaki* fairly glistening in the sun, accompanied by four courtesans, watch a festival performance at the "Tōjin temple" (*Tōjin-dera*) of two bearded *Tōjin*, their shaggy eyebrows visible beneath the broad brims of their hats; the two dance on a stage draped with the carcasses of beasts—most likely dogs, accompanied by another bearded *Tōjin* who plays music on a *shō*.[123] In Saikaku, at least, though—so far as I can tell—he never used the term, *ketōjin*, "Japanese" have clean-shaven faces and pates, while *tōjin* are hairy, bearded creatures.

---

121   *Rakuchū rakugai-zu byōbu* (pair of six-panel screens, gilt and color on paper, Museum of Fine Art, Boston); *Rakuchū rakugai-zu byōbu* (pair of six-panel screens, gilt and color on paper, private collection, Imai-chō, Nara Prefecture); *Chōsen tsūshinshi byōbu* (ca. 1682, six-panel screen, color on paper, Amagasaki Board of Education).

122   For a convenient reproduction of this illustration from *Kōshoku ichidai otoko*, see Asō, Itasaka, and Tsutsumi (1957, 47:21).

123   *Shoen ōkagami* (Edo and Osaka, 1684). I have used the facsimile edition, Ihara (1684/1974, 232–233).

FIGURE 84
Two clean-shaven,
sakayaki-wearing Japanese
cross paths with bearded,
hat-wearing Chinese in
the Maruyama
prostitution quarter of
Nagasaki. Ihara Saikaku,
Kōshoku ichidai otoko,
illustrated by Hishikawa
Moronobu, Edo, 1684.

In all this, of course, Japanese artists could not fail to picture the queue itself.
Saikaku's Nagasaki *Tōjin* were all hatted, and iconographically owe more to
the representation of Korean embassies, or Tatar hunters, in the iconographic
tradition—recall, Saikaku, had not likely left Osaka to travel to Nagasaki and
observe the "Chinese," nor had the publishing industry of Nagasaki got under
way—than to observation of Chinese in their Nagasaki "habitat." But after
about 1720, Nagasaki publishers such as Bunkindō and Toshimaya, put out print
after print of "Chinese" in the town, both at "home," and out on the town—
often disporting themselves in the Maruyama district. Often, as in Bunkindō's
"The Qing at a Banquet," some of the Chinese are portrayed hatless, side-view
or three-quarters rear to the viewer, to display the queue clearly. In Toshimaya's
"Interior of a Chinese Home," mustachioed, queued Chinese men lounge about
at home, their shaved sides and unshaved pates on display—two of them seem
to keep the queue out of the way by coiling it around their scalps. (Figs. 86, 87)[124]

---

124   These two prints are reproduced in Mody (1939/1969, plates 73 and 55).

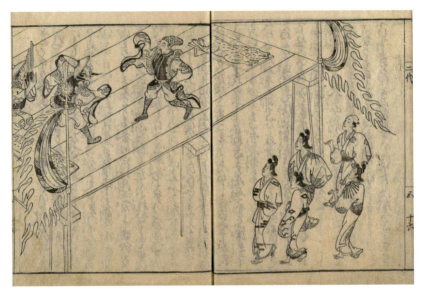

FIGURE 85   A clean-shaven, sakayaki-wearing Japanese dandy, with four courtesans in
tow, watch bearded Chinese dancers performing on a stage. The boar carcass
stage left further emphasizes the alienness of the Chinese by pointing to
their meat-eating habits. Ihara Saikaku, *Shoen ōkagami* (1684/1974).

FIGURE 86   Unsigned, "The Qing at a Banquet." Woodblock print published by Bunkindō,
Nagasaki, n.d., Mody (1939/1969), Plate 73.

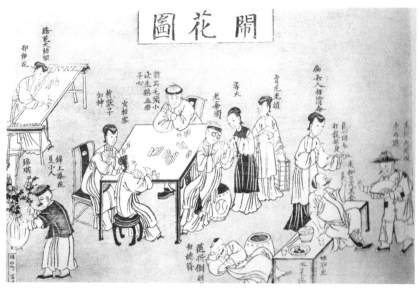

FIGURE 87   Unsigned, "Bawdy House." Woodblock print published by Toshimaya, Nagasaki, n.d., Mody (1939/1969), Plate 73.

Beyond the somewhat fanciful world of Nagasaki prints, scholars, too, in their representations of "Qing-ese," were often equally fascinated by the queue. In what was perhaps the first modern Japanese attempt at a universal encyclopedia, *Wakan sansai zue* (1713), Terajima Ryōan offered an annotated visual taxonomy of the "people of strange/foreign lands" (*ikoku jinbutsu*). Ryōan, perhaps constrained by his reliance on the taxonomy of his late-Ming exemplar, *Sancai tuhui*, represented the "people" of each "country" pictorially in a supra-historical male type, in contrast to the male-female couples of the *Bankoku jinbutsu zu* of 1647,[125] and so was not ethnographically precise about "Chinese"—or any other people. His timeless visual "China" (*Shintan; Morokoshi; Shina*), had no room for distinctions of *Dai-min*, or *Dai-shin*, showing only an ideal-type scholar-official, robed and capped, who might as easily have been Tang as Ming (Fig. 88). We cannot see his hairstyle, but he is indeed mustachioed, and wears a three-pronged style beard iconographically—if fancifully—associated with *Tōjin*. Likewise, Ryōan's Tatar (*Dattan*) exemplum,

---

125   Terajima (1713). See also facsimile edition, Terajima (1970). There are two modern print editions, both occasionally unreliable: Endō (1980) and Shimada, Takeshima, and Higuchi (1985–1991), which represents China (Shintan; Morokoshi) but neither Da-min nor Dai-shin.

FIGURE 88
"Shintan," i.e., a "Chinese" man, in
Terajima (1712, vol. 13).

is thickly whiskered, as are the Ryukyuan, Ezo, and Jurchen—and most other—foreign types.[126]

In his ethnographic comments on China, however, which take minimal account of dynasties, Ryōan carefully notes in the Qing section that with the transition from Ming to Qing, "The emperor is a Tatar.... The Nanjingese [a metonym for Chinese generally] now wear their hair on the sides of their heads following the Tatar custom...." Then separately, in his section on Tatars, Ryōan is more specific: "However, the Mongol custom is to shave the nape of the neck, and thence around to the forehead, [leaving the hair's] shape in a square, and binding the hair in the very center. They call this a *qiechouer* (J., *kyōkyūji*; Mongol., *kökyl*). *Nowadays, everyone follows this custom in China.*"[127] Clearly, by Ryōan's time, Japanese had fairly detailed knowledge of Manchu tonsorial

126   Shimada, Takeshima, and Higuchi (1985–1991) represents Japanese in a wide variety of status, gender, and occupation, and reduces China to a single—male—"type," subverting the model, *Sancai tuhui*, which represented *Chinese* in their full variety of occupations, status, and gender, but foreigners in a one-to-country type.

127   Terajima (1980, 246, 257); Terajima (1970, 1:204, 214). Emphasis added. The Manchu term is *sonçoho*, which is unrelated; my thanks to Victor Mair for help in locating the Mongol term (which means a tuft of horse's mane or bird's feathers standing up on the creature's head—transcribed here) and the Manchu.

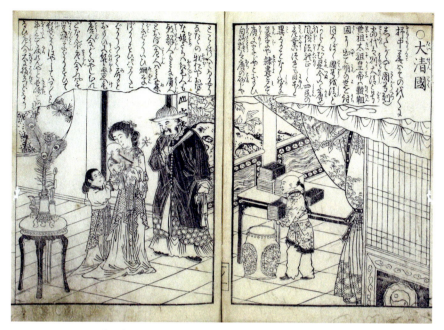

FIGURE 89   A Qing family depicted at home. The bearded mustachioed father and the
             bare-headed son display the tonsorial regime imposed by the Manchus. Shunkōen
             & Okada (1799).

practices, and of the inscription of Manchu hegemony on now-docile Chinese
bodies. This knowledge, as we saw above, had also penetrated the world of the
Nagasaki print, and through the diffusion of these prints, had become fairly
common knowledge throughout Japan.

The *Ehon ikoku ichiran* (Illustrated Survey of Foreign (Strange) Lands),[128]
while verbally less delicate, is visually far more explicit. This work, published
in 1799, is a brief *National Geographic*-esque ethnography of the peoples of
fifty-two of the world's countries, most organized along the principle of "type"
family portraits (Fig. 89). It opens with "the Qing-ese" family—a couple with
three children—at home (vol. 1). The text, which is extremely brief, does not
address matters of the body, but the picture speaks volumes: the father's queue
is visible behind his fur-brimmed "Tatar" hat, and his face sprouting five lush
tufts of whiskers; the couple's young son, though, is hatless, and turned so
we can see that the top of his head is completely shaved clean, except for a
round patch of hair at the back of his crown, and a queue already down to
his waist. Mother, daughter, and infant stand in a cluster, under the father's

128   Shunkōen and Okada (1799).

gaze. The men of the "Tatar" family, too (vol. 2), appear in a variety of poses that show off their fur-trimmed hats and thickly bearded faces, or turn away from the viewer, for a good, almost "ethnographic" gaze at the way the queue is plaited and laid. "Korea" is represented, not by a family, but by two military officers with remarkably untamed hair and beards, looking out to sea through a telescope; on "Taiwan," "The people are base because it is a tropical country, and go about naked. Coxinga, i.e., Zheng Zhilong, subdued the island," we are told, and shown the naked, *fur-covered* natives of Taiwan bowing and cowering before a heroic, Coxinga-as-Japanese-warrior (with a moustache, to be sure). The "barbarians" were getting hairier!

Ehon ikoku ichiran conveyed nearly all its information through illustrations, with only minimal verbal text, but that same year, Nakagawa Tadateru published his much more substantial, focused, encyclopedia of Qing customs, *Shinzoku kibun*.[129] In the public bath, heavily bearded, mature men, whose queues have grown long, keep them dry by winding them around their scalps; a younger boy, his queue not yet that advanced, lets it dangle down his back. (Fig. 90) In the illustrations of agriculture and industry, the viewer gazes upon a boy harvesting rice with his bearded, hat-wearing elders; he works hatless, so the view can gaze upon his queue, here wound around his scalp to keep it from getting tangled in his work; other boys, threshing, milling, and winnowing rice (Fig. 91), or working the water-wheel give the reader further views of the queue, while an illustration of "The Queue, the Skull-cap, and [Women's] Hair-bun" in the section on "Headgear Formalities" gives further views (Fig. 92), and an accompanying text provides a detailed description of the coming-of-age ceremony, when boys are first queued, and girls' hair first bound up. "Nowadays, in the age of the Qing, the ancient capping ceremonies [marking boys' coming of age] have disappeared, and are no longer practiced ... nor is there a fixed age for girls to put the first combs in their hair.... At the time of a [boy's] coming of age (Nakagawa uses the Japanese term, *genpuku*) ... they call a barber ... and leaving a circle of hair in the very middle of the head, he shaves off everything else ... combing the hair into three strands.... This is called the *bentsū*; they bind the tip of the hair with a cord of scarlet (*akamoegi*) color, and wear a cap over it."[130]

Though "real" foreigners were a relatively rare sight outside Nagasaki in the Edo period, Japanese created faux-*tōjin* in a variety of ways. One of these, as

---

129 Nakagawa (1799); reprint Son and Muramatsu (1966–1969). References are to the Son and Muramatsu edition.
130 Son and Muramatsu (1966–1969, 2:71–73). Nakagawa's description includes details on the profession of barbering in Qing China, even down to prices.

FIGURE 90 Chinese men at the public bath, posed and depicted to emphasize the Manchu-imposed tonsorial regime. Nakagawa (1799, 2).

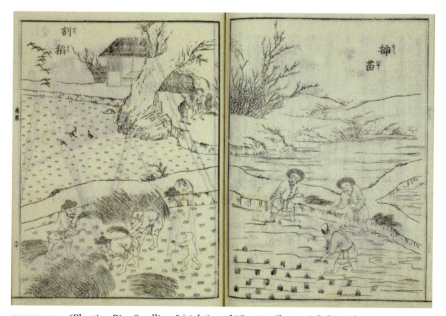

FIGURE 91 "Planting Rice Seedlings" (right), and "Cutting Sheaves" (left). Nakagawa (1799, 2).

FIGURE 92   "The Queue, the Flowered Skull-Cap, and Hair-bun," from Nakagawa (1799, 3).

noted above, was to identify certain products with "the foreign," and clothe peddlers of those products as "*tōjin*." Prominent among these was the peddler of "Korean" or "Chinese" candy: Since pharmaceutical products were a major import item, and since both disease and its cure had long been associated with "the foreign," medicines and lozenges—not only ginseng—refashioned as "foreign" had a special market appeal. Hanabusa Itchō, mentioned above, portrayed such a "Candy-man" (Figs. 70–71) whom he supplied with a blatant-ly "false" tie-on beard: It was important for "readers" of his print to know that this candy-man is a Japanese *playing* the *Tōjin*, rather than a "real" Chinese, so he is decked out in an array of iconographic keys that the "literate reader" of his text will decode in that way. The false beard tells us that something's up; the frills at his ankles and waist are iconographic markers of Other with roots in early Buddhist iconography. But the feet are the giveaway: our "Chinese Candy-man" wears *Japanese* straw sandals, which tell the "reader" what the game is.

Another Itchō painting (Figs. 93–94), the "*Tōjin* Quartermaster" (*Makanai Tōjin*), in the same collection, plays the same game. He depicts what at first glance appears to be the supply officer of a Korean embassy to Japan,[131] in a

---

131   Son and Muramatsu (1966–1969, 2:5a–6b). See also the 1765 version by Shōshōken (Buckingham Collection #65.594, Art Institute of Chicago).

FIGURE 93   After Hanabusa Itchō, "Makanai Tōjin" (The Foreign Quartermaster), in
Hanabusa (1770, vol. 2). Suzuki Rinshō's line drawing emphasizes the quartermaster's facial hair more than Itchō's original.

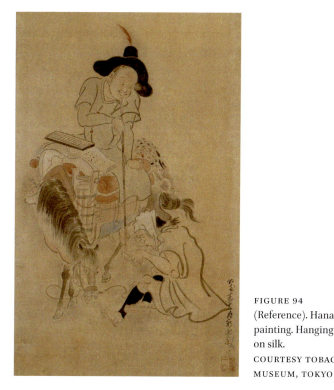

FIGURE 94

(Reference). Hanabusa Itchō's original
painting. Hanging scroll, ink and color
on silk.

COURTESY TOBACCO AND SALT
MUSEUM, TOKYO

hodgepodge of signs for Other mixed with cues telling us it is all a masquerade. The most flagrant cue, perhaps, is the quite ridiculous false beard tied to the quartermaster's ears. Itchō is deliberately mixing his signs: The moment we decide it is a "real" foreigner, something pops up to tell us we are wrong. What's likely going on here, is that he is depicting what would become a stock figure in *matsuri* performances of "*Tōjin* parades," from the Kantō to the Kansai, whose false beard—making him a *hige-Tōjin*—was a required part of his costume. The *makanai Tōjin* reappears, for example, in festivals in Kawagoe (Musashi Province), Tsu (Ise Province) and Tsuchiura (Hitachi Province),[132] and Katsushika Hokusai's choice to represent the "Sannō Matsuri" in his collection of prints of famous sights in Edo, *Tōto shōkei ichiran* (1800; Fig. 95) is likewise a "quartermaster" from the Kōjimachi performance, "Korean Parade," complete with waxed moustache and false beard.[133]

Not only for special roles like that of the "Quartermaster," but for nearly all the roles in the "foreigner" parades and dances that became a fixture in festivals from one end of Japan to the other in the seventeenth through nineteenth centuries, splendid false beards that would have been the envy of Hideyoshi became a required sign of the Othering of these performers. There are examples too numerous to catalogue, so I will take but three: The effigy of the "King of Korea," who was carried around Ōgaki (Mino Province) as part of the "Korean parade" of Takeshima-chō in the local Hachiman festival, the bearded masks that are part of the "*Tōjin* dance" (*Tōjin odori*) performed by the residents of Wakebe-chō in Tsu (Ise Province) at the annual Hachiman festival, and the outrageously false beards of the revelers from Kōjimachi, in their "Korean parade" performance in the Sannō Festival, as depicted in a mid-nineteenth century guide to the annual cycle of events in Edo (Fig. 96).[134] In each case, the beard—along with a cluster of other markers of alienness—are essential parts of "becoming Other," much like the tasseled Fez caps worn by Shriners in Independence Day parades all across the United States, that tell us they are (make-believe) "Turks."

As Japanese became—or fancied themselves—less and less hirsute, contrastive representations of relatively hairless "Japanese" selves and ever-hairier "others" became increasingly common, in pictorial, performative, and narrative

132 *Tsuchiura go-sairei no zu* (n.d., color on paper, Tsuchiura Municipal Museum); *Kawagoe Hikawa sairei emaki* (1826, color on paper, Kawagoe Municipal Museum). The *Hachiman sairei no shidai* (ca. 1854–60) recording performance costumes for the annual Hachiman festival in the town of Tsu, reproduced in Fukuhara (2003, 138–149), describe performers "dressed as *Tōjin* ... with false beards" (*tsukuri-hige nite*).

133 Katsushika Hokusai, "Sannō matsuri," in Katsushika (1800).

134 Saitō (1837/1980–1982, 2:110–111).

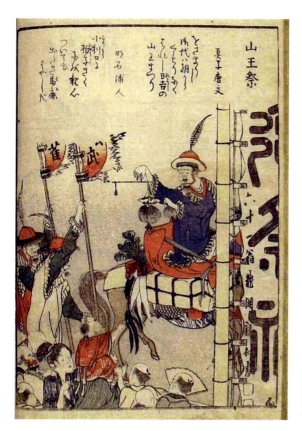

FIGURE 95

Katsushika Hokusai, *Sannō matsuri*, in Hokusai (1800), portrays a Japanese reveler in the role of the "Chinese quartermaster" as part of a masquerade "Korean parade," one of the most popular performances in Edo's great Sannō Festival. The man and his attendant flag bearers wear false beards.

FIGURE 96   Book illustration of Kōjimachi's "Korean Parade" in the Sannō Festival. All the men masquerading as Koreans wear long false beards, like the elephant handler in this detail, emphasizing the alienness of facial hair in the Japanese tonsorial regime. Saitō (1855).

FIGURES 97 & 98   Ambassador Kim Igyo (left) and military officer Hŏ Sŭng (right, "said to be
221.2 cm tall") are depicted as outlandishly hirsute, with lush, long beards
and bushy eyebrows in a scroll of portraits of members of Korean embassy
of 1811. Unsigned, *Bunka-do Chōsen tsūshinshi jinbutsu zukan* (ink & color
on paper, 1811).
COURTESY SIN KISU COLLECTION, OSAKA MUSEUM OF HISTORY

media. A print of circa 1748 is characteristic: Ishikawa Toyonobu (1711–1785;
Fig. 35) shows "A Korean Smoking," writing classical Chinese poetry in the air
with the smoke from his pipe. The print is laden with iconographic codes of
"otherness," including an especially thick, lush moustache and side-whiskers, a
dangling beard, and thick, bushy eyebrows. But most remarkable of all, I think,
is the man's hand: It is densely furred and clawed, the true *ketōjin*![135]

Even more radically "hairy barbarians," however, were those portrayed in
an official (i.e., bakufu-commissioned) set of "portraits" of the personnel of
the Korean mission of 1811 (Figs. 97 & 98). This series of paintings shows each
of the principal members of the embassy in official garb, some from the front,
others in rear or three-quarter views. Each face sports a set of eyebrows and
whiskers that might as easily have graced the visage of a Commodore Perry
print of forty years later! Here, the hairiness of the imagined "barbarian" has
gone wild![136]

Yet the hairiness of the barbarian is most vivid when set against the well-
ordered, properly inscribed, clean-shaven face and *sakayaki* of a Japanese hero,
and this is what Takizawa Bakin and Katsushika Hokusai have provided in the
illustrations for Bakin's masterpiece, *Chinsetsu yumiharizuki* (Takizawa 1807–
1811). This is a long fiction of exploits of the hero Minamoto no Tametomo,

---

135   Ishikawa Toyonobu, *A Korean Smoking*, (*benizuri-e*, 66.7 × 15.0 cm, British Museum acquisition number 1906.12–20.45), reproduced in Lawrence Smith (1988, 58).

136   *Chōsen tsūshinshi jinbutsu zu* (1811, color on paper, 30.3 × 984.0 cm, collection Tokyo
National Museum). See reproductions in Tokyo National Museum (1985, 13). A second
example of this work is in the Sin Kisu collection, Osaka Historical Museum.

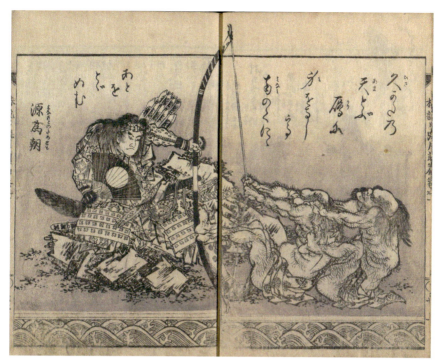

FIGURE 99   Katsushika Hokusai, frontispiece for Takizawa Bakin, *Chinsetsu yumiharizuki* (Takizawa 1807–1811, v. 1).

who was banished to the southern island of Ōshima for his part in the Hōgen Incident (1156), and who, in Japanese legend, was transformed into the founder of the Ryukyuan royal line. In the opening visual (Fig. 99), Hokusai shows us Tametomo, as Japanese warrior-hero, contesting the camellia-wood bow with a native of the islands. Tametomo, though historically he would have been as hirsute as the Japanese warrior in the *Bankoku jinbutsu zu* of 1647, seen above, while his nearly naked "Ryukyuan" counterpart is covered with hair from head to toe.[137]

8   Tying Up Loose Ends

Japanese ethnicities and identity(ies) were contested and in flux, being re-constructed and reinscribed not only in domestic practice, but in discourses of difference that marked "foreign bodies" as excluded others against which

---

137   Takizawa (1811/1958–1961, 61:72).

a "Japanese-ness" might be clear. As I have argued elsewhere, the crisis of ethnicity that—I believe—characterizes Edo-period discourse, is fundamentally different from the *Wa-kan* (Japan & China) dialectic of earlier years, that David Pollack has discussed, and that is played out on a different field from the scholarly and theological debates of Confucian and Nativist ideologues.[138] The collapse of both the Buddhist "Three-Kingdoms" cosmology of "Our-Land, the Continent, and Tenjiku" required a radical re-differentiation of what was "Japanese" from what I call "proximate others," in the face of the "radical alterities" suddenly posed by Europeans, Africans, and other Others from the mid-sixteenth century onwards.

The inscription of new, positively formulated "Japanese" identities likewise entailed the counter-inscription of new formulations of "excluded others," and it was in that process, I believe, that new ethnic pejoratives were summoned forth. The "hairy barbarian"—later transvalued to signify "Euro-Americans"—was an artifact of ethnic crisis vis-à-vis China, Korea, and other "proximate" or familiar others, in the mid seventeenth-century. The particular product—*ketōjin*—may have been fortuitous, but it has discursive roots in the changing cultural practices of mid-century Japan and China, as much as in popular discursive practices.

The continuing importance of tonsorial practice as a site for the articulation and contestation of ethnicity(ies) in Japanese culture is underscored by popular efforts to affect "foreign" hairstyles, in the years after the visit of a Korean embassy in 1748, for example, when the bakufu repeatedly attempted to suppress the wearing of cross-ethnic hairstyles: "In recent years, many of the townsfolk have taken to adopting foreign ways, in particular, doing up their hair in foreign hairstyles...."[139] which was prohibited—except in festival performances. Yet not all Japanese found "foreign" hairstyles attractive, for as one wag wrote in a satirical verse in *faux* classical Chinese, "The strange/foreign hairstyles of the [Korean ambassadors'] pages have no charm at all."[140]

The emergence, first of hair color, then of hairstyles, and ultimately, of the many varieties of hirsuteness as a site for the articulation of identities in seventeenth-century Japanese discourse, as represented in the emergence of *ketōjin* and *higetōjin* rhetoric, verbal, visual, and performative, underscores the crisis of identity inherent in the century of the Tokugawa and Qing settlements (here

---

138   Pollack (1986), Nakai (1980), and Harootunian (1980) look closely at the problem of "China" in elite discourse. Jansen (1980, 1992) looks at the "China problem" more broadly, in all levels of culture, elite and street.

139   Takayanagi and Ishii, ed. (1958, 295 [doc. 875]).

140   The original text: *Shōdō no uruwashikarazaru ihatsu sugata*, a passage from "Sajiki hihan," in Tsuji Jihei, *Ezu-iri Chōsen raihei-ki zen*, MS, 1748 (MS copy, 1764, private collection).

taken broadly to run from the mid-sixteenth to mid-seventeenth centuries). In Japanese discourse, the male face in a "state-of-nature" was transformed from manliness into "unshaved"-ness, resistance to authority, and hence barbarous foreignness, in the face of the universalization of shaving in Japanese practice. Neither a simple Wa-kan dichotomy, nor a tripartite Sangoku cosmology of Wagachō, Kara and Tenjiku, could adequately resolve or rationalize the "conceptualizations of the exotic and the domestic ..., [which] are inextricably intertwined,"[141] in Japanese discourse as elsewhere. The emergence and articulation of the *ketōjin* and *higetōjin* are signs of that struggle to reformulate comfortable distance between conceptions of a Japanese "self" and a newly numerous universe of exotic "others."

---

141   Boon (1982, 154). See also Boon (1990) on the of the constitution of an "un"-state through the practice of its negation.

CHAPTER 7

The Mountain That Needs No Interpreter:
Mt. Fuji and the Foreign

That mountain, Fuji!
O Chinamen! If you've any feelings,
Take one more journey, to admire its drifting snow!

attributed to Tōjin-kō ("Lord Tōjin"), 1669[1]

• • •

Everyone says that Chinamen write well…. Who knows? Their lousy brushwork can't be worth much. Having Fuji praised [by foreigners] is just a pain.

ŌTA NANPO, 1764[2]

• • •

---

1 *Fuji no yama/Tō no monodomo/kokoro araba/ima hitotabi no/miyuki medenan.* Yūsōan (1669) parodies the classic poetry collection *Hyakunin isshu* (ca. 1235). "Yūsōan" is a nom de plume for an otherwise unidentified satirist; no other work appears under this signature. For facsimile editions of *Inu hyakunin isshu*, see NSSSS, 30:456–480; Watanabe (1977). The best study of the *Hyakunin isshu* is Mostow (1996). The target of Yūsōan's satire is *Hyakunin isshu*, Poem 26, by "Lord Teishin" (Fujiwara no Tadahira, 880–949), "O autumn leaves/on the peak of Ogura Hill/If you have a heart/O would that you would wait/for one more imperial progress" (in Mostow 1996, 220; *Ogura-yama/mine no momiji-ba/kokoro araba/ima hitotabi no/miyuki matanamu*). Yūsōan translates Ogura Hill, which lay to the west of Kyoto, to Mt. Fuji; appropriates outright the third and fourth lines of Tadahira's poem; and puns on *miyuki*, written phonetically in the source poem, and generally read as 御幸, "imperial progress"; Yūsōan's version writes it with the *kanji* for the homophone 深雪, meaning "deep snow." Yūsōan's play on Tadahira's conceit that the insentient autumn leaves might be moved to sentiment implies that foreigners are ordinarily unfeeling, but that even they would be moved by the sight of Mt. Fuji's snowy mantle. He also translates Tadahira's *ima hitotabi no* ("one more time") to a homophone meaning "one more trip."

2 Ōta (1985, 1:351).

Foreigners bring tribute: The one mountain that needs no interpreter.
Anonymous poet, *Haifū yanagidaru*, 1811[3]

..
.

Parody and subversion of classical texts and images were a favorite literary and artistic pursuit in early modern Japan. Writers, readers, artists and publishers alike delighted in a *Phony Tale* [*of Ise*] or *Twenty-four Japanese Paragons of Unfiliality*.[4] So when the parodist Yūsōan (??–??) assumed the persona of "Lord Tōjin" (Tōjin-kō), poetically bringing foreigners to admire Japan's most famous mountain, illustrating the poem with a small parade of foreigners passing the foot of Mt. Fuji (Fig. 100), he was, to say the least, in good company.

One of a hundred invented poets in the satiric *Inu hyakunin isshu* (A Hundred Dogs, One Poem Each, 1669), Lord Tōjin assumed readers' knowledge not only of the *Hyakunin isshu* (A Hundred Poets, One Poem Each) source poem by Lord Teishin (Fujiwara no Tadahira, 880–949), but of illustrations of the source poem like one from a later Kyoto edition, showing an aristocrat's retinue passing Mt. Ogura.[5] The illustrator echoes the poem's conceit that anyone with feeling—even a foreigner—would be moved by the majestic snow-capped form of Mt. Fuji (Fig. 100); he parodies the stock depiction of Ariwara no Narihira gazing upon Mt. Fuji in *Ise Stories* (Fig. 101), but with the retinue marked iconographically as a group of Tōjin, led by a Japanese groom, passing the foot of the mountain. One of the *Tōjin* points upward, drawing the attention of his companions to the lofty peak.

---

3 Anonymous, in *Haifū yanagidaru*, 50, 16. See Okada, ed. (1976–1984), 4: 195.

4 *Nise* [phony] *monogatari*, ca. 1630, attributed to Karasumaru Mitsuhiro, is a send-up of the tenth-century Japanese poem-tale *Ise monogatari*, in Maeda and Morita (1965, 151–230); see also Mostow & Tyler (2010). Ihara Saikaku (1686/1953) satirizes the Chinese *Ershisi xiao* ("Twenty-Four Paragons of Filial Piety," J. *Nijūshi kō*), a Yuan dynasty (1271–1368) collection of didactic tales of Chinese paragons of filial widely read in early modern Japan; six Japanese print editions are known from the seventeenth century alone.

5 Poem 26, *Ogura-yama/mine no momiji-ba/kokoro araba/ima hitotabi no/miyuki matanamu* (O autumn leaves/on the peak of Ogura Hill,/if you have a heart,/would that you wait/for one more royal progress), Mostow (1996, 220). See the illustration from *Kogata hyakunin isshu zōsan-shō* (Kyoto: Kyōto Shorin, 1746), reproduced in Mostow (1996, 221). The illustration also parodies illustrated versions of *Ise monogatari*, which represents its hero riding "down to the east" past the foot of Mt. Fuji.

FIGURE 100 & 101　A group of *Tōjin* admiring Mt. Fuji as they travel past it towards Edo, in an illustration from Yūsōan's *Inu hyakunin isshu* (left), a parody of the late Heian/early Kamakura poetry collection, *One Hundred Poets, One Poem Each*. The inscription is a comic verse attributed to "Lord Tōjin," reading, "That mountain, Fuji!/O Chinamen! If you've any feelings,/Take one more journey, to admire its drifting snow!" parodying a *Hyakunin isshu* poem celebrating a quite different mountain, by "Lord Teishin." The illustration parodies a long visual tradition depicting Ariwara no Narihira's "journey to the East" (*Azuma kudari*), from the early Heian-period poem-tale, *Ise Stories* (*Ise monogatari*), such as the illustration at right, from the first print edition of *Ise Stories*, 1608).

The notion that people might come from abroad just to visit Mt. Fuji, that the "greatest mountain in all the world" (*sangoku-ichi no yama*) spoke not only to Japanese but to foreigners as well, was not new in the seventeenth century.[6] But any link between Mt. Fuji and the foreign, which was only a minor trope in earlier discourse, took on new and powerful valences in early modern discourse that have significant implications for our understanding of the formation of early modern and modern Japanese public discourse and popular

---

6　According to Kobayashi (2007, 72) *Sangoku denki* (ca. 1432), a medieval collection of Buddhist didactic tales (*setsuwa*), is the earliest identification of Mt. Fuji as *sangoku-ichi*.

ideology.[7] However minor or occasional a trope the conceit of intercourse between Mt. Fuji and the foreign in ancient and medieval discourse, the two merged in intimate converse quite early in the seventeenth century, and that conversation deepened and broadened throughout the early modern era. The outlines of that imagined communion between Mt. Fuji and the foreign have continued to shape popular discourse, as has the mobilization of the mountain as a domestic and global metonym for Japan itself, right down to the present day. That imagined communion with the mountain is the concern of the discussion that follows.

This satiric poem and the woodblock illustration that visualizes the poem, that is, are but one among countless instances in which Mt. Fuji imagery, both verbal and visual, was juxtaposed with representations of foreign peoples and distant lands in early modern discourse. But precisely how did foreigners know about Mt. Fuji in the first place? What brought them to cross the seas and parade past, gazing up in admiration? And, if those Tōjin indeed had "any feelings," was admiration the only sentiment that Mt. Fuji might arouse in them? What, that is, did Japanese discourse propose that Mt. Fuji and the foreign meant to each other and what, in turn, did that discourse mean to Japanese themselves?

1 National Symbols, Found and Made

Widely recognized symbols of shared identity and common purpose are as essential to a nation as proclaiming clear—and clearly recognized—geographic and human boundaries (the latter, citizenship or subjecthood) or creating a national language.[8] National symbols recognized as readily abroad as at home, however, seem most often to be manmade: the Great Wall of China, the Eiffel Tower, and the Statue of Liberty come readily to mind.

Mt. Fuji is in this sense anomalous—a "natural" feature of the Japanese landscape rather than part of the built environment. The majestically sloping, snow-capped cone of Mt. Fuji is without doubt the most widely recognized natural-feature-as-national-symbol of Japan, as readily identified with "Japan"

---

7 I distinguish here between the "foreign," or earthly Other, and the other-worldly Other, for linkage between Mt. Fuji and the other world was a long-established conceit. It was the place from which Kaguya-hime departed to return to her other-worldly home in *Taketori monogatari*, the site where the heavenly creature descended and danced in the *nō* play *Hagoromo*.

8 See especially Anderson (1992) for a stimulating discussion focused on the role of language and print capitalism in the emergence of national identity; Thongchai (1994) for a pioneering analysis of the cognitive dimensions of spatiality in the invention of the nation.

as the manmade "Rising Sun" flag. Indeed, no comparable geographic feature elsewhere comes readily to mind that so completely symbolizes a particular country, and no other country is so identified with a particular feature of the natural landscape.

Mt. Fuji's status as national symbol, however, is neither so timeless nor so natural as the mountain itself. Mt. Fuji as imagined is "made"—a discursive site constructed upon the mountain. Moreover, just as the recognition of the status of the Great Wall both at home and abroad as a Chinese national symbol is a quite modern development,[9] the construction of Mt. Fuji as a core symbolic site of Japanese national identity is a relatively recent, and ongoing, process.[10]

Before the seventeenth century, when both formal cultural production and its largely elite audience were centered in Kyoto and the capital region, the distant Mt. Fuji, though recognized as a "sacred mountain" (*reizan*), was essentially a peripheral symbol, a boundary marking the outer limits of the emperor's civilizing influence and the eastern limit of ethnic and cultural "Japan."[11] *Ise monogatari*, an early Heian poem-tale of the culture hero Ariwara no Narihira, sets Mt. Fuji as backdrop to Narihira's "descent into the [barbarous] east" (*azuma kudari*). Mt. Fuji was at the limits of Japan, rather than central to it. Indeed, Mt. Fuji was so alien to the courtier audience of *Ise monogatari* that the narrator had to recast it in terms more familiar to a Kyoto-centered culture: "If we compare that mountain (Fuji) to something here [in the capital], it's as tall as Mt. Hiei stacked up twenty-fold, its shape rather like a pile of salt."[12]

---

9   Waldron (1990, esp. 194–226).

10   Here I differ with Kawata (2008, 7), who argues that Mt. Fuji only came to symbolize Japan after the emergence of an "international self-consciousness that sprouted due to the opening of [Japan]" in the mid-nineteenth century. As will be seen below, the early modern discourse of Mt. Fuji was itself steeped in notions of Japan in international context.

11   By "formal cultural production," here, I mean production embodied in physical form— written, painted, sculpted, or built—as distinguished from, for example, oral literature, dance, and other performance forms that, however complex or sophisticated, are not committed to written form.

12   Sakakura, Ōtsu, Tsukishima, Abe, and Imai (1957, 117). Mostow & Tyler (2011, 35) render this line, "To compare the sight to something closer to home, the mountain was as high as twenty Mount Hieis piled on one another, and it looked like a heap of salt." Scholars generally date *Ise monogatari* in its current form to Fujiwara no Teika (1162–1241), who collated and copied the text a great number of times" (Mostow & Tyler 2011, 5), but conjecture that it includes material composed as early as the late ninth century. For an excellent reproduction of this scene in the thirteenth-century (?) illustrated scroll version, see *Bessatsu Taiyō: Fuji* (Winter 1983): 38–39; more readily available is *Nihon emaki-mono zenshū*, vol. 17 (Kadokawa, 1980), color fig. 4; b-w fig. 41; English explanation by Shirahata Yoshi, 7–8. The association of *azuma* with alien, wild, rustic, and barbarous customs was a recurrent trope in courtier discourse from the Heian era onward, fixed in terms like

Mt. Fuji was likewise the eastern limit of Prince Shōtoku's (574–622) legend-ary peregrinations, as depicted in the eleventh century *Illustrated Life of Prince Shōtoku*; beyond the mountain were only "eastern barbarians (*emishi*).[13]

Aliens, the excluded Other, we have seen, were also peripheral to visual rep-resentations of Japanese identity before the sixteenth century. Other appeared in Japan more frequently in literary setting—one thinks of the Koryŏ sooth-sayer who foretells Prince Genji's future—yet literature, too, largely kept Other "out there" rather than in Japan. Until Iberians burst into East Asia—and into Japanese consciousness—in the mid-sixteenth century, aliens were almost en-tirely absent from representation of Japanese settings in the visual arts, though there were countless depictions of "Chinese" in a "China" imagined or remem-bered and of Japanese travelers to China. After the arrival of the Europeans, however, as we have seen, images of the Alien deluge the ports, alleys, and highways in a new genre of painting, today called Nanban ("southern barbar-ian") art; the art of depicting the Other, especially, but not only, in Japanese surroundings.[14]

I focus in this chapter on the interplay of these two motifs, foreigners/for-eign lands and Mt. Fuji, in the art and popular culture of early modern Japan. Particularly, I shall examine the dialogical relationship in which Foreigner was employed in part to catalyze a transvaluation of Mt. Fuji, while Mt. Fuji became a mechanism to situate the Foreign in a *particular* relationship to Japan. I shall argue that from the late seventeenth century onward, a continuous, but evolv-ing, dialogue emerged, in virtually every medium of expressive popular cul-ture, between a "Fuji" that stood as icon for "Japan" and equally iconic aliens. This dialogue was based on a rhetoric that argued in both verbal and nonver-bal terms an assumption of Japanese primacy and the subordination, indeed subjugation, of the foreign. While the rhetoric allowed for a simple, lyric alien admiration of Mt. Fuji's (Japan's) sublimity, it will be seen in examining the

---

     azuma ebisu—"eastern barbarians"—which came also to denote the "wild" samurai of eastern Japan; the *Vocabulario da Lingoa de Iapam* (Nagasaki, 1603) defines an *azuma votoko* (*azuma-otoko*; "man of azuma") as a "man of the east; a base person; or a bumpkin." Doi et al. (1980, 45).

13   See *Shōtoku Taishi eden* (Nara, 1969; Kikuchi, 1973).

14   Izumi (1988) makes a strong case for representations of Chinese in Japanese settings as precursors of the Nanban genre in fifteenth- and sixteenth-century works that no longer survive. For a stimulating study of the construction of China in the Japanese literary tradi-tion, see Pollack (1986)'; for Pollack, an undifferentiated "China" constituted Japan's sole, unitary Other, leaving no room for other Others, as it were, in Korea, Manchuria, and so forth. Pollack examines Japanese painting in Chinese styles, along with literature, but not Japanese portrayal of "Chinese" or other aliens in the visual arts per se. On Nanban art, see Cooper (1971) and Okamoto (1977).

terms of debate that the rhetoric became more militant toward the last years of the Edo era and that it peaked at moments of crisis—even into the twentieth century—in particularly virulent, aggressive formulations.

2   The Rise of Mt. Fuji

Though it had long held pride of place as Japan's greatest mountain, it was only in the Edo period, especially after about 1700, that Mt. Fuji metamorphosed from remote boundary outpost between Culture and Barbarity, to a central symbol through which Japan represented itself, both to itself, and to others. Other, of course, was not solely responsible for this central transvaluation: Edo's establishment as the center of national politics in the seventeenth century and its gradual displacement of Kyoto and Osaka as the dominant center of cultural production and arbiter of taste were clearly the main engines of this transvaluation.[15] As part of this process, Mt. Fuji was made to speak to the Foreign, to emphasize its Otherness, while reducing the distance separating Mt. Fuji (Japan) from the Foreign, bringing the Foreign into the orbit of Mt. Fuji (Japan), and subordinating the Foreign to the mysterious, universal powers of the sacred mountain.

The explosive growth of Mt. Fuji piety, which in the eighteenth and nineteenth centuries became immensely more popular than it ever had been, helped to generate interest, on the one hand, in making ever-greater claims for Mt. Fuji's numinous reach, and on the other, a rapidly expanding market for images of Mt. Fuji.[16] What had been primarily a cult of a small number of itinerant *yamabushi* (mountain holy men) burgeoned from the 1760s into a popular cult, in some areas rivaling that of the Ise Shrine. Fuji preachers (*oshi*) roamed the country promoting the god of Mt. Fuji. Fuji-cult confraternities (*Fuji-kō*) proliferated, sponsoring mass pilgrimages to the sacred mountain; they built "Fuji mounds" (*Fujizuka*) all over the Kantō plain and elsewhere that

---

15   Ikezawa for example, notes that "The unique character of early modern literary works that took Mt. Fuji as their subject, not visible in other eras, is intimately linked to the city of Edo." (2000, 236).

16   For a brief English-language review of the cultural valuation of Mt. Fuji, see Tyler (1981). For an introduction to the emergence of Fuji pietism in the Edo period, see Tyler (1984). Kakugyō (1541–1646) and Jikigyō (1671–1733) were instrumental in the (re)popularization of Fuji piety in the Edo period. For an introduction to recent Japanese scholarship on the Fuji cult, see Hirano (1987), especially chapters by Iwashina Shōichirō ("Fuji-kō" [71–95]) and Hirano ("Fuji to minzoku" [97–109]) and the bibliography of studies of the Fuji cult (354–357).

were as large as fifteen to twenty meters tall, using lava chunks from the mountain itself, making vicarious pilgrimage possible for those too poor or frail—or for women, who were normally barred from the sacred slopes—to visit the mountain itself.[17] And volcanic cones from Kagoshima in the south to Hirosaki in the north took the nickname "the Mt. Fuji of such-and-such a place." This growing cult of Mt. Fuji must be kept in mind, for it is there that the transformation of Mt. Fuji to national symbol derives its greatest power; the dialogue with the Other is but a field on which that transformation was articulated.

However, this dialogue between Fuji and Foreigner as it relates to the transformation of Fuji from a symbol of boundary to a symbol of nation is also representative of a transvaluation in Japanese discourse of Japan itself. What had been a "small country on the periphery" of East Asia (*hendo shōkoku*) in medieval thought, as Narusawa Akira has argued, was refashioned into a competitor for centrality in East Asia, displacing even China, as I have shown elsewhere and as others have noted as well.[18]

Mt. Fuji's symbolic status, like all symbolisms, was socially and culturally constructed in a process that took place in a particular historical context. And by the same token, the significance of the Other, of the foreigner, and of the iconography in which it was represented were constructed over time in similar fashion. Although visual representations of Other in Japan are scarce prior to the late sixteenth century, as noted above, literary and performative representations are fairly common, and it was these representations more than actual contact with foreigners that informed popular notions of Other. From at least the late sixteenth century, and probably much earlier, Japanese regularly recreated Other in festival performance as well, in both organized coordinated fashion and in spontaneous (if culturally constrained) enactments, much like those we are familiar with in Mardi Gras and Carnaval. Therefore, my principal concern in this discussion is to articulate attitudes toward Japanese "ethnic" or

---

17   *Oshi* were specialists that served one particular cult site exclusively; they were generally bound to the site by a complex set of what we might call licensing arrangements and frequently had long-standing relationships with the inns to which they steered their pilgrims. Other *oshi* proselytized for Ise, Kumano, and other cult sites as well as Mt. Fuji. See especially Iwashina (1983), esp. Chapter 3, "Edo no Fuji-kō," on both the confraternities and the professional religious who served them. For a more recent discussion, focused primarily on the activities of the Fuji cult *oshi*, Takano (1992).

18   On medieval Japanese self-representation as an isolated periphery, see especially Narusawa (1978); on the transformation of Japan from periphery to center in Japanese thought, see Toby (1984 & 1985), Arano (1988) and Takagi (1992), which has since appeared in English in revised form as Takagi (2004).

"national" self and Other in a dialogic relationship of Fuji and Foreigner in the iconography of Edo-period art and popular culture.[19]

The development of iconographies is a large, complex, and important subject; the iconography of Mt. Fuji is well studied, though rarely with reference to the mountain's ideological significance.[20] In this discussion, I shall occasionally refer back to these earlier iconographic traditions of both Fuji and Other but focus primarily on their intertwinement in the Edo period. The ironic juxtaposition of Fuji and Foreigner in iconography and performance transformed the significatory value of each but especially helped, I would argue, to advance popular notions of Japanese sacrality and centrality (Japan as "Land-of-the-gods" [*shinkoku*] or "Central-kingdom" [*chūgoku; chūka*]) that had long since made strong inroads on elite ideology. Ultimately such rhetoric served to strengthen popular belief in Japanese exceptionalism, in Japanese superiority to other peoples, and in Japanese prerogatives to dominate neighboring peoples, thus helping generate images that promoted popular support for Japanese expansionism.

The effacement of Chinese and Koreans from representations of the domestic landscape began to change in the late sixteenth century, however. In the Nanban period, it became increasingly common for Japanese artists to depict foreigners in specific, identifiable sites in Japan, for these new, strange aliens were the focus of great interest. These Iberian visitors and their variegated entourages of Africans, Indians, and Southeast Asians, in port at Nagasaki, and on the streets of the capital, became a popular theme for painters—who were undoubtedly responding to specific commissions from their powerful patrons. Occasionally they also included one or two Chinese figures among the other Others depicted aboard ship or engaged in trade onshore, yet Chinese or Korean figures remained rare in Nanban art.[21]

---

19   There are dangers, of course, in using either "ethnic" or "national" in the context of seventeenth- to early-nineteenth-century Japan. Both are partially apt and partially infelicitous, and neither alone is adequate.

20   A good introduction to the development of Mt. Fuji iconography is Naruse (1982, 1983b, 1983a). For an illustrated history of Fuji iconography, see Yamato (1980), the catalog of an exhibition of Mt. Fuji in Japanese painting. Naruse was curator for that exhibition; his articles may be read as a commentary on the exhibit. A classic, though dated, study of Mt. Fuji in the visual arts is Sawada (1928). More recently, Earhart (2011, 15–21; 99–130), and Lippit (2012, ch. 2). I know of no serviceable study of the iconography of Other in Japanese art.

21   See, for example, the Chinese figure seated on the foredeck of the punt dockside in Nagasaki, and two others on the wharf in the pair of unsigned Nanban screens in the collection of the Cleveland Museum, in *Kinsei fūzoku zufu 13: Nanban* (Shōgakukan, 1974), 36–37. The scarcity of Chinese among the Nanban is typified by the fact that these three

In the 1590s, however, Hideyoshi's Korean campaigns (1592–1598) deployed tens of thousands of samurai to the battleground, and consequently unprecedented numbers of Japanese from all over the country found themselves in face-to-face encounters with both Koreans and Chinese.[22] These encounters took place at home as well, for the war brought equally unprecedented numbers of Koreans to Japan, primarily as war prisoners. By war's end, tens of thousands of Koreans were scattered across Japan, from one end to the other.[23] In 1591, Hideyoshi began construction of a massive castle at Nagoya, in northwestern Kyushu, to serve as his command headquarters for the invasion; by the beginning of the war, the castle was the heart of a sprawling, bustling town containing the mansions of Tokugawa Ieyasu, and over 120 more of Hideyoshi's greatest vassals.

Sometime around 1593, Hideyoshi commissioned Kanō Mitsunobu (1561–1602) to paint a panoramic view of Nagoya Castle and the surrounding town, which he executed in a quasi-cartographic, bird's-eye view that looked across the harbor to the sprawling castle rising in the background.[24] Mitsunobu depicts a parade of Chinese diplomats, led by a vanguard of Japanese samurai, approaching the castle along a street that leads from the harbor, where three large Japanese warships lie at anchor; smaller tenders are moored at the dock. On a side street, Mitsunobu adds two Japanese in Nanban dress deep in conversation—perhaps a nod to Hideyoshi's well-known love of Nanban fashion. The Chinese are but a detail in the grand sweep of the cityscape, but they—not to mention the Japanese spectators along their route—are by far the largest group of figures in the entire composition—and the most colorful, as well.

The dialog of Fuji and Other has archaic roots, though the rhetoric we shall be examining was not fully articulated until the eighteenth century. As a *reizan*, Mt. Fuji had evoked alien and otherworldly associations from very early times: *Taketori monogatari* ("The Tale of the Bamboo Cutter," late 9th-early 10th c.) recounts the tale of Kaguya-hime, a heavenly princess of such beauty that

are the only identifiably Chinese figures (i.e., conforming to Japanese conventions for the representation of Chinese) among over 300 figures in the three Nanban screens reproduced in this volume.

22   There is a large corpus of both Korean and Japanese scholarship on the war. For a recent concise, but reliable history of Hideyoshi's invasions, see Kitajima (1995). See also Ch'oe (1974); Ikeuchi (1987); Sanbō Honbu (1924); Yi (1967); Yi (1999).

23   The definitive study of Korean war prisoners in the campaigns of the 1590s is Naitō (1976).

24   *Hizen Nagoya-jō zu byōbu*, ink and color on paper, Nagoya-jō Hakubutsukan. See *Kokka*, no. 915 (1968) for a full-color reproduction and several research articles about the Nagoya screen. *Rakuchū rakugai* screens, bird's-eye urban panoramas of Kyoto and its surroundings, emerged as an important new genre in the sixteenth century. See McKelway (2006) for an important new discussion of the urban panorama genre.

she inspires a parade of suitors during her brief sojourn on earth. When she is recalled to her capital on the moon, she leaves the imperial envoy "the elixir of immortality (*fushi no kusuri*)" as a parting gift. Bereft, the emperor spurns immortality, sending an envoy to "the summit of a mountain in the province of Suruga," the tallest peak and hence closest to heaven, to burn "the elixir of immortality" there; the smoke rises quickly to heaven. To commemorate the volcanic smoke of *fushi* rising to the Other world, the mountain was named with the homophonous "Fuji."[25]

A peak as lofty and perfectly formed as Mt. Fuji was surely a gateway to heaven—and not only in the purely fictional world of *Taketori*. As early as the eleventh century, as noted above, Prince Shōtoku was depicted ascending to heaven over Mt. Fuji. In *nō* drama, too, Mt. Fuji is an intersection between this world and others; between Japan and the foreign. An angel dances before the mountain in the *nō* play *Hagoromo*, while in *Fujisan* a Tang Chinese journeys to Japan seeking the elixir of immortality found only at Mt. Fuji.[26]

3   On a Clear Day You Can See Forever: Mt. Fuji and the Ambit of the Gods

As noted above, the Korean campaigns of the 1590s were a transformative moment in the mutual awareness of Japanese and Koreans; the echoes of that transformation still ring through the popular and scholarly discourse of both countries today, more than four centuries later.[27] Even the discourse of Mt. Fuji and the Foreign took a decisive new turn, inspired by the (often heavily embellished) exploits of one of the generals who had led Hideyoshi's armies in Korea, Katō Kiyomasa (1562–1611).[28]

---

25   *Taketori monogatari*, 10, in Sakakura, Ōtsu, Tsukishima, Abe, and Imai (1957, 5, 66) or Horiuchi and Akiyama (1997, 75–76).

26   For *Hagoromo*, see Yokomichi and Omote (1960–1963, 2:326–329); for *Fujisan*, see Nonomura (1988, 58–60). Both plays are credited to Zeami. *Fushi*, "not to die," is written with the same *kana* as Fuji, the mountain's name; this sort of word play is common in *nō* plays.

27   Some important studies of the enduring transformations in Japanese culture, consciousness, and memory emerging from the Korean campaigns are Abe (1965); Ch'oe (1994); Ikeuchi (1999); Hino (1991, 265–304); Haboush (2016).

28   Japanese biographies of Kiyomasa tend to the hagiographic; the classic is Nakano (1909/1979), which was published on the eve of the 300th anniversary of Kiyomasa's death; a more recent treatment is Araki (1989). If Kiyomasa came to be revered in Japan, in Korea he came to personify the brutality of the Japanese armies. Maliangkay (2007)

FIGURE 102
Map of Korea showing Katō
Kiyomasa's route into Hamgyŏngdo,
across the Tumen into "Orankai,"
and then along the course of the
Tumen River to Sŏsura, where he
"saw" Mt. Fuji.

As commander of the east-route army during the first invasion, Kiyomasa was one of those leading the first assault, landing in Pusan on 1592/4/14 (24 May). Korea was unprepared for an attack, and the Japanese armies moved quickly from one victory to the next; they took the capital of Hansŏng (Seoul) on 5/3 (12 June) and Kaesŏng on 5/29 (7 July). From Kaesŏng, Kiyomasa's army turned northeast and fought its way up the coast, taking Hamgyŏngdo (Hamgyŏng Province)—though he would not hold it for long (Fig. 102).

On 7/23 (30 August), Kiyomasa took the district capital of Hoeryŏng, only a few miles from the Tumen River, the boundary between Korea and the Jurchen lands beyond—though even the Korean side of the river was compared to distant Japanese islands such as "Hachijōjima and Iōgashima, a place where

---

discusses several Korean folk songs (minyo) in which Ch'ŏngjong (the Korean pronunciation of "Kiyomasa") is the villain.

criminals are sent into exile."[29] As he reported that same day to Hideyoshi's aide, Natsuka Masaie, "I learned that two Korean royal princes were in the southern part of [Hamgyŏngdo], so I searched the entire frontier wilderness, and found the Korean king's heir apparent [and many others] holed up in a fortification called Hoeryŏng. I no sooner attacked, than the fortress surrendered.... I have taken them all prisoner."[30]

Then, on 7/27 (3 September), according to accounts widely circulated in Edo-period Japan, Kiyomasa crossed the Tumen River from Hamgyŏngdo into what is now Jilin Province in northeast China, a region that Japanese would know as "Orankai."[31] This marked the limits of Japanese success: They were soon forced to retreat and ultimately would return to Japan seven years later, never achieving Hideyoshi's dreams of conquest and territorial aggrandizement. Kiyomasa spent the better part of a month reconnoitering the trans-Tumen area, advancing through Longjing to Juzijie before turning back and reentering Hamgyŏngdo on 8/22 (27 September).

Like so much of Kiyomasa's life, his campaign in Hamgyŏngdo and Orankai is clouded in the heroic legend that accrued to him, a legend first shaped by his vassal, Shimokawa Heidayū, in his *Kiyomasa Kōrai-jin oboegaki* ("Memoir of Kiyomasa's exploits in the Korea Campaigns"), a dozen years after his lord's death in 1611.[32] We pick up Shimokawa's account with Kiyomasa in Hoeryŏng:

---

29   *Kiyomasa Kōrai-jin oboegaki*, quoted in Kitajima (1982, 110).

30   Kiyomasa to Natsuka Masaie, Tenshō 20/7/23, quoted in Kitajima (1982, 111).

31   The historicity of Kiyomasa's foray across the Tumen River, and the location of the "Orankai" referred to in these accounts, has been debated since the early eighteenth century. The mid-Edo period scholar Kawaguchi Seisai (1703–54) challenged the account in its entirety, writing that although the *Chōsen seibatsu-ki* (Hori 1659) says "Kiyomasa reached deep into [Orankai], there is no evidence that he got that far; I have always doubted the account. I asked Amenomori Hōshū [1668–1755, Tsushima Confucian scholar and specialist on Korean affairs]. He said, 'Korean dialect calls the entire untamed frontier region Orankai; it is not the fixed name of a particular place....'" Kim (2010, 126). Kim Sidŏk accepts this view, and argues that Kiyomasa only "neared the Orankai frontier," but did not actually cross into what is now Jilin Province. On the other hand, Nakamura Hidetaka (1965–1967), 2: 106, Nakamura (1980), Kitajima (1990, 64; 300; 323–325; 387), Nukii Masayuki (1996, 196–197), and Nakano Hitoshi (2008, 65–68), accept Kiyomasa's foray across the Tumen into Orankai as historical fact. Whether or not Kiyomasa actually crossed the Tumen, however, Edo-period popular discourse—except for a few scholars—held the accounts to be true. Kawaguchi is most likely referring to Hori (1659), but several printed or manuscript works titled *Chōsen seibatsu-ki* circulated at the time.

32   Shimokawa's account, written ca. 1624, was first published in 1669. Shimokawa (1669/1970). Fukunishi (2012, 234–263) catalogs nearly four hundred Shinto and Buddhist sites where Kiyomasa is enshrined as a deity.

Though Kiyomasa's armies numbered ten thousand horsemen, he left troops at every town he had taken, so when he arrived at Hoeryŏng (Hoireku), there were only eight-thousand-odd.... Kiyomasa wondered if there might be a prince or some such [in the town], so he resolved to enter the town. He wanted see if the person holed up there was actually the [prince] or only an imposter.... [After he took the town] Kiyomasa took the two brother princes and all the rest captive and put them under guard....

Kiyomasa used interpreters to inquire about the situation in Orankai. They told him there were many archers in Orankai ... but Kiyomasa responded that he would send in Japanese archers [against them].... He was told that there was an outpost (*bansho*) about four and one-half *ri* [ca. 18 kilometers] from Hoeryŏng, and from there it was a day's march to the capital of Orankai.... Early the next morning, he arrived at his camp before an array of thirteen [enemy] fortifications. As is the custom in foreign lands [*ikoku*], they were well-fortified in front, but to the rear they relied only on the mountains and some stone walls, which didn't look like much of a defense. So Kiyomasa sent the [men he'd conscripted from] Hoeryŏng to attack from the front, while he sent his Japanese troops around to [attack from] the mountains in the rear.... They used iron crowbars to tear down the stone works, and rushed down from the mountainside firing their muskets. All the Orankai troops fled ...

Kiyomasa then withdrew five or six *ri* back toward Korea and made camp on a hillside. He was planning to return to his base in Korea the following day, when an Orankai force of untold thousands of men attacked [his position].... They attacked with such ferocity, and in such numbers, that [Kiyomasa] was in dire straits. But perhaps *because Japan is the land of the gods* (*Nihon shinkoku yue nite sōrō ya*), there was a sudden downpour that day, and it rained in faces of the Orankai troops so fiercely that they could not attack and had to withdraw. The following day, [Kiyomasa] made it back to his camp in Kuisŏng, in Korea....

After five days' encampment in Kuisŏng to rest his men and horses, [Kiyomasa] marched five days east to a place called Sŏsura [a port at the mouth of the Tumen], where he heard of a general of the north country named Serutōsu ....[33] [Kiyomasa] captured Serutōsu. Serutōsu was about

---

33 Arai Hakuseki doubted that "Serutōsu" actually existed, and began trying to explain him and the entire myth of Kiyomasa in Orankai as a textual confusion. See Arai Hakuseki, *Hankanpu* (1716) in Arai (1905–1907, 1:546). Ikeuchi (1914–1936, 1:254–255) agrees with Hakuseki's identification of "Serutōsu" as Han Kuksŏng, the military inspector (*chŏlttosa*

fifty-four or fifty-five years of age; he was about six *shaku* five *sun* (197 cm;
6' 5½") tall, a large man with a thick beard. Serutōsu said he had heard
that Japanese had come to the area and had encamped in this place.... We
took him easily. We also captured an interpreter named Gotō there. This
Gotō was cast up here in Sŏsura when his fishing boat out of Matsumae
in Japan (i.e., Hokkaido) had been blown here in a storm. He had been
here for twenty years and was fluent in Orankai language, Korean, and
Japanese. He was [such] a talented interpreter that Kiyomasa cherished
him and gave him the name "Jirō," calling him "Gotō Jirō."

"When the weather is fair," [Jirō said], "*you can see Mt. Fuji from Sŏsura,*
as if it were really close by. From there, you can see Mt. Fuji in the southwest, [so] I think we are due north of Matsumae."[34]

Shimokawa's account is noteworthy in several respects. As he tells it, Kiyomasa
survived his trans-Tumen adventure "because Japan is the land of the gods,"
who sent a storm to his aid when confronted with an enemy attacking in over-
whelming numbers. Protected by the Japanese gods, Kiyomasa returns safely
to his base on the Korean side of the Tumen. There, his interpreter—a man
from "Matsumae, in Japan," who has been marooned in the Orankai region for
twenty years—says that if he looks out from Orankai on a clear day, he will
see Mt. Fuji rising from the southwestern horizon, across the sea. Just as important, this vignette of Kiyomasa's transmarine Mt. Fuji sighting became the
template for further retellings of the legend for the remainder of the Tokugawa
period, and beyond into the Meiji era.[35]

It goes without saying, of course, that Mt. Fuji is not visible from the
mouth of the Tumen River, some 1,050 kilometers (650 miles) distant, nor
from Matsumae.[36] (Fig. 103) Mt. Fuji, at 3,776 meters (12,388 feet), is the tall-

---

節度使) of northern Hamgyŏngdo Kiyomasa captured at Sŏsura. "Serutōsu" and "Seishū-
ura" are quite plausible Japanese phonetic transcriptions of "*chŏlttosa*" and "Sŏsura." Arai
and Ikeuchi are likely correct that "Serutōsu" is a fiction—as is the sighting of Mt. Fuji
but the fiction itself has a cultural reality, which is what we confront here. Thus, when the
Kiyomasa legend was taken up by modern nationalist writers—and artists, as we shall
see—at times of crisis, they found it convenient to accept both Serutōsu and the legend
of Kiyomasa gazing at Mt. Fuji from afar. See, e.g., Wada (1943, 106).

34   Shimokawa, *op. cit.* (emphasis added). Quoted from Kimura (n.d., vol. 1). Furuhashi (n.d.
     vol. 2; Furuhashi 1924, 341), and Shimokawa Heidayū (1669/1970, 302), give virtually iden-
     tical accounts. The legend of Kiyomasa seeing Mt. Fuji from Orankai evolved through
     multiple retellings over the course of the Edo period. See Kim (2010), esp. Ch. 4.

35   E.g., Ōta (1782); Terasawa (1790); Akizato (1800); Takeuchi & Okada (1797–1802).

36   The maximum distance from which Mt. Fuji is visible at sea level—assuming, of course,
     that the skies between are perfectly clear and nothing obstructing the view—is ap-
     proximately 220 km. On an exceptionally clear day, Mt. Fuji is visible as far west as

est mountain in Japan, and when midwinter skies are exceptionally clear it is visible for a great distance—more than 200 kilometers (124 miles)—at sea level.[37] Furthermore, of course, Mt. Fuji is south*east* of Sŏsura, rather than "southwest." If Kiyomasa had in fact seen a mountain that looked like Mt. Fuji to his *southwest*, it would have had to be a peak on Korea's eastern coast, but no east-coast mountain even remotely fits the morphology of Mt. Fuji.[38]

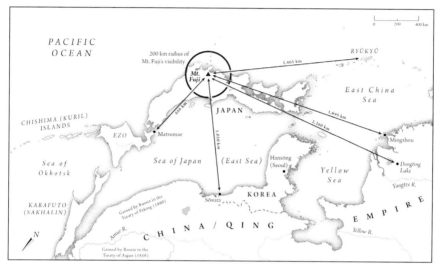

FIGURE 103   Map of Mt. Fuji's radius of visibility—assuming no intervening obstacles, such as the Japan Alps—and distances to places where Edo-period textual and pictorial discourse claimed the mountain was visible.

Futami-ga-ura and the lowlands along Ise Bay but no farther; to the east, it can be seen along the northern reaches of the Hitachi coast (Ibaraki Prefecture) and parts of southern Fukushima. A Mt. Fuji-centered vision emerges in Edo-period discourse, nicely symbolized by Akiyama Nagatoshi's *Fujisan jūsan-shū yochi no zenzu* (Edo, 1842, Rare Books and Special Collections, University of Illinois Library), a map of Mt. Fuji and the thirteen provinces of Japan from which it can be seen. To be visible from the Orankai coast, by my calculations, Mt. Fuji would have to be about 175 km high.

37   Mt. Fuji is occasionally visible from even greater distances, at higher elevations: On 22 September 2014 an amateur photographer photographed the summit of Mt. Fuji from a mountaintop on the eastern outskirts of Kyoto, a distance of about 265 km. *Mainichi shinbun*, 2014/09/23.

38   Korea's mountainous east coast arcs southwestward from the mouth of the Tumen for about 180 kilometers (112 miles) to a cape south of Kalmo, North Hamgyŏng Province (40°50'29"N, 129°44'48"E), which is the last point on an unobstructed direct line—over the horizon—SW from the mouth of the Tumen. The east coast mountains are the product of block movements resulting from compressive stress, tilting, and block movements; none are volcanic cones. On the geology of Korea, Tateiwa (1960); coordinates from *Google Earth* (2013.03.13).

Whatever mountain it was that Kiyomasa actually saw from Sŏsura—assuming any factual basis for this legend—it was not Mt. Fuji. But it matters little whether this was a case of mistaken identity or a completely apocryphal yarn, for the tale of Kiyomasa seeing Mt. Fuji from either Orankai or Korea quickly embedded itself as cultural reality in the fabric of Japanese popular belief. Interpreting myth and legend is always a tricky business, but this account of Kiyomasa's exploits in Orankai and the northern reaches of Hamgyŏngdo seems to evoke quite clear messages.

First, by invoking the divinity of Japan (*shinkoku*, "land of the gods") as the power that saved Kiyomasa and his army when they were hopelessly outnumbered, Shimokawa's account attributes to the Japanese gods the power to reach beyond the "sixty-six provinces" of the homeland and protect Japanese far beyond the seas—toward the ubiquity of their power. In doing so, he implicitly evokes the "divine winds" (*kamikaze*), the storms called up by the Japanese gods to destroy the invading Mongol fleets in 1274 and 1281.

And second, by linking the extended reach of the Japanese gods to the extended visibility of Mt. Fuji—it is invocation of those very gods that preserves Kiyomasa to fight another day, to make it safely back to his base in Hamgyŏngdo, and see Mt. Fuji—the story both centers the projection of Japanese divine authority on Mt. Fuji and subliminally asserts two corollaries: on the one hand, that the power of Japan's gods extends everywhere Mt. Fuji is visible and, on the other, that the entire ambit of the gods' power ought properly to be ruled by Japan. Mt. Fuji, the greatest of Japan's many sacred mountains, looks across the sea on Kiyomasa's project and guarantees its success.

The legend of Kiyomasa grew after his death, especially after his heirs were dispossessed by the shogun in 1632—the reasons are unclear—and he became a popular cult figure believed to bring "martial success without limit."[39] The legend that he saw Mt. Fuji from Orankai (or Korea; the precise location varies with the retelling) also took on a life of its own, making its way into the popular imagination in both textual and visual representation.[40] As we shall

---

39   Saitō (1834–1835/1966–1968), 3: 71. *Edo meisho zue* was a popular, influential Edo guidebook; this passage is from the section on Saishō Gakurinji, a Nichiren sect Buddhist temple in Edo said to have been founded by one of the Korean princes Kiyomasa took captive. There was a monthly pilgrimage to the shrine to Kiyomasa within the temple precincts. Saitō (1837/1972–1974, 2: 132). There were similar shrines to Kiyomasa in Kumamoto, his castle town in western Kyushu, and in Maruoka (modern Yamagata Prefecture), where his son was buried. Fukunishi (2012), a study of the cult of Kiyomasa, catalogs nearly four hundred shrines and temples dedicated to Kiyomasa.

40   Versions of the legend, both visual and textual, appeared frequently in Meiji-era accounts of the Korean campaigns and biographies of Kiyomasa, some of them written by

see below, the legend of Kiyomasa and Mt. Fuji metamorphosed in succeeding decades and centuries from simple hero tale to a sort of scientific truth. The legend has, at its core, two simple ideological assertions: First, Mt. Fuji is visible to unimaginable distances beyond the seas—the "fact" that Kiyomasa saw it from the mouth of the Tumen does not exclude the possibility of an even more distant prospect. Second, and perhaps of greater ideological potency, the amuletic power of Mt. Fuji's numen extends everywhere the mountain is visible, just as it protects Kiyomasa and ensures his victory.

Returning to the bit of doggerel with which we began, if Mt. Fuji could inspire normally unfeeling foreigners to endure the long "journey to admire its drifting snow," perhaps they came from afar precisely because they could see Mt. Fuji from their distant country and were drawn by its majesty to come and "admire." But what, if any, were the limits of the mountain's visibility—and its numinous ambit?

4   Universal Mt. Fuji as "Scientific" Truth

The trope of Mt. Fuji's near-universal visibility made its debut as part of the hagiographic tale of a Japanese hero fighting on distant foreign shores. The legend of Kiyomasa, Serutōsu, and the sighting of Mt. Fuji from an encampment along the Tumen River is of course blatantly apocryphal and was rejected by some Edo-period scholars as fantasy. Yet the tale nonetheless circulated widely from the 1660s on, both in hagiographic biographies of Kiyomasa and in more complete accounts of Hideyoshi's invasion of Korea. The episode began as legend, perhaps, but quickly made the transition to scholarly truth toward the end of the seventeenth century.

Mt. Fuji got a boost in this transition from Matsushita Kenrin (1637–1703), a Kyoto physician and historian, whose magnum opus, *Ishō Nihon-den* ("Foreign accounts of Japan"), was an attempt to resolve contradictions between Chinese and Korean historical accounts of Japan and the Japanese record—which he generally took as true.[41] One of the Korean texts Kenrin quoted extensively, and examined with great interest, was Sin Sukchu's *Haedong chegukki*, a

---

respected, influential historians, e.g., Rai San'yō's 1827 *Nihon gaishi* (Rai 1979–1981, 89–90); Fukuchi Gen'ichirō (Fukuchi 1891, 52).

41   Matsushita Kenrin, *Ishō Nihon-den*, 7 vols. (Settsu Kitanomidō [Osaka]: Mōrita Shōtarō, 1693). In *Ishō Nihon-den*, Kenrin compiles and annotates accounts of Japan in dozens of Chinese and Korean texts. There is a facsimile edition in 2 vols. (Kokusho Kankōkai, 1975), as well as two modern reprints: in Mozume (1927–1929, 12:187–953); and *Kaitei shiseki shūran*, vol. 24 (Sumiya Shobō, 1968). All citations are to the 1968 edition, which is the

fifteenth-century political, diplomatic, economic and geographic gazetteer of Japan and the Ryukyuan kingdom.[42] The *Haedong chegukki* (Accounts of the Lands East of the Sea) account incorporates a number of historically important maps of Japan and the Ryukyus, which are valuable sources for the history of both Japanese and Korean cartography.[43] Kenrin reproduces all of Sukchu's maps except the one of the Ryukyus, but comments on only one, his "Map of the Mainland of Japan" (K., *Ilbon-guk pondo ji t'o*; J., *Nihon-koku hondo no zu*, Figs. 101 & inset).[44]

Mt. Fuji is the only mountain shown in the *Haedong chegukki* map of Japan, depicted as a towering spike rising from the border between Suruga and Izu provinces to the south, and Shinano Province to the north.[45] Even in the cartographic canons of the fifteenth century, the *Haedong chegukki* Japan map embodies a number of empirical errors—pardonable, perhaps, since Sin Sukchu

FIGURE 104   "Map of the Main Country of Japan" (detail, Eastern Japan), from Sin Sukchu, *Haedong chegukki* (Sin 1521), depicts a towering Mt. Fuji, with the note, "Mt. Fuji: Forty *li* high; snow all four seasons" (inset). (*Chōsen shiryō sōkan*, vol. 2).

---

most widely available, but in each case, I have verified the text against the original 1693 edition, using the copy in the collection of the Shiryō Hensansho, University of Tokyo.

42   Sin Sukchu, *Haedong chegukki* (Hansŏng [Seoul], 1512), edition in the collection of the Historiographical Institute, Tokyo University. I have used the edition prepared by Tanaka (1991), which includes both the original text in Chinese and an annotated translation into Japanese.

43   On the *Haedong chegukki* maps, see Nakamura (1965–1970, 1:339–380); Tanaka (1988).

44   The maps were redrawn—whether by Kenrin or by a draftsman is not certain—for the printing blocks for *Ishō Nihon-den*, and the differences between Kenrin's maps and those in the original Korean editions offer interesting insights into the extent of Kenrin's understanding of the maps. Those differences, however, do not affect the current discussion.

45   For a reproductions, Sin (1991, 380–3810; Robinson (2012, 20).

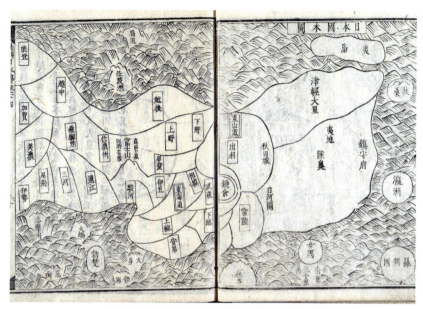

FIGURE 105   Matsushita Kenrin (1693) reproduces Sin's map, and comments that, "This
map of Japan is distorted and inaccurate. But when it says 'Mt. Fuji is forty
li high; there's snow on it [in all] four seasons,' it is very close to the truth."
(Matsushita 1975, v. 2).

never ventured beyond Kyoto.[46] Mt. Fuji straddles the Suruga-Kai provincial
boundary and at its summit is about 55 kilometers from the nearest point on
the Suruga-Shinano border.

Kenrin treated the *Haedong chegukki* maps just as he did the other foreign
texts he examined in his work, first reproducing the parts he deemed germane
to "Japan" and then commenting on the texts when they seemed to conflict
with Japanese accounts. Kenrin's comment on Sin Sukchu's map of Japan
focused almost entirely on the representation of Mt. Fuji. "This map of Japan

---

46   The *Haedong chegukki* map is based on one or more contemporary Japanese maps in
the genre known as the "Gyōki style" (*Gyōki-shiki*, after the seventh- and eighth-century
Buddhist monk Gyōki, who is credited with originating the genre). The genre emphasizes
the relative positionality of provinces as they lay along the medieval highway system linking them to the capital. Rather than attempting to approximate the shape of each province, therefore, provinces have somewhat amorphous shapes—which Japanese scholars
sometimes liken to dumplings or rice bales—resulting in a depiction of Japan shaped
like a *dokko* (Skt., *vajra*), a Buddhist ritual implement. On "Gyōki-style" Japan maps, see
Kuroda (2001). On the relationship between the *dokko* and the shape of Japan in "Gyōki-
style" maps, see Kuroda (2003, 28–46).

is distorted and inaccurate. But when it says 'Mt. Fuji is forty *li* high, there's snow on it [in all] four seasons,' it is very close to the truth." If Kiyomasa and his scout could see Mt. Fuji from far-off Sŏsura "as if it were right up close," Kenrin reasoned, then Sin Sukchu's reckoning that the mountain was forty *li* (approx. 157 km/96 mi.) high must be right on the money. How else could it be visible from such a distant shore?[47]

In 1713, Kenrin's contemporary, the encyclopedist Terajima Ryōan (1654–17??) likewise proclaimed Mt. Fuji's manifest visibility from Orankai as a geographical truth, incorporating the legend of Kiyomasa and Serutōsu sighting Mt. Fuji from Manchuria in his glosses on Fuji in the "Mountains" section of his great encyclopedia, *Wakan sansai zue*. In fact, Ryōan simply repeated almost verbatim what Kenrin had written twenty-five years earlier.[48]

Kenrin's close friend Kaibara Ekiken (1630–1714) accepted the notion that Kiyomasa had seen one of Japan's mountains from Orankai, but didn't believe it was Mt. Fuji; according to Hayashi Shihei (1738–93), Ekiken thought Kiyomasa must have seen Kaimondake, a 924 m (3,031') volcanic peak in southern Satsuma Province, about 1,250 km due south of Sŏsura, even farther from Kiyomasa's vantage point than Mt. Fuji. Shihei himself, on the other hand, advanced Mt. Rishiri (1,721m/5,646 ft), a volcanic island off the west coast of the Sōya Peninsula in Ezo (today's Hokkaido) as his candidate for what Kiyomasa had "seen." Mt. Rishiri, at least, had the advantage of being marginally closer to Sŏsura (about 910 km), but no more visible from there than Mt. Fuji—or any other mountain in Japan.[49]

Academic writers like Kenrin and Ryōan gave a veneer of scholarly, even empirical imprimatur to the conceit that Mt. Fuji's lofty peak was visible

---

47 Some Koreans apparently thought Mt. Fuji was even taller. Im Suhan, Second Ambassador on the 1711 embassy to Japan, wrote in his log of the journey to Edo, "They say [Mt. Fuji] is seventy or eighty *li* from base to summit." Im Suhan & Yi Pang'ŏn, *Tongsa ilgi*, quoted in Horiguchi (1996, 89).

48 Terajima (1712, 56: 14a.)

49 Hayashi (1975, 39): "After Katō Kiyomasa defeated Chosŏn, charged into Orankai, and burned its capital, he climbed a high mountain and gazed to the east, where Japan's Mt. Fuji was visible. Kiyomasa and his troops marveled at this. Kaibara Atsunobu (Ekiken) said that the mountain must be Kaimon[dake] in Satsuma. Another theory is that it was Mt. Daisen in Hōki [Province]. My view is that they are all wrong. The mountain in question must have been Rishiri, in the sea west of Ezo." The "Map of Ezo (*Ezo-koku zenzu*) appended to Shihei's *Sangoku tsūran zusetsu* (Hayashi 1786) depicts Rishiri, a volcanic island about 41 km (26 mi) SW of Wakkanai, the cone rises to 1,721 m (5,646 ft.), in the trefoil-peaked convention used for Mt. Fuji. I have been unable to locate the passage Shihei cites from Kaibara Ekiken identifying Kaimon-dake as the peak Kiyomasa "saw" from Orankai. Yamazaki (1854, 3: 9b), quoted in Kim (2012, 169–170) argues for Rishiri.

across the seas, subtly asserting an extension of Japan's sacred moral territory to far-off Tartary and setting new boundaries for Japan. Illustrators, artists, and writers pursued the theme along two axes. First, they embodied the legend of Kiyomasa seeing Fuji from distant shores in paintings and prints and in new versions of both Kiyomasa's biography and stories of Hideyoshi's Korean invasions, tales that continued to be published as historical truth well into the twentieth century. Second, they extended the trope of Mt. Fuji's miraculously distant visibility to ever farther shores and to other points of the compass, ultimately rendering Mt. Fuji the universal mountain and *axis mundi*.

5   Mt. Fuji's Growing Reach

The range of Mt. Fuji's power was not limited to the direction of Tartary; in the eighteenth and nineteenth centuries, its ambit gradually expanded, reaching all the "foreign lands" anticipated for Japanese expansionism in the somewhat unsystematic designs of late-eighteenth-century expansionists such as Hayashi Shihei: Ezo to the north, Ryūkyū to the south, and the East Asian mainland to Japan's west.[50] Among the most insistent and inventive apostles of Mt. Fuji's near-universal visibility was Katsushika Hokusai (1760–1849), a devotee of the Mt. Fuji cult and one of the most prolific artists of the late Edo period.[51] In 1832, Hokusai executed a woodblock-printed series of "Eight Views of the Ryukyus" (*Ryūkyū hakkei*) for the publisher Nishimuraya Yohachi, himself an organizer of Fuji-cult confraternities.[52]

---

50   Hayashi (1943–1944, 2:633–711).

51   Mt. Fuji appears in an untold number of Hokusai's artistic output of paintings and prints, both as principal subject and as distant, seemingly incidental scenery. Katsushika (1934, vol. 3) and his earlier series of thirty-six polychrome prints of Mt. Fuji (Katsushika 1931) are the best known of these. See also Henry D. Smith (1988). As Nishiyama Matsunosuke has recently observed, "The[se] two celebrated works by Hokusai were probably, in a sense, by-products of [the] great tide of Fuji-worship sweeping through the city of Edo" in the 1830s (Nishiyama 1993, xix [English], 23 [Japanese]). Thus, any reading of Hokusai's interest in Mt. Fuji as subject must allow for the possibility that he was merely an astute exploiter of the commercial possibilities afforded by the Fuji-fervor of his age. Kanō (1994, 81) points out that Nishimuraya Yohachi, Hokusai's publisher, was the organizer of a Fuji confraternity (*kō*) and suggests that Hokusai may have been an affiliate of one of these confraternities.

52   Nishimuraya, *Ryūkyū hakkei* (1832, Edo, collection New York Metropolitan Museum of Art); available online at http://fromto.cc/hosokawa/diary/2004/20040723-naha4/. Hokusai had no more seen the Ryukyus than he had Orankai; he derived—plagiarized—his "views" from a Chinese gazetteer, Zhou Huang's *Liuqiuguozhi lue* ("Abbreviated Gazetteer of the Land of Ryukyu," 3 vols., Qianlong 22 = 1757).

With a Ryukyuan embassy scheduled to visit the shogun at Edo in 1832, Hokusai and Nishimuraya, ever astute businessmen, hopped on the anticipated demand for Okinawa memorabilia and at the same time sought to exploit the fever pitch in Fuji pietism.[53] Hokusai had been interested in the Ryukyus at least since 1808, when he illustrated Takizawa Bakin's *Chinsetsu yumiharizuki*, a fabulist retelling of a legendary twelfth-century Japanese conquest of the Ryukyus.[54] Hokusai cleverly reworked eight landscapes from a mideighteenth-century Chinese gazetteer of the Ryukyus that had been reprinted in Japan just the year before; of the "Eight Views of the Ryukyus" included in his set, three rendered Mt. Fuji unmistakably visible in the far, far background. (Figs. 106, 107, 108) In one of them, Mt. Fuji's snowy crown is clearly visible above the mountain's reddened slopes. Here, truly, is "a snowy peak that needs no interpreter," even at a distance of 1,500 kilometers.

The Ryukyus had been a thriving maritime kingdom in medieval times and a quasi-independent tributary of Japan for 270 years from 1609 to 1879 (but also a vassal state of Ming and Qing China). A decade after the Meiji Restoration, Japan imposed a final "disposition" (*shobun*) of the Ryukyus, incorporating the islands into the Japanese homeland as "Okinawa Prefecture" in 1879 and integrating the Okinawan royal family into the domestic Japanese nobility. Though much modern scholarship treats Ryukyu as if it had been part of Japan even in the Edo period, it was neither wholly "independent," on the one hand, nor "part of" *either* Japan or China. Rather, it was *all three*, and more: It was an "independent kingdom" that was, at the same time, "tributary" to *both* Beijing and Edo while also being an offshore possession of the daimyo of Satsuma.[55]

---

53 For a sense of the demand, see Matsura (1979–1981, 302, 323). Yokoyama (1981, 4:464–465) counts fifteen different books and pamphlets about the Ryukyuan embassy published in 1832. Hokusai's is not on the list.

54 Takizawa (1807–1811) is reprinted in an annotated edition, with Hokusai's illustrations, in Gotō (1958–1962).

55 Jurgis Elisonas falls into this fallacy in an attempt to preserve the notion that Japanese "seclusion policies" defined Japan from the early seventeenth century. See "The Inseparable Trinity: Japan's Relations with China and Korea," and "Christianity and the Daimyo," chapters 6 and 7 of Hall 1991, esp. 300–301. Though a vigorous scholarly debate continues over the status of the early modern Ryukyus, both within and without the Edo-period political and diplomatic order, a scholarly consensus has emerged in Japan in the last fifteen years that Edo-period Japan was not a "closed country," whatever it was, and that we must either discard entirely the notion of *sakoku*, as I have argued (as have Asao Naohiro, Arano Yasunori, Maehira Fusaaki, Tsuruta Kei, etc.) or keep the term but completely redefine it, as has Katō Eiichi. Elisonas does neither. On "*Ryūkyū shobun*," see especially Oguma (2014, 15–35).

FIGURES 106–108   Katsushika Hokusai's "Eight Views of the Ryukyus" series (L–R): "Clear
Atumn Weather at Chōkō" (*Chōkō shūsei*); "Sacred Spring at Castle
Mountain" (*Jōgaku reisen*); "Banana Garden at Chūtō" (*Chūtō shōen*).
(Edo, 1832)

The confusion over the nature and sovereignty of Ryūkyū was so great that debate continued well into the nineteenth century as to whether it might not in fact be the same as the mythic Dragon Palace beneath the sea, whose name could also be pronounced "Ryūkyū."[56] This confusion, and perhaps some none-too-gentle satiric intent, provoked Chikamatsu Monzaemon to write, in a puppet play parodying the recent visits of both Ryukyuan and Korean ambassadors to Edo, "Is the Dragon Palace /Ryūkyū Japan's territory, or China's (*Morokoshi*)? ... It's hard to know where the Dragon Palace belongs."[57] Hokusai resolves the ambiguities of Ryukyu's status by rendering Mt. Fuji as visible from the Ryukyus; he seems to suggest that it is within the mountain's numinous orbit and, by the same logic as the legend of Kiyomasa in Orankai, actually part of "Japan."

Not content to stop with the Ryukyus, Hokusai adumbrated an even more encompassing sense of Mt. Fuji's power, commenting in a few brushstrokes on a canonical monochrome painting of Mt. Fuji attributed to Sesshū Tōyō (1420–1506) and on the expanded reach of the mountain's vector beyond even Orankai and Ryūkyū. (Fig. 109) Sesshū's *Mt. Fuji, Miho, Seikenji* has had an immense impact on the subsequent development of Mt. Fuji iconography,

56   See Yokoyama (1987, chapter 3), for treatment of the identity of the Dragon King's Palace (Ryūgū) and Ryūkyū in Edo-period discourse.

57   *Taishokan*, in Chikamatsu (1928, 7:458, 470). Here, Chikamatsu puns on the word 龍宮 which, though normally pronounced *ryūgū*, can also be pronounced a homophone for 琉球, i.e., Ryūkyū. Taishokan brilliantly satirizes the dual vassalage of Ryūkyū to both Japan and China through the metaphor of a fabulous jewel which the Tang emperor Xuanzong sent to Japan in the early eighth century. The *Menkō-fuhai no tama* ("the ever-facing, never-spurning jewel") contained an image of the bodhisattva Kannon (Skt., Avalokiteśvara; Ch., Guanyin). Just as Ryūkyū sent tribute to both China and Japan, playing the good vassal to whichever was watching, so too the jewel: no matter what direction one looked at the jewel, Kannon always faced the observer and never looked away.

FIGURE 109 "Mt. Fuji, Seikenji, Miho-no-Matsubara," attributed to Sesshū Tōyō, was the most influential depiction of Mt. Fuji in the Edo period. The widespread belief that Sesshū painted it during his sojourn in China, 1467–69, contributed to the conceit that Mt. Fuji was visible from foreign lands.
COURTESY EISEI BUNKO, TOKYO

establishing for future artists a canonical triad of Mt. Fuji looming in the distance, viewed across an improbable vista, with the pagoda and temple buildings of Seikenji at the left foreground, just the tip of the spit of land known as Miho-no-Matsubara at the right foreground, and Kiyomi Bay between and Tago-no-ura beyond.[58]

Sesshū, a Zen monk-painter, traveled in China from 1467 to 1469 to visit important Buddhist temples, study, and meet Chinese painters. In part because Sesshū's *Mt. Fuji, Miho, Seikenji* bears a colophon by the Chinese Zhan Zhonghe, it was widely believed in the Edo period that Sesshū had executed the work during his stay in China and brought the painting back with him on his return to Japan.[59] The Kyoto aristocrat Konoe Iehiro, for example, discussing Sesshū's

58 The painting has been in the Hosokawa collection for several centuries, and is now in the Eisei Bunko, the Hosokawa archives, in Tokyo. See Naruse (1983b, 1983a) and Sawada (1928). For discussion see Lippit (1993), pp. 141–151; Lippit (2012), pp. 77–82. Seikenji, a Rinzai Zen temple on the Tōkaidō, midway between Edo and Nagoya, was founded in 1261.

59 Shimao Arata cites a "legend" (*densetsu*) that, "A disciple of Sesshū who traveled to Ming copied this painting and colophon [in] China, and came back to Japan with it." (TNM, 2002: 266). Naruse Fujio (1980: 19), noting that Zhan, a Ningbo literatus, interacted socially with Japanese visitors to the city, but that since Zhan's "Active period was the 1510s, it is likely that some third party took the painting to Ming China, where he obtained Zhonghe's colophon." Lippit (2003: 148–149 & 2012:) does not directly address the question of whether Sesshū executed the original painting while he was in China, or at home in Japan. But he speculates that since Zhan was not active until nearly a half-century after Sesshū's sojourn in China, perhaps the work was "taken by a disciple or close acquaintance [of Sesshū] to China during the sixteenth century to be inscribed."

œuvre with a companion after tea in the early summer of 1726, said, "I [once] asked Yōboku to make a copy of the picture of *Mt. Fuji that Sesshū had painted while in China*; it is in Lord Hosokawa Etchū's collection."[60]

Later scholarship has identified Zhan as active only after ca. 1510, after Sesshū's death. Scholars now believe the surviving work is a copy, and that after Sesshū's death someone, most likely one of his students, took the painting to China in order to acquire a colophon.[61] Whether the work was *ever* in China— that is, whether Sesshū painted it there—or someone took it there to obtain a colophon may never be known, but the *belief* that Sesshū painted it during his two-year Ming sojourn was a constant cultural fact, part of what Walter Benjamin would later call the "aura" of the work.[62]

Hokusai had no doubt at all that Sesshū was in China when he painted his Mt. Fuji masterpiece. Not only that, there was no need for Sesshū to rely on his memory of the mountain in order to execute a perfect Mt. Fuji: Sesshū just looked up over the horizon and painted what he saw. In a provocative composition in his sketchbooks (Fig. 110), Hokusai depicts a classic trope of both Chinese and Japanese literati painters: a group of Confucian gentlemen in a small boat floating on the waters of a broad lake, probably intended as a parody of conventional scenes of West Lake in Hangzhou. Hokusai's sketch is too small to be certain, but the conventions of such a scene would have us assume the men are drinking and composing poetry. But not all of them are so occupied. Hokusai's caption announces that one of these men is "Sesshū paint[ing]

---

60 Yamashina Dōan, *Kaiki*, entry of Kyōho 11/4/21 (12 May 1726), quoted in Nakabe Yoshitaka (2004), p. 155 (my italics). On Iehiro (1667–1736), scion of a distinguished noble lineage and a former imperial regent (*sesshō*) and prime minister (*daijō daijin*), was a noted calligrapher, tea master, and collector; see Nakai (1988), p. 308. Yōboku (Kanō Tsunenobu, 1636–1713), head of the Kanō line of artists, handled the shogun's most important painting projects, such as commissions for Edo Castle and the imperial palace, or screens for presentation to the king of Korea. Hosokawa Etchū-no-kami Nobunori (1676–1732), was daimyo of Kumamoto. Sesshū's painting remains today in the Hosokawa collection, the Eisei Bunko, Tokyo.

61 Shimao Arata, note on *Fuji Miho Seikenji-zu*, in *Sesshū: botsugo 500 nen*, 265–266. The colophon ends with a tantalizing reference to the legend of the heavenly feather-garment (*hagoromo*), best known the eponymous *nō* play, which is set on Miho-no-Matsubara and replete with Mt. Fuji imagery. This raises the question of how Zhan knew about the *hagoromo* legend. Lippit (2012: 80) suggests that a friend of Sesshū took the copied painting to China, and "most likely brought a prepared text for Zhan to write out, accounting for the obligatory and systematic way in which the inscription touches upon the most familiar [Japanese] associations of the site."

62 Benjamin (1968, 221).

FIGURE 110   Katsushika Hokusai, "Sesshū paints Fuji [while] in China," visualizes the
              painter on a boat on an unnamed Chinese lake, most likely West Lake or
              Lake Dongting, rendering a Mt. Fuji rising in the distance—visible all the
              way from China. (Katsushika, 1814–1878, 10: 18b).

Fuji [while] in China" (*Sesshū, Tōdo ni Fuji o egaku*).[63] The mountain, in all
its snow-capped majesty, rises far above the Chinese mountains in the middle
distance, dwarfing them and reminding viewers that Mt. Fuji is the "greatest
mountain in all the world" (*sangoku-ichi no yama*).

In a few simple brushstrokes, Hokusai had greatly extended Mt. Fuji's range
of visibility, to the Southern Song (1127–1279) capital of Hangzhou, 2,000 kilometers southwest, or the even the more distant Lake Dongting, 2,550 kilometers

---

63   Katsushika (1814–1878, 10: 18b); for a reprint edition, see Nagata (1986, 2:282). Hangzhou
      and West Lake (Ch., *Xihu*), about 140 km. NNW of Ningbo, has long been a canonical *topos*
      for Chinese painters. Hokusai's cartoon may parody a "West Lake" attributed to Sesshū
      now in the Seikadō Bunko Art Museum, Tokyo; a copy by the obscure Edo-period artist
      Shōtetsu is in the Tokyo National Museum collection. TNM (2002), pp. 125, 267. Sesshū
      passed several months in Ningbo, about 140 km from Hangzhou, during his sojourn in
      China, 1467–1468 sojourn in China. Shimao (2002): 219.

to the southwest. A comic poet of the 1830s summed it up: "As far away as China you can see it: Mt. Fuji!" (*Morokoshi made miyuru—Fuji no yama!*).[64]

Nor was the conceit that Sesshū had painted his canonical scene of Mt. Fuji while gazing at it from China original with Hokusai. Nearly seventy years earlier Kawamura Minsetsu (1767) had coupled a depiction of Sesshū standing at the bow of a Chinese vessel emerging from between the rocks flanking entry to "the port of Mingzhou" (Ningbo), and gazing across the sea to at Mt. Fuji looming in the distance, above the clouds. (Fig. 111) Minsetsu attributes the composition to a painting by Kano Tan'yū (1602–1674), but more likely had based himself on a painting on the same theme by Kano Norinobu (1692–1731), which he had turned into a mirror-image of the original. (Fig. 112)

FIGURE 111   "The Port of Mingzhou," in Kawamura Minsetsu (1767) riffs on the conceit of the limitless range from which Mt. Fuji is visible, depicting a lone figure standing on the foredeck of a Chinese ship emerging from the rocky mouth of Mingzhou Harbor, and shielding his eyes to gaze at Mt. Fuji beyond the sea. Kawamura's caption attributes his to "the brush of [Kanō] Tan'yū-sai," though it corresponds to no known work by the master, but rather to a painting by Kanō Norinobu (1692–1731), Fig. 102. Mingzhou was Sesshū Tōyō's port of embarkation on his return to Japan in 1469.

64   Okada (1984, 931). The poet writes "Fuji no yama," "Mt. Matchless"; "Mt. Peerless."

FIGURE 112   Kanō Norinobu (1692–1731) clearly anticipates the composition of
              Kawamura Minsetsu's depiction of Sesshū gazing of Mt. Fuji from the
              mouth of the harbor at Mingzhou—though the title on the box in which
              the painting is stored reads "Departing Pusan Harbor." (hanging scroll,
              color on paper, Shin Kisu Collection, Osaka Rekishi Hakubutsukan).

To the northeast, as well, Mt. Fuji seemed to rise higher, to be visible from ever
more distant vantage points. An early nineteenth century artist proposed pictorially that if one gazed out from Mt. Fuji, one could see as far as southern
Ezo. (Fig. 113) The artist offered a panoramic view of Matsumae, the outpost
in southern Ezo that was the heart of Japanese colonial efforts in the north,
painted in a bird's-eye view that placed the viewer in the skies southwest of
Mt. Fuji, gazing down past the unmistakable crest of the snow-capped peak at
the port of Hakodate and the fortifications at Matsumae.[65]

The rhetorical extension of Mt. Fuji's reach, its visibility from ever-more-
distant climes, confirmed the further conceit that it was the axis mundi, the
point around which the cosmos revolved—that it was indeed the universal
source of vitality and the origin of all beings. As Matsuzono Umehiko wrote
in 1860, a *kōshin* year (fifty-seventh in the sixty-year zodiac cycle), the one year
in each 60-year cycle when the mountain, from which women were otherwise
barred, was open to all who wished to climb the sacred peak: "To begin with,

---

65   Of course the referent was at the same time Mt. Iwaki (1675 m), visible on clear days from
      Matsumae, just 87 km to the north. According to *Wakan sansai zue* (Terajima 1712, Ch. 65),
      "Because [Mt. Iwaki] resembles the form of Mt. Fuji; it is called the Mt. Fuji of the North"
      (*Oku-Fuji*). (6-panel folding screen, color on paper, 157 × 364.8 cm, Matsumae-chō Kyōdo
      Shiryōkan)

FIGURE 113   "Matsumae Screen," rather than viewing Mt. Fuji from Matsumae, presents a
                birds-eye view of Matsumae as if looking past the summit of Mt. Fuji. (6-panel
                screen, color on paper, 157 × 364.8 cm, Matsumae-chō Kyōdo Shiryōkan)

ever since the formation of Heaven and Earth, Mt. Fuji has been the source
of all things; therefore, it is a Sacred Peak inherently endowed with the Five
Elements, and different from all others. It is a Mountain of Spiritual Power
without peer throughout the world."[66]

Contemporary cartographers, too, often visualized Mt. Fuji as the axis
mundi, none more strikingly than the *Bankoku jinbutsu zue* (Illustrated peoples of the world, at left, Figs. 114 & 114 detail), a woodblock printed single-
sheet world map dating from the last years of the Edo period. Rising from the
Japanese islands, at the very center of the map, is a majestic Mt. Fuji so large it
even dwarfs the country on which it sits (detail, right). People in nearby lands
labeled "Ezo" and "Korea" seem to stare across the intervening space, gazing
worshipfully from afar at the sacred mountain that sustains the world.

6   If the Mountain Won't Come ...: Drawing the Other to Japan

The legend of Kiyomasa posits that Mt. Fuji is visible beyond the seas and has
the wondrous power to move even foreigners to "take one more journey, to admire [Mt. Fuji's] drifting snows." As artists and writers integrated the repeated
parades of foreign diplomatic entourages along the Tōkaidō into their repertoire, depictions of Tōjin—sometimes unmistakably "Korean" or "Ryukyuan,"
sometimes generic Tōjin—they articulated a rhetorical juxtaposition of

---

66   Matsuzono Umehiko, *Fujisan michi shirube* (1860), with illustrations by Gyokuransai
        Sadahide, quoted in Aoyagi (2002, 18).

FIGURE 114   "Map of the World and its Peoples" situates Mt. Fuji at the center (detail,
                right), emphasizing its presumed function as the *axis mundi* mountain.
                COURTESY ŌSHIMA AKIHIDE

Mt. Fuji and foreigners that increasingly asserted the subliminal or overt message that it was the ineffable beauty and numinous potency of the mountain itself that brought the Other to Japan. The assertion that Mt. Fuji had the power of positive attraction, drawing Other to admire or even worship, emerged as an important element in both the ideological and the cultic discourse of the middle and later years of the Edo period.

The notion that Mt. Fuji could draw the Other to Japan was not unique to Edo period discourse, as we saw earlier in the *nō* play *Fujisan*—but this was attributed only to the happenstance that the elixir of "immortality" might be found there, not to the appeal of the mountain itself. In the middle to later decades of the seventeenth century, however, a rhetoric emerged positing that Mt. Fuji drew foreigners to Japan, that they came to admire the mountain and even to worship it. Among the earliest to invoke that trope was the poetaster Yūsōan, author of the *Inu hyakunin isshu* of 1669, whose doggerel satirized Fujiwara no Tadahira while he visually invoked Ariwara no Narihira's *azuma kudari*. (See Fig. 101)

Yūsōan's "Lord *Tōjin*" proposes that foreigners are so moved by the beauty of Mt. Fuji that they will cross the seas simply to admire the mountain's ineffable form. His illustrator, too, evokes established canons for representing Narihira's journey "down to the east," the lone hero on horseback surrounded by attendants who accompany him on foot.

Great retinues of "Chinamen"—Korean and Ryukyuan embassies, actually—with samurai escorts and porters numbering more than 1,000 paraded past Mt. Fuji on their way to Edo twenty-three times in the seventeenth and eighteenth centuries, including a parade of 371 Koreans who made their way up and down the Tōkaidō in 1682, just a few years after the appearance of *Inu*

FIGURE 115   Panoramic view of the canonical Mt. Fuji, Seikenji (on the hill above
              the town) and Miho-no-Matsubara (foreground, left), centered on the
              Tōkaidō post station of Okitsu. The human activity focuses on a Korean
              embassy procession through Okitsu, and the crowds of spectators
              gathered to watch, but the scene is dominated by the looming form of
              Mt. Fuji, from whence the Koreans seem to have come. ("Okitsu Screen,"
              unsigned six-panel screen, ca. 1682).
              COURTESY AMAGASAKI KYŌIKU IINKAI

FIGURE 116
Hanabusa Itchō, untitled *hashira-e*, ca. 1711–1719, depicting a mounted Korean
flag-bearer transfixed by Mt. Fuji, whose silhouette rises above the clouds far above.
(Ink and color on paper, signed Hokusō'ō (private collection).

hyakunin isshu. A contemporary panoramic screen painting (Fig. 115) depicts
the Korean procession in the setting of Mt. Fuji, Miho-no-Matsubara, and
Seikenji that had been canonical since the time of Sesshū.[67] The screen offers a
bird's-eye view, looking across the piney spit of Miho-no-Matsubara (lower left
foreground), the bay of Tago-no-ura, the Tōkaidō highway, and the compound
of Seikenji, to the mountain's gently curving, snow-mantled peak rising majestically in the distance.

---

67   A combination of internal ethnographic and stylistic evidence suggests that the screen
      dates to the immediate aftermath of the Korean embassy of 1682.

The parade of Koreans, led and followed by its Japanese escort—as if to envelop its Otherness—marches along the Tōkaidō, rounds a hillside just below Mt. Fuji, and parades through the post town of Okitsu, where crowds of spectators have gathered to watch. The panorama allows the viewer to infer, perhaps, that the Koreans have just "admire[d Mt Fuji's] drifting snow"; only two or three members of the retinue appear to look back over their shoulders at the mountain itself.

Here, the dialogue of Fuji and the Foreign is removed from the mediation of Edo and brought closer to the potential of a direct rhetorical relation. Yet compositionally, the foreigners are doubly encapsulated: First, they are surrounded by a Japanese military escort, whose vanguard will lead them off to Edo and whose rearguard separates them from the mountain itself; second, the composition fences them into an oval area in the center of the screen—the post town of Okitsu—within which they remain surrounded by their escort and Japanese onlookers. The "Foreigners" do not touch "Fuji." And further, the dialogue of Fuji and the Other is mediated by the mountain's accumulation of poetic and artistic associations over nearly a millennium—Mt. Fuji, Miho-no-Matsubara, and Seikenji form an iconographic trinity at the center of the *nadokoro* tradition.[68] Seikenji, moreover, the "temple up the hill" in Statler's *Japanese Inn*, regularly served as lodgings for Korean and Ryukyuan embassies whenever they passed; the temple is filled with relics and souvenirs of the Koreans' visits and was popularly identified with the Foreign for that reason.[69]

If Mt. Fuji and Other had largely ignored each other in the Amagasaki screen, however, Hanabusa Itchō (1652–1724) forced the Other to look up and notice Mt. Fuji. Late in his career, after his return from eleven years' exile on Miyakejima (1698–1709), Itchō executed several paintings on themes related

68   A *nadokoro* is a famed scenic site, generally one with poetic associations.

69   Oliver Statler, *Japanese Inn* (Random House, 1961). On the association of Seikenji with Korean embassies, see Ri Jinhi (Yi Jinhŭi) (1987, 207–214); Kim (1985, 324–333). The association of Seikenji with Korean embassies in the popular imagination is symbolized by Hokusai's early-nineteenth-century depiction of the Tōkaidō post town of Yui showing a Korean, accompanied by two formally dressed samurai and a tonsured Japanese Buddhist priest sitting on the veranda of a temple. The priest prepares ink for the Korean, who inscribes the characters "Seikenji" on a plaque (collection Ōta Kinen Bijutsukan, Tokyo). See Ikuta Shigeru (1993, pl. 95; Ōta Kinen Bijutsukan, 1985, pl. 175). Hokusai was surely inspired by the plaque over the main gate of Seikenji, proclaiming it a "famous place on the Tōkaidō" (J., *Tōkai meiku*; K., *Tonghae myŏnggu*); the plaque is written in the hand of Hyŏn Kŭmgok, a member of the Korean embassy of 1711. The corridors of Seikenji are literally festooned with plaques inscribed with poetry composed by Koreans who stayed there in the seventeenth and eighteenth centuries.

to visiting Korean embassies, not to mention his many depictions of Mt. Fuji.[70] In a remarkable "pillar painting" (*hashira-e*, left), a format that emphasizes and exploits an extreme verticality, Itchō portrays a mounted Korean flag-bearer from the rear. (Fig. 116) The flag-bearer has stopped in his tracks, his neck craned all the way back as he looks toward the skies. Above him stretches an expanse of bare white paper, suggesting an enveloping mist or cloud; but the viewer follows the rider's gaze up through the mist, beyond the darkening clouds, to see that he is transfixed by a Mt. Fuji that floats above the clouds, outlined against the gray skies.

The exaggerated verticality of Itchō's composition underscores the be-lief that Mt. Fuji is the tallest mountain in the world; its minimalist reduc-tion seems to break through the mediation of region, to escape from Japanese military escorts and gawking onlookers and place the Other—the Korean—in direct dialogue with Mt. Fuji itself. The rider, whose "Korean" identity is estab-lished by his flag, his hat and clothing, and his bearded face, is riveted to the spot by the mountain and its majesty. And to the contemporary cognoscenti—Itchō's patron for this work surely was one—the rising-dragon motif on the rider's flag announces him as the standard-bearer of the Korean king. Not only has the Other come to the mountain; Itchō has fashioned a rhetoric implying that the king of Korea himself has come—vicariously, embodied in a fetish—to admire the "greatest mountain in the world."

A half-century later, as another Korean embassy made its way to Edo—to bring "tribute," according to popular Japanese belief—Suzuki Harunobu (1724–1770) reprised Hanabusa Itchō's vertical composition of mounted Koreans beneath the majestic form of Mt. Fuji but incorporated more explic-itly the tripartite *nadokoro* frame of Fuji, Seikenji, and Miho-no-Matsubara—as was done in the Amagasaki screen. (Fig. 117) Harunobu, one of the great eighteenth-century print masters, published an untitled print set at almost exactly the same deeply valenced site, Miho no Matsubara, that Itchō had cho-sen and that likewise placed the Other—Koreans—in direct dialogue with the mountain.[71]

---

70   On Itchō, see Kobayashi (1988), Kobayashi and Sakakibara (1978), and Wattles (2013).

71   Suzuki Harunobu, *Untitled hashira-e*. This print is not listed in David Waterhouse's cata-log of Harunobu's works, in *Ukiyo-e shūka, Bosuton Bijutsukan hokan I* (Shōgakukan, 1979). My thanks to Roger Keyes for bringing it to my attention and providing me with a color transparency. We have been unable to identify the provenance of the print. Harunobu executed at least four other *benizuri-e* prints on Korean embassy themes in 1764, when the visit of a Korean embassy to Edo excited popular interest. One, *Tōjin to mago no moraibi* ("*Tōjin* and stable boy exchanging a light with their pipes," *hosoban*, Library of Congress call no. FP2-JPD, no 2138), also depicts a mounted Korean and a groom lighting their

FIGURE 117
Suzuki Harunobu, untitled woodblock print, ca. 1764,
places two mounted Korean military officers in the
foreground, with Mt. Fuji, an anachronistic view of
Seikenji, and Miho-no-Matsubara in the distance.
(polychrome woodblock print; photograph courtesy
of Roger Keyes).

FIGURE 118   Illustration in a guidebook published to take advantage of
popular interest in the Korean mission of 1748 shows the
embassy procession as it marches past the foot of Mt. Fuji.
The last figure in the line of march is made to proclaim that,
"Mt. Fuji is the world's greatest mountain" (*Fuji no yama
wa sangoku-ichi ja*). (*Chōsenjin dai-gyōretsu ki*, 1748; Kyoto
University Library).

Two Koreans pause to rest their horses and enjoy a smoke on the foreground shore, while their horse-driver adjusts a straw horseshoe on the dapple-gray pony. Here, Harunobu has captured two Koreans (their hats, shoes, and facial hair, eyebrows, and eye shapes, as well as their clothing, mark them iconographically as "not-Japanese") separated from the implied great parade, resting astride their mounts for a smoke. Behind them in the distance, smokeless, however, the sacred three-peaked mountain looms above the clouds.[72] In the middle ground between Fuji and Foreign, an expanse of water, some pines and a single hut, and a temple—Seikenji—at the foot of the mountain catch our eye.

Harunobu has removed his Foreign-and-Fuji dialogue from the confines of Edo (and Harunobu was an Edoite himself) and by doing so has extended the range of its significatory power to include all Japan. But he has done more than that. Through the device of *mitate*, often rendered "parody," or "travesty," he has also embedded Fuji-Foreign discourse more deeply in the Japanese cultural realm, for he has inscribed the Foreign in the long iconographic tradition of Mt. Fuji, borrowing both the setting and the poses—travelers at rest beneath the Mountain—of the "Descent into the barbarous East" (*azuma kudari*) from the *Ise monogatari*, itself an immensely popular motif for eighteenth-century artists.[73]

The association with Ariwara no Narihira's *azuma kudari* is not in the least surprising, on its face, for like Narihira, Korean and Ryukyuan diplomatic entourages traveled the length of Japan, from Kyushu through the imperial capital and on "down into the East" to visit the shogun in Edo. Perhaps Harunobu hit upon the idea because of a *rakusho* (lampoon) of over a decade earlier. Then, in 1747—with a Korean embassy due in Edo the next year—a wag suggested that the entertainments presented for the diversion of the shogun at New Year

pipes. The other three are in the Museum of Fine Arts Boston: *Chōsenjin gyōretsu* (Korean Parade, acq. no. 11-30408), an untitled Mounted Korean Flag-Bearer, (acq. no. 54-347), and an untitled Mounted Korean Youth (acq. no. 521.4421).

72   Although there have been several traditions of representing Mt. Fuji, including three-, four-, and eight-peaked forms, a three-peaked depiction that had evolved by the Kamakura period (1185–1333) became the standard representation dominating the iconography of Mt. Fuji, depicting the mountain's summit as being comprised of three domed peaks, each of the same curvature and altitude. The standard pattern was displaced by a variety of representations again in the eighteenth century. For an analysis, see Naruse (1983b).

73   On *mitate* in Harunobu's work, see Tanabe (1990). Tanabe notes that Harunobu's prints were often made to order for circles of *tsū* (connoisseurs) and that those of his prints that were marketed often sold at a premium that placed them beyond the reach of most buyers, so it is unclear how widely this print circulated. But the issue here is the range of utterances, whether verbal or pictorial, possible in the discursive field of Harunobu's day.

would culminate in a performance of "Koreans coming to court" (*Chōsenjin raichō no shidai*). The same wag suggested that the *kyōgen* (i.e., kabuki) program in the Fifth Month would feature Chikamatsu Monzaemon's *Tenjin-ki* (1714), a five-act puppet drama in which the fictionalized visit of a Chinese embassy to ninth-century Japan is a key element of the plot, transforming the final act into *Chōsenjin azuma-kudari*—"The Koreans' Descent into the East!"[74]

Harunobu adopts elements of the iconography associated with Sesshū Tōyō's (1420–1506) *Fujisan Miho-no-matsubara Seikenji zu*, familiar to every Edo-period artist, embedding the Other simultaneously in the verbal, visual, and performative traditions of Mt. Fuji representation. The Seikenji depicted in the middle distance, between the distant Mt. Fuji and the Koreans in the foreground, is not the Seikenji of Harunobu's day but of Sesshū's—the five-storied pagoda shown here was destroyed in Hideyoshi's campaigns of 1590 against the Hōjō and was never rebuilt. Harunobu's deliberately archaizing strategy, therefore, brings the foreigners to Mt. Fuji and subordinates them not only to the sacred mount but to the full force of Japan's literary and artistic traditions.

The conceit that Mt. Fuji was the greatest mountain in the world and drew men from afar—none of these visitors were women—to gaze, admire, and even worship its potent numen seemed only to accelerate over the course of eighteenth century and to claim, as seen above, an expanding spatial reach. A two-page illustration in one of the many pamphlets printed in anticipation of the spectators expected to gather to watch the Korean ambassadorial events of 1748, *Chōsenjin dai-gyōretsu ki daizen*, portrayed the embassy parading past the snow-capped peak, much the same setting as shown in the Amagasaki Screen—but eliding such distracting details as Seikenji, Miho, and even the spectators. (Fig. 118) A Korean at the very end of the procession is made to remark, "Mt. Fuji is the world's greatest mountain!" (*Fuji no yama wa sangoku-ichi no yama ja!*), subliminally suggesting that it was admiration of Mt. Fuji as much as diplomatic duties that brought the Koreans to Japan.[75]

Fifteen years later, on the eve of the next Korean mission's arrival, the notion that Mt. Fuji beckoned foreign worshippers caught the imagination of Osaka artist Kitao Tokinobu as well. His *Chōsenjin raihei gyōretsu* (Osaka, 1763), an illustrated pamphlet published nearly a year in advance of the Koreans' arrival,

---

74   Yano (1984–1985, 316–318). *Tenjin-ki*, in Matsuzaki and Hara (1993–1995, 91:401–476), explains the exile of Sugawara no Michizane in 901 as the result of a scheme between his nemesis at court, Fujiwara no Tokihira, and an ambassador from China to frame Michizane in a phony plot to sell out Japan.

75   *Chōsenjin dai-gyōretsu ki daizen* (1748, Kyō Teramachi, Kikuya Shichirōbei collection Kyoto University Library).

opens with an imaginative depiction of "The Great Ship from the Continent," its sails billowing, its pennants stretched taught in the wind.[76] The Koreans are shown coming from the gates of a "Chinese-looking" royal city on the shores of Korea to deliver their king's letter to the shogun on board ship in "The Korean Embassy of State Raises Anchor." Their destination is shown on the next page: The vanguard of their Japanese military escort parades the Tōkaidō past the massive but graceful form of Mt. Fuji, which looms over a two-page spread captioned, "It Stands in Solitary Splendor in the Space Between the White Clouds." Only then does the "Parade of the Koreans" commence, as if making a pilgrimage to the mountain.

Nowhere does the verbal or visual rhetoric of Kitao's work suggest that the Korean visit bears the least relation to the shogun or his government: The only motivations suggested for their visit are a tradition of Korean tribute that dates from the subjugation of Korea in the age of the earliest, legendary "emperors" of Japan, referred to in the one-page "How Korea Began Paying Tribute" at the end of the slim volume, and the far more powerful rhetorical pull of Mt. Fuji "in solitary splendor in the space between the clouds." Tokimasa, moreover, as an Osaka artist, had no reason to be motivated by Edoite fantasies of the power of Mt. Fuji. Taking this rhetorical stance, therefore, underscores both the spreading impact of the mountain as a national symbol and the didactic power throughout the country of the conceit that Mt. Fuji spoke directly to foreigners, beckoning them to Japan.

Early in the eighteenth century, Edo surpassed Osaka and Kyoto as the center of the publishing industry and was home to most popular writers and artists. As Edo's dominance in cultural production grew, Edo popular culture became, in large measure, national popular culture. After the turn of the eighteenth century, Edoites turned increasingly to Mt. Fuji as a symbol of their city and promoted the mountain as a core national symbol more strongly than ever before, in part, I believe, as an assertion of Edo's own cultural primacy.[77] During this period, Mt. Fuji, a peripheral cult site and cultural symbol since earliest times, went international in Edo. The mythos of Katō Kiyomasa, the illustrated doggerel of *Inu hyakunin isshu*, and Hanabusa Itchō's pillar-format depiction of foreigners admiring *Sangoku-ichi no meizan*, "the greatest mountain in the world," took on for Edoites a new power and meaning amid a rising tide of Mt. Fuji piety.

---

76   Kitao (1763).

77   The city plan of Edo was laid out to exploit sight lines to Mt. Fuji to the west and Mt. Tsukuba to the northeast.

During the visit of the Korean mission of 1748, or shortly after the mission left Edo, Hanegawa Tōei[78] executed a remarkable painting on commission from the shogun's brother, Tokugawa Munetake, depicting Koreans—or Japanese masquerading as Koreans in festival procession—returning from their audience with the shogun at Edo Castle, parading along Honchō-dōri.[79] (Fig. 119) Contemporary Japanese, as we have seen, widely regarded the Koreans as tribute-bearing visitors from a foreign vassal state. Hanegawa's masterful composition exploits the techniques of single-point perspective to show the parade flowing like a human river through the streets of downtown Edo beneath the snow-capped Mt. Fuji, as if it had been Mt. Fuji that brought them to the shogun's castle—the masonry wall at the background—and thence into the town. Honchō-dōri, the street they march along, was oriented as a sight line to Mt. Fuji in the initial Edo town plan; by focusing on Mt. Fuji and eliding Edo Castle, the artist exploited this sight line both to underscore the links between the sacred peak and the commoners' city of Edo and to suggest, subliminally,

---

78   Little is known about "Hanegawa Tōei," almost certainly a pseudonym; his true identity is unknown. This painting and a woodblock print version of it (Fig. 119) are the only works bearing Hanegawa's signature (*Hanegawa Tōei hitsu*, "brush of Hanegawa Tōei"). A second painted version (private collection) is also signed *Hanegawa Tōei hitsu*, but both the painting and the signature are clearly by a different hand.

79   Hanegawa Tōei, *Chōsenjin raichō-zu* (hanging scroll, color on paper, collection Kobe Municipal Museum), in TNM (1985, 5); Hanegawa, *Ukie Chōsenjin* (*yoko ō-ōban* print, Matsukata Collection, Tokyo National Museum), in ibid., p. 31. It was this painting that first alerted me to the rhetorical pairing of Mt. Fuji and the Other. Hanegawa's work is most likely modeled on an unsigned, untitled painting in the Hayashibara Art Museum which, however, does not show Mt. Fuji in the distance. There are numerous reiterations, both straightforward and satiric, of the Hayashibara painting and Hanegawa's composition, both paintings and prints; all except the Hayashibara version depict Mt. Fuji in the distance, testifying to the popular appeal of the theme and composition. To date, I have identified at least fourteen distinct versions, nine paintings and five prints, the latest of which dates to ca. 1770. Just what each depicts is of particular interest, as several versions have been read as realistic, even journalistic, depictions of the "actual appearance" of the historical 1748 Korean embassy as it passed through Edo. Kishi Fumikazu, for example, says that the Hanegawa painting and print, "certainly depict the 1748 Korean embassy … and have a strong flavor of reportage of a historical event" (1992, 242). The Hanegawa painting was apparently done for a grandson of the shogun, Tayasu Kojirō, who died in 1753. See Oka (1992, 57ff), who likewise regards this as "a sort of for-the-record painting" (*kirokuga*), which "depicts the tenth Korean embassy, of 1748." I too, until challenged by Kuroda Hideo, initially read Hanegawa's painting as a journalistic depiction of the 1748 embassy. (Toby 1984) Close reading shows that some examples in this series are at pains to "represent" an actual Korean procession, some to show a festival masquerade, and others to confuse the issue. See Toby & Kuroda (1994b, 32–33). See also Toby (2008a).

FIGURE 119   Hanegawa Tōei, "Koreans in Perspective," ca. 1748. (Hanegawa Tōei, *Chōsenjin ukie*, yoko-ōōban print; Tokyo National Museum).

that the foreign envoys were returning from a pilgrimage to Mt. Fuji, not from an audience at the Castle.

Even the location in central Edo where Hanegawa situated his ambiguously Other/masquerade Other parade was redolent with associations of Otherness. Honchō, the ward through which the parade passes—clearly identified by the inscription (*Honchō ni-chōme*) on the large water cask at the intersection—was the heart of Edo's pharmacopoeia-wholesalers' district, and the finest medicines came from abroad. The shops lining the way, festooned in bunting, marketed Korean ginseng, powdered Chinese deer antler, and myriad other highly prized but exotic pharmaceuticals, including a popular lozenge known variously as *Tōjin ame, Chōsen ame*, and *Kanjin ame* ("*Tōjin*, Korea, or Korean lozenges").[80] Itinerant Tōjin *ame* peddlers often costumed themselves in plumed hats, baggy trousers, and voluminous neck, wrist, and ankle frills and called to customers with the sound of the *charumera*, a wind instrument long identified with the Tōjin code.

The notion that Mt. Fuji might draw foreigners across the seas and speak to them in unmediated fashion, communicating its sacred power even to

---

80   Yao (2008); Saeki Akiko (2012).

barbarians, is not, I hasten to add, a reading I impose arbitrarily on Harunobu's and Tokinobu's visual compositions but one that emerges from contemporary verbal texts as well. An anonymous doggerel poet of a slightly later day celebrated the universality of Fuji's voice:

> Foreigners bring tribute: The one mountain that needs no interpreter.
> *Raichō ni*   *Tsūji mo iranu yama hitotsu*[81]

In the traditions of Japanese poetry, a good line might be used over and over, and this one was re-used frequently: Mt. Fuji, all agreed, spoke directly and universally, transcending the constraints of language: this mountain needed *no* interpreter. Indeed the conceit that Mt. Fuji evoked the admiration of foreigners was so deeply entrenched by the 1760s that the cynical Ōta Nanpo (1749–1823), who would later celebrate just that admiration in his colophons for Maruyama Ōzui's *Mt. Fuji*, ultimately found it tiresome indeed. (Fig. 128)[82] As he wrote in a satiric poem in rhyming faux classical Chinese, perhaps shortly after a Korean mission had left for home,

> Everyone says Chinamen write well.   *Mina iu: Tōjin sho o yoku mono o kaku to,*
>
> Who knows? Their lousy brushwork   *Tareka shiran—akuhitsu zeni ni narazaru koto,*
> can't be worth much. Having Fuji
> praised [by foreigners] is just a pain.   *Fujisan   homerarete,   kaette meiwaku.*[83]

---

81   The original: *Raichō ni tsūji mo iranu yama hitotsu.* Okada (2984), 50: 16. Another poet writes, "Foreigners come bearing tribute: This snowy peak needs no interpreter" (*Raichō ni tsūji iranu yuki no mine;* ibid., 79:6, 8; 94:3). The notion that certain things are so universal they need no interpreter appears a century earlier in Chikamatsu's *Tenjinki* (1714): When a visiting Chinese ambassador is offered a bribe, he counts the money as the narrator comments, "When [Fujiwara no Tokihira] quietly hands over [the five-hundred *ryō*], even the *Tōjin* needs no interpreter." Chikamatsu (1993–1995, 91: 419–420).

82   Maruyama Ōzui, *Mt. Fuji*, hanging scroll, ink on paper (197.8 × 57.5 cm), ca. 1820 (Minneapolis Institute of Arts, The Christina N. and Swan J. Turnblad Memorial Fund, 78.21; see Fig. 128, below). Nanpo, signing himself "Shokusanjin," added two colophons, the second of which reads, "Even Chinamen (*Tōjin*) must come all the way here if they want to see the greatest mountain in the world." Nanpo later (?) reprised the second colophon on Mori Tetsuzan's (1775–1841) undated "Mt. Fuji"; and in 1860, Kanagaki Robun and Utagawa Yoshitora (1860/1961) incorporated both Nanpo's colophons into an illustration of Rutherford Alcock's journey to Mt. Fuji (see below, at n. 103).

83   Ōta Nanpo, "Gekan no Tōjin Chōsen ni kaeru o okuru," in *Neboke Sansei bunshū* (Edo and Osaka, 1767), in Hamada, Nakano, Hino, and Ibi (1985–1990, 1:351). "Gekan no Tōjin Chōsen ni kaeru o okuru" is a *kyōshi*, a comic poem in faux literary Chinese—at least on

Whether Nanpo approved or not, however, the discourse clearly asserted that Mt. Fuji could speak directly, with "no interpreter," to Japanese and foreigner alike, not merely drawing them as travelers to the foot of the mountain, as Itchō, Harunobu and other artists asserted, but compelling them as pilgrims come to worship. In the mid-1830s, Katsushika Hokusai, that most prolific of print artists, published his ambitious *One Hundred Views of Mt. Fuji* (*Fugaku hyakkei*), a work printed and reprinted in numerous editions. Several of the "Views" have implications for our understanding of Hokusai's reading of the relationship between what Marius Jansen has termed "Japan and its world," but "Raichō no Fuji" (Foreigners Paying Tribute to Fuji," Fig. 120) is of particular salience here.[84]

Hokusai depicts a Korean embassy's entourage passing the sacred mount. Several firmly established iconographic elements signify their general Otherness (plumed hats, ruffled collars, musical instrumentation) or their particular Koreanness (especially the two long-braided youths [K, *sodong*; J, *shōdō*: "young boys"; "pages"]). The gaze Hokusai imposes on his viewers is that of a Japanese traveler along the Tōkaidō highway, looking out from the entryway of an inn, indicated by the two carefully shaped piles of sand (which coincidentally reiterate the curved slopes of the mountain) and the vertical wooden plaque that announces—on the face we cannot see—the name of the highest-ranking guests, most likely a daimyo on his way to or from Edo.[85]

---

the surface—conforming to the rhyme scheme of a "regulated poem" (*lüshi*). However, Nanpo adds a gloss directing readers to parse it in Japanese, to quite hilarious effect. Hezutsu Tōsaku (Tatematsu Tōmō), a contemporary of Nanpo's, claims that he wrote the poem when Nanpo was seventeen (i.e., 1765), a year later than the time of the Korean mission. See *Shin'ya meidan*, in Mori et al. (1980, 1:142). Tōsaku, if written with different characters, means "plagiarist"; on the other hand, Nanpo wrote a preface to *Shin'ya meidan* in 1795, after Tōsaku's death. Nakano, Hino, and Ibi (1993, 20) accept Tōsaku's claim, though they did not mention it in the *Nanpo zenshū*. Whether written by Nanpo or Tōsaku, the poem remains a complex comment on the Korean visit, which provoked positive interest, peasant protests, and the dialog of Fuji and the foreign.

84 Katsushika (1834–35, 3: 5b–6a); Jansen (1980).

85 These sand mounds (*morisuna*), whose "precise significance is unclear" to Henry D. Smith (1988, 214), apparently originated as a symbolic "expression of entryway" in Muromachi architecture but evolved in the Edo period into an intrinsic part of cleaning and purifying waterways and highways in preparation for the passage of an exalted personage. As the "final touch" in preparing the road, *morisuna* (or salt mounds, *morishio*) was expressive of the relationship between ruled and ruling classes. *Morisuna* or *morishio* likewise announced visibly that all preparations to offer hospitality (*chisō*) were complete and in this context are still seen at the entrances to many upscale Japanese restaurants. For an insightful discussion of the cultural meanings of *morishio* and *morisuna*, see Kurushima (1986). Though *bakufu* precedent has clear specifications about the inn where the three senior members of the Korean embassy stayed ("Except for the lodgings of the Three

FIGURE 120   Hokusai's fanciful rendering of a Korean embassy procession marching past
               Mt. Fuji, as all eyes turn to gaze up at the mountain's snow-draped slopes.
               The Fuji-shaped cones in the foreground, the vertical placard, and the three
               Japanese spectators (the shaved pates) imply that the viewer is seated in an
               official inn (*honjin*). The pennants fancifully proclaim that the Koreans are
               "bringing tribute" (*raichō*) to the mountain, replicating the title of the scene,
               Raichō no Fuji, i.e., "Tribute-bearers at Mt. Fuji." At the time of this render-
               ing, it had been seventy years since the last Korean mission to Edo—when
               Hokusai was five *sai*: the artist had never seen a mission himself. (Katsushika
               Hokusai, *Fugaku hyakkei*, 3 vols., Edo, 1834; vol. 3, private collection).

Three Japanese men, samurai in semi-formal garb, see the Koreans on their
way. Seated between the sand piles and the Korean procession they remind
us—as if Mt. Fuji were not sufficient—who (what) constitutes the "Japanese"
and underscore the alienness of these passing Others.

Hokusai's Koreans, however, do not merely pass Mt. Fuji, as those in the
Amagasaki screen did, decorations to a landscape, not even bothering to look
up. No, indeed! Rather, reprising the rapt gaze of the Korean in Hanabusa

---

Ambassadors, do not prepare mounded sand"), it is more likely that Hokusai here intends
to convey that a daimyo or other high-ranking Japanese is the inn's guest. Orders of the
sixth month of 1719, in Hayashi (1913/1967, 1:508). These orders stood as precedent for later
embassies in 1748 and 1764, the last to visit Edo. See ibid., 1:518, 528.

Itchō's pillar painting, they gaze worshipfully, as one, at the sacred form of Fuji, written "Matchless," which consumes the background. Their pennants, moreover, proclaim them "bearers of tribute" (*raichō*).[86] Just as Koreans and Okinawans had been represented as if on pilgrimage to worship the dynastic founder at Nikkō in the *Tōshōgū engi* scrolls of Kanō Tan'yū, Sumiyoshi Jokei, and Sumiyoshi Gukei in the 1640s,[87] Hokusai presented them as worshippers drawn from across the seas by the universal reach of the mountain's sacred power.

The conceit of Mt. Fuji's power to attract the Other, to cast its spell beyond the seas, and to broaden the boundaries of Japanese "transformative power" to attract the Other to Japan from across the seas was not limited to Edoites like Hokusai or adopted Edoites like Gennai. The Osaka artist Kitao Tokinobu, as we saw above, implied pictorially that the goal of the upcoming Korean mission of 1764 was to admire Mt. Fuji's splendor.

7   Preserve and Protect

The universal reach of Fuji's voice, the admiration, the worship of Mt. Fuji all across the world, found further literary expression in *Furyū shidōken-den*, Hiraga Gennai's raucous and wildly popular Gulliverian farce of 1769.[88] Gennai, an immigrant from Shikoku to Edo, may well be parodying the pretensions of Fuji devotees, yet he evokes the realm of the possible in notions of Fuji's power.

Halfway through the fiction—the episode spans the transition from Book 1 to Book 2—Gennai's intrepid comic hero Fukai Asanoshin (Mr. Shallow Deepwell) finds himself at the court of the Chinese emperor, Qianlong (r. 1736–1796). The emperor commands Asanoshin to relate his travels, and after listening for a few minutes opines, "It's a wide world out there, but surely there's not a mountain the equal of the Five Peaks of China." Asanoshin responds, "It's as your Majesty says, that amongst the mountains of the world, the Five Peaks are Number One; but in my homeland of Japan, there's a famous mountain called

---

86   Actual Korean embassies did not carry regalia emblazoned with the slogan *raichō*, nor did Koreans intend "tribute" to Japan. These were, however, common Japanese constructions placed on the motivation of foreigners sending emissaries to the shogun, as I have noted elsewhere (1984, chapter 5; 1985).

87   On the representation of Korean visits in 1636, 1643, and 1655, to the shogunal shrines at Nikkō as "worship" (*sanpai*) and its ideological import, see Toby (1984, chapters 3 and 5).

88   In Nakamura Yukihiko, ed., *Fūrai sanjin-shū* (NKBT, vol. 55, Iwanami Shoten, 1961): 204–206. Note that Gennai's farce was published just as the Fuji cult was gathering momentum.

Fuji, 'Second-to-None';[89] it's taller than the Five Peaks; it's crowned with eight peaks; in all the four seasons, the snow never melts." On hearing Asanoshin's boast, the emperor replies:

> Long ago, a Japanese artist named Sesshū came to Our country and painted a picture of that mountain.... Until now we always thought it was a painter's fantasy (*esoragoto*), that it couldn't be greater than the Five Peaks. But now, listening to you, I realize that Mt. Second-to-none is greater than any other mountain in the world.... Ruling the 400 Provinces [of China] I wanted for nothing; but now, without my own Mt. Second-to-none, it's all emptiness. I'll command the entire realm to send workmen to build me my own Mt. Second-to-none.... Since you know what Mt. Fuji should look like, you oversee [the project].... Build me Mt. Fuji at once!

Qianlong finally decides to send Asanoshin back to Japan to make a papier-mâché duplicate of Mt. Fuji and bring it to China. When the Japanese gods learn that a "foreign country" (*ikoku*) is planning to steal Mt. Fuji, they gather at the sacred peak to consult: "We should follow the ancient precedent [from the 13th century], when the Mongols attacked Japan: Order the Wind God and the Rain God to smash the Chinese ships on the high seas immediately!" The winds blew down from Fuji, from all the gods of Japan, destroying 30,000 Chinese ships and drowning thousands of Chinese crewmen.

It was not simply that the gods had saved Mt. Second-to-None from the Chinese emperor's grasp. In fact, Mt. Second-to-None had protected Japan from Chinese invasion, and not just this once: It was Mt. Fuji, as venue for the gathering of the gods, that had saved Japan twice before when the Mongols attacked. Mt. Fuji's physical and numinous superiority to all other peaks was manifest even in China, proclaiming the universal appeal of its sacral power to attract admiration—even worship—from abroad. But perhaps more important, the awesome power of Mt. Fuji to subdue and repel the unwanted Other made itself manifest—a power that would gain appeal in later years, as a mounting fear of threat from abroad engulfed Japan.

Over the following century, Japanese artists and writers rehearsed and elaborated the Mt. Fuji themes adumbrated in Gennai's farce: notions that Mt. Fuji's loftiness and sanctity made it (nearly) universally visible, *extending* the moral and sovereign boundaries of Japan and the legitimate reach of Japanese

---

89   Fuji, is written here with characters meaning "not two," which I have translated here as "Second-to-None," as in the name of the modern confectioner Fujiya. Alcock renders this as "Mt. Matchless."

control; that it had the power to *attract* the alien, to call aliens to admire and worship; and that it had as well the power to *protect* Japan from enemies and *repel barbarians who threatened Japan.* I shall now examine the iconographic elaboration of these three themes in the work of late-Tokugawa (and some mid-Meiji) artists.

8   Kiyomasa Redux

The tale of Katō Kiyomasa's overseas encounter with Mt. Fuji during the first invasion of Korea in 1592, was integrated into the legend of Kiyomasa, apotheosized as a culture hero in Edo-period popular culture.[90] While Hideyoshi's armies were driven from Korea, after two major campaigns spread over seven years, in Japanese popular consciousness at least the Korean campaigns were a great Japanese victory that had "restored" proper relations between Japan and its subordinate, tributary vassal-state, Korea.

One diarist, writing in 1748, explained the reason foreigners began to bring tribute to Japan:

> In ancient times [the legendary] Empress Jingū had attacked [Korea, conquered it], and turned it into Japan's pet dog by force of arms. Thereafter, for generations, they submitted tribute [*nyūkō*] to our country. But [since the founding of the Chosŏn dynasty], they'd become lax about bringing tribute to our country, so Prince Toyotomi sent an army of several tens of thousands across the sea [to Korea].... The King [of Korea] fled across the Yalu River to Ming.... This angered Katō Kiyomasa, who captured two [Korean] royal princes and over 1,300 other prisoners.... [Later,] Korea sued for peace, and Tōshōgū [Tokugawa Ieyasu] returned all the prisoners.... Awed by this virtuous grace, an embassy came to pay court.... From ancient to recent times, the limitless light of [Japan's] Martial Prestige (*bui*) has shone brilliantly from the Mulberry Land (*Fusō*, a poetic name for "Japan"), sending the brightly shining, morally transforming virtue [*ka*] of [Japan's] pacification far beyond the seas to Korea.[91]

---

90   On the cult of Kiyomasa, Fukunishi (2012).

91   Kozono (1748/1800). The view expressed here, that these were "tribute" embassies sent because Korea was subjugated, first by the Empress Jingū and again by Kiyomasa (or Hideyoshi), was a common Edo-period reading of the meaning of Korean embassies. The claim that "Tōshōgū returned all the prisoners" taken in the Korean campaigns is exaggerated. The precise number taken to Japan as prisoners is uncertain, but the best estimate is on the order of 20,000 (Naitō 1976), but the best estimates place the number who made it

The Qianlong Emperor had only "heard" of Mt. Fuji's majesty and seen it in Sesshū's picture, but Serutōsu reported seeing the physical Fuji from Tartary, 1,045 km northwest of Mt. Second-to-None! Just as Japanese intellectuals and shogunal publicists argued that it was the "winds of virtue" that summoned barbarians to trade, that Japan had successfully "contested the center," displacing China as the moral center of East Asia and the whole world, popular discourse suggested that the sacred form of Mount Fuji, emergent symbol of all Japan, was visible around the world—or at least, across the seas.[92]

Kiyomasa's visual encounter with Mt. Fuji from Orankai became a stock trope in both verbal and visual popular discourse, spurred, at least in part, by publication of three illustrated accounts of Hideyoshi's exploits, *Ehon buyū Taikōki, Ehon Chōsen gunki,* and *Ehon Taikōki,* between 1790 and 1802, each of which embellished the legend with a two-page illustration of Kiyomasa's long-distance encounter with Mt. Fuji.[93] The first of these, a rather crude, cluttered illustration in *Ehon buyū Taikōki* (Fig. 121), depicts Kiyomasa and a few of his men on the Korean or Orankai coast; Kiyomasa, on horseback, raises a hand to shade his eyes from the sun, and gazes at massive Mt. Fuji beyond the sea, rising above the clouds. The caption identifies the scene as the land of the "Tatars" (Jurchen; J., *Jochoku*), and reads, in part, "Mt. Fuji is visible from here; the men's thoughts turned to returning home."[94] The figure presumably

---

home to Korea, either as repatriates or escapees, at between 6,100 and 6,300 (Nakao (2000, 201–203), and 7,500 (Yonetani, 1999). Many were sold as slaves to European traders, who took them not only to Southeast Asian slave markets but to Europe as well. Kitajima (1995, 259–270).

92   On this displacement of China, and the emergence of a "Japan-centered" vision of the dichotomies of civilized and barbarian, moral/political center and periphery in Edo-period Japanese discourse, see Toby (1985).

93   Terasawa (1790); Takeuchi & Okada (1797–1802); Akizato (1800). *Ehon Taikōki* was banned in 1804, the printing blocks confiscated and destroyed, following an incident earlier in the year when *ukiyo-e* prints portraying Toyotomi Hideyoshi by Kitagawa Utamaro and Utagawa Toyokuni—thought to be inspired by *Ehon Taikōki*—were deemed to have violated bakufu censorship laws that proscribed works that discussed historical samurai figures active any time from the 1570s to the present. *NKBD*, 1: 371. For a full transcription of Terasawa (1790), see Kim (2008).

94   As printed, not only does the illustration show Kiyomasa looking away from Mt. Fuji; the left and right panels of the illustration in Terasawa (1789) do not register correctly. The illustrator visualizes the caption's reference to on the roofs of Orankai houses by depicting a house festooned with drying kelp, but as printed, the two halves of the house are at the opposite margins, with Kiyomasa between them. Only by reversing the panels as I have done here does the illustration make sense: The two halves of the house align perfectly, as do the clouds or mist at the lower margin and the middle of the frame. The caption (*kakiire*), however, only scans grammatically and syntactically as printed.

FIGURE 121   A helmeted, mounted Katō Kiyomasa gazes at Mt. Fuji from the Orankai coast, from Terasawa Masatsugu, *Tales of Martial Valor and Great Success, Illustrated*. To my knowledge, this is the earliest visualization of the legend of Kiyomasa's transmarine encounter with the mountain. The narrative, written across the sky, informs us that Kiyomasa's guide, "Guided by Serutōsu, renamed Jirō, Kiyomasa saw Mt. Fuji in the southwest, which caused the men to think of returning home." Serutōsu/Jirō's clothes, fur collar and "Chinese" beard sign him as foreign; his shaved pate as Japanese. (*Ehon buyū taikō-ki*, Kyoto: Hishiya Jihei, 1790; National Diet Library) I have corrected the block-carver's error that reversed the left and right halves of the image; otherwise the composition does not scan.

representing Serutōsu is seated on the ground in a posture of deference; his beard and fur collar suggest he is a Tatar—or that he has gone native.

The illustrations of this scene in both *Ehon Chōsen gunki* (Fig. 122) and *Ehon Taikōki* (Fig. 123) are sparer and more skillfully executed; they eliminate some extraneous figures and move the kelp-festooned house to one corner, heightening the focus on Kiyomasa—now on a camp stool—Serutōsu, shown wearing a grass skirt (a sign of primitivity, or of having "gone native"), and much more economically rendered Mt. Fuji. Both identify the scene as "Seishū" (Sŏsura). Only *Ehon Taikōki*'s rendering shows Kiyomasa in the tall, arching "court-cap helmet" (*eboshi kabuto*) that had become his trademark, though Akizato does add pennants and a battle standard (*umajirushi*) with his "snake-eye" logo.

FIGURE 122   Akizato Ritō reworks Terawasa's rendering of Kiyomasa's sighting of Mt. Fuji.
              Akizato (1800).

FIGURE 123   Okada Gyokuzan's rendition of Kiyomasa sighting Mt. Fuji from the Korean
              coast. Takeuchi & Okada (1797–1802, pt. 6, vol. 2).

For Hokusai, like Kiyomasa, it wasn't merely that Mt. Fuji "needed no interpreter" to be heard abroad; Mt. Second-to-None was visible beyond the seas. The legend of Kiyomasa only implicates Japanese—Kiyomasa himself, and his interpreters Gotō Jirō and Serutōsu—as seeing Mt. Fuji from the northern Korean frontier; there is no claim that the Korean princes he had captured shared this miraculous vision. Hokusai, however, by suggestion, brings the princes back into the frame: "Orankai no Fuji" depicts two figures, both not only signed unmistakably Other but each also as a sort of Other distinct from his companion, at the door of a crude, thatched sod hut on the rocky coast of Tartary (Fig. 124).[95] They look off across the sea and gaze up wonderingly, even worshipfully at the pure form of the sacred summit, floating above the clouds. The caption identifies the setting as Orankai, and the figures are clothed in garb which, in Edo-period iconography, signifies the Other. The one at the right shows an elegant, aristocratic face framed in an elaborate coiffure, a circle of gold dangling from his earlobe; he wears luxurious, many-layered robes, a trimming of fur at the wrists. The second figure, smaller and more rudely dressed, is clearly a servant, laden with baggage. The minimalist title, "Mt. Fuji from Orankai," suggests that Kiyomasa's legendary encounter with Mt. Fuji from across the sea had so thoroughly permeated popular consciousness—at least among the reading public—that the scene required no further explanation.

Kiyomasa-ki and *Wakan sansai zue* merely reported that Serutōsu said he "could see Fuji." In Hokusai's "Mt. Fuji from Orankai" (Fig. 116) two figures in alien dress, perhaps intended to depict one of the Korean princes Kiyomasa had captured earlier in the campaign, accompanied by a servant, actually did see Fuji, and they gazed as far-off worshippers. The implication of an increasing Japanese sovereign range waiting to be realized and of people waiting eagerly, reverently to greet that sovereignty is difficult to miss. Hokusai's rendition of Other gazing on Mt. Fuji from Orankai reflects, in part, a mounting sense of foreign forces that threatened Japan from all sides that became ever more urgent from the late eighteenth century onward. Many writers and artists— not just adherents of the Fuji cult, like Hokusai—took up this mythic topos, announcing to their audiences across Japan that Mt. Fuji's visibility, and the

---

95   Katsushika (1834–1835, 3: 8b). Hokusai may have been prompted to produce this composition by a *senryū* (comic verse) published in 1833, *Chōsen no/ōji kokora ni/Orankai*, which may be parsed, "Korean prince/ain't he/around here?" with *Orankai* doing double duty as both a toponym and a verb. Okada (1974, 581); cf. Kimura (1982, 64–65), who notes the virtual simultaneity of the unsigned *senryū* and Hokusai's "Orankai no Fuji." Henry D. Smith notes that the notion of Mt. Fuji's "visib[ility] from the continent is revealing as a mark of Japan's evolving national consciousness" (1988, 215). As I hope I have made clear, much more remains to be said on this question.

FIGURE 124
"Orankai no Fuji," in Katsushika
Hokusai, *Fugaku hyakkei*
(Katsushika 1834, 3: 8b).

implied reach of Japanese moral, or perhaps political, territory ranged far beyond Japan's immediate shores.

Some sixty years later, a popular artist translated the Kiyomasa legend's
conceit of a Fuji visible on the continent into a vision fit for a nation whose
martial vigor was newly revived, and stood on the brink of reclaiming Korea
by conquest for Japanese sovereignty.[96] Watanabe Nobukazu dispenses with
both Serutōsu and captive Korean princes to give us Kiyomasa resplendent in
full battle array, astride his charger at the Korean front. Kiyomasa's helm is blazoned with the Rising Sun, and he shields his eyes from the blinding rays of
another Rising Sun: for Fuji's sacred form rises majestic across the sea, backed
by the glow of a morning sunrise. (Fig. 125) As his men point to the peak rising
across the sea, we can almost hear them announce to Kiyomasa, and to the

---

96   Nobukazu (pseud. of Watanabe Jirō, fl. late nineteenth c.), *Katō Kiyomasa Chōsen yori
      Fujisan o nozomu* (triptych polychrome print, dated 1893. Collection, Nagoya Shiritsu
      Hakubutsukan). Nobukazu was best known for his prints of the Sino-Japanese War.

FIGURE 125   Watanabe Nobukazu published his "Katō Kiyomasa Gazes upon Mt. Fuji from
Korea" in 1893, amid the buildup to what would erupt the following year as the
Sino-Japanese War. Polychrome triptych print, 1893.
COURTESY HIDEYOSHI & KIYOMASA MUSEUM, NAGOYA

Meiji imperial forces poised for the impending Sino-Japanese War, "Mt. Fuji
guarantees Japan's victory; Korea is ours."[97]

Nobukazu's composition reprises the scene as depicted in *Ehon Taikō-ki* and
numerous other illustrated books from the 1780s and 1790s, but also reflects an
growing appetite for images of Kiyomasa as well as of the legendary conquest
of Korea by the mythical "Empress Jingū," and the trope of gazing at Mt. Fuji
from across the seas.[98] The episode of Kiyomasa viewing the mountain had
been popularized in widely marketed polychrome prints published at least
four previous times since 1860, and Fukuchi Ōchi had incorporated the scene
into a play that opened at Tokyo's *Kabuki-za* in November 1891:[99]

---

97   Other evocations of Kiyomasa's purported heroics, equating them with the mythical
      conquest of the Three Kingdoms of Korea by the "Empress Jingū" (*Jingū Kōgō Sankan
      seibatsu*), were current by the early 1860s. See, e.g., Yoshitoshi, *Kiyomasa Sankan taiji zu*
      (1864, triptych), reprinted in Konishi (1977, 2:22–23).

98   Takeuchi (1789). See below, p. 273.

99   Fukuchi (1891): 52–52. Precursor prints include Utagawa Yoshitora, "Ten'an nenjū Satō
      Kazue-no-suke Masakiyo Bokkai-koku seisen no hi, kaigan yori Fuji no yama o miru
      zu" (1860; Fig. 137), Toyohara Kunihiro, "Mitate Fuji jūrokkei" (1876), Mizuno Toshikata,
      "Nihon ryakushi zukai: jinnō jūgodai" (1885), and Utagawa Kunisada, "Kiyomasa Chōsen
      yori Nihon no Fuji o miru zu" (1887). Yoshitora print, collection of the author; Kunihiro,
      Toshisada and Kiyomasa prints, Tōyō Keizai Daigaku Toshokan collection, at www.tku
      .ac.jp/~library/korea/KOREA.html (accessed 2014/021/01).

Katō: Jirō, this is Orankai, right?

Gotō [Serutōsu]: As your lordship says. This place is called Seishūho [Sŏsura], on the southern border of Orankai. When the weather is fair you can see Mt. Fuji in Japan exceptionally clearly off to the southwest as if it was right up close. You should be able to see it today.

So saying he turned to face Katō and said:

Gotō: Look over there, my lord. There, that mountain you see far off above the sea, if you look at the clear gaps between the clouds, is Mt. Fuji in Japan.

So saying, as he pointed a finger [toward it], Katō [Kiyomasa] doffed his helmet and stood, gazing far across the waves at Mt. Fuji:

Katō: Hmm. Of course! I can worship Mt. Fuji from here. I landed in Korea, and I thought we'd been marching northwestward ever leaving the royal capital [Hansŏng, i.e., Seoul). Have we now come around to Japan's southwest!? That's where my lord the Taikō [Hideyoshi] is!

So saying he sat on the ground, shaded his eyes with his hand, and gazed worshipfully in the direction of Mt. Fuji.[100]

Yet in the end, it was as much the power of Mt. Fuji to "repel the barbarian" and to "protect" Japan that most engaged artist, pamphleteer, and publicist in the last decades of the Edo period. From the 1770s on, Japanese increasingly saw themselves surrounded by an ever-more-hostile "barbarian" threat, coming first from the north—hence the *Matsumae byōbu* to mark boundaries now contested by the Russians—but then, more dangerously, from the South and Southwest in the form of Euro-American encroachments. This eventually coupled with a renewed focus on the emperor to generate the "revere-the-emperor-and-repel-the-barbarian" discourse of the mid-nineteenth century.[101] The rising tide of foreign pressure provoked a spate of books and pamphlets, some published as early as the Bunka era (1804–1818), more than a decade before Aizawa Seishisai's *Shinron* (1825), that recalled the Empress Jingū's mythic conquest of Korea; the glorious, divinely aided victory repelling the Mongol invaders in the thirteenth century; and Katō Kiyomasa's "heroic" exploits in Korea in the 1590s.[102] Recall that Hiraga Gennai had invoked the memory of

100   Fukuchi (1891): 52–52.
101   The classic study is Keene (1952); an important newer study is Wakabayashi (1986).
102   *Hotei-ban Kokusho sōmokuroku*, 9 vols. (Iwanami Shoten, 1989), lists numerous works; for
       example, Wakabayashi Kazumitsu, Ishida Gyokuzan, and Ishida Gyokuhō, *Kiyomasa shin-
       denki* (1812); Uyū Sanjin and Utagawa Kuniyoshi, *Kiyomasa ichidai-ki*, 5 vols. (1840); Muro
       Kiso, *Katō Kiyomasa den* (1851); Tamenaga Shunsui and Utagawa Kuniyoshi, *Kiyomasa
       ichidai-ki*, 3 vols. (1864); Yano Gendō, *Jingū Kōgō go-denki*, 2 vols. (1858); Sangetsu-an

Japan's salvation from the Mongols by the *kamikaze*, the "winds of the gods," to save Mt. Fuji from the Qianlong Emperor's plot.

Many continued to emphasize Mt. Fuji's positive attraction, the mountain's ability to excite wonder and reverence, to draw Other to Japan to worship the mountain in its beauty, the mountain that riveted Itchō's Korean rider or the passing Korean entourage in Hokusai's "*Raichō no Fuji.*" But increasingly, a different, more awesome Mt. Fuji moved to the fore, the wrathful Mt. Fuji of Hiraga Gennai's playfully surreal imagination that possessed both consciousness of distant threats to Japan and the power to repel or destroy any who approached with malign intent.

When the long-imagined foreign threat materialized in 1853, when Commodore Matthew C. Perry's fleet of "Black Ships" (*kurofune*) steamed into Uraga Bay, demanding access to Japan, artists and authors turned to the amuletic power of Mt. Fuji to repel the approaching alien. The print artist Kagehide, for example, invoked the boar-hunting expedition of the 12th-century shogun Minamoto no Yoritomo on the "skirts of Mt. Fuji" (*Fuji no suso no makigari*), portraying Perry and his troops fleeing before the shogun's onslaught, charging down the slopes of the mountain.[103] The following year, another artist invoked Yoritomo's hunt when a Russian ship hove into the mouth of the Ajigawa river in Osaka, only a few miles from the imperial capital of Kyoto; though the artist does not depict the mountain *in* the print, he titles it, "The Military Encampments for the Hunt on the Skirts of Mt. Fuji."[104]

Another such author and artist was Ishikawa Masumi, whose *Mōzokki* (Record of the Mongol Pirates)[105] appeared in 1858. Only five years had passed since Commodore Perry's fleet had sailed into Edo Bay and forced a treaty on the reluctant *bakufu*—quickly followed by treaties with Russia, England, France, and Holland. That very year, the bakufu had committed itself to creating a new treaty port in Yokohama. For more than two centuries, the *bakufu* had been able to control foreigners, or at least to give the appearance of such power; as that power evaporated, a palpable sense of crisis overtook Japan and dominated public discourse.

Shujin and Katsushika Daito, *Sankan taiji zue*, 5 vols. (1841); Issa, *Sankan-jin* (1811). Miyachi Masato (1985, 42) notes another surge of publications celebrating Hideyoshi's "punishment of Korea" (*Chōsen seibatsu*), in which "the people were repeatedly reminded of images of Japan's 'glorious accomplishments' of the Japanese state in former times."

103   Kachōrō Kagehide, "Fuji no suso no makigari zu," polychrome triptych print, 1853, reproduced in Konishi (1977. 2–3).

104   Unsigned, "Fuji no makigari jin-tori no zu," polychrome triptych print, 1854, reproduced in Konishi (1977, 22–23).

105   Ishikawa (1858, 4: 17b–18a).

Ishikawa's text is a product of this critical moment. It should be no surprise, therefore, that Ishikawa turned for a talisman to a moment in the past when the gods had saved Japan from an earlier foreign threat, the Mongol invasions of the thirteenth century. *Mōzokki* is largely a reworking of familiar material, the text and illustrations following closely the *Mongol Invasion Scrolls* that were commissioned by a samurai who participated in Japan's defense against the Mongols. One of Ishikawa's illustrations is new, however, harking back to an incident of 1275, when the Kamakura bakufu executed five Mongol ambassadors from the Great Khan.[106] (Fig. 126) The execution of the Mongol ambassadors was of little interest to Suenaga, whose scroll focuses entirely on his own military exploits and his debt to the Kamakura official Adachi Yasumori. But it was a moment of great interest to Ishikawa, whose primary concern was how Japan might best resist the rising "barbarian" onslaught of his own day.[107] His talismanic invocation of the divinely assisted victory over the Mongols was widely echoed in the 1850s and 1860s. Ishikawa arrays the severed heads of the Mongol ambassadors on the beaches of Yui, under the protective gaze of Mt. Fuji, in an invocation of Mt. Fuji as the agent of Japan's salvation that resonated across a broad range of media.

Ishikawa, like Hiraga Gennai before him, associated that earlier moment of Japan's salvation from foreign threat to Mt. Fuji's awesome majesty, portraying the heads of the Mongol five ambassadors exposed on the beaches of Yui, where the envoys might gaze blindly, perhaps even worshipfully and apologetically, at the sacred mountain that had the power to protect Japan from barbarian attack. *Jōi*—"repel the barbarians"—was the rallying cry of many of Ishikawa's contemporaries, not only for those who found it a convenient way to arouse imperial loyalist and anti-*bakufu* sentiment but for thousands of others sincerely concerned about Japan's vulnerability.

Only two years later, Mt. Fuji's power to "repel the barbarians," the goal of anti-foreign activists for the past seven years, seemed to receive divinely oracular confirmation once more from the mountain itself. In 1860 the British minister to Japan, Rutherford Alcock, told the *bakufu* that he wanted to climb the sacred peak. Alcock viewed his proposal as a test of western diplomats' recently won treaty "right to travel freely in any part of the Empire of Japan," a right

---

106 Tōkyō Daigaku Shiryō Hensansho, comp. (1963, 5:211); Jingū Shichō (1981–1985, 26: 911). Compare *Kadokawa Nihon chimei daijiten* Hensan Iinkai (1978–1991, 14: 562), identifying the execution ground at Tatsunokuchi as part of the present-day city of Fujisawa.

107 Very little is known about Ishikawa. Since his only other extant work is a collection of poetry in the thirty-one syllable *waka* mode that experienced a revival among those of nativist (*kokugaku*) leanings, one wonders if he was involved in *kokugaku* himself.

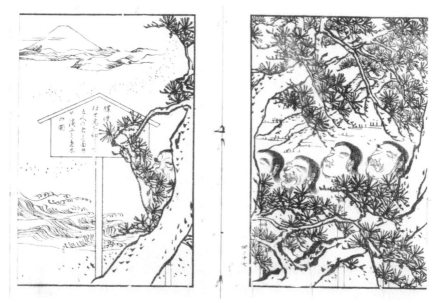

FIGURE 126   The severed heads of the five ambassadors from the Mongol emperor are
exposed on the sands of Yui Beach, outside Kamakura, under the watchful
gaze of Mt. Fuji. (Ishikawa Masumi, *Mōzokki* [Ishikawa 1858], Tokyo University
Library).

that Japanese officials strove mightily to prevent diplomats from exercising.[108]
Although he was warned that the late-summer storm season made ascent
dangerous, Alcock insisted and in early September received permission for his
expedition.

Alcock's desire to climb Mt. Fuji constituted the realization of generations of
popular discourse crediting the mountain with a universal appeal that "needs
no interpreter," drawing people from all over the world as pilgrims and admirers. Kanagaki Robun (1829–1894), one of the most widely read literary humor-
ists of the nineteenth century, both reflected and enhanced the mythos in his
1860 satire, *A Comic Pilgrimage to Mt. Fuji*,[109] which presented a view of "The
Parade of the English Minister and His Retinue Traveling along the Tōkaidō to

---

108   Article 1 of the "Treaty between the United States and Japan," signed on 29 July 1858, in
        Beasley (1967, 183). Under the most-favored-nation clause of the Anglo-Japanese treaty
        signed a month later, this provision extended to British diplomats as well, and Alcock as-
        serts this clearly in his memoir (1863, 1:396).

109   Kanagaki (1860/1961), vol. 9. 1860 was the *kōshin* [senior metal/monkey] year in that
        zodiac cycle, which meant that for the first time in sixty years, women were permitted to
        climb Mt. Fuji. Robun undoubtedly anticipated that the crescendo of popular interest in
        Fuji pilgrimage would translate into strong sales for his lighthearted parody.

Climb Mt. Fuji, in … the Autumn of This Year of [1860]." (Fig. 127)[110] The procession presents a hodgepodge of stereotypical figures from the rapidly evolving visual discourse of the post-Perry period, which had recently been stimulated by the opening of the foreign settlement in Yokohama, but Robun situates Alcock's desire to make a pilgrimage to the mountain explicitly in the evolving discourse of Mt. Fuji as the most beautiful mountain in the world that had the power to draw admirers from abroad by quoting in full a colophon Ōta Nanpo had added to Maruyama Ōzui's Mt. Fuji painting of decades before. (Fig. 128)

Alcock's ascent of Mt. Fuji went smoothly enough, and at the summit his aide Lt. Robinson measured the altitude, latitude, and longitude of the mountain. The party then proceeded down "Mt. Matchless," as Alcock called it (a fair rendition of one of the mountain's many names), but as they descended, the weather worsened rapidly and they found themselves in "a thick Scotch mist,

FIGURE 127   An illustration from Kanagaki Robun, *Kokkei Fuji-mōde* (1860). The caption at the upper right reads, "Illustration of the travels of English *minisutoru* (minister) [Alcock] along the Tokaido to climb Mount Fuji, mid-seventh month, autumn of this *koshin* year (1860)." The remaining captions in Chinese and Japanese are "In Praise of Mt. Fuji, by Professor Sleepyhead," i.e., Ōta Nanpo's colophons from Maruyama Ōzui's "Mt. Fuji" (See Fig. 125).

---

110   *Tō kōshin no aki, shichigatsu chūjun Eikoku no Minisutoru* [in phonetics] *shujū Fuji tozan Tōkaidō ryokō no zu.*

FIGURE 128

Maruyama Ōzui, "Mt. Fuji," with two colophons by Ōta Nanpo. The first is a faux genealogy of the mountain. The second reads, "Even Chinamen (*Tōjin*) must come all the way here if they want to see the greatest mountain in the world."

COURTESY OF THE MINNEAPOLIS INSTITUTE OF ART

which soon changed into a drenching rain" and barely "escaped the typhoon." By the time his entourage reached the Tōkaidō station of Kanagawa, on their way back to Edo, he "heard that, when they were visited by the typhoon there, the report was circulated that it was a sign of the anger of the gods at the foreigner profaning the sacred precincts of their stormy home."[111]

These reports were more than local; they were national. Indeed, they had been anticipated by knowledgeable people all around the country who had heard of Alcock's intention. A domain counselor from Mito Domain, Toda Tadanori, predicted on 7/21 that if Alcock climbed Mt. Fuji, "the God of the Mountain will surely be furious, and I fear that he will send a great wind to destroy the bumper crop now ripening nicely.... This will cause great hardship." Three days later, he noted that "the people have been enraged [that the English Barbarian Alcock was to climb Mt. Fuji], and say there's no doubt the Mountain Deity will not allow the barbarous curs to approach. The last few days people

---

111   Alcock (1863, 1:427–428). Their measurements were off considerably; they put the crater at 13,977 feet and the highest peak at 14,177 feet. The official measurement of the mountain is 12,389 feet (3,776 m).

have been selling all sorts of broadsides [*kawaraban*] [about this] ... and itin-
erant preachers of the Fuji cult are all absolutely opposed, warning that ...
[Alcock's party] will surely die a weird death before they reach the Fifth Stage."
Twelve days later, Toda wrote of the "Great Typhoon of the 24th, uprooting a
myriad trees; the winds were fiercer [at Mt. Fuji] than anywhere else. From
the start [people] had said the God of the Mountain would strike them." A
Sendai samurai and an innkeeper from Yui both echoed the same thoughts.
"The gods must be angry that impure foreigners have climbed to the summit
of the Incomparable Mountain, the most famous in all Japan, a land of sacred
mountains."[112]

The flames of xenophobic rumor were fanned by broadsides. Publishers in
Edo, as Toda had noted, were always quick to catch a timely, exciting story. One
such *kawaraban* of late 1860 (Fig. 129) shows Alcock and his party being blown
away by the wrathful god of the mountain, portrayed as a *tengu* (a winged,
hawk-beaked demon): "In the seventh month of this year, the aliens said they
wanted to climb Mt. Fuji. When the aliens climbed Mt. Fuji, they'd got to about
halfway [between] the seventh [and eighth] stages, when suddenly it seemed
to cloud over, and the winds came up.... A voice from the clouds said: 'This is
the sacred mountain of Japan. Aliens! Go down the mountain at once,' and
they were blown down the mountain."

Another *kawaraban* has Alcock and his "barbarian" companions grov-
eling in abject apology before the glowering *tengu*-deity at the foot of Mt.
Matchless while storm clouds gather at the summit. (Fig. 130) Here, the barbarians themselves apologize: "We had heard that Mt. Fuji is the greatest
mountain in the world. We begged for permission to climb the mountain.
But because this was not in accord with the will of the Honorable Protector
Deity of the Mountain, the Honorable Mountain went wild; thus we have
caused great hardship to many provinces. We have been spared our lives by
the exceptional grace of the god of the mountain, and for this we are profoundly grateful. Henceforth, we will never climb Mount Fuji again ... and we
apologize for having come to Japan."

In the face of Mt. Fuji's awesome power, the foreigners abased themselves
and promised to leave Japan forever—at least in the wishful thinking embodied in these *kawaraban*. The contemporary print artist Utagawa Yoshimori

---

112   These passages are from Toda's diary, *Mito hanshi Toda Tadanori zakki*, I, held in Ishin
       shiryō-hikitsugi-bon, 11-ho/305–1. The second passage quoted is an anonymous comment
       recorded by the Sendai samurai Sakurada Ryōsuke, *Saibikan manpitsu*, 5 vols. (MS, collec-
       tion Hōon-kai, Sendai), entry of Man'en 1/8/21. The comments of the Yui innkeeper, Koike,
       are recorded in his *Nendai-ki*, a copy of which is held by the Historiographical Institute,
       Tokyo University. I am grateful to Prof. Miyachi Masato for these references.

FIGURE 129   The *tengu* deity of Mt. Fuji (atop the rain cloud) calls up a
storm to blow Rutherford Alcock and his party down off the
slopes of Mt. Fuji. (Unsigned monochrome printed broadside
(*kawaraban*), 1860, in Kinoshita & Yoshimi, 1999, 89).

FIGURE 130   Alcock and his party grovel before the "god of the mountain,"
apologize for having even come to Japan, and for desecrating
Mt. Fuji, "the greatest mountain in the world." (Unsigned
monochrome printed broadside (*kawaraban*), 1860, in
Nishimaki, 1978, 2: 82).

(1830–1884) recuperated the image of Alcock trembling before the mountain's fearsome, if beautiful, form in his, *"Matchless: Famed Mountain of Japan,"* published in the year of Alcock's ascent.[113] (Fig. 131) Yoshimori's unidentified European figure—surely Alcock—stares up at a distant Mt. Fuji in abject terror, his eyes wide as saucers, his mouth distorted with fear; before him, a Chinese servant (?) has fallen to his knees, tremulously peering up at the mountain through a telescope. The print makes no explicit claims that Mt. Fuji will protect Japan or drive the foreigners away, but in the context of contemporary discourse, such as Ishikawa Masumi's depiction of the decapitated Mongol envoys or the *kawaraban* and rumors about the mountain's divine retribution against Alcock, there is little doubt that Yoshimori's audience would have recognized the message, now no more than a wish, that Mt. Fuji was Japan's protector deity, and would drive away the foreign threat.

9 Conclusion

The power of Mt. Fuji, "Matchless," to extend the divine grace of Japan's gods beyond the seas, to attract foreigners and cause them worshipfully to approach Japan and Mt. Matchless; to protect Japan from barbarian attack and ultimately to repel and to subjugate the barbarian was elaborated in a continuing dialogue between Mt. Fuji and the Alien that grew increasingly articulate and explicit over the last century of the Edo period. As discourses differentiating Japan from Other became more urgent in the final years of Edo's rule, the recourse to Mt. Fuji, Ise, and other sacred symbols became more insistent as well. But Mt. Fuji's distinct silhouette and well-developed iconography suited it better to the task than other, less readily visualized symbols of Japanese identity.

The transformation of Mt. Matchless from a peripheral to a central symbol of Japanese identity was not merely a condition of this dialogue of Fuji and the Foreign, nor was Mt. Fuji by any means the sole venue where Japanese discourses on the Foreign, and wishful dreaming of the subjection of the Foreign to Japanese will, were played out. But they were unquestionably mutually reflexive processes, to paraphrase Robert Darnton, of "a [nation] representing itself to itself" by keeping "a close watch on [its] borders … defin[ing, defending, and even expanding] itself negatively, by reference to … hostile [barbarians]."[114]

---

113   Ikkōsai (1860). I have used the copies in the Yuasa Hachirō Collection, International Christian University and the Kanagawa Prefectural Museum.
114   Darnton (1985, 124, 128).

FIGURE 131
Utagawa Yoshimori, "Matchless: Famed Mountain of Japan" (1860), celebrates the abject terror that grips Alcock at the mere sight of Mt. Fuji, mobilizing the mountain as an ally in the drive to "expel the barbarians" (*jōi*).
COURTESY OF THE KANAGAWA PREFECTURAL MUSEUM

The parable of the Qianlong Emperor, like the windstorm of rumors and *kawaraban* surrounding Alcock's ascent of Mt. Fuji, expressed Mt. Fuji's sacred powers to attract, to protect, and to repel the barbarian. The universal visibility of Mt. Matchless was represented best in the verbal and visual articulation of the legend of Kiyomasa the conqueror, whose conquest of Korea carried him to the limits of Japanese sovereignty, as far as the cast of the sacred mountain's shadow. These articulations didn't merely represent great, if imaginary, victories over foreign foes of the past. Rather, they recalled—recuperated in the present—pretended archaic extensions of Japanese authority to subjugate the Foreign.[115]

The imposition of coevality between the archaic and the present, between the sacred (e.g., the Empress Jingū, the god Sumiyoshi) and the profane, make it possible to invoke Mt. Fuji in service of multiple goals: not only resistance to foreign aggression but also to the discursive expansion of Japan's sacred,

115   Cf. Fabian (1983, 30–35).

sovereign boundaries beyond the seas—as far as Fuji's form is visible—and subjection of the foreign. Thus, the rhetoric of Fuji, "Mount Matchless," contributed quite directly to an accelerating drumbeat of expansionist rhetoric in the last decades of the shogunate and through the Meiji era, beginning with calls to conquer Korea (*Seikan-ron*, i.e., "advocacy of conquering Korea") and culminating in the Sino-Japanese and Russo-Japanese wars.

It is no accident, then, that we find the legend of Kiyomasa gazing on Mt. Fuji from the coasts of the Korean frontier revived and amplified in the nineteenth century. The growing sense of military threats from all sides was palpable. Russian inroads in northern Ezo and American whalers landing at will on the Pacific coast, not to mention increasingly frequent diplomatic approaches and even aggressive forays by the English and Americans at Nagasaki were all cause enough for alarm caused alarm. Yet these were only a prelude to the shocking news of China's defeat in the Opium War, the Perry mission, and the opening of ports to foreign trade and residence.

The pressing foreign question in the last years of the eighteenth century was the increasingly insistent and aggressive inroads Russia was making in northern Ezo, where a provocative report of impending Russian invasion, occasional armed clashes between Russians and Japanese, and Russian demands for trading rights in Japan had sparked a brushfire of fears both in the *bakufu* and in the broader public.[116] Authors, artists, and publishers intervened in—or capitalized on—this agitated discourse, producing an outpouring of books and prints and staging theatrical works and festival performances, evoking past overseas heroism, both historical and purely imaginative.

Just as Hiraga Gennai and Ishikawa Masumi, writing in quite different literary genres and in different historical moments, had credited the amuletic power of Mt. Fuji with the rout of the Mongol invasions of the thirteenth century, Japanese turned increasingly to talismans of celebrated—if perhaps mythic—conquests of the heroic past. Most prominent among these were "Empress Jingū conquering the three Korean kingdoms," the victory over the Mongols, and the Korean campaigns of the 1590s–imagined as a heroic Japanese victory and personified by Katō Kiyomasa and exemplified in Kiyomasa's overseas encounter with Mt. Fuji.

---

116   Howell (1995) and Walker (2001) on early modern Ezo; more broadly on eighteenth- and nineteenth-century xenophobia, see Wakabayashi (1986). Among the classic treatments, Donald Keene's chapter on "Tales from Muscovy" in his *The Japanese Discovery of Europe* (1952), has lost none of its saliency, particularly with regard to the spreading public consternation about a threat from the north.

In the vanguard of this revival of themes of overseas conquest in literature, performance, and visual art was Takeuchi Kakusai's reworking of the biography of Toyotomi Hideyoshi (1536–1598), architect of the Korean invasions. His *Ehon Taikō-ki* (Illustrated biography of Hideyoshi), illustrated by the leading Osaka print artist of the day, Okada Gyokuzan (1737–1812), lavished loving attention on Katō Kiyomasa's exploits during the Korean campaigns, especially his foray into Orankai. Gyokuzan's realization of Kiyomasa on the shores of Orankai, gazing across the waves at Mt. Fuji was to become canonical in nineteenth-century discourse. (Fig. 118)

Gyokuzan depicts Kiyomasa on horseback, in full battle array on a small sandy beach among the craggy rocks along the Orankai coast, surrounded by a detachment of his men, lancers, standard-bearers, and foot soldiers. The tall lacquered helm, an *eboshi-kabuto* brandishing golden horns and blazoned with his circular crest, were thoroughly familiar to visually literate readers in the late Edo period as identifying marks of Kiyomasa.[117] Kiyomasa shields his eyes from the rising sun, his sight guided across the waves by two men, one quite obviously a soldier in Kiyomasa's army, the other, signed as a barbarian beyond civilization (with unkempt beard and unbound hair, no hat, no shoes, wearing rough garments), who point to the wondrous sight of Mt. Fuji rising majestically beyond the storm-tossed sea. The second barbarian, kneeling on the sand before Kiyomasa, is shown gesticulating and speaking—most likely Serutōsu or "Gotō Jirō," explaining to the general that "when the sky is clear, you can see Mt. Fuji, right up close."

It is a relatively simple matter to identify utterances, interventions in the discourse; it is rather more difficult to gauge how a particular utterance, such as Gyokuzan's visualization of the Kiyomasa-meets-Mt. Fuji episode, was received and interpreted by its audience, not to mention assessing the depth or breadth of the audience. In this case, however, we have the opportunity to follow the effect of Gyokuzan's masterly illustration, for it came to redefine Kiyomasa and Mt. Fuji in much the way visualization of Marilyn Monroe has been forever altered by Andy Warhol's silk-screen rendition of the actress.

Thirty years later, nineteen devotees of the Mt. Fuji cult in Yashiro Village, Hitachi Province, who were at the same time members of a peasant confraternity formed to support pilgrimage to the shrines at Ise, immortalized their pilgrimage of 1830 by commissioning a large *ema* (votive plaque) and donating

---

117   Kabuki costumery for the role of "Katō Masakiyo," a thinly disguised name for Kiyomasa as a dramatic persona, featured the helmet and crest. See, for example, two prints by Hokushū depicting Nakamura Utaemon III as Masakiyo in *Hachjijin shugo no honjō*, in Keyes and Mizushima (1973, 66–69).

it for perpetual display in their local Fuji Shrine. Despite their destination—most likely because it was more distant and would allow them to spend more time in the relative freedom of the road—the face of their *ema* said nothing about the shrines at Ise. Rather, befitting presentation to a Fuji cult shrine, they hired artist who signed himself Setsuzan Ganshō (??–??) to paint a Mt. Fuji scene.[118] (Fig. 132) The pilgrims would, of course, have passed Mt. Fuji both outbound and returning from their journey to Ise, so their choice is doubly unsurprising. But what does surprise, until one considers the atmosphere of gathering foreign threat, is that the result—whether specified in the commission or chosen by the artist is unclear—was a realization in color of the monochrome book illustration of three decades earlier.[119]

Setsuzan greatly simplified the composition by eliding superfluous figures, as well as the houses and trees that cluttered the book illustrations. He reduces the scene to its essentials: An oversized Kiyomasa, the grass-skirted Serutōsu/Jirō figure kneeling before him and pointing across the waves to guide Kiyomasa's gaze to the mountain, and a minimalist Mt. Fuji floating in the distance above the horizon. But by simplifying the composition, Setsuzan in fact created a more effective evocation of Mt. Fuji's power.

The true significance of Setsuzan's representation of Kiyomasa gazing on Mt. Fuji, however, is not simply that this otherwise obscure artist has improved on Gyokuzan. Rather, the choice of theme by a group of peasants in the hinterland and the absence of any verbal elaboration on the visual text provide an invaluable index to the reception and propagation of the legend of Kiyomasa's encounter with Mt. Fuji in Orankai. Setsuzan's composition offers the viewer no written guide to the program of the painting or the identity of the figures depicted. Reading Setsuzan's *ema* in tandem with Hokusai's almost precisely contemporaneous *Orankai no Fuji* and the 1833 *senryū*, *Chōsen no/ōji kokora ni/*

---

118   I have been unable to identify the artist. Two other artists active in the early 19th century used the name Setsuzan, but neither was alive when this *ema* was painted. See Roberts, (1976), pp. 107; 183.

119   Setsuzan's composition shares some features of the illustrations in Terasawa (1789), Akizato (1800) and Takeuchi & Okada (1797–1802). Setsuzan follows Akizato's overall composition, with Kiyomasa to the left and Mt. Fuji to the right. He shows Kiyomasa seated on a camp stool, and Serutōsu wearing a grass skirt, as in Akizato; on the other hand, he depicts Kiyomasa in the "court-cap helmet" (*eboshi kabuto*) decorated with the "snake-eye" (*janome*) crest seen only in Okada's illustration. Finally, Setsuzan's Kiyomasa raises his right hand to his brow to shield his eyes from the sun, a feature seen only in Terasawa. It is likely that the legend of Kiyomasa's sighting of Mt. Fuji had fairly wide currency in Hitachi in the early Tenpō era (1829–1844), for at that same time, Kawaguchi Chōju (1831), a scholar in the Mito domain, which comprised most of Hitachi Province, included the tale in his account of what he deemed Japan's historical conquests of Korea.

FIGURE 132   Setsuzan Ganshō, *Ema* (votive plaque), 1830, depicting Katō Kiyomasa gazing across the sea at Mt. Fuji, pointed out to him by the kneeling Serutōsu. The absence of any caption or explanatory text testifies to the degree to which the legend of Kiyomasa's transmarine encounter with the mountain had become deeply embedded in popular discourse—at least among devotees of the Mt. Fuji cult. Ganshō borrows from both Akizato's and Gyokuzan's rendering of the scene: From the former, the positioning of Kiyomasa at the left; the kneeling Serutōsu in grass skirt (a sign of barbarism), and Mt. Fuji to the right. From the latter, he takes Kiyomasa's signature "court-cap helmet." Pigment on wood.
COURTESY OF FUJI JINJA, YASHIRO VILLAGE, RYŪGASAKI CITY, IBARAKI PREFECTURE

Orankai (Ain't those Korean princes here in Orankai), both of which elide even Kiyomasa himself, leads to the conclusion that both artists and the *senryū* poet assumed an audience that was broadly familiar with the narrative of Kiyomasa, the captive Korean princes and Serutōsu, and their distant vision of Mt. Fuji.[120]

A decade earlier the print artist Yashima Gakutei (1786?–1868) had likewise simplified the composition of this scene, and played with the theme of Kiyomasa seeing Mt. Fuji from Orankai, in a New Year's print of 1819 (Fig. 133). He places a readily recognizable Kiyomasa—wearing his iconic deer-antlered "court-cap helmet," seated on a rocky foreign shore in a roundel, and shading his eyes as he gazes out to sea. He sees Mt. Fuji, however, in separate square composition, a canonical view from Miho-no-Matsubara, as if Kiyomasa were

120   *Supra*, n. 94.

FIGURE 133
Yashima Gakutei depicts Katō Kiyomasa in
a roundel, seated on rock outcroppings in
Orankai or Korea, gazing at Mt. Fuji. A *kyōka*
(31-syllable comic verse) in the brocade
at the right reads, "Even in foreign lands/
they ask, 'Is that Fuji?'/I want to stroke/
my shaved-off beard/Spring in Japan." (*Ikoku
ni mo/Fuji no ari ya to/sori tote no/hige o
nadetaki/Hi-no-moto no haru*). New Year's
print for 1819. This is the earliest single-sheet
woodblock print I have seen on the theme of
Kiyomasa's overseas sighting of Mt. Fuji.
COURTESY CHAZEN MUSEUM OF ART,
UNIVERSITY OF WISCONSIN, MADISON

looking across Tago Bay from the continent! The caption to the right reads,
Ikoku ni mo/Fuji no ari ya to/sori tote/hige o nadetaki/Hi-no-moto no haru
("Even in foreign lands/they ask, 'Is that Fuji?'/I want to stroke my shaved-off
beard/Spring in Japan.")

The legend of Kiyomasa's overseas engagement with Mt. Fuji also engaged
painters moving in the most exalted social and political circles. The "Yamato-e
revival" (*fukko yamato-e*) painter Ukita Ikkei (1795–1859) and his son Yoshinari
(a.k.a. Shōan, d. 1893), whose imperial loyalism and involvement in anti-baku-
fu politics landed both in an Edo prison cell in 1858, collaborated to paint the
scene of Kiyomasa and Serutōsu (in Tōjin garb and hairstyle) on the shores
of Orankai gazing across the sea at Mt. Fuji.[121] (Fig. 134) Ikkei and Shōan, like
Setsuzan, are reprising the composition of the scene in *Ehon Taikō-ki* and *Ehon
Chōsen gunki*, but reducing it to the essentials: Kiyomasa astride his horse,
wearing his court-cap helmet; Serutōsu kneeling on the shore, pointing at the
distant Mt. Fuji. Ikkei's strong ties to the imperial court and nobility hint at
the degree to which the legend of Kiyomasa in Orankai had permeated even
the most elite levels of late-Edo society, and the political valences that pulsed
through it.

My choice to return at the end to visualizations of a heroic Kiyomasa on
foreign shores, gazing across the sea to a talismanic Mt. Fuji that juts its perfectly formed summit through the clouds, stems not just from a desire to link

---

121   [Ukita] Ikkei & [Ukita] Shōan, *Kiyomasa Fuji o haisuru no zu*, ink and color on silk (40 ×
       62 cm, collection of the Nagoya-shi Hideyoshi Kiyomasa Kinenkan). On Ikkei, Roberts
       (1976, 53); Tsuji (1980); for Shōan's dates, http://www.shibunkaku.co.jp/biography/search_
       biography_number.php?number=2146. Accessed 2016.02.29.

FIGURE 134   Ukita Ikkei & Ukita Shōan, "Kiyomasa Gazes on Mt. Fuji from
                Orankai" (undated). Placement of the signatures and seals
                suggests that Shōan painted the scene of Kiyomasa on the
                Orankai coast, while Ikkei inscribed the image of Mt. Fuji in
                the distance across the sea. Ikkei and Shōan, father and son,
                were deeply involved in the "expel the barbarians" (*sonnō jōi*)
                movement swirling around the imperial court in the 1850s,
                and likely saw this image as an icon in the cause. (Nagoya-shi
                Hideyoshi Kiyomasa Kinenkan).

Mt. Fuji discourse in the waning of the early modern order—the *bakumatsu*
years[122]—to roots reaching down to its beginnings. Perhaps more significant, it
joins the early modern discourse of Mt. Fuji and the Other to modern discourses of militarism, expansionism, and empire, to both the domestic and international politics of the late nineteenth and early twentieth centuries. Illustrated
books, both explicitly fictional and overtly factual or historical, kabuki, and
jōruji plays and festival performances in which Kiyomasa figured, were popular entertainments throughout the nineteenth century, bringing the Kiyomasa
legend to a wide audience.[123]

   Mt. Fuji was invoked repeatedly at moments when either "repelling the
barbarian" or extending the empire abroad—especially to Korea—was an
issue of burning urgency. In the wake of the Perry expedition print artists and

---

122   Some historians use the term *bakumatsu* ("end of the *bakufu*") narrowly to refer to the
      fifteen years from the arrival of Commodore Perry's fleet in 1853 to the fall of the *bakufu*
      in 1868. Others use it more broadly, to include the slow unraveling of the regime over a
      period of thirty or forty years.
123   By my reckoning, based on a keyword search of the Kokuritsu Bungaku Kenkyū Shiryōkan's
      online databases, at least twenty-three works of fiction, history, and drama appeared in
      the last eight decades of Tokugawa rule in which Kiyomasa figures as either the hero or in
      an important supporting role.

publishers got into the act, producing numerous polychrome prints (*nishiki-e*) on the theme of Kiyomasa gazing at Mt. Fuji from foreign soil. The earliest such commercial print I have found to date, predating the Perry mission, is a Kuniyoshi work of 1849 in which an armored "Fujiwara Masakiyo," seated on a camp stool on a beach, gazes across the waves at the silhouette of Mt. Fuji on the horizon. (Fig. 135) The caption reads, in part, "He invaded the territory of Orankai, and from the seashore there he gazed at Mt. Fuyō (i.e., Fuji) in the Imperial Land [of Japan]. His followers were overwhelmed with thoughts of home."[124] Kuniyoshi reprised the episode six years later, in a print depicting Mt. Fuji only barely visible above the horizon. (Fig. 136 & 136 detail)

FIGURE 135

Utagawa Kuniyoshi, "Fujiwara Masakiyo," in the series *Heroes of the Taiheki* (1847), is just one of many iterations of the legend of Kiyomasa sighting Mt. Fuji from the Orankai/Korean coast published in the final years of the Tokugawa bakufu, a theme that evoked legends of martial valor and overseas conquest. The long caption reads, in part, "He invaded the Orankai region and from the coast there he gazed at Mt. Fuyō (Fuji) in the Imperial Land (i.e., Japan). His troops were overcome with thoughts of home."

TOKYO METROPOLITAN LIBRARY

---

124   "Fujiwara Masakiyo," in the series *Taiheiki eiyū den* (Biographies of the heroes of the *Taiheiki*).

FIGURE 136   Utagawa Kuniyoshi, "Watōnai," from the series *Wakan jun Genji* (1853), depicts Kiyomasa in the guise of Watōnai (i.e., Coxinga) gazing across the sea at Mt. Fuji (det., rt.), barely visible on the horizon at the right edge. It was not uncommon to mix Kiyomasa and Coxinga metaphors in festival performances; both were revered as heroes of foreign conquest, and both were associated with a legend of besting a tiger.

In the aftermath of Alcock's 1860 ascent to the summit, as hot-blooded (and hot-headed) advocates of "revering the emperor and expelling the barbarian" embarked on a campaign of random attacks against foreigners,[125] Utagawa Yoshitora (fl. ca. 1850–1880) published a lavishly colored triptych depiction of

---

125   Henry Heusken, interpreter to the American consul, was assassinated by *sonnō jōi* samurai on 15 January 1861 (Man'en 1/12/5), for example, and on 5 July 1861 (Bunkyū 1/5/28), Mito samurai attacked the Edo residence of British minister Rutherford Alcock. "Bokkai" (Ch., *Bohai*; K., *Parhae*), a state stretching across the northern Korean peninsula and southeastern Manchuria, was a successor to the state of Koguryŏ, which had been destroyed in 668 by an alliance between the state of Silla and the Tang empire.

FIGURE 137   Utagawa Yoshitora, "In the Ten'an era [857–859] Satō Kazue-no-suke
              Masakiyo Sees Mt. Fuji from the Coast of Parhae on the Day He Attacked
              Parhae." Polychrome triptych print, 1860. Collection of the author.

Kiyomasa, in his thinly disguised theatrical persona of "Satō Masakiyo," gazing
on Mt. Fuji from the coast of "Bokkai" (Fig. 137).[126]

Just months earlier, a Russian flotilla had landed by force on Tsushima and
built a small hut on shore. Since Tsushima was the stepping-off point for Japan's
trade with Korea, news of this clash may have been the immediate stimulus to
Yoshitora's choice of "Bokkai" as setting for his scene. Perhaps equally important was a rising tide of discourse urging the "conquest of Korea," an argument
heard from former students of the late Yoshida Shōin (d. 1859) in both Chōshū
and in Tsushima.[127] Just three years later, a consortium of Edo, Kyoto, Osaka
and Nagoya publishing houses put out a household encyclopedia (*setsuyōshū*)
that included a "Map of Korea" (Fig. 138); just up the east coast from Pusan it

---

126   Official censorship proscribed direct representation of Kiyomasa and many other histori-
       cal figures in fiction and on stage, yet accepted thinly disguised transpositions of name
       and plot. Just as Katō Kiyomasa became "Satō Masakiyo," Toyotomi (formerly Hashiba)
       Hideyoshi was renamed "Mashiba Hisayoshi"; the most famous example is the refashion-
       ing of Ōishi Kuranosuke, leader of the Akō vendetta of 1701–1702, as "Ōboshi Yuranosuke"
       in the play *Kanadehon chūshingura*. The most thorough discussion of censorship in
       publishing is Kornicki (1998, 320–362); for censorship in the Edo-era theater, see Shively
       (1955 & 1982); on censorship of prints, Thompson (1991). As Kornicki (1998, 332) observes,
       "Although there is no extant edict explicitly banning books dealing with Hideyoshi and
       [his son] Hideyori, in practice such books invariably got their authors and publishers into
       trouble." The publication of Takeuchi (1797–1802), *Ehon taikōki*, provoked a ban on "all
       references to warriors active from 1573 onwards" (Kornicki, 1998, 342), which of course
       included Kiyomasa.
127   Kimura (1993).

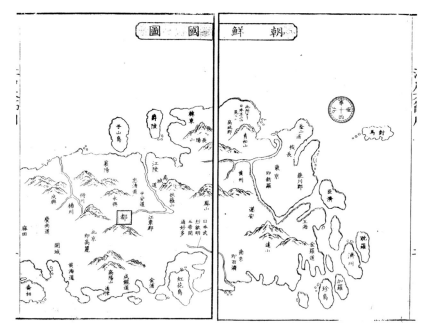

FIGURE 138   "Map of Korea," from *Edo dai-setsuyō kaidai-kura* (Takai, Nakamura &
                  Kikukawa 1863), with a notation on the east coast of Korea that, "From
                  here on can see Japan's Mt. Fuji."

pictured a mountain, *Ch'ŏngsongsan*, above which was the legend, "From here one can see Japan's Mt. Fuji."[128]

After the Meiji Restoration, the argument over Korea took on new urgency. For many, it was an opportunity to assuage the sense of helplessness in the face of the western powers by flexing Japan's muscles against a weaker opponent. In 1873, in fact, the fledgling government split over the question of whether (or when) to invade Korea; the defeated hawks left the government and metamorphosed into either rebels against the state or leaders of an insistent opposition movement under the banner of "freedom and people's rights."[129] In part as a balm to those critics and an escape valve for pressure from angry samurai, the government sent a punitive expedition against Taiwanese aborigines in 1874. The following year the government dispatched a naval expedition to provoke a confrontation with Korea, creating the pretext to extract from Korea in 1876 an "unequal treaty," with guarantees of Japanese extraterritoriality and most-

128   Takai et al. (1863). Ch'ŏngsongsan, Ch'ŏngsong County, North Kyŏngsang Province.
129   Conroy (1960), though dated in other respects, remains the best extended English-language treatment of the early Meiji debates over "conquering Korea."

favored-nation status—precisely the conditions of their own treaties with the western powers that so angered Japanese.

In this atmosphere Katō Kiyomasa's exploits in Korea—inflated with the passage of time and accretion of new apocrypha—and his supposed sighting of Mt. Fuji from the northeast Korean coast, took on added appeal. Immediately after the Restoration Utagawa Yoshitora, who had executed a triptych depicting Kiyomasa gazing across at Mt. Fuji (Fig. 137), published "Record of Famous Battles: The Conquest of Korea," illustrating the cover with a fiercely martial Kiyomasa looking across at Mt. Fuji. (Fig. 139) The preface, paired with a depiction of a towering Mt. Fuji, echoed Edo-period discourse, proclaimed that,

> Korea in ancient times comprised the "Three Han" (J., *Sankan*), named Silla, Paekche and Ko[gu]ryŏ. It was later renamed *Chōsen*. Ever since Empress Jingū, consort of the fifteenth sovereign, conquered it, the Three Han were subordinate to the Imperial Land [Japan], and never failed to send tribute. Whenever that country was attacked, Japan sent aid many times. But after the Genpei Wars [of 1180–1185], they lost their propriety, and in the Kōan era [1278–1287] they served as the vanguard of the Mongol [invasion] and became the enemy of Japan. During the reign of the Ashikaga, there were troublesome relations, but they did not follow Japanese ceremonies. Therefore Lord Toyo[tomi] Hideyoshi sent a military force to chastise [Korea], and they have been Japan's vassals [ever since].[130]

Other print artists instantly saw the potential for associating the "gunboat diplomacy" of 1875–1876 to force Korea into a modern treaty with Katō Kiyomasa's legendary heroism of three centuries before. Satō Toyotada (??–??) executed a lurid triptych battle scene entitled "Katō Kazue-no-Kami Kiyomasa Crosses the Sea to Korea and Shines the Light of [Japan's] Imperial Prestige Abroad."[131] And with Kiyomasa already mobilized, of course, Mt. Fuji could not be far behind. Toyohara Kunihiro's realization of the legend, "Parody Thirty-six Views of Fuji: Korean Harbor," in which a half-naked, half-blackened, and barbarized Serutōsu timorously guides Kiyomasa's gaze, assimilates Kuroda Kiyotaka, commander of the 1876 expedition, to the image of Kiyomasa. Kunihiro sees

---

130   Utagawa (1869).
131   "Katō Kazue-no-kami Kiyomasa Chōsen-koku ni tokai shite kōi o kaigai ni kagayakasu zu," Chōsen Nishiki-e Korekushon, Tōkyō Keizai Daigaku Library http://repository.tku.ac.jp/dspace/bitstream/11150/1272/1/U018.GIF, accessed 2018/09/14.

FIGURE 139
Scene of Katō Kiyomasa gazing at
Mt. Fuji from Korea adorns the front
cover of Utagawa Yoshitora, *Kōmyō
kassen-ki Chōsen seibatsu* (Tokyo,
1869).
COURTESY MAREGA COLLECTION,
UNIVERSITÀ PONTIFICIA
SALESIANA

no need even to identify his man, clearly expecting that culturally literate view-ers of his print were prepared to make the necessary association.[132]

The Kanghwa Treaty of 1876 that emerged from Kuroda's gunboat diplomacy transformed not only Japanese-Korean relations but all multilateral relations in Northeast Asia, placing Japan on a collision course with China and Russia over their competing interests in Korea. By the early 1890s, repeated minor clashes between Japanese and Chinese military detachments in Korea had growing segments of the Japanese public calling for decisive action; the ter-centenary of Hideyoshi's Korean campaigns added nostalgia to the mix.

Again, Katō Kiyomasa legendary heroics were mobilized in the outpouring of pro-war propaganda and popular sentiment that began long before hostili-ties seemed likely. As early as 1891, for example, parishioners of the Aso Shrine in Kiyomasa's former castle town of Kumamoto offered an *ema* depicting the

---

132 "Mitate Fuji jūrokkei: Chōsen minato," 1876, Chōsen Nishiki-e Korekushon, Tōyō Keizai
   Daigaku Library.

legendary moment Kiyomasa gazed upon Mt. Fuji from Orankai.[133] And within weeks of the formal declaration of war on 1 August 1894 a prominent publishing house rushed to print with a biography of Kiyomasa in a popular series that targeted the youth market; over the next fifteen years, at least three more biographies appeared.[134] Watanabe Nobukazu (fl. 1890s), best known for his polychrome prints visualizing the great battles of the Sino-Japanese War, completely effaces the presence of the Other—even Serutōsu—in his reiteration of this by now quite famous episode in Japan's imaginative history. (Fig. 131) The invocation of Mt. Fuji as both a protective and potentially aggressive metaphor for the nation and its divinely manifest destiny, thus, has continued into the modern era as a trope of Japanese invincibility.

Even in our own time, Mt. Fuji has continued to inform vocabularies for the attempted subjection of the foreign in the Pacific War and in the "trade war" beyond. Now, however, it is not merely Japanese who "construct" both Fuji and the readings Japanese think foreigners place on Mt. Matchless; The Other, too, readily mobilized Mt. Fuji as a symbol of the Japanese threat at the height of the Japanese "bubble economy" of the 1980s and early 1990s.

The cover of *Fortune International*'s June 1990 issue mobilized Mt. Fuji as a symbol of the threat of Japan's economic and technological might.[135] In a take-off on the famous *New Yorker* cover that gazes across the absurdly limitless spaces of midtown Manhattan's West Side and a broad Hudson River, *Fortune* gazes across a shrunken Manhattan, Hudson River and American "Midwest," running thence to a silicon-chip labeled "Palo Alto," to a Pacific Ocean narrower than the Hudson and a looming Mt. Fuji superimposed on an Imperial Japanese Navy sunburst (the sun also rises from the West?),[136] from which a shark-toothed, tiger-eyed Japanese auto leads the charge of Seiko, Sony, Nikon, and Fuji products that flow from the sacred, demonic mountain. Now, Other also reads Fuji, offering Japan new meanings, new readings of Mt. Fuji.

---

133   *Ema*, Jinnai Aso Shrine, Tatsuta-Jinnai-Chō, Kumamoto City, reproduced in Kumamoto Hakubutsukan (2005), p. 27.

134   Emi Suiin (1894) appeared as Hakubunkan's *Shōnen Bunko* (Youth Library), vol. 31. Other late-Meiji biographies, anticipating the 300th anniversary of Kiyomasa's death, include Tsukahara Jūshien, *Katō Kiyomasa* (Sakura Shobō, ca. 1907); Nakano Yoshitarō, ed., *Katō Kiyomasa-den* (Ryūbunkan, 1909); Yamaji Aizan, *Katō Kiyomasa* (Min'yūsha, 1909); Saitō Kazunori & Tsuchiya Kazumasa, *Katō Kiyomasa kō den: zen-go hen* (Kinkōdō Shoseki, 1910). Kurokawa Masamichi (1910/1911) published a collection of Kiyomasa's "instructions" in a series of ethics texts for *The Japan Educational Library*.

135   *Fortune International*, January 26, 1990.

136   *The New Yorker*, March 29, 1976.

Antiphonals of Identity

Three Riffs from Langston Hughes:[1]

1. I wonder if white folks ever feel bad,
   Waking up in the morning, lonesome and sad.

2. When you turn the corner and run into yourself,
   Then you know that you have turned all the corners that are left.

3. From river to river,
   Uptown and down,
   There's liable to be confusion,
   When a dream gets kicked around.
   You talk like they don't kick dreams around downtown,
   But I expect they do. But I'm talking about Harlem to you.

Langston Hughes, whose insights, cadences, and turns of phrase have inspired me since childhood, throughout his provocative and illuminating oeuvre invariably "ran into [him]self" through encounters with his own excluded others, others of race, class, gender, and, occasionally, of gender orientation. Hughes's poetry rests, or, more accurately, is restless, atop an antiphonal structure of binary alterities—black/white, male/female, adult/child, hip/square, "uptown and down"—that give form both to his world and ours.

In these essays I have likewise approached the construction of identity through images in the funhouse mirrors of the Other, looking at its inseparable twin, its essential mirror, the production of what Freud called "petty difference." In concert with Hughes, Freud, Laing, and Genet, with Tan'yū and Itchō, Harunobu, and Hokusai, with Akinari, Chikamatsu, Gennai, and Nanpo, I have sought that discourse of identity in reflected images of imagined difference.

I have proceeded in these chapters from the initial observation that the global encounter of the sixteenth century provoked a crisis of identity in Japanese culture and consciousness—as it did among many peoples around

---

1 Langston Hughes, 1958 (recording); 1959 (print). "Same in Blues," 270f; "Comment on Curb," 271; "Final Curve," p. 136. There are a few small differences between the poems in print, and as Hughes recites them on the recording.

© KONINKLIJKE BRILL NV, LEIDEN, 2019 | DOI:10.1163/9789004393516_010

the world: Longstanding structures of binary alterity predicated on a *sangoku*, or "three countries," cosmology imploded under the knowledge that this brave new world comprised *bankoku*—a myriad of countries. If the impact of encounter shattered the mirrored Other embedded in *sangoku* cosmologies, the challenge for seventeenth-century and later discourse was to construct a new cosmos of plural others and to fill it with enough specificity to establish and maintain an array of excluded, negated characteristics—the cultural indicia of being not-Japanese, the geographic indicia of being not-Japan.

That is, I have focused principally on the representation of the excluded other, the not-Japan and not-Japanese imagined to be "out there," working from the outside inward—yet stopping, one might protest, before truly illuminating what that discourse assumes to be the core identity of "Japan" or "Japanese." The resulting methodological unease is that only an empty center appears to remain—something Barthes seemed to charge was, in any case, all there was.[2]

I do not, of course, believe that the center was in any way empty. At the same time artists, writers, street performers, and so on were sketching the lineaments of what it meant to be outside a Japan/Japanese identity, of course, other stars in the constellation of early modern Japanese discourse—from Yamazaki Ansai, Keichū, Kaibara Ekiken and his friend Matsushita Kenrin, to Ueda Akinari, Motoori Norinaga, and Hirata Atsutane—were busily articulating a framework of positive statements about the "included self" (if that phrase may stand to represent the excluded other's "excluded other"). These broad and deep currents of introspective—yet assertive and aggressive—discourse are often subsumed under the rubric of "nativism" or "national learning" (two competing renderings of the notion of *kokugaku*).[3]

For nativists, of course, the Other was among their most vital concerns; one modern scholar suggests that, "One of the most conspicuous features of nativist thought in eighteenth century Japan was its vilification of Buddhism and Confucianism as 'foreign' creeds alleged to have had a deleterious impact upon the national character."[4] But for nativists it was of far, far greater urgency to delineate the content, the indicia of the included, the claimed national self. They often proceeded from assumptions of equivalency between themselves and the divine origins they posited for Japan and its people, from a belief in

---

2   Barthes (1982).
3   Some of the most provocative recent English-language monographs on the varieties of Edo-period Nativism include Wakabayashi (1986); Harootunian (1988); Nosco (1990); Burns (2003); McNally (2005).
4   Nosco (1990, 41).

what Peter Dale has called "the myth[s] of Japanese uniqueness," to a set of qualities and purposes divinely imbued in both the "sacred country" (one possible rendering of *shinkoku*) and the people (*aohitogusa*) who sprouted like the grasses from its sacred soil.

The community between originary Japanese and the native pantheon that nativists from Keichū to Atsutane sought to establish through re-reading ancient texts thought to predate the accretion of linguistic and moral overlays from abroad (e.g., Chinese language; Buddhism and Confucianism) itself proceeded from an axiomatic Othering of China, Korea, and Tenjiku. At the turn of the eighteenth century, for example, Matsushita Kenrin and Kaibara Ekiken argued, from a distinctly nativist perspective, that, in Kenrin's words, their contemporaries were unable to access "the true meaning of the ancients," because through centuries of reading Chinese letters (*kanji*), Japanese "had ultimately become accustomed to reading books and writing texts as if it were natural, and with the passage of time, things are now different, and errors and foreign meanings have crept into [the Japanese language] so that it is impossible to distinguish the sources of Japanese words ..." Worse still, the overlay of "foreign meanings" had corrupted current understanding, and led to "errors of both meaning and principle appearing in the interpretation of our nation's histories."[5]

A quarter-century later, when Kada Azumamaro (1669–1736) proposed establishing a "school of national learning" (*kokugaku*), he picked up the arguments Kenrin and Ekiken had advanced, arguing that, "If the old words are not understood the old meanings will not be clear; if the old meanings are not clear, the old learning will not revive." And the culprit was the intervening layers of alien ideas, words, and practices: "Everywhere now Confucian studies are followed, and every day the Buddhist teachings flourish more. 'Humanity' and 'righteousness' have become household words; even common soldiers and menials know what is meant by the [Chinese] *Book of Songs*. In every family they read [Buddhist scriptures]; porters and scullery-maids can discuss [the core Buddhist notion of] Emptiness.... Most lamentably, however, the teachings of our Divine Emperors are steadily melting away, each year more conspicuously than the last...."[6]

Nativists pursued a dual strategy, that is, for the privileged qualities of self-identity could only be articulated by strategies of what Freud had called "petty difference," by explicit and implicit juxtaposition with the excluded Other. In

---

5   Matsushita (1700), in Ekiken-kai (1910–1911, 1: 1); Kaibara (1700).
6   Kada, "Petition for the Establishment of a School of National Learning," in Tsunoda, de Bary, and Keene (1958, 510–514).

R. D. Laing's quite apposite formulation—though Laing's interest is primarily individual, rather than collective identity formation—this is a dialectic of "counterfeiting" and "collusion":[7]

> Every relationship implies a definition of self by other and other by self.... A person's 'own' identity cannot be completely abstracted from his identity-for-others....
>
> Consider this as a game of *counterfeiting a relationship*. Peter or Paul may try to *establish an identity for himself by achieving a particular identity for the other*.... Peter needs Paul to be a certain person in order for Peter to be the person he wishes to be....
>
> Collusion is always clinched when self finds in other that other who will 'confirm' self in the false self that self is trying to make real, and vice versa. The ground is then set for a prolonged mutual evasion of truth and true fulfillment. Each has found an other to endorse his own false notion of himself and to give this a semblance of reality.

Scholars both in and beyond Japan have focused on literary, philosophical, or religious strands of nativism, and especially on nativists' articulation of "counterfeit" Japanese identities, far more than their modes of "achieving a particular identity for the other." I have therefore focused the essays brought together here all the more strongly on that "identity for others" as constructed in political and ideological, literary and performative, and especially visual discourse—precisely to bring into focus the "Other" side of that discourse of identity formation.

In the visual and performing arts, as we have seen, the discourse of identity formation was instantiated in representation of direct Japanese engagements with Other, in ways not seen before Iberian irruption of the middle to late sixteenth century, and the invasion of Korea in the 1590s. Until then, Other had been comfortably "out there," and consequently far less problematic. Bringing the Other into Japan, juxtaposing the representation of Other with depictions of Self, however, demanded the articulation of difference at a level of detail not seen in earlier visual discourse—not merely difference between Self and Other as unitary tropes, but the complex differentiation of Other into the diverse peoples of a "myriad lands" (*bankoku*).

Medieval mapmakers, we have also seen, had kept Other comfortably "out there" when visualizing and mapping "Japan." The very earliest extant maps of Japan most often represented a group of islands surrounded on by seemingly endless seas, or marked the maritime limits with *terrae peligrosae* like

---

7   Laing (1969, 69f; 93). Emphasis in original.

Rasetsu-koku and *Gandō*; representation of "Japan," that is, was curiously in-curious about what lay beyond the "azure fields of the sea" (*ao-unabara*) all around.[8] At the same time, the *mappae mundi* of medieval discourse, taking its cue more from Buddhist *sangoku* cosmologies than Confucian cosmologies of a "central kingdom" surrounded by tributaries and barbarous regions, rep-resented a universe in which the known world of "China" (*Shintan*) was small, and largely undifferentiated—"Korea" went entirely unnoticed.

The Iberian irruption and Hideyoshi's Korean campaigns permanently moved the locus of identity discourses, which had once been safely "out there," to venues on-shore, "in here," in Japan. What had been a relatively straight-forward binary of *Wagachō* and *Shintan*—with a nod to an essentially mythic *Tenjiku*, the third 'country' in a *Sangoku* universe—rapidly morphed to a con-frontation with the limitless potential alterities presented in the brave new world of *bankoku*. The fragmentation of that binary opposition to a unitary Other, into a bricolage of *jinrui*—Anthropos—comprising countless sorts of Others, "black and white, gold and brown,"[9] that had to be systematized, cat-egorized, and—ultimately—reduced to a familiar set of codes and identities. The variegated Anthropos produced and classified in seventeenth-century Japanese discourse was proto-ethnographic, though perhaps it should not thought of as "racial," "ethnic," or "national," concepts inaccessible at the time.

It may be appropriate, however, to think of this as a "proto-ethnic" or "proto-national" turn in Japanese discourse, steps on "Japan's" path to producing "the geo-body of a nation."[10] That is, by constructing a protective hedge of alterities just beyond the immediate boundaries of the emergent proto-national Self, the discourse produced an interior identity between territory, people, and their customs—of the body, of diet, of language—that was defined in opposi-tion to those excluded Others.

More than the Iberian encounter, of course, and the consequent fragment-ing of Japan's Others was required to produce the proto-national Japanese "geo-body." The conjunction of new discourses of collective identity, however, with a new regime of political unification and the achievement of both do-mestic and international peace—a common ideologically produced epithet for the age was "Great Peace throughout the Realm" (*tenka taihei*)—and with new media for the dissemination of a popular culture reaching from one end

---

8   Not all medieval Japan maps occluded lands beyond the seas. In an early fourteen cen-
     tury map, Japan is protected against all other lands by a guardian serpent looped around
     the archipelago; another, likely reflecting the impact of the failed Mongol invasions of the
     late thirteenth century, arrays alien lands—some of them anachronistic—like an open
     folding fan. For a discussion, see Kuroda (2003).

9   Hughes (1958, 272; 1959).

10   Thongchai (1994).

of the "realm" to the other, was an indispensable condition for the production
of that new geo-body.

Most important was the rapid advance of both literacy and print capitalism,
and the concomitant emergence of a diverse, national array of reading publics.
While a few printed texts had been produced in Japan from at least the middle
of the eighth century, most were either amulets, or luxurious, expensive religious texts meant more to be possessed than to be read. Indeed, Buddhist
monasteries were the most important producers of printed texts prior to the
"Great Peace."[11] But it was the growth of urban markets, a money economy, and
literate publics in the seventeenth century that produced the essential conditions for the birth of the geo-body: the possibility of sharing identical texts and
images from one end of Japan to the other.

These images provided what Tamar Garb has called a "crucial point of differentiation," and "a referent in relation to which the specificity" of Japanese
identities were "demarcated and defined."[12] The mimetically produced Other
of art and urban performance generated a coherent inventory of stock imagery, replicated across media and appropriated to subsume Japan's Others in a
framework of difference that buttressed collective self-identities that endured
well beyond the demise of the early-modern order.

As Japanese artists, writers, and ordinary folk dressed myth and legend in
the raiment of alterity thus fashioned—tales of "Empress Jingū's" mythic conquest, or transformations of Hideyoshi's debacle in Korea into heroic victory—
"were mediated via these stock images of" Korean/Tōjin diplomatic parades
to produce popular belief in a Japan to which Other was subordinate and, indeed, subservient.[13] As we have seen above in examining the deployment of
Mt. Fuji in juxtaposition to the Other—especially as invested in the trope of
Katō Kiyomasa gazing upon the mountain from "Orankai"—what was at stake
was not mere innocent entertainment, but what Linda Nochlin has termed the
"inscription of value in imagery,"[14] the production of an Other that would play
a role scripted to sustain desired Japanese notions of the proto-national Self.

It is therefore no coincidence that as Japanese of all stations became increasingly obsessed by external threats that seemed to crescendo from the
last third of the eighteenth century until the downfall of the early modern
order—a collapse due in large measure to the inability of the bakufu to cope
with very threat, to "expel the barbarians"—they increasingly turned to the

---

11   Kornicki (1998, 114–125) give a concise introduction to the forms and uses of printing in
      pre-1600 Japan.
12   Garb (1995, 20).
13   Garb (1995, 21).
14   Nochlin (1995, 12).

familiar stock of images of Other, and nostalgic, if often completely fanciful, tales of the subjugation of Other, as an amuletic source of comfort. Publishers both pandered to the obsession and fanned the flames book and print, producing a rising tide of xenophobic material often couched in the very same visual and verbal vocabulary that may have been merely amusing in earlier times.

Beyond Mt. Fuji, late Edo authors, artists, and publishers drew on the lexicon, grammar, and rhetoric of Self and Other articulated and refined since the seventeenth century, to address the foreign crisis in varied ways. My initial interest in this was sparked by the seemingly simple question, how did two-and-a-half centuries of overtly peaceful, amicable, and, for the most part, mutually satisfactory relations between Japan and Korea morph in the nineteenth century into a discourse that authorized Japanese aggression and invasion, political manipulation, and ultimately the colonization of Korea? Was there in the popular culture a subtext to the superficially innocent, playful Tōjin performances seen in so many festivals across Japan? In the hundreds of images of "Koreans?" When Japanese spectators turned out by the thousands to watch visiting Korean dignitaries, or patronized a costumed itinerant peddler, false beard and all, selling *Tōjin* candy, what did they see?

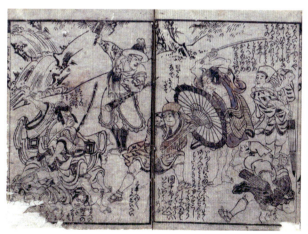

FIGURES 140 & 141   Torii Kiyonaga, *Meidai higashiyama-dono* (1778). The title puns
                       on "Higashiyama-dono," a sobriquet of the 8th Ashikaga shogun,
                       Yoshimasa. Here, *Higashiyama* is written with characters 干菓子山,
                       "Dry-candy Mountain," and the story turns on the making and peddling
                       of *sankan-ame*, a form of "China-candy" (*Tōjin-ame*). At left, the
                       candy-maker/peddler is a clean-shaven (i.e., Japanese) man who wears
                       the high-crowned hat associated with Korean military officers, has
                       ruffles on the hem of his coat, his shoulders and wrists, and carries a
                       large *charumera*; in his left hand, he holds the false beard that he wears
                       when peddling his wares. At right, a pennant advertises "Sankan-ame."

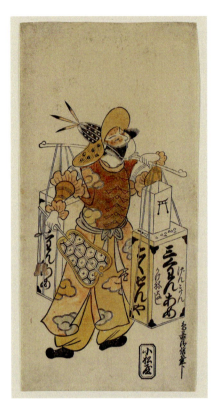

FIGURE 142
Torii Kiyonobu I, "The Actor Ōtani Hiroji I
as the Candy-seller Kokusen'ya," *benizuri-e*,
ca. 1717. The case in the foreground bears the
legends, "*Sankan-ame, genkin, kakene nashi*"
(Sankan candy, cash, no discounts), and
"Kokusen'ya" ("Coxinga"). "Sankan" was one of
Coxinga's sobriquets. His shoes and hat, and
the ruffles on his sleeves signify the "Chinese"
side of his identity. This print was published
at the end of the first run of *The Battles of
Coxinga* on the Osaka stage.
BOSTON MUSEUM OF FINE ART

1   One Costume/Many Scripts

The annual festival in Kon-no-ura, a fishing hamlet on the Bizen shores of the
Inland Sea, mobilizes two mimetic "Chinese boys" (*Karako*) to appease the
local epidemic deity (*ekijin; yakushin*), a "wicked deity" (*akushin*)—who is also
believed to have come from abroad—enshrined on a hilltop at the center of
the village.[15] The dance is performed by two young boys who, after ritual pu-
rification, are made up and dressed in frilled "Chinese" garb, to a musical accompaniment provided by a group of adult men on flutes and drums. The boys
are possessed or inhabited by the deity (*kamigakari*), and their feet are not
allowed to touch bare ground—they are carried from their homes to every site
where they perform. After offering their dance to the *ekijin*, they are carried on
a circuit of other sacred sites in the hamlet, offering the dance to the healing

---

15   Unless otherwise noted, the ethnographic material in this section is drawn from my
        October 1989 field notes.

FIGURE 143   Two young boys dressed as *Karako* (Chinese boys) offer the *Karako odori* to the deity of the Ekijin Shrine, atop a small hill overlooking the hamlet of Kon-no-ura, which is now part of Setouchi-shi, Okayama Prefecture.

Buddha Yakushi, and finally at a large bench-like boulder known as the "sitting-rock" (*koshikake-iwa*), before returning to the shrine council's meeting house.

Kon-no-ura, a section of the "Town of Ushimado" [Ushimado-chō] when I visited in the 1980s and 1990s—merged into Ushimado in one of the rounds of forced mergers since the Meiji Restoration—was a distinct village in the Edo period, west of the port town of Ushimado, and completely cut off to land access.[16] Residents speak of Kon-no-ura as an "isolated on-land island" [*riku no kotō*]; Ushimado was a small port town just east of Kon-no-ura, where Korean embassy convoys often put in for the night.

16   Kon-no-ura was part of "Ushimado-chō" when I made field visits in 1989–1990; in the latest round of "city-town-village mergers" (*shi-chō-son gappei*), Ushimado-chō was itself merged into the newly created "Setouchi City." Ushimado-chō survives as an administrative district within Setouchi City, but "Kon-no-ura" does not appear on the city's homepage, at http://www.city.setouchi.lg.jp/. The central government in Tokyo has mandated several mergers of small local governments into larger administrative units. The first of these, in 1889, reduced the number of local governments by 78%, from 71,314 to 15,859; postwar mergers in the 1950s and 1960s further reduced these to 4,472 cities, towns, and villages. The latest round of mergers, in 2005, has left only 2,395 units of local government, just over 3.3% of the number at the time of the Meiji Restoration. (http://ja.wikipedia .org/wiki/)

It is not clear when or how the dance originated, but it has been a central ritual in pacifying the malevolent spirits that might otherwise bring disease to the village. Local oral tradition from the late 19th century holds that the dance was performed regularly until the early 19th century, but then fell into disuse until being revived in the Meiji period.[17] Today, the village explains on its Website, "Oral tradition has it that the [Karako] dance originated either in a dance performed for Korean embassies when they stayed at Ushimado on their way to and from Edo, or that it was learnt from the Korean envoys, but since there are no detailed sources, the actual origins aren't certain."[18] A number of modern scholars—both Japanese and ethnic Koreans—interpret the dance as philo-Korean.[19] Similar claims have been made for mimetic Tōjin performances in festivals around Japan—that they were invariably evocations of Korean embassies, and at the same time, manifestations of admiration (*shōkei*) for Korea and its culture.[20]

The question of origins, though tempting, is often hedged about with thorny problems. In this case it is driven in part by the flawed exclusionary argument that the *Karako-odori* does not fit the usual canons of Japanese dance, where pairs' dances are uncommon.[21] While this may be true of "Japanese dance" (*Nihon buyō*), as narrowly defined, a category invented in modern times to cordon off pure, native dance from imported genres, it is not at all true of what one might call "dance *in* Japan." From the Heian court to the Edo-period entertainment quarter, the repertoires of most Japanese dance genres—*bugaku* (classical court dance) and *Nō; nagauta* and *gidayū-bushi*—include paired dances. more-or-less continuously since at least the Nara period (710–794).[22]

---

17   Nishikawa (1982, 109).

18   "Karako odori," at http://www2.cc22.ne.jp/~otoya/7-sonohoka/7-08karako/7-08karako .html.

19   Ri (1976, 121–128; 1979, 52–61; 1987, 125–129); Shin (2002, 44 & 123–125).

20   See Toby (2004) for an extended discussion. Im (2004, 179), for example, argues an exclusively Korean filiation for Tōjin and Karako performances: "Thus, the [Sino-Japanese character] *tō/kara* of 'Tōjin' and 'Karako' signifies Korea and not China. *Therefore, the Tōjin and Karako dances [performed in Japan] are not Chinese dances; they are Korean dances transmitted [to Japan] by Korean embassies.*" (emphasis added)

21   This is the heart of the argument advanced by Sin Kisu (1999; 2002); Sin, *et al.* (1993–1996).

22   Murasaki Shikibu, for example, opens Chapter 7 of the *Genji*, "Beneath the Autumn Leaves," with Genji and his friend Tō no Chūjō performing "Blue Sea Waves" before the emperor and his favorite consort. Murasaki (1993–1997, 1: 271); for an English translation see Murasaki (2002, 135). Murasaki's contemporary, Sei Shōnagon, writes of 'Bird dances.... *Rakuson* is danced *a deux*, [the performers] striking their knees to the floor. Sei (1958, 250; cf. 1967, 1: 189). See Hirano, *et al.* (1989, *passim*) for paired dances, variously termed *ninin-mai* (two-person dance), *aimai* (paired dance), etc., across the genres. On the other hand, in an illustration in Ihara (1684/1974) the protagonist, an Osaka dandy with an entourage

And *bugaku* was hardly confined either to the court or to ancient times. Rather, *bugaku* has been integral to both Shintō and Buddhist rites since the sixth century, at least, and would have been familiar to Japanese of all stations in the early modern era. Paired dancers performed to the accompaniment of *Kyōunraku*, a work associated with Prince Shōtoku (574–622), as part of the memorial rites at Tōshōgū on the twenty-first anniversary of Tokugawa Ieyasu's death.[23] Similarly, the paired *bugaku* dance *Karyōbin* was performed in rites at Hōryūji, outside Nara, on the 1380th anniversary of Prince Shōtoku's death, while *Enbu*, another paired *bugaku* dance, is still performed at the Ise Shrine, dedicated to the imperial ancestor deity Amaterasu.[24]

Affirmative claims that the Kon-no-ura *Karako* dance derives from Korean dances rest almost entirely on two brief notes from the diary of Sin Yuhan's visit in 1719, as an official in the Korean embassy of that year. While waiting for a break in the weather in Tsushima, "It was raining when we reached the place beneath towering cliffs where our ships were moored. Several officials were seated on a rock ledge drinking wine; they had the musicians play their drums, flutes and soprano oboes (K., *piri*); we sang songs to match the music, while two pages did a paired dance, waving their garments wildly. They were rather like the beauties of the Royal Court. All present felt as if it were a performance in the [ancient Chinese state of] Chu." Later in their journey, "In the evening," at the port of Hyōgo, "I went out with Kang Jach'ŏng to a place on the shore where they'd laid a board deck; we had the musicians play their drums and flutes, and had two pages do a paired dance. Crowds of Japanese gathered like clouds ..."[25]

This explanation, however, founders when examined closely. First, not only does Sin Yuhan make no mention of dancing during the embassy's stay in Ushimado; no diarist from the eight earlier and two later Korean missions hints at dancing there, nor does Sin's account suggest that Japanese might have witnessed any Korean dances in that port. In addition, the argument overlooks

---

of geisha, watches two bearded men in *Tōjin* garb dancing on a stage in the precincts of a Buddhist temple.

23   Kano Tan'yū & Tenkai (1641, 4), reproduced in Kawakami (1998, 14). According to the *Tokugawa jikki*, the rites were held on Kan'ei 13/4/17 (1636/5/21), the twentieth anniversary—by Japanese count—of Tokugawa Ieyasu's death.

24   For *Karyōbin* at Hōryūji, www.asukanet.gr.jp/umayado/horyuji/goshouki/bugaku/bugaku .html; for the Ise *Enbu* performance, www.isesyoyu.co.jp/jinguu/bugaku/2001haru-kagura .htm.

25   Kang, trans. (1974, 58; 106). "Soprano oboes": the *piri* (J., *hichiriki*; Ch., *bili*) is a double-reed wind instrument, about 18 cm. (7") long, with a pitch range from F' to A"; "paired dance" is my imperfect translation for J. *taibu* (Ch., *duiwu*; K., *taemu*). The state of Chu ruled parts of south China from the fall of the Tang in 907, until conquered by the 'Southern Tang' in 951.

the repertoire of classical court dance (*bugaku*), which, as noted above, includes dances for pairs, as well as quartets and sextets, of dancers. By the seventeenth century, *bugaku* had been incorporated into the rituals of a number of major Shinto shrines around the country; if for that reason alone, Occam's razor should point us in that direction, rather than imagining a "Korean" model for which no direct evidence exists.[26] And more to the point, it requires us to ignore the physical, social, economic, and political geography of Kon-no-ura, and fails to take into account the relationship between the performance offered to the local deities, on the one hand, and the identities and history of the deities on the other.

As noted above, Kon-no-ura was a fishing village, accessible only by boat until a tunnel was carved through the surrounding collar of hills. Ushimado, a busy Inland Sea port from early times,[27] was a frequent port of call for Korean embassy flotillas as they sailed to and from Osaka, before heading inland to Kyoto and Edo. But one wonders why a nearby fishing village the Koreans never visited would commemorate an event that may have affected them only as a spectacle sailing past, and by generating demands for corvée labor.

It is important, rather, to read the dance in the context of its ritual objects, the deities to whom it is offered, and the anticipated outcomes of the prayer it instantiates. Disease deities (*ekijin*) were worshipped primarily in the spirit of Tevye's toast to the Tsar, to "keep [him] far away from here!" *Ekijin* cults are thought to have roots as boundary cults, protecting communities from epidemics—believed to be invasive external threats to the community or the country—and consequently to require the invocation of curative deities of similarly foreign origin. Effigies, as well as painted or printed images of the Chinese cult figure known as Shōki (Ch., Zhongkui) the "demon-queller" in Japan, for example were used from early times to ward off smallpox, while the Ox-head King (Gozu Tennō, the focus of the Gion cult, and originally a deity originating in the Chinese border region of Xinjiang) was invoked not only to

---

26   The two major sub-genres of *bugaku*, however, are explicitly identified as foreign—*Tōgaku* (Tang [Chinese] music) and *Komagaku* (Koguryŏ [Korean] music)—and the dancers' costumes are festooned with the signs of Otherness, particularly ruffles. For a brief introduction see Gamō Mitsuko, "Bugaku," in *Kokushi daijiten*, 12: 26–28.

27   A seventh or eighth century poet celebrated Ushimado in a short poem included in the *Man'yōshū*, the earliest collection of Japanese poetry (*MYS*, Book 11, No. 2731): "The thundering waves of Ushimado echo across the islands. Yet perhaps I shall not see my love when he calls."

ward off epidemic, but insects that could blight agriculture, and other malevolent spirits from outside.[28]

What these cults have in common, therefore, is the inherent need to communicate with "foreign" deities, whose familiar world was not Japan, but a "China" of Japanese construction—the world of the *Tōjin* and *Karako*. The *Karako* of Kon-no-ura, like the Tōjin mobilized in *Namode* dances throughout the Nara region and elsewhere praying for rain to the thunder deity (*raijin*)—who is also the undersea dragon deity (*ryūjin*)—are efficacious in part because they are "Chinese," and can communicate with deities whose realm is iconographically and folklorically constructed as "Chinese."[29] Further, and especially salient in understanding the range of significations available in the Kon-no-ura festival, is the sequential identification of Raijin not only with Ryūjin, but with water deities' potency in warding off disease.[30]

Moreover, the climactic dance offering in Kon-no-ura at the "sitting rock," in my view, roots the ritual even more firmly in mythic and folkloric structures of confrontation with Other, and not only as defense against the threat of disease. The "sitter" on that rock, in local belief, was the mythic Empress Jingū, who rested there on the return route from her "conquest of Korea." Intrinsic to the narrative is the submission of the kings of Silla and Paekche to the "empress," and their promise henceforth to send tribute to Japan—a trope that resurfaces frequently in popular Edo-era narratives explaining the reasons Korea was again sending missions to Japan (see below), and in some variants, Jingū also brought Korean princes back to Japan as captives. It makes more sense, that is, to understand the *Karako* performance before the "sitting rock" less as "admiration" for Korea inspired by the embassies, than as a re-presentation of Jingū's mythic "conquest of Korea."

This was the local explanation of the rite until the 1970s,[31] and comports well with other associations of the myth of Empress Jingū's Korean exploits

---

28   For a brief note on the Shōki cult in Japan, and its origins in Tang-dynasty Chinese legend, see Tanahashi (1986). On Gion and the cult dedicated to the disease deity Ox-head King (Gozu Tennō), see Shibata (1984); Mayumi (2000).

29   Several *ema* in the Nara region depict *amagoi* (or *namode*) dancers in Tōjin garb. I am grateful to Ueki Yukinobu for introducing me to these *ema*, and for sharing his encyclopedic knowledge of Edo period folklore. On *Namode odori* in Tenri City, just east of Nara, Tenri-shi (1977–1979, *Shiryō-hen* 1, *passim*). On the identification of the Dragon King as a rain and water deity, see, e.g., Yanagita (1941/1962–1975).

30   The folklorist Ōshima Tatehiko (2003, 154), finds that for example, "Broadly across [Japan], especially in summer, festivals for water and river deities were also conducted to prevent severe epidemic," citing the Gion and Tsushima festivals, both of which focused on a deity from abroad, Gozu Tennō.

31   Nishikawa (1982, 109).

with local lore;[32] it is this "traditional" understanding that numerous modern scholars are at pains to refute, and to substitute a "correct" tradition tying the dance to visiting Korean embassies. This was confirmed by members of the "Association for Preservation of the *Karako* Dance" (*Karako-odori Hozon-kai*) in Kon-no-ura in conversations in 1990.[33] We were well into our second magnum of sake at the time, which may have licensed a bit more frankness, when I inquired about the notion that the dance both derived from and celebrated Edo-era Korean embassies, and about possible connections to the "Empress Jingū." One of the men remarked that they'd never even heard of "Korean embassies" until an ethnic Korean activist had "corrected our erroneous historical understanding" (*machigatta rekishi ninshiki*), and that until then he'd always believed that the referent was the Empress Jingū. Another chimed in that although some people say the empress is only a figure in myth, the priest at the nearby Hachiman Shrine[34] had told him that she was an actual historical figure, and that he, too, believed this. Indeed, until the 1970s, villagers' own public explanation was that, "It is the dance of two princes of Silla that Empress Jingū brought back after her conquest of the Three Korean Kingdoms."[35]

Kon-no-ura's deployment of *Karako* in its annual festival reminds us—if any reminder is necessary—that texts and performances, signs and signifiers, are rarely univocal, that they invariably offer multiple meanings. Every audience, every reader, comes to the text from a different angle, bringing a different store of experience, knowledge, and expectations, and consequently comes away from the text with a different reading. Every performance, even of the same text, is unique; even successive performances by the same actors, on the same stage, may reveal different meanings in the text.

In Kon-no-ura, for example, one might read different, though related, significations into the *Karako* dances at the Ekijin Shrine and the Yakushi Temple.

---

32   Hayashi Razan, *Honchō jinja-kō*, quoted in Nishikawa (1982, 93), links the toponym "Ushimado" to the Jingū myth: "While Empress Jingū was sailing past Bizen, a great ox appeared and tried to capsize her ship. At that moment, the great deity Sumiyoshi appeared in the form of an old man, and threw the ox down. The place was therefore called *Ushimarobi* ("ox-throwing"), but the pronunciation has morphed to *Ushimado*."

33   Field interviews, October 1990.

34   Hachiman became identified in the Heian period as the deified form of "Empress Jingū's son, "Emperor Ōjin," with whom she was pregnant during her Korean expedition. Kanda (1985, 43). On the Hachiman cult more broadly, Nakano (1983); in English, Guth (1985).

35   See also Ri (1976, 53). See also Kariya (1973, 1: 17), who explains that, "Tradition has it that when the Empress Jingū returned from her expedition against the Three Korean [kingdoms], she was pleased to seat herself on this rock on the shore, and here watched as children she'd brought back from that country danced. This is the [dance] now offered at the Autumn Festival of the Susano-o Shrine in Kon-no-ura."

Both deploy "Chinese boys" as intercessors in dialog with "foreign" deities, whose other-world "Chinese" identities require an interpreter or "native speaker" to understand their petitioners. The dance at the epidemic deity's shrine provides amuletic means to drive the deity away, to keep it "far away from here"; at the Yakushi hall, what is outwardly the same dance invites the Healing Buddha's protection—from the very same epidemic deity it is at the same time supposed to keep away. And at the "sitting rock," the boys meta-morphose into shamanic invocations of Empress Jingū and her mythic Korean conquest, performing as princes who surrendered to her and promised tribute and fealty forevermore. Even were the undocumented assertions of an origin in dances performed by personnel in a Korean embassy true, despite evidence to the contrary, none of the stories enacted by these mimetic "Chinese boys" refers to the embassies.

2 Capturing "Korea"

Just as the context of McCarthyism is essential to understanding the inten-tionalities underlying Miller's *The Crucible*, context selectively infuses *Karako* and *Tōjin* performances with particular significations, from among the poly-semic inventory of the sign itself. In Kon-no-ura alone, at least three distinct significations are invoked, each derived from its own narrative sources. Each venue where *Karako/Tōjin* mimesis was deployed invoked narratives specific to either the deity celebrated or the history of locality and community enacting the performance. And, like Kon-no-ura, many communities adapted the mi-metic content of the performance to the local narrative.

The merchant ward of Wakebe-chō, for example, in the port and castle town of Tsu, on the east coast of the Kii Peninsula, offered two separate mi-metic *Tōjin* performances in the annual official festival (*goyō matsuri*) initi-ated in 1635, on the order of the daimyo, Tōdō Takatsugu. Takatsugu had built a grand shrine to the god Hachiman as the protector deity of the town, and commanded the merchant wards to participate in the annual festival.[36] The cult of Hachiman celebrates a deity associated since the ninth century with the mythical "Emperor Ōjin," who, as son of the "Empress Jingū," is intimately implicated in myths of an ancient "conquest of Korea."[37] Indeed, among the

---

36 Tsu-shi Bunkazai Hogo Iinkai (1991, 8); Fukuhara (2005, 21).
37 According to the *Kojiki* and the *Nihon shoki*, "Empress Jingū" was about to deliver the future Ōjin when she embarked on her invasion of the "Three Korean states" (*Sankan*), so she blocked her birth canal with a stone to delay the prince's arrival until her return

most important rites at the originary Hachiman shrine in Usa, on the eastern shores of Kyushu, are "performances that reenact [Empress Jingū's] mythical conquest of Korea."[38]

Although the oldest surviving visual record depicts costumes and regalia more in keeping with conventional representation of European referents than "Chinese,"[39] still earlier contemporary texts describe Wakebe-chō's performances as mimesis of *Tōjin*.[40] Since *Tōjin* could denote almost any foreigner,[41] one should in any not case not look for empirical precision in these mimetic representations. What is clear, however, is that at some point in the early Edo period, Wakebe-chō re-clothed its performance in the visual vocabulary of Korean embassies to Japan, a parade of men in faux Korean garb, flying giant pennants emblazoned with soaring, swooping dragons, and other insignia associated with Korean embassies.

Yet Tsu is well off the route the Korean embassies followed, nor is it on the highways taken by the Ryukyuans or the Dutch. The closest Korean envoys came to Tsu was the town of Nagoya, about seventy kilometers to the northeast. But Tsu had its own, much stronger link to Korea: The first daimyo, Tōdō Takatora (1556–1630) had commanded a fleet in Hideyoshi's Korean campaigns

---

to Japan. For English translations of the *Kojiki* and *Nihon shoki* texts, Philippi (1969, 262–263); Aston (1896/1956, 224–253). On the history of the Empress Jingū myth and legends, Tsukaguchi (1980); on the Hachiman cult, Nakano (1975; 1985; 2002) in English, Bender (1978; 1979; 1980), Kanda (1985, 35–47 *et passim*), and Law (1994). For the core texts of the Hachiman cult, the *Hachiman gudō-kun*, see Sakurai, Hagiwara, and Miyata (1975, 168–273).

38   Law (1994, 349).

39   *Tsu Hachiman sairei emaki* (see Figs. 38, 39, 40). Sugawara (2005) argues that the scroll cannot predate 1673, based on datable architectural details in the painting. The marchers are represented in a mixture of signs signifying both Iberian and Dutch referents, with a smattering of more conventionally "Chinese" figures.

40   Yamanaka Tametsuna (1656/1968). The same dissonance occurs in verbal and visual representation of other early seventeenth-century festivals can be seen, for example, in festivals in Kyoto on the seventh anniversary of Hideyoshi's death (1604), and Wakayama on the seventh anniversary of Ieyasu's death (1622). See above, Chapter Four.

41   Recall that the German physician Engelbert Kaempfer (1727/1906, 2: 357) reported that on his journeys between Nagasaki and Edo in 1690–1692, "young boys, who are childish all-over the world, would run after us, call us names, and crack some malicious jests or other, levell'd at the Chinese, whom they take us to be. One of the most common, and not much different from a like sort of a compliment, which is commonly made to Jews in Germany, is, *Toosin bay bay* (*Tōjin baibai*), which in broken Chinese, signifies, Chinese, have ye nothing to truck?"

of the 1590s, and brought hundreds of war prisoners back with him as captives to Japan.[42]

This places Wakebe-chō's Korean masque in the Tsu Hachiman festival in a quite different light. Read against the backdrop of what the daimyo unquestionably regarded as his father's heroic military achievements in the Korean campaigns, one notices that the principal figure in the parade is not—as it was in the great Sannō and Kanda festivals in Edo, for example—assigned the role of an "ambassador" riding on a palanquin, but as a "Korean general" (*Chōsen taishō*) proceeding on foot, marching with more than one hundred others also mumming "Korean" characters. (Fig. 37) The seventy-eight *Tōjin* identified in the earliest surviving order of march (*shidai-gaki*) proceed, however, as captives under a Japanese military escort.[43]

In Tsu, that is, the stage was a celebration of the god Hachiman, in a festival sponsored by descendants of a daimyo whose reputation rested, in part, on military exploits during an invasion of Korea that was itself seen as a reprise of "Empress Jingū's conquest," and who returned from the war with hundreds of captured Korean prisoners. The performance on that stage featured a mimesis of captive Koreans, led by a general, all under Japanese military guard. This script cannot be reconciled with a subtext of admiration or affection (*shōkei*) for Korea and Koreans. Rather, the script and stage only make sense as evocations of imagined past conquests of Korea, even of irredentist visions of recovering a Korea divinely ordained to be a Japanese tributary state. As Shimokawa Heidayū, one of Katō Kiyomasa's early hagiographers put it:

> From ancient times, since the time of Empress Jingū and Emperor Ōjin, the Three Korean Kingdoms (*Sankan*) have offered tribute to Japan. This custom has, however, been lost in recent times (*kindai*), and so as a eulogy to the late Lord Hachiman, [Hideyoshi] ordered the dispatch of troops to Korea. Kiyomasa received orders to lead the attack, to capture the Korean king, and force them once more to offer tribute to Japan.[44]

---

42 Among Takatora's prisoners was the Confucian scholar-official Kang Hang (1567–1618), who was captured off the Ch'ŏlla coast while commanding a supply convoy for the Ming vice-commander Yang Yuan. See Kitajima (1985. 262); Sin and Murakami (1991, 37–46).

43 The first record of Wakebe-chō's performance, dated 1656, counts 115 men in the parade: seventy-eight *Tōjin*, under guard by twenty-five Japanese guards, with six Wakebe-chō elders. Yamanaka (1656/1968); Fukuhara (2005, 22; 23). This early record does not, however, specifically name the chief figure a "general," but only as a "senior officer" (*jōkan*), a term that can indicate either military or civilian officials.

44 *Kiyomasa Kōraijin oboegaki*, in *Zokuzoku Gunsho ruijū* (Circa 1625?, 295).

Although neither the *Kojiki* nor the *Nihon shoki* mentions it, later versions of the legend of "Empress Jingū," including some recorded by participants in Hideyoshi's invasion, claimed that,

> When in ancient times the Empress Jingū decided to put down for-
> eign countries (*ikoku*), the foreigners surrendered instantly. When the
> Empress heard this, she returned from Ch'ungju [where she had been
> encamped] to Japan, and at once inscribed upon a stone stele, "The king
> of China (*Morokoshi*) is Japan's dog." Down to our own day, the folk hand
> down this story orally. And now, here encamped here in Ch'ungju, I won-
> der where the stone is that the Empress wrote upon?[45]

Read against popular beliefs like these, both widely known texts and local ac-counts, the performances in Kon-no-ura, Tsu, and elsewhere around the coun-try take on a profoundly different coloration, less admiring and affectionate, and far more ominous and threatening.

At yet another Hachiman festival, in the castle town of Ōgaki, which Korean embassies regularly traversed on their way to and from Edo, the chief figure in the float put out by the neighborhood of Takeshima-chō, beginning in 1658, was a crowned, bearded effigy of a Korean general (*taishō*), whose parade be-gins with "purify the road" pennants, and ends with a pennant reading, "King of Korea" (*Chōsen ō*)![46] Interestingly, in 1874, the year after the Meiji govern-ment decided to postpone indefinitely a proposed invasion of Korea, the Ōgaki Korean performance was banned—not to be revived until 1972—per-haps because of fears that it would further provoke the outraged proponents of invasion.[47]

Late Edo publishers put out dozens of books and prints between 1850 and 1868 evoking the mythic conquest of Korea by the "Empress Jingū," the thirteenth-century rout of the Mongol invaders, or what was recalled as the glorious, victorious campaigns of Hideyoshi's armies in Korea in the 1590s.[48]

---

45   Shukuro Shungaku, *Shukuro-kō*, quoted in Kitajima (1995, 60). Most variants of the myth
       refer to the "great king of Silla" or "king of Ko[gu]ryŏ" (*Shiragi no daiō; Kōrai no ō*).

46   Gifu City Museum of History (1992, 90).

47   Kyōto Bunka Hakubutsukan, ed. (2001, 240). The chief effigy in the performance was re-
       identified as the Shinto deity Sarutahiko, who is not especially identified with foreign
       conquest.

48   E.g., Tsurumine & Hashimoto (1854); Ishikawa (1858). In addition to illustrating *Kiyomasa
       ichidai ki* (Tamenaga & Tsukioka, 1864), in 1863–64 alone, Tsukioka Yoshitoshi also pro-
       duced at least four polychrome triptychs of Hideyoshi's 'conquest' of Korea: *Sankan
       taiji Shishū kassen-zu* (The Battle of Chinju in the Conquest of the Three Korean States,
       1863); *Sankan taiji zu* (Conquest of the Three Korean States, 1863); *Masakiyo Sankan*

FIGURE 144   Mizuno Toshikata. "Nihon ryakushi zukai jinnō jūgodai." Polychrome triptych print, ca. 1895. Tōyō Keizai Daigaku Library.

(Fig. 144) As Miyachi Masato has observed, "After [Commodore Matthew C.] Perry's arrival, chronicles in the genre of Hideyoshi's 'Conquest of Korea' were published, once more stirring up visions of the 'glories' of the Japanese state in earlier times, a testimony to the ethnic and national consciousness of the time."[49]

Semiotic overlays, moreover, blended the myth of Empress Jingū with the legend of Katō Kiyomasa's exploits in Korea to produce fantasies of former conquest and Korean tributary subordination that kept dreams of Korean conquest at a boil in late Edo and early Meiji times.[50] Long before the Perry expedition rent the "public transcript" of bakufu pretenses of "barbarian-quelling" powers, popular writers and artists had linked the Empress Jingū myth and the Hideyoshi invasions to the ideological script of Korean subservience to Japan—both to the potency of indigenous deities, and to the "awesome brilliance" (go-ikō) and "martial splendor" (bui) of the shogun's regime.

---

taiji zu (Masakiyo's Conquest of the Three Korean States, 1864). See *Mui-an no shosai*, www.muian.com (accessed 2010/04/28); Yoshitoshi's *Mashiba Hisayoshi-kō Nagoya-jin sakite* (Lord Mashiba Hisayoshi [i.e., Hideyoshi] reviews his generals at Nagoya Castle, 1865), in the Tokyo Keizai University Library's 'Korea in *Nishiki-e* Collection,' www.tku.ac.jp/~library/korea/No06 (accessed 2010/04/28). In total, the 'Korea in *Nishiki-e* Collection' holds seventeen 'Korean conquest' themed prints dating from the pre-Meiji 1860s alone—and over one-hundred more between 1868 and 1895.

49   Miyachi (1985, 42).

50   On the late-Edo ideological argument for what its proponents saw as the re-conquest of Korea, see Kimura (1993). On the early Meiji 'conquer-Korea' debate, see Conroy (1960).

Guidebooks peddled to the spectators jamming the shores and roadsides along the route of Korean embassies had explained the coming of the foreigners in just such terms:

> Korea is the ancient countries of Koguryŏ, Silla and Paekche. These three were called the "Three Han" (J. *sankan*; K., *samhan*). Each of the three countries had its own king. And they attacked each other, contesting their relative standing. They did not submit to our country, and they were disloyal to Great Tang [China], so the Empress Jingū attacked the Three Han, and made them submit to Japan.... Later, one could not be sure if the Three Han would be disloyal, or subservient. And even though they failed to submit tribute, they were not punished for it. Then, in the Bunroku era (1592–1596) the Taikō, Lord Hideyoshi, personally rode forth to Nagoya [in Kyushu], and with Katō Kiyomasa and Konishi Yukinaga as his commanding generals, he attacked and defeated Korea, making it forever a slave to Japan. At the first, they brought tribute annually, but as time passed they were granted a gracious reprieve, and [their tribute obligation was reduced] so that they now only come to Our Country on the occasion of a joyous Japanese occasion.[51]

Many contemporary guidebooks reprised the same story, with minor differences in wording;[52] the conceit that Hideyoshi's armies had been victorious in Korea, and were a re-production of Empress Jingū's conquest, had become as well-established in popular memory as the legend of George Washington and the cherry tree in American folklore. This view was reinforced in a wide range of popular media, including *jōruri* and *kabuki* plays reprising both Empress Jingū's and Hideyoshi's 'conquests' of Korea—productions often timed to profit from intense public interest generated by the anticipated arrival or recent departure of a Korean embassy.[53]

---

51   *Chōsen raichō monogatari* (1748) preface. Watanabe's contemporary Kozono Hōfuku, of whom little is known, was more explicit about the connection between the "failure" of Korea to send tribute, and Hideyoshi's motives for invading: "When Yi Sŏnggye became king of Korea, he overthrew Koryŏ, and changed the name of the country to Chōsen. Ever since, the Yi clan has continued its rule of Korea. *Because they stopped sending tribute to Our Country*, Lord Toyotomi sent a great army of many tens of thousands across the sea...." Kozono (1748, preface; my italics).

52   *Chōsen-jin raichō monogatari* (1748); *Chōsen-jin dai-gyōretsu ki* (1763).

53   Suda (2010) makes a similar point about the idea of Korea as a Japanese tributary in the Edo-period imaginary, drawing primarily on 'Korea' themed *jōruri* and *kabuki* performances to gauge popular mentalities. He argues that the theater was, in McLuhan's terms "hot media," and a "cultural hegemon" (*bunka-teki hasha*). I don't disagree with

Thus, when Councillor (*karō*) Watanabe Zen'emon, of the Yodo domain, through which every Korean embassy passed on its way from Osaka to Kyoto, recorded his impressions of the embassy of 1748—not for publication, but simply for his private use—he drew from the common store of tropes circulating in the world of print, picture and performance. His opening lines could as well be a summary of the guidebook just quoted:

> Now, amongst the many glories (*ikō*) of our land, one which still shines today is that Korea sends tribute to the "Origin of the Sun" (*Hi-no-moto*). This is entirely due to the fact that not only did the Empress Jingū defeat them through [her] divine powers, but Lord Toyotomi's valorous anger [in once more chastising Korea] rekindled that blinding light through later ages, down to the present. Truly this is Japan's glory.[54]

In reprising mythic (Empress Jingū) and pseudo-historical (Toyotomi) visions of Korean conquest, subordination and tribute in his private—at least, unpublished—writings, Watanabe and other contemporary memoirists drew from a common store of tropes circulating in a wide range of print and other popular media that went well beyond the occasional spectator's guide to this, or any other, Korean embassy. The trope of Korea as a Japanese vassal was central to popular historical narratives, to festival masquerades, and to *jōruri* and *kabuki* plays reprising both Empress Jingū's and Hideyoshi's 'conquests' of Korea—productions often timed to profit from intense public interest generated by the anticipated arrival or recent departure of a Korean embassy.[55] The conceit that Hideyoshi's armies had been victorious in Korea, and were a reproduction of Empress Jingū's conquest, had become as well-established in popular memory.

The metamorphosis of policy and popular discourse into active jingoism and expansionism in late 19th century Japan was not, of course, the inevitable product of Edo period discourse or practice, but of a complex set of domestic

---

Suda's conclusions—which echo arguments I have made here and elsewhere, e.g., Toby (2004)—about popular conceptions of Korea, but think he is too quick to read the scripts as palimpsests of popular belief.

54 Watanabe (1748).

55 Suda (2010) makes a similar point about the idea of Korea as a Japanese tributary in the Edo-period imaginary, drawing primarily on 'Korea' themed *jōruri* and *kabuki* performances to measure gauge popular mentalities. He argues that the theater was, in McLuhan's terms 'hot media,' and a 'cultural hegemon' (*bunka-teki hasha*). I don't disagree with Suda's conclusions—which echo arguments I have made here and elsewhere, e.g., Toby (2004)—about popular conceptions of Korea, but think he is too quick to read the scripts as palimpsests of popular belief.

and international forces. Not least among these were the 'restorationist' claims of the Meiji state, which represented itself as recovering the original, archaic glory of a Japan whose moral and political axis was an imperial house governing in an uninterrupted 'single line for countless generations' (*bansei ikkei*). In the face of palpable danger from Western imperialism, and a sense of humiliation at the hands of the West, the temptation to recover past 'glory' abroad by reprising the 'Korean conquests' of Jingū and Hideyoshi may have been too strong to resist.

Kido Takayoshi, Itō Hirobumi and other Restoration leaders, after all, had been students of the charismatic teacher Yoshida Shōin (1830–1859), who preached an ideological mix peppered with dreams of once more conquering Korea. Kido himself suggested precisely such a course just weeks after the Restoration to Sanjō Sanetomi, one of the triumvirate of nobles heading the new government.[56] But arguments within the Government, whether Kido's 1868 suggestion of a Korean campaign, or Saigō Takamori's in 1873—the so-called *Seikan-ron* (Conquer Korea debate), were couched in terms of recovering Jingū's and Hideyoshi's somehow 'lost' conquests. Yet mythic discourses of Korea as a former tributary certainly not only rendered enabled, but potentially authorized dreams of a future conquest.

All this underscores the point that the Edo-era imaginary of Other was much more than an assemblage of simple popular tropes. Rather, it was *productive* and *generative* of discourses that shaped ideological and political debate well beyond the chronological frame of a foreign embassy's brief visit to Edo, the masquerades offered to entertain local deities, or peddlers of "Three-Korean Kingdoms Candy" (*Sankan-ame*) Images of Korea and Koreans, Ryukyu and Ryukyuans, China and Chinese, constructed by engaging the Other in early modern popular discourse continued long after the Meiji Restoration—perhaps even today—to shape identities and inform action, that is, to be *consequential*. The resonance with both national beliefs, embodied in ancient myth, oral lore, and contemporary literature, and local practice like these festivals, preserved popular imaginaries of foreign conquest and Korean subservience. They served, from the late eighteenth century into the twentieth, to legitimize future dreams of aggression against Korea as recovery of lost possessions divinely ordained as subject to Japan and its gods.

---

56   Kido (1967), 1: 159; Kido (1983–86), 1: 167–168.

Bibliography

Note: The great majority of Japanese and Korean publishers are based in Tokyo and Seoul, respectively. I have therefore listed place of publication only for Korean or Japanese books published elsewhere; otherwise I omit place of publication, except where ambiguity might result, or publishers have gone out of business.

HHCJ — *Haehaeng ch'ongjae* (4 vols., Chōsen Kosho Kankōkai, 1914).

JAS — *Journal of Asian Studies.*

KB — *Koten bunko* (670+1 vols., Koten Bunko, 1947–2003).

NKBD — Ichiko Teiji & Noma Kōshin, ed. 1983–1985. *Nihon koten bungaku daijiten.* 6 vols. Iwanami Shoten.

NKBT — *Nihon koten bungaku taikei* (102 vols., Iwanami Shoten, 1957–69).

NKD — *Nihon kokugo daijiten* (13 vols., Shōgakukan, 2000–2002).

NST — *Nihon shisō taikei* (67 vols., Iwanami Shoten, 1970–82).

NSSSS — *Nihon shomin seikatsu shiryō shūsei.* Tanigawa Ken'ichi, ed. (30 vols. San'ichi Shobō, 1968–1984).

SNKBT — *Shin Nihon koten bungaku taikei* (105 vols., Iwanami Shoten, 1989–2001).

TNM — Tokyo National Museum.

Abe Yoshio. 1965. *Nihon Shushi-gaku to Chōsen.* Tōkyō Daigaku Shuppankai.

Agrawal, Nayda. 2015. "Sikh Soldier in U.S. Army Allowed to Keep His Beard." *Huffinton Post.* huffingtonpost.com/entry/sikh-solider-beard_us_566ed513e4b011b83a6bcb2b (accessed 2016.03.03).

Akasaka Norio. 1985. *Ijin-ron josetsu.* Sunagoya Shobō.

Akizato Ritō. 1800. *Ehon Chōsen gunki.* 10 vols. Kyoto & Edo: Izumoji Bunjirō & Matsumoto Heisuke.

Akizuki Toshiyuki. 1999. *Nihon hoppen no tanken to chizu no rekishi.* Sapporo: Hokkaidō Daigaku Tosho Kankōkai.

Alcock, Rutherford. 1863. *In the Capital of the Tycoon: A Narrative of Three Years' Residence in Japan.* 2 vols. Longman, Green, Longman, Roberts, & Green.

Alpers, Svetlana. 1995. *The Making of Rubens.* Yale University Press.

Amino Yoshihiko. 1992. *Shokunin uta-awase.* Iwanami Shoten.

Amino Yoshihiko. 1993. "Shokunin uta-awase kenkyū o meguru 2, 3 no mondai." In Iwasaki Yoshie *et al.*, ed. (1993).

Amino Yoshihiko. 2000. *"Nihon" to wa nani ka.* Kōdansha. (*Nihon no rekishi,* vol. 00).

Anderson, Benedict. 1992. *Imagined Communities: Reflections on the Origin and Spread of Nationalism.* Rev. ed., Verso.

Anonymous. 1666. *Nihon bunkei zu*. Kyoto: Yoshida Tarōbei.

Anonymous. 1846. *Ukiyo no arisama*. *NSSSS*, vol. 11.

Aoyagi Masanori & Ronald Toby, ed. 2002. *Kanryū suru bunka to bi*. Kadokawa Shoten.

Aoyagi Shūichi. 2002. *Fugaku tabi hyakkei: kankō chiiki-shi no kokoromi*. Kadokawa Shoten.

Arai Hakuseki. 1905–1907. *Arai Hakuseki zenshū*. 6 vols. Kokusho Kankōkai.

Araki Seishi. 1989. *Katō Kiyomasa*. Ashi Shobō.

Araki Yōichirō. 1993. "Ezo no koshō/hyōki o meguru shomondai (dai-gokai): hyōki 'Mōjin' 'Ezo' no kigen to koshō Emishi to no musubitsuki." In *Hirosaki Daigaku kokushi kenkyū* 95: 56–75.

Arano Yasunori. 1988. *Higashi Ajia no naka no kinsei Nihon*. Tōkyō Daigaku Shuppankai.

Arano Yasunori, Ishii Masatoshi, & Murai Shōsuke, eds. 1992–1993. *Ajia no naka no Nihon-shi*. 6 vols. Tōkyō Daigaku Shuppankai.

Arisaka Michiko. 2011. "Kinsei no bunjin to ikoku." In *Ibunka kōryū-shi no saikentō: Nihon kindai no 'keiken' to sono shūhen*, Hirota Masaki & Yokota Fuyuhiko, ed. Tokyo: Heibonsha.

Ashkenazi, Michael. 1993. *Matsuri: Festivals of A Japanese Town*. University of Hawai'i Press.

Asō Isoji, Itasaka Gen, & Tsutsumi Seiji, eds. 1957. *Saikaku shū*. 2 vols. *NKBT*, 46–47.

Aston, W. G., tr. 1896/1956. *Nihongi: Chronicles of Japan from the Earliest Times to AD 697*. George Allen & Unwin.

Axtell, James. 1991. *Imagining the Other: First Encounters in North America*. American Historical Association.

Ayusawa Shintarō. 1953. *Mateo Ritchi* [Matteo Ricci] *no sekai-zu ni kan suru shiteki kenkyū: kinsei Nihon ni okeru sekai chiri chishiki no shuryū*. Yokohama: Yokohama Shiritsu Daigaku (*Yokohama Shiritsu Daigaku kiyō*, Series A-4 ; No. 18).

Baddeley, G. F. 1917. "Father Matteo Ricci's Chinese World-Maps, 1584–1608." *The Geographical Journal*. 50, 4 (October): 254–270.

Barnhill, David Landis. 2005. *Bashō's Journey: The Literary Prose of Matsuo Bashō*. State University of New York Press.

Baroni, Helen. 2000. *Obaku Zen: The Emergence of the Third Sect of Zen in Tokugawa Japan*. University of Hawai'i Press.

Barth, Frederick, ed. 1969. *Ethnic Groups and Boundaries: The Social Organization of Culture Difference*. Little, Brown.

Barthes, Roland. 1982. *Empire of Signs*. Translated by Richard Howard. Hill and Wang.

Batten, Bruce. 2003. *To the Ends of Japan: Premodern Frontiers, Boundaries, and Interactions*. University of Hawai'i Press.

Baxandall, Michael. 1985. *Patterns of Intention: On the Historical Interpretation of Pictures*. Yale University Press.

Beasley, W. G. 1967. *Select Documents on Japanese Foreign Policy, 1853–1868.* Oxford University Press.

Bender, Ross. 1978. "Metamorphosis of a Deity: The Image of Hachiman in Yumi Yawata." In *Monumenta Nipponica* 33, 2: 165–178.

Bender, Ross. 1979. "The Hachiman Cult and the Dōkyō Incident." In *Monumenta Nipponica* 34, 2: 125–153.

Bender, Ross. 1980. "The Political Meaning of the Hachiman Cult in Ancient and Early Medieval Japan." Ph.D. dissertation. East Asian Languages and Cultures, Columbia University.

Benedict, Ruth. 1946. *The Chrysanthemum and the Sword: Patterns of Japanese Culture.* Houghton Mifflin Co., 1946.

Benjamin, Walter. 1968. *Illuminations.* Harry Zohn, trans.; Hannah Arendt, ed. Harcourt Brace Janovich, Inc.; repr., Schocken Books, 1969.

Benvenisti, Meron. 1988. "Two Generations Growing Up in Jerusalem," *The New York Times*, October 16, 1988.

Berry, Mary Elizabeth. 1982. *Hideyoshi.* Harvard University Press.

Berry, Mary Elizabeth. 1994. *The Culture of Civil War in Kyoto.* University of California Press.

Berry, Mary Elizabeth. 2006. *Japan in Print: Information and Nation in the Early Modern Period.* University of California Press.

Bird, Isabella. 1881. *Unbeaten Tracks in Japan: An Account of Travels in the Interior Including Visits to the Aborigines of Yezo and the Shrine of Nikko.* 2 vols. G. P. Putnam.

Bird, Isabella. 1898/1986. *Korea and Her Neighbours: A Narrative of Travel with an Account of the Recent Vicissitudes and Present Position of the Country.* 2 vols. John Murray/C.E. Tuttle Co.

Bloch-Smith, Elizabeth. 2003. "Israelite Ethnicity in Iron I: Archaeology Preserves What Is Remembered and What Is Forgotten." *Journal of Biblical Literature* 122.3: 401–425.

Boon, James A. 1982. *Other Tribes, Other Scribes: Symbolic Anthropology in the Comparative Study of Cultures, Histories, Religions, and Texts.* Cambridge University Press.

Boon, James A. 1990. *Affinities and Extremes: Crisscrossing the Bittersweet Ethnology of East Indies History, Balinese Culture, and Indo-European Allure.* University of Chicago Press.

Boon, James A. 1994. "Circumscribing Circumcision/Uncircumcision: An Essay in the History of Difficult Description." In Schwartz (1994): 556–585.

Boot, W. J. 2000. "The Death of a Shogun: Deification in Early Modern Japan." In *Shinto in History: Ways of the Kami*, ed. John Breen & Mark Teeuwen. Curzon, 2000: 144–166.

Boscaro, Adriana, & Lutz Walter. 1994. "Ezo and Its Surroundings through the Eyes of European Cartographers." In Lutz Walter, ed. *Japan: A Cartographic Vision*, 84–90. Prestel-Verlag.

Bourdieu, Pierre. 1977. *Outline of a Theory of Practice*. Cambridge University Press.

Boxer, C. R. 1951. *The Christian Century in Japan, 1549–1650*. University of California Press.

Bray, Francesca. 1997. *Technology and Gender: Fabrics of Power in Late Imperial China*. University of California Press.

Bromberger, Christian. 2008. "Hair: From the West to the Middle East Through the Mediterranean." *The Journal of American Folklore* 121 (482:) 379–99.

Brotton, Jerry. 1997. *Trading Territories: Mapping the Early Modern World*. Reaktion Books.

Brower, Robert H. & Earl Miner. 1961. *Japanese Court Poetry*. Stanford University Press.

Brown, Philip. 1993. *Central Authority and Local Autonomy in the Formation of Early Modern Japan: The Case of Kaga Domain*. Stanford University Press.

Bucher, Bernadette. 1981. *Icon and Conquest: Analysis of the Illustrations of de Bry's Great Voyages*. Basia Miller Gulati, transl. University of Chicago Press.

Burke, Peter. 1997. *Varieties of Cultural History*. Cornell University Press.

Burke, Peter. 2001. *Eyewitnessing: The Uses of Images as Historical Evidence*. Reaktion Books.

Burns, Susan. 2003. *Before the Nation: Kokugaku and the Imagining of Community in Early Modern Japan*. Duke University Press.

Byrd, Ayana & Lori L. Tharps. 2014. "When Black Hair Is against the Rules." *The New York Times*, April 30.

Cartos. 1575. *Cartos que los Padres y Hermanos de la Compania de Iesus*. MS, Biblioteca Nacional, Madrid, ref. no. R-6654.

Cheng, Weikun. 1998. "Hair and Society: Social Significance of Hair in South Asian Traditions." In *Politics of the Queue: Agitation and Resistance at the Beginning and End of Qing China*. Alf Hiltbeitel and Barbara D. Miller, ed. State University of New York Press, pp. 123–142.

Chikamatsu Monzaemon. 1711/1985–1994. *Taishokan*. In Chikamatsu Zenshū Kankōkai (1985–1994, vol. 8).

Chikamatsu Monzaemon. 1711/1993–1995. *Taishokan*. In Matsuzaki *et al.*, ed. *Chikamatsu jōruri shū* (2 vols., SNKBT, vols. 91–92), 91: 326–397.

Chikamatsu Monzaemon. 1714/1993–1995. *Tenjinki*. In Matsuzaki *et al.*, ed. *Chikamatsu jōruri shū* (2 vols., SNKBT, vols. 91–92), 91: 399–467.

Chikamatsu Monzaemon. 1715/1985–1994. *Kokusen'ya kassen*. In Chikamatsu Zenshū Kankōkai (1985–1994, 9 : 628–748).

Chikamatsu Monzaemon. 1715. *Kokusen'ya kassen zashiki-ayatsuri otogi gunki*. 5 vols. Katei Bunko, Tokyo University Library.

Chikamatsu Monzaemon. 1717/1985–1994. *Kokusen'ya gonichi kassen*. In Chikamatsu Zenshū Kankōkai (1985–1994, 10: 1–126).

Chikamatsu Monzaemon. 1719/1925–1928. *Honchō sangokushi*. In Fujii Otoo, ed. (1925–1928), vol. 8.

Chikamatsu Monzaemon. 1719/1985–1994. *Honchō sangokushi*. In Chikamatsu Zenshū Kankōkai (1985–1994, 11: 1–110).

Chikamatsu Monzaemon. 1722/1985–1994. *Tōsen-banashi ima Kokusen'ya*. In Chikamatsu Zenshū Kankōkai (1985–1994, 12: 319–414).

Chikamatsu Zenshū Kankōkai, comp. 1985–1994. *Chikamatsu zenshū*. 17 vols. Iwanami Shoten.

Chinese Text Project. http://ctext.org/.

Chino Kaori. 1993. *Jū~jūsan seiki no bijutsu* (*Nihon bijutsu no nagare*, vol. 3). Iwanami Shoten.

Chino Kaori. 2003, "Gender in Japanese Art." In *Gender and Power in the Japanese Visual Field*. Joshua S. Mostow, Norman Bryson & Maribeth Graybill, eds. University of Hawai'i Press, pp. 17–34.

Chiyoda Toshokan, ed. 1970. *Kanda matsuri: sono shūhen*. Chiyoda-ku.

Ch'oe Kwan. 1994. *Bunroku-Keichō no eki (Jinshin-Teiyū waran): bungaku ni kizamareta sensō*. Kōdansha.

Ch'oe Yŏnghŭi. 1974. *Imjin waeran*. Sejong Taewang Kinyŏm Saŏphoe.

Chŏng Ŭnji. See Jung Eunji, below.

Chōsen-jin dai-gyōretsu ki taizen. 1763. Kyōto Teramachi: Kikuya Shichirōbei. (reissue of *Chōsen-jin raichō monogatari*, 1748, under new title).

Chōsen-jin raichō monogatari. 1748. Kyōto Teramachi: Kikuya Shichirōbei.

Chow, Kai-wing; Kevin M. Doak & Poshek Fu, eds., 2001. *Constructing Nationhood in Modern East Asia*. University of Michigan Press.

Clark, Timothy, Donald Jenkins, & Osamu Ueda. 1994. *The Actor's Image: Printmakers of the Katsukawa School*. Princeton University Press.

Coaldrake, William. 1996. *Architecture and Authority in Japan*. Routledge.

Collegio de Iapam da Companhia de Iesus. 1603. *Vocabulario da Lingoa de Iapam*. Nagasaki.

Conroy, Hilary. 1960. *The Japanese Seizure of Korea, 1868–1910: A Study of Realism and Idealism in International Relations*. University of Pennsylvania Press.

Cooper, Helene. 2014a. "Army's Ban on Some Popular Hairstyles Raises Ire of Black Female Soldiers." *The New York Times*, April 20.

Cooper, Helene. 2014b. "Hagel Seeks Review of Military Policies on Hairstyles." *The New York Times*, April 29.

Cooper, Michael. 1974. *Rodrigues the Interpreter: An Early Jesuit in Japan and China.* John Weatherhill.

Cooper, Michael. 1965. *They Came to Japan: An Anthology of European Reports on Japan, 1543–1640.* University of California Press.

Cooper, Michael, ed. 1971. *The Southern Barbarians: The First Europeans in Japan.* John Weatherhill.

Cortazzi, Hugh. 1986. *Isles of Gold: Antique Maps of Japan.* John Weatherhill.

Crossley, Pamela Kyle. 1997. *The Manchus.* Blackwell Publishers.

Dale, Peter M., 1986. *The Myth of Japanese Uniqueness.* Routledge and Kegan Paul.

Darnton, Robert. 1985. *The Great Cat Massacre, and Other Episodes in French Cultural History.* Vintage.

Davies, R.R. 1996. "Presidential Address: The Peoples of Britain and Ireland 1100–1400. III. Laws and Customs." In *Transactions of the Royal Historical Society,* 6.3: 1–23.

Davis, Julie Nelson. 2007. *Utamaro: Ukiyo-e Images of Women in Late Eighteenth-Century Japan.* University of Hawai'i Press.

de Bary, William T. & Irene Bloom, comp. 1999. *Sources of Chinese Tradition.* 2nd ed., Columbia University Press.

de Bry, Theodor. 1593. *Dritte Buch Americae, darinn Brasilia durch Johann Staden auss eigener Erfahrung in Teutsch Beschrieben: item Historia der Schiffart Ioannis Lerij in Brasilien, welche e selbst publiciert hat, jetzt von newem verteutscht, durch Teucrium Annaeum Priuatum, C.: vom Wilden vnerhörtem wesen der Innwoner von allerley frembden Gethieren und Gewächsen, sampt einem Colloquio, in der Wilden Sprach: alles von newem mit künstlichen Figuren in Kupffer gestochen vnd an Tag geben, durch Dieterich Bry Von Lüttich, jetzt Burger zu Franckfurt am Mayn.* Franckfurt am Mayn: Venales reperiu[n]tur in officina Theodori de Bry. Rare Books & Special Collections, University of Illinois Library.

de Fonblanque, Edward Barrington. 1863. *Niphon and Pe-che-li; or Two Years in Japan.* London: Saunders, Otley and Co.

Delaney, Carol. 1994. "Untangling the Meanings of Hair in Turkish Society." *Anthropological Quarterly* 67 (4): 159–72.

Dening, Greg. 1994. "The Theatricality of Observing and Being Observed: Eighteenth-Century Europe 'Discovers' The ?-Century 'Pacific.'" In Schwartz, ed. (1994): 451–483.

Desmond-Harris, Jenee. 2009. "Why Michelle's Hair Matters." In *Time* (Sept. 7, 2009): 55–57.

Dewa no Jō. 1665. *Usa Hachiman no yurai* (The history of the god Hachiman), in Yokoyama (1954).

Dikötter, Frank. 1998. "Hairy Barbarians, Furry Primates, and Wild Men: Medical Science and Cultural Representations of Hair in China." In *Politics of the Queue: Agitation and Resistance at the Beginning and End of Qing China.* Alf Hiltbeitel & Barbara D. Miller, ed. State University of New York Press, pp. 51–74.

Doak, Kevin M. 2001. "Narrating China, Ordering East Asia: The Discourse on Nation and Ethnicity in Imperial Japan." In Chow *et al.*, 2001, pp. 85–113.

Doi Tadao, Morita Takeshi & Chōnan Minoru, trans. 1980. *Hōyaku Nippo jisho.* Iwanami Shoten. Translation of Collegio de Iapam da Companhia de Iesus (1603).

Doi Tsugiyoshi, ed. 1978. *Kanō Tan'yū; Mitsunobu (Nihon bijutsu kaiga zenshū).* Shūeisha.

Dolce, Lucia. 2007. "Mapping the 'Divine Country': Sacred Geography and International Concerns in Mediaeval Japan." In Remco E. Breuker ed., *Korea in the Middle: Korean Studies and Area Studies: Essays in Honour of Boudewijn Walraven.* Leiden: CHWS Publications, pp. 288–312.

Douglas, Mary. 1966/1984. *Purity and Danger: An Analysis of the Concepts of Pollution and Taboo.* Ark Paperbacks.

Dower, John W. 1986. *War without Mercy: Race and Power in the Pacific War.* Pantheon Books.

Dubrow, Heather. 1982. *Genre.* Methuen.

Duffy, Seán. 1997. "The Problem of Degeneracy." In *Law and Disorder in Thirteenth-Century Ireland*, ed. James Lydon. Dublin: Four Courts Press, pp. 87–106.

Earhart, Byron H. 2011. *Mount Fuji: Icon of Japan.* The University of South Carolina Press.

Edmonds, Richard Louis. 1985. *Northern Frontiers of Qing China and Tokugawa Japan: A Comparative Study of Frontier Policy.* University of Chicago Department of Geography Papers, vol. 213.

Eiyū. 1965. *Teiō hennen ki.* In Kuroita Katsumi, ed., *Shintei zōho Kokushi taikei* (60 v., Yoshikawa Kōbunkan, 1964–67), vol. 12.

Eizō Bunka Kyōkai. 1979. *Edo jidai no Chōsen tsūshinshi.* Mainichi Shinbunsha.

Ejima Kiseki. 1717. *Kokusen'ya Minchō taiheiki.* In Nagatomo Chiyoji *et al.*, ed. *Hachimonjiya-bon zenshū* (23 vols., Kyūko Shoin, 1999–2000), 6: 375–473.

Ejima Kiseki. 1717/1933. *Kokusen'ya Minchō taiheiki.* In *Kiseki Jishō kessaku-shū (Teikoku bunko*, vol. 8), Hakubunkan, 1933.

Ekiken-kai, comp. (1910–1911) *Ekiken zenshū.* 8 vols. Ekiken Zenshū Kankō-bu.

Elison, George. 1973. *Deus Destroyed: The Image of Christianity in Early Modern Japan.* Harvard University Press.

Elison, George. 1981. "Toyotomi Hideyoshi: Bountiful Minister." In George Elison & Bardwell Smith, eds., *Warlords, Artists, and Commoners: Japan in the Sixteenth Century.* University of Hawai'i Press.

Elisonas, Jurgis. 1991. "The Inseparable Trinity: Japan's Relations with China and Korea." In *The Cambridge History of Japan.* Vol. 4, *Early Modern Japan*, 235–300. Ed. J. W. Hall. Cambridge University Press.

Ema Tsutomu. 1976. "Fūzoku shijō yori mitaru hige." In *Ema Tsutomu chosakushū 4: Sōshin to keshō.* Chūō Kōronsha.

Emi Suiin. 1894. *Katō Kiyomasa*. Hakubunkan.

Endō Shizuo, ed. 1980. *Wakan sansai zue*. NSSSS vols. 28–29.

Endō Masatoshi. 1985. "Sakayaki." In *Kokushi daijiten*, 6: 292.

Enkōan. See Kōriki Tanenobu.

Enomoto Yazaemon. 2001. *Enomoto Yazaemon oboegaki: kinsei shoki shōnin no kiroku*.
   Ōno Mizuo, ed. Heibonsha.

Entenmann, Robert E. 1974. "De Tonsura Sino-Tartarica: The Queue in Early Ch'ing
   China." Unpublished seminar paper, Harvard University.

Fabian, Johannes. 1983. *Time and the Other: How Anthropology Makes its Object*.
   Columbia University Press.

Fernandez, James W. 1984. "Convivial Attitudes: The Ironic Interplay of Tropes in an
   International Kayak Festival in Northern Spain." In Edward M. Bruner, ed., *Text,
   Play, and Story: The Construction and Reconstruction of Self and Society*, 199–229.
   American Ethnological Society.

Firth, Raymond. 1973. *Symbols, Public and Private*. Cornell University Press.

Forman, Ross G. 2013. China and the Victorian Imagination: Empires Entwined.
   Cambridge University Press.

Fortune, Robert. 1863. *Yedo and Peking: A Narrative of a Journey to the Capitals of Japan
   and China*. London: J. Murray.

Foucault, Michel. 1970. *The Order of Things: An Archaeology of the Human Sciences*.
   Pantheon Books.

Foucault, Michel. 1995. *Discipline and Punish: The Birth of the Prison*. 2nd ed., Vintage
   Books.

Freud, Sigmund. 1953–1974. *The Standard Edition of the Complete Psychological Works
   of Sigmund Freud*. James Strachey, trans. & ed., 24 vols. (The Hogarth Press and The
   Institute for Psychoanalysis, 1953–1974).

Freud, Sigmund. 1961. *Civilization and Its Discontents*. James Strachey, trans.
   W.W. Norton.

Fujii Jōji. 2007. "Futatsu no Shōhō Nihon-zu," in Fujii *et al.* 2007.

Fujii Jōji *et al.* 2007. Fujii Jōji, Sugiyama Masaaki & Kinda Akihiro, ed., *Daichi no shōzō:
   ezu/chizu ga kataru sekai*. Kyōto Daigaku Gakujutsu Shuppankai.

Fujii Otoo, ed. 1925–1928. *Chikamatsu zenshū*. 12 vols. Ōsaka: Asahi Shinbunsha.

Fujita Yūji. 1993. "Jiminzoku chūshin-shugi no ni-ruikei: 'bunmei'-gata to 'senmin'-
   gata," in *Shisō*, 832: 106–129.

Fujitani, Takashi. 1996. *Splendid Monarchy: Power and Pageantry in Modern Japan*.
   University of California Press.

Fukuchi Ōchi. 1891. *Taikō gunki Chōsen no maki: engeki kyakuhon*. Kinkōdō.

Fukuhara Toshio. 2003. "Tsu Hachiman-gū sairei no shiryō to gazō: Bakumatsu sōchō
   no ichi jirei." *Kokuritsu Rekishi Minzoku Hakubutsukan Kenkyū kiyō* 98: 133–156

Fukuhara Toshio. 2005. "*Seiyō zakki* ni miru Tsu Hachiman-gū sairei gyōretsu no kōsei." In *Tsu shimin bunka*. No. 32 (March): 21–23.

Fukuhara Toshio. 2006. "Kinsei Nagoya Tōshōgū sairei no hennen shiryō gosairei kyūki." In *Shaji shiryō kenkyū* 8: 2–26.

Fukui Kenritsu Hakubutsukan, ed. 1994. *Ema Gallery*. Fukui-shi: Fukui Kenritsu Hakubutsukan, 1994.

Fukunishi Daisuke. 2012. *Katō Kiyomasa shinkō: hito o kami ni matsuri shūzoku*. Iwata Shoin.

Furukawa Koshōken. 1789. *Tōyū zakki*. In *NSSSS*, 3: 439–533.

Furuhashi Yūgen. n.d. *Kiyomasa ki* (MS copy, Shiryō Hensanjo, Tokyo University).

Furuhashi Yūgen. 1924. *Kiyomasa ki*, reprinted in *Zoku gunsho ruijū*, vol. 23, pt. 1. Zoku Gunsho Ruijū Kanseikai.

Gächter, Othmar. 2010. "Sikhism: An Indian Religion in Addition to Hinduism and Islam." *Anthropos* 105 (1): 213–22.

Gamō Mitsuko. 1991. "Bugaku." In *Kokushi daijiten* (1979–1996). 12: 26–28.

Garb, Tamar. 1995. "Modernity, Identity, Textuality," in Nochlin & Garb (1995, 20–30).

Geertz, Clifford. 1980. *Negara: The Theatre State in Nineteenth-Century Bali*. Princeton University Press.

Geertz, Clifford. 1983. *Local Knowledge: Further Essays in Interpretive Anthropology*. Basic Books, Inc.

Genet, Jean. 1960. *The Balcony (Le balcon): A Play in Nine Scenes*, trans. Bernard Frechtman New York: Grove Press.

Gerhart, Karen M. 1999. *The Eyes of Power: Art and Early Tokugawa Authority*. University of Hawai'i Press.

Gifu City Museum of History, ed. 1992. *Chōsen tsūshinshi: Edo jidai no shinzen gaikō*. Exh. cat. Gifu Shiritsu Rekishi Hakubutsukan.

Godley, Michael R. 1994. "The End of the Queue: Hair as Symbol in Chinese History." In *East Asian History* 8: 53–72.

Gombrich, E. H. 1969. *Art and Illusion: A Study in the Psychology of Pictorial Representation*. Bollingen Series/Princeton University Press.

Gordon, Leonard. 1965. "Japan's Abortive Colonial Venture in Taiwan, 1874." *Journal of Modern History*, no. 37.2: 171–185.

Grapard, Allan G. 1992. *Protocol of the Gods: A Study of the Kasuga Cult in Japanese History*. University of California Press.

Ghufran, Nasreen. 2001. "The Taliban and the Civil War Entanglement in Afghanistan." *Asian Survey* 41 (3): 462–87.

Guo Moruo. 1979. *Zheng Chenggong*. Shanghai Wenyi Chupan-she.

Guth, Christine. 1985. *Shinzō: Hachiman Imagery and Its Development*. Council on East Asian Studies, Harvard University.

HHCJ. 1914. *Haehaeng ch'ongjae*. 4 vols. Keijō (Seoul): Chōsen Kosho Kankōkai.

Haboush, JaHyun Kim, ed. 2009. *Epistolary Korea: Letters in the Communicative Space of the Chosŏn, 1392–1910*. Columbia University Press.

Haboush, JaHyun Kim. 2016. *The Great East Asian War and the Birth of the Korean Nation*. Columbia University Press.

Hall, Francis. 1992. *Japan through American Eyes: The Journal of Francis Hall, Kanagawa and Yokohama, 1859–1866*. Ed. F. G. Notehelfer. Princeton University Press.

Hall, John W. 1955. *Tanuma Okitsugu, 1719–1788, Forerunner of Modern Japan*. Harvard University Press.

Hall, John W. 1966. *Government and Local Power in Japan, 500–1700: A Study Based on Bizen Province*. Princeton University Press.

Hall, John W. 1974. "Rule by Status in Tokugawa Japan." *Journal of Japanese Studies* 1, no. 1: 34–50.

Hamada Giichirō, comp. 1968. *Edo Senryū jiten*. Tōkyōdō Shuppan.

Hamada Giichirō, Nakano Mitsutoshi, Hino Tatsuo, & Ibi Takashi, eds. 1985–1990. *Ōta Nanpo zenshū*. 20 vols. Iwanami Shoten.

Hanabusa Itchō. 1770. *Itchō gafu*. 3 vols. ed. Suzuki Rinshō. Edo: Nishimura Sōshichi.

Hanzawa Emiko. 1996. "*Enkōan nikki* ni miru kinsei Nagoya kōkan geinō bunka ni kan-suru ichi kōsatsu." In *Ongaku kenkyū*, 8: 53–104.

Haraguchi Torao & Robert Sakai. 1975. *The Status System and Social Organization of Satsuma: A Translation of the Shūmon Tefuda Aratame Jōmoku*. Tokyo University Press.

Harley, J. Brian. 1989. 1988. "Silences and Secrecy: The Hidden Agenda of Cartography in Early Modern Europe." In *Imago Mundi*, 40: 57–76.

Harley, J. Brian. "Deconstructing the Map". In *Cartographica*, 26, 2: 1–20.

Harootunian, Harry D. 1980. "The Functions of China in Tokugawa Thought." In Akira Iriye, ed., *The Chinese and the Japanese: Essays in Political and Cultural Interaction*, 9–36. Princeton University Press.

Harootunian, Harry D. 1988. *Things Seen and Unseen: Discourse and Ideology in Tokugawa Nativism*. University of Chicago Press.

Harrison, John. 1953. *Japan's Northern Frontier: A Preliminary Study in Colonization and Expansion, with Special Reference to the Relations of Japan and Russia*. University of Florida Press.

Hasegawa Settan. 1823. *Hyaku Fuji no zu*. MS copy of Kawamura (1767), National Diet Library.

Hashimoto Asao, ed. 1990–1992. *Ōkura Toramitsu kyōgen-shū*. 4 vols. KB.

Hata Awagimaru, Murakami Teisuke & Mamiya Rinzō. ca. 1801/1969. *Ezo seikei zusetsu*. *NSSSS*, 4: 545–638.

Hatano Jun. 1988. "'Edo tenka sairei-zu byōbu' no kenchiku to kōsō." In *Kokka*, 4.4 (Nov.): 29–37.

Hayashi Akira, ed. 1913/1967. *Tsūkō ichiran*. 8 vols. Kokusho Kankōkai; reprint, Osaka: Seibundō.

Hayashi Razan. 1918. *Hayashi Razan bunshū*. 2 vols. Kyoto: Kyōto Shiseki-kai.

Hayashi Shihei. 1782. *Nihon enkin gaikoku no zenzu*. MS map, Sendai City Museum.

Hayashi Shihei. 1786. *Sangoku tsūran zusetsu*. 1 vol. + 4 maps. Edo: Suharaya Ichibei.

Hayashi Shihei. 1787–1791. *Kaikoku heidan*. 3 vols. Sendai: Ishida Eisuke & Kamata Sakichi, in Yamagishi & Sano (1978–1979), 1: 77–288.

Hayashi Shihei. 1943–1944. *Sangoku tsūran zusetsu*. In Yamamoto Yutaka, ed., *Hayashi Shihei zenshū*. 2 vols. Seikatsusha.

Hayashi Shihei. 1979. *Sangoku tsūran zusetsu*. In Yamagishi & Sano, eds. (1978–1979), vol. 2, *Chiri*.

Hayashida Yoshio. 2003. *Tei-shi Taiwan-shi: Tei Seikō sandai no kōbō jikki*. Kyūko Shoin.

Heldt, Gustav. 2008. *The Pursuit of Harmony: Poetry and Power in Early Heian Japan*. Ithaca: East Asia Program, Cornell University, 2008.

Hertz, J.H., ed. 1961. *The Pentateuch and Haftorahs*. London: Soncino Press.

Hiltbeitel, Alf & Barbara D. Miller, eds. 1998. *Hair: Its Power and Meaning in Asian Cultures*. State University of New York Press.

Hino Tatsuo. 1991. "Kinsei bungaku ni arawareru ikoku-zō." In Asao Naohiro, ed., *Nihon no kinsei 1 sekai-shi no naka no kinsei*, 265–304. Chūō Kōronsha.

Hiraga Gennai. 1961. *Furyū Shidōken den*. In *Fūrai sanjin shū*. NKBT, 55.

Hirai Yasusaburō, ed. 1980. *Sendai matsuri ezu*. Sendai: Hōbundō.

Hirano Eiji, ed. 1987. *Fuji Sengen shinkō. Minshū shūkyō-shi sōsho*, 15. Yūzankaku.

Hirano Kenji, *et al.*, comp. 1989. *Nihon ongaku daijiten*. Heibonsha.

Hong Ujae. 1655. *Tongsarok*. In HHCJ (1914), 4: 250–413.

Hōreki monogatari (1764). NSSSS, 27: 279–319.

Hori Masaoki (Hori Kyōan). 1659. *Chōsen seibatsu-ki*. 9 vols. Kyoto: Yamatoya Ihei.

Horiguchi Ikuo. 1996. "Shōtoku shinbō Chōsen tsūshinshi to Fujisan no shi" in *Nihon shisōshi*, 49: 88–105.

Horiuchi Hideaki & Akiyama Ken, eds. 1997. *Taketori monogatari; Ise monogatari*. SNKBT, 17.

Horowitz, Elliott. 1997. "The New World and the Changing Face of Europe." *Sixteenth Century Journal*, 28.4: 1181–1201.

Hoshino Yoshinao. 2010. *Inō Tadataka: Nihon o hajimete hakatta guchoku no hito*. Yamakawa Shuppansha.

Hostetler, Laura. 2001. *Qing Colonial Enterprise: Ethnography and Cartography in Early Modern China*. Chicago & London: University of Chicago Press, 2001.

Howell David L. 1995. *Capitalism from Within: Economy, Society, and the State in a Japanese Fishery*. University of California Press.

Howell David L. 2005. *Geographies of Identity in Nineteenth-Century Japan*. University of California Press.

Howell David L. 2009. "The Girl with the Horse-Dung Hairdo," In *Looking Modern: East Asian Visual Culture from Treaty Ports to World War II*, ed. Jennifer Purtle & Hans Bjarne Thomsen. University of Chicago Press, pp. 203–219.

Howland, Douglas R. 1996. *Borders of Chinese Civilization: Geography and History at Empire's End*. Duke University Press.

Hoyanagi Mutsumi. 1974. *Inō Tadataka no kagaku-teki gyōseki*. Kokin Shoin.

Hughes, Langston. 1958. *The Weary Blues*. Polygram Records.

Hughes, Langston. 1959. *Selected Poems of Langston Hughes*. Alfred A. Knopf.

Hur, Namlin. 2000. *Prayer and Play in Late Tokugawa Japan: Sensōji and Edo Society*. Harvard University Asia Center.

Hwang Mallang. 1624. *Tongsarok*. In *HHCJ* (1914). 49–115.

Ichiko Teiji, ed. 1958. *Otogizōshi*. *NKBT*, 38.

Ichiko Teiji & Noma Kōshin, ed. 1983–1985. *Nihon koten bungaku daijiten*. 6 vols. Iwanami Shoten.

Ichinose Naoyuki. 1960. *Nihon no gūwa*. Hōbunkan.

Igarashi Satomi. 2003. *Ainu emaki tanbō: rekishi dorama no nazo o toku*. Sapporo: Hokkaidō Shinbunsha.

Ihara Saikaku. 1682. *Kōshoku ichidai otoko*. Osaka: Akitaya Ichibei. National Diet Library.

Ihara Saikaku. 1682/1971. *Kōshoku ichidai otoko*. (Osaka edition). In *KB*, vol. 290.

Ihara Saikaku. 1684. *Kōshoku ichidai otoko*, illustrated by Hishikawa Moronobu. 8 vols., Edo: Kawasaki Shichirōbei.

Ihara Saikaku. 1684/1949. *Kōshoku ichidai otoko: Edo-ban*. In *KB*, vols. 28–29.

Ihara Saikaku. 1684. *Shoen ōkagami*. 8 vols. Edo & Osaka: Mikawaya Kyūbei & Ikedaya Saburō'emon.

Ihara Saikaku. 1684/1974. *Shoen ōkagami*. Facsimile, ed. Yasuda Fumiko. (Vol. 3 of the Saikaku volumes of *Kinsei bungaku shiryō ruijū*). Benseisha, 1974.

Ihara Saikaku. 1686/1953. *Honchō nijū fukō*. Facsimile, ed. Yoshida Kōichi. *KB*, vol. 70. Koten Bunko, 1953.

Ihara Saikaku. 1689. *Hitome tamaboko*. 4 vols., Osaka: Kariganeya Shōzaemon.

Ihara Saikaku. 2000–2007. *Shinpen Saikaku zenshū*. Shinpen Saikaku Zenshū Henshū Iinkai, ed. 16 vols. Bensei Shuppan.

Iizawa Fumio. 1979–1996. *Sekisui-zu*. In *Kokushi daijiten* (1979–1996), 8: 298–299.

Ikeda Fumi & Niwa Rieko, ed. 2014. *Nozoite bikkuri Edo kaiga: kagaku no me, shikaku no fushigi*. (Suntory Museum of Art, 2014).

Ikeda Kikan. 1963. See Sei Shōnagon, 1963.

Ikegami, Eiko. 1995. *The Taming of the Samurai: Honorific Individualism and the Making of Modern Japan*. Massachusetts: Harvard University Press.

Ikeuchi Hiroshi. 1914–1936. *Bunroku Keichō no eki*. 2 vols. Minami Manshū Tetsudō Kabushiki Kaisha & Tōyō Bunko.

Ikeuchi Hiroshi. 1987. *Bunroku-Keichō no eki*. 3 vols. Yoshikawa Kōbunkan.

Ikeuchi Satoshi. 1991. "Kinsei kōki ni okeru taigai-kan to 'kokumin.'" In *Nihon-shi kenkyū*, 344: 95–125.

Ikeuchi Satoshi. 1999. *Tōjin-goroshi no sekai*. Kyoto: Rinsen Shoten.

Ikeuchi Satoshi. 1998. *Kinsei Nihon to Chōsen hyōryūmin*. Kyoto: Rinsen Shoten.

Ikezawa Ichirō. 2000. *Edo bunjin-ron: Ōta Nanpo o chūshin ni*. Kyūko Shoin, 2000.

Ikuta Shigeru, ed. 1993. *Edo ga unda sekai eshi "Dai Hokusai ten" zuroku*. Exh. cat. 2 vols. Asahi Shinbunsha.

Im Tonggwŏn. 2004a. *T'ongsinsa wa munhwa chŏnp'a: Tangin(ja) yong kwa cherye haengnyŏl ŭl chungsim ŭro*. Minsogwŏn.

Im Tonggwŏn. 2004b. *Chōsen tsūshinshi to bunka denpa: karako odori/Tōjin odori to sairei gyōretsu o chūshin ni*. Takeda Akira, trans. Dai'ichi Shobō.

Imao Tetsuya. 1984. "Kokusen'ya kassen," in Ichiko & Noma (1983–1985, 2: 568–569).

Inagaki, Hisao. 1984. *A Dictionary of Japanese Buddhist Terms*. Kyoto: Nagata Bushodo.

Inui Katsumi, Koike Masatane, Shimura Arihiro, Takahashi Mitsugu & Torigoe Bunzō, ed. 1986. *Nihon denki densetsu daijiten*. Kadokawa Shoten.

Isaacson, Walter. 2017, *Leonardo da Vinci*. Simon & Schuster.

Ishihara Michihiro. 1942. *Tei Seikō*. Sanseidō.

Ishihara Michihiro. 1945. *Minmatsu-Shinsho Nihon kisshi no kenkyū*. Fuzanbō.

Ishihara Michihiro. 1986. *Kokusen'ya*. Yoshikawa Kōbunkan.

Ishii Ryōsuke, ed. 1959–1961. *Tokugawa kinrei-kō*. 11 vols. Sōbunsha.

Ishii Ryōsuke, ed. 1961. *Hanpōshū 2 Tottori-han*. Sōbunsha.

Ishii Ryōsuke, ed. 1962. *Hanpōshū 3 Tokushima-han*. Sōbunsha.

Ishikawa Masumi. 1858. *Mōzokki*. Pref. dated 1856; 5 vols. Edo, Kyoto, Osaka & Nagoya: Suharaya Mohei *et al*. Tokyo University Library.

Itasaka Yōko. 1979. "Koshōken no Hayashi Shihei hihan," in *Kinsei bungei*, 31: 20–30.

Itō Hideo. 1997. *Kami no rekishi*. Hokusōsha.

Iwama Kaori. 2012. "Kansei-do fukko dairi ni okeru Konmei-chi no sōji no fukugen katei: Uramatsu Kozen to Tosa Mitsusada no kan'yo." *Setsudai jinbun kagaku* 19: 35–65.

Iwasaki Hitoshi. 1988. "'Edo tenka sairei-zu byōbu' no kōsatsu: sairei-shi no kanten kara." In *Kokka*, 4, 4 (Nov.): 21–28.

Iwasaki Yoshie, Amino Yoshihiko, Takahashi Kiichi & Shiomura Kō, eds. 1993. *Nanajū ichiban shokunin uta-awase, Shinsen kyōka-shū, Kokin ikyoku-shū*. SNKBT, 61.

Iwashina Koichirō. 1983. *Fuji shinkō: Edo shomin no sangaku shinkō*. Meicho Shuppan.

Izumi Mari. 1988. "Tōsen-zu no keishō: Taishokan-zu byōbu o megutte." *Firokaria* 5 (March): 102–129.

Jansen, Marius B. 1980. *Japan and Its World: Two Centuries of Change*. Princeton University Press.

Jansen, Marius B. 1992. *China in the Tokugawa World*. Harvard University Press.

Jingū Shichō, ed. 1981–1985. *Koji ruien*. 5th edition. 56 vols. Yoshikawa Kōbunkan.

Jung Eunji (Chŏng Ŭnji). 2003. "Edo jidai ni okeru Chōsen tsūshinshi no fukushoku." In *Fukushoku bunka gakkai-shi*, 4.1: 15–29.

Jung Eunji (Chŏng Ŭnji). 2004. "Chōsen tsūshinshi no fukushoku: emaki ni miru fukushoku hyōgen no hensen katei o megutte." In *Kokusai fukushoku gakkai-shi*, 26: 14–30.

Jung Eunji (Chŏng Ŭnji). 2006a. "Kusumi Morikage hitsu 'Chōsen tsūshinshi gyōretsuzu byōbu' ni miru fukushoku no kōsatsu." *Nihon kasei gakkai-shi* 57(5): 309–322.

Jung Eunji (Chŏng Ŭnji). 2006b. "Kokusho denmei-rei ni miru Chōsen tsūshinshi no fukushoku to Tokugawa shōgun-ke no fukushoku." *Zenkindai ni okeru higashi Ajia sangoku no bunka kōryū to hyōshō: Chōsen tsūshinshi to Yonhaengsa o chūshin ni*, ed. Liu Jianhui. Kyoto: Kokusai Nihon Kenkyū Sentā, 2006, pp. 285–308.

Jung Eunji (Chŏng Ŭnji). 2006c. "Chōsen tsūshinshi no fukushoku: emaki ni miru fukushoku hyōgen no hensen katei o megutte." *Kokusai fukushoku gakkai-shi* 26: 14–30.

Jung Eunji (Chŏng Ŭnji). 2009a. "Chōsen tsūshinshi no fukushoku ni kansuru kenkyū. Tokyo, Nihon Joshi Daigaku. Ph. D. dissertation.

Jung Eunji (Chŏng Ŭnji). 2009b. "Tenna-do Chōsen tsūshinshi kō: fukushoku ni miru Nihon koyū no nijū seiji kōzō e no taiō." *Nihon kasei gakkai-shi* 57(5): 309–322.

Kaempfer, Engelbert. 1727. *A History of Japan, Together with a Description of the Kingdom of Siam*. 2 vols. London (Gale Cengage Learning Eighteenth Century Collections Online, accessed 22/12/2016).

Kaempfer, Engelbert. 1727/1906. *A History of Japan, Together with a Description of the Kingdom of Siam*. Trans. J. G. Scheuzer. 3 vols. London/reprint, Glasgow: James L. MacLehose & Son.

Kaempfer, Engelbert. 1727/1999. *Kaempfer's Japan: Tokugawa Culture Observed*. Trans. Beatrice Bodart Bailey. University of Hawaii Press.

Kaibara Ekiken. 1700. *Nihon shakumyō*. 3 vols. Kyoto: Nagao Heibei.

Kamo no Chōmei. (1956). *Hōjōki*. KB, vol. 105. KB.

Kan Jeon [Kang Chaeŏn]. 2002. *Chōsen tsūshinshi ga mita Nihon*. Akashi Shoten.

Kanagaki Robun & Utagawa Yoshitora. 1860–1861. *Kokkei Fuji mōde*. 10 vols., Edo: Fuyōdō.

Kanagaki Robun & Utagawa Yoshitora. 1961. *Kokkei Fuji mōde*. ed. Okitsu Kaname. KB, vols. 162; 164.

Kanda, Christine Guth. (1985). *Shinzo: Hachiman Imagery and Its Development*. Council on East Asian Studies, Harvard University.

Kang Chaeŏn, trans. 1974. *Kaiyūroku* [Sin Yuhan, *Haeyurok*]. Heibonsha.

Kang Hongjung. 1624. *Tongsarok*. In *Haehaeng ch'ongjae* (1914), vol. 2.

Kano Hiroyuki. 1991. *Nadokoro*. Vol. 5 of *Kinsei fūzoku zufu*. Kyoto: Tankōsha.

Kano Hiroyuki. 1994. *Katsushika Hokusai hitsu gaisen kaisei: "Akafuji" no fōkuroa*. Heibonsha.

Kano Hiroyuki, Yamaji Kōzō & Fujii Kenzō. 2005. *Kinsei sairei/Tsukinami fūzoku emaki.* Osaka: Tōhō Shuppan.

Kanwatei Onitake. 1805–1806. *Kyūkanchō.* 3 vols. Edo: Kanaya Matabei & Kimura Kōzō.

Kadokawa Nihon Chimei Jiten Hensan Iinkai. 1978–1991. *Kadokawa chimei jiten.* 51 vols. Kadokawa Shoten.

Kariya Eishō. 1973. *Ushimado fūdo monogatari.* 2 vols. Okayama: Nihon Bunkyō Shuppan.

Kashiwara Shōzō. 1922. *Hatamoto to machi yakko.* Kokushi Kōshū-kai.

Katsushika Hokusai. 1800. *Tōto shōkei ichiran* (Edo, 1800). 2 vols. Art Institute of Chicago collection.

Katsushika Hokusai. 1814–1878. *Hokusai manga.* 15 vols. Nagoya & Edo: Eirakuya Tōshirō & Kakumaruya Jinsuke.

Katsushika Hokusai. 1831. *Fugaku sanjū-rokkei.* Series of thirty-six woodblock prints. Edo: Nishimuraya Yohachi.

Katsushika Hokusai. 1834–1835. *Fugaku hyakkei.* 3 vols. Nagoya: Eirakuya Tōshirō; Edo: Kakumaru Jinsuke, Nishimura Yohachi & Nishimura Yūsuke.

Kawaguchi Chōju. 1831. *Seikan iryaku.* Reprinted in Mito-gaku Taikei Kankōkai, comp. 1940–1941. *Mito-gaku taikei.* 8 vols. Mito-gaku Taikei Kankōkai. Vol. 4.

Kawakami Shigeki. 1998. *Bugaku shōzoku.* (*Nihon no bijutsu*, no. 383). Shibundō.

Kawamura Hirotada. 1984. *Edo bakufu sen kuni-ezu no kenkyū.* Kokon Shoin.

Kawamura Hirotada. 1990. *Kuni-ezu.* Yoshikawa Kōbunkan.

Kawamura Hirotada. 2003. *Kinsei Nihon no sekai-zō.* Perikansha.

Kawamura Hirotada. 2005a. *Kuni-ezu no sekai.* Kashiwa Shobō.

Kawamura Hirotada. 2005b. "Ikoku jōhō to shuppan: sekai chizu o chūshin ni." *Edo bungaku* 32: 26–39.

Kawamura Minsetsu. 1767. *Hyaku Fuji.* Edo, Kyoto & Osaka: Suharaya Mohei *et al.*

Kawashima Masao. 1985. "Ryūkyū no ichi to geinō." In Geinō-shi Kenkyūkai, ed. *Nihon geinō-shi.* 6 vols. Hōsei Daigaku Shuppan-kyoku. 4: 115–176.

Kawata Akihisa. 2008. "Fujizu no kindai." In Yamanashi Kenritsu Bijutsukan, ed., *Fujisan: kindai ni tenkai shita Nihon no shinboru.* Exh. cat. Kofu: Yamanashi Kenritsu Bijutsukan, 7–13.

Keene, Donald. 1951. *The Battles of Coxinga: Chikamatsu's Puppet Play, Its Background and Importance.* Taylor's Foreign Press.

Keene, Donald. 1952. *The Japanese Discovery of Europe, 1720–1830.* Stanford University Press.

Keene, Donald. 1955. *Anthology of Japanese Literature.* Grove Press.

Keyes, Roger, & Keiko Mizushima. 1973. *The Theatrical World of Osaka Prints.* David R. Godine and the Philadelphia Museum of Art.

Kido Takayoshi. 1967. *Kido Takayoshi nikki.* 3 vols. (*Nihon Shiseki Kyōkai sōsho*, vols. 74–76). Tōkyō Daigaku Shuppankai.

Kido Takayoshi. 1983–86. *The Diary of Kido Takayoshi*. Sydney D. Brown & Akiko Hirota, tr. 3 vols., University of Tokyo Press.

Kikuchi Isao. 1991. *Hoppō-shi no naka no kinsei Nihon*. Azekura Shobō.

Kikuchi Isao. 1999. *Etorofutō: tsukurareta kokkyō*. Yoshikawa Kōbunkan.

Kikuchi Isao. 2013. *Ainu to Matsumae no seiji bunka-shi: kyōkai to minzoku*. Azekura Shobō.

Kikuchi Jun'ichi. 1973. *Shōtoku Taishi eden* (*Nihon no bijutsu*, vol. 91). Shibundō.

Kim Ingyŏm. 1974. *Iltong chang'yu ga*. Han'guk Muhŏn Yŏngusŏ, ed. Asea Munhwasa.

Kim Ingyŏm. 1999. *Nittō sōyū-ka: hanguru de tuzuru Chōsen tsūshinshi no kiroku*. Takashima Shizuo, tr. Heibonsha.

Kim Kwangch'ŏl. 1999. *Chū-kinsei ni okeru Chōsen-kan no sōshutsu*. Azekura Shobō.

Kim Seryŏn. *Haesarok*, in *Haehaeng ch'ongjae* (1914), vol. 2.

Kim Sidŏk. 2009. "Kokuritsu kokkai toshokan-zō *Ehon buyū Taikōki* honkoku to kaidai." *Kokubungaku Kenkyū Shiryōkan kiyō* 35: 209–240.

Kim Sidŏk. 2010. *Ikoku seibatsu senki no sekai: Kan hantō, Ryūkyū rettō, Ezochi*. Kasama Shoin.

Kim Sidŏk. 2015. "Jinshin sensō wa dono yō ni egakareta ka: Edo chūki no ehon; ukiyo-e o chūshin ni." In Tanaka Yūko, ed., *Nihonjin wa Nihon o dō mite kita ka: Edo kara miru ji'ishiki no hensen* (Kasama Shoin), pp. 164–190.

Kim Ŭihwan. 1985. *Chosŏn t'ongsinsa ŭi palchach'ui*. Chŏng'ŭm Munhwasa.

Kim Young-bong (1997). "Chōsen tsūshinshi no Nihon ni okeru ongaku ensō." *Firokaria* 14: 140–155.

Kimura Matazō. n.d. *Kiyomasa-ki*. MS copy, 2 vols., Tokyo University Library.

Kimura Naoya. 1993. "Bakumatsu no Nitchō kankei to Seikanron." *Rekishi hyōron* 516: 26–37.

Kimura Yaeko. 1982. "Musha-e no sokumen." *Tōkyō Toritsu Chūō Toshokan kenkyū kiyō* 13: 61–94.

Kinda Akihiro, Ishigami Eiichi, Kamada Motokazu & Sakaehara Towao, eds. 1996. *Nihon kodai shōen zu*. Tōkyō Daigaku Shuppankai.

King, Geoff. 1996. *Mapping Reality: An Exploration of Cultural Cartographies*. St. Martin's Press.

Kinoshita Masahiro. 1985. *Kawagoe matsuri to dashi: Motomachi ni-chōme no baai*. Kawagoe-shi Bunkazai Hogo Iinkai.

Kirishitan monogatari. 1639. In *Zokuzoku Gunsho Ruijū* (17 vols., Zoku Gunsho Ruijū Kanseikai, 1969–1978), 12: 531–550.

Kishi Fumikazu. 1992. "Enkyō 2-nen no pāsupekutivu: Okumura Masanobu-ga 'ō-ukie' o megutte." *Bijutsushi* 132: 228–246.

Kitabatake Chikafusa. *Jinnō shōtōki; Masukagami*. NKBT, vol. 87. Iwasa Tadashi, ed. Tokyo: Iwanami Shoten, 1965.

Kitabatake Chikafusa. *A Chronicle of Gods and Sovereigns: Jinnō Shōtōki of Kitabatake Chikafusa*. H. Paul Varley, trans. Columbia University Press, 1980.

Kitabayashi Kōji. 2014. "Kyōto kara Fujisan no sanchō totta! Nishi no genkai, 261 kiro." *Asahi Shimbun*, 2014/09/22.

Kitagawa Tadahiko. 1984. "Higeyagura." In Ichiko & Noma (1983–1985, 5: 157).

Kitajima Manji. 1982. *Chōsen nichinichi-ki; Kōrai nikki: Hideyoshi no Chōsen shinryaku to sono rekishi-teki kokuhatsu*. Soshiete.

Kitajima Manji. 1990. *Toyotomi seiken no taigai ninshiki to Chōsen shinryaku*. Azekura Shoten.

Kitajima Manji. 1995. *Toyotomi Hideyoshi no Chōsen shinryaku*. Yoshikawa Kōbunkan.

Kitajima Manji. 2000. "'Nihon wa kami no kuni' to wa dō iu koto ka: shinkoku shisō to sono rekishi-teki keifu." *Rekishi hyōron* 604: 78–88.

Kitajima Masamoto. 1977. *Kinsei no gunzō*. Yoshikawa Kōbunkan.

Kitao Sekkōsai (Tokinobu). 1763. *Chōsenjin raihei gyōretsu*. Ōsaka Kōraibashi: Fujiya Yahei. Imanishi Collection, Tenri Library.

Kobanawa Heiroku, ed. 1988. *Kōshin shinkō*. Vol. 17 of *Minshū shūkyō-shi sōsho*. Yūzankaku, 1988.

Kobayashi Fumiko. 2007. "'Sangoku-ichi' no Fuji-no-yama: Nihonjin no kokka ishiki to Fujisan to no kakawari o kangaeru tansho toshite," in Amano Kiyoko & Sawanobori Hirosato, ed., *Fujisan o meguru Nihonjin no shinsei*. Hōsei Daigaku Kokusai Nihon-gaku Kenkyūjo, pp. 71–90.

Kobayashi Kentei. 1710. *Sekai bankoku chikyū-zu*. Single-sheet printed map. Osaka: Ikedaya Shinshirō & Sagamiya Senzaemon. Collection Kobe City Museum. Reproduced in Kōbe Shiritsu Nanban Bijutsukan Zuroku Henshū Iinkai (1972), 5: 79.

Kobayashi Shigeru. 1967. "Tokugawa jidai ni okeru Chōsen tsūshinshi no sukegō mon-dai: Yodo han o shūshin ni." *Chōsen gakuhō* 43: 49–82.

Kobayashi Shigeru. 1981. *Kinsei hisabetsu buraku kankei hōrei-shū*. Akashi Shoten.

Kobayashi Tadashi. 1988. *Hanabusa Itchō*. (*Nihon no bijutsu*, no. 260.) Shibundō.

Kobayashi Tadashi & Sakakibara Satoru. 1978. *Morikage/Itchō*. (Vol. 16 of *Nihon bijutsu kaiga zenshū*.) Shūeisha.

Kōbe Shiritsu Bijutsukan. 1994. *Kochizu korekushon: Kōbe Shiritsu Bijutsukan*. Kobe: Kōbe-shi Supōtsu Kyōiku Sentā.

Kōbe Shiritsu Nanban Bijutsukan zuroku Henshū Iinkai, comp. 1972. *Kōbe Shiritsu Nanban Bijutsukan zuroku*. 5 vols. Kobe: Kōbe Shiritsu Nanban Bijutsukan.

Kodama Kōta, ed. 1990. *Chōsenjindō mitori ezu*. 2 Vols., Tōkyō Bijutsu.

Koike Masatane. 1984. "Kanwatei Onitake." In *NKBD*, 2: 97–98.

Kojima Kyōko. 1984. "Emishi, Ezo, 'Mōjin' no imi: Ezo-ron joshō." In *Takeuchi Rizō Sensei kijū kinen ronbunshū, 1, ritsuryō-sei to kodai shakai*. Tōkyōdō Shuppan.

Kokuritsu Rekishi Minzoku Hakubutsukan. 2012. *Gyōretsu ni miru kinsei: bushi to ikoku to sairei to*. Exh. cat. Kokuritsu Rekishi Minzoku Hakubutsukan.

Kokushi daijiten. 1979–1996. 15 vols. Yoshikawa Kōbunkan.

Kōma Miyoshi, ed. 1994. *Sengaikyō: Chūgoku kodai no shinwa sekai*. Kōdansha.

Komatsu Kazuhiko. 1985. *Ijin-ron: minzoku shakai no shinsei*. Seidosha.

Komatsu Shigemi & Kanzaki Mitsuharu, ed. 1994. *Tōshosha engi*. In *Zokuzoku Nihon emaki taisei, denki/engi-hen*, vol. 8, Chūō Kōronsha.

Kondō Jūzō. 1905. *Kondō Seisai zenshū*. 3 vols., Kokusho Kankōkai.

Konishi Shirō, ed. 1977. *Nishiki-e Bakumatsu Meiji no rekishi 1 kurofune raikō*. Kōdansha.

Korean National Museum. 1986. *Chosŏn sidae t'ongsinsa*. Exh. cat. Korean National Museum.

Kōriki Tanenobu. 1756–1831. *Enkōan nikki*, in *Nagoya sōsho sanpen*, vol. 14 (Nagoya-shi Kyōiku Iinkai, 1986).

Kornicki, Peter. 1998. *The Book in Japan: A Cultural History from the Beginnings to the Nineteenth Century*. Brill.

Kornicki, Peter. 2006. "Manuscript, Not Print: Scribal Culture in the Edo Period." *Journal of Japanese Studies* 32.1: 23–52.

Koyama Hiroshi. 1960–1961. *Kyōgen-shū*. 2 vols. Vols. 42–43 of *NKBT*.

Kozono Hōfuku. 1748/1800. *Senpei bunchin*. MS copy, 1800. Historiographical Institute Collection, Tokyo University.

Kreiner, Josef. 1994. "Ezo and Its Surroundings through the Eyes of European Cartographers." In Lutz Walter, ed. *Japan: A Cartographic Vision*, 77–83. Prestel-Verlag.

Kuhn, Philip A. 1990. *Soulstealers: The Chinese Sorcery Scare of 1768*. Harvard University Press.

Kujō Kanezane. 1969. *Gyokuyō*. 3 vols., Kokusho Kankōkai.

Kujō Michifusa. n.d. *Michifusa kō ki*. 10 vols. MS copy, Shiryō Hensanjo collection, Tokyo University.

Kuksa P'yŏnch'an Wiwŏnhoe & Chosŏn T'ongsinsa Munhwa Saŏphoe Chiphang Wiwŏnhoe, comp. 2005. *Chosŏn sidae t'ongsinsa hangnyŏl*. Kuksa P'yŏnchán Wiwŏnhoe & Chosŏn T'ongsinsa Munhwa Saŏphoe Chiphang Wiwŏnhoe.

Kumamoto Hakubutsukan. 2005. *Ema hakken: shirarezaru Kumamoto no isan*. Kumamoto Hakubutsukan Kōkogaku Dōkōkai, comp. & pub.

Kung Minbong. 1982. "Chosŏn t'ongsinsa poksik ŭi il-yŏn'gu." M.A. thesis, Ehwa Women's University.

Kungnip Chung'ang Pangmulgwan, comp. 1986. *Chosŏn sidae t'ongsinsa*. Samhwa Ch'ulp'ansa.

Kungnip Chung'ang Pangmulgwan, comp. 2002. *Koryŏ-Chosŏn ŭi taeoe kyoryu*. Kungnip Chung'ang Pangmulgwan.

Kuroda Hideo. 1977. "Edo bakufu kuni-ezu, gōchō kanken (1) Keichō kuni-ezu gōchō ni tsuite." *Rekishi chiri* 93, no. 2: 71–94.ō

Kuroda Hideo. 1980. "Edo bakufu kuni-ezu, gōchō kanken (2) genson Keichō-Shōhō-Genroku kuni-ezu no tokuchō ni tsuite." *Tōkyō Daigaku Shiryō Hensanjo-hō*, 15: 1–21.

Kuroda Hideo. 1982. "Kan'ei Edo bakufu kuni-ezu shōkō: Kawamura ronbun no hihanteki kentō." *Shikan* 107: 49–62.

Kuroda Hideo. 1986a. "Kuni-ezu ni tsuite no taiwa." *Rekishi hyōron* 433: 27–39.

Kuroda Hideo. 1986b. *Kyōkai no chūsei, shōchō no chūsei*. Tōkyō Daigaku Shuppankai.

Kuroda Hideo. 1987. "Komoru, tsusumu, kakusu," in Asao Naohiro, *et al.*, ed., *Nihon no shakai-shi*, 8: 169–206. Iwanami Shoten.

Kuroda Hideo. 1988. *Kaiga shiryō no yomikata. (Shūkan Asahi hyakka Nihon no rekishi bessatsu, rekishi no yomikata*, 1). Asahi Shinbunsha.

Kuroda Hideo. 1990. "Otogizōshi no kaiga kōdo: sashie no sekai o yomu tame ni." In Kuroda Hideo, Satō Masahide & Furuhashi Nobutaka, eds., *Otogizōshi: monogatari, shisō, kaiga*, 216–298. Perikansha.

Kuroda Hideo. 1993. *Ō no shintai ō no shōzō*. Heibonsha.

Kuroda Hideo. 1994. "Tōjin ameuri: amasa to ikoku/ikai." in Kuroda & Toby, 1994.

Kuroda Hideo. 1996. "Hidetada no miyo-hajime to Genna kuni-ezu." Unpublished MS.

Kuroda Hideo. 2000. *Chūsei shōen ezu no kaishakugaku*. Tōkyō Daigaku Shuppankai.

Kuroda Hideo. 2001. "Gyōki-shiki 'Nihon-zu' to wa nani ka?" In Kuroda Hideo, Mary Elizabeth Berry, & Sugimoto Fumiko, eds., *Chizu to ezu no seiji bunka-shi*, 3–77. Tōkyō Daigaku Shuppankai.

Kuroda Hideo. 2003. *Ryū no sumu Nihon*. Iwanami Shoten.

Kuroda Hideo. 2010. *Edo-zu byōbu no nazo o toku*. Kadokawa Shoten.

Kuroda Hideo. 2011. *Minamoto Yoritomo no shinzō*. Kadokawa Shoten.

Kuroda Hideo. 2012. *Kokuhō Jingoji sanzō to wa nanika*. Kadokawa Shoten.

Kuroda Hideo & Ronald P. Toby. 1994. *Gyōretsu to misemono*. Vol. 17 of *Asahi hyakka Nihon no rekishi bessatsu: rekishi o yominaosu*. Asahi Shinbunsha.

Kuroda Hideo, Mary Elizabeth Berry, & Sugimoto Fumiko, eds. 2001. *Chizu to ezu no seiji bunka-shi*. Tōkyō Daigaku Shuppankai.

Kurokawa Masamichi, ed. 1910/1911. *Katō Kiyomasa okitegaki*. Dōbunkan.

Kurushima Hiroshi. 1986. "Morisuna, makisuna, kazari teoke, hōki: kinsei ni okeru 'chisō' no hitotsu to shite." *Shigaku zasshi* 95, no. 8: 1346–1378.

Kurushima Hiroshi. 2012. "Gyōretsu ni miru kinsei no 'ikokujin' ninshiki." *Kokuritsu Rekishi Minzoku Hakubutsukan kenkyū hōkoku* 104: 103–122.

Kuwabara Jitsuzō. 1913. "Shinajin benpatsu no rekishi." In Miyazaki Ichisada *et al.*, ed., *Kuwabara Jitsuzō zenshū*. 6 vols., Iwanami Shoten, 1968. 1: 441–453.

Kyōto Bunka Hakubutsukan, ed. 2001. *Kokoro no kōryū: Chōsen tsūshinshi—Edo jidai kara 21 seiki e no messēji*. Exh. cat. Kyoto: Kyōto Bunka Hakubutsukan & Kyōto Shinbunsha.

Kyōto-shi Rekishi Hakubutsukan, ed. 2010. *Yodo Watanabe-ke shozō Chōsen tsūshinshi kankei monjo*. Sōsho Kyōto no shiryō, vol. 11. Kyōto-shi Rekishi Shiryōkan.

Laing, R. D. 1969. *Self and Others*. 2nd ed. Pantheon.

Laslett, Peter. 1966. *The World We Have Lost*. Scribner.

Lattimore, Richmond (1959). "Introduction to the *Oresteia*." *The Complete Greek Tragedies*. D. Grene & R. Lattimore, eds. Chicago, University of Chicago Press. 1: 1–31.

Law, Jane Marie. 1994. "Violence, Ritual Reenactment, and Ideology: The 'Hojo-e' (Rite for Release of Sentient Beings) of the Usa Hachiman Shrine in Japan." In *History of Religions*, 33, 4: 325–357.

Lenneberg, E. H. 1964. *Animal Categories and Verbal Abuse in the Study of Language*. MIT Press.

Lévi-Strauss, Claude. 1961. *A World on the Wane*. Trans. John Russell. Criterion Books.

Lewis, James B. 2003. *Frontier Contact between Chosŏn Korea and Tokugawa Japan*. Routledge.

Lewis, Martin W., & Wigen, Kären E. 1997. *The Myth of Continents: A Critique of Metageography*. University of California Press.

Lillehoj, Elizabeth. 1996. "Tōfukumon'in: Empress, Patron, and Artist." *Woman's Art Journal* 17. 1: 18–34.

Lillehoj, Elizabeth. 2007. "A Gift for the Retired Empress." In Elizabeth Lillehoj, ed., *Acquisition: Art and Ownership in Edo-Period Japan*. Warren, CT: Floating World Editions, pp. 91–110.

Lillehoj, Elizabeth. 2011. *Art and Palace Politics in Early Modern Japan, 1580s–1680s*. Brill.

Lippit, Yukio. 2012. *Painting of the Realm: The Kano House of Painters in 17th-Century Japan*. University of Washington Press.

Liu Mingzhuan, ed. 2003. *Zhongguo jindai wenhua de jieguo yu chongjian: Zheng Chenggong*. Tainan: Tainan City Government.

Livingston, Paisley. 1996. "Arguing over Intentions." *Revue Internationale de Philosophie* 198: 615–633.

Lurie, David. 2011. *Realms of Literacy: Early Japan and the History of Writing*. Harvard University Asia Center.

Maeda Kingorō & Morita Takeshi, eds. 1965. *Kanazōshi*. NKBT, 90.

Makihara Norio. 2008. *Bunmei-koku o mezashite (Nihon no rekishi, v. 13)*. Shōgakukan.

Maliangkay, Roald. 2007. "Them Pig Feet: Anti-Japanese Folk Songs in Korea." In Remco E. Breuker ed., *Korea in the Middle: Korean Studies and Area Studies: Essays in Honour of Boudewijm Walraven*, 175–203.

Mamiya Kotonobu, comp. 1972–1979. *Henshū chishi biyō tenseki kaidai*, in Tōkyō Daigaku Shiryō Hensanjo, ed., *Dai Nihon Kinsei Shiryō*. Tokyo Daigaku Shuppankai.

Marshall, Alison R. 2011. *The Way of the Bachelor: Early Chinese Settlement in Manitoba*. UBC Press.

Masuda, Koh. 1974. *Kenkyūsha's New Japanese-English Dictionary*. 4th ed. Kenkyūsha.

Matar, Nabil. 1999. *Turks, Moors, and Englishmen in the Age of Discovery*. Columbia University Press.

Matsuda Rokuzan. 1865. *Dai Nihon saizu*. Kyoto: Shimabayashi Sensuke *et al.*

Matsue Shigeyori. 1638/1943. *Kefukigusa*. Shinmura Izuru & Takenouchi Waka, ed. Iwanami Shoten.

Matsumae Shima-no-kami. 1700. *Matsumae gōchō*, in *Zoku-zoku gunsho ruijū*, vol. 9. Zoku Gunsho Ruijū Kanseikai, 1969, pp. 323–325.

Matsura Seizan. 1979–1981. *Kasshi yawa zokuhen*. 8 vols. Ed. Nakamura Yukihiko & Nakano Mitsutoshi. Heibonsha.

Matsushita Kenrin. 1693. *Ishō Nihon-den*. 3 vols. Settsu Kitanomidō (Osaka): Mōrita Shōtarō.

Matsushita Kenrin. 1700. "Nihon shakumyō jo." In Kaibara (1700); also in Kaibara (1910–1911), 1: 1.

Matsushita Kenrin. 1927–1929. *Ishō Nihon-den*. In Mozume (1927–1929, 12: 187–953).

Matsushita Kenrin. 1968. *Ishō Nihon-den*. In *Kaitei shiseki shūran*, vol. 24 (Sumiya Shobō).

Matsushita Kenrin. 1975. *Ishō Nihon-den*. (2 vols., Kokusho Kankōkai).

Matsuzaka Toshio. 2005. "Furukawa Koshōken," in Takeuchi Makoto et al., ed., *Kinsei jinmei daijiten*, p. 873. Yoshikawa Kōbunkan.

Matsuzaki Hitoshi & Hara Michio, eds. 1993–1995. *Chikamatsu jōruri shū*. SNKBT, vols. 91–92.

Mayumi Tsunetada. 2000. *Gion shinkō: Shintō shinkō no tayōsei*. Ebisu Kōshō Shuppan.

McKelway, Matthew P. 2006. *Capitalscapes: Folding Screens and Political Imagination in Late Medieval Kyoto*. University of Hawai'i Press.

McKinney, Meredith. 2007. See Sei Shōnagon.

McNally Mark. 2005. *Proving the Way: Conflict and Practice in the History of Japanese Nativism*. Harvard University Asia Center.

Melville, Herman. 1851. *Moby-Dick or The White Whale*. Boston: Harper & Brothers, Publishers; London: Richard Bentley.

Meyerhoff, Barbara. 1986. "Life Not Death in Venice." In Victor W. Turner & Edward M. Bruner, eds., *The Anthropology of Experience*. University of Illinois Press.

Minamoto Munetaka. 1861. *Hōketsu kenmon zusetsu*. MS copy, 3 vols., National Diet Library.

Mitamura Engyo. 1975–1978. *Mitamura Engyo zenshū*. 28 vols. Chūō Kōronsha.

Mitani Hiroshi. 1997. *Meiji ishin to nashonarizumu: Bakumatsu no gaikō to seiji hendō*. Tōkyō Daigaku Shuppankai.

Mitani Hiroshi. 2006. *Escape from Impasse: The Decision to Open Japan*. International House of Japan.

Miyachi Masato. 1985. "Bakumatsu Ishin-ki no kokka to gaikō." In *Kōza Nihon rekishi 7 kindai 1*. Tōkyō Daigaku Shuppankai.

Miyazaki Fumiko. 2008. "Gaikokujin no Fuji tozan ni taisuru bakumatsu Nihonjin no taiō." In *Fujisan bunka kenkyū* 9–10, (2008): 13–32.

Mizuno, Norihito. 2009. "Early Meiji Policies Towards the Ryukyus and the Taiwanese Aboriginal Territories " *Modern Asian Studies*, 43.3: 683–739.

Mody, N. H. N. 1939/1969. *A Collection of Nagasaki Colour Prints and Paintings, Showing the Influence of Chinese and European Art on That of Japan*. Kobe: Private Printing; reprint: Charles M. Tuttle & Co.

Mogami Tokunai. 1790/1969. *Ezo-koku fūzoku ninjō no sata*. NSSS 4: 439–484.

Mogami Tokunai. 1808/1969. *Totō hikki*. NSSS 4 : 589.

Montaigne, Michel de. 1987. *The Complete Essays*. Trans. M. A. Screech. Penguin Books.

Moretti, Laura. 2010. "Kanazōshi Revisited: The Beginnings of Japanese Popular Literature in Print." *Monumenta Nipponica* 65.2: 297–356

Mori Senzō, *et al.*, eds. 1980. *Shin'ya meidan*. In *Zoku Enseki jisshu*. 3 vols. Chūō Kōronsha.

Morohashi Tetsuji, comp. 1955–1960. *Dai Kan-Wa jiten*. 13 vols. Taishūkan.

Morris, Ivan I. 1967. See Sei Shōnagon.

Morris-Suzuki, Tessa. 1994. "Creating the Frontier: Border, Identity, and History in Japan's Far North." *East Asian History*, vol. 7.

Morris-Suzuki. 1998. *Re-Inventing Japan*. M. E. Sharpe.

Morris-Suzuki. 2004. "Rethinking 'Japan': Frontiers and Minorities in Modern Japan." *International House of Japan Bulletin* 24.1: 1–19.

Morrison, Toni. 1993. *The Bluest Eye*. Alfred A. Knopf, Inc.

Morrison, Toni. 1992. *Playing in the Dark: Whiteness in the Literary Imagination*. Vintage Books.

Mostow, Joshua S. 1996. *Pictures of the Heart: The* Hyakunin isshu *in Word and Image*. University of Hawai'i Press.

Mostow, Joshua S & Royall Tyler, trans. 2010. *The Ise Stories: Ise Monogatari*. University of Hawai'i Press.

Mozume Takami, ed. 1927–1929. *Shinchū kōkoku-gaku sōsho*. 12 vols. Kōbunko Kankōkai.

Mun Konghǔi. 1998. "Nishikie/nishikie-shinbun ni miru Chōsen/Chūgoku e no manazashi: Kōkadō Jiken kara Nisshin Sensō made." *Ōsaka Jinken Hakubutsukan kiyō* 2: 29–51.

Murai Shōsuke. 1985. "Chūsei Nihon rettō no chiiki kūkan to kokka." In *Shisō*, 732: 36–58.

Murai Shōsuke. 1988. *Ajia no naka no chūsei Nihon*. Azekura Shobō.

Murai Shōsuke. 1993. *Chūsei wajin den*. Iwanami Shoten.

Murai Shōsuke. 1995. *Higashi Ajia ōkan*. Asahi Shinbunsha.

Murakami Naojirō, trans. 1938–1939. *Dejima Rankan nisshi*. 3 vols. Bunmei Kyōkai.

Muramatsu Kazuya. 1966. "Shinzoku kibun oboegaki," in Shuto Daigaku Tōkyō Toshi Kyōyō Gakubu Jinbun Shakai-kei, *Jinbun gakuhō*, 53 (March): 1–46.

Murasaki Shikibu. 1960. *The Tale of Genji*. Translated by Arthur Waley. Modern Library.

Murasaki Shikibu. 1993–1997. *Genji monogatari*. Ed. Yanai Shigeshi, *et al.* 5 vols. NKBT, vols. 12–23.

Murasaki Shikibu. 2001. *The Tale of Genji*. Translated by Royall Tyler. Penguin Classics.

Murase, Miyeko. 1986. *Tales of Japan*. Oxford University Press.

Muroga Nobuo. 1974. "Nihon no chizu no ayumi: josetsu." In Muroga *et al.* 1974, pp. 4–7.

Muroga Nobuo, Oda Takeo & Unno Kazutaka, ed. 1974. *Nihon kochizu taisei*.

Mutō Sadao, ed. 1987–1988. *Kinsei waraibanashi-shū*. 3 vols., Iwanami Shoten.

Nagata Seiji, ed. 1986–1987. *Hokusai manga*. 3 vols. Iwasaki Bijutsusha.

Naguib, Saphinaz-Amal. 1990. "Hair in Ancient Egypt." *Acta Orientalia* 51: 7–26.

Naitō Akira, ed. 1978. *Nihon byōbu-e shūsei ikkan rakuchū rakugai*. Kōdansha.

Naitō Seisan. 1975–1976. *Chōshū zasshi*. 12 vols. Nagoya: Aichi-ken Kyōdo Shiryō Kankōkai. (original MS, 100 vols., Hōsa Bunko, Nagoya).

Naitō Shunpo. 1976. *Bunroku Keichō no eki ni okeru hiryonin no kenkyū*. Tōkyō Daigaku Shuppankai.

Nakabe Yoshitaka. 2004. 'Kaiki ni arawareru Kanō-ha sakuhin,' in *Kinsei Kyōto no Kanō-ha ten*. Kyōto Bunka Hakubutsukan, pp. 152–156.

Nakagawa Tadateru. 1799. *Shinzoku kibun*. 13 vols. Edo, Osaka & Kyoto: Okadaya Kashichi et. al.

Nakagawa Tadateru. 1966. *Shinzoku kibun*. 2 vols. Ed. Son Hakujun & Matsumura Kazuya. Tōyō Bunko, vols. 62; 70. Heibonsha.

Nakagawa Tadateru. 2006. *Qingsu jiwen*. Fang Ke & Sun Xuanling, tr. Beijing: Zhonghua Shuju.

Nakai, Kate W. 1980. "The Naturalization of Confucianism in Tokugawa Japan: The Problem of Sinocentrism." *Harvard Journal of Asiatic Studies* 40.1: 157–199.

Nakai, Kate W. 1988. *Shogunal Politics: Arai Hakuseki and the Premises of Tokugawa Rule*. Council on East Asian Studies, Harvard University (Harvard East Asian Monographs, no. 134).

Nakamura Hidetaka. 1965–1970. *Nissen kankei-shi no kenkyū*. 3 vols. Yoshikawa Kōbunkan.

Nakamura Hidetaka. 1980. "Ōrankai," in *Kokushi daijiten* (1979–1996), 2: 932–33.

Nakamura Jūsuke. 1786/1931. "Saruwaka bandai butai," in Ihara Seisei'en, ed., *Chūko Edo kyōgen shū* (Shun'yōdō, 1931 [*Nihon gikyoku zenshū*, vol. 1]): 277–434.

Nakamura Tekisai. 1666. *Kinmō zui*. 20 vols., Kyoto: Yamagataya Shigeru.

Nakamura Yukihiko, ed. 1961. *Fūrai sanjin-shū*. NKBT, 55.

Nakanishi Hiroshi. 2014. "Fujisan: Kyōto kara mieru ... hatsu no shōko shashin toreta!" *Mainichi shinbun*, 2014/09/22.

Nakano Hatayoshi. 1975. *Hachiman shinkō-shi no kenkyū*. Expanded edition, 2 vols. Yoshikawa Kōbunkan.

Nakano Hatayoshi. 1983. *Hachiman shinkō*. Yūzankaku Shuppan (*Minshū shūkyō-shi sōsho*, vol. 2).

Nakano Hatayoshi. 1985. *Hachiman shinkō*. Hanawa Shobō.

Nakano Hatayoshi. 2002. *Hachiman shinkō jiten*. Ebisu Kōshō Shuppan.

Nakano Hitoshi. 2008. *Bunroku-Keichō no eki.* (*Sensō no Nihonshi*, vol. 8) Yoshikawa Kōbunkan, 2008.

Nakano Katarō, ed. 1909/1979. *Katō Kiyomasa-den.* Ryūbunkan; reprint, Kumamoto: Seichōsha.

Nakano Mitsutoshi, Hino Tatsuo & Ibi Takashi, eds. 1993. *Neboke Sensei bunshū, Kyōka saizō shū, Yomo no aka.* SNKBT, 84.

Nakao Hiroshi. 2000. *Chōsen tsūshinshi to Jinshin waran.* Akashi Shoten.

Nakayama Hisao. 2009. "'Onaji hatake no Onitake Issaku Tsukimaru' kō: Jippensha Ikku no kōyū kankei sono ta." In *Bungaku ronsō* (Tōyō Daigaku Bungakubu Nihon Bungaku-bunka-ka). 80: 100–111.

Nanba Matsutaro, Muroga Nobuo & Unno Kazutaka. 1973. *Old Maps in Japan.* Trans. Patricia Murray. Sogensha Inc.

Nanban bijutsu sōmokuroku (*yōfū-ga hen*). 1997. Published as *Kokuritsu Rekishi Minzoku Hakubutsukan kenkyū hōkoku*, no. 75.

Napier, A. David. 1992. *Foreign Bodies: Performance, Art, and Symbolic Anthropology.* University of California Press.

Nara Kokuritsu Hakubutsukan, ed. 1969. *Shōtoku Taishi eden.* Tōkyō Bijutsu.

Narusawa Akira. 1978. "Hendo Nihon." In *Gekkan hyakka*, nos. 194, 195 (Nov.; Dec.).

Naruse Fujio. 1982. "Nihon kaiga ni okeru Fuji-zu no tenkei-teki hyōgen ni tsuite." *Bijutsushi* 112 (March): 115–130.

Naruse Fujio. 1983a. "Fuji no e no rekishi." *Bessatsu Taiyō: Fuji* (Winter): 67–74.

Naruse Fujio. 1983b. "Fuji no kaiga: Kamakura jidai kara gendai made." *Bessatsu Taiyō: Fuji* (Winter): 35–65.

Nelson, John K. 1996. *A Year in the Life of A Shinto Shrine.* University of Washington Press.

Nelson, Sarah M. 1998. "Bound Hair and Confucianism in Korea." In *Politics of the Queue: Agitation and Resistance at the Beginning and End of Qing China*, Alf Hiltbeitel and Barbara D. Miller, ed. State University of New York Press, pp. 105–21.

Niditch, Susan. 2008. *"My Brother Esau Is a Hairy Man": Hair and Identity in Ancient Israel.* Oxford University Press.

Nihon kankei kaigai shiryō Iezusu-kai shokan-shū genbun-hen. 2 vols. 1994–1995. Tōkyō Daigaku Shiryō Hensanjo.

Nihon kankei kaigai shiryō Iezusu-kai shokan-shū yakubun-hen. 2 vols. 1990–1991. Tōkyō Daigaku Shiryō Hensanjo.

Nihon Kinsei Seikatsu Ebiki Minami Kyūshū-hen Hensan Kyōdō Kenkyū-han, ed. 2018. *Nihon kinsei seikatsu ebiki Minami Kyūshū-hen.* Yokohama: Kanagawa Daigaku Nihon Jōmin Bunka Kenkyūjo Hi-moji Shiryō Kenkyū Sentā.

Nihon kiryaku. 1964. *Kokushi taikei*, vols. 10–11. Yoshikawa Kōbunkan.

Nihon kokugo daijiten Henshū Iinkai, comp. 2000–2002. *Nihon kokugo daijiten*, 2nd ed. Shōgakukan.

Nishikawa Hiroshi.1982. *Okayama to Chōsen*. Okayama: Nihon Bunkyō Shuppan.

Nishikawa Joken. 1708. *Zōho ka'i tsūshō kō*. 5 vols. Kyoto: Umemura Ya'emon & Furukawa Saburōbei.

Nishikawa Joken. 1720a. *Nihon suido kō*. Kyoto: Ryūshiken Ibaraki Tazaemon.

Nishikawa Joken. 1720b. *Shijūni-koku jinbutsu zusetsu*. 2 vols. Edo: Enbaiken Zōhan.

Nishikawa Joken. 1928–1931. *Nihon suido kō*. In Takimoto Seiichi, ed., *Nihon keizai taiten*. 54 vols., Shishi Shuppansha, 4: 535–542.

Nishiki Bunryū. 1701. *Kokusen'ya tegara nikki*. In Nagatomo Chiyoji, ed., *Nishiki Bunryū zenshū*. 3 vols. Koten Bunko, 1991 (*Kinsei bungei shiryō*, 21, pts 1–3), 1: 57–108; 3: 9–29.

Nishimaki Kōzaburō, ed. 1978. *Kawaraban shinbun*. 4 vols., Heibonsha (*Taiyō korekushon* series).

Nishimura Tei. 1958. *Nanban bijutsu*. Kōdansha.

Nishiyama Matsunosuke. 1993. "Hokusai and Edo." In *"Dai Hokusai ten" zuroku: Edo ga unda sekai no eshi*. 2 vols. Asahi Shinbunsha. 2: xvii–xx.

Nochlin, Linda & Tamar Garb, eds. (1995). *The Jew in the Text: Modernity and the Construction of Identity*. Thames and Hudson.

Noguchi Takehiko. 1991. *Edo no heigaku shisō*. Chūō Kōronsha.

Nonomura Kaizō, ed. 1988. *Yōkyoku nihyaku-gojūban shū*. Akao Shōbundō.

Nosco, Peter, ed. 1984. *Confucianism and Tokugawa Culture*. Princeton University Press.

Nosco, Peter. 1990. *Remembering Paradise: Nativism and Nostalgia in Eighteenth-Century Japan*. Harvard University Press.

Nukii Masayuki. 1996. *Toyotomi seiken no kaigai shinryaku to Chōsen gihei kenkyū*. Aoki Shoten.

Ōba Osamu. 1967. *Edo jidai ni okeru Chūgoku mochiwatari-sho no kenkyū*. Suita: Kansai Daigaku Tōzai Gakujutsu Kenkyūjo.

Ōba Osamu. 1994. *Edo jidai ni okeru Chūgoku bunka juyō no kenkyū*. Kyoto: Dōbōsha Shuppan.

O'Brien, Suzanne G. 2008. "Splitting Hairs: History and the Politics of Daily Life in Nineteenth-Century Japan" in *JAS*, 67. 4: 1309–039.

Oda Takeo, Muroga Nobuo & Unno Kazutaka, eds. 1975. *Nihon kochizu taisei, sekai-zu hen*. 2 vols. Kōdansha.

Odaka Toshio, ed. 1966. *Edo waraibanashi shū*. NKBT, vol. 100. Iwanami Shoten.

Oguma, Eiji. 2014. *The Boundaries of 'the Japanese' Volume 1: Okinawa 1818–1872—Inclusion and Exclusion*. Translated by Leonie R. Strickland. Melbourne: Trans Pacific Press.

Ōhara Rieko. 1988. *Kurokami no bunkashi*. Tsukiji Shokan.

Ohnuki-Tierney, Emiko. 1987. *Monkey as Mirror: Symbolic Transformations in Japanese History and Culture*. Princeton University Press.

Ōji Toshiaki. 1996. *Echizu no sekaizō*. Iwanami Shoten.

Oka Yasumasa. 1992. *Megane-e shinkō*. Chikuma Shobō, 1992.

Okada Hajime, ed. 1976–1984. *Haifū yanagidaru zenshū sakuin-hen*. 13 vols., Sanseidō.

Okamoto Ryōichi. 1977. *The Nanban Art of Japan*. Weatherhill.

Ōkawa Nobuyoshi, ed. 1926. *Dai Saigō zenshū*. 3 vols. *Dai Saigō zenshū* Kankōkai.

Okazaki Yoshie. 1943–1950. *Nihon geijutsu shichō*. 5 vols. Iwanami Shoten.

Okinawa-ken Kyōiku Iinkai Bunka-ka and Ryūkyū Kuni-ezu Shiryō Henshū Iinkai, eds. 1992–1994. *Ryūkyū kuni-ezu shiryō*.

Okudaira Shunroku. 1991. *Rakuchū rakugai-zu to Nanban byōbu*. Shōgakukan. (*Shōgakukan gyararī: Shinpen meihō Nihon no bijutsu*, vol. 25).

Ōkurashō, ed. 1922–1925. *Nihon zaisei keizai shiryō*. 11 vols. Geirinsha.

Oldstone-Moore, Christopher. 2016. *Of Beards and Men: The Revealing History of Facial Hair*. University of Chicago Press.

Ōno Mizuo, ed. 2001. *Enomoto Yazaemon oboegaki: kinsei shoki shōnin no kiroku*. Heibonsha.

Ono Takeo. 1975. *Edo no hakurai fūzoku*. Tenbōsha.

Ooms, Herman. 1985. *Tokugawa Ideology: Early Constructs, 1570–1680*. Princeton University Press.

Orikuchi Shinobu. 1954–1959. *Orikuchi Shinobu zenshū*. 32 vols. Chūō Kōronsha.

Ōsaka Jinken Hakubutsukan. 1999. *Kami no mibun-shi*. Ōsaka Jinken Hakubutsukan.

Ōshima Akihide. 2009. *'Sakoku' to iu gensetsu*. Mineruva Shobō.

Ōta Gyūichi. 1702. *Kōrai-jin oboegaki*. Kyoto: Umemura Ichirōbei.

Ōta Kinen Bijutsukan, ed. 1985. *Katsushika Hokusai ten*. Ōta Kinen Bijutsukan.

Ōta Nanpo. 1784/1985. *Koitsu wa Nippon*. In Kimura Yaeko *et al.* ed., SNKBT, 83: 211–226.

Ōta Nanpo. 1985. *Neboke sensei shū*. In Hamada Giichirō, ed., *Ōta Nanpo zenshū*. 21 vols. Iwanami Shoten.

Ōtake Susumu. 1996. *Satsuma Naeshirokawa shinkō*. Kagoshima: Ōtake Susumu.

Ōtani Ryūkichi. 1932. *Tadataka Inō: The Japanese Land-Surveyor*. S. Iwanami, Publisher.

Ōtsu Tōru. 2001. *Michinaga to kyūtei shakai*. Kōdansha.

Ōtsuki Fumihiko. 1891/1984. *Daigenkai*. Fuzanbō; new edition, 1984.

Ozawa Hiromu & Maruyama Nobuhiko. 1993. *Edo-zu byōbu o yomu*. Kawade Shobō Shinsha.

Oze Hoan. 1996. *Taikōki*. Ed. Hinoyama Teruhiko & Emoto Hiroshi. *Shin Nihon koten bungaku taikei*, vol. 60. Iwanami Shoten.

Paine, Robert Treat, & Alexander Soper. 1955. *The Art and Architecture of Japan*. Penguin Books.

Paku Chun'iru (Pak Ch'unil). 1992. *Chōsen tsūshinshi shiwa*. Yūzankaku Shuppan.

Parker, Kathleen. 2013. "Michelle Obama's Wings." In *The Washington Post* (Op-Ed), February 26.

Pastreich, Emanuel. 2011. *The Observable Mundane: Vernacular Chinese and the Emergence of a Literary Discourse on Popular Narrative in Edo Japan*. Seoul: SNU Press.

Pflugfelder, Gregory M. 2012. "The Nation-State, the Age/Gender System, and the Reconstitution of Erotic Desire in Nineteenth-Century Japan," in *JAS*, 71.4: 963–974.

Philippi, Donald L., trans. 1969. *Kojiki*. Princeton University Press & University of Tokyo Press.

Pirandello, Luigi. 1958. *Six Characters in Search of An Author*. Trans. Frederick May. Heinemann.

Plath, David W. 1980. *Long Engagements: Maturity in Modern Japan*. Stanford University Press.

Pollack, David. 1986. *The Fracture of Meaning: Japan's Synthesis of China from the Eighth through the Eighteenth Centuries*. Princeton University Press.

Rabinow, Paul, ed. 1984. *The Foucault Reader*. Pantheon.

Rai San'yō. 1979–81. *Nihon gaishi*. 3 vols., Iwanami Shoten (*Iwanami bunko*).

Ravina, Mark. 1999. *Land and Lordship in Early Modern Japan*. Stanford University Press.

Raz, Jacob. 1992. *Aspects of Otherness in Japanese Culture*. Institute for the Study of Languages and Cultures of Africa and Asia, Tokyo University of Foreign Studies.

Ri Jinhi (Yi Jinhŭi). 1976. *Richō no Chōsen tsūshinshi: Edo jidai no Nihon to Chōsen*. Kōdansha.

Ridgeon, Lloyd. 2010. "Shaggy or Shaved? the Symbolism of Hair Among Persian Qalandar Sufis." *Iran & the Caucasus* 14 (2). Brill: 233–63.

Ridgeon, Lloyd. 1979. "Karako odori to Chōsen yama." In Eizō Bunka Kyōkai, ed. 1979: 51–68.

Ridgeon, Lloyd. 1987. *Edo jidai no Chōsen tsūshinshi*. Kōdansha.

Roberts, Laurance P. *A Dictionary of Japanese Artists*. Weatherhill, Inc.

Roberts, Luke S. 1998. *Mercantilism in a Japanese Domain: The Merchant Origins of Economic Nationalism in 18th-Century Tosa*. Cambridge University Press.

Robinson, Kenneth R. 2012. "Mapping Japan in Chosŏn Korea: Images in the Government Report *Haedong Chegukki*." *Korean Studies* 36: 1–30.

Ryū Kaori. 1990. *Danpatsu: kindai higashi Ajia no bunka shōtotsu*. Asahi Shinbunsha.

Ryūtei Tanehiko. 1811/1902. *Tōjin-wage ima Kokusen'ya*. In Kōdō Tokuchi, ed. *Tanehiko tanpen kessaku-shū*. Hakubunkan.

Saeki Akiko. 2012. "Tōjin ameuri kō." *Tōyō Daigaku Daigakuin kiyō* (*Bungaku Kenkyūka/Kokubungaku*), 49: 81–95.

Safire, William. 1988. "People of Color." *The New York Times Magazine* (20 Nov): 20.

Sahlins, Marshall. 1985. *Islands of History*. University of Chicago Press.

Said, Edward. 1978. *Orientalism*. Pantheon Books.

Saitō Gesshin. 1835. *Edo meisho zue*. 20 vols. Edo: Sawaki Isaburō, Asakura Ihachi, & Tomita Rokuzaemon.

Saitō Gesshin. 1834–1835/1966–1968. *Edo meisho zue*. Ed. Suzuki Shōzō. 6 vols. Kadokawa Shoten.

Saitō Gesshin. 1837. *Tōto saiji-ki*. Edo: Suharaya Mohei & Suharaya Ihachi..

Saitō Gesshin. 1837/1972–1974. *Tōto saiji-ki*. Edo; reprint, 3 vols., Heibonsha.

Sakai, Tadao. 1970. "Confucianism and Popular Educational Works." In W. T. de Bary & Irene T. Bloom, eds., *Self and Society in Ming Thought*, 331–366. Columbia University Press.

Sakakibara Satoru. 1988. "'Edo tenka sairei-zu byōbu' ni tsuite." In *Kokka*, 4, 4 (Nov.): 11–20.

Sakakura Atsuyoshi, Ōtsu Yūichi, Tsukishima Hiroshi, Abe Toshiko & Imai Gen'e, eds. 1957. *Taketori monogatari, Ise monogatari, Yamato Monogatari*. NKBT, 9.

Sakamoto Mitsuru, Sugase Tadashi & Naruse Fujio, ed. 1990. *Nanban bijutsu to yōfūga*. (*Genshoku Nihon no bijutsu*, 20). Shōgakukan.

Sakamoto Tarō, ed. 1965–1967. *Nihon shoki*. NKBT, 67–68.

Sakumi Yōichi. 1996. *Ōedo no tenka matsuri*. Kawade Shobō Shinsha.

Sakurai Tokutarō, Hagiwara Tatsuo & Miyata Noboru, ed.1975. *Jisha engi*. NST, 20.

Sanbō Honbu, ed. 1924. *Nihon senshi: Chōsen eki*. Kaikōsha.

Sano Midori. 1997. *Fūryū, zōkei, monogatari: Nihon bi-ishiki no kōzō to yōtai*. Sukaidoa.

Satō Hiroo. 1995. "Shinkoku Shisō." In *Nihonshi kenkyū*, 309: 1–30.

Satō Hiroo. 2006. *Shinkoku Nihon*: Chikuma Shobō.

Satō Masayuki. 2004. *Rekishi ninshiki no jikū*. Chisen Shokan.

Satō Yukiko. 2001. *Edo no e'iri shōsetsu*. Perikansha.

Sawada Akira. 1928. "Fuji no bijutsu." In Kanpei Taisha Sengen Jinja, ed., *Fuji no kenkyū*. Vol. 4. Kokin Shoin.

Scheiner, Irwin, ed. 1974. *Modern Japan: An Interpretive Anthology*. Macmillan.

Schwartz, Stuart, ed. 1994. *Implicit Understandings: Observing, Reporting, and Reflecting on the Encounters between Europeans and Other Peoples in the Early Modern Era*. Cambridge University Press.

Scott, James C. 1990. *Domination and the Arts of Resistance: Hidden Transcripts*. Yale University Press.

Sei Shōnagon. 1958. *Makura no sōshi*, in Ikeda Kikan & Akiyama Bin, ed., *Makura no sōshi; Murasaki Shikibu nikki*. NKBT, 19.

Sei Shōnagon. 1963. *Zenkō Makura no sōshi*. Ikeda Kikan, comp. Shibundō.

Sei Shōnagon. 1967. *The Pillow Book of Sei Shōnagon*. Ivan I. Morris, tr. 2 vols., Columbia University Press.

Sei Shōnagon. 2006. *The Pillow Book*. Meredith McKinney, tr. Penguin Classics.

Seki Akiko. 2012. "Tōjin ame-uri kō." *Tōyō Daigaku Daigakuin kiyō* (*Bungaku Kenkyū-ka/ Kokubungaku*) 49: 81–95.

Shakespeare, William. 1974. *The Riverside Shakespeare*. G. Blakemore Evans *et al.*, ed. Houghton Mifflin Company.

Shange, Ntozake. 1992, "The Desert," *The New York Times*. (24 May).

Shibata Minoru. 1984. *Goryō shinkō*. Vol. 5 of *Minshū shūkyō-shi sōsho*. Yūzankaku.

Shigetomo Ki. 1958. *Chikamatsu jōruri shū*. 2 vols. (NKBT, vols. 49–50), Iwanami Shoten.

Shinoda Jun'ichi, ed. 1986. *Chikamatsu Monzaemon shū.* (*Shinchōsha Nihon koten shūsei*, vol. 75) Shinchōsha.

Shimao Arata. 2002. "Shi-teki Sesshū-zō," in TNM (2002): 218–225.

Shimizu, Yoshiaki, ed. 1988. *Japan: The Shaping of Daimyo Culture.* Exh. cat. The National Gallery.

Shimokawa Heidayū. ca. 1669/1970. *Kiyomasa Kōrai-jin oboegaki.* In *Zokuzoku gunsho ruijū*, vol. 4: 293–330.

Shin Kisu. 1999. *Chōsen tsūshinshi: hito no ōrai, bunka no kōryū.* Akashi Shoten.

Shin Kisu. 2002. *Chōsen tsūshinshi ōrai: Edo jidai 260-nen no heiwa to yūkō.* Akashi Shoten.

Sin Kisu & Murakami Tsuneo. 1991. *Jusha Kan Han to Nihon.* Akashi Shoten.

Sin Sukchu. 1512. *Haedong chegukki* (Hansŏng [Seoul]), Collection of the Historiographical Institute, Tokyo University. See also Tanaka (1991).

Sin Yuhan. *Haeyurok*, in HHCJ (1941), vol. 1.

Sin Yuhan. 1974. *Kaiyūroku (Haeyurok).* Trans. Kang Chaeŏn. Heibonsha.

Sin Yuhan. 1975. *Haeyurok.* In *Kug'yŏk HHCJ.* 11 vols. Minjok Munhwa Ch'ujinhoe & Tamgudang.

Shin Kisu & Nakao Hiroshi, eds. 1993–1996. *Taikei Chōsen tsūshinshi.* 8 vols. Akashi Shoten.

Shintani Hiroshi. 1982. "Chikujō-zu byōbu." *Kokka*, 89.1: 19–27.

Shiratori, Kurakichi. 1929. "The Queue among the Peoples of North Asia." In *Memoirs of the Research Department of the Toyo Bunko (The Oriental Library)* 4: 1–70.

Shively, Donald. 1955. "Bakufu versus Kabuki." In *Harvard Journal of Asiatic Studies.* 18, 3–4: 326–356.

Shively, Donald. 1964–65. "Sumptuary Regulation and Status in Early Tokugawa Japan." In *Harvard Journal of Asiatic Studies.* 25: 123–164.

Shōnyo (1966–1968). *Tenbun nikki*, published as *Ishiyama Honganji nikki* (2 vols. + 2 index vols.). Osaka: Seibundō.

Shunkōen Hanamaru & Okada Gyokuzan. 1799. *Ehon ikoku ichiran.* 5 vols. Osaka: Kawaguchi Sōbei, Ōnishi Jinshichi & Matsumoto Heishirō.

Skinner, G. William. 1957. *Chinese Society in Thailand: An Analytical History.* Cornell University Press.

Smith, Henry D. II, ed. 1988. *Hokusai: One Hundred Views of Mt. Fuji.* George Braziller, Inc.

Smith, Lawrence, ed. 1988. *Ukiyoe: Images of Unknown Japan.* British Museum Publications, Ltd.

Smith, Richard J. 1996. *Chinese Maps.* Oxford University Press.

Smith, Robert J. 1974. *Ancestor Worship in Contemporary Japan.* Stanford University Press.

Son Hakujun & Muramatsu Kazuya. 1966–1966. *Shinzoku kibun.* 2 vols. Vols. 62 and 70 of *Tōyō Bunko.* Heibonsha.

Son Kyŏngja & Kim Yongsuk. 1984. *Chōsen ōchō Kankoku fukushoku zuroku*. Rinsen Shoten.

Sonehara Satoshi. 1996. *Tokugawa Ieyasu shinkoku-ka e no michi: chūsei Tendai shisō no tenkai*. Yoshikawa Kōbunkan.

Sonehara Satoshi. 2008. *Shinkun Ieyasu no tanjō: Tōshōgū to Gongen-sama*. Yoshikawa Kōbunkan.

Sørensen, Preben Meulengracht. 1983. *The Unmanly Man: Concepts of Sexual Defamation in Early Northern Society*. Trans. Joan R. Turville-Petre. Odense University Press.

Sorimachi, Shigeo. 1978. *Catalog of Japanese Illustrated Books and Manuscripts in the Spencer Collection of the New York Public Library*. Rev. ed. The Kōbunsō.

Stager, Lawrence E. 1998. "Forging an Identity: The Emergence of Ancient Israel." In Michael D. Coogan, ed., *The Oxford History of the Biblical World*, 123–175. Oxford University Press.

Staden, Hans. 1557. *Warhaftige Historia und beschreibung eyner Landtschafft der Wilden Nacketen, Grimmigen Menschfresser-Leuthen in der Newenwelt America gelegen*. Marpurg: Kolb.

Staden, Hans. 2008. Neil L. Whitehead & Michael Harbsmeier, tr. *Hans Staden's True History: An Account of Cannibal Captivity in Brazil*. Duke University Press.

Staples, Brent. 2014. "Eurocentric Beauty Ideals in the Military." *The New York Times*, May 1.

Stewart, Susan. 1989. "Antipodal Expectations: Notes on the Formosan 'Ethnography' of George Psalmanazar." In George W. Stocking, ed., *Romantic Motives: Essays on Anthropological Sensibility*, 44–73. University of Wisconsin Press.

Struve, Lynn. 1984. *The Southern Ming, 1644–1662*. Yale University Press.

Suda Tsutomu. 2010. "Edo jidai minshū no Chōsen/Chōsenjin-kan: jōruri; kabuki to iu media o tsūjite." In *Shisō*, 1029: 151–169.

Sugimoto, Etsuko Inagaki. 1966. *A Daughter of the Samurai*. Charles E. Tuttle, Publishers.

Sugimoto Fumiko. 1994. "Kuni-ezu". In *Iwanami kōza Nihon tsūshi 12 kinsei 2*. Iwanami Shoten.

Sugimoto Fumiko. 1999. *Ryōiki shihai no tenkai to kinsei*. Yamakawa Shuppansha.

Sugiya Yukinao. 1827. *Ka'i jinbutsu zu*. The Spencer Collection, New York Public Library.

Sumiya Kazuhiko *et al*. 1987. *Ijin, kappa, Nihonjin: Nihon bunka o yomu*. Shin'yōsha.

Suzuki Keizō, ed. 1994. *Yūsoku kojitsu daijiten*. Yoshikawa Kōbunkan.

Suzuki, Keiko, 2007. "The Making of *Tōjin*: Construction of the Other in Early Modern Japan. In *Asian Folklore Studies*, 66.1/2: 83–105.

Suzuki Susumu, ed. 1971. *Edo-zu byōbu*. Heibonsha.

Tachibana no Narisue. 1966. *Kokon chomonjū*. Nagazumi Yasuaki & Shimada Isao, ed. In *NKBT*, vol. 84.

Taigai Kankeishi Sōgō Nenpyō Henshū Iinkai, ed. 1999. *Taigai kankeishi sōgō nenpyō*. Yoshikawa Kōbunkan.

Taira Shigemichi. 1977. *Hayashi Shihei sono hito to shisō*. Sendai: Hōbundō Shuppan.

Takafuji Harutoshi. 1996. *Nikkō Tōshōgū no nazo*. Kōdansha.

Takagi Shōsaku. 1992. "Hideyoshi, Ieyasu no shinkoku-kan to sono keifu: Keichō 18-nen 'Bateren tsuihō no fumi' o tegakari to shite." *Shigaku zasshi* 101, no. 10: 1–26.

Takagi Shōsaku. 2004. "Hideyoshi's and Ieyasu's Views of Japan as a Land of the Gods and Its Antecedents: With Reference to the 'Writ for the Expulsion of the Missionaries' of 1614." *Acta Asiatica* 87: 59–84.

Takagi Takayoshi. 2011. *Kinsei Nihon hoppō-zu kenkyū*. Sapporo: Hokkaidō Shuppan Kikaku Sentā.

Takai Ranzan, Nakamura Tsunetoshi & Kikukawa Eizan. 1863. *Edo dai setuyō kaidai-gura*. Edo, Kyoto, Osaka & Nagoya: Izumoji Manjirō *et al*.

Takamaki Minoru. 1992. *Kinsei Tōhoku chihō ni okeru toshi to sairei no kenkyū*. Heisei 3-nendo Kagaku Kenkyū-hi Hojo-kin (Ippan Kenkyū C) Kenkyū Seika Hōkokusho.

Takimoto Seiichi, ed. 1928–1931. *Nihon keizai taiten*. 54 vols., Shishi Shuppansha, 1929–1931.

Takano Toshihiko. 1992. "Idō suru mibun: shinshoku to hyakushō no aida." In Asao Naohiro, ed., *Nihon no kinsei, 7: mibun to kakushiki*, 345–377. Chūō Kōronsha.

Takase Baisei. 1677/1969. *Haikai ruisen-shū*. Vol. 1 of *Kinsei bungei sōkan*. Sen'an Noma Kōshin Sensei Kankō Kinen-kai. (Facsimile of original edition, Kyoto: Teradaya Yoheiji, 1677).

Takayama Yatai Hozonkai, ed. 1959. *Takayama matsuri yatai to sono enkaku*. Takayama: Takayama Yatai Hozonkai.

Takayanagi Shinzō & Ishii Ryōsuke, ed. 1958. *Ofuregaki Kanpō shūsei*. Iwanami Shoten.

Takeda Akira. 1984. "Sengaikyō," in *NKBD*, 3: 632–633.

Takeda Mariko. 2005. *Sakoku to kokkyō no seiritsu*. Tokyo: Dōseisha.

Takeshima Atsuo. 1996. "Kinsei no ikoku/ikokujin ron: *Wakan sansai zue* ni miru ikoku/ikokujin." *Kokubungaku kaishaku to kanshō* 61.10: 97–102.

Takeuchi Kakusai & Okada Gyokuzan. 1797–1802. *Ehon Taikōki*. 84 vols. Osaka, Kyoto & Edo: Katsuoya Rokubei *et al*.

Takizawa Bakin. 1807–1811. *Chinsetsu yumiharizuki*. 29 vols., Edo: Hirabayashi Shōgorō & Nishimura Genroku.

Takizawa Bakin. 1811/1958–1961. *Chinsetsu yumiharizuki*. Ed. Gotō Tanji. 2 vols. *NKBT*, 60–61.

Tamenaga Shunsui & Utagawa Yoshitoshi. 1864. *Kiyomasa ichidai ki*. 3 vols., National Diet Library Collection.

Tanabe Masako. 1990. "Suzuki Harunobu no zugara shakuyō: mitate no shukō to shite no saihyōka." *Bijutsushi* 39, no. 1 (February): 66–86.

Tanahashi Masahiro. 1986. "Shōki." In Inui, *et al*. (1986), p. 458.

Tanaka Takeo. 1959. "Kenmin-sen bōeki-ka, Kusuha Sainin to sono ichizoku." In *Nihon jinbutsu-shi taikei*, vol. 2, *Chūsei*, ed. Satō Shin'ichi, 193–225. Asakura Shoten.

Tanaka Takeo. 1988. "*Kaitō shokokki* no Nihon-zu Ryūkyū-zu ni tsuite." *Kaiji-shi kenkyū*
    45: 1–36.

Tanaka Takeo, ed. 1991. *Kaitō shokokki: Chōsenjin no mita chūsei Nihon to Ryūkyū.*
    Iwanami Shoten.

Tanaka Takeo. 1996. *Higashi Ajia kōtsū-ken to kokusai ninshiki.* Yoshikawa Kōbunkan.

Tanaka Yoshitada. 1979. *Waka-matsuri no hanashi.* Wakayama: Tanaka Yoshitada Sensei
    Shōju Kinen-kai.

Tanno Kaoru. 1994. *Nanban fukushoku no kenkyū.* Yūzankaku.

Tashiro Kazui. 1990. "Chōsen tsūshinshi gyōretsu emaki no kenkyū: Shōtoku gannen
    (1711) no emaki shitate o chūshin ni." *Chōsen gakuhō* 137.

Tateiwa, Iwao. 1960. "Outline of the Geology of Korea." In *International Geology Review,*
    2.12: 1053–1070.

Tejapira, Kasian. 1992. "Pigtail: A Pre-History of Chineseness in Siam." *Sojourn: Journal
    of Social Issues in Southeast Asia.* 7.1: 95–122.

Tenkai & Kano Tan'yū. 1640. *Tōshōsha engi emaki.* MS. 5 vols., ink, color & gold leaf on
    paper. Rinnōji Collection, Nikkō.

Tenri-shi. 1976–1979. *Tenri-shi shi.* 8 vols. Tenri-shi.

Terajima Ryōan. 1712. *Wakan sansai zue.* 105 vols. Osaka: Okada Saburōemon, Torikai
    Ichibei, Shibukawa Sei'emon, Matsumura Kyūbei & Ōnogi Ichibei.

Terajima Ryōan. 1970. *Wakan sansai zue.* 2 vols. Tōkyō Bijutsu.

Terajima Ryōan. 1980. *Wakan sansai zue.* 2 vols. Endō Shizuo, ed. *NSSSS,* vols. 28–29.

Terajima Ryōan. 1985–1991. *Wakan sansai zue.* Shimada Isao, Takeshima Atsuo Higuchi
    Motomi, eds. 18 vols. Heibonsha.

Terajima Ryōan. 1998. *Wakan sansai zue.* 2 CD-ROM set. Ōzora-sha.

Terao Yoshio. 1986. *Tei Seikō: Minmatsu no fūun-ji.* Tōhō Shoten.

Terasawa Masatsugu. 1790. *Ehon buyū Taikōki.* 3 vols. Kyoto: Hishiya Jihei.

Thompson, Sarah E. 1991. "The Politics of Japanese Prints." In Thompson & Harootunian
    (1991): 29–91.

Thompson, Sarah E, & Harootunian, H[arry] D. *Undercurrents in the Floating World:
    Censorship and Japanese Prints.* The Asia Society Galleries.

Thongchai Winichakul. 1994. *Siam Mapped: A History of the Geo-Body of a Nation.*
    University of Hawai'i Press.

Toby, Ronald P. 1984. *State and Diplomacy in Early Modern Japan: Asia in the Development
    of the Tokugawa Bakufu.* Princeton University Press.

Toby, Ronald P. 1985. "Contesting the Centre: International Sources of Japanese
    National Identity." *International History Review* 7, no. 3: 347–363.

Toby, Ronald P. 1986. "Carnival of the Aliens: Korean Embassies in Edo-Period Art and
    Popular Culture." *Monumenta Nipponica* 41, no. 4: 415–456.

Toby, Ronald P. 1990. "Leaving the Closed Country: New Models for Early-Modern
    Japan." *Trans. International Conf. of Orientalists in Japan* 35: 213–221.

Toby, Ronald P. 1994a. "Gaikō no gyōretsu: ikoku gaikō kenbutsunin." In Kuroda Hideo & Ronald P. Toby, 1994.

Toby, Ronald P. 1994b. "The Indianness of Iberia and Changing Japanese Iconographies of Other," in Schwartz (1994): 323–351.

Toby, Ronald P. 1995. *Foreigners, Fierce and Festive*. Richmond, IN: Media Production Group.

Toby, Ronald P. 1996a. "Chōsenjin gyōretsu-zu no hatsumei: *Edo-zu byōbu*, shinshutsu *Rakuchū rakugai-zu byōbu* to kinsei shoki no kaiga ni okeru 'Chōsenjin-zō' e." In Shin Kisu and Nakao Hiroshi, eds., *Taikei Chōsen tsūshinshi*, 1: 120–129. 8 vols. Akashi Shoten.

Toby, Ronald P. 1996b. "Watōnai no sakayaki/Dattan no benpatsu." *Sōbun* (April).

Toby, Ronald P. 1997. "'Ketōjin' no tōjō o megutte: kinsei Nihon no taigai ninshiki/tashakan no ichi sokumen." In Murai Shōsuke, Satō Shin, and Yoshida Nobuyuki, eds., *Kyōkai no Nihonshi*, 245–291. Yamakawa Shuppan.

Toby, Ronald P. 1998a. "Imaging and Imagining Anthropos." *Visual Anthropology Review* 14, 3: 19–44.

Toby, Ronald P. 1998b. "The Race to Classify." *Anthropology Newsletter* 39, 4: 55–56.

Toby, Ronald P. 2001a. "Kinsei no 'Nihon-zu' to 'Nihon' no kyōkai." In Kuroda, *et al.* ed. 79–102.

Toby, Ronald P. 2001b. "Rescuing the Nation from History: The State of the State in Early-Modern Japan." *Monumenta Nipponica* 56, no. 1: 197–237.

Toby, Ronald P. 2001c. "Three Realms/Myriad Countries: An 'Ethnography' of Other and the Re-Bounding of Japan, 1550–1750," in Chow *et al.* 2001, pp. 15–45.

Toby, Ronald P. 2002. "Kan-Nihonkai no Fugaku enbō," in Aoyagi & Toby, ed. (2002).

Toby, Ronald P. 2004. "'Heiwa gaikō' ga hagukunda shinryaku; Seikanron." In Yoshida Mitsuo, ed., *Nikkanchū no kōryū: hito mono bunka*. Yamakawa Shuppansha, pp. 195–213.

Toby, Ronald P. 2005. "Mind Maps and Land Maps: Toward A Cognitive Geography of 'The Village' in Tokugawa Japan." In Yamaji Hidetoshi and Jeffrey E. Hanes, eds., *Image and Identity*. Kobe University Press.

Toby, Ronald P. 2008a. "The Originality of the 'Copy': Mimesis and Subversion in Hanegawa Tōei's *Chōsenjin ukie*." In Rupert Cox, ed., *The Culture of Copying in Japan: Critical and Historical Perspectives*. Routledge, pp. 71–110.

Toby, Ronald P. 2008b. *'Sakoku' to iu gaikō* (*Nihon no rekishi*, v. 9). Shōgakukan.

Toby, Ronald P. 2008c. "*Edo-zu byōbu* no wasurerareta Chōsenjin," in *Chōsen tsūshinshi ten zuroku* (Shimonoseki Museum): 12–18.

Toby, Ronald P. 2011. "Mibun hyōgen." In Sugimoto Fumiko *et al.*, ed. *Ezu-gaku nyūmon*. Tōkyō Daigaku Shuppankai, pp. 26–29.

Toby, Ronald P. 2016. "Kanō Masunobu-hitsu *Chōsen shisetsu kantai-zu byōbu* no kaiga retorikku," tr. Matsushima Jin, in *Kokka*, 121.6: 9–25.

Toby, Ronald P. & Kuroda Hideo. 1994a "Gyōretsu no gaidobukku." In Kuroda & Toby, 1994.

Toby, Ronald P. & Kuroda Hideo. 1994b. "Iwayuru *Chōsenjin raichō-zu* o yomu." In Kuroda & Toby, 1994.

Tōdaiji zoku yōroku. n.d. In *Zokuzoku gunsho ruijū*. Vol. 11.

Todorov, Tzvetan. 1985. *The Conquest of America*. Harper & Row.

Tōin Kinkata. 1656. *Shūgaishō*. 3 vols. Murakami Kanbei, 1656. National Diet Library Collection.

Tokugawa jikki. 1964. 10 vols. Yoshikawa Kōbunkan.

Tōkyō Chigaku Kyōkai, ed. 1998. *Inō-zu ni manabu*. Asakura Shoten.

Tōkyō Daigaku Shiryō Hensanjo, comp. 1963. *Shiryō sōran*. 17 vols. Tōkyō Daigaku Shuppankai.

Tōkyō Daigaku Shiryō Hensanjo. 1989–1993. *Dai Nihon kinsei shiryō Kondō Jūzō Ezochi kankei shiryō*. 4 vols. + suppl.; 10 maps. Tōkyō Daigaku Shuppankai.

Tokyo National Museum. 1985. *Tokubetsuten Chōsen tsūshinshi: kinsei 200 nen no Nikkan bunka kōryū*. Exh. cat. TNM.

Tokyo National Museum. 2002. *Sesshū: botsugo 500-nen*. Exh. cat. TNM.

Tōkyō Shiyakusho. 1939. *Tenka matsuri*. Tōkyō Shiyakusho.

Tōnei Genshin (Arai Seisai). 1805/1969. *Tōkai Santan*. In NSSSS, 4: 23–44.

Torii Kiyonaga. 1778. *Meidai higashiyama-dono*. 3 vols. npd.

Torres, Cosme de. 1598/1972. *Cartas que os Padres e Irmãos da Campanhia de Iesus*. Yūshōdō.

Toshi-shi Kenkyūkai, ed. 2002. *Dentō toshi to mibun-teki shūen*. Yamakawa Shuppansha. (*Nenpō toshishi kenkyū*, no. 10).

Tsuji Jihei. 1748. *Ezu-iri Chōsen raihei kiroku*. MS copy, 1764. Private collection.

Tsuji Nobuo. 1980. "Ukita Ikkei to sono daihyō saku 'Konkai sōshi emaki' ni tsuite." In Yamane Yūzō, ed., *Zaigai Nihon no shihō* (11 vols., Mainichi Shinbunsha, 1979–1981), 6: 111–117.

Tsuji Nobuo. 1988. "'Edo tenka sairei-zu byōbu' no tokushū ni tsuite." In *Kokka*, 4, 4 (Nov.): 2–10.

Tsukada Takashi, ed. 2010. *Mibun-teki shūen no hikakushi: hō to shakai no shiten kara*. Seibundō.

Tsukada Takashi *et al*., ed. 1994. *Mibun-teki shūen*. Buraku Mondai Kenkyūjo Shuppanbu.

Tsukada Takashi *et al*., ed. 2000. *Shirīzu kinsei no mibun-teki shūen*. 6 vols., Yoshikawa Kōbunkan.

Tsukada Takashi *et al*., ed. 2007. *Shirīzu kinsei no mibun-teki shūen*. 6 vols., Yoshikawa Kōbunkan.

Tsukaguchi Yoshinobu. 1980. *Jingū Kōgō densetsu no kenkyū*. Sōgensha.

Tsukamoto Akira. 1996. "Jingū Kōgō densetsu to kinsei Nihon no Chōsen-kan." In *Shirin*, 79, 6: 1–33.

Tsukamoto Manabu. 1983. *Shōrui o meguru seiji: Genroku no fōkuroa*. Heibonsha.

Tsukamoto Manabu. 1986. *Kinsei saikō: chihō no shiten kara*. Nihon Editā Sukūru.

Tsurumine Shigenobu & Hashimoto Gyokuran (Utagawa Sadahide). 1854. *Ehon Chōsen seibatsu ki*. 20 vols. Tokyo University Library.

Tsunoda, Ryusaku; de Bary, Wm. Theodore; Keene, Donald, comp. 1958. *Sources of Japanese Tradition*. Columbia University Press.

Tsu-shi Kyōiku Iinkai, ed. 1991. *Tsu-shi no bunkazai*. Tsu: Tsu-shi Kyōiku Iinkai.

Tyler, Royall. 1981. "A Glimpse of Mt. Fuji in Legend and Cult." *Journal of the Association of Teachers of Japanese*. Vol. 16, no. 2: 140–165.

Tyler, Royall. 1984. "The Tokugawa Peace and Popular Religion: Suzuki Shōsan, Kakugyō Tōbutsu, and Jikigyō Miroku." In Nosco, ed. (1984): 92–119.

Tyler, Royall, trans. 2001. *The Tale of Genji*. Penguin Classics.

Uberoi, J.P. Singh. 1967. "On Being Unshorn." In *Sikhism and Indian Society*. Simla: Indian Institute of Advanced Study, pp. 87–100.

Ujiie Mikito. 1995. *Bushidō to erosu*. Kōdansha.

Ukai Nobuyuki. 1661. *Minshin tōki*. 10 vols. Kyoto.

Ukai Nobuyuki. 1717. *Minshin gundan Kokusen'ya chūgi den*. 19 vols. Kyoto & Edo: Tanaka Shōbei & Nakamura Shinshichi.

Umeda Yukio & Hayashi Yoshikazu. 1983. *Kaihō Yūsetsu: shokunin ezukushi*. Kyōwa Kikaku.

Unno Kazutaka. 1990. "Nihon-zu." In *Kokushi daijiten*, 2: 201–204.

Unno Kazutaka. 1994. "Cartography in Japan." In J. B. Harley & David Woodward, ed. *The History of Cartography, Vol. 2 Book 2: Cartography in the Traditional East and Southeast Asian Societies*. University of Chicago Press, pp. 346–477.

Uramatsu Mitsuyo. 1993. *Daidairi-zu kōshō*. 3 vols. (*Kojitsu sōsho*, vols. 26–28, ed. Zōtei Kojitsu Sōsho Henshūbu. Yoshikawa Kōbunkan.

Vaporis, Constantine N. 1989. "Post Stations and Assisting Villages: Corvée Labor and Peasant Contention." *Monumenta Nipponica* 41, no. 4: 377–414.

Vaporis, Constantine N. 1994. *Breaking Barriers: Travel and the State in Early Modern Japan*. Harvard University Council on East Asian Studies.

Vaporis, Constantine N. 2008. *Tour of Duty: Samurai, Military Service in Edo, and the Culture of Early Modern Japan*. University of Hawai'i Press.

Wada Masao. 1943. *Katō Kiyomasa*. Chōbunkaku.

Wagatsuma, Hiroshi. 1967. "The Social Perception of Skin Color in Japan." In *Daedalus*. 96: 407–443.

Wakabayashi, Bob Tadashi. 1986. *Anti-Foreignism and Western Learning in Early-Modern Japan: The New Theses of 1825*. Harvard University Council on East Asian Studies.

Wakabayashi, Haruko. 2009. "The Mongol Invasions and the Making of the Iconography of Foreign Enemies: The Case of *Shikaumi jinja engi*." In *Tools of Culture: Japan's*

Cultural, Intellectual, Medical, and Technological Contacts in East Asia, 1000s–1500s. Andrew Edmund Goble, Kenneth R. Robinson & Haruko Wakabayashi, eds. Association for Asian Studies. pp. 105–34.

Wakeman, Frederic, Jr. 1975. "The Great Enterprise: The Manchu Reconstruction of Imperial Order in Seventeenth-Century China." In Wakeman & Carolyn Grant, ed., *Conflict and Control in Late Imperial China.* University of California Press, pp. 43–85.

Wakeman, Frederic, Jr. 1985. *The Great Enterprise: The Manchu Reconstruction of Imperial Order in Seventeenth-Century China.* 2 vols. University of California Press.

Waldron, Arthur. 1990. *The Great Wall of China: From History to Myth.* Cambridge University Press.

Walker, Brett. 1997. "Matsumae Domain and the Conquest of Ainu Lands: Ecology and Culture in Tokugawa Expansionism." Ph.D. diss., University of Oregon.

Walker, Brett. 2001. *The Conquest of Ainu Lands: Ecology and Culture in Japanese Expansion, 1590–1800.* University of California Press.

Walker, Brett. 2007. "Mamiya Rinzō and the Japanese Exploration of Sakhalin Island: Cartography and Empire." *Journal of Historical Geography*, 33: 283–313.

Walter, Lutz. 1994. "A Typology of Maps of Japan Printed in Europe (1595–1800)." In Lutz Walter, ed. *Japan: A Cartographic Vision.* Prestel-Verlag.

Wang Qi. 1607. *Sancai tuhui.* Repr., 3 vols., Shanghai: Shanghai Guji Chupanshe, 1988.

Watanabe Ichirō & Suzuki Junko. 2010. *Zusetsu Inō Tadataka no chizo o yomu.* Kawade Shobō Shinsha.

Watanabe Morikuni, ed. 1977. *Nise monogatari; Inu hyakunin isshu; Shucharon; Shuheiron. (Kinsei bungaku shiryō ruijū, Kanazōshi-hen,* vol. 26). Benseisha.

Watanabe Takao. 1997. "Inō Tadataka no zenkoku sokuryō to genchi no taiō ni tsuite: dai-ichiji—dai-goji sokuryō o chūshin ni." In Tōkyō Chigaku Kyōkai, ed. *Inō Tadataka ni manabu.* Asakura Shoten.

Watanabe Zen'emon. 1748. *Chōsen-jin raihei-ki.* 3 vols. MS. Kyoto University Museum. See Kyōto-shi Rekishi Shiryōkan, 2010.

Wattles, Miriam. 2013. *The Life and Afterlives of Hanabusa Itchō, Artist-Rebel of Edo.* Vol. 10 Japanese Visual Culture. Brill.

Weems, The Rev. M.L. 1800?. *A History of the Life and Death of General George Washington.* 3rd. ed., Philadelphia: Jon Bigren, n.d..

Wheelwright, Carolyn. "A Visualization of Eitoku's Lost Paintings at Azuchi Castle." In George Elison & Bardwell Smith, ed., *Warlords, Artists, and Commoners: Japan in the Sixteenth Century.* University of Hawai'i Press, pp. 87–111,

White, James W. 1995. *Ikki: Social Conflict and Political Protest in Early Modern Japan.* Cornell University Press.

Wigen, Kären. 1992. "The Geographic Imaginary in Early Modern Japanese History: Retrospect and Prospect." In *JAS*, 51, no. 1: 3–29.

Wigen, Kären. 2010. *A Malleable Map: Geographies of Restoration in Central Japan, 1600–1912*. Berkeley: University of California Press.

Williams, Patricia J. 2009. "The Politics of Michelle Obama's Hair." In *The Daily Beast* (Sept. 28, 2009, http://www.thedailybeast.com/blogs-and-stories/2008-10-09/the-politics-of-michelle-obamas-hair/).

Wilson, Noell. 2010. "Tokugawa Defense Redux: Organizational Failure in the 'Phaeton' Incident of 1808." *Journal of Japanese Studies* 36.1: 1–32.

Wood, Denis. 1992. *The Power of Maps*. The Guilford Press.

Xu Zaiquan & Wang Weiming, ed. 1999. *Zheng Chenggong yanjiu*. Beijing: Zhongguo Shehui Kexue Chupan-she.

Xuefu chuanbian. 1607. 10 vols. Beijing.

Yabuta Yutaka *et al.*, ed. 2010–2011. *"Edo" no hito to mibun* (6 vols., Yoshikawa Kōbunkan).

Yamagishi Tokuhei & Sano Masami, eds., 1978–79. *Shinpen Hayashi Shihei zenshū, 1 heigaku*. Dai'ichi Shobō.

Yamamoto Iwao. 1994. "Shinzoku kibun kō," *in Utsunomiya Daigaku Kyōiku Gakubu kiyō, dai-ichibu*, 44.1 (March): 55–68.

Yamamoto Tsunetomo. 1974. *Hagakure*. In Saiki Kazuma, Okayama Taiji & Sagara Tōru, eds., *Mikawa monogatari; Hagakure. NST*, 26.

Yamamuro Kyōko. 1992. *Ōgon Taikō*. Chūō Kōronsha.

Yamanaka Tametsuna. 1656/1968. *Seiyō zakki*. Suzuki Toshio & Noda Seiichi, ed. Tsu: Mie-ken Kyōdo Shiryō Kankōkai.

Yamato Bunkakan. 1980. *Fuji no e: Kamakura jidai kara gendai made*. Exh. cat., Nara: Yamato Bunkakan.

Yamazaki Hisanaga. 1854. *Chōsen seitō shimatsu ki*. 5 vols. Edo: Izumiya Zenbei; Osaka: Akitaya Ta'emon; Kyoto: Izumodera Bunjirō.

Yanagita Kunio. 1941/1962–1975. "Ryūō to mizu no kami." In *Teihon Yanagita Kunio shū*. 36 vols. Chikuma Shobō. 27: 350–354.

Yanai Shigeshi *et al.*, ed. 1993. *Genji monogatari* (5 v., *Shin Nihon koten bungaku taikei*, vols. 19–22), Iwanami Shoten, 1993.

Yano Takanori, ed. 1984–1985. *Edo jidai rakusho ruijū*. 3 vols. Tōkyōdō Shuppan.

Yao Keisuke. 2008. "Kinsei ni okeru ame no seihō to Sankan-ame." *Kitakyūshū Shiritsu Daigaku Bungakubu kiyō* 72: 37–46.

Yi Changhŭi. 1999. *Imjin waeransa yŏn'gu*. Asea Munhwasa.

Yi Hyŏngsŏk. 1967. *Imjin chŏllan-sa*. Imjin Chŏllansa Kanhaeng Wiwŏnhoe.

Yi Wŏnsik. 1997. *Chōsen tsūshinshi no kenkyū*. Kyoto: Shibunkaku.

Yokomichi Mario & Omote Akira, eds. 1960–1963. *Yōkyoku*. 2 vols. *NKBT*, 40–41.

Yokota Fuyuhiko. 2011. "Konketsuji tsuihō-rei to ijin yūkaku no seiritsu: 'sakoku' ni okeru 'jinshu shugi' saikō." In *Ibunka kōryū-shi no saikentō: Nihon Kindai no 'keiken' to sono shūhen*, Hirota Masaki & Yokota Fuyuhiko, ed. Tokyo: Heibonsha.

Yokoyama Manabu. 1981. "Ryūkyū-mono to Ryūshi raihei." In *Edo-ki Ryūkyū-mono shiryō shūsei*. 4 vols. Honpō Shoseki.

Yokoyama Manabu. 1987. *Ryūkyū-koku shisetsu torai no kenkyū*. Yoshikawa Kōbunkan.

Yokoyama Shigeru, ed. 1954. *Kojōruri-shū (Dewa no Jō shōhon)*. *KB*, vol. 79. KB.

Yokoyama Toshio. 1987. *Japan in the Victorian Mind: A Study of Stereotyped Images of a Nation, 1850–1880*. Macmillan.

Yonekura Michio. 1995. *Minamoto Yoritomo-zō: chinmoku no shōzōga*. Heibonsha.

Yonemoto, Marcia. 1995. "Mapping Culture in Eighteenth-Century Japan." Ph.D. dissertation, University of California, Berkeley.

Yonemoto, Marcia. 2000. "Envisioning Japan in Eighteenth-Century Europe: The International Career of a Cartographic Image." In *Intellectual History Newsletter*. 22: 17–35.

Yonemoto, Marcia. 2003. *Mapping Early Modern Japan: Space, Place, and Culture in the Tokugawa Period, 1603–1868*. University of California Press.

Yonetani Hitoshi. 1999. "Kinsei Nitchō kankei ni okeru sensō horyo no sōkan," in *Rekishi hyōron*, 595: 28–41.

Yoshida Kōichi, ed. 1971. *Kōshoku ichidai otoko*. *KB*, vol. 290.

Young, Robert. 1990. *White Mythologies: Writing History and the West*. Routledge.

Yuan Minxi, Xia Lin & Zheng Yizou, comp. 1957. *Zheng Chenggong shiliao haokan*. Taibei: Haidongshanfang.

Yun Jihye. 2005. "Edo kaiga ni egakareta Chōsen tsūshinshi no gakutai." (Shimane Kenritsu Daigaku) *Sōgō seisaku ronsō*, 10: 73–89.

Yun Jihye. 2008. "Kinsei Nihon no kaiga sakuhin ni okeru Chōsen tsūshinshi no egaki-kata: gakutai to sono ishō ni chūmoku shite." *Bigaku*, 59.1: 57–70.

Yusōan. 1669. *Inu hyakunin isshu*. (Facsimile eds., Beisandō, 1919; NSSSS, 30: 456–480).

Zeami Motokiyo. 1931. "Fujisan," in Sanari Kentarō, ed., *Yōkyoku taikan*. 7 vols. Meiji Shoin, 1931, 4: 2683–2696.

Zhou Huang. 1727. *Liuqiu guozhi lue* ("Abbreviated Gazetteer of the Land of Ryukyu"). 6 vols. Fujian.

Zhou Huang. 1832. *Ryūkyū kokushi ryaku* (6 vols., Edo: Izumoji Tomigorō). Japanese repr. of Zhou 1727.

Zhu Xie. 1956. *Zheng Chenggong*. Shanghai: Xin-Wenyi Chupan-she.

Index